# THE WHOLE

PEOPLE • MATERIALS • GUIDELINES • TECHNOLOGY

# LIBRARY

OPERATIONS • FUNDING • STAFF DEVELOPMENT

# HANDBOOK 2

ISSUES • DIVERSITY • THE INTERNET • LIBRARIANA

**CURRENT DATA, PROFESSIONAL ADVICE, AND
CURIOSA ABOUT LIBRARIES AND LIBRARY SERVICES**

compiled by George M.
Eberhart

AMERICAN LIBRARY ASSOCIATION
Chicago and London 1995

Cover designed by Richmond Jones

Text and graphics designed by Priority Publishing

Composition by Priority Publishing using Aldus PageMaker and Corel Draw! with a Unity 1000 laser printer

Printed on 40-pound Precision Offset, a pH-neutral stock, and bound in 10-point C1S cover stock by Edwards Brothers, Inc.

The paper used in this publication meets the minimum requirements of American National Standard for Information Sciences—Permanence of Paper for Printed Library Materials, ANSI Z39.48-1992. ∞

**Library of Congress Cataloging-in-Publication Data**

Eberhart, George M.
  The whole library handbook 2: current data, professional advice, and curiosa about libraries and library services / compiled by George M. Eberhart.
      p.   cm.
  Includes index.
  ISBN 0-8389-0646-X (alk. paper)
  1. Library science—United States—Handbooks, manuals, etc.
  2. Libraries—United States—Handbooks, manuals, etc.   I. American Library Association.  II. Title.  III. Title: Whole library handbook two.
  Z665.2.U6E23   1995
  020'.973—dc20                                                           94-42091

Printed in the United States of America.

99   98   97   96   95        5   4   3   2

# CONTENTS

## Preface

# The Whole Library Handbook 2

### George M. Eberhart

SEQUELS SHOULD BE EASY, but they're not. Especially when the author/compiler seeks to produce a work as beloved and indispensable as the first was intended to be. A couple of years daydreaming about how to improve the package and what new material to include have resulted in a full year of late-night selecting, scanning, and scheming to put together a superior, not a sloppy, sequel.

I believe *The Whole Library Handbook 2* satisfies my requirements. But don't discard your earlier edition! At least 88% of *WLH2* is completely new or revised, and some excellent lists, guidelines, and essays from the first edition just did not fit—even with 32 additional pages. I will still consult my copy of the first *WLH* whenever I want to alphabetize Portuguese surnames, figure out what to do with my old books, or photocopy without (much) damage.

Here are some highlights of what I had to make room for in *WLH2*: an expanded list of useful addresses, telephone numbers, and e-mail addresses; providing quality bookmobile service; how to handle unruly teens; 84 library uses for the Internet; 50 things librarians can do to save the earth; choosing a mass deacidification process; special products for the print-impaired patron; and how to photograph your library.

As in the first edition, please keep in mind that many of the selections are only extracts or summaries of much longer articles, books, or guidelines. If you find the extract useful, then consult the original for even more insight and advice. In many cases I had to restrict my borrowings to a fraction of what I would have reprinted had there been room. The *Whole Library Handbooks* serve as first-stop, all-in-one reference books, but you should have the source material on your shelves for in-depth study.

A mere 514 pages cannot contain everything the compleat librarian might require. Nor can one mortal editor predict all the protean needs of late-20th-century professionals. So, if there is to be a *Whole Library Handbook 3*, I will once again need your help. If you know of a checklist, a glossary, a how-to guide that you find indispensable, or interesting facts and concepts of the kind presented here, please write and tell me so that it can be shared with others. Or, if I have overlooked a certain topic due to unconscious editorial preference, let me know. Send everything to: *The Whole Library Handbook*, c/o Art Plotnik, ALA Editions, 50 E. Huron Street, Chicago, IL 60611-2795; or e-mail me at: U12576@uicvm.uic.edu.

Finally, I would like to thank the many people who contributed their time and writings to this project. Some who made a special effort to provide information and data include: Mary Jo Lynch, ALA Office for Research and Statistics, who put extra effort into ensuring that the basic figures were accurate and representative; Margaret Myers, ALA Office for Library Personnel Resources; Prudence Dalrymple, ALA Office for Accreditation; all of the ALA division directors who were flooded with permission requests; Linda J. Knutson, executive director of LITA, who offered guidance on library technology; Ed Valauskas and Rob Carlson, who inducted me into the arcane mysteries of the Internet; Janet Russell, for preparing the index; Norman Stevens, Billy Wilkinson, and Fred Duda, whose combined knowledge of popular culture and libraries should be preserved and made a part of the National Information Infrastructure; all the famous librarians and music librarians who shared their favorite books and music; all the interested readers who sent suggestions for future editions; and the many people I had to annoy in order to extract grants, awards, and e-mail information from them.

I also want to thank all those authors of articles and books whose research and experiences deserved to be enshrined in a volume like this one; and everyone who served on the many committees charged with developing standards, guidelines, checklists, and tip sheets. You should all be added entries in *The Whole Library Handbook 2* tracings!

Once again, my deepest appreciation to Art Plotnik, who was instrumental in crafting the content and scope of both *WLH* volumes; to my wife, Jennifer Henderson, who had to listen to long orations on the epistemology of sequels; to our cats, Andy and Noodles, who had to put up with piles of books and photocopies in their favorite observation posts; and to the purchasers of the first *Whole Library Handbook*—may you find even more information, enlightenment, and whimsey in this volume.

# Author note

GEORGE M. EBERHART served for 10 years (1980–1990) as editor of *College & Research Libraries News*, the monthly news magazine of the Association of College and Research Libraries, a division of the American Library Association. With his wife Jennifer he owns Priority Publishing, a home-based desktop publishing and graphic arts business. He is the author of *UFOs and the Extraterrestrial Contact Movement: A Bibliography* (Scarecrow, 1986), *Monsters* (Garland, 1984), and *A Geo-Bibliography of Anomalies* (Greenwood, 1980), and the editor of *The Roswell Report: A Historical Perspective* (Center for UFO Studies, 1991). For the Chicago-based J. Allen Hynek Center for UFO Studies he is the associate editor of the *International UFO Reporter* and the managing editor of the *Journal of UFO Studies*, the only peer-reviewed scientific journal in the field. He holds a bachelor's degree in journalism from Ohio State University (1973) and an MLS from the University of Chicago (1976).

# LIBRARIES

1

# Some basic figures

*by Mary Jo Lynch*

**MANY OF THE FIGURES** given here are from surveys published by the National Center for Education Statistics (NCES): *Academic Libraries, 1992* (1994), *Public Libraries in the United States, 1992* (1994); and *Statistics of Public and Private School Library Media Centers, 1985–1986* (1987). Additional sources are cited where appropriate.

## How many libraries are there?

Libraries of various types exist in all parts of the United States, and there is no official source that counts them all every year. The following count is based on the surveys cited above for academic and public libraries. Figures for school libraries come from *School Library Media Centers in the United States: National Data, 1990–91* (NCES, 1994). Figures for special libraries, armed forces libraries, government libraries, and Canadian libraries come from the 1994–95 *American Library Directory* compiled by the R. R. Bowker Company.

| Libraries in the United States | | |
|---|---|---|
| College and university libraries | | 3,274 |
| Public libraries | | 8,946* |
| Branches | 7,035 | |
| Buildings | 15,981 | |
| School library media centers | | 97,975 |
| Public schools | 76,544 | |
| Private schools | 21,431 | |
| Special libraries | | 10,059 |
| Armed forces libraries | | 442 |
| Government libraries | | 1,864 |
| **TOTAL** | | **122,560** |

\* This is the number of administrative units. Many libraries have one or more branches, totalling 7,035 nationally. Thus, the total number of buildings is 15,981.

| Libraries in Canada | | |
|---|---|---|
| College and university libraries | | 504 |
| Public libraries | | 794 |
| Branches | 949 | |
| Buildings | 1,743 | |
| Special libraries | | 1,354 |
| Government libraries | | 400 |
| **TOTAL** | | **3,052** |

These libraries are often involved in cooperative organizations through which they share collections, technology, and staff expertise. The most recent national survey found that approximately 760 networks and cooperatives existed in the United States at that time *(Survey of Library Networks and Cooperative Library Organizations, 1985–1986,* NCES, 1987). Most college, university, and public libraries and many school libraries belong to at least one and many participate in more than one.

## How much are they used?

The 3,274 **college and university libraries** submitting "attendance" figures to the National Center for Education Statistics for 1989–1990 reported that more than 13,093,800 people visited these libraries in a typical week. During 1991–1992, more than 180,300,000 items circulated from academic libraries. Another 48,400,000 were used in reserve collections.

The 1992 NCES report on **public libraries** shows 773,236,000 "visits." This is an increase of 14% over the figure in the 1991 report. In 1992, the average circulation for public libraries was 6.4 items per capita. The total number of items circulated nationally from public libraries in 1992 was over 1,555,482,000, an increase of 6% more than the figure reported in 1991.

The 1985 NCES survey estimated that for the 73,352 **public school library media centers** in the United States:

- more than 42.4 million students visited all libraries per week;
- each student averaged 1.2 visits to the library per week.

During the 1984–1985 school year, all public school libraries in the United States:

- circulated a total of more than 38,300 items per week;
- circulated an average of 523 items per school per week.

Most **private schools** have small enrollments and are less likely to have a library. The 1985 NCES survey estimated that:

- of the 13,216 private schools with less than 300 students, 69% had libraries;
- of the 5,970 private schools with 300 or more students, 93% had libraries.

The same survey showed that for the 19,186 private school library media centers in the United States:

- more than 5.3 million students visited all libraries per week;
- each student averaged 1.2 visits to the library per week.

## Who uses public libraries?

It is fairly obvious who uses college and university libraries and who uses school library media centers—students and faculty associated with those institutions. But who uses public libraries? Answers come from the 1991 National Household Education Survey sponsored by the National Center for Education Statistics (NCES). Surveyors conducted about 12,600 interviews with adults on their own activities and about 14,000 interviews with adults on the activities of children aged 3–8.

Fifty-three percent of *adults* reported that they used a public library at least once in the past year. When considered in terms of standard demographic categories, the percent of adults who reported using the library at least once in the past year is as follows:

### Sex

| Male | 47% | Female | 57% |
|------|-----|--------|-----|

### Age

| 18–24 | 65% | 40–49 | 58% |
|-------|-----|-------|-----|
| 25–29 | 55% | 50–64 | 42% |
| 30–39 | 62% | 65+ | 34% |

### Urbanicity

| Nonmetropolitan areas | 43% | Metropolitan areas | 36% |
|-----------------------|-----|--------------------|-----|

### Race/Ethnicity

| White/non-Hispanic | 55% | Black/non-Hispanic | 42% |
|--------------------|-----|--------------------|-----|
| Hispanic | 38% | Other races | 52% |

### Education

| Less than high school | 17% | College | 71% |
|-----------------------|-----|---------|-----|
| High school | 44% | Graduate or | |
| Vocational/technical | 69% | professional | 80% |

### Income

| Less than $10,000 | 32% | $30,001–$40,000 | 57% |
|-------------------|-----|-----------------|-----|
| $10,001–$15,000 | 43% | $40,001–$50,000 | 63% |
| $15,001–$20,000 | 42% | $50,001–$75,000 | 66% |
| $20,001–$25,000 | 48% | Above $75,000 | 70% |
| $25,001–$30,000 | 52% | | |

### Labor Force Status

| Employed | 58% | Unemployed | 48% |
|----------|-----|------------|-----|
| Not in labor force | 43% | | |

*Children* have always been a large percentage of the users in many public libraries. In the 1991 Household Survey, adults were asked how often 3- to 8-year-olds visited a public library. The percentage of children in various demographic groups who had been there at least once in the past year were as follows:

### Sex

| Male | 73% | Female | 75% |
|------|-----|--------|-----|

### Age

| 3- to 4-year-olds | 64% | 7- to 8-year-olds | 82% |
|-------------------|-----|-------------------|-----|
| 5- to 6-year-olds | 76% | | |

### Race/Ethnicity

| White/non-Hispanic | 78% | Black/non-Hispanic | 67% |
|--------------------|-----|--------------------|-----|
| Hispanic | 59% | Other races | 72% |

### Household Income

| | | | |
|---|---|---|---|
| $10,000 or less | 62% | $40,001–$50,000 | 83% |
| $10,001–$20,000 | 66% | $50,001–$75,000 | 85% |
| $20,001–$30,000 | 71% | above $75,000 | 87% |
| $30,001–$40,000 | 79% | | |

### Parents' Highest Education

| | | | |
|---|---|---|---|
| Less than high school | 49% | College | 87% |
| High school | 64% | Graduate or | |
| Vocational/technical | 80% | professional | 92% |

## The traditional library

*Ownership.* For many years, librarians have acquired, organized, and helped people use collections of printed materials, primarily books and serials (i.e., magazines, journals, newspapers). Audiovisual materials and microforms were added in the 20th century. Although electronic resources are revolutionizing library service today, collections of print, audiovisual, and microform material are still the bedrock of library service.

The 3,274 **college & university libraries** reporting to NCES in the fall of 1992 held a total of 749,428,719 volumes of books, bound serials, and government documents. Collections ranged in size from 146 libraries with less than 5,000 volumes to 152 with 1,000,000 or more. The 3,274 academic libraries held 6,965,855 serial subscriptions and material in several other formats including:

- 865,000,000   microform units
- 34,744,000   cartographic items
- 9,492,000   audio items
- 2,926,000   film and video items

Of the 8,946 **public libraries** in the United States included in the 1992 NCES report, more than half had collections of less than 25,000, but 170 had collections of 500,000 or more. These libraries held a total of 642,525,000 book and serial volumes and received 1,959,000 serial subscriptions. These libraries also hold material in many nonprint formats including:

- 22,641,000   audio items
- 6,778,000   video items

Book collections in **public school library media centers** range from less than 2,000 in 3% of the public schools to over 30,000 in 1%. The average public school library in 1985 had:

- 8,466   volumes
- 20.3   volumes per pupil
- 921   audiovisual titles
- 34   periodical subscriptions

The average **private school library** had:

- 5,615   books
- 869   items of audiovisual and other materials
- 19   periodical subscriptions

*Access.* For many years, libraries of all types have borrowed materials for their clients from other libraries through a cooperative arrangement known as interlibrary loan. Guidelines and forms devised by ALA facilitate this service. During the academic year 1991–1992, **academic libraries** in the United States:

- provided more than 7,987,000 items to other libraries
- received more than 5,304,000 items from other libraries

In 1992, the 8,946 **public libraries** in the United States:

- provided more than 6,749,000 items to other libraries
- received more than 7,125,000 items from other libraries.

In the figures just given, the number of items provided is not equal to the number received for each type of library. This is due to several factors such as lending across library types (including types for which no statistics are available).

In recent years, there have been many changes in interlibrary loan services. Photocopying technology, telefacsimile technology, and the development of commercial document delivery services have had major impacts on the volume and speed of traffic. Other factors are the increasing cost of serial publications and the increasing availability of electronic indexes to those publications. A recent study of interlibrary loan in 76 of the largest research libraries in the United States and Canada found that 60% of filled transactions were for nonreturnable copies rather than original items.

## Answers to questions

Librarians find answers to questions or help library users do so. During 1992, the 7,729 **public libraries** in the United States reporting to NCES on this topic answered more than 227,997,000 reference questions. The 3,274 **academic libraries** reporting in the fall of 1990 answered a total of 1,766,823 reference questions in a typical week.

The 145 **medical school libraries** in the United States and Canada reported a total of 3,302,784 reference questions answered in 1991–92. Each medical school library averaged 27,072 questions.

## The automated library

Between 1970 and 1990, library automation became widespread in the United States. Single-function systems came first, using computers to manage cataloging, or circulation, or acquisitions, or serials. In the 1980s, integrated systems were developed, using a single bibliographic database to support multiple library operations, including online public access catalogs (OPACs). Many different vendors are involved and the systems may be based on microcomputers, minicomputers, or mainframes.

The annual *Library Journal* article on the automated system marketplace estimates that revenues in 1993 for micro- and minicomputer-based systems worldwide was $377,000,000. About two-thirds of the systems were installed in the United States and Canada. As of 1993, the number of such systems installed worldwide was 63,936 with 11,172 installed in 1993. Installations in 1993 that could be assigned to a specific type of library and type of platform were as follows:

| Academic Libraries | | School Libraries | |
|---|---|---|---|
| Microcomputers | 236 | Microcomputers | 6,909 |
| Minicomputers | 246 | Minicomputers | 158 |
| Public Libraries | | Special Libraries | |
| Microcomputers | 442 | Microcomputers | 582 |
| Minicomputers | 222 | Minicomputers | 137 |

# The electronic library

Automating library functions has changed the traditional library, especially for those who staff it. But for those who use libraries, a much more profound change is under way with the increasing use of computer and telecommunications technologies to provide information.
Online bibliographic databases were a first step, with searches of remote sources available in many libraries since the early 1980s. Today, databases are available in several other forms for use on local computers. According to the July 1993 edition of the 2-volume *Gale Directory of Databases*, the number of publicly available databases in various categories was as follows:

- 5,200 online
- 1,433 CD-ROM
- 710 diskette
- 611 magnetic tape

More detail on the industry that produces CD-ROM databases and other CD-ROM products is found in the *CD-ROM Factbook*. This source credits libraries with playing a major role in the development of this industry, which was expected to capture $4.2 billion in revenue in 1993. Among its products used by libraries are indexes, dictionaries, encyclopedias, directories, and full-text collections of periodical articles.
The November 1993 *Factbook* reports that 4,422 titles are available and shows 1993 output by type and subject as follows:

### 1993 titles by subject

| | | | |
|---|---|---|---|
| Science and technical | 774 | Medicine | 229 |
| Arts and humanities | 430 | General | 546 |
| Legal | 215 | Business | 290 |
| Social sciences | 504 | | |

### 1993 titles by type

| | | | |
|---|---|---|---|
| Images | 380 | Index | 493 |
| Reference | 1,076 | Full text | 651 |
| Source | 1,406 | Numeric | 135 |
| Mix of types | 130 | Software | 114 |

# The Internet

The Internet is a worldwide interconnected network of networks. Counts vary, but a June 1994 article in the *New York Times* gave the following statistics on involvement with the Internet:

- 135+ countries
- 32,400+ networks
- 2,200,000+ computers
- 25,000,000+ users

```
Rice CMS Gopher 2.4.2                              info.e)
19/26
                              U.S. Geological Survey (USGS)
<menu>       Reference
<menu>       Regulations
<menu>       Search of GopherSpace - Veronica
<menu>       The UofI Weather Machine
type h       USGSHome.html
<menu>       WAIS Gateway
<document>   lynx_it
<menu>           special collections
```

It is said to be growing at a rate of 10% to 15% each month.
More than 800 catalogs of libraries from all over the world were available on the Internet as of July 1994, but that is only one of the important connections between the Internet and libraries. Because vast amounts of information are stored on computers connected to the Internet, a connection to the Internet

greatly increases the amount of information librarians can provide to library users. Three types of sources are well described in the *Directory of Electronic Journals, Newsletters and Academic Discussion Lists,* published by the Association of Research Libraries. The 4th edition (May 1994) includes:

- 443 journals and newsletters (74 refereed)
- 1,785 academic discussion lists

Journals and newsletters have long appeared in print and their electronic cousins are similar. Discussion lists are a new form of information exchange. Messages on the topic of a specific list are automatically sent to everyone who has subscribed to the list. Responses can be sent to the whole list or to the original author only. The directory mentioned above organizes scholarly lists under 63 topics ranging from Art to Weather.

Electronic journals, newsletters, and discussion lists are just a small part of the resources available through the Internet. The rest is not as well organized, but a sizable number of guidebooks and workshops exist to help librarians and other explorers. For more information on the Internet, see Chapter 8.

*Source:* Mary Jo Lynch, ALA Office for Research and Statistics.

# National Libraries

# The Library of Congress: The nation's library

THE LIBRARY OF CONGRESS is the nation's library. Its services extend not only to members and committees of the Congress but to the executive and judicial branches of government, to libraries throughout the nation and the world, and to the scholars and researchers and artists and scientists who use its resources. This was not always the case. When President John Adams signed the bill that provided for the removal of the seat of government to the new capital city of Washington in 1800, he created a reference library for Congress only. The bill provided, among other items, $5,000 "for the purchase of such books as may be necessary for the use of Congress—and for putting up a suitable apartment for containing them therein."

The first books were ordered from England and shipped across the Atlantic in 11 hair trunks and a map case. The Library was housed in the new Capitol until August 1814, when British troops invaded Washington and put the torch to the Capitol Building, and the small collection was lost. Within a month former President Thomas Jefferson, living in retirement at Monticello, offered as a replacement his personal library, accumulated over a span of 50 years. As Minister to France, Jefferson had spent many afternoons at bookstalls in Paris, "turning over every book with my own hands, putting by everything which related to America, and indeed whatever was rare and valuable in every science." His library was considered one of the finest in the United States.

In offering his library to the Congress Jefferson wrote, "I do not know that it contains any branch of science which Congress would wish to exclude from their collection; there is, in fact, no subject to which a Member of Congress may not have occasion to refer." After considerable debate Congress in January 1815 accepted Jefferson's offer, appropriating $23,950 for the collection of 6,487 books. Thus the foundation was laid for a great national library.

The Main Reading Room of the Library of Congress.

## Buildings and facilities

The Library of Congress complex on Capitol Hill includes three buildings. The Thomas Jefferson Building, executed in Italian Renaissance style, is the oldest of these. Heralded as the largest and costliest library structure in the world when it was completed in 1897, it is elaborately decorated with splendid sculpture, murals, and mosaics created by 50 American artists. The building's Great Hall includes towering marble columns, murals and mosaics, statuary, and stained glass, portraying themes relating to learning, knowledge, and the many pursuits of civilization. Restored to its original magnificence, the Main Reading Room now boasts state-of-the-art information technology. The 236 reader desks are wired so that laptop computers can be used for electronic notetaking; readers can search any of 10 CD-ROM indexes on a local area network installed at the room's perimeter.

In the Computer Catalog Center, 58 computer terminals are available for researchers. Of these, 18 are ACCESS terminals using touch-screen technology to welcome novice or infrequent users to the Library's online public access catalog. The center also includes six personal computers that permit screen-by-screen capture of information to disk.

To make the Main Reading Room's resources more available to visually impaired researchers, the Library has installed a Kurzweil machine offering eight voices as well as a personal computer equipped with a 19-inch screen and printer to display and print in large type.

The John Adams Building, in art deco style, faced with white Georgia marble, was opened in 1939. Bas relief sculptures on its large bronze doors represent 12 historic figures credited with giving the art of writing to their people. Ezra Winter's murals of the *Canterbury Tales* decorate the building's fifth-floor reading room.

The white marble James Madison Memorial Building, dedicated on April

24, 1980, more than doubled the Library's available Capitol Hill space. The building houses the memorial to the nation's fourth President, James Madison, as well as eight reading rooms, offices, and storage areas for the Library's special-format collections, which number more than 88 million items.

## From papyrus to lasers

Collections of the Library include more than 98 million items covering virtually every subject in formats that vary from papyrus to optical disk. These materials stretch along 575 miles of shelves and are being acquired at a rate of 10 items a minute. The Library has 29 million books and pamphlets in 470 languages and more than 43 million manuscripts, among them such treasures of American history and culture as the papers of presidents, notable families, writers, artists, and scientists. The Library has the world's largest and most comprehensive cartographic collection—almost 4 million maps and

atlases, dating to the middle of the 14th century—and a 7-million-piece music collection that includes autograph scores, correspondence of composers and musicians, flutes from throughout the world, and rare Stradivarius instruments, with Tourte bows.

The Library's 12 million prints and photographs provide a visual record of people, places, and events in the United States and in many foreign countries. Master photos, fine prints, works of popular and applied graphic arts, and documentary photographs are included. Approximately 75,000 serial titles are received annually; 1,200 newspapers are held in the Library's permanent collections, with some dating back to the 17th century. There are also 100,000 motion picture titles, 80,000 television broadcasts, 500,000 radio transcriptions, and more than 1.5 million other sound recordings, as well as about 10 million microforms.

Throughout the Library buildings manuscripts, rare books, prints, and maps from collections are exhibited. On permanent display are such priceless treasures as the Library's copy of the Gutenberg Bible, one of three surviving examples printed on vellum and perfect in all respects, and the Giant Bible of Mainz, an illuminated manuscript executed by hand at about the time the Gutenberg Bible was printed. Also on permanent display is a copyright exhibit that traces the history of copyright through landmark cases.

Keeping pace with the technological age, the Library is becoming "a library without walls." The Global Library Project uses cable television to take stories based on Library collections to the classroom. LC Direct is making access to the Library's bibliographical database available by computer to state libraries. By converting collections of artifacts into electronic format, American Memory shares the Library's unique multimedia holdings with libraries across the nation.

## Services to Congress

The Library of Congress provides numerous services that directly or indirectly benefit all Americans. A primary role is to serve as the research and reference arm of the Congress. Through the Congressional Research Service (CRS), a department established more than 75 years ago, the Library provides legislators with the information they need to govern wisely and effectively. The staff of CRS answers about 600,000 inquiries a year, ranging from simple requests for data to highly complex in-depth studies. In addition, CRS prepares bill digests, summaries of major legislation, and other reference tools to help members and their committees stay abreast of the daily flow of legislation. The CRS staff of 800 ranges from civil engineers and oceanographers to labor arbitrators and experts on Soviet rocketry. Their most important function is to provide objective, unbiased information to the Congress.

The staff of the Law Library, a department created by an Act of Congress more than 150 years ago, is the research arm of the Congress for questions regarding foreign law. The Law Library answers congressional requests for analyses of foreign legislation and legal developments. Congressional requests also come in the form of translations of foreign laws, which are handled by the Law Library's legal specialists, proficient in 50 different languages.

## Scholarly resources

As its most important service to the scholarly community the Library of Congress makes its vast resources available to the public. Scholars, writers, teachers, artists, journalists, students—anyone beyond high school pursuing serious research—may use the Library's reading rooms. Readers may use computer terminals to search the Library's databases for new titles, for sources of information on a variety of subjects, and for legislative histories.

The uses of the Library's resources are as varied as its collections. For example, a graduate student doing a comparative study of American writers may go to the Manuscript Reading Room to examine the papers of Walt Whitman and Archibald MacLeish. A violinist  may use the Music Reading Room to study the notations on an original score of a Mozart string quartet. To gather background material for a spy story set in Eastern Europe, a novelist may refer to the reference collections of the Main Reading Room, the European Division, and the Government Publications, Newspaper, and Current Periodical Reading Room. An information specialist researching the history of software development may go to the Machine-Readable Collections Reading Room.

For those who are not able to visit the Library a number of special services are available. Through its interlibrary loan program the Library extends the use of its books and other research materials to scholars working at academic, public, or other libraries across the country. The service is intended to aid scholarly research by making available unusual materials not readily accessible elsewhere. Through the Library's Photoduplication Service the public may purchase photographs, photostats, facsimile prints, and microfilms of research materials by mail (subject to copyright or other restrictions), fax, and in some cases, electronic mail.

In 1993 the Library established a new online information system, LC MARVEL (Library of Congress Machine-Assisted Realization of the Virtual Electronic Library), that can be accessed over the worldwide computer network known as the Internet. Internet users can download text and graphic information on the Library's exhibits, catalogs, and services and on Congress and the entire federal government.

## Cultural programs

Chamber music concerts, poetry readings, films, lectures, and symposia are presented throughout the year in the Library's 500-seat Coolidge Auditorium, the adjacent Whittall Pavilion, the Mary Pickford Theater, and the Mumford Room. The auditorium will be closed for renovation, reopening sometime in 1995. Events will continue at other locations, however.

Through its Interpretive Programs Office, the Library exhibits examples of the treasures in its collections, including prints and photographs, maps, musical scores, rare books, and manuscripts. Some of the exhibitions travel to libraries and museums across the nation.

Especially popular is the lunchtime concert series sponsored by the Library's American Folklife Center. Once a month, from May through October, musical groups representing a variety of folk traditions perform on the Neptune Plaza in front of the Library's Jefferson Building.

The Center for the Book in the Library of Congress is a catalyst for stimulating public interest in books, reading, and the printed word. Its symposia, exhibits, and publications are supported by tax-deductible contributions from individuals and corporations. "A Nation of Readers," "Read More About It," "Explore New Worlds—Read!" and "Books Change Lives" are reading promotion themes used nationally and by affiliated Centers for the Book in 24 states.

# Library of Congress 1993 fact sheet

IN FISCAL YEAR 1993, the Library of Congress—

*Welcomed* 1,065,771 users and visitors.

*Held* 104,834,652 items, including:

16,055,353 books and serials cataloged in the Library of Congress classification system.

88,779,299 items in the nonclassed collections. These included:

12,752,983 books in large type and raised characters, incunabula, monographs and serials, music, bound newspapers, pamphlets, technical reports, and other printed material.

2,161,976 audio materials, such as discs, tapes, and other recorded formats.

43,226,412 total manuscripts.

4,247,049 maps.

9,793,544 microforms.

16,597,335 visual materials. This total included 994,188 moving images, 13,904,668 photographs, 82,040 posters, 362,670 prints and drawings, and 1,253,769 other visual materials.

*Registered* 564,894 claims to copyright. Answered 505,598 inquiries through the Copyright Office.

*Completed* 615,913 research assignments for the Congress through the Congressional Research Service.

*Conducted* public tours for 27,954 general visitors and arranged programs, available in 25 languages, for 6,264 professional visitors.

*Coordinated* 363 special events through Special Events Office.

*Circulated* more than 21,826,000 disc, cassette, and braille items to more than 764,800 blind and physically handicapped patrons.

*Had* more than 26,000,000 records in computer databases.

*Employed* a staff of 5,033 employees.

*Operated* with a total fiscal 1993 appropriation of $334,448,000.

*Source:* Library of Congress.

# The National Library of Canada

THE NATIONAL LIBRARY OF CANADA is a federal institution located in Ottawa, whose main role is to acquire, preserve, and promote the published heritage of Canada for all Canadians, now and in the years to come. The Library houses the most comprehensive collection of Canadiana in the world—books, periodicals, sound recordings, and other materials.

## Some facts and figures

The National Library's online system, DOBIS, contains approximately 8,200,000 unique bibliographic records and has access to another 1,000 databases relevant to Canadian studies.

The National Library of Canada receives more than 30,000 Canadian periodicals on a regular basis.

Each year the National Library acquires about 55,000 new Canadian items.

Each year the Reference and Information Services Division responds to about 100,000 inquiries.

Each year the Interlibrary Loan Service lends about 270,000 items and circulates about 400,000 volumes in more than 30 Canadian heritage languages.

The National Library builds its collections through:

*Legal deposit.* Collection building at the National Library depends largely on the cooperation of Canadian publishers. Since 1953, the National Library Act has required Canadian publishers to deposit copies of their publications at the National Library including periodicals, sound recordings, educational kits, microforms and videos. *Agreements.* The National Library receives federal and provincial government publications through directives and agreements negotiated with each issuing agency. *Purchases.* The National Library uses its annual book budget to buy directly from publishers, through agents and vendors, from antiquarian book dealers and individuals in Canada and around the world. *Gifts.* Many people from all walks of life have donated individual titles or entire personal collections to the Library. *Exchanges.* The National Library has many exchange arrangements with institutions throughout the world to obtain publications not available from commercial sources.

## Services

The Canadian Book Exchange Centre offers a service to all Canadian libraries for the distribution and exchange of publications that are deemed surplus by some institutions but are of use to others.

The Library collects sheet music, scores, books, sound recordings, and archival materials that reflect Canada's musical heritage. Recognized as one of the major resources for music research in Canada, the Music Division provides in-depth reference, referral, and consultative services to libraries and organizations in Canada and abroad.

The Library's Rare Book Collection focuses on pre-Confederation Canadian imprints (1752–1867) and early books on Canada and North America published elsewhere. The Rare Book Room also houses Canadian limited editions, *livres d'artistes* received on legal deposit, and examples of private press publications from other countries.

The Multilingual Biblioservice provides more than 400,000 books in 32 heritage languages and makes them available through the Canadian public library network. The collection consists of materials for leisure reading (novels, biographies and classics) and material on popular topics such as crafts, sports, cooking, and child care. Rotation of deposits ensures access to constantly changing collections. Books are also available on interlibrary loan from the special large-print and books-on-cassette collections.

The Library Development Centre makes available for research books, periodicals, reports, documents, and databases concerning Canadian and international library and information science. Clients include staff from libraries in every province and territory, members of the Canadian publishing and cultural communities, and the international library community.

*Source:* National Library of Canada.

# Academic Libraries

# The biggest university research libraries, 1992–1993

THE FOLLOWING FIGURES are based on an index developed by the Association of Research Libraries (ARL) to measure the relative size of its university library members. The five categories used in the rankings were determined by factor analysis of 22 categories of quantitative data and represent the elements in which ARL university libraries most resemble one another. The index does not attempt to measure a library's services, quality of collections, or success in meeting the needs of users. The five data elements are: number of volumes held, number of volumes added (gross), number of current serials received, total operating expenditures, and number of professional and support staff.

This rank order table is only for 108 university library members of ARL, which has 11 nonuniversity library members. Nonuniversity libraries are not gauged by the same index formula as the universities, and are sufficiently different that it would be misleading to incorporate them into the table.

ARL does not claim that this ranking incorporates all the factors necessary to give a complete picture of research library quality. However, it is a measuring device that has proven reliable over the years for specific internal and comparative purposes.

*Volumes in library* does not include microforms, manuscripts, audiovisual and computer resources, maps, or certain other items central to research library collections and services. It includes government documents in some (but not all) cases. It is thus not a complete indicator of library resources.

*Total staff* includes professional, nonprofessional, and student assistants; however, only the first two groups are used to calculate the rank score.

*Total expenditures* include money spent on materials purchases, salaries, and general operations, but does not include capital expenditures for buildings, expenditures for plant maintenance, and some kinds of computing and administrative services; these are often part of the main university budget and not directly allocated to the library. However, such additional expenditures are crucial to an effective library and reflect the total commitment of an institution to providing and preserving research information.

1

| | Rank | Volumes in library | Volumes added | Current serials | Total staff | Total expenditures[1] |
|---|---|---|---|---|---|---|
| Harvard University | 1 | 12,505,537 | 245,643 | 96,357 | 1,129 | $57,978,016 |
| Yale University | 2 | 9,327,219 | 163,217 | 52,971 | 590 | 33,176,000 |
| University of California-Berkeley | 3 | 7,961,724 | 144,157 | 89,730 | 758 | 32,381,956 |
| University of California-Los Angeles | 4 | 6,390,409 | 175,991 | 94,612 | 527 | 29,346,248 |
| University of Illinois at Urbana-Champaign | 5 | 8,281,456 | 185,593 | 91,026 | 493 | 19,668,417 |
| University of Toronto | 6 | 6,406,524 | 185,478 | 41,103 | 646 | 30,991,448 |
| Columbia University | 7 | 6,386,712 | 139,073 | 65,000 | 604 | 27,158,173 |
| University of Texas | 8 | 6,835,983 | 173,891 | 51,689 | 627 | 22,428,945 |
| Stanford University | 9 | 6,250,671 | 142,839 | 46,397 | 606 | 35,801,401 |
| Cornell University | 10 | 5,579,629 | 173,428 | 61,015 | 585 | 28,027,033 |
| University of Michigan | 11 | 6,699,359 | 128,765 | 70,691 | 571 | 27,842,889 |
| University of Washington | 12 | 5,248,347 | 143,303 | 54,517 | 512 | 24,754,045 |
| Indiana University | 13 | 5,438,850 | 191,185 | 39,929 | 474 | 20,831,961 |
| University of Wisconsin, Madison | 14 | 5,424,299 | 118,122 | 46,651 | 519 | 24,065,100 |
| University of Minnesota | 15 | 5,008,637 | 129,858 | 52,015 | 458 | 24,534,429 |
| University of Pennsylvania | 16 | 4,099,548 | 264,165 | 33,024 | 378 | 19,827,081 |
| University of Chicago | 17 | 5,578,937 | 135,778 | 45,613 | 384 | 17,492,376 |
| Princeton University | 18 | 5,081,114 | 122,674 | 30,656 | 389 | 20,713,519 |
| Pennsylvania State University | 19 | 3,421,370 | 133,805 | 31,707 | 507 | 20,339,945 |
| University of North Carolina at Chapel Hill | 20 | 4,059,441 | 112,493 | 38,288 | 415 | 18,082,240 |
| Ohio State University | 21 | 4,693,081 | 110,647 | 33,010 | 431 | 18,021,179 |
| Rutgers University | 22 | 3,441,294 | 83,431 | 32,564 | 469 | 23,603,845 |
| University of Virginia | 23 | 3,948,504 | 109,970 | 44,349 | 352 | 16,391,905 |
| Duke University | 24 | 4,234,985 | 110,504 | 32,732 | 358 | 17,346,777 |
| University of British Columbia | 25 | 3,347,672 | 122,953 | 22,787 | 410 | 19,807,345 |
| University of Alberta | 26 | 3,389,394 | 152,561 | 21,972 | 350 | 16,160,087 |
| University of Arizona | 27 | 4,018,071 | 114,197 | 28,662 | 359 | 16,152,251 |
| New York University | 28 | 3,273,708 | 68,472 | 28,689 | 434 | 21,042,947 |
| Arizona State University | 29 | 2,922,157 | 102,389 | 32,241 | 361 | 16,106,184 |
| Northwestern University | 30 | 3,642,790 | 78,204 | 37,424 | 343 | 15,857,232 |
| University of California-Davis | 31 | 2,659,270 | 81,558 | 50,298 | 324 | 15,231,633 |
| University of Georgia | 32 | 3,131,402 | 82,911 | 47,993 | 335 | 13,593,007 |
| University of Pittsburgh | 33 | 3,122,798 | 89,968 | 24,991 | 369 | 15,672,214 |
| University of Iowa | 34 | 3,317,265 | 69,383 | 40,047 | 283 | 14,050,389 |
| University of Kansas | 35 | 3,193,850 | 81,733 | 33,047 | 321 | 13,130,657 |
| Johns Hopkins University | 36 | 3,012,364 | 68,001 | 21,172 | 319 | 17,923,556 |
| University of Southern Calif. | 37 | 3,168,969 | 76,861 | 24,832 | 311 | 15,478,970 |
| University of California-San Diego | 38 | 2,241,696 | 78,173 | 24,414 | 367 | 15,623,336 |
| University of Florida | 39 | 3,022,768 | 51,877 | 24,191 | 402 | 14,577,203 |
| University of Hawaii | 40 | 2,718,618 | 89,339 | 36,592 | 246 | 12,107,103 |
| Michigan State University | 41 | 2,939,376 | 88,695 | 27,876 | 289 | 12,956,601 |
| McGill University | 42 | 2,766,775 | 68,580 | 18,524 | 321 | 13,989,375 |
| Wayne State University | 43 | 2,752,167 | 88,868 | 24,468 | 252 | 12,532,336 |
| State University of New York at Buffalo | 44 | 2,797,145 | 87,882 | 22,593 | 263 | 12,092,366 |
| Texas A&M University | 45 | 2,154,600 | 121,069 | 16,187 | 355 | 12,398,022 |
| University of Colorado | 46 | 2,504,405 | 78,943 | 27,727 | 241 | 13,501,424 |
| Washington University (Mo.) | 47 | 2,979,934 | 63,708 | 18,601 | 293 | 13,524,921 |
| Emory University | 48 | 2,212,507 | 68,136 | 22,842 | 257 | 14,255,332 |
| Georgetown University | 49 | 1,965,113 | 61,493 | 24,763 | 273 | 14,134,147 |

[1]Figures for Canadian libraries are expressed in U.S. dollars.

| | Rank | Volumes in library | Volumes added | Current serials | Total staff | Total expenditures |
|---|---|---|---|---|---|---|
| University of Maryland | 50 | 2,231,552 | 63,163 | 19,433 | 336 | $14,211,800 |
| Laval University | 51 | 1,987,510 | 72,304 | 16,975 | 265 | 12,903,464 |
| University of Kentucky | 52 | 2,515,874 | 59,923 | 26,889 | 302 | 11,017,533 |
| University of Connecticut | 53 | 2,442,215 | 89,838 | 16,924 | 232 | 13,257,582 |
| University of Miami | 54 | 1,875,556 | 84,325 | 18,890 | 257 | 12,265,696 |
| University of Western Ontario | 55 | 2,104,301 | 63,855 | 18,770 | 262 | 12,568,328 |
| Massachusetts Institute of Technology | 56 | 2,320,524 | 59,646 | 21,136 | 236 | 11,703,150 |
| York University (Ontario) | 57 | 2,011,251 | 65,483 | 19,312 | 258 | 12,175,242 |
| Vanderbilt University | 58 | 2,085,652 | 66,068 | 16,357 | 279 | 12,400,106 |
| University of Missouri | 59 | 2,630,419 | 58,017 | 22,688 | 248 | 9,800,337 |
| University of Utah | 60 | 2,345,111 | 76,056 | 19,572 | 304 | 11,458,576 |
| University of New Mexico | 61 | 1,859,848 | 47,229 | 21,795 | 311 | 13,391,678 |
| University of California-Santa Barbara | 62 | 2,126,774 | 53,221 | 24,325 | 240 | 11,447,525 |
| Boston University | 63 | 1,895,723 | 57,344 | 28,512 | 250 | 10,802,180 |
| University of Illinois at Chicago | 64 | 1,782,637 | 47,339 | 21,119 | 265 | 12,311,435 |
| University of South Carolina | 65 | 2,576,311 | 53,490 | 19,232 | 234 | 10,587,879 |
| University of Notre Dame | 66 | 2,252,029 | 63,451 | 21,727 | 214 | 9,037,724 |
| University of Tennessee | 67 | 2,021,903 | 64,811 | 18,881 | 255 | 10,395,983 |
| Dartmouth College | 68 | 1,992,074 | 83,844 | 20,143 | 184 | 10,154,627 |
| Brown University | 69 | 2,606,259 | 59,299 | 13,533 | 255 | 11,215,205 |
| Purdue University | 70 | 2,076,302 | 67,814 | 14,139 | 261 | 10,627,758 |
| University of Cincinnati | 71 | 1,947,773 | 49,562 | 19,574 | 272 | 11,831,437 |
| Brigham Young University | 72 | 2,262,029 | 69,112 | 17,698 | 291 | 11,540,081 |
| Syracuse University | 73 | 2,572,485 | 45,932 | 16,477 | 256 | 9,876,449 |
| University of Nebraska | 74 | 2,164,254 | 59,585 | 21,671 | 219 | 9,194,016 |
| Auburn University | 75 | 2,140,856 | 83,564 | 21,611 | 196 | 7,817,308 |
| Temple University | 76 | 2,189,431 | 52,069 | 15,699 | 238 | 10,882,911 |
| University of Massachusetts | 77 | 2,575,292 | 64,875 | 15,546 | 191 | 9,260,118 |
| University of Delaware | 78 | 2,119,899 | 50,639 | 20,941 | 218 | 9,716,097 |
| Howard University | 79 | 1,905,110 | 37,576 | 25,564 | 211 | 9,599,571 |
| Iowa State University | 80 | 1,994,376 | 42,218 | 21,547 | 208 | 12,005,617 |
| Louisiana State University | 81 | 2,709,757 | 56,559 | 16,169 | 218 | 8,966,596 |
| Florida State University | 82 | 2,028,509 | 53,599 | 18,420 | 240 | 8,754,797 |
| Queen's University | 83 | 1,937,296 | 60,973 | 14,800 | 205 | 9,561,602 |
| University of California-Irvine | 84 | 1,598,488 | 45,389 | 17,550 | 219 | 12,247,934 |
| Tulane University | 85 | 1,943,858 | 58,415 | 16,934 | 195 | 8,805,861 |
| University of Southern Illinois | 86 | 2,248,064 | 57,508 | 17,047 | 214 | 8,956,072 |
| University of Rochester | 87 | 2,812,892 | 42,243 | 12,885 | 214 | 9,277,901 |
| University of Oregon | 88 | 2,024,323 | 45,650 | 17,914 | 217 | 10,233,298 |
| Virginia Polytechnic Institute and State University | 89 | 1,849,994 | 55,284 | 18,288 | 194 | 9,350,312 |
| North Carolina State University | 90 | 1,485,041 | 48,781 | 18,086 | 229 | 10,413,684 |
| University of Oklahoma | 91 | 2,430,404 | 52,258 | 17,400 | 193 | 8,429,979 |
| University of Waterloo | 92 | 1,716,502 | 49,962 | 16,196 | 175 | 9,238,348 |
| Oklahoma State University | 93 | 1,705,986 | 87,031 | 17,553 | 183 | 7,892,909 |
| State University of New York at Stony Brook | 94 | 1,848,618 | 42,158 | 16,952 | 205 | 10,374,810 |
| Washington State University | 95 | 1,717,764 | 38,711 | 24,038 | 188 | 9,207,768 |
| University of Saskatchewan | 96 | 1,547,741 | 60,922 | 13,820 | 181 | 8,369,785 |
| McMaster University | 97 | 1,654,619 | 40,396 | 14,921 | 192 | 9,447,302 |
| University of Manitoba | 98 | 1,609,237 | 39,003 | 11,928 | 222 | 9,933,876 |
| University of Alabama | 99 | 1,949,073 | 49,502 | 16,164 | 188 | 7,937,213 |
| Colorado State University | 100 | 1,505,169 | 63,724 | 20,868 | 153 | 7,769,201 |
| University of Houston | 101 | 1,754,375 | 49,696 | 14,437 | 207 | 8,872,227 |

| | Volumes Rank | Volumes in library | Current added | Total serials | Total staff | Total expenditures |
|---|---|---|---|---|---|---|
| Kent State University | 102 | 2,139,129 | 42,074 | 11,146 | 228 | $8,811,149 |
| Rice University | 103 | 1,794,602 | 57,507 | 13,725 | 142 | 8,284,248 |
| University of Guelph | 104 | 2,058,632 | 46,902 | 12,945 | 155 | 7,201,213 |
| Case Western Reserve University | 105 | 1,802,042 | 37,874 | 14,344 | 187 | 8,625,221 |
| State University of New York at Albany | 106 | 1,748,697 | 37,336 | 16,039 | 175 | 7,641,624 |
| University of California-Riverside | 107 | 1,682,006 | 41,850 | 13,621 | 171 | 7,493,525 |
| Georgia Institute of Technology | 108 | 1,771,934 | 35,415 | 11,381 | 111 | 5,327,085 |

Source: Association of Research Libraries, *ARL Statistics 1992–1993* (Washington, D.C.: ARL, 1994).

# Data from non-ARL university libraries, 1993

THE FOLLOWING STATISTICS are from North American research universities and doctorate-granting institutions that are not members of the Association of Research Libraries. Data were compiled by the ALA Association of College and Research Libraries. Institutions are arranged by number of volumes in the library and not by a ranking similar to the ARL list.

| | Volumes in library | Volumes added | Current serials | Total staff | Total expenditures |
|---|---|---|---|---|---|
| Université de Montréal | 2,245,482 | 62,675 | 16,993 | 325 | $14,784,470 |
| Southern Methodist University | 2,197,215 | 50,896 | 4,784 | 169 | 7,953,395 |
| Claremont Colleges | 1,843,798 | 44,278 | 4,215 | 87 | 4,632,684 |
| Texas Tech University | 1,833,798 | 54,905 | 17,413 | 203 | 8,240,504 |
| Bowling Green State University | 1,798,711 | 41,054 | 7,602 | 173 | 6,680,179 |
| University of Wisconsin-Milwaukee | 1,785,170 | 42,447 | 8,239 | 141 | 6,472,004 |
| West Virginia University | 1,706,768 | 21,746 | 11,099 | 196 | 6,436,817 |
| Ohio University | 1,642,952 | 54,503 | 22,485 | 173 | 8,073,409 |
| Fordham University | 1,574,042 | 30,368 | 12,677 | 111 | 5,363,261 |
| North Texas State University | 1,557,017 | 38,789 | 10,525 | 173 | 5,255,824 |
| University of Windsor | 1,529,092 | 84,100 | 7,080 | 124 | 6,042,601 |
| Baylor University | 1,510,111 | N/A | 9,171 | 139 | 5,839,078 |
| State University of New York at Binghamton | 1,471,424 | 43,921 | 9,443 | 143 | 7,064,754 |
| Miami University | 1,438,750 | 31,261 | 7,294 | 154 | 5,230,094 |
| University of Ottawa | 1,433,318 | 34,963 | 11,014 | 218 | 9,998,070 |
| University of Arkansas, Fayetteville | 1,392,403 | 36,088 | 16,540 | 160 | 6,413,929 |
| Northern Illinois University | 1,354,657 | 28,348 | 13,215 | 182 | 6,555,258 |
| St. Louis University | 1,338,931 | 36,590 | 13,183 | 159 | 6,776,870 |
| Catholic University | 1,321,879 | 25,945 | 8,961 | 96 | 3,010,764 |
| Boston College | 1,318,437 | 41,913 | 14,619 | 209 | 10,126,555 |
| Loyola University (Chicago) | 1,309,832 | 48,310 | 11,843 | 197 | 10,478,770 |
| George Washington University | 1,291,356 | 32,637 | 8,020 | 156 | 9,664,566 |
| Kansas State University | 1,276,462 | 34,213 | 9,609 | 136 | 5,988,983 |
| Oregon State University | 1,246,307 | 29,249 | 18,800 | 127 | 6,975,424 |
| Illinois State University | 1,237,815 | 30,861 | 9,600 | 172 | 5,672,678 |
| College of William and Mary | 1,203,718 | 35,539 | 10,133 | 108 | 6,186,800 |

| | Volumes in library | Volumes added | Current serials | Total staff | Total expenditures |
|---|---|---|---|---|---|
| University of Louisville | 1,196,410 | 39,482 | 12,131 | 181 | $9,240,108 |
| Georgia State University | 1,185,801 | 33,554 | 11,157 | 167 | 5,785,624 |
| Utah State University | 1,177,282 | 42,769 | 13,994 | 98 | 4,524,203 |
| Indiana State University | 1,160,450 | 32,465 | 5,663 | 102 | 3,400,862 |
| St. John's University | 1,148,601 | 35,552 | 15,034 | 187 | 8,939,056 |
| University of Vermont | 1,105,649 | 28,523 | 17,229 | 129 | 5,983,855 |
| Western Michigan University | 1,104,251 | 37,934 | 10,016 | 134 | 5,798,373 |
| University of Wyoming | 1,096,703 | 29,449 | 16,090 | 117 | 4,793,237 |
| University of Denver | 1,078,325 | 22,705 | 4,796 | 87 | 2,694,311 |
| University of California-Santa Cruz | 1,065,529 | 30,364 | 9,663 | 136 | 7,269,342 |
| Hofstra University | 1,063,772 | N/A | 2,786 | 116 | 5,404,796 |
| Lehigh University | 1,059,491 | 37,744 | 10,994 | 85 | 4,872,023 |
| University of New Brunswick | 1,045,147 | 20,362 | 5,839 | 108 | 4,405,337 |
| Ball State University | 1,041,232 | 26,926 | 5,703 | 177 | 5,972,284 |
| Virginia Commonwealth University | 1,030,463 | 49,238 | 9,932 | 162 | 8,132,962 |
| University of New Hampshire | 1,024,911 | 25,174 | 7,000 | 117 | 4,136,855 |
| Northern Arizona University | 1,023,658 | 36,945 | 5,398 | 104 | 4,206,868 |
| University of Rhode Island | 1,019,029 | 30,996 | 9,759 | 95 | 4,705,571 |
| Memphis State University | 986,699 | 15,222 | 9,218 | 125 | 4,566,437 |
| Brandeis University | 938,072 | 25,476 | 7,142 | 92 | 4,314,302 |
| Portland State University | 930,693 | 26,444 | 11,132 | 98 | 5,149,681 |
| University of Missouri, Kansas City | 925,453 | 22,240 | 8,583 | 112 | 3,437,074 |
| New Mexico State University | 924,614 | 24,326 | 8,389 | 140 | 4,395,913 |
| University of Akron | 897,779 | 34,902 | 4,826 | 110 | 4,450,593 |
| University of Texas at Arlington | 897,292 | 47,566 | 8,035 | 151 | 5,283,433 |
| University of Mississippi | 896,517 | 23,643 | 9,131 | 93 | 4,035,700 |
| University of South Florida | 880,261 | 21,926 | 4,452 | 147 | 5,132,705 |
| University of Southern Mississippi | 868,477 | 15,540 | 4,770 | 88 | 3,273,209 |
| University of Nevada, Reno | 861,089 | 28,946 | 12,914 | 119 | 6,165,158 |
| Mississippi State University | 859,306 | 17,316 | 7,189 | 88 | 3,748,632 |
| Cleveland State University | 856,978 | 29,454 | 6,918 | 89 | 4,056,084 |
| University of North Dakota | 847,181 | 14,099 | 8,673 | 63 | 2,353,428 |
| Marquette University | 846,978 | 28,343 | 6,054 | 104 | 4,873,540 |
| University of North Carolina, Greensboro | 830,530 | 24,996 | 5,525 | 95 | 4,247,851 |
| Carnegie-Mellon University | 828,109 | 25,522 | 4,061 | 112 | 4,533,313 |
| University of Maine at Orono | 826,648 | 31,571 | 14,590 | 84 | 4,333,979 |
| University of Idaho | 805,139 | N/A | 10,296 | 72 | 3,188,469 |
| Clemson University | 797,997 | 32,978 | 6,831 | 124 | 5,911,903 |
| Texas Woman's University | 782,573 | 6,351 | 3,072 | 76 | 2,399,409 |
| University of Tulsa | 762,925 | 22,369 | 7,756 | 87 | 3,651,342 |
| Texas Christian University | 748,887 | 25,381 | 3,637 | 75 | 3,396,807 |
| Northeastern University | 738,193 | 48,349 | 8,698 | 184 | 7,804,915 |
| University of Alaska | 703,051 | 14,412 | 5,926 | 99 | 4,711,539 |
| Old Dominion University | 655,677 | 24,014 | 6,792 | 84 | 3,955,155 |
| University of Montana | 649,993 | 13,039 | 4,656 | 64 | 3,065,536 |
| American University | 598,386 | 16,853 | 4,877 | 100 | 4,054,819 |
| Florida Atlantic University | 592,131 | 33,282 | 4,670 | 124 | 3,690,452 |
| University of New Orleans | 591,545 | 10,197 | 5,909 | 72 | 2,603,881 |
| University of Missouri, St. Louis | 583,134 | 14,215 | 8,995 | 67 | 2,587,833 |
| University of San Francisco | 577,404 | 17,666 | 2,409 | 36 | 2,248,758 |
| Middle Tennessee State University | 576,751 | 16,039 | 3,528 | 70 | 2,835,533 |
| University of Maryland, Baltimore County | 567,159 | 23,995 | 4,114 | 60 | 3,158,453 |
| Tufts University | 565,082 | 15,874 | 2,424 | 74 | 3,568,981 |
| Andrews University | 554,440 | 11,771 | 2,957 | 52 | 1,924,049 |
| East Texas State University | 533,621 | 8,120 | 2,166 | 67 | 1,690,868 |

| | Volumes in library | Volumes added | Current serials | Total staff | Total expenditures |
|---|---|---|---|---|---|
| Montana State University | 515,214 | 22,027 | 5,078 | 62 | $3,144,920 |
| Clark University | 505,307 | 9,529 | 1,891 | 41 | 1,759,947 |
| California Institute of Technology | 498,812 | 13,145 | 4,600 | 65 | 4,347,207 |
| Idaho State University | 498,786 | 12,565 | 3,383 | 61 | 2,401,230 |
| University of Texas at Dallas | 498,661 | 24,376 | 2,918 | 64 | 4,233,186 |
| Drexel University | 493,537 | 7,381 | 4,126 | 56 | 2,328,955 |
| Duquesne University | 491,509 | 13,132 | 2,112 | 87 | 1,637,373 |
| South Dakota State University | 474,903 | 12,226 | 3,052 | 40 | 2,014,194 |
| Adelphi University | 473,098 | 14,102 | 3,514 | 88 | 3,591,450 |
| Drake University | 463,492 | 9,070 | 2,600 | 43 | 1,805,000 |
| North Dakota State University | 455,338 | 10,466 | 5,345 | 68 | 2,350,114 |
| University of Missouri, Rolla | 447,229 | 6,682 | 1,394 | 29 | 1,312,994 |
| University of South Dakota | 445,215 | 12,273 | 2,687 | 38 | 1,818,280 |
| University of the Pacific | 432,661 | 7,093 | 2,504 | 41 | 1,617,196 |
| Tennessee Technical University | 383,616 | 13,157 | 3,799 | 57 | 2,027,403 |
| Pepperdine University | 351,175 | 8,256 | 1,421 | 51 | 2,229,373 |
| Louisiana Technical University | 349,780 | 7,344 | 2,627 | 52 | 1,838,020 |

*Source:* Library Research Center, Graduate School of Library and Information Science, University of Illinois at Urbana-Champaign, *ACRL University Library Statistics, 1992–1993* (Chicago: ALA Association of College and Research Libraries, 1994).

# Biggest academic library collections in 1849

| Institution | Volumes held |
|---|---|
| Harvard | 68,000 |
| Yale | 47,700 |
| Brown | 30,200 |
| Georgetown | 26,100 |
| Bowdoin | 21,500 |
| South Carolina | 18,400 |
| Virginia | 18,400 |
| Princeton | 16,000 |
| Union | 14,600 |
| Dickinson | 14,500 |
| Amherst | 13,700 |
| Columbia | 12,700 |
| Vermont | 12,300 |
| North Carolina | 12,300 |
| Wesleyan | 11,100 |
| Williams | 10,600 |
| Franklin | 10,300 |
| Hamilton | 10,300 |
| Waterville | 8,500 |

*Source:* Kenneth J. Brough, *Scholar's Workshop: Evolving Conceptions of Library Service* (Urbana: University of Illinois Press, 1953), pp.14–15. ©1953, 1981 by the Board of Trustees of the University of Illinois. Used with permission of the University of Illinois Press.

# Academic libraries, 1990

ACCORDING TO A 1990 SURVEY by the Integrated Postsecondary Education Data System:

- In 1990, total operating expenditures for libraries at the 3,274 institutions of higher education totaled $3.3 billion.
- The three largest individual expenditure items were salaries and wages, $1.7 billion (52.0%); current serial subscription expenditures, $549 million (16.8%); and print material expenditures, $402 million (12.3%).
- The libraries of the 488 doctoral-granting institutions (14.9% of the total institutions) accounted for $1.9 billion (58.0%) of the total operating expenditure dollars at all college and university libraries.
- The number of volumes held at all academic libraries at the end of fiscal year 1990 totaled about 717 million.
- Libraries at institutions granting doctoral degrees held about 437 million volumes (61.0%) of the total volumes for all academic libraries.
- The total number of full-time equivalent (FTE) staff members in college and university libraries equaled about 100,000, including about 26,000 librarians and other professional staff, 42,000 other paid staff, 30,000 student assistants, and 1,400 staff who contributed their services.
- Libraries at institutions granting doctoral degrees accounted for 52,000, or half of FTE staff at all academic libraries.
- Academic libraries had 199 million circulation transactions; 80.4% from general collections, and 19.6% from reserve collections.
- Libraries at institutions granting doctoral degrees accounted for more than half of this total circulation, with 105 million circulation transactions.

*Source:* National Center for Education Statistics, *Academic Libraries: 1990* (Washington, D.C.: U.S. Gov't Printing Office, December 1992). 57p.

# Learning resources programs in two-year colleges: Basic and additional services

THIS CHECKLIST IS TAKEN FROM Appendixes A and B of the draft *Standards for Community, Junior, and Technical College Learning Resources Programs* (1994).

## Checklist of basic learning resources center (LRC) services and activities

Listed below are specific services that are considered to be normal and basic library services in two-year college learning resources or emerging program budgets. This list may not include future or emerging technologies and services. Inclusion does not mean that an institution should have every activity or service listed.

**1**

**Acquisitions, cataloging, maintenance, preservation, and/or circulation of:**
- Audiovisual materials/ programs
- Books
- College archives including institutional publications
- Computer programs
- Government documents
- Laser optical (CD-ROM) resources
- Local history materials
- Microforms
- Periodicals
- Special collections

**Computer systems management and maintenance:**
- Computer programs
- Gateway and Internet access
- Integrated automation systems
- Local area networks (LANs) and wide area networks (WANs)
- Public access computers

**Equipment services:**
- Equipment inventory, scheduling, and distribution
- Equipment maintenance and repair
- Equipment specifications and purchase
- Group viewing services
- Public access listening/ viewing area

**Instructional services:**
- Bibliographic instruction courses
- Bibliographies
- Computer literacy
- Copyright consultation
- Group orientation
- Individualized

instruction and/or self-paced learning assistance
- Instructional design and development
- Media orientation and instruction
- Online databases searching
- Point-of-use guides, pathfinders, and study guides
- Reference service
- Reserve materials
- Staff development
- Telephone reference

**Production services:**
- Audio duplication, editing, and recording
- Copy machines, paper and microforms
- Drymounting and lamination
- Graphic layout and design
- Interactive video
- Multimedia
- Photography and darkroom
- Satellite communications downlink
- Scripting
- Teleconference services
- Telecourse and distance learning distribution
- Transparencies and slides
- Video duplication, recording, and editing

**Resource sharing services:**
- Bibliographic networks
- Gateway services
- Interlibrary loan (ILL)
- Internet
- Reciprocal borrowing
- Rental and free-loan materials
- Union catalogs of local resources

## Checklist of additional services components

This list includes services that require capital funds, space, personnel, and operating budgets in excess of those recommended as basic in the *Standards for Community, Junior, and Technical College Learning Resources Programs* (1994).

**Community Services.**
**Curriculum:**
  • Library technician
    education
  • Bibliographic instruction
    courses
**Faculty development.**
**Government documents depository.**
**Joint-use:**
  • Museum
  • Other academic library
  • Public library
  • School library
**Laboratories:**
  • Career
  • Learning development
  • Literacy
  • Self-paced learning
  • Testing

  • Tutoring
**Literacy programs.**
**Printing:**
  • College catalogs
  • Copy services (not self-
    serve)
  • Literary or other
    academic college
    publications
  • Print shop
**Student ID service.**
**Television/radio:**
  • Radio broadcast
  • Satellite uplink
  • Telecourse administration
  • Telecourse production
  • Television broadcast
  • Television station/Radio
    station administration

## Library space

Since some public higher education regulatory agencies issue space formulas for campus facilities, building planners should investigate guidelines that exist in their state early in the planning process. The following is an example of a state-mandated formula.

**Example: California Community Colleges Facilities Standards—Library Space**
(from *Title 5: California Code of Regulations, Section 57030*)
Note: This table is an example of California Standards.

All library space shall be computed by assignable square feet (ASF) for library functions as specified in the subdivisions of this section. Square feet are "assignable" only if they are usable for the function described. Areas such as the main lobby (excluding card catalog area), elevators, stairs, walled corridors, restrooms, and areas accommodating building maintenance services are not deemed usable for any of the described functions.

| Stack space | = | .1 ASF x Number of Bound Volumes | | |
|---|---|---|---|---|
| | | Number of Volumes: | | |
| | | Initial Increment = 16,000 volumes | | |
| | | Additional Increments: | | |
| | | (a) Under 3,000 DGE* | = | +8 volumes per DGS** |
| | | (b) 3,000–9,000 DGE | = | +7 volumes per DGS |
| | | (c) Above 9,000 DGE | = | +6 volumes per DGS |

| Staff Space | = | (140 ASF x Number of FTE staff) + 400 ASF | | |
|---|---|---|---|---|
| | | Number of FTE staff: | | |
| | | Initial Increment = 3.0 FTE | | |
| | | Additional Increments: | | |
| | | (a) Under 3,000 DGE | = | +.0020 FTE staff per DGS |
| | | (b) 3,000–9,000 DGE | = | +.0015 FTE staff per DGS |
| | | (c) Above 9,000 DGE | = | +.0010 FTE staff per DGS |

Reader Station Space= 27.5 ASF x Number of reader stations
Number of reader stations:   Initial Increment = 50 stations

Additional Increments:
(a) Under 3,000 DGE  =  +.10 stations per DGS
(b) 3,000–9,000 DGE  =  +.09 stations per DGS
(c) Above 9,000 DGE  =  +.08 stations per DGS

| Total Space | = | Initial Increment = 3,795 ASF |
| | | Additional Increments: |
| | | (a) Under 3,000 DGE  =  +3.83 ASF per DGS |
| | | (b) 3,000–9,000 DGE  =  +3.39 ASF per DGS |
| | | (c) Above 9,000 DGE  =  +2.94 ASF per DGS |

For audiovisual and programmed instruction activities associated with learning resource functions, additional areas sized for individual needs but not exceeding the following totals for the district as a whole.

| Total Space | = | Initial Increment = 3,500 ASF |
| | | Additional Increments: |
| | | (a) Under 3,000 DGE  =  +1.50 ASF per DGS |
| | | (b) 3,000–9,000 DGE  =  +0.75 ASF per DGS |
| | | (c) Above 9,000 DGE  =  +0.25 ASF per DGS |

\* Day-Graded Enrollment  =  use FTES
\*\* Day-Graded Student  =  use FTES

*Source: Standards for Community, Junior and Technical College Learning Resources Programs* (Chicago: ALA Association of College and Research Libraries, 1994). 14p.

# Public Libraries

## Public library records

Most bookmobiles ........................................ St. Louis County (Mo.) Library: 18
Most branches ............................................ County of Los Angeles (Calif.) PL: 86
Highest director's salary ......................... Los Angeles (Calif.) PL: $110,000
Highest entry-level salary ...................... County of Los Angeles (Calif.) PL: $49,032
Most reference transactions ................... Miami-Dade (Fla.) PL System: 5,784,641
Most interlibrary loans to others ........... Hutchinson (Kan.) PL: 134,611
Most interlibrary loans from others ...... Kern County (Calif.) Library: 96,035
Most expenditures per capita ............... Middle County (N.Y.) PL: $108.30
Most materials expenditures
    per capita ......................................... Lisle (Ill.) Library District: $13.45
Highest registrations as % of
    population ....................................... R.P. Flower Memorial Library, Watertown
        (N.Y.): 225.1%
Highest circulation per registered
    borrower ........................................... Warren (Mich.) PL: 126

*Source: Statistical Report '94: Public Library Data Service* (Chicago: ALA Public Library Association, 1994). 155p.

# The 20 largest public libraries

THE NUMBER OF VOLUMES a library owns is not a measure of the quality of library service. However, volume counts do have a certain fascination. The following are the largest public libraries in North America, according to 1994 data. (San Francisco PL, which ranked 4th in 1993, was not included in the 1994 data.)

New York (N.Y.) Public Library (The Research Libraries) ............ 10,534,818
Queens Borough (N.Y.) Public Library .................................. 9,271,960
Free Library of Philadelphia (Pa.) .................................... 6,687,777
Carnegie Library of Pittsburgh (Pa.) .................................. 6,409,300
Boston (Mass.) Public Library ......................................... 6,319,206
Chicago (Ill.) Public Library ......................................... 6,037,756
County of Los Angeles (Calif.) Public Library ........................ 6,006,780
Brooklyn (N.Y.) Public Library ........................................ 5,859,444
Los Angeles (Calif.) Public Library ................................... 5,000,000
Public Library of Cincinnati and Hamilton County (Ohio) ........... 4,542,300
Houston (Tex.) Public Library ......................................... 4,020,637
Buffalo & Erie County (N.Y.) Public Library .......................... 3,924,898
Bibliothèque de Montréal, Quebec ...................................... 3,442,992
Miami-Dade (Fla.) Public Library System ............................. 3,350,200
King County (Wash.) Library System .................................... 2,861,159
Cleveland (Ohio) Public Library ....................................... 2,759,613
Rosenberg Library, Galveston, Tex. .................................... 2,680,261
Detroit (Mich.) Public Library ........................................ 2,672,754
Enoch Pratt Free Library, Baltimore, Md. ............................ 2,668,228
Fairfax County (Va.) Public Library ................................... 2,524,377

Source: Statistical Report '94: Public Library Data Service
(Chicago: ALA Public Library Association, 1994). 155p.

# Key dates in public library history

**ca. 240 B.C.**—The first public library in Athens was established in a gymnasium (the Ptolemaion) on the initiative of Ptolemy Philadelphus.

**37 B.C.**—Asinius Pollio founded the first public library in Rome, combining Varro's collection with that of Sulla's.

**1258**—Thirty-six libraries open to the public existed in Baghdad at the time of the Mongol invasion.

**1656**—Captain Robert Keayne endowed his collection for a public library in Boston on the condition that the town authorities provide a building to house it.

**1731**—Benjamin Franklin founded the Library Company of Philadelphia as the first American subscription library.

**1774**—The Library Company of Philadelphia made its resources available to the members of the First Continental Congress.

**1787**—The first free public library was founded in Newington, Conn.

**1800**—One of the first endowed town libraries, the Hale Donation Library, was established in Coventry, Conn.

**1827**—A municipally supported juvenile library was established in Lexington, Mass.

**1833**—Peterborough, N.H., established the first municipally supported, free public library.

1834—The first general library in Chicago, the Chicago Lyceum, was established.

1835—New York enacted a state law permitting tax-supported, free library service in each school district through a school district library to be used by the general public.

1848—Boston became the first city in the United States to levy a tax for the establishment of a public library.

1849—The first public subscription library in California was organized in Monterey.

1886—The first Carnegie library grant was to the Allegheny Library (now a part of Pittsburgh), Pa.

1890—Cleveland Public Library became the first large public library to adopt an unrestricted open access policy.

1905—The first horse-drawn library wagon was created by Mary Lemist Titcomb, librarian of the Washington County Free Library, Hagerstown, Md.

1912—The first motorized bookmobile was established by the Washington County Free Library. It was an International Harvester Autowagon with a specially built body for carrying books.

*Sources:* George S. Bobinski, *Carnegie Libraries: Their History and Impact on American Public Library Development* (Chicago: American Library Association, 1969); Luciano Canfora, *The Vanished Library* (London: Hutchinson Radius, 1989); Paul Dickson, *The Library in America: A Celebration in Words and Pictures* (New York: Facts on File, 1986); D. N. Marshall, *History of Libraries: Ancient and Mediaeval* (New Delhi: Oxford & IBH, 1983); Elizabeth W. Stone, *American Library Development, 1600–1899* (New York: H.W. Wilson, 1977).

# Public opinion on the role of the public library

TWO NATIONWIDE GALLUP POLLS were undertaken in 1992, sampling 1,000 members of the general public and 300 community opinion leaders. Both groups were asked to evaluate the importance to their communities of each of the public library roles that appear in the *Planning and Role Setting for Public Libraries* manual published by ALA. The results were reported by Dr. George D'Elia, associate professor in the Carlson School of Management at the University of Minnesota.—*GME.*

Public library roles were evaluated in terms of their importance to the community using the categories "not important," "slightly important," "moderately important," or "very important."

## Sample of 1,000 members of the general public

| Public library role | % responding "very important" |
|---|---|
| Formal education support center | 88% |
| Independent learning center | 85% |
| Preschoolers' door to learning | 83% |
| Research center | 68% |
| Community information center | 66% |
| Reference library—business | 55% |
| Public workplace | 52% |
| Popular materials library | 51% |

| Public library role | % responding "very important" |
|---|---|
| Reference library—personal | 48% |
| Community activities center | 41% |

## Sample of 300 community opinion leaders

| Public library role | % responding "very important" |
|---|---|
| Formal education support center | 88% |
| Preschoolers' door to learning | 81% |
| Independent learning center | 78% |
| Community information center | 65% |
| Research center | 56% |
| Popular materials library | 53% |
| Reference library—business | 47% |
| Community activities center | 46% |
| Reference library—personal | 38% |
| Public workplace | 38% |

*Source:* George D'Elia, *The Roles of the Public Library in Society: The Results of a National Survey* (Evanston, Ill.: Urban Libraries Council, 1993). 225p. Reprinted with permission.

# How the states rank, 1991

DATA ON PUBLIC LIBRARY operating expenditures, local income, circulation and reference transactions, and staff expenditures are given for 1991. The rankings were compiled by the National Data Resource Center of the National Center for Education Statistics using data submitted in July 1992 to NCES through the Federal State Cooperative System for public library data (FSCS).

| State | Operating Expenditures | Per Capita | Rank | Rank for Local Income | Rank for Circulation Transactions | Rank for Reference Transactions | Rank for Total Staff $ |
|---|---|---|---|---|---|---|---|
| D.C.* | $21,615,000 | $35.62 | 1 | 1 | 49 | 3 | 1 |
| N.Y. | 546,215,009 | 30.36 | 2 | 7 | 23 | 2 | 2 |
| Alaska | 16,415,123 | 28.64 | 3 | 2 | 30 | 35 | 5 |
| Ohio | 307,297,856 | 28.34 | 4 | 49 | 1 | 6 | 6 |
| N.J. | 206,384,309 | 27.35 | 5 | 3 | 33 | 22 | 3 |
| Ct. | 82,752,410 | 27.20 | 6 | 5 | 15 | 13 | 4 |
| Md. | 118,087,065 | 25.52 | 7 | 11 | 2 | 1 | 7 |
| Wash. | 115,248,329 | 23.79 | 8 | 6 | 3 | 9 | 8 |
| Ind. | 117,148,315 | 22.80 | 9 | 9 | 5 | 18 | 14 |
| Ill. | 231,292,666 | 22.72 | 10 | 4 | 20 | 11 | 11 |
| Wyo. | 10,160,118 | 22.40 | 11 | 8 | 8 | 40 | 10 |
| Mass. | 123,749,490 | 21.36 | 12 | 13 | 22 | 20 | 9 |
| Minn. | 90,057,819 | 20.58 | 13 | 14 | 4 | 8 | 12 |
| Colo. | 67,540,321 | 20.51 | 14 | 10 | 17 | 17 | 16 |
| Hawaii | 21,488,698 | 19.39 | 15 | 51 | 31 | 12 | 18 |
| Wisc. | 94,002,947 | 19.10 | 16 | 16 | 10 | 15 | 15 |
| Va. | 112,512,178 | 18.79 | 17 | 20 | 19 | 10 | 17 |
| R.I. | 17,444,256 | 18.63 | 18 | 23 | 26 | 51 | 13 |
| Ore. | 47,456,708 | 17.86 | 19 | 15 | 6 | 23 | 20 |
| Calif. | 532,218,934 | 17.54 | 20 | 17 | 38 | 7 | 21 |
| Kan. | 33,202,726 | 17.41 | 21 | 12 | 7 | 5 | 22 |
| N.H. | 18,846,582 | 17.40 | 22 | 21 | 18 | 29 | 19 |
| Nev. | 19,719,075 | 16.41 | 23 | 18 | 34 | 24 | 23 |
| Ariz. | 59,394,016 | 16.38 | 24 | 19 | 24 | 14 | 26 |

| State | Operating Expenditures | Per Capita | Rank | Rank for Local Income | Rank for Circulation Transactions | Rank for Reference Transactions | Rank for Total Staff $ |
|---|---|---|---|---|---|---|---|
| Utah | $27,061,521 | $15.71 | 25 | 26 | 11 | 16 | 24 |
| Mich. | 144,551,444 | 15.51 | 26 | 29 | 37 | 21 | 25 |
| Mo. | 73,157,929 | 15.50 | 27 | 22 | 21 | 37 | 30 |
| Maine | 15,454,475 | 15.40 | 28 | 32 | 16 | 28 | 27 |
| Nebr. | 19,609,442 | 15.38 | 29 | 24 | 13 | 25 | 28 |
| Fla. | 192,979,132 | 15.09 | 30 | 25 | 39 | 4 | 33 |
| Iowa | 40,151,214 | 14.42 | 31 | 27 | 9 | 33 | 31 |
| N.Mex. | 16,227,461 | 14.24 | 32 | 30 | 28 | 46 | 32 |
| Idaho | 11,233,457 | 13.62 | 33 | 33 | 14 | 26 | 34 |
| S.Dak. | 7,653,731 | 13.59 | 34 | 28 | 12 | 41 | 29 |
| Vt. | 7,112,686 | 13.24 | 35 | 38 | 27 | 42 | 40 |
| Pa. | 147,918,401 | 12.92 | 36 | 39 | 42 | 31 | 35 |
| La. | 53,269,321 | 12.62 | 37 | 31 | 40 | 34 | 37 |
| Okla. | 31,708,401 | 12.37 | 38 | 34 | 29 | 27 | 36 |
| N.C. | 79,577,728 | 12.01 | 39 | 35 | 35 | 38 | 38 |
| Ga. | 78,393,094 | 11.62 | 40 | 41 | 45 | 39 | 39 |
| Ala. | 39,934,735 | 9.88 | 41 | 40 | 47 | 45 | 44 |
| N.D. | 5,482,776 | 9.73 | 42 | 44 | 25 | 30 | 46 |
| S.C. | 33,716,345 | 9.67 | 43 | 42 | 48 | 47 | 43 |
| Tex. | 149,885,800 | 9.53 | 44 | 36 | 43 | 19 | 41 |
| Del. | 6,312,110 | 9.48 | 45 | 45 | 44 | 44 | 42 |
| Ky. | 33,387,345 | 9.16 | 46 | 43 | 36 | 49 | 47 |
| Mont. | 7,188,512 | 9.02 | 47 | 37 | 32 | 43 | 45 |
| W.Va. | 16,132,543 | 8.38 | 48 | 50 | 41 | 32 | 49 |
| Miss. | 19,619,842 | 7.62 | 49 | 47 | 51 | 48 | 50 |
| Tenn. | 41,095,717 | 7.44 | 50 | 46 | 50 | 36 | 48 |
| Ark. | 14,872,707 | 6.75 | 51 | 48 | 46 | 50 | 51 |

*The NCES includes data for the District of Columbia to be comprehensive, but the Public Library of the District of Columbia might more legitimately be compared to other large cities.

Source: State Rankings of Selected Public Library Data, 1991
(Washington, D.C.: National Center for Education Statistics, July 1993).

Fullerton (California) Public Library, circa 1929.

# School Libraries

## Schools that need libraries

ACCORDING TO A 1990–91 SURVEY conducted by the National Center for Education Statistics, only 86.8% of private schools in the United States offered library services to their students, compared with 93.7% of public schools. The types of schools that were least likely to have a library fell into these categories:

Public schools with less than 150 students in urban fringe areas or large towns (53.8%)
Public schools with less than 150 students in the central city (68.6%)
Combined elementary and secondary public schools in urban fringe areas or large towns (71.9%)
Combined elementary and secondary public schools in the central city (73.9%)
Private schools with less than 150 students in the central city (74.9%)
Private schools with less than 150 students in rural areas or small towns (79.0%)
Private schools with less than 150 students in urban fringe areas or large towns (79.9%)
Elementary private schools in rural areas or small towns (81.1%)
Private schools with 20% or more minority enrollment in urban fringe areas, large towns, rural areas, or small towns (82.1%)
Private schools with 20% or more minority enrollment in the central city (83.0%)
Combined elementary and secondary private schools in the central city (83.9%)
Public schools with less than 150 students in rural areas or small towns (84.4%)

*Source:* National Center for Education Statistics, *Schools and Staffing in the United States: A Statistical Profile, 1990–91* (Washington, D.C.: U.S. Gov't Printing Office, July 1993). 204p.

## The school library media program

THE SCHOOL LIBRARY media program is an integral part of the school curriculum and provides a wide range of resources and information that satisfies the educational needs and interests of students. Materials are selected to meet the wide range of students' individual learning styles. The school library media center is a place where students may explore more fully classroom subjects that interest them, expand their imagination, delve into areas of personal interest, and develop the ability to think clearly, critically, and creatively about the resources they have chosen to read, hear, or view.

The school library media center provides a setting where students develop skills they will need as adults to locate, analyze, evaluate, interpret, and communicate information and ideas in an information-rich world. Students are encouraged to realize their potential as informed citizens who think critically and solve problems, to observe rights and responsibilities relating to the generation and flow of information and ideas, and to appreciate the value of literature in an educated society.

The school library media program serves *all* of the students of the community—not only the children of the most powerful, the most vocal or even the majority, but all of the students who attend the school. The collection includes materials to meet the needs of all learners, including the gifted, the reluctant readers, the mentally, physically, and emotionally impaired, and those from a diversity of backgrounds. The school library media program strives to maintain a diverse collection that represents various points of view on current and historical issues, as well as a wide variety of areas of interest to all students served. Though one parent or member of the school community may feel a particular title in the school library media center's collection is inappropriate, others will feel the title is not only appropriate but desirable.

The school library media center is the symbol to students of our most cherished freedom—the freedom to speak our minds and hear what others have to say. School boards are urged to reaffirm the importance and value of the freedom to read, view, and listen. Students have the right to develop the ability to think clearly, critically, and creatively about what they have chosen to read, hear, or view.

## Library media programs in education

School library media specialists are an integral part of the total educational team that prepares students to become responsible citizens in a changing global society. In today's information age, an individual's success, even existence, depends largely on the ability to access, evaluate and utilize information. Library media specialists are leaders in carrying out the school's instructional program through their separate but overlapping roles of information specialist, teacher, and instructional consultant.

*The National Goals for Education* and *America 2000* challenge our nation to make education a top priority in preparing students to compete in the worldwide marketplace and make informed decisions about problems facing society. To guarantee every young person an equal and effective educational opportunity, officials must provide each school with library media facilities and resources to meet curriculum needs. Officials must also ensure that each school's staff includes library media professionals and support personnel to carry out the mission of the instructional program.

The ability to locate and use information in solving problems, expanding ideas, and becoming informed citizens depends on access to adequate library media facilities, appropriate resources and qualified personnel. Recent studies, such as Keith Curry Lance's *The Impact of School Library Media Centers on Academic Achievement* (Castle Rock, Colo.: Hi Willow Research and Publishing, 1993), show a strong positive correlation between library media programs and student achievement.

Administrators, teachers, school board members, parents, and community members are urged to recognize the power of information and the critical need for strong, professionally staffed library media programs so all students may become effective users of information.

*Sources:* ALA American Association of School Librarians statements:
*Sample Statement on the Role of the School Library Media Program* (1990);
and *Position Statement on the Value of Library Media Programs in Education* (1993).

# Facilities

# Planning library buildings: Ten practical considerations

*by Kate W. Ragsdale*

LIBRARIANS RARELY RECEIVE FORMAL TRAINING in planning a new library building or a major library building renovation. Even the terminology used by architects and builders is unfamiliar to us. We do not have a crystal ball to guide us in visualizing the needs of our institutions 20 years into the future. We do not know how technology will change the way we provide access to information. So how do we manage to be successful in handling the complex responsibility of planning library buildings? We devour the library literature; we consult with others who have had experience in planning library buildings; we learn from architects and university facility planners (who in turn learn from us); we share information informally through electronic mail—and we make some mistakes.

Here are ten practical tips, not necessarily in order of priority, to assist librarians who, in addition to their other responsibilities, find themselves planning a college or university library building. Of course, each building project is unique, but there are fundamental issues that apply to many, if not all, academic library construction projects.

1. **Hire an interior designer.** The services of a designer are important for both major library renovations and new library construction. We all know that designers coordinate colors, select finishes, and choose wall and floor coverings—all fundamental to the ambiance of the building. But architects, too, are often adept at making these selections. So why insist on a designer?

Reference desk area, Eric and Sarah Rodgers Library for Science and Engineering, University of Alabama, Tuscaloosa. Under construction.

The additional services provided by a designer can make a significant difference in the quality of the finished product. Matching furniture design with the needs of the library, the designer lays out the arrangement of the furnishings within the space available. A designer's expertise in this phase of the project alone can save the librarian hours and hours of time and also help to prevent mistakes in the furniture selection process. The designer knows how much space to allow at the front of a file cabinet so that the drawers can be pulled out easily, or between study tables so that the chairs will not strike each other. A designer helps the librarian deal with issues of functionality in work room and office furnishings; is familiar with reliable manufacturers and products; is able to write specifications if bids must be let; is on-site to troubleshoot when the furnishings are installed; and deals with the vendors to solve problems.

Many architectural firms employ their own interior designers, a situation that enhances effective communication among the librarian, the architect, and the designer throughout the project.

In the interest of economy, university and college administrators may suggest that an interior designer is an unnecessary luxury. If this should happen, the librarian might offer a compromise by suggesting that something else in the project could be deleted to free up funds to hire the services of a designer.

2. **Remember the library signs.** Early in the planning process make certain that the signs are to be a part of either the building contract or the interior design/furnishings contract. Amazingly enough, it is possible that the signage system will be overlooked by the architect.

Unless they design libraries, hospitals, airports, or other public buildings, architects may be oblivious to the need for effective signage in library buildings. And sometimes architects balk at the multitude of signs needed to direct library users because they think the signs will interfere with the design of the building.

The librarian is the logical person to de-

Reference desk area, Rodgers Library, its first week open.

velop a list of signs (directional, room numbers, building directory, and so forth) needed in the building. Although it is easier to draw up a list of signs once the building is partially completed, sometimes this list must be compiled even before construction begins. In this case, the librarian, using the drawings as a guide, must simply conceptualize. A visit to nearby libraries and hospitals can be useful in gathering information and ideas about appropriate signs for the library.

3. **Include the book detection system in the building contract.** The technical nature of book detection systems plus competitiveness in the book security system business in general combines to make it wise to include this system as a part of the building contract. The architect will gather information directly from vendors concerning the features of book detection systems, thereby relieving the librarian of the stress of serving as a liaison.

It is, of course, the responsibility of the librarian to alert the architect to desirable features in a book security system, to the need for compatibility with systems in other libraries on campus, and to preferences among the available book detection systems and installation options.

4. **Pay careful attention to the accessibility of the building.** In spite of requirements of the Americans with Disabilities Act (ADA), and civil rights laws for persons with disabilities passed prior to the ADA, important issues

of accessibility may be overlooked, even in planning a new building. The ADA is specific in requiring that all new construction completed after January 1, 1993, must be accessible to users with disabilities.

Increasingly, architects understand the issues that librarians raise concerning accessibility. But architects may be looking only at requirements actually spelled out by the law rather than at fairly simple, maybe even inexpensive, adjustments which make it easier for patrons with disabilities to use the building.

One way to ensure careful attention to the accessibility of the building is to seek suggestions from library patrons with disabilities. Giving these library users the opportunity to review drawings and/or to visit the site as the building is being constructed, and to make suggestions as the project progresses, will go a long way toward making certain that the completed library building is truly accessible.

5. **Take lots of photos throughout the project.** Be sure that photos are taken on a regular basis—the "before" shots, the ground breaking, all stages of construction, vendors making installations, committees planning for the move, the move process itself, the building dedication ceremony.

It is surprising how useful photos, even those taken by an amateur, turn out to be. Photos are a great way to keep the library staff and users informed of the progress of construction; for promotional displays and articles; for a scrapbook entry in the John Cotton Dana public relations competition; for the library archives; for displays during the building dedication; as mementos for library staff and donors.

At the end of the project, arrange to have a professional photographer (e.g., the university photographer) take artistic exterior and interior shots of the building, highlighting the best features of the building. These photos may be used in applying for an architectural award (such as an AIA/ALA-LAMA Library Building Award) or submitted to journals that annually feature library architecture (such as *American Libraries* and *Library Journal*).

6. **Be prepared to compromise on items that are not vital to library service and to stand firm on the ones that are.** Know the difference and make sure that the architect does, too. Giving up some shelving to cut costs is a compromise that might be feasible; additional shelving can be installed later as it is needed. And while decorative elements may be attractive, eliminating some of these items probably will not affect the level of library service. Examples of design features that librarians might actively promote are floor loads which are capable of handling future compact shelving and having only one public entrance/exit for the building.

Flexibility is an important attribute for library building planners; however, it is equally important for librarians to speak out on issues that will affect the level of service for library users.

7. **Join the architect on weekly site inspections as soon as the finishes begin.** It is important for the librarian to visit the site often during the entire project, but observation almost daily once the painting, carpeting installation, and trim finishes are being completed can be time well spent. Make arrangements to accompany the architect on weekly inspections as the project nears its end; also, help to develop the punch list.

Attention to detail throughout the final weeks can ensure a better product—and a much, much shorter punch list.

8. **Be generous in estimating the amount of time you will spend on the project, and plan to accommodate your other responsibilities.** Librarians who plan new and renovated buildings are also juggling other responsibilities; actually, this is true of almost everyone who is working on the project— the architect, the designer, the vendors, the subcontractors, the campus planners. The project superintendent on the site may be the only key person who is working full time on this one project.

With this in mind, the librarian will have to make arrangements to share responsibilities during this period or to delay other projects for a while. Extra student assistants or temporary staff members may be needed to fill in; adjusting schedules and responsibilities with supervisors and coworkers during the construction project may need to be considered.

Dealing with the many hours spent on planning new or renovated library buildings is one of the most difficult aspects of the project. This management issue should be handled directly from the beginning to help to maintain a positive attitude toward the new building and toward those who are planning it.

9. **As much as possible, follow up informal communication in writing.** The complexity of a building project contributes to lapses in communication, and circulating notes and memos can clear up misunderstandings before costly mistakes occur.

The files for a building project can be voluminous, in part because it is useful to make sure that communication (a casual conversation in person, a telephone conversation, agreements at a meeting) is followed up in writing and that copies are forwarded to everyone concerned. Written communication of all approved change orders is especially important since these changes do not appear on the drawings.

At the beginning of each building project, an established line of communication should be explained to everyone involved. Librarians must conform to the recognized line of communication. At the outset, arrangements should be made for sending copies of written correspondence, and librarians must make sure that they are a part of this loop.

The new Eric and Sarah Rodgers Library for Science and Engineering, University of Alabama, Tuscaloosa.

10. **Keep complete files on each building project.** Once the project is complete, library staff think that they will never forget even the most minute details of how to move a library, how to write bid specifications for ordering equipment, how to launch a public relations campaign for the new library, how to schedule library services during a move. But details fade as routines are once again assumed.

It is a good idea to ask each committee or individual responsible for an aspect of the project to develop a final report which includes methodology used, examples, mistakes made, and suggestions for better implementation during the next construction project. These files will assist the library in planning the next building venture, and they are also helpful when other libraries ask for assistance in planning a building.

The above tips are not in any particular order; each can contribute to the success of a construction project. We librarians muddle our way through the process of planning library construction. Each time we do it, we get better at it. Our success may be based in part on our eagerness to assist each other as well as to learn from one another.

*Source:* Kate W. Ragsdale, "Planning Library Buildings: Ten Practical Considerations," *College & Research Libraries News* 54 (June 1993): 318–21.

# Sensible signage

*by Carol R. Brown*

A SUCCESSFUL SIGN SYSTEM is one that can be learned easily and is truly helpful to the user of the library. Here are some guidelines:

1. Consistency is essential to the development of an effective sign system. It allows the user to learn the system quickly and easily. Signs that serve the same function throughout the building, such as those giving instructions or those identifying specific departments, should have the same shape, size, layout, type size, and placement (height, location on the wall, etc.).

2. The sign system should be logical. Directions should be given in a progression from the general to the specific. Levels of information should be established so that some messages receive more emphasis than others.

3. Signs should use terminology consistently—only one term should be applied to any one area, service, etc. The words used should be as descriptive as possible and easily recognized by the public. Avoid using jargon that is familiar only to the staff.

4. Redundancy should be avoided. Too many signs, all providing the same message, can be as bad as no sign at all.

5. Signs should be placed appropriately at decision points in the building—at the entrance to the library, by elevators or stairs, at the end of a hall.

6. The text of a sign should be clearly and accurately written in order to communicate the intended message effectively. The phrases used and the length of the lines of text should be short, so the sign can be easily read and understood. The tone should be appropriate for promoting good public relations.

7. Signs should work well in relation to the architecture of the library. The dimensions of signs should be in proportion to the scale of the building. The colors and materials should coordinate with the colors and finishes of the building. Place signs where they will not be obscured by parts of the building, fixtures, or furnishings.

8. Signs should be made in accordance with the principles of good design. These principles pertain to typeface, size and spacing of letters and lines, contrast, use of symbols, and color. (Information about the effective design of signs can be found in a number of books.)

9. As the situation in the library changes, signs should be changed promptly to reflect the new conditions.

*Source:* Reprinted from Carol R. Brown, *Selecting Library Furniture: A Guide for Librarians, Designers, and Architects,* 2d ed. (Phoenix: Oryx Press, December 1994). Used by permission of Carol R. Brown and the Oryx Press.

# Library signs

*by Jackie Kinder and Catherine Eckman*

## Preliminary planning for good library signage

- Walk through the building and try to experience it from the user's perspective.
- Look at the building's floor plans for ideas about where signage is needed.
- Determine what the most frequently asked directional questions are.
- Ask for input from other library staff.
- Determine what type of signs are needed (service points: circulation, reference; facilities: copiers, phones, restrooms; directional: getting around the building, getting around a floor, getting out of the building).
- Look at sign catalogs and samples for ideas.
- Determine sign format (moulded-injected letters, hanging signs, signs mounted on walls, painted-on signs, or a combination of these).
- Select the type of lettering to be used.
- Select colors to be used for lettering and background.
- Determine how large signs and lettering should be.
- Determine what signs should say (this should be consistent throughout the library, including library handouts).
- Determine the number of signs needed.

## Visibility

- Signs for major service points should be visible from the entrance if possible.
- Signs should be visible from a reasonable distance.
- Signs should be visible from any direction.
- A building cross section sign should be visible from the entrance to help orient the user to the building.

## Aesthetics

- Signs should not clash with the building's decor or purpose.
- Signs should be numerous enough to ensure that users find what they need, but not so many as to appear visually overwhelming or cluttered.

## Maintenance/costs

- Signs should be difficult to deface or vandalize.
- Signs should be easy and inexpensive to update or change.
- Signs should be durable.
- Signs should be easy to clean.
- Cost of signs should include installation.

## User-friendliness

- Signs should be easy to read.

- "You Are Here" indicators in contrasting colors should be used on building cross sections and floor plans.
- Building cross sections should be located in stairwells and both inside and outside of elevators.
- Floor plans should not be so detailed as to be confusing to the user.
- Exit signs should be clearly marked.
- Braille signs should be included.

*Source:* Jackie Kinder and Catherine Eckman, "Where Do I Go from Here?" *College & Research Libraries News* 54 (February 1993): 79–80.

# Regulations and codes

*by Dianne Lueder and Sally Webb*

LIBRARIES ARE PUBLIC BUILDINGS and as such must exercise care to maintain a facility that is safe for library users and staff members. The building and equipment must also be safeguarded to protect the public investment and to assure that library operations will continue uninterrupted.

People generally think of libraries as safe places, but unsafe conditions can develop if proper maintenance and housekeeping are not practiced on a regular basis. Accidents that result from poor maintenance procedures can threaten the financial well-being of the library because of potential lawsuits. Maintenance procedures that violate state and local health and fire-prevention codes pose the threat of fines, lost hours of service, and, in the event of a fire, huge financial loss.

State and local governments routinely adopt building codes and standards that pertain to structural safety and fire protection. Life-safety codes, occupational safety and health codes, indoor air-quality standards, and licensing and inspection regulations apply to library operations. It is the obligation of the library administration to be aware of these requirements and to incorporate them into library maintenance policy and procedure.

The following are a few of the codes that apply to library building maintenance. Additional regulations might exist, so you should verify others that apply to your facility.

### Asbestos
*Jurisdiction:* OSHA regulations specify work practices dealing with asbestos. EPA rules govern the handling and disposal of asbestos in abatement actions. State regulations vary and may be more stringent than federal requirements.

### Boilers and pressure vessels
*Jurisdiction:* Office of the State Fire Marshal. Boiler-insurance company inspection.

### Building construction or repair
*Jurisdiction:* State and local building codes. Building Officials and Code Administrators (BOCA) *Basic National Building Code* includes established construction standards often adopted as part of local codes by reference to same.

Other standard building codes include the International Conference of Building Officials' *Uniform Building Code* and the *Standard Building Code* published by the Southern Building Code Congress International. Fire protection, life-safety, and electrical codes are incorporated into these building codes.

**1**

### Electrical
*Jurisdiction:* Local building and fire/life-safety codes. Insurance company inspection. The *National Electrical Code* published by the NFPA as Code No. 70 is a recognized authority on electrical installation requirements. (Building inspectors, electrical contractors, and insurance inspectors use these guidelines.)

### Elevators
*Jurisdiction:* State or local codes and licensing (regular inspection required for licensing).

### Employee safety and health
*Jurisdiction:* Federal OSHA regulations. State occupational safety and health codes. These safety codes cover a wide array of concerns such as safety of ladders and scaffolds; safe handling of hazardous materials; accident prevention; fire, safety, and emergency procedures; eye and face protection; insect and vermin control, etc.

*Specifically:* State laws relating to employee occupational safety and health or 29 C.F.R. §§ 1900–1910.

### Fire protection
*Jurisdiction:* Local fire-prevention/life-safety codes. Office of the State Fire Marshal. The NFPA provides established building fire-protection codes that are often incorporated into local codes.

*For libraries see specifically: NFPA 101: Life Safety Code; NFPA 910: Protection of Libraries and Library Collections; NFPA 10: Standard for Portable Fire Extinguishers; NFPA 13A: Inspection, Testing and Maintenance of Sprinkler Systems.* Any others which may apply to the specific fire suppression, detection, and alarm systems.

### Indoor-air quality (office environment)
*Jurisdiction:* Not clearly established. OSHA regulates air quality in the work setting, but standards cited relate generally to a manufacturing environment. State occupational safety and health laws may apply. EPA has an ongoing investigation into indoor-air-quality concerns, but it does not have established jurisdiction. NIOSH, a division of the U.S. Department of Health and Human Services, conducts indoor-air-quality investigations upon request as part of the Health Hazard Evaluation Program. When conducting these evaluations, NIOSH uses guidelines for air quality established by ASHRAE.

*Specifically: ASHRAE Standard 62-1989: Ventilation for Acceptable Indoor Air Quality; ASHRAE Standard 55-1981: Thermal Environmental Conditions for Human Occupancy.*

### Pesticides
*Jurisdiction:* The EPA under rules and regulations of the Federal Environmental Pesticide Control Act.

### Plumbing
*Jurisdiction:* State and local building codes.

### Radon
*Jurisdiction:* The EPA and state departments of Environmental Protection or Nuclear Safety can provide information on radon contamination. No current federal regulations require testing or corrective action for radon contamination in public or commercial buildings.

### Sanitation/food service and rest rooms
*Jurisdiction:* Local municipal, county, or state codes usually prevail. Occupational safety and health regulations, state or federal, regulate the sanitary

working conditions for employees.

**Water and sewer**
 *Jurisdiction:* State and local codes and U.S. Public Health Service and EPA standards.

*Source:* Dianne Lueder and Sally Webb, *Administrator's Guide to Library Building Maintenance* (Chicago: American Library Association, 1992). 202p.

# The sick (library) building syndrome

*by Matthew J. Simon*

WE EXPECT A LOT FROM OUR LIBRARY BUILDINGS, but we don't expect them to make us sick. We expect them to keep us warm and our users expect them to be good places to read and study. Our staff expect to be comfortable while they are doing their work. Beyond that, the library's collections must be preserved. If we have computers or telecommunications equipment, they, too, must be housed and operated within a specific range of temperature and humidity. Why is it then, that sometimes things go wrong, and our buildings do not do what they are supposed to do?

## What is a sick building?

The term "Sick Building Syndrome" or "SBS" generally refers to "modern buildings throughout the world whose occupants display symptoms such as: (a) irritation of the eyes, nose, and throat; (b) dry sensations in the mucosa and the skin; (c) erythema; (d) mental fatigue; and (e) the perception of weak but persistent odors." The term itself is of fairly recent origin. Prior to articles published in 1981, there is little mention of the terms or discussions about the problems of Sick Building Syndrome or indoor pollution. Since that time, however, hundreds of articles have appeared focusing on medical, legal, engineering, psychological, and other aspects.

Research into the causes and cures of Sick Building Syndrome grew out of increasing concern about pollution that occurs outdoors, and the recognition that pollution can also occur in the work place and in the home. There was also a growing awareness that the chemical and microbial factors found indoors were little understood, and that methods for testing and analysis that worked well outdoors had little validity in an enclosed environment.

Little writing in the library professional literature has dealt with sick library buildings. This is surprising because they most definitely do exist and because library administrators, as a group, are knowledgeable about the impact of the environment on books and other collection media. Because our buildings have immediate impact on the ability of staff to work and patrons to use the facilities and collections, a sick building can negate the finest array of services. But those of us who are seeking to understand problems with our buildings must rely on the articles that appear in scientific, engineering, or general management publications.

## Medical considerations

In the United States, most people spend less than 10 percent of their waking time out-of-doors. It is known that people who work inside are exposed to many pollutants at higher concentrations than when they are working outside. When complaints of ill health are ascribed to indoor pollution, many different factors must be examined in order to achieve a correct identification of the problem, its causes, and possible solutions. From a medical standpoint, research is needed into indoor air pollution that centers on the identification of vectors and causative agents that may make people sick; establishing benchmarks of their susceptibility; and then attempting to identify remedies.

Different individuals exhibit a wide range of susceptibilities. Age is a primary determinant; the very young and the elderly tend to react to pollutants more strongly than the rest of the population. People who suffer from allergies or who suffer from asthma react strongly to indoor pollutants. Smokers have a demonstrably greater susceptibiiity to pollutants than do nonsmokers (even though the nonsmokers may complain more vociferously). Several factors, which by themselves would not present a significant risk, may work together to create a health hazard. For example, a primary component of cigarette smoke is the carcinogen, benzene. The presence of benzene in the bloodstream also seems to act as a catalytic agent or accelerator by increasing the body's reaction to other contaminants. An investigator, therefore, must not only attempt to identify the possible pollutants, but must also be able to understand possible interactions between them. The questions of age and susceptibility are further complicated by the issue of chronic and transient effects. Sources of pollution may be of temporary duration. The pollutants themselves may have a transient effect on people. The symptoms or illnesses may be of short duration and clear up without any chronic effect. Therefore, the mere suspicion of SBS should not be a prelude to highly involved toxicological and epidemiological studies that can cost thousands of dollars and, in the end, may result in imprecise answers.

## Engineering considerations

The medical aspects of Sick Building Syndrome are closely tied to the engineering of the building. In 1987, the Conservation Foundation stated that

> The indoor air pollution problem has been exacerbated, especially in recent years, by a number of trends. More chemicals have been used in a variety of consumer and office products and building materials. Most new houses, office buildings, mobile homes, and prefabricated housing units have been built much tighter or sealed thereby reducing ventilation.

"Tight Building Syndrome" or "Sealed Building Syndrome" occurs in buildings with windows that do not open, which rely exclusively on mechanical systems for ventilation. A large percentage of the requests for indoor air evaluations come from workers who work in sealed buildings. Individual health factors are examined against questions of exposure time to different agents, the exposure levels, and the rate of air circulation.

Significant efforts have been made to identify the causes of sickness. The federal government continually works to identify different sources of pollution and to establish standards through the EPA and other agencies. However, those efforts are compromised by the continuous introduction of new chemicals and products. Progress is being made but success varies widely depending upon the compound suspected, its prevalence in the work place, and the severity of the health effects.

## Why are there sick library buildings?

Libraries have the same potential as other buildings to make people very sick. A number of articles list the chemical and microbiological agents most frequently identified as the causes of indoor sickness.

Unfortunately for our staffs and users, a large number of them are commonly found in libraries. In testimony before the House of Representatives, Dr. James Melius of the National Institute for Occupational Safety and Health (NIOSH) described the most common sources of pollution and symptoms:

- Contamination from outside the building, such as exhaust from a neighboring garage.
- Contamination from building materials (a surprising number that are toxic). This is a problem that has increased dramatically as new insulating materials, adhesives, and curing agents have been introduced in construction.
- Contamination from copying machines. Machines that are not externally vented can release ozone, trinitrofluorenone, and methyl alcohol into the work space.
- Hypersensitivity pneumonitis. Libraries are dust reservoirs and the dust provides a safe, nourishing haven for a variety of mites and bacteria. In addition, air conditioners breed *Legionella*, and office workers and patrons spread infection.
- Contamination from chemicals used in building maintenance. This is a particular problem if directions for mixing and application are not scrupulously followed. In libraries, a variety of chemicals are used in preservation work and other activities that can be dangerous if used without skin and eye protection, or in inadequately ventilated areas.
- Inadequate ventilation is found to be the principal cause in over half of the investigations conducted by NIOSH.

In addition, other factors actively influence staff and users' sense of physical well-being. These include the building's lighting, the level and type of noise, the furnishings, and the density of humans working in a confined space. Of these, human density is the most direct factor, as crowded conditions facilitate the spread of contagion. The conditions of crowding are exacerbated if the work environment is hot and humid, which encourages the growth of bacteria and other microbial agents.

## Issues of management concern

Managers should suspect Sick Building Syndrome if more than one-fifth of a building's occupants complain about symptoms such as headache, nausea, eye irritation, or sore throat; if the symptoms continue for more than two weeks; and if those people experiencing the symptoms feel relief upon leaving the building. For managers, the health and safety of the building's occupants are the immediate concern. Some problems may cause little more than temporary discomfort while others pose significant long-term threats to health and safety. Managers must also be concerned about issues such as productivity. Staff who do not feel well, and who suspect that their work place is making them sick, may not be productive. In addition, some pollutants that are common to libraries can actually increase nervousness and cause short-term memory loss.

SBS also has significant economic cost. Occasionally the cause can be readily identified and corrected. However, it is far more common to find the syndrome and no clearly defined causal factor. In such cases, specialists may have to be hired to conduct air samplings, to perform epidemiological studies, to interview and examine staff or patrons, and to examine the building and its Heating, Ventilating and Air Conditioning (HVAC) systems. Such ventures do not always have positive outcomes. In many cases, the cause of the sickness cannot be identified with any certainty. In addition, when staff become aware that a study is going on they may assume that there is a significant problem, increasing the sense of anxiety described above. If a cause is found, the cost of remedy may be significant—particularly if it requires redesign and correction of HVAC systems or addition of barriers and other protective structures. Legal and statutory requirements must be considered. Discussing staff complaints with unions or OSHA can require a great deal of management time. If civil or criminal actions are initiated by or on behalf of staff or users, legal fees and occasionally monetary damages must be paid.

## Strategies for remedy and prevention

Much work has been done over the last ten years to treat sick buildings. A number of strategies have been developed that are effective, but the best is one that will satisfy the building's occupants and costs the least amount of time and money.

**Low-cost: staff initiated.** The decision to recognize that a potential health problem exists should be carefully considered by management. Many of the most basic complaints can be handled informally by staff working independently or in committees. A surprising number of complaints can be handled with no or minimal cost. For example, cigarette smoke has long-term health risks for smokers and for people who live and work around smokers. Dr. James Melius stated that the minimum level of ventilation of 5 cubic feet per minute (cfm) of outdoor air per person should be immediately increased to 20 cfm if smoking is permitted in the office. In addition, dry cleaning chemicals brought into the work place on clothing have been identified in many SBS complaints as the primary cause of illness. Tetrochloroethylene, the primary component, can cause headache and nausea in very low concentrations. Staff should be encouraged to air out drycleaned garments to permit evaporation of the fluid before bringing them into the office.

In physical plant maintenance, many common cleaning chemicals, as well as the compounds used by exterminators, have well-documented health risks. Their use in buildings should be carefully controlled and eliminated if possible. Storage of volatile organic chemicals must be carefully monitored to make sure that containers are leakproof and vaporproof.

**Mid-cost: management initiated.** Management is able to initiate (or at least request) a variety of strategies that may eliminate illness if the low-cost strategies do not work. Of primary importance is recognition that dust-borne contamination is a continuing problem in libraries. Susceptibility to dust, or more accurately, to the mites and organisms that live in dust, increases with exposure. Upgrading the frequency and effectiveness of cleaning can reduce the incidence of asthma attacks and allergic reactions. A related issue is the establishment of regular preventive maintenance of air handling equipment. It is very important to change filters as prescribed by the manufacturer. Even well-designed systems will fail if the filters are clogged. The increasingly common practice of "cycling" fresh air ventilation often results in modest energy cost savings and a considerable increase in the number of complaints about stagnant air or stuffiness. If complaints of this nature are being received or if telltale paper strips begin to be seen around air vents, providing constant air exchange may eliminate the problem.

Occasionally, staff may have to work with substances that have risk. If this cannot be avoided, schedules should be set that minimize the length of exposure (contaminants can build up in body tissue over time). Also, staff must be educated in the proper use of volatile chemicals or poisons, and must be required to wear protective garb such as goggles, gloves, masks, or smocks.

Unfortunately, health complaints attributed to the building may have little to do with the building itself. Staff may transfer their anger toward management or coworkers into complaints that are expressed as problems with the physical environment. In such cases, one-to-one interviews with the staff are a very important step because they may help a manager determine if the complaint is building-related or if it originates from another source. In many organizations, the need for an effective problem reporting and staff complaint resolution process is overlooked in the day-to-day tumult of the job. Additionally, a tour of the library or library building from basement to top floor on a weekly basis can help identify problem areas. If this list is regularly reviewed by management with the knowledge of staff, work orders can be initiated or requests for capital budget items can be discussed with the organization's executive officer or board.

**High-cost: top management initiated.** If problems persist and solutions are either not apparent or are beyond staff capabilities or the library's operating budget, it is necessary to bring in consultants. Frequently, state and local governments maintain an office that considers environmental affairs. Alternatively, NIOSH will provide assistance. In 1987, NIOSH published "Guidance for Indoor Air Quality Investigations" (in *Indoor Air Quality: Selected References* (Cincinnati, Ohio: U.S. Dep't of Health & Human Services, National Institute for Occupational Health)). This booklet provides assistance, including a description of NIOSH's experience regarding air quality problems. More important is a "self-evaluation of indoor air quality problems" that is extremely useful in assessing the type and severity of the problem, and in telling managers where to look for possible causes. Lastly, the booklet provides a listing of indoor air quality consultation services.

**Repair, redesign, and replacement of existing systems and facilities.** Many of the most persistent problems involve poorly designed or inadequately sized HVAC systems. Correction of HVAC problems can cost a great deal of money and take years to implement. If analysis leads to identification of a specific cause, and if readily available and inexpensive remedies do not work, then a reexamination of the building and its systems is required. The consulting engineer may make specific recommendations about changing the size and functionality of the HVAC system. However, the changes may also require physical alteration of work spaces and a thorough disruption of work schedules and routines while the changes are being made.

**Remodeling and new construction.** Most outbreaks of Sick Building Syndrome occur in new construction or renovation. Library planners have always been concerned with layout and functionality, but such concerns carry little weight if staff and users cannot work comfortably and safely. Attention to the design details in HVAC and other systems is critical if the factors that can lead to SBS are to be minimized. Questions about the minimal requirements for a new building's systems should be thought through in looking for the minimum common denominators. What is needed to operate a facility and keep staff productive and users satisfied if there is a power failure?

- The ability of staff to control and manipulate their work environment is a very important determinant in user satisfaction. If the budget permits, individual controls for temperature and air exchange should be permitted in the offices and workrooms.
- Active air filtration systems are very important in libraries since they reduce the amount of dust that is deposited on and generated by library materials, and the chance of microbial and allergic reaction. From a health perspective, "they remove many pollutants at the same time, obviating the need to have a complete understanding of the mixtures and concentrations present in the indoor environment and the hazards they present."
- Many of the chemicals that make people sick evaporate fairly rapidly. To accelerate this process, many construction managers

now "pre-age" buildings. This involves the "'baking out' of new buildings by elevating interior temperatures for a period prior to occupancy." However, there is some debate about this practice.

- Holding the mechanical system designers to strict adherence of federal, state, and local guidelines is strongly recommended.
- Specifications for furnishings and carpeting, too, must be carefully reviewed to eliminate the use of formaldehyde, fiberglass, asbestos, oil-based carpet adhesives, etc.

Plumbing systems must be designed to remove water and waste effectively, and avoid the possibility of conditions that can encourage mold, bacteria, and fungus growth. All have the potential for causing illness, if the organisms, their waste, or spores are transmitted into the air inside a building.

Savvy managers will recognize that every building has the potential for becoming a sick building. Even if the design and construction are faultless, once a building is in use factors may be introduced that can have significant health consequences. The most obvious problems, such as smoking, the use of noxious cleaning solvents, or liquid process photocopiers in unvented work areas, can be solved quite easily. Also, most managers may request increased building and HVAC maintenance, which can reduce the incidence of dust. These activities should be part of a regular and systematic review by library staff of the effectiveness of plant maintenance operations.

Managers should also realize that contaminants, as well as complaints from staff, can come from many different sources. Buildings—particularly new buildings whose air systems have not been fully balanced—are easy targets. Staff may express their resentment toward management, or express their dissatisfaction by complaining about physical distress that may have little to do with the true conditions in the building.

The least expensive remedies should be tried first. If these do not succeed, more expensive strategies, beginning with a detailed self-study, should be tried. Knowledge that even new and recently renovated buildings often exhibit Sick Building Syndrome should alert facilities planners to ask questions about system capabilities and the use of volatile organic compounds in the manufacture of furnishings and building materials. In new construction, the old adage "Plan for the best, but expect the worst" applies.

*Source:* Matthew J. Simon, "The Sick (Library) Building Syndrome,"
*Library Administration and Management* 4 (Spring 1990): 87–91.

# Quality bookmobile service without going broke

*by Carol Hole*

MY LIBRARY HAS HAD FOUR DIRECTORS in six years. I asked each new director: "Should I go for maximum circulation, or serve those who need us the most?" Every one of them said, "maximum circulation!" But then they added, "Ah . . . but . . . be sure to serve those who need us, too."

I thought they were copping out, but now I see they were right. The most responsible way to use the taxpayer's dollar is to go for big circulation. Your friendly, local government officials (who love you so dearly) are less likely to see your bookmobile as a "frill" and cut it out of the budget.

Then you can also serve the needy people. You just put their stop on the same day you go to a popular stop nearby, and say, "Really, it's costing us almost nothing to serve them, since we had to go right past there anyway." Sneakiness pays off.

This worked so well for me that after several years of threatening to cut the bookmobiles, my County Commissioners gave up. They couldn't handle the letters and phone calls. Being popular is your best guarantee that you'll still be there to serve the needy.

I'm sorry to tell you that this means that your key to good bookmobile service is cost per circulation. That doesn't sound as inspiring as taking culture to the country, but it's vital. Because if your cost per circulation is much higher than the Main Library's, you're going to have a hard time justifying keeping that bookmobile on the road.

So how can you lower costs, and still give terrific service?

## Lowering costs

1. **Look at where you stop.** Even a small bookmobile eats dollars, so it makes no sense to send your bookmobile to nursing homes or the homebound: Those people can't get up the bookmobile steps. If you use a regular van with a wheelchair ramp in the back, you can wheel a booktruck right to their bedside if necessary, and it only takes one person to do it.

Same goes for jails, unless all inmates can come out to the bookmobile. And they hardly ever can.

For the same reason, I'm horrified at the number of bookmobiles that go house-to-house, or stop for one or two families. That's a shameful waste of taxpayers' money. After I conducted a workshop for the bookmobile librarians in South Carolina, one guy came up afterward and said, "It's okay for my bookmobile to go house-to-house, because we get our gas free."

"How the heck do you manage that?" I asked.

"Oh, we get it from the county garage."

Who did he think was paying for that gas—the tooth fairy?

It's irresponsible to ignore costs that don't come out of the library budget. Nothing's free if the taxpayer is paying for it, and house-to-house service is very, very expensive.

We've known for years that if you build a new library, your circulation will always double, but *only if you build it on a main street.* The same goes for bookmobile stops: they won't attract circulation if they aren't visible. Painting them white helps, but it's amazing how people can fail to see a 30-foot bookmobile parked in plain sight.

Put your bookmobile stop on a main road, someplace where people have to go anyway—grocery stores and post offices are good. Please! Not inside a trailer park or housing project. Only the people who live there will use it. Pick a central spot.

I can hear some of you thinking, "If we do that, the kids won't be able to get there." Right. That's because you're going out between 3 and 5 in the afternoon. Naturally the kids can't get there. Mom isn't home from work yet, and they're not allowed to ride their bikes on the highway.

So you go after 5:00 when Mom can drive the kids to the bookmobile. That way, Mom gets to check out books too.

Nobody likes working evenings. But if you don't, you might as well scratch your bookmobile, because (let's face it) in modern America, parents work. You can find a few places where people are home before 5, but not many.

When I took my bookmobiles off an 8:00–5:00 house-to-house schedule and started going to fewer, longer stops, circulation went from 25,000 to over 120,000 a year. The way we used to hop around like grasshoppers, you could be in the bathroom and miss the bookmobile. Now we stay put long enough for people to find us.

Some of the bookmobiles owned by the Topeka (Kan.) Public Library in the 1950s.

2. **Hookups.** A great way to lower costs. You can put a mobile home hookup on a pole for $150 to $200. At mobile home parks, they cost nothing: you just borrow one of theirs.

Most rural towns will gladly pay for a hookup to ensure that bookmobile service keeps coming. Get your Friends to pay for some, or budget a few each year, but get them. They'll pay for themselves the first year, because you won't have to run your generator. Fewer trips to the gas pump, no cloud of stinking exhaust, and no noise. You won't believe the difference in staff morale until you've worked on a bookmobile where you can actually hear youself think.

We figure hookups save us $5,000 to $10,000 a year in gas, plus lower maintenance bills.

3. **Scheduling.** There are a million ways to schedule bookmobiles: Experiment and see what works for you. Four ten-hour days allow longer routes and evening stops, plus maintenance days. Weekly stops are easier for patrons to remember. If you stagger shifts, one group can take the bookmobile out; later, group two drives out in a car and takes over. This gets more mileage out of your bus. Some libraries leave the bookmobile out overnight, while the staff goes home by car. Next day they return and drive a couple of miles to the next stop. It saves a lot of gas. You can even leave the bookmobile in one spot all day or all week.

My bookmobiles are on a "fifth day" schedule. Stops may be on first and third Mondays, second and fourth Tuesdays, and so forth. So if there is a fifth Monday (or whatever) in the month, there is no run scheduled for that day. We can catch up on in-house work, take vacations, and schedule maintenance. When I told another librarian this recently, she said, "Don't tell me you're still on that old fifth day schedule!" as if we were desperately old-fashioned.

The fact is, very little in libraries is really new. Everything has been tried by somebody, someplace. She thought fifth days were old hat just because her library had dropped them for something else. Fine. The question is, what works for you?

4. **Schedule for the convenience of the public, not this staff.** Yes, Virginia, that means evenings and weekends.

5. **Don't change your schedule very often** (once you get one that works). Give word of mouth a chance. It takes at least one year, and maybe five years, to build a stop to maximum potential.

6. **Make routes economical.** At some libraries, the bookmobiles drive all

the way back to the main library for lunch. That's a no-no. Schedule so you hit A on the way to B and C on the way home.

7. **Stop charging fines.** They cost more to collect than you make, and fines prevent more people from returning books than they encourage. They're bad public relations, too.

8. **Load efficiently.** Build a loading dock or extension if you must, but get some way to wheel a booktruck directly onto your bookmobile so you can speed up loading and rotating the collection.

9. **Get an easy-to-clear circulation system** like Recordak or any system where you just take out the T-slip and the book is ready to check out again. Don't waste hours recording books.

10. **Don't overspecialize service.** When I go on a bookmobile and the aisle is full of bags and boxes, I know what they are: Mrs. Jones's romances, Mr. Smith's westerns, and so on. You know how it is: You get in the habit of bringing extra goodies for your best customers. Don't. You can't afford the time. Specialized service rewards the staff, because Mrs. Jones is so grateful, but it's unfair to other patrons. Let Mrs. Jones get her books off the shelf like everybody else. Tell her your mean old library director won't let you give some people special service. Having to take the heat is why library directors get paid such fantastic salaries.

11. **Get on the same circulation system as Main.** It's amazing how this improves communication with the main library staff. Get them to do your overdues; it's much cheaper to centralize the process.

12. **Use the fewest possible staff**—usually two, except on very small bookmobiles. Be careful, though. A single person may not be safe in some places or in emergencies, and it may create substitution problems.

13. **Train all staff to think about cost cutting.** They'll have better ideas than you do because they know their jobs better.

14. **Use the smallest possible vehicle.** Don't send a 30-foot bus to a five-patron stop. In fact, you shouldn't send a 30-foot bus anywhere unless you have a really busy stop. We have one that circulates 1,000 books each time, so we need a big bus. But a step van with one staff member can handle up to 50 books an hour.

## Improving service

Okay, so you've used these and any other ideas you could locate to cut costs. Now, how do you keep service so good people will beat on your doors?

1. **Motivate staff.** The main duty of a manager is to appreciate the staff. They're doing the work. You can't do it for them. All you can do is make sure they know that you, personally, appreciate it.

If you go home and hand my list of so-called improvements to your staff with instructions to implement them, you'll create bad service. Why? Because you're implying that they're doing a lousy job now; whereas they, like everybody else, are already doing the best they can. If they aren't, they don't have a problem; you do. Unless people have been made to feel bad about themselves, they will always do a good job. Always. Ask any psychologist.

Better yet, read *In Search of Excellence*. If you apply the principles in that book, I guarantee your service will improve.

A boss's main duty is to appreciate the staff. Encourage and reward innovation and experimentation. If an experiment fails, you've gained priceless knowledge of what doesn't work. Tell your staff they're great. Notice anything they do well and praise it; they will surprise you.

2. **Subscribe to** *Mobile Ideas* **and contribute to it.** It's the only outreach journal we've got. For heaven's sake, encourage it! Do you want to spend the rest of your life reading articles about computers?

3. **Talk to other outreachers.** Take a phone survey around your state and

find out what others are trying. It might work for you.

4. **Do "Management by Walking Around."** There's an old saying that the best fertilizer for land is the owner's foot. None of us wants to hear that. We're so behind in office work that we don't want to "waste time" visiting bookmobile stops. Fess up—How many of you are library directors? And how many have visited a bookmobile stop in the last three months? You've got to go out! And when you go, no matter what idiotic thing they're doing, don't criticize. Let them tell you what the problems are. They'll be so glad you're interested you won't be able to shut them up. And next time you make a suggestion they'll accept it, because you'll understand the system and your suggestion will be workable and will solve a problem they pointed out.

The best thing I've done for staff morale in a year happened because two of my staff were up for job reclassification and pay raises. At 4:00 one day I got word the raises were approved. My desk was piled high, but I jumped in the car and drove to two bookmobile stops to tell the staff involved.

So they got the word three hours before they'd have gotten it anyway. Big deal. Why did I bother? Because they also got the message that I cared. They've been busting a gut to prove they deserve that raise ever since.

5. **Get rid of your separate bookmobile collection.** Give the main library staff whatever bribes and guarantees you must, but work out a system that allows you to pull books from Main shelves and load then on the bookmobile without having to check them out. It can be done. With a computer, it's easy. Without one, you have to work out a system for catching reserves on the bookmobile. At my library, the bookmobiles are searched for reserves daily.

Do it however you can, but do it! If you don't, bookmobile patrons are second-class citizens who get the same books over and over. They deserve the same service as all other patrons.

6. **Work your tail off to make sure people get the books they want.** That's the one area where any amount of time and money is worth investing. My library has a really amazing tradition of practically killing themselves to get what the patron wants. Start a tradition like that at your library.

7. **Understand your community.** Consult city/county planning departments, the regional planning council, the health planning council, and (above all) the school system. If you don't understand zoning and school bus schedules, you can forget after-school stops. Schedule evening and weekend stops for heavy-use areas.

8. **Carry what people really want.** In every library there are two groups: the elitists (or snobs) and the democrats (or slobs). I am a slob. I have a staff member who is sure that someday a person will come on his bookmobile panting to read *Paradise Lost*. It ain't gonna happen.

On a small bookmobile, there's no excuse for carrying anything that's not in real demand. Don't be a snob. No matter how much you think people ought to want to read the classics, they won't. And it's not our job to censor patrons' reading. If they want Harlequin romances and Michael Jackson books, that's what you should carry.

9. **Publicize.** This is hard. You must have printed schedules and distribute them all over the place—not just in the library. If a local station will broadcast schedules, great, but you need printed ones, too. Use the newspaper, posters near stops, and permanent "Bookmobile Stop" signs. (Get them made by your road department; they're very cheap.)

When you've done all that, the best publicity is still word of mouth. Next best is direct mail. Get your Friends to mail a flyer to routes near slow stops, using their bulk mailing permit. For $50 you can cover two rural routes. Even your Friends can afford that. And it gets unbelievable results.

*Source:* Carol Hole, "Producing Quality Bookmobile Service without Going Broke," *Rural Libraries,* vol.6, no.1 (1986): 19–30. Reprinted with permission.

## The bad old days

ONE OF THE MOST PRESTIGIOUS libraries in medieval Europe was the Sorbonne, a theological college founded in Paris about 1250 by Robert de Sorbon. The 36 members of the college had their own keys to the library, but for its time, the Sorbonne had a liberal access policy and allowed visiting scholars and other officials the use of its noncirculating collection. Here are the regulations issued in 1321 for using the room:

1. Robes and caps required.
2. No children or illiterates admitted.
3. Respectable learned men may enter if introduced by a member; their "valets" must remain outside.
4. Each member keeps his own key and loans it to no one.
5. Neither fire nor light permitted at any time.
6. No books issued without the permission of the Society.
7. A book should be laid upon a desk only after the dust has been removed.
8. No writing in or other abuse of a book.
9. Whether writing or reading, no bothering of others by talking or walking.
10. Maximum silence, as would be appropriate to premises "sacred and august."
11. Condemned books are available to professors of theology only—for use in line of duty only.
12. The professor is not to read such works for curiosity, lest he be poisoned.
13. Violators of that restraint are to be reprimanded.

*Source:* Sidney L. Jackson, *Libraries and Librarianship in the West: A Brief History* (New York: McGraw-Hill, 1974). 489p. Reprinted with permission.

## The five laws of academic library science

*by Maurice B. Line*

1. Books are for collecting.
2. Some readers their books.
3. Some books their readers.
4. Waste the time of the reader.
5. The library is a growing mausoleum.

*Source:* Review, *College & Research Libraries* 40 (1979): 557–58.

# The five laws of library science

*by S. R. Ranganathan*

1

1. Books are for use.
2. Every person his or her book.
3. Every book, its reader.
4. Save the time of the reader.
5. A library is a growing organism.

*Source:* S. R. Ranganathan, *The Five Laws of Library Science*
(1st ed., Madras: Madras Library Association, 1931).

# Who was Ranganathan?

*by R. N. Sharma*

BORN ON AUGUST 9, 1892, S. R. Ranganathan may most commonly be remembered for his formulation of laws. In 1929 he felt that librarianship lacked a set of unifying, guiding principles and set down his five laws of library science.

In 1925 he introduced the Colon Classification, a radical departure from the Dewey Decimal and Library of Congress Classification systems. In 1934 he published the *Classified Catalogue* code which showed that an analytico-synthetic approach is useful irrespective of what scheme for classification is used for developing a structured subject index.

After spreading his reforms throughout India, Ranganathan was active in international librarianship from 1948 until his death on September 27, 1972. A visionary, he predicted in the 1950s that computers would play an important part in libraries and that online catalogs would replace the card catalog in all types of libraries. He coined such terms as "facet," "phase," "isolate," "librametrics," and "chain procedure," and his ideas on bibliographic instruction, faculty status, and internships for librarians have become popular in Western countries. During his lifetime he wrote 62 books and more than 2,000 articles on all aspects of library science.

At its 1992 Midwinter Meeting, the Council of the American Library Association passed two resolutions in honor of Ranganathan. One said that the "ALA on the birth centennial of an international giant, S. R. Ranganathan, expresses the gratitude of its members to him for his contributions, many years of dedication and outstanding services to the promotion of international librarianship."

*Source:* R. N. Sharma, "Books Are for Use: Ranganathan Centennial Year,"
*College & Research Libraries News* 53 (September 1992): 504.

# A salute to Ranganathan

*by Lee W. Finks*

WHAT IS IT ABOUT RANGANATHAN? What makes so many of us love and admire him? The great Indian librarian was honored around the world in 1992 to celebrate the 100th anniversary of his birth on August 9. But while we may have a vague awareness of the famous "Five Laws" (and perhaps even his theories about classification systems), most Americans would have to admit that his direct impact on our libraries has been limited.

Yet love and admire him we do. Eugene Garfield, founder of the Institute for Scientific Information, wrote that Ranganathan is "without question, one of the luminaries of library science" and has had a "revolutionary impact on international classification theory." K. G. B. Bakewell in his article in the *ALA World Encyclopedia* called him "one of the immortals of library science." And Michael Gorman, editor of *AACR2* and currently dean of library services at California State University, Fresno, referred to him as "the unquestioned giant of 20th-century library science."

## Intellectual high spots

In 1981, I paid tribute to the Five Laws on the occasion of the 50th anniversary of their first publication, calling them, among other things, one of the few intellectual high spots I had encountered in library school. Ranganathan inspired me at a time when I was searching for some philosophical underpinning for all of the practical, mundane details that my teachers were trying to cram into my head.

I am a teacher now myself, and I still appreciate the power of idealism in our efforts to professionalize our students. Ranganathan's Five Laws can fill an otherwise empty spot as a foundation for reflecting on our mission. As I said in that earlier article, they are just right for such a purpose: simply stated, obviously wise, somehow romantic and charming in an exotic sort of way, and with the intellectual strength to stand alone.

## Possessed by librarianship

The stature and character of the author himself also contribute to the appeal of Ranganathan's ideas. Shiyali Ramamrita Ranganathan (1892–1972) was originally a professor of mathematics who was pressed into library service at Madras University in the 1920s. He went abroad to study librarianship at the University College of London, working under the renowned W. C. Berwick-Sayers, and returned to India as a man possessed. He lived and breathed librarianship for the rest of his long and remarkable career.

He was known as the Father of Indian Librarianship for his work in organizing professional associations, developing his country's regional and national library plans, and organizing schools of library science at three major Indian universities.

He was a prolific writer, turning out an impressive stream of books and articles on all aspects of the field. And he developed what is almost certainly the most elegant and ingenious library classification system to date: the Colon Classification, an "analytico-synthetic" scheme of facets, isolates, and fundamental categories that is still the delight of classification students.

He was also a devout Hindu and a mystic, and his writings are filled with a sense of *dharma*, the cosmic law that binds together all things in their mutual destiny. In his book on the Five Laws, he speaks of "the spirit of the library," a vital force that persists through time and reality, through books, ideas, and our thirst for knowledge, to create eternally the climate in which a library will live and flourish. He even goes on to quote, in Sanskrit, from the Bhagavad-Gita, comparing the spirit of the library to the "inner person" of Krishna:

वासांसि जीर्णानि यथा विहाय नवानि गृह्णाति नरोऽपराणि ।
तथा शरीराणि विहाय जीर्णान्यन्यानि संयाति नवानि देही ॥

नैनं छिन्दन्ति शस्त्राणि नैनं दहति पावकः ।
न चैनं क्लेदयन्त्यापो न शोषयति मारुतः ॥

अच्छेद्योऽयमदाह्योऽयमक्लेद्योऽशोष्य एव च ।
नित्यः सर्वगतः स्थाणुरचलोऽयं सनातनः ॥

This is translated, in part:

> He is eternal, all-pervading,
> steadfast and immovable;
> he is the same for ever.

Such mysticism and subjectivity were also evident in Ranganathan's passionate commitment to a highly personal approach in reference service. His faith is sublimely expressed at the end of a discussion of the need for close intellectual contact between librarians and our patrons. We must never abandon them to our nonhuman tools, he says, but rather should whisper to them as they come among us:

> take my hand,
> for I have passed this way
> And know the truth.

It is in just such mysticism and such idealism that Ranganathan's strong appeal lies. How compelling to believe that this brilliant man could—perhaps through some arcane Eastern way of understanding—recognize the kernel, the essence, the distillation of our professional mission and present it to us in the form of five simple canons. And how appealing to have our instincts buttressed by the knowledge that this prophet of librarianship was also the creator of elegant classification systems and theories of indexing that are still studied today, as well as the pragmatic force behind an entire great nation's library development.

Irresistible. Ranganathan, we hail you.

*Source:* Lee W. Finks, "A Centennial Salute to Ranganathan," *American Libraries* 23 (July/August 1992): 593–94.

# Insight into Ranganathan

**EXTRACT FROM A LETTER of S. R. Ranganathan to M. S. Venkataramani:**

Those that have only fractional intuition will have to do much intellectual work before intuition is spontaneously released for a short while. It is during this short period that most of the discoveries, inventions, formulation of fundamental laws, etc., are made. But after the intuitive spell passes away, these very persons will have to follow up the results of intuition by persistent intellectual work. The industry of such people is immeasurable. Newton is a historical example. Our mathematician, Ramanujan, was an example within my knowledge. After the intellect pursues the problem doggedly for a time, suddenly intuition will push aside the intellect and he will directly see "some new result." Then he will spend sleepless nights in following up the consequences of that new result. I have given some anecdotes illustrating this in my book, *Ramanujan: The Man and Mathematician* (Asia Publishing House).

In my case, in the present subject of my interest, I have had split moments of experience of intuition. My Five Laws of Library Science were "seen" in this new way. My own other postulates, forming the foundation of my theory of library classification were seen like that. I had to slave a good deal to understand the why and wherefore of certain facts of experience. But the intellect had done its best; it appears for a split second and gives the postulates. Once they are handed over by intuition, my intellect had to work out their implications for days and days with hardly any sleep, for example, continuously for a few days. My theory of library classification published as *Prolegomena to Library Classification* has been worked out in this way.

After a person is bathed in intuition even for a split second he rises above his body as it were. The intellect works for long days without any exhaustion developing in the body.

It is this experience during the last 45 years that accounts, for example, for the near ecstasy into which I fell when you called on me the other day. My wife and yourself were showing concern about my physical health and protested that I should not talk any longer. But I persisted because enormous energy came over me. My sleep was very pleasant. At 5:00 a.m., the write-up that you wanted came out whole as an egg.

After the Burning of the Witches, the West tabooed, so to speak, any talk of mysticism. Though there are still a few mystics in the West—I knew some of them—they dare not show themselves out. Therefore, the West regards mysticism as a branch of Philosophy, which is a purely intellectual one.

*Source:* Girja Kumar, *Ranganathan, Dewey and C. V. Raman: A Study in the Arrogance of Intellectual Power* (New Delhi: Vikas Publishing House, 1991). 147p.

# Writing a local library history

*by John V. Richardson Jr., Steve Fisher,*
*Betty Hanson, and Holley R. Lange*

## Ten steps

1. Identify all relevant primary and secondary source material relating to the library (see below for a brief listing of the various types of sources).
2. Identify any local histories or archival collections which will allow you to set your library's history in the context of its community.
3. Read other local library histories as models for your own work. Donald G. Davis and John M. Tucker, *American Library History: A Comprehensive Guide to the Literature* (Santa Barbara, Calif.: ABC-CLIO, 1989), contains some excellent examples for all types of libraries.
4. Read other sources which give you a sense of the development of libraries and the environmental context during the time period you are covering so that you can set your library in context.
5. Immerse yourself in your local source material.
6. Establish a chronology of critical events and people in the history of the library.

7. Identify time periods within the chronology.
8. Consider these periods as the basis for the chapters of your local history.
9. Write drafts of your chapters, documenting how you know what you know (footnotes, references, or bibliography) and circulate these to critical readers for their comments.
10. Publish your work so that it can contribute to the growing body of knowledge about the development of libraries.

### Primary source materials

1. Board minutes.
2. Annual reports and departmental reports.
3. Collection development statements, donation records, accession books, circulation records, and any public service policy statements.
4. Correspondence (letter books).
5. Photographs.
6. Local/national newspaper and journal articles.
7. Personal papers of librarians and support staff.
8. Oral histories of senior/retired staff as well as long-time library users.
9. Earlier local histories, published or in manuscript.
10. Precursor organizations (minute books of women's clubs, Sunday School libraries).
11. Published biographies or memoirs.
12. Student papers from colleges and universities with an interest in your library.
13. Blueprints and other architectural material relating to library construction.

Some locations for primary source materials include the state library, your local institution's archives, and local historical societies.

*Source:* John V. Richardson Jr., Steve Fisher, Betty Hanson, and Holley R. Lange, *Guidelines for Writing Local Library Histories* (Chicago: ALA Library History Round Table, 1994). 2p.

The Future

# ALA's long-range communications plan, 1990–2000

## The decade of the librarian

GOALS
- Librarianship will be perceived as *the* information profession.
- Librarians and ALA will be recognized as authorities on key information issues.
- ALA will have greater visibility with members and the public.
- ALA members will enjoy greater visibility and support for their

profession and institutions, more respect from the public, and increased self-esteem.
- Librarians will be perceived as leaders fighting for information issues.
- Librarians will be effective spokespersons for their profession and institutions.
- Libraries will be well-used and supported.

OBJECTIVES
- Focus ALA's public information program on key issues and messages of importance to the profession and public.
- Increase visibility of ALA and librarians to nonlibrary audiences using a variety of media.
- Identify and respond to emerging issues in a timely way.
- Support ALA leadership and librarians at all levels in speaking out effectively for their profession and association.

KEY MESSAGES
Librarians are fighting for . . .
- Literacy and reading.
- The First Amendment.
- Access to information and your right to know.
- Excellence in education.

KEY AUDIENCES
- Decision makers and influencers: Congress, state and local officials, community leaders, and library boards.
- Educators: associations, administrators, and faculty.
- General public: taxpayers, parents, minorities, senior citizens, children, future librarians.
- Librarians: ALA members and nonmembers, Friends of Libraries groups, trustees, library advocates, and White House Conference on Library and Information Science delegates.
- Financial backers: Prospective donors, current donors, and supporters.

*Source:* ALA Public Information Office.

# Future personnel projections

THOSE ATTENDING THE 20th ALA Office for Library Personnel Resources anniversary reception at the 1993 ALA Annual Conference offered these projections for the future:

- Librarianship will adopt a new paradigm in which all employees function as managers or are self-managed.
- A major issue will be how to achieve quality performance in collaborative organizational models.
- Recognition of the importance and interdependency of professionals in customer service will grow.
- ADA compliance—title employment, job descriptions, etc., will remain an important issue.
- Achieving equity and diversity will continue to be problems.
- A different type of person will be recruited into the profession. He or she will have a greater variety of cultural/ethnic background and different ideas of what library/ information service can be—more creative, articulate, energetic.

- The cost of educating personnel will affect the type of individual entering the profession.
- Questions about training will loom large: How will our personnel be trained? In graduate programs? On the job? By big corporations?
- Librarians will focus primarily on ways to make library customers more effective in their own search for knowledge and information.
- Education will shift increasingly to libraries and away from universities (returning to the original apprenticeship model prior to Dewey).
- There will be more temporary and contract employees than permanent employees in certain kinds of libraries, although American society may revolt against this.
- Telecommuting and independent librarianship will grow. The librarian will be independent and will have a "portfolio" of activities relating to the provision of information to clients via electronic media and transfer.

*Source:* "Future Projections: What Personnel Issues Will Affect Librarianship in the Next Twenty Years?" *Library Personnel News* 7 (November-December 1993): 5.

# What's wrong with libraries?

AT THE ALA MIDWINTER MEETING IN DENVER in January 1993, CRISES Press sponsored a flip-chart for anonymous graffiti responding to the question "What's Wrong with Libraries?" Here are librarians' unexpurgated replies.

- It's too hard to keep things and give them away at the same time!
- We're not libraries—we're the information stores—the 7-11 of information!
- The computers (the modern substitute for the card catalog) are down half the time.
- Librarians are factory workers with fancy titles—the work is routine and management is hostile.
- (Referring to above quote) If true, sounds like you're prime management material!
- The "greed factor" is alive and well in libraries—administrators get all the money!
- Librarians take themselves far too seriously at ALA committee meetings—lighten up!
- ALA does not need to meet twice a year!
- (Referring to above quote) Some organizations such as the National Lawyers Guild have major meetings every 18 months, then two or three smaller ones in between. This also solves the problem of always having large meetings in summer in large conference cities that may have poor summer weather. We should learn to use (not just store) our information. Why do we go to Dallas and New Orleans and Miami in the summer? A quick look at a source like *Climate of U.S. Cities* would tell any intelligent person that's a stupid idea.
- (In reply to the above quote) Money! If you think hotel rates are high, consider what they'd be during "seasons"—maybe ALA should go to Fall/Spring?

- Need to learn to be "people-people" not "book-people" . . . from a people person.
- Not enough libraries make this kind of material available to their users. Self-censorship??!!
- (In response to above quote) We have met the enemy and he is us!—Pogo the Librarian.
- Librarians do not think big enough.
- Libraries do not get the financial support to do the job they want/need to do.
- They are designed and operated for librarians, not the people who use them!
- The profession is too "inner-directed"—need to get out and talk/work with other people professions. We've got a lot of expertise—but how many people know it?
- No one knows librarians ARE educated professionals—we need a MASSIVE publicity campaign to regain respect for libraries.
- (In response to above quote) Hear, Hear!
- PAY.
- Too many male administrators and too many female foot soldiers.
- There is not enough political sophistication/activism on the part of librarians. We are in the middle of the information revolution, yet the vendors are getting rich off it, and we are still begging for the crumbs. Every librarian should have political activism written into her job description. We are too wise to be so passive.
- (In response to the above quote) AMEN!
- Librarians should also not censor so much in their selection. Knowledge should be free.
- Not enough library staff.
- Our users need to see both or many sides of the issues. More talk gives better ideas!
- Amendment 1—Colorado.
- Too many committees—too much duplication!
- The controversial materials need to be selected and made accessible to library users more often and more aggressively.

*Source:* "What's Wrong with Libraries?" *Librarians at Liberty* 1, no.1 (June 1993): 4–5.
Reprinted with permission.

# Musts for the research library by 2000

*by Richard M. Dougherty and Carol Hughes*

IN JUNE 1992, the Research Libraries Group sponsored a workshop on "Preferred Library Futures: Charting the Paths," led by Richard M. Dougherty, University of Michigan, and Penny Griffith, consultant. Thirty-two people, from six groups with a stake in the future of research libraries, met to consider what strategies might be pursued to transform the library and other elements of the campus information environment. These were their recommendations:

From the perspective of university library directors:
- become more adept at providing information; become managers of knowledge; increase the library's education role; attract staff who

possess disciplinary strengths as well as technical literacy;
- preserve the library as a place where people can meet, interact, and work; continue to focus on preservation of print information sources as well as electronic sources;
- become a technology leader and not a follower; become more active as producers of information; focus on access rather than ownership and acquisitions; work collaboratively with many other stakeholder groups;
- provide environments that are fluid enough to accommodate change; be cost effective.

**From the perspective of consortia and foundation officers:**
- assume that resources will continue to be scarce;
- do a better job of prioritizing; give more consideration to risk-benefit choices; make distinctions about services (or risk bankruptcy); give up illusions that information is free and access is equal; ameliorate stratification;
- invest in technology to continue to be a supplier; does the library play a role in changing the performance and quality evaluation of faculty?
- do a better job of defining the purpose of linkages among institutions; e.g., define what is meant by resource sharing;
- involve other sectors of the campus in efforts to change;
- make a case that the public benefits in order to make a case for more resources;
- make distinctions at the institutional level about research and teaching, and between individuals who have grants and those who don't.

**From the perspective of the faculty:**
- be involved in teaching students; help faculty teach the use of technology to unprepared students;
- provide access to all; provide a different information environment to support research with economic value;
- play a more active role in scholarly communication; take over the publishing function; scan texts, distribute electronic texts; play a more direct role in communicating through discipline-oriented invisible colleges;
- the campus must provide an infrastructure that supports technology; must be willing to continue reinvesting in technology; stop buying some items on paper.

**From the perspective of the publishers:**
- the library must not be a warehouse but provide access; librarians need to be more effective at cooperating with other institutions; have a perspective that embraces all information formats; be more selective in what is bought and in services provided; be better marketers; be willing to offer some services free while charging for others; be more active as intermediaries between users and information providers and scholars and information resources;
- the campus requires a campus information system, which requires a larger share of the campus budget; librarians need to be more actively involved in allocating campus information dollars; librarians need to lead in university environments.

**From the perspective of information technology managers:**
- be client-centered; provide services so that faculty need not come

to a building; retain the good things and values libraries currently possess, e.g., contact with faculty and connections with the humanities; be a nexus between librarians and computer consultants but not necessarily an organizational nexus;

- librarians need to be part of the leadership group; become more technologically sophisticated;
- recognize the common ground between libraries and information technology; become fully integrated with information technology either as part of a single infrastructure or as service providers; develop common structures; develop a new breed of middle managers in both libraries and information technology units; develop a common language and mutual respect; develop a new class of information professional.

**From the perspective of the administrators:**
- be affordable; require no increase in total dollar share of resources spent; no increase in space;
- increase efficiency of getting at information through better cataloging and organization;
- effect a genuine merger between information technology and the library that moves away from a competitive stance;
- become an information center; serve all kinds of clients; establish their own organization to sell scholarly output; stimulate collaboration between providers and scholars;
- improve library education—current professionals are not trained well enough; need more subject preparation; achieve a better understanding of what scholars need;
- provide access to information of any type anywhere; acquire rights to use, but not acquire, information on speculation that it might be needed later; provide proportionately more access than ownership;
- do not publicize the number of volumes in college statistics; instead emphasize access to information that can be provided;
- campuses need to change faculty attitudes toward the library; change the concept of publication; reassess what should be required with publication and the format of publication; protect privacy and honor copyright in an electronic environment; reassess the criteria used to gauge faculty productivity.

*Source:* Richard M. Dougherty and Carol Hughes, *Preferred Library Futures II: Charting the Paths* (Mountain View, Calif.: Research Libraries Group, February 1993). 27p. Reprinted with permission.

# PEOPLE

2

# Who works in libraries?

*by Mary Jo Lynch*

LIBRARIES HIRE LIBRARIANS AND OTHER professionals, paraprofessionals, clerical and technical personnel. The 3,274 college and university libraries responding to a 1992 survey reported a total of 95,837 paid staff (full-time and full-time equivalent of part-time) for the academic year 1991–92. Of the total staff in academic libraries, 27% are librarians and other professionals, 30% are student assistants, and 42% are other paid staff.

The almost 8,946 public libraries reporting to NCES for 1992 employ a total of 109,933 paid staff (full-time and full-time equivalent of part-time). Of the total number of staff in public libraries, 22.3% hold master's degrees from graduate library education programs accredited by ALA.

For 1990–1991, public and private schools reported a total of 144,368 paid staff (full-time and full-time equivalent of part-time) in library media centers. Of the total number of staff, 57% are certified school library media specialists.

The following figures provide an estimate of employment in academic, public and school libraries as of 1992:

|         |                                   |
|---------|-----------------------------------|
| 133,081 | Librarians and other professionals |
| 219,734 | Support staff                     |
| 352,815 | Total persons employed            |

Comparable figures for employment in special libraries (e.g., libraries serving businesses, scientific and government agencies, and nonprofit organizations) are not available from any one source. However, the Special Libraries Association counts among its personal members almost 12,000 who work in such libraries.

*Source:* Mary Jo Lynch, ALA Office for Research and Statistics; National Center for Education Statistics, *Academic Libraries, 1992* (1994); National Center for Education Statistics, *Public Libraries in the United States, 1992* (1994); National Center for Education Statistics, *Schools and Staffing in the United States: A Statistical Profile, 1990–91* (1993).

# What job categories are there?

IN ADDITION TO FORMAL TRAINING and education, skills other than those of librarianship may have an important contribution to make to the achievement of superior library service. There should be equal recognition in both the professional and support ranks for those individuals whose expertise contributes to the effective performance of the library.

The table on the next page suggests a set of categories and defines basic requirements and responsibilities for professional and support staff.

The titles recommended here represent categories or broad classifications, within which it is assumed that there will be several levels of promotional steps. Specific job titles may be used within any category: for example, catalogers, reference librarians, children's librarians would be included in either the "Librarian" or (depending upon the level of their responsibilities and qualifications) "Senior Librarian" categories; department heads, the director of the library, and certain specialists would presumably have the additional qualifications and responsibilities which place them in the "Senior Librarian" category.

## Categories of library personnel—Professional

Senior Librarian/Senior Specialist
*Requirements:* In addition to relevant experience, education beyond the M.A. (i.e., a
master's degree in any of its variant designations: M.A., M.L.S., M.S.L.S., M.Ed.,
etc.) as: post-master's degree; Ph.D.; relevant continuing education in many forms.
*Responsibility:* Top-level responsibilities, including but not limited to administration;
superior knowledge of some aspect of librarianship, or of other subject fields of
value to the library.

Librarian/Specialist
*Requirements:* Master's degree.
*Responsibility:* Professional responsibilities including those of management, which
require independent judgment, interpretation of rules and procedures, analysis of
library problems, and formulation of original and creative solutions for them
(normally utilizing knowledge of the subject field represented by the academic
degree).

## Categories of library personnel—Support staff

Library Associate/Associate Specialist
*Requirements:* Bachelor's degree (with or without coursework in library science); *or*
bachelor's degree, plus additional academic work short of the master's degree (in
librarianship for the Library Associate; in other relevant subject fields for the
Associate Specialist).
*Responsibility:* Support responsibilities at a high level, normally working within the
established procedures and techniques, and with some supervision by a
professional, but requiring judgment, and subject knowledge such as is represented by a full, four-year college education culminating in the bachelor's degree.
Library Technical Assistant/Technical Assistant
*Requirements:* At least two years of college-level study; *or* A.A. degree, with or without
Library Technical Assistant training; *or* post-secondary school training in relevant
skills.
*Responsibility:* Tasks performed as support staff to Associates and higher ranks,
following established rules and procedures, and including, at the top level,
supervision of such tasks.
Clerk
*Requirements:* Business school or commercial courses, supplemented by in-service
training or on-the-job experience.
*Responsibility:* Clerical assignments as required by the individual library.

2

Where specific job titles dictated by local usage and tradition do not make
clear the level of the staff member's qualification and responsibility, it is
recommended that reference to the ALA category title be used parentheti-
cally to provide clarification. For example: Reference Assistant (Librarian);
Head Cataloger (Senior Librarian); Library Aide (Library Technical Assistant).

The title "Librarian" carries with it the connotation of "professional" in the
sense that professional tasks are those which require a special background
and education. This is the basis by which the librarian identifies library needs,
analyzes problems, sets goals, and formulates original and creative solutions,
integrating theory into practice, and planning, organizing, communicating,
and administering successful programs of service to users of the library's
materials and services. In defining services to users, the professional recognizes potential users as well as current ones, and designs services that will
reach all who might benefit from them.

"Librarian" therefore should be used only to designate positions in
libraries that utilize the qualifications and impose the responsibilities suggested above. Positions that are primarily devoted to the routine application
of established rules and techniques, however useful and essential to the
effective operation of a library's ongoing services, should not carry the word
"Librarian" in the job title.

The salaries for each category should offer a range of promotional steps sufficient to permit a career-in-rank. The top salary in any category should overlap the beginning salary in the next higher category, in order to give recognition to the value of experience and knowledge gained on the job.

Inadequately supported libraries or libraries too small to be able to afford professional staff should nevertheless have access to the services and supervision of a librarian. To obtain the professional guidance that they themselves cannot supply, such libraries should promote cooperative arrangements or join larger systems of cooperating libraries through which supervisory personnel can be supported. Smaller libraries that are part of such a system can often maintain the local service with building staff at the Associate level.

The *Clerk* classifications do not require formal academic training in library subjects. The assignments in these categories are based upon general clerical and secretarial proficiencies. Familiarity with basic library terminology and routines necessary to

*Career Lattice:* The movement among staff responsibilities is not necessarily directly up, but often may be lateral to increased responsibilities of equal importance. Each category embodies a number of promotional steps within it, as indicated by the gradation markings on each bar. The top of any category overlaps in responsibility and salary the next higher category.

adapt clerical skills to the library's needs is best learned on the job.

The *Technical Assistant* categories assume certain kinds of specific "technical" skills; they are not meant simply to accommodate advanced clerks. While clerical skills might well be part of a Technical Assistant's equipment, the emphasis in an assignment should be on the special technical skill. For example, someone who is skilled in handling audiovisual equipment, or at introductory data processing, or in making posters and other displays might well be hired in the Technical Assistant category for these skills, related to librarianship only to the extent that they are employed in a library. A *Library Technical Assistant* is a person with certain specific library-related skills—in preliminary bibliographic searching for example, or utilization of certain mechanical equipment—the performance of whose duties seldom requires a background in general education.

The *Associate* categories assume a need for an educational background like that represented by a bachelor's degree from a good four-year institution of higher education in the United States. Assignments may be such that library knowledge is less important than general education, and whether the title is *Library Associate* or *Associate Specialist* depends upon the nature of the tasks and responsibilities assigned. Persons holding the B.A. degree, with or without a library science minor or practical experience in libraries, are eligible for employment in this category. Titles within the Associate category that are assigned to individuals will depend upon the relevance of their training and background to their specific assignments.

The Associate category also provides the opportunity for persons of promise and exceptional talent to begin library employment below the level of professional (as defined in this statement) and thus to combine employment in a library with coursework at the graduate level. Where this kind of work/study arrangement is made, the combination of work and formal study should provide 1) increasing responsibility within the Associate ranks as the individual moves through the academic program, and 2) eligibility for promotion, upon completion of the master's degree, to positions of professional responsibility and attendant reclassification to the professional category.

The first professional category—*Librarian*, or *Specialist*—assumes responsibilities that are professional in the sense described above. A good liberal education plus graduate-level study in the field of specialization (either in librarianship or in a relevant field) are seen as the minimum preparation for the kinds of assignments implied. The title, however, is given for a position entailing professional responsibilities and not automatically upon achievement of the academic degree.

The *Senior* categories assume relevant professional experience as well as qualifications beyond those required for admission to the first professional ranks. Normally it is assumed that such advanced qualifications shall be held in some specialty, either in a particular aspect of librarianship or some relevant subject field. Subject specializations are as applicable in the *Senior Librarian* category as they are in the *Senior Specialist* category.

Administrative responsibilities entail advanced knowledge and skills comparable to those represented by any other high-level specialty, and appointment to positions in top administration should normally require the qualifications of a *Senior Librarian* with a specialization in administration. This category, however, is not limited to administrators, whose specialty is only one of several specializations of value to the library service. There are many areas of special knowledge within librarianship which are equally important and to which equal recognition in prestige and salary should be given. Highly qualified persons with specialist responsibilities in some aspects of librarianship—archives, bibliography, reference, for example— should be eligible for advanced status and financial rewards without being forced to abandon for administrative responsibilities their areas of major competence.

*Source: Library Education and Personnel Utilization* (Chicago: American Library Association, 1976).

# Guide to library
# placement sources

*by Margaret Myers*

### General sources of library jobs

**CLASSIFIED ADS** are regularly found in *American Libraries, Chronicle of Higher Education, College & Research Libraries News, Library Journal,* and *Library Hotline*. State and regional library association newsletters, state library journals, and foreign library periodicals are other sources.

The *New York Times* Sunday "Week in Review" section carries a special section of ads for librarian jobs in addition to the regular classifieds. Local newspapers, particularly the larger city Sunday editions, often carry job vacancy listings in libraries for both professional and support staff.

A number of position openings appear as announcements on the library-related electronic listservs on the Internet, although these are interspersed with other news items. This is undoubtedly a growing trend.

## Specialized library associations and groups

Other organizations assist library job seekers with advertisements or placement services. Only a short listing with address and phone number is found here; further information may be obtained from the organization itself, or from a more complete listing available from ALA's Office for Library Personnel Resources.

**Advanced Information Management,** 444 Castro St., Suite 320, Mountain View, CA 94041; (415) 965-7799.

*Affirmative Action Register,* 8356 Olive Blvd., St. Louis, MO 63132.

**American Association of Law Libraries,** 53 W. Jackson Blvd., Suite 940, Chicago, IL 60604; (312) 939-4764.

*American Libraries,* "Career LEADS," 50 E. Huron St., Chicago, IL 60611; (312) 280-4211.

**ALA/Office for Library Personnel Resources,** 50 E. Huron St., Chicago, IL 60611; (312) 280-4277.

**American Society for Information Science,** 8720 Georgia Ave., #501, Silver Spring, MD 20910-3602; (301) 495-0900.

**Art Libraries Society of North America,** 4101 Lake Boone Trail, Suite 201, Raleigh, NC; (919) 787-5181.

*Asian/Pacific American Libraries Newsletter,* c/o Anna Wang, Ohio State University, 124 Main Library, 1858 Neil Avenue Mall, Columbus, OH 43210-1286; (614) 292-6151.

**Association for Educational Communications and Technology,** Placement and Referral Service, 1025 Vermont Ave., Suite 820, Washington, DC 20005; (202) 347-7834; fax (202) 347-7839.

**Association for Library and Information Science Education,** 4101 Lake Boone Trail, Suite 201, Raleigh, NC 27607; (919) 787-5181.

*Black Caucus Newsletter,* c/o George C. Grant, Editor, Rollins College, 1000 Holt Ave., #2654, Winter Park, FL 32789; (407) 646-2676; fax (407) 646-1515.

**C. Berger and Company,** 327 E. Gundersen Dr., Carol Stream, IL 60188; (708) 653-1115, (800) 382-4222.

**Canadian Association of Special Libraries and Information Services,** c/o Job Bank Coordinator, 266 Sherwood Dr., Ottawa, Ontario, Canada K1Y 3W4; (613) 728-9982.

*Catholic Library World,* 9009 Carter St., Allen Park, MI 48101.

*Chinese-American Librarians Association Newsletter,* c/o Meng-Xiong Liu, Clark Library, San Jose State University, 1 Washington Square, San Jose, CA 95119-0028; (408) 924-2817; fax (408) 924-2701.

*Chronicle of Higher Education,* 1255 23d St., N.W., Suite 700, Washington, DC 20037; (202) 466-1000; fax (202) 296-2691.

*College & Research Libraries News,* ALA/Association of College & Research Libraries, 50 E. Huron St., Chicago, IL 60611; (312) 280-2513.

**Council for International Exchange of Scholars,** 3007 Tilden St., N.W., Suite 5M, Washington, DC 20008-3097; (202) 686-7877.

**Council on Library/Media Technical Assistants,** c/o Membership Chair, Ruth

A. Tolbert, Central Indiana ALSA, 1100 W. 42d St., #305, Indianapolis, IN 46208.

*Feliciter,* 200 Elgin St., Suite 602, Ottawa, Ontario, Canada K2P 1L5; (613) 232-9625.

**Gossage Regan Associates, Inc.,** 25 W. 43d St., New York, NY 10036; (212) 869-3348; fax (212) 997-1127.

*Indiana Jobline,* Central Indiana ALSA, 1100 W. 42d St., #305, Indianapolis, IN 46208; (317) 926-6561; modem (317) 924-9584.

*Institutional Library Mailed Jobline,* c/o Gloria Spooner, State Library of Louisiana, P.O. Box 131, Baton Rouge, LA 70821; (504) 342-4931; fax (504) 342-3547.

**International Association of School Librarianship,** P.O. Box 1486, Kalamazoo, MI 49005.

**International Schools Services,** P.O. Box 5910, Princeton, NJ 08543; (609) 452-0990.

**Labat-Anderson, Inc.,** 2200 Clarendon Blvd., Suite 900, Arlington, VA 22201; (703) 525-9400.

**The Library Co-Op, Inc.,** 3840 Park Ave., Suite 107, Edison, NJ 08820; (908) 906-1777, (800) 654-6275.

**Library Fellows Program,** c/o Robert P. Doyle, American Library Association, 50 E. Huron St., Chicago, IL 60611; (312) 280-3200.

**Library Management Systems,** 4730 Woodman Ave., Suite 330, Sherman Oaks, CA 91423; (818) 789-3141, (310) 277-9012, (714) 251-1020, (619) 456-4083.

*Library Mosaics,* P.O. Box 5171, Culver City, CA 90231; (310) 410-1573.

*MLA News,* Medical Library Association, 6 N. Michigan Ave., Suite 300, Chicago, IL 60602-4805; (312) 419-9094.

**National Faculty Exchange,** 4656 W. Jefferson, Suite 140, Fort Wayne, IN 46804.

*Overseas Opportunities for Educators,* U.S. Department of Defense, Dependents Schools, 2461 Eisenhower Ave., Alexandria, VA 22331-1100.

**Peace Corps,** 1990 K St., N.W., 9th Floor, Washington, DC 20525; (202) 606-3010.

**Pro Libra Associates, Inc.,** 6 Inwood Place, Maplewood, NJ 07040; (201) 762-0070, (800) 262-0070.

*SCANsheet,* School Library Career Awareness Network, School of Information Studies, Syracuse, NY 13244; (315) 443-2740.

**Society of American Archivists,** 600 S. Federal, Suite 504, Chicago, IL 60605; (312) 922-0140.

*SpecialList,* Special Libraries Association, 1700 18th St., N.W., Washington, DC 20009-2508; (202) 234-4700.

**U.S. Information Agency,** Special Services Branch, 301 4th St., S.W., Washington, DC 20547.

---

### Librarians on leadership

**Richard DeGennaro, librarian, Widener Memorial Library, Harvard:**
It's a question of age and experience. Young people, as they enter the profession, are so concerned about doing things right that they don't pay attention. . . . it takes age, experience and self-confidence to come to the conclusion that maybe what we are doing is not the right thing and there is need to change. . . . Some people are born with that; some of us have to work at it and develop it.

*Source:* Brooke E. Sheldon, *Leaders in Libraries: Styles and Strategies for Success* (Chicago: American Library Association, 1991), 93p.

# Library joblines

LIBRARY JOBLINES GIVE recorded telephone messages of job openings.
Most tapes are changed once a week, although individual listings may be
repeated. The majority are for professional jobs only.

| Jobline sponsor | Job seekers call | |
| --- | --- | --- |
| American Association of Law Libraries | (312) 939-7877 | |
| Arizona Dept. of Library, Archives & Public Records | (602) 275-2325 | (Arizona only) |
| British Columbia Library Association | (604) 430-6411 | (B.C. only) |
| California Library Association | (916) 443-1222 | (in north) |
| | (818) 797-4602 | (in south) |
| California Media & Library Educators Association | (415) 697-8832 | |
| Colorado State Library | (303) 866-6741 | (Colorado only) |
| Connecticut Library Association Jobline | (203) 645-8090 | (Conn. only) |
| Delaware Division of Libraries | (800) 282-8696 | (in-state) |
| | (302) 739-4748 | (out-of-state) |
| Drexel University College of Information Studies | (215) 895-1672 | |
| State Library of Florida | (904) 488-5232 | (Florida only) |
| Library Jobline of Illinois | (312) 828-0930 | (professional) |
| | (312) 828-9198 | (support) |
| Indiana Statewide Library Jobline | (317) 926-6561 | |
| State Library of Iowa | (515) 281-6788 | (Iowa only) |
| Kansas State Library Jobline | (913) 296-3296 | |
| Kentucky Job Hotline | (502) 564-3008 | |
| Maryland Library Association | (410) 685-5760 | |
| Medical Library Association | (312) 553-4636 | |
| Metropolitan Washington Council of Governments | (202) 962-3712 | |
| Michigan Library Association | (517) 694-7440 | |
| Missouri Library Association Jobline | (314) 442-6590 | |
| Mountain Plains Library Association | (800) 356-7820 | (regional only) |
| | (605) 677-5757 | |
| Nebraska Job Hotline | (800) 307-2665 | (in Nebraska) |
| | (402) 471-2045 | |
| New England Library Jobline | (617) 738-3148 | (regional only) |
| New Jersey Library Association | (609) 695-2121 | |
| New York Library Association | (800) 252-6952 | (in New York) |
| | (518) 432-6952 | |
| North Carolina State Library | (919) 733-6410 | (N.C. only) |
| Ohio Library Council Jobline | (614) 225-6999 | (Ohio only) |
| Oklahoma Dept. of Libraries Jobline | (405) 521-4202 | |
| Oregon Library Association | (503) 585-2232 | (regional only) |
| Pacific Northwest Library Association | (206) 543-2890 | (regional only) |
| Pennsylvania Jobline | (717) 234-4646 | |
| Pratt Institute SLIS Job Hotline | (718) 636-3742 | |
| Special Libraries Association | (202) 234-3632 | |
| Special Libraries Association, N.Y. Chapter | (212) 740-2007 | |
| Special Libraries Association, San Andreas-<br>San Francisco Bay Chapter | (415) 856-2140<br>(415) 391-7441 | |
| Special Libraries Association, S.Calif. Chapter | (818) 795-2145 | |
| Texas Library Association Job Hotline | (512) 328-0651 | |
| Texas State Library Jobline | (512) 463-5470 | |
| University of South Carolina College of Library<br>and Information Science | (803) 777-8443 | |

Virginia Library Association           (703) 519-8027   (Virginia only)
University of Western Ontario         (519) 661-3543

*Source:* ALA Office for Library Personnel Resources, 1994.

# Where MLS librarians are in public libraries

**2**

*by Mary Jo Lynch and Keith Curry Lance*

**EVERY PUBLIC LIBRARY HAS A LIBRARIAN** and every librarian has an MLS. Right? Wrong. If you accept the official American Library Association (ALA) policy on the appropriate professional degree for a librarian, only 41.1% of public libraries had qualified librarians in 1990. This situation is not really news to a lot of people. Many guessed that it was true. But statistics now available from the Federal-State Cooperative System for Public Library Data (FSCS) enable us to support those guesses with facts!

The FSCS is a system that involves the annual collection of data from public libraries by state library agencies, submission of these data on diskette to the National Center for Education Statistics (NCES), and compilation of the data into a national report produced annually by the NCES. This article describes data on public library staff in the 1990 FSCS report and suggests what the data might mean, especially for state library agencies, library associations, and library educators.

The phrase "MLS librarian" is a shorthand for persons who have master's degrees from graduate library education programs accredited by the ALA. Several years ago, ALA officially proclaimed that this degree is "the appropriate professional degree for librarians" (ALA Policy Manual 54.2). Despite this policy, the authorities that employ staff in public libraries frequently give the title of librarian to people with widely varying credentials. In some states, the practice is authorized by certification requirements that do not specify the MLS. In other places, the practice is a manifestation of the all-too-common assumption that anyone responsible for a library is a librarian.

During the process of determining what statistics to collect for the FSCS, it was decided to include data elements that could be used to document the situation just described. The following data elements are included among the forty-one that each state library agency collected from public libraries in the state for reporting to the FSCS in 1990:

- Librarians with master's degrees from programs accredited by the ALA;
- All employees holding the title of librarian;
- All other paid employees; and
- Total paid employees.

The FSCS report for 1990 contains data on 8,978 public libraries in the United States. (Data for the 6,562 branches are included but are not reported separately.) Ninety-seven percent of the 8,978 libraries responded to the item "total paid employees." Ninety-five percent responded to the item "all employees holding the title of librarian," and 89 percent provided data on "librarians with master's degrees from programs accredited by the ALA." The missing 11% were mostly in two states where the state library agency did not collect data on that item: Alabama and Illinois. In future years, those two states are expected to add the item to the state form. However, the data

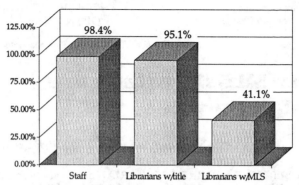

**Figure 1.** Percentage of public libraries with different types of paid staff, 1990.
Source: NCES.

available now are complete enough to give a reasonably accurate picture.

The report of FSCS data for 1990 displays a variety of statistics about the staffing of public libraries. For example:

- 108,246 persons are employed in public libraries.
- 34,082 of the 108,246 (31%) have the title of librarian.
- 21,305 of the 108,246 (20%) have the MLS.
- 73,186 "other paid staff" are employed in public libraries.

Those data are displayed by state and by size of population in the FSCS report for 1990.

A table in that report shows the number of paid full-time equivalents (FTE) staff in public libraries by ranges—from the 141 libraries reporting "none" to the 154 reporting "100 or more." These data were used to create the first bar in Figure 1, which shows that 98.4% of public libraries reported paid FTE staff. The second and third bars in Figure 1 were created from data that are not displayed in the paper report but are available on diskette. Those two bars present a very revealing picture of public library staffing. Note that although more than 95% of responding libraries reported some "employees holding title of librarian," only 41.1% reported any "librarians with master's degrees from programs accredited by the ALA."

Where are those libraries without MLS librarians? Data on the FSCS diskette were used to create Figures 3 and 4, which show where they are in terms of population of legal service area and state. To put the data in context, it is important to consider first the distribution of public libraries in the United States by size of "population of legal service area." That phrase was defined for the FSCS to mean "the number of people in the geographical area for which a public library has been established to offer services and from which (or on behalf of which) the library derives income plus any areas served under contract for which the library is the primary service provider."

Of the 8,978 libraries for which data are presented in the 1990 report, 8,888 (99%) reported on population legal service area. Figure 2 displays that data, thus illustrating an important fact about public libraries in the United States: Many libraries serve small populations (5,457 or 61% serve populations of less than 10,000) while only a few serve large populations (444 or 5% serve populations more than 100,000). Most of the people in the United States are served by those 444 libraries. Still, a good number of people in this country are served by the 5,457 libraries serving populations of less than 10,000 and those places have a strong hold on the popular image of what a public library should be. The public libraries depicted in fiction, biography, and the media are often in small towns.

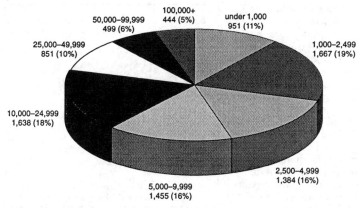

**Figure 2.** Public libraries by population of legal service area, 1990. Source: NCES.

Figure 3 shows the percentage of libraries with MLS librarians by population ranges. Here the picture is very different. Only a few of the libraries serving populations of less than 10,000 have MLS librarians, while all libraries serving populations of 100,000 or more employ them.

The matter of where those libraries are by state is more complex. First, it must be recognized that the two states noted earlier (Alabama and Illinois) did not provide any data on this topic (MLS librarians) for 1990. It is also important to understand that libraries in some states are organized so that there are no independent libraries serving the smaller population ranges. One table in the 1990 report displays by state the number of libraries serving eleven ranges of "population of legal service area." While most states have some libraries in all ranges, some states show no libraries below a certain range. Two states—Georgia and Maryland—have no libraries serving populations of less than 10,000. The cutoff point is 5,000 for four states (Arizona, Louisiana, Mississippi, and South Carolina), 2,500 for three states (Delaware, Tennessee, and Virginia), and 1,000 for another three states (Kentucky, New Jersey, and Wyoming). None of these states are in Figure 4, which shows eleven states reporting that more than 80% of the public libraries in the state have no MLS librarians. Figure 4 also shows the high percentage of libraries in those eleven

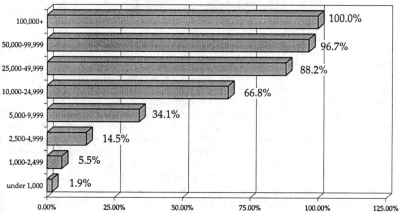

**Figure 3.** Percentage of public libraries with MLS librarians by population range, 1990. Source: NCES.

states serving populations of less than 10,000.

What do these data mean and what, if anything, should be done? Thinking about these questions raises three very controversial issues: education, elitism, and economics. The education of librarians has been controversial since Melvil Dewey's time and is especially so today when every aspect of librarianship is changing rapidly and the social role of many other professions is also changing. The importance of the MLS for public library staff has been challenged in the library press. The character and content of education for librarianship were much discussed during the years of work that preceded the acceptance of ALA's revised standards for accreditation.

| State | % with no MLS librarians |
| --- | --- |
| Nebraska | 92.1% |
| Iowa | 88.6% |
| Montana | 88.2% |
| North Dakota | 87.3% |
| Kansas | 86.9% |
| South Dakota | 85.7% |
| Idaho | 85.3% |
| Vermont | 84.3% |
| Maine | 84.1% |
| Utah | 81.2% |
| Alaska | 81.5% |

Note: MLS = master's degree from program accredited by American Library Association.

**Figure 4.** Percentage of public libraries reporting no MLS librarians in top 11 states, 1990. Source: NCES.

The charge of elitism is difficult to counter when the nature of professional work in libraries has never been clear and is less so today as technology is changing what staff do in libraries. Good arguments for the value of the MLS have been offered for years but are even more cogent today. The complexities of physical and intellectual access to information in the age of the electronic library obviously demand a high level of expertise.

Finally, the economic facts of life are such that libraries serving small populations have a small tax base and usually cannot afford to pay the salary expected by an MLS librarian. It is unrealistic to expect that every public library will have such a person on its staff, and it is also unnecessary thanks to computer and telecommunication technologies.

What response to these data is realistic? Here are a few ideas to get the discussion started. To begin with, it may be useful to consider the question: When is a library not a library? In a letter to the editor of *Library Journal* (June 1992), Oregon state librarian Jim Scheppke suggested that we have many "pseudo libraries" in the United States because staffing and budgets are inadequate. Scheppke recommended serious reconsideration of the 1990s concept of "larger units of service."

These data heighten the importance of work performed by state library agencies and regional library systems to provide leadership from MLS librarians to the non-MLS staff who are running almost 60% of the public libraries in the country. State library agencies sometimes are criticized for not putting federal aid directly into library budgets but using it instead for statewide services, consultant services, and support of systems. These data show one reason why those state and system services are needed. Although economics may preclude employing an MLS librarian in every library, good planning at the state and regional levels can ensure that every library receives advice and other services from MLS librarians. What responsibility does the profession at large have for ensuring that the work that systems and state library agencies do in support of small public libraries is done and done well? This support is in danger now as state library agency budgets suffer and federal funds are short, and system services are easy targets for cuts.

For state and national library associations, these data demonstrate the need for materials in all media and events of various types that provide learning opportunities for library staff who do not have the MLS. Those people may or may not become members of the association. But improving their skills is essential to progress in library service. If that is the goal of an association, attention must be paid to people who are directing local libraries no matter what their qualifications.

For library school faculty, the implications of the data are less clear. One could argue that the data indicate a large market for graduate library education. But it may not be realistic to assume that library staff without the MLS would acquire the degree even if distance education brought programs close to them. Library schools may need to consider how they educate MLS librarians to work with library directors who lack the degree. Also, there may be a market not for education leading to the MLS, but for something better suited to the needs and resources of small population groups. Is this appropriate territory for graduate library education programs? Or is the need better served by other agencies?

There are many possibilities for discussion and debate. The challenge is to use these data to understand and improve public library service in the United States.

*Source:* Mary Jo Lynch and Keith Curry Lance,
"M.L.S. Librarians in Public Libraries: Where They Are and Why It Matters,"
*Public Libraries* 32 (July/August 1993): 204–7.

# Assessing the need for staff development

*by Charles E. Kratz*

SUCCESSFUL STAFF DEVELOPMENT PROGRAMS are relevant to the needs of the staff. A library can determine its staff needs by conducting a needs assessment. This is the process by which an organization asks its staff what they need to do their jobs better and, from the answers, determines a plan of action. The process may range from a simple survey to a complex investigation. Properly done, a needs assessment can be the foundation upon which a strong staff-development program is built.

A needs assessment can:
- Assist management in planning staff-development activities.
- Identify organizational and individual needs and help prioritize those needs.
- Identify training needs based on the goals of the organization.
- Identify attitudes concerning new services, skills, or technologies.
- Identify future opportunities for the organization.
- Identify performance gaps, i.e., when an individual's work performance does not meet expectations.
- Determine the cause of certain performance problems and identify possible solutions.
- Determine whether a need is the result of a training problem, such as a skills deficit, or a nontraining issue, such as policy clarification.
- Provide a checklist of needs for trainers.

## Preparing for the needs assessment

Determine *who* will be responsible for conducting the needs assessment.
Obtain *management support*. This may be the single most important step in

the preparation for a needs assessment. It sends the message to the staff that you are serious about wanting the program to be responsive to their needs.

Obtain *employee support*. Emphasize the positive outcomes. Without employee support, the response you receive may not be completely candid.

Determine if an *external consultant* is needed for any phase of the assessment.

Gather *background information*. Search through documentation from previous assessments that measure competence, and deficiency in service. Look at the organization's goals and objectives. Seek out information concerning change and its impact on the organization. Identify past attempts to improve operations, programs, and services.

Identify *expenses,* including the staff time spent on planning, preparation, and implementation and the cost of materials, supplies, and printing.

Identify *people* on your staff who can help move the process forward—those with an understanding of the problem(s), experience in training, and knowledge of available funds.

Identify *constraints*—time, cost, political, and personnel—that might hinder the process.

## Defining the goals and objectives

Define the *purpose and scope* of the assessment, the aspects to be analyzed, and the expected outcome.

Relate this effort to the overall goals of the organization.

## Conducting the needs assessment

Examine data collected prior to the assessment, such as attitude surveys, job descriptions, performance appraisals, work samples, and performance standards.

Identify what new *data* are needed; identify specific questions that need to be answered.

Determine the *best time* to conduct an assessment and how long it will take to complete.

Design an effective *data-gathering method* for your organization. Use questionnaires and surveys, interviews, observations, reviews of written resources, task and competency surveys, focus groups, assessment centers, informal discussions, and advisory committees. Design an approach or method for gathering data from employees at different levels of the organization.

Determine if the assessment will be administered by in-house or external sources.

Identify the population—what department and which employees will be involved in the process.

Identify the *budgeted amount* available to cover costs incurred in the process.

Consider various *sampling strategies*. Before any approach is used on the entire staff, it is a good idea to test it with a sample group.

Listen carefully, avoid personal *bias*, and emphasize *accuracy* in gathering data. Determine whether the information collected will remain *confidential*.

*Verify* the content of the documentation, identifying any inconsistent responses. Analyze the gathered information to determine *priorities* for training and program planning. Distinguish between training and nontraining problems.

*Source:* Anne Grodzins Lipow and Deborah A. Carver, *Staff Development: A Practical Guide* (Chicago: ALA Library Administration and Management Association, 1992). 104p.

# Librarian salaries in 1994

*by Mary Jo Lynch*

**BETWEEN 1993 AND 1994,** the average salary for librarians increased an average of 3.65% for all six positions surveyed (director, deputy director, department or branch head, reference librarian, cataloger, children's or young adult services librarian). The figure is slightly higher than the increase in comparable occupations reported by the U.S. Bureau of Labor Statistics (BLS) in the June 1994 *Monthly Labor Review.* Civilian workers in private industry, state and local government received an average 3.2% increase in the twelve months ending in March 1994. White collar workers received an average increase of 3.3% for the same time period.

The percentage increases for 1994 librarian salaries shown in Table 1 were greater than in 1993, when they varied from –2.1% to +3.9%.

The 1994 survey showed that the mean of salaries paid is highest in large public libraries for director and deputy, associate, or assistant director and lowest for both in four-year colleges. For department and branch head, the mean is highest in two-year colleges and lowest in medium-sized public libraries. For the other two common positions, the mean is always highest in two-year colleges and lowest in four-year colleges. For the position found only in public libraries (children's or young adult services librarian) the mean of salaries paid is higher in large public libraries.

In most cases, salaries are highest in the North Atlantic region, followed by the West and Southwest. This is the second year in a row that the West and Southwest have not had the largest percentage of highest mean salaries—a pattern that prevailed in all earlier years of this survey. The lowest mean salary was in the Southeast more than 92% of the time. This pattern is similar to what has been observed in all previous surveys since 1982.

**Table 1. Rank order of position titles by mean salary, 1993–1994**

| Title | 1994 Salary | 1993 Salary | % |
|---|---|---|---|
| Director | $55,672 | $53,331 | +4.4 |
| Deputy/Associate/Assistant Director | 48,659 | 47,070 | +3.4 |
| Department or Branch Head | 40,544 | 39,352 | +3.0 |
| Reference/Information Librarian | 34,233 | 33,001 | +3.7 |
| Cataloger or Classifier | 33,928 | 32,582 | +4.1 |
| Children's/Young Adult Services Librarian | 33,588 | 32,530 | +3.2 |

*Source:* Mary Jo Lynch, Margaret Myers, and Jeniece Guy,
*ALA Survey of Librarian Salaries, 1994* (Chicago: American Library Association, 1994). 55p.

**Table 2. Median salaries for academic library positions, 1993–1994**

| | |
|---|---|
| Dean, library and information sciences | $73,168 |
| Director, library services | 50,500 |
| Director, learning resources center | 40,500 |
| Director, educational/media services center | 37,797 |
| Chief public services librarian | 36,811 |
| Chief technical services librarian | 36,324 |
| Acquisitions librarian | 34,695 |
| Reference librarian | 33,721 |
| Catalog librarian | 32,270 |

*Source:* College and University Personnel Association.

### Table 3. Annual salaries for beginning public librarians, 1994

| Public libraries serving | High | Low | Mean |
|---|---|---|---|
| over 1,000,000 | $49,032 | $21,306 | $28,126 |
| 500,000 to 999,999 | 37,669 | 20,748 | 26,665 |
| 250,000 to 499,999 | 32,441 | 16,879 | 25,381 |
| 100,000 to 249,999 | 44,492 | 16,000 | 24,842 |
| 50,000 to 99,999 | 37,648 | 14,868 | 24,562 |
| 25,000 to 49,999 | 34,728 | 10,500 | 23,994 |
| 10,000 to 24,999 | 32,000 | 11,500 | 22,964 |
| 5,000 to 9,999 | 30,000 | 12,740 | 22,084 |
| under 5,000 | 23,000 | 1,800 | 13,391 |

*Source: Statistical Report '94: Public Library Data Service* (Chicago: ALA Public Library Association, 1994).

### Table 4. Median salaries of special librarians by region, 1992–1994

| Census Division | 1992 Salary | 1994 Salary | % |
|---|---|---|---|
| Middle Atlantic | $42,724 | $45,000 | 5 |
| Pacific | 42,000 | 42,800 | 2 |
| New England | 40,000 | 40,987 | 2 |
| South Atlantic | 39,600 | 40,000 | 1 |
| East North Central | 38,000 | 38,600 | 2 |
| West South Central | 35,000 | 38,000 | 9 |
| East South Central | 35,000 | 36,500 | 4 |
| West North Central | 34,980 | 36,025 | 3 |
| Mountain | 34,155 | 35,500 | 4 |

*Source: SLA Biennial Salary Survey, 1995* (Washington, D.C.: Special Libraries Association, 1994). 72p.

### Pop quiz

**Instructions:** Check the box next to the correct answer for each of the following questions.

1. $43 million is:
   - Arnold Schwarzenegger's estimated gross earnings for 1991–92.
   - The total salaries, wages, and benefits earned by more than 1,700 Coloradans employed in public libraries during 1991.
   - Both of the above.

2. $62 million is:
   - Estimated gross earnings for 1991–92 by New Kids on the Block.
   - The sum of a) total salaries, wages, and benefits earned by more than 1,700 Coloradans employed in public libraries during 1991, and b) total salaries and wages earned by more than 900 Coloradans employed in academic libraries in 1990.
   - Both of the above.

3. $51 million is:
   - Michael Jackson's estimated gross earnings for 1991–92.
   - Estimated salaries and wages earned by Coloradans employed in public library school media centers in 1991.
   - Both of the above.

Answers: Just as you feared.

*Source: Fast Facts: Recent Statistics from the Library Research Service*
(Colorado State Library, Library Research Service), September 15, 1992. Reprinted with permission.

**Table 5. Mean salaries for health science librarians by type of institution, 1992**

| Type of institution | Number of respondents | Mean |
|---|---|---|
| Academic Medical Center (AMC) | 550 | $42,581 |
| Hospital affiliated with AMC | 429 | 35,223 |
| Hospital not affiliated with AMC | 541 | 31,157 |
| College/university library | 140 | 44,596 |
| Business/industry | 78 | 44,200 |
| Cancer | 7 | 46,310 |
| Chiropractic | 12 | 32,766 |
| Dental | 12 | 40,115 |
| Government | 70 | 44,725 |
| Library/information science school | 9 | 37,950 |
| Medical or health sciences association | 32 | 38,671 |
| Medical society | 21 | 36,668 |
| Military | 19 | 37,186 |
| Nursing | 30 | 31,458 |
| Osteopathic | 16 | 37,412 |
| Pharmacy | 10 | 43,769 |
| Podiatry | 3 | 38,988 |
| Psychiatric | 47 | 34,269 |
| Public health/health administration | 15 | 36,326 |
| Public library | 15 | 34,170 |
| Self-employed | 11 | 43,584 |
| Vendor of library materials/services | 21 | 47,157 |
| Veterans Administration | 58 | 39,755 |
| Veterinary/animal institute | 12 | 38,835 |
| Other | 86 | 36,063 |
| Multiple | 8 | 36,873 |
| No response | 4 | 29,701 |
| TOTAL | 2,256 | 37,670 |

*Source: MLA 1992 Salary Survey* (Chicago: Medical Library Association, 1992). 39p.
© by the Medical Library Association. Reprinted with permission.

# Salary administration:
# What to put in the personnel manual

*by Charles E. Kratz and Valerie A. Platz*

A LIBRARY PERSONNEL MANUAL should specify how an employee's salary level is set, the conditions that may affect it, deductions that may be made before the employee receives a paycheck, how the employee receives the paycheck, and other information related to salary administration. The following outline offers guidelines for library managers and staff concerned with preparing that section of the manual.

## General procedure for determining salaries

*Identify* the persons or office authorized to set salaries, such as: 1) the state legislature, county commissioners, city council, or other legislative body; 2) the state library, board of regents, board of trustees, or corporate policy council; or 3) any other person or office.

*Name* the persons or office responsible for recommending salary levels and explain related procedures. Identify ordinances, charter provisions, or other legal regulations that affect salary levels and cite the sources.

*Explain* how unions or employee organizations participate in the process. *Explain* how often the salary structure is reviewed for pay equity consideration. Describe how evaluation tools are used to make pay equity comparisons. Describe policy or procedures that ensure pay equity for each position in comparison to similar positions in the city, state, region—including the procedure utilized to bring existing positions up to parity, and examples of libraries or other organizations used for comparison.

## Salaries and factors related to take-home pay

*State* the salary ordinance or official pay schedule. Include the frequency of update. Show the range of pay for each grade or position classification in the library. Explain any variations, such as flat-rate pay for executives, pay for part-time employees, merit exempt, or employees contracted for specific periods of time. Explain probationary employment periods in relation to salary schedules. Identify salary level considerations made when rehiring former employees.

*Explain* the application of official salary schedules to employees' paychecks. Describe how the authorized salary is adapted to monthly, biweekly, or weekly pay periods, as applicable. Describe merit increases, longevity pay, or other increases, including:

1. Normal frequency and percentage of merit or annual increments.
2. Circumstances under which a salary raise is given if not as an annual increment, such as salary compensation based on performance measures or expectations.
3. Circumstances under which increases may be withheld.
4. Conditions under which special raises may be granted.
5. Refer to your manual's chapter on "Personnel Actions."

*Explain* any raise given upon satisfactory completion of a probationary period.

*Describe* cost-of-living raises. Identify the persons or office authorized to grant cost-of-living raises, and the conditions under which cost-of-living raises are granted (frequency, basis of percentages or increments, position ranges affected). Explain the effect that a cost-of-living raise will have on salary ranges or schedule.

*Explain* the schedule and payment of salary during leaves of absence. Refer to your manual's chapter on "Leaves of Absence." Explain how inclement weather or emergency closings may affect schedule and payment of salary.

*Identify* salaries that are subsidized, that is, not paid from regular income but from grants received by the library (explain whether positions that are paid from grant funds have full benefits, tenure, or temporary employee status), endowment funds (explain any special provisions attached to positions paid from endowment funds), or other sources.

## Deductions made from salary before paycheck is received by employee

**Identify mandatory deductions.**

1. *Federal taxes,* including income tax (name the persons or office responsible for providing forms and information concerning federal income tax) and Social Security tax. Identify the class of employees, such as part-time or temporary, who are not required to pay Social Security taxes. Specify the library's contribution to the individual's Social Security account and indicate the persons or office responsible for providing information concerning the tax.
2. *State taxes.* If there is state income tax, provide the same information as for federal tax. Specify whether or not taxes are withheld for other jurisdic-

tions for those employees who live in one and work in another.

3. *Local taxes.* If there is local income tax, provide the same information as for federal tax.

4. *Insurance.* If participation in a health, disability, or other insurance plan is mandatory, list the premium deductions. If participation in a health, disability, or other insurance plan is voluntary, include insurance in the section on "Voluntary deductions" below.

5. *Mandatory retirement plan or fund,* including retirement plan deductions, the library's contribution to an employee's retirement plan, the category or class of job positions (such as part-time or intermittent) where employees are not required to pay into the retirement plan, and the persons or office responsible for providing information and forms. Refer to your manual's chapter on "Retirement benefits."

6. *Garnishment of wages:* the policy and procedure upon which an employee's paycheck is garnished due to court action.

### Identify voluntary deductions.

1. *Deferred compensation plans.* The definition and explanation of benefits or service to the employee, the persons or office responsible for providing information and forms, and the procedure for authorizing deductions.

2. *Savings bonds.* Define and explain benefits or service to the employee, the persons or office responsible for providing information and forms, and the procedure for authorizing deductions.

3. *Employee unions.* Identify the union(s) that represent library employees, the persons or office responsible for providing information and forms, and the procedure for authorizing deductions. If union membership is mandatory, include in the section on "Mandatory deductions" above. See also the contract or memorandum for the understanding and description of union functions.

4. *Credit union.* Specify the types of deductions that are available utilizing the credit union, the persons or office responsible for providing information and forms, and the procedure for authorizing deductions.

5. *Reimbursement plans or accounts such as health or dependent care.* Identify the persons or office responsible for providing information and forms, the procedure for authorizing deductions, and the procedure for participating in the program (for receiving reimbursement).

6. *Voluntary retirement or savings plan(s).*

7. *Donations to charitable, political, or nonprofit funds or organizations.* Identify the charity drive in which the institution participates, the calendar schedule of event and deduction schedule, the procedure for authorizing deductions, the procedure for authorizing deductions for other organizations such as political action committees (PACs), and the persons or office responsible for providing information and forms.

## Pay cycles and schedule of paydays

*Explain* the frequency of paydays and when paychecks are issued. Give the official schedule of paydays and cite any differences between pay cycles, such as for part-time and full-time employees. Explain how the cycle is adapted to weekends or holidays. Cite any policy for acceleration of payday for an employee in case of emergency or hardship.

## Payroll forms

*Identify* forms that need to be completed routinely for generation of paycheck, such as time sheets. Explain the frequency with which each form is to be completed and to which persons or office it must be sent.

## Distribution of paychecks

*Identify* the persons or office responsible for the distribution of paychecks. Describe the methodology employed for distribution of paychecks. Cite the policy or procedure for missing or incorrect paychecks.

*Describe* special arrangements that may be made to obtain a paycheck: distribution at location other than the normal place, direct deposit, disposition of paycheck for an employee on leave, or an employee who has resigned or been terminated. See also the section on "Separation pay" below.

## Premium and hazard pay

*Explain* the purpose of premium or hazard pay and cite policy and authority under which the special pay is granted, such as a law or city/county charter, or a contract or memorandum of understanding with employee organizations.

*List* the circumstances, occasions, or positions for which premium or hazard pay is granted, such as: working overtime, working holidays or Sundays, working a night schedule, call-back of employee off schedule, hazardous working conditions, or inclement weather or emergency conditions.

*Name* the persons or office authorized to grant premium or hazard pay. Explain the basis for computing premium or hazard pay, such as whether or not it is a percentage above the normal rate of pay. Include non-pay provisions such as compensatory time. Refer to your manual's chapter on "Leaves of Absence."

## Compensatory leave

*Explain* the purpose of compensatory leave and how it is earned. Explain the differences between earning compensatory time and earning overtime pay. Cite policy and authority under which compensatory time is granted, and the procedure for recording time earned.

## Additions to paycheck

*Describe* additions to the standard paycheck, such as travel, parking, and office expense reimbursements. Name the persons or office responsible for facilitating reimbursement of expenses. Describe the appropriate forms needed for reimbursement. Cite the time frame requirements, and explain whether the reimbursement is added to the paycheck total or distributed separately.

## Separation pay

*Name* the persons or office responsible for providing forms and information concerning separation pay. Describe forms that need to be completed or provisions that need to be addressed by the employee for the creation of a separation paycheck.

*Explain* the provisions or benefits that comprise the separation pay. Include accumulated leave, contractual compensation, stipends, etc. Explain any deductions taken from separation paycheck for reasons of fines, property usage, theft of equipment, noncompliance with contractual agreements, etc. Explain the time frame for the creation of a severance paycheck.

*Describe* how separation paychecks are distributed. Explain whether distribution is conditional upon any procedures or actions, such as surrender of keys or identification badge. Refer to your manual's chapter on "Separation from service, or termination of employment."

*Explain* provisions and procedures for pay that are arranged when an employee dies. Refer to your manual's chapter on "Death of an employee."

## Federal tax W-2 forms

*Name* the position or office that provides forms and information concerning W-2 forms. Explain the procedure and time frame for distribution of W-2 forms to employees.

*Source:* Charles E. Kratz and Valerie A. Platz, *The Personnel Manual: An Outline for Libraries* (Chicago: American Library Association, 1993). 96p.

# Librarians: Racial, ethnic, and gender statistics

A 1991 SURVEY by the American Library Association revealed the following ethnic and racial profile of American librarians:

| Number and percentage of public and academic librarians by race and ethnic group | | |
|---|---|---|
| American Indian/Alaskan Native | 91 | 0.4% |
| Asian/Pacific Islander | 889 | 3.8% |
| Black | 1,451 | 6.3% |
| Hispanic | 419 | 1.8% |
| White | 20,264 | 87.7% |
| TOTAL | 23,114 | 100.0% |

Women made up nearly three-quarters of all public and academic librarians in 1991:

| Number and percentage of librarians by gender | | |
|---|---|---|
| Female | 16,907 | 73.2% |
| Male | 6,205 | 26.8% |
| TOTAL | 23,114 | 100.0% |

Women constitute a higher percentage of public librarians than academic librarians (79.1% to 65.0%). Conversely, males are found to a greater extent in academic libraries than public libraries (34.2% to 20.9%).

A higher percentage of public librarians are black (7.2%) than academic librarians (5.0%). A higher percentage of the academic librarians are Asian/Pacific Islander (5.0% as compared to 3.0% in public libraries). There is less difference in the percentage of Hispanic librarians in academic and public libraries (1.5% in academic and 2.0% in public). There is a sizable difference between male and female whites working in academic libraries—56.5% white females to 31.4% white males—while public libraries are made up of 68.8% white females and 18.7% white males.

The distribution of men and women in the various racial and ethnic groups parallels the overall distribution of men and women in the total sample, except for a larger percentage of Hispanic males and a smaller percentage of black males. The minority group with the largest percentage of women is black—82.0%. The minority group with the smallest percentage of females is Hispanic—68.2%.

Female librarians are 86.9% white, 0.4% American Indian/Alaskan Native, 4.0% Asian/Pacific Islander, 7.0% black, and 1.7% Hispanic. Male librarians are 89.8% white, 0.4% American Indian/Alaskan Native, 3.5% Asian/Pacific Islander, 4.2% black, and 2.1% Hispanic.

The percentage of females in top management in public libraries is higher than that of males (66.4% to 33.6%). In academic libraries, the distribution of top management has shifted since 1985 when the survey was last taken. At that time, males had a slight majority in top management; however, in 1991, 52.8% of top management is female and 47.2% is male.

The racial and ethnic distribution of top management shows a greater percentage of whites than among librarians as a whole (92.0% of upper-level managers are white vs. 87.7% overall).

Within each racial and ethnic group, females constitute a larger percentage than males in both public library and academic library top managers. Women comprise 65.6% of whites in top management in public libraries and 51.4% of whites in top management in academic libraries.

The percentage of blacks who are branch and department heads is slightly larger than their representation in the total work force, while the percentage of Hispanics is the same. The percentage of American Indian/Alaskan Natives and Asian/Pacific Islanders is slightly smaller than in the profession at large. These figures suggest that Hispanics have fared better and American Indian/Alaskan Natives have made less progress in moving into middle management since the 1985 survey.

At the branch and department head level, the distribution of males and females is almost the same as the total work force: 74.3% of branch and department heads are female compared with their 73.1% total representation, and 25.7% are males, compared with a 26.9% overall distribution. This is considerably higher than the overall percentage of top female managers (59.4%) and raises questions as to what happens to the females who are in middle management positions but do not move to the top management positions. Female branch and department heads are found in a greater percentage in public libraries than in academic libraries—80.3% in public libraries are female compared to 65.4% in academic libraries.

At the entry level, there is a slightly higher percentage of females (77.6%) compared to the overall distribution of females in the profession (73.1%). The percentage is higher for public librarians (80.6% entry level) and lower for academic librarians (69.4%).

There is a higher percentage of Asian/Pacific Islanders, Hispanics, and whites at the entry level than in the total work force. The percentage for blacks is roughly the same, while the entry-level percentage for American Indian/ Alaskan Natives is lower than for the profession at large (this could be a side-effect of the low number (6) of entry-level respondents to the survey).

Entry-level librarians were 81.7% female in 1985, compared to 77.6% in 1991. All minority groups in the entry-level category remained almost constant, showing less than 1% change since 1985.

A survey of U.S. library and information studies education programs in 1991–1992 provides racial, ethnic, and gender data for the 4,295 students awarded ALA-accredited master's degrees in that academic year: American Indian/Alaskan Native (0.1%), Asian/Pacific Islander (3.1%), black (3.3%), Hispanic (2.0%), and white (91.5%). Female graduates were 79.4% of the total.

Interestingly, the proportion of doctorates granted was greater for each minority group except for American Indian/Alaskan Natives, who had no doctoral graduates that year: Asian/Pacific Islander (3.7%), black (9.2%), and Hispanic (5.6%). Females also dominated the doctorates with 68.5%. All of the Ph.D. degrees awarded to blacks went to female students. This was not true in the 1990–1991 academic year, when one of the six doctorates granted to black students went to a black male.

*Source: Academic and Public Librarians: Data by Race, Ethnicity & Sex, 1991* (Chicago: ALA Office for Library Personnel Resources, 1991). 14p. *Degrees and Certificates Awarded by U.S. Library and Information Studies Education Programs 1990–1991 and 1991–1992* (Chicago: ALA Office for Library Personnel Resources, 1993). 1p.

# Part-time librarians

### by Elizabeth Hogue and Lorene Sisson

MOST PART-TIME LIBRARIANS ARE part-time by choice, and most are women who are not the sole support of their household, according to our 1990 survey (see Figure 1). A great number of part-time librarians who responded to the survey worked in public libraries (see Figure 2). After public libraries, nearly a third of the respondents were most likely to work in college and university libraries or community and junior college libraries. Fewer responses were associated with special libraries, county and regional libraries, school libraries, and other types of libraries.

Most part-time librarians (77.4%) did not supervise other employees (see figure 3). However, some did have supervisory positions (8.9%), or in rare instances, others held middle- and upper-level management positions, such as department head (2.7%), assistant or associate director (1.4%), or director (7.5%). There were three survey responses labeled "other" (2.1%) for which the researchers were unable to determine the type of responsibility.

More than 70% of respondents work in public-service positions rather than technical services, automation systems, or administration. More than half (51.3%) of the respondents reported working in reference. Part-time librarians were less likely to work in administration (7%), in youth services (7.6%), in adult services (8.2%), or in cataloging and classification (8.2%).

---

**Highest education level achieved:**

156 listed a master's degree

7 listed a bachelor's degree

2 listed a high school diploma

87% are **not** sole income earners of the household

- 95% are female*
- 90% are white
- The average age of the respondents who answered was 43
- 83% work part-time by choice
- 37% work 20 hrs/wk, 29% work 19 or less hrs/wk, 24% work 21 hrs/wk or more
- 56% indicated that benefits were not comparable to full-time

| Average salary | | # respondents |
|---|---|---|
| per hour = | $13.37 | 98 |
| per year = | $18,262.60 | 42 |
| per month = | $1,336.83 | 18 |

*167 total respondents

Figure 1. Salaries and working conditions of the typical part-time librarian.

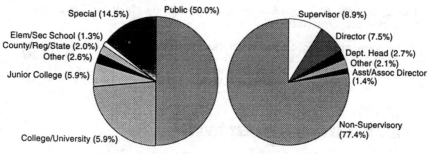

Figure 2. Type of library.       Figure 3. Type of responsibility.

Nearly a fifth (17.3%) of the respondents were distributed among eight remaining types of work, which was labeled "other."

Part-time librarians reported their salaries as hourly, monthly, or yearly wages (see Figure 1). Hourly wages ranged from $5 to $33 per hour. The mean rate of pay was $13.37 per hour. Monthly wages ranged from $541 to $2,700 per month. The mean rate of pay was $1,337 per month. Yearly wages ranged from $10,000 to $35,000 per year. The mean rate of pay was $18,262 per year.

Benefits were not comparable to full-time librarians in 56% of survey responses (see Figure 1).

The number of hours worked per week ranged from 3 to 35. Most librarians (37%) worked 20 hours per week. Some librarians (29%) worked a range of 3 to 19 hours per week while one-third (33%) worked a range of 21 to 35 hours per week.

The part-time librarians surveyed have many years of experience in the profession, but the length of time within their current part-time positions was markedly less in the majority of the responses. The part-time librarians reported a range of six months to thirty-seven years in the profession with 66% reporting ten years or more, while 33% reported less than ten years. These librarians reported working in their current part-time positions within a range of one month to 28 years. A large percentage (61%) worked less than five years.

Nearly 40% of respondents had another part-time job. Of those, almost half had a position in another library. Less than 5% of respondents now have paraprofessional positions in addition to their part-time librarian positions; however, more than half (56%) of the total respondents had been at one time a paraprofessional. The majority of respondents work in California, New York, and Illinois. Every region of the United States, including Washington, D.C., and Canada, was represented. An overwhelming number of the respondents (93.4%) had attained their master's degree, usually in library science (see Figure 1).

Respondents wrote explanatory notes listing advantages and disadvantages of part-time employment. In their view, flexible schedules, more personal time, less job stress, and less involvement in office politics are incentives to remain part-time. On the other hand, the lack of commensurate benefits and/or salaries, the inaccurate image of part-timers, the information and communication problems, the limited professional development, and the lack of career opportunities rank high as disadvantages.

Future career plans for the majority of respondents include continuing part-time or increasing to full-time, based upon aspects of the librarian's personal and professional life. Some librarians indicated that personal matters would dictate whether they continue as part-time professionals. Others indicated the lack of ability to remain part-time due to professional demands by their administrators or colleagues.

This research study compiled and analyzed information on the job responsibilities, working conditions, and career goals of part-time librarians in all types of libraries. Survey respondents were solicited in 1990 via announcements posted in six professional journals. Respondents were sent the survey instrument, which they volunteered to fill out. Over 165 part-time librarians representing academic, public, and special libraries responded to issues such as salary, benefits, hours of work, and advantages and disadvantages of part-time careers in the library profession.

The findings from this exploratory survey affect all members of the profession. The respondents expressed the need for comparable compensation and benefits, respect from their colleagues, and recognition for their contributions. Administrators may use these findings to explore relevant employer issues. Peers can derive useful information related to desirable working conditions for their colleagues. Additional research needs to be done on a larger scale across the nation to obtain a greater representative sample.

*Source:* Elizabeth Hogue and Lorene Sisson, "Part-Time Librarians: Jewels of the Profession," *Library Personnel News* 7 (March-April 1993): 7–8.

# Preparing for accreditation

*by Patricia Ann Sacks and Sara Lou Whildin*

ACADEMIC LIBRARIANS ARE OFTEN CALLED UPON to assist in the process of preparing for reviews of external agencies responsible for accrediting their colleges or universities. Accreditation is a voluntary, self-regulatory process for encouraging and assisting institutions of higher education to evaluate and improve their educational endeavors.

The library should seize the accreditation visit as an opportunity for consultancy, affirmation of direction, and new perspectives. The central question the evaluator seeks to answer is, "Does it work?" That is, does a given library program function effectively in light of the library's and the institution's stated goals? The atmosphere should not be one of inspection, examination, accountability, and fault finding. To avoid such an atmosphere in responding to the accreditation visit, the library utilizes the following strategy:

1. Anticipate that the review will be based on the library section in the review or self-study document; in particular on the key recommendations and implementation plans and processes contained in the conclusion of the library's self-study report.
2. Focus on the library's stated objectives and its effectiveness in meeting them in its dialogue with the accrediting team.
3. Maintain complete open communication with the accrediting team members.
4. Expect the accrediting team to understand the library's mission, goals, and related activities as articulated in the self-study document.

In addition, the library is advised to engage in the following activities in response to the visit:

1. Recommend a librarian be one of the members of the visiting accrediting team. In making this recommendation, the library should be knowledgeable about the accrediting agency's policies and practices regard-

ing team membership, and be in touch with the officers of its parent institution about their requisites for team membership. If a librarian is not on the visiting team, identify the team member who will be primarily responsible for reviewing the library.

2. Select and make available related library documents for background files accessible to the evaluation team. Identify and prepare to distribute any key document that may be in demand by team members. When the library is a focus of the accrediting report, or if the library is "atypical" in comparison to its peers, and the institution's report to the accrediting agency cannot include the library's full report and/or background documents, ask the institution's steering committee to mail the full report and background documents to the appropriate team member at least one month before the team visit.

3. Seek an opportunity to meet with the accrediting team members and campus colleagues in a social setting.

4. Share information about the evaluation visit and schedules with the library staff to prepare them to greet the visitors and offer them assistance.

5. Be readily available for meetings with team members and arrange individual or group staff meetings in response to team requests.

6. Attend the oral preview of the team's evaluation report, and discuss the preview with library staff and academic officers.

7. Review the accrediting agency's evaluation report and advise on library-related contents.

8. Assist the institution in responding to the agency's formal accrediting action requiring follow-up reports or special visits with a library emphasis.

To increase the usefulness of the accrediting reviews, the library should consider:

1. Addressing key concerns expressed by the library's users as a first priority.

2. Initiating implementation of key recommendations identified in the self-study report prior to accrediting visits and reports.

3. Identifying matters that will require the understanding and support of the institution's decision makers and communicating with this audience. The plan for involving these persons should identify who the decision makers will be, what information they will need, and when the information will be needed. Evaluations are more likely to be used if they relate to decision makers' concerns, are communicated clearly and concisely with an assessment of their impact, and are presented both verbally and in written form.

4. Linking the accrediting agency's evaluations with the library's and the institution's planning and resource allocation processes. It is important for the results to be linked to these decision-making processes, but unreasonable to expect the recommendations to be implemented in their "pure form." The results should be reviewed with multiple perspectives.

5. Communicating the library's response to the library's audiences. Accrediting reviews occur in a social and political environment in which various groups have vested interests in the evaluation process. If the results are to be used by these groups, communication among them is essential.

6. Maintaining flexibility to accommodate change in the accreditation process. It is impossible to design an accrediting review process that anticipates all the issues that need to be addressed and all the constitu-

encies that need to be consulted. Recommendations and their priority ordering will need to be adjusted in the implementation process to adapt to changing environments and to cultivate expectations at a reasonable level.

When the review results are used, basic concerns about the consequences of their application will surface. In fact, these concerns often appear in the design stage of the evaluation review and effect, sometimes negatively, the design itself. Assumptions about decreasing budget support, eliminating a subject collection responsibility or service, and changing personnel are viewed as negative and threatening. They create distrusts and resentment. These situations should be recognized as common conditions in organizations undergoing change.

*Source:* Patricia Ann Sacks and Sara Lou Whildin, *Preparing for Accreditation: A Handbook for Academic Librarians* (Chicago: American Library Association, 1993). 84p.

# Tips for librarians planning for accreditation visits

1. Make sure you have all relevant materials available from your regional accrediting agency. These may include criteria or standards, guides for self-study, or other publications prepared for aspects of self-study. Read them and note those sections which pertain to the library.
2. Press for adequate representation of the library on the steering committee as well as other relevant committees.
3. Take the self-study process seriously. It should be an opportunity for the library staff to reflect, learn, and grow. The process can be an opportunity for an internal planning effort. It can also be a learning experience about the library for your institution's faculty.
4. Make sure you understand your institution's mission and goals and can demonstrate how the library helps to fulfill them.
5. All accrediting agencies are stressing accountability and outcomes assessment. The accrediting visit is a golden opportunity for your library to assess its outcomes. *Note.*—ACRL's *Measuring Academic Library Performance: A Practical Approach* (Chicago: ALA, 1991) contains field-tested, easy-to-use output measures that can help you with this.
6. Your self-study should be cogent, clear, and explicit. Avoid generalities and hyperbole. Brevity is a virtue.
7. Highlight your library's strengths. However, be assured that no institution or library is perfect and that the visiting team will not expect perfection. Be honest about your library's shortcomings, but also be prepared to discuss your strategies for overcoming them.
8. Go beyond the traditional library plaint of "need more money, more books, more staff." Everyone's already heard that.
9. Educational equity and diversity in your collection and staff should be noted as appropriate.
10. Your self-study should not just include traditional items such as number of volumes or hours open, but should reflect changes in libraries such as networking, resource sharing, expedited document delivery, etc.
11. Make certain that the accreditation team has access to documentation that supports the claims made in the self-study.

12. A scrapbook of all library publications—including bibliographic instruction handouts, bookplates, programs—is helpful for the team to examine.
13. Press your institution to ask for a librarian to be on the visiting team.
14. Take the opportunity to use the visiting team as consultants. Ask their ideas for solving problems; they likely won't offer unless asked.
15. Finally, consider the possibility of serving as an evaluator for your regional agency. You'll learn and your colleagues will profit.

Based on contributions from accreditation veterans: Mignon Adams, Keith Cottam, Ron Leach, Alice Schell, David Walch, and Joan Worley.

Source: "Tips for Librarians Planning for Accreditation Visits,"
College & Research Libraries News 53 (July/August 1992): 447.

# ALA presidents

| | | | | |
|---|---|---|---|---|
| Justin Winsor | 1876–1885 | George H. Locke | 1926–1927 |
| William Frederick Poole | 1885–1887 | Carl B. Roden | 1927–1928 |
| Charles Ammi Cutter | 1887–1889 | Linda A. Eastman | 1928–1929 |
| Frederick Morgan Crunden | 1889–1890 | Andrew Keogh | 1929–1930 |
| Melvil Dewey | 1890–July 1891 | Adam Strohm | 1930–1931 |
| Samuel Swett Green | July–Nov. 1891 | Josephine Adams Rathbone | 1931–1932 |
| William Isaac Fletcher | 1891–1892 | Harry Miller Lydenberg | 1932–1933 |
| Melvil Dewey | 1892–1893 | Gratia A. Countryman | 1933–1934 |
| Josephus Nelson Larned | 1893–1894 | Charles H. Compton | 1934–1935 |
| Henry Munson Utley | 1894–1895 | Louis Round Wilson | 1935–1936 |
| John Cotton Dana | 1895–1896 | Malcolm Glenn Wyer | 1936–1937 |
| William Howard Brett | 1896–1897 | Harrison Warwick Craver | 1937–1938 |
| Justin Winsor | July–Oct. 1897 | Milton James Ferguson | 1938–1939 |
| Herbert Putnam | Jan.–Aug. 1898 | Ralph Munn | 1939–1940 |
| William Coolidge Lane | 1898–1899 | Essae Martha Culver | 1940–1941 |
| Reuben Gold Thwaites | 1899–1900 | Charles Harvey Brown | 1941–1942 |
| Henry James Carr | 1900–1901 | Keyes D. Metcalf | 1942–1943 |
| John Shaw Billings | 1901–1902 | Althea H. Warren | 1943–1944 |
| James Kendall Hosmer | 1902–1903 | Carl Vitz | 1944–1945 |
| Herbert Putnam | 1903–1904 | Ralph A. Ulveling | 1945–1946 |
| Ernest Cushing Richardson | 1904–1905 | Mary U. Rothrock | 1946–1947 |
| Frank Pierce Hill | 1905–1906 | Paul North Rice | 1947–1948 |
| Clement Walker Andrews | 1906–1907 | Errett Weir McDiarmid | 1948–1949 |
| Arthur Elmore Bostwick | 1907–1908 | Milton E. Lord | 1949–1950 |
| Charles Henry Gould | 1908–1909 | Clarence R. Graham | 1950–1951 |
| Nathaniel Hodges | 1909–1910 | Loleta Dawson Fyan | 1951–1952 |
| James Ingersoll Wyer | 1910–1911 | Robert Bingham Downs | 1952–1953 |
| Theresa West Elmendorf | 1911–1912 | Flora Belle Ludington | 1953–1954 |
| Henry Eduard Legler | 1912–1913 | L. Quincy Mumford | 1954–1955 |
| Edwin Hatfield Anderson | 1913–1914 | John S. Richards | 1955–1956 |
| Hiller Crowell Wellman | 1914–1915 | Ralph R. Shaw | 1956–1957 |
| Mary Wright Plummer | 1915–1916 | Lucile M. Morsch | 1957–1958 |
| Walter Lewis Brown | 1916–1917 | Emerson Greenaway | 1958–1959 |
| Thomas Lynch Montgomery | 1917–1918 | Benjamin E. Powell | 1959–1960 |
| William Warner Bishop | 1918–1919 | Frances Lander Spain | 1960–1961 |
| Chalmers Hadley | 1919–1920 | Florrinell F. Morton | 1961–1962 |
| Alice S. Tyler | 1920–1921 | James E. Bryan | 1962–1963 |
| Azariah Smith Root | 1921–1922 | Frederick H. Wagman | 1963–1964 |
| George Burwell Utley | 1922–1923 | Edwin Castagna | 1964–1965 |
| Judson Toll Jennings | 1923–1924 | Robert Vosper | 1965–1966 |
| Herman H. B. Meyer | 1924–1925 | Mary V. Gaver | 1966–1967 |
| Charles F. D. Belden | 1925–1926 | Foster E. Mohrhardt | 1967–1968 |

| | | | |
|---|---|---|---|
| Roger McDonough | 1968–1969 | Carol A. Nemeyer | 1982–1983 |
| William S. Dix | 1969–1970 | Brooke E. Sheldon | 1983–1984 |
| Lillian M. Bradshaw | 1970–1971 | E.J.Josey | 1984–1985 |
| Keith Doms | 1971–1972 | Beverly P. Lynch | 1985–1986 |
| Katherine Laich | 1972–1973 | Regina Minudri | 1986–1987 |
| Jean E. Lowrie | 1973–1974 | Margaret E. Chisholm | 1987–1988 |
| Edward G. Holley | 1974–1975 | F. William Summers | 1988–1989 |
| Allie Beth Martin | 1975–April 1976 | Patricia Wilson Berger | 1989–1990 |
| Clara Stanton Jones | July 1976–1977 | Richard M. Dougherty | 1990–1991 |
| Eric Moon | 1977–1978 | Patricia G. Schuman | 1991–1992 |
| Russell Shank | 1978–1979 | Marilyn L. Miller | 1992–1993 |
| Thomas J. Galvin | 1979–1980 | Hardy R. Franklin | 1993–1994 |
| Peggy A. Sullivan | 1980–1981 | Arthur Curley | 1994–1995 |
| Elizabeth W. (Betty) Stone | 1981–1982 | Betty J. Turock | 1995–1996 |

# ALA treasurers

| | | | |
|---|---|---|---|
| Melvil Dewey | 1876–1877 | Edward D. Tweedell | 1920–1927 |
| Charles Evans | 1877–1878 | Matthew S. Dudgeon | 1927–1941 |
| Melvil Dewey | 1878–1879 | Rudolph H. Gjelness | 1941–1947 |
| Frederick Jackson | 1879–1880 | Harold F. Brigham | 1947–1949 |
| Melvil Dewey | 1880–1881 | R. Russell Munn | 1949–1952 |
| Frederick Jackson | 1881–1882 | Raymond C. Lindquist | 1952–1956 |
| James Lyman Whitney | 1882–1886 | Richard B. Sealock | 1956–1960 |
| Henry James Carr | 1886–1893 | Arthur Yabroff | 1960–1964 |
| George Watson Cole | 1893–1895 | Ralph Blasingame | 1964–1968 |
| Edwin Hatfield Anderson | 1895–1896 | Robert B. McClarren | 1968–1972 |
| George Watson Cole | 1896 | Frank B. Sessa | 1972–1976 |
| Charles Knowles Bolton | 1896–1897 | William Chait | 1976–1980 |
| Gardner Maynard Jones | 1897–1906 | Herbert Biblo | 1980–1984 |
| George Franklin Bowerman | 1906–1907 | Patricia Glass Schuman | 1984–1988 |
| Anderson Hoyt Hopkins | 1907–1908 | Carla J. Stoffle | 1988–1992 |
| Purd B. Wright | 1908–1910 | Ann K. Symons | 1992–1996 |
| Carl B. Roden | 1910–1920 | | |

Nathaniel Hodges

Josephine Rathbone

Mary U. Rothrock

Robert Downs

Emerson Greenaway

Lillian M. Bradshaw

Edward G. Holley

Clara Stanton Jones

# ALA executive secretaries

| | | | |
|---|---|---|---|
| Melvil Dewey | 1879–1890 | (Edward C. Hovey, executive officer) | |
| William E. Parker and | | | 1905–1907 |
| Mary Salome Cutler | 1890–July 1891 | Chalmers Hadley | 1909–1911 |
| Frank Pierce Hill | 1891–1895 | George Burwell Utley | 1911–1920 |
| Henry Livingston Elmendorf | 1895–1896 | Carl H. Milam | 1920–1948 |
| Rutherford Platt Hayes | 1896–1897 | Harold F. Brigham (interim) | |
| Melvil Dewey | 1897–1898 | | July–Aug. 1948 |
| Henry James Carr | 1898–1900 | John MacKenzie Cory | 1948–1951 |
| Frederick Winthrop Faxon | 1900–1902 | David H. Clift | 1951–1958 |
| James Ingersoll Wyer | 1902–1909 | | |

# ALA executive directors

| | | | |
|---|---|---|---|
| David H. Clift | 1958–1972 | Peggy Sullivan | 1992–1994 |
| Robert Wedgeworth | 1972–1985 | Elizabeth Martinez | 1994– |
| Thomas J. Galvin | 1985–1989 | | |
| Linda F. Crismond | 1989–1992 | | |

# Librarians of Congress

| | | | |
|---|---|---|---|
| John J. Beckley | 1802–1807 | Herbert Putnam | 1899–1939 |
| Patrick Magruder | 1807–1815 | Archibald MacLeish | 1939–1944 |
| George Watterston | 1815–1829 | Luther H. Evans | 1945–1953 |
| John Silva Meehan | 1829–1861 | L. Quincy Mumford | 1954–1974* |
| John G. Stephenson | 1861–1864 | Daniel J. Boorstin | 1975–1987 |
| Ainsworth Rand Spofford | 1864–1897 | James H. Billington | 1987– |
| John Russell Young | 1897–1899 | | |

*The only Librarian of Congress with an MLS.

Directors

# Time management in public libraries

*by Helen M. Gothberg*

DIRECTORS OF LARGER PUBLIC LIBRARIES were solicited to provide data on their time-management practices. A questionnaire was sent out asking how time was allocated for traditional management activities, delegation of authority, leadership style, rankings of time wasters, and information about the respondents. Analysis of the data shows the following major issues: the use of committees, and gender and age differences in authority delegation involving younger and less experienced managers. Also, overall indications are that library directors possess the necessary skills to meet the new demands; however, attention must be paid to new organizational patterns.

**Table 1. Public Library Directors:
Percent of Time Spent on Management Activities**

| Hours per week | 0-3 | 4-7 | 8-11 | 12+ |
| --- | --- | --- | --- | --- |
| Planning | 20.6 | 39.4 | 27.4 | 21.6 |
| Reporting (internal and external) | 15.2 | 43.2 | 22.7 | 18.9 |
| Supervising | 34.1 | 39.4 | 16.7 | 9.8 |
| Budgeting | 42.6 | 37.3 | 12.3 | 7.8 |
| Personnel work | 48.5 | 34.1 | 9.8 | 7.6 |
| Meetings with administrators* | 20.5 | 23.5 | 3.8 | 3.2 |
| Meetings with library administrators | 12.4 | 40.2 | 31.8 | 15.6 |
| Library committees | 62.1 | 25.8 | 6.4 | 5.7 |
| Professional committees | 77.3 | 17.4 | 5.3 | 0.0 |
| External fundraising | 65.9 | 21.3 | 6.4 | 6.4 |

*Data for this item less than reliable because of a printing error.

**Table 2. Public Library Directors:
Ranking of Top Ten Time Wasters**

| Rank | Time Wasters |
| --- | --- |
| 1 | Telephone interruptions |
| 2 | Meetings (scheduled and unscheduled) |
| 3 | Drop-in visitors |
| 4 | Attempting too much at once and estimating time unrealistically |
| 5 | Inability to say no |
| 6 | Inadequate, inaccurate, or delayed information |
| 7 | Crises (personal and/or staff) |
| 8 | Indecision and procrastination |
| 9 | Cluttered desk and personal disorganization |
| 10 | Leaving tasks unfinished |

*Unranked Time Wasters:*
   Confused responsibility and authority
   Ineffective delegation and involvement in routine and detail
   Lack of objectives, priorities, and deadlines
   Lack of, or unclear communications or instructions
   Lack of self-discipline

*Source:* Helen M. Gothberg, "Time Management in Public Libraries,"
*Public Libraries* 30, no.6 (November/December 1991): 350–57.

# Management by wandering around

*by Paul John Cirino*

SEVERAL YEARS AGO A LIBRARY was designated as one of the most distinguished public libraries in the country, based on a university research study. The director received a very complimentary letter from a venerable library academic in which he asked the director to explain, in further detail, some of the unique features of the library. One of the things that was mentioned in the director's answer was that this library's administration had practiced MBWA (Management By Wandering Around) long before management consultant Tom Peters had ever identified it as such in his book, *In Search of Excellence*. The library director received in return a letter filled with pleasantries, in which Professor X asked, "By the way, what is MBWA?" Mind you, this gentleman had written a well-regarded work on library administration that had been used for many years by library school students and library administrators.

Library directors usually spend a great deal of their time at various committee meetings and library conferences. They spend little time studying the skills of leadership and even less time practicing them in their institutions. Library directors need to spend more time in their libraries practicing MBWA. This means that they have to get off their comfy chairs, and out of their offices. They have to bring themselves to the staff and to the customers, so that they can directly find out what's really happening. The library director who sits in the office all day waiting for people to bring in problems is missing the boat. Most staff members will not run the gauntlet of their fellow employees and knock on the boss's door to discuss a problem.

The library director must constantly wander around the library, informally talking to the staff and the public alike. A relaxed, friendly atmosphere should prevail. This requires a high level of interpersonal skills. If handled incorrectly, MBWA can cause employees to feel that they are being over-supervised, feeling that the boss is always on their backs. If practiced skillfully, MBWA will convey to your employees the feeling that you are concerned about them and their problems. This will not only serve to boost morale, but will provide you with a priceless flow of information about potential improvements and innovations. The employee that might be afraid to come to your office would be happy to tell you how to improve the library in the informal atmosphere that might prevail at the morning coffee break.

Wandering around also helps to keep the library director in closer contact with the public. I often wander around our buildings and chat with our customers. Most of the time they think I am just another customer, and so are very happy to offer their true opinions on our service. It is also a good practice to work at different jobs in different departments of the library from time to time. This not only helps to give you a better idea of what the customers are asking for, but provides you with your subordinates' perspective on what each person's job is actually like. These informal procedures are far more effective than any formal surveys that could be undertaken.

MBWA is just another form of leadership in practice. Successful military leaders do not become so by remaining aloof from their troops. They are constantly in contact with their troops, and will lead them into battle, should that be necessary. Military bureaucrats will be serving tea and passing reports at high level staff meetings. They may rise to prominent places in the military bureaucracy, but they will never be successful leaders by my standard. When things are running smoothly, bureaucrats will flourish. When the going gets rough, only true leaders will rise to the top.

I am constantly asked why I refuse to attend the plethora of useless conferences, meetings, and other such nonsense that seems to delight so many of our colleagues. My answer is always the same. "I can't afford the time. I'm too busy running my library. You ought to try it some time." A little leadership will go a long way toward improving any library. As Tom Peters says, "At least if you're out of your office wandering around, you won't be in your office writing a lot of useless memos and otherwise making it more difficult for the people who actually have to get the work done."

*Source:* Paul John Cirino, *The Business of Running a Library: A Handbook for Public Library Directors* (Jefferson, N.C.: McFarland & Co., 1991). 176p. Reprinted with permission.

# To whom does the director report?

**SIXTY-EIGHT PUBLIC LIBRARIES** in the Urban Libraries Council were asked that question in 1993. Here are their responses:

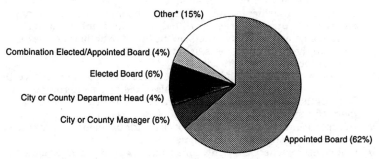

"Other" included the mayor; city manager and appointed board; mayor, county judge-executive, and library commission; county chair of commissioners; appointed commission; assistant city manager; city manager and appointed advisory board; mayor and appointed board.

*Source: Staffing Survey Results* (Evanston, Ill.: Urban Libraries Council, June 1993). 247p. Reprinted with permission.

# Who are trustees?

*by Lorraine M. Williams*

### Qualities of a good board member

**GOOD TRUSTEESHIP STARTS** with good board members, and there are certain ingredients that go into the making of a good board member, regardless of the type of board. There are as many differences among library trustees as you would tend to find among any part of the population. Some profiles have been done which document these. Yet there is a basic "profile" they all share. Library boards, social agency boards, or even profit-making corporate boards (where directors are financially compensated for their time and expertise) require the same qualities in their members. One organization that has spent a lot of time examining board membership is the National Charities Information Bureau in New York City. According to the bureau, good board members:

1. Are dedicated to helping others and modest in the light of their responsibilities as board members.
2. Approach their responsibilities in the spirit of a trustee on behalf of contributors, their intended beneficiaries, and the public at large.
3. Stand up for their convictions, even at the cost of misunderstanding or disapproval in business or social life.
4. Back up other board members and staff, rising to their defense when they are unjustly criticized or attacked.
5. Treat staff as a partner in a high calling, maintaining overall supervision and control but not interfering with day-to-day administration.
6. Avoid being overawed by others on the board, whether they be executive staff; tycoons of business, labor or society; professionals in social work, education, medicine, etc.
7. Welcome information and the best available advice, but reserve the right to arrive at decisions on the basis of their own judgment.
8. Respect the right of other board members and of staff to disagree with them and to have a fair hearing of their points of view.
9. Accept as routine that decisions must be made by majority vote and will at times go against one or more members.
10. Criticize, when necessary, in a constructive way, if possible suggesting an alternative course.
11. Recognize that time and energy are limited and that overcommitment may prove self-defeating.
12. Endeavor to keep disagreements and controversies impersonal and to promote unity.
13. Maintain loyalty to their agency, within a higher loyalty to the welfare of the community and humanity as a whole.

Don't be discouraged by the list. Remember, it is describing the ideal board member. Brian O'Connell, an expert in the area of volunteer development, quotes the *Wall Street Journal* as saying the ideal board member "is a man or woman with the versatility of Leonardo da Vinci, the financial acumen of Bernard Baruch, and the scholarly bent of Erasmus." I would add one more to the list: the patience of Job.

## Qualities of a good leader

O'Connell, in exploring the performance of board members who emerge as formal or informal leaders, has some revealing insights to share. He found that such leaders exhibit the following characteristics to a much greater extent than the average board member:

1. the ability to start and end every analysis and evaluation (the question before the board) with the standard of "what is right"
2. fairness, and giving credit to others for their contribution
3. a combination of toughness and sensitivity
4. reliability
5. controlled ambition
6. flexibility
7. enthusiasm
8. humor

It goes without saying that people with these characteristics do not limit the exercise of such qualities to the board room. They maintain that kind of approach to all areas of human interaction, whether it be family, business, or social life. In looking over O'Connell's list, think to yourself, how did I handle the last contentious issue that cropped up in my life? How would I measure up as a potential leader?

Because the leadership role is so vital in enabling a strong and dedicated library board to carry through its responsibilities, it is worth spending more time looking at the implications of O'Connell's list. On the standard of "what is right," O'Connell shares his experience with us:

> One of the significant lessons I've learned is that when I let other factors intervene, such as timidity, ambition, wanting to please, and all the other things that come to the fore when we're asked to speak our minds, I generally end up using poor judgment. On the positive side, there have been times when, for one persuasive reason or another, I did not want to take on a hassle or be in the minority, but I persisted and subsequently learned that by following the rule of doing what was right, my point was won or at least respected, and to have done otherwise would have been wrong in every respect.

How familiar this seems to us, and how utterly human. One of the difficult tasks in library trusteeship is having to make choices among competing "rights." Does one ultimately have priority over the others? Sometimes a decision that seems politically right, for example, the choice of a site for a new library, may not be right from a service point of view. Or sometimes we are faced with the option of beginning a new service that is trendy and bound to attract media and public support, or using the monies to bolster or even initiate a service that is desperately needed by some segment of our users and that has been sitting in the wings for a long while. Sometimes it is not terribly clear which "right" choice has priority.

Decisions of this kind are basically ethical decisions. What ultimately should be the guiding factor in choosing? For that answer we go right back to the definition of the word "trust," implied at the beginning of this chapter. Whatever supports the development of our library users as citizens has to be the final criterion in making the right decision. It is amazing how, when that yardstick is painstakingly applied to every possible choice, the right answer becomes much clearer.

## The "old boys' club"

Whether we choose the right answer, once we have identified it, is another question. Good leadership for our library board increases our chances of choosing wisely. This is why the "old boys' club" view of what a library board is has become totally inappropriate. So is its variation, namely, "You scratch my back; I'll scratch yours." Because we as library trustees are appointed politically, it is hard to avoid that kind of mentality. It is an immature approach; it is elitist; it perpetuates a web of reciprocity from which it is very difficult to escape. Finally, it destroys our very purpose, because it concentrates attention on the library trustee rather than on the community the trustee serves.

One member of a large urban board recounts her attempts to break into this old boys' milieu when first appointed to her board. It seemed that all decisions were made with a formula approach. Nothing was ever considered in the light of its distinctive situation, but everything was lumped into some generic category, such as complaints, personnel, or service. She said that she almost didn't have to go to meetings any more, because she knew that a problem would be solved in one of three or four standard ways, depending on how it was categorized. When she tried to raise the possibility that a particular problem was different, she was smiled at indulgently and the pat solution was applied to the problem.

It would have been tempting for her to graduate to the "club" as her seniority on the board grew and let newcomers experience what she had gone through. However, this woman was tough, and she knew that the clique approach was really creating a stagnant board, too wrapped up in its chumminess to see how truly unresponsive it was to the community. She bided her time, refused to keep quiet, and slowly, as members retired from the board, she began to earn a position of respect. Eventually she ended up as chairperson and gave a dynamism to the role that had been sadly missing for years.

## A matter of ethics

In the last decade, the need for ethics education in professional, government and business life has moved into the limelight, sometimes spurred on by scandalous betrayals of public trust. Not surprisingly, the field of librarianship has had to rethink its code of ethics as well. Trustees have been taking a look at how their ethical obligations might be set down, too. In the Winter 1990 edition of the *ALTA Trustee Digest*, there is a two-page treatment of the topic. One section deals with a proposed code of ethics for Louisiana trustees. The main points are listed below:

## The code of ethics

1. Trustees in the capacity of trust imposed upon them shall observe ethical standards with absolute truth, integrity, and honor.
2. Trustees in the age of intense and ever increasing technological advances must promote just and equal library service at the highest level possible to their community, to all citizens regardless of race, creed, color, or age. To accomplish this it is absolutely necessary to cooperate with other libraries in the state and with the State Library.
3. Trustees must avoid situations in which personal interests might be served or financial benefits gained at the expense of library users, colleagues or the institution.
4. It is incumbent upon any trustee to disqualify himself/herself immediately whenever even the appearance of a conflict of interest exists.
5. Trustees must distinguish clearly in their official statements between their personal philosophies and attitudes and those of the institution. Trustees must acknowledge and support the formal position of the board even if they personally disagree.
6. Trustees must respect the confidential nature of library records and of housekeeping business and must be able to distinguish these records from the records the library keeps for public accounting. Trustees also must be aware of and in compliance with the laws governing freedom of information and those safeguarding the rights of privacy of the patrons served.
7. Trustees must be prepared by a policy of the board to support to the fullest the efforts of librarians to resist censorship of library materials by groups or individuals.
8. Trustees as policy makers are clearly distinguished from the director who is the administrator. All complaints from staff and/or patrons must be courteously referred to the proper library authority. Trustees must refrain absolutely from individual actions, statements or comments which might undermine the authority of the director.
9. Trustees who accept appointment to a library board are expected to perform all of the functions of library trustees by working harmoniously with the board, accepting the will of the majority vote without trying to dominate the board or other board members or to neglect any share of the board's work.
10. To the extent permitted by budgetary provisions trustees should participate in state and national library trustee organizations in order to

strengthen and broaden their individual understanding of the duties of trustees and, because of informed knowledge, better serve the public library.

Before we move from this general overview of trusteeship, I'd like to issue a challenge to readers. Many trustees refer to their director and staff as "the professionals." Let's take a look at the qualities considered essential in order to qualify as a "professional" and see if we can learn anything about injecting more professionalism into our approach to trusteeship. The list, as it appeared in a recent journal article, had seven characteristics. The ones which could act as role models for trustees are as follows:

- The professional has a strong commitment to the field. (If we don't feel this about libraries, we shouldn't be on the board.)
- The professional has a specialized body of knowledge and skills. (This is where the necessity of on-the-board training is so necessary, either in-house, through seminars and conferences, or reading the literature on library trusteeship.)
- The professional makes decisions on the basis of general principles and theories applied to specific cases. (The mission statement of our library, its goals and objectives and the basic philosophy behind public libraries, reflected on in the light of our own and others' life experience, are what trustees base decisions on.)
- The professional is assumed to have a service orientation, implying the use of expertise on behalf of . . . the client and an absence of self-interest. (The goals of the library system come before any personal goals, and all trustee work is done on behalf of the community, not for self-aggrandizement.)
- Professionals form associations. . . . (Trustees have associations, both state and federal. To be serious about trusteeship is to be an ardent supporter of our Trustee Association.)

An attempt to draw parallels here may be judged as "straining at the seams." However, the more I see and hear of library trustees across the United States and Canada, the more I realize that there is such a thing as a "professional trustee." The quality shines through. You'll recognize it when you see it.

*Source:* Lorraine M. Williams, *The Library Trustee and the Public Librarian: Partners in Service* (Metuchen, N.J.: Scarecrow Press, 1993). 167p. Reprinted with permission.

# Top 10 things every good library trustee should do

*by Malcolm Hill*

10. Give a speech about your library. Rotary Clubs, PTAs and other groups are always looking for programs, and the world won't know what your library has to offer unless you tell them.
9. Go visit another library and steal a good idea from it.
8. Don't ever stop learning. It's hard enough to keep up even when you work at it. Seek out learning opportunities that will help make you a better trustee.
7. Be ACTIVE! Being a trustee means more than just going to the board meetings every month. Write a letter to the governor about state aid.

Take the editor of your local paper to lunch.

6. Spend your money wisely. Don't hoard it. Your funding bodies didn't give you tax money so that you could put it in the bank. They are buying *service* from you.

5. Never forget that it's the public's library, not the board's. On the other hand, remember that the *board* governs the library, not the staff, not the town board, and not the Friends of the Library.

4. Pay your staff a decent wage. They work hard, sometimes in less than ideal conditions, and their pay rates almost everywhere are pretty bad.

3. Have a plan for your library. If you don't know where you're going, any road will get you there.

2. Embrace change. Welcome it. Create it.

1. Have fun! As a trustee or a librarian, you should love what you're doing, and it should be obvious to everyone.

*Source: Mid-York Library System Reporter,* November 1993, p.1. Reprinted with permission.

# Qualifications of killer trustees

### by Paul John Cirino

THE CHIEF FUNCTIONS OF A LIBRARY BOARD are to learn what are the appropriate objectives for the library in the community, and to secure funds that will make their attainment possible. However, quite the opposite is true in many cases. Horror stories abound. Here's a tongue-in-cheek scenario that many of our embattled library directors can surely identify with.

Sometimes the library can appear to be a smooth-running, efficient operation. Like any institution, there is always room for improvement, but, basically, the operation seems to meet acceptable standards. Staff morale is good and turnover is low. Services are of high quality and wide variety. But don't let that fool you. Those underworked, overpaid civil servants must be doing something wrong.

So here's your chance! Become a library trustee and shake them out of their complacency. After all, we know it takes a public-spirited citizen like you to keep these lazy louts from further bilking the public. Here are some helpful hints on how to go about obtaining this position and performing your vital function.

First of all, don't run for election on your qualifications. The less you have, the better. Don't have experience as a manager, a business person or a professional person, or anything else that might contribute to your worth in the position. There are too many college educated intellectuals running things anyway. If you don't have to be elected, but rather appointed by the mayor or some other politicians, your political connections, not your qualifications, are what count. This may very well be the first step in your quest for higher office.

And secondly, campaign on negative issues. Nit-pick. Magnify every fault. Some good examples are: "Every time I come into the library, the staff is always standing around doing nothing; the staff is overpaid; I never get the books I want in time; taxes are already too high." It doesn't matter. Anything will do. The taxpayers and the politicians will love it. You're a shoo-in.

Congratulations! You've made it. You're a library trustee. Now you're ready for phase two in your quest for truth and justice and to provide your community with better library service.

*One.* Come to the library often to observe the activities of the staff. Don't just remain in the public areas. Wander through the work areas, too. Try to make staff members feel as uncomfortable and ill at ease as possible. After all, you're a trustee now. Start exercising your authority. Besides, what does the library director know about supervision? They're only a librarian. If they knew what they were doing, the staff wouldn't be doing so little. This is sure to keep staff members on their toes.

*Two.* Expect the director to be available whenever you call or come to the library. There is never any reason for them to be out of the building, and nothing is more important than catering to your every desire. If they're at a meeting, out sick or on vacation, make remarks like "He's never here" or "What are we paying her for?" Do this in earshot of the public and the staff, whenever possible. Generally show disbelief that the director has the audacity to be at the library any fewer than 24 hours a day, 7 days a week. For your tax money, you expect nothing less than total devotion. This is sure to keep the director from goofing off.

*Three.* Take credit for all the new ideas that work, and blame the staff for those that don't. This is a sure morale booster. Pretty soon they'll be so afraid to act that they won't even make the most minor decisions without consulting you. That's real control.

*Four.* Ask your director embarrassing and demeaning questions in front of the public and the staff. Always keep them on the defensive. The humiliation will do them good. Undermining their authority will show who is really the boss.

*Five.* Question every administrative decision, no matter how minor. Ask justification for every hiring or firing. Find out why that filing cabinet was needed, and why it needed a lock—and—ugh—who chose that color? Remember, no decision, no matter how small, should escape your purview. After all, you are a trustee.

*Six.* Agree with every critic of the library. They are the voters in the next election. After all, everyone knows that angry taxpayers have a clearer understanding and perspective of the library's operations than the director and staff. They're only looking out for their self interest. Besides, if you were to back up the director, he or she might not look for another job and we all know that frequent staff turnover, especially at the top, keeps the library from becoming stodgy and complacent.

*Seven.* Hold surprise board meetings and don't invite the director. That way you will be sure not to be influenced in any way by expert advice. The director doesn't have the best interests of the library at heart, but only wishes to increase the bureaucratic empire. It's much easier this way. The director won't annoy you by questioning your benign decisions. Keeping them in the dark should help to further their encroaching paranoid state.

*Eight.* Scoff at the accomplishments of the director and staff. When you are shown charts or graphs demonstrating the library's level of efficiency, laugh and make remarks like, "Statistics can be made to show anything," or "Statistics don't lie, but liars can use statistics." Show them that nothing they do is ever good enough. This will serve to destroy their motivation and transform them into the lifeless bureaucrats you knew they were anyway. This attitude will come in extremely handy at salary increase time. You don't have to reward the staff for their accomplishments, because you have already established that they haven't made any.

*Nine.* Reject all your director's requests for adequate staff. There's too much fat, anyway. No matter the justification to prove otherwise, always claim the library is overstaffed. Don't forget, statistics can be made to show anything. Also, when the public complains about poor service, you can blame it on incompetence, and not on a shortage of personnel. No matter what, you can't lose.

*Ten.* Don't base the director's salary on the worth of that person to the library. If they maintain high staff morale and run an efficient operation, providing quality services at bargain prices, downplay that. Forget about their years of experience and educational level. Don't compare their salary level with other government officials, or private sector managers with similar responsibilities. Instead, keep salary discussions on a purely personal level. What you get paid and what you got for a raise is what's important. You represent the average citizen in the community and what makes the director think he or she has a right to do any better than the average citizen?

(*Note*—This line of logic is not to be used for those who are themselves highly paid professionals or executives. In those instances, you must point out that there is absolutely no similarity between your level of education and the work you do and that of a library director. How could a lowly librarian ever consider receiving remuneration remotely comparable to yours?)

*Source:* Paul John Cirino, *The Business of Running a Library*
(Jefferson, N.C.: McFarland & Co., 1991). 176p. Reprinted with permission.

# Friends Groups

# Friends of the library

*by Sandy Dolnick*

FRIENDS ARE A NECESSARY part of life for institutions as well as for people. Support and recognition are important elements of any friendship. Friends of the Library groups can and should supply these elements to all libraries while they represent the library to the community. The potential effectiveness of a group of citizens with no vested interest cannot be overestimated. The library, which is often taken for granted, can multiply its support by the community if it is willing to establish and perpetuate a Friends organization.

Friends
of
Libraries
U.S.A.

Inflation and changes in public attitudes toward government spending have brought intense pressures to bear upon library budgets. In many cases, Friends of the Library groups, by raising funds from private sources or by providing volunteer labor, have made it possible for the library to continue services that would otherwise have been terminated.

The initial reasons for having a support group differ among libraries and communities but generally include:

**Money.** Friends groups have traditionally raised funds for projects or acquisitions in excess of the general library budget.

**Services.** There is no limit to the services that a dedicated volunteer group can provide, short of substituting members for specialized staff.

**Public relations.** Each Friend is a walking public relations vehicle for the library.

**Advocacy.** An informed, active citizen lobby can be the strongest weapon the library has.

**Community involvement.** An organized Friends group is living proof of the library's value to the community.

The rationale for a Friends group may change over time. A group that begins as a purely social organization, for example, may shift its orientation as the library's needs grow.

Friends of Libraries, therefore, are many different things to many different communities. They all may be defined as groups of citizens that are associated on behalf of libraries.

The interest in Friends groups grows steadily. Every year the American Library Association receives more queries about them. Friends of Libraries U.S.A., a national organization, was formed to further the growth of new groups and to exchange information among existing ones.

## The ten commandments

Certain principles, if adhered to and reviewed annually, will develop a nurturing atmosphere and pleasant environment for Friends and library staff. These ten commandments were learned through the combined experiences of hundreds of groups.

1. The library director must want a Friends group. If this is not the case, do not proceed any further. There is no use in continuing.
2. The library staff must be willing to work with Friends—at least that part of the staff that must come into contact with the Friends.
3. All parties involved must realize that a time commitment is involved, and that a successful group is no accident. The activity level of the group will determine the amount of time involved; if there is only one book sale a year to worry about, for example, there will be minimal time involved *once the group is organized.*
4. The library must agree which of its resources (e.g., space, staff time, paper, and telephone) will be used by the Friends.
5. A committed core group must exist. This core group may be only two or three people.
6. The authority to which the library director reports must be aware of the Friends group.
7. Communication must be open to all groups involved in the use of the library; the Friends should not have an exclusionist policy.
8. All those involved in the Friends must realize that the Friends group does not make library policy, which is the function of the trustees.
9. The library must decide, in discussion with the Friends, the roles it wishes the group to play: advocates, social, fundraising, volunteers or a combination. These roles change as needs change, so they should be reviewed annually.
10. All those involved must understand that trustees and Friends have separate functions, and liaisons should be developed between the two groups. Money raised by the Friends should be disbursed by them as they see fit according to information on the library's needs.

Groups being organized should be able to check off each item listed above; established groups will find this list a good yearly evaluation. By renewing its goals each year, a group can retain the vitality of a new organization and reap the benefits of experience.

## Services to the community

Literacy program newsletter
Christmas open house
Produce and host television series or radio show
Book sales

Exhibit booth at county fair
Volunteers for the blind
High school essay contest
Parade float
Outreach program at retirement center
Film program for elderly in public housing
Oral history
Teachers' tea
Newcomers' day
Survey on library use
Shut-ins brought to the library for National Library Week lunch to meet staff
and the mayor
Librarian sent to ALA conference
Help for "mother's morning out"
Storyphone
Rare book appraisals
Community calendar

## Services to the library

Legislative Day
Clerical help
Coffee and refreshments at programs
Christmas decorations
Tours of library
Clipping and setting up magazine file
Displays
Grounds and shrubs maintenance
Painting shelving
Mailings assistance
Piano tuning
Memorial gift procedure maintenance
Article clipping for vertical file
Free paperback book exchange
Typing
Book mending
Library switchboard operation
Newspaper indexing
Microfilm indexing
Telephoning
Bags to carry art reproductions

## Purchases for the library

Videotapes, audiotapes
Film programs
Special audiovisual equipment
Matching funds for Reading Is Fundamental grant
Books

## Funds to increase endowment

Special furnishings
Rare books
Printing
Hospital book carts
Repair of rare books

Elevator for handicapped
Fiscal agent for humanities grant
Building repair
Security system
Rental book collection
Copy machine
Large-print books
Landscaping
Shades
Computer hardware and software
Magazine subscriptions
Compact discs
Laser printer

2

*Source:* Sandy Dolnick, *Friends of Libraries Sourcebook*
(Chicago: American Library Association, 1990).

# Support staff networks

*compiled by Meralyn Meadows*

**MANY ASSOCIATIONS EXIST** for library support staff. The following list was compiled by Meralyn Meadows for the ALA Support Staff Interests Round Table.

**Alabama Library Association, Paraprofessional Roundtable,** Clevelyn Alexander, Mobile Public Library, 701 Government Street, Mobile, AL 36602; (205) 434-7073; fax (205) 434-7571.

**American Library Association, Support Staff Interests Round Table,** Margaret Myers, ALA, 50 E. Huron St., Chicago, IL 60611; (312) 280-4277.

**Arizona Library Technicians and Paraprofessionals,** Mary McKee, Marcos de Niza High School, 6000 S. Lakeshore Dr., Tempe, AZ 85283; (602) 838-8200, x227; fax (602) 491-7985.

**Arkansas Library Paraprofessional Roundtable,** Sherryl Robinson, University Libraries, University of Arkansas at Fayetteville, Fayetteville, AR 72701; (501) 767-9371; fax (501) 767-3427.

**California Library Association, Support Staff Round Table,** Betty Baker, Bruggemeyer Memorial Library, 318 S. Ramona Ave., Monterey Park, CA 91754-3312; (818) 307-1366; fax (818) 288-4251.

**Colorado Library Association, Paralibrarian Division,** Jackie Konselman, University of Colorado at Colorado Springs, Austin Bluffs Parkway, Box 7150, Colorado Springs, CO 80933; (719) 593-3523; fax (719) 528-5229.

**Connecticut Library Association, Library Technical Assistants Section,** Gina Antolini, Meriden Public Library, 105 Miller St., Meriden, CT 08540; (203) 238-2344; fax (203) 238-3647.

**Council on Library/Media Technicians,** Linda J. Owen, President, Rivera Library, University of California, Riverside, CA 92517-5900; (909) 787-3780; fax (909) 787-3285.

**District of Columbia Association of Library Technicians,** Nicole M. Robinson, c/o Ross, Dixon & Masback, 601 Pennsylvania Ave., N.W., Washington, DC 20004; (202) 662-2957; e-mail: nrobi@class.org.

**Florida Library Association, Library Paraprofessional Caucus,** Jean Glaze, 1500 S.W. 1st St., #3, Ft. Lauderdale, FL 33312; (305) 357-7419.

**Georgia Support Staff and Paraprofessional Resources Interest Group (SPRIG),** James E. Camp, Cobb County Public Library System, 266 Roswell St., S.E., Marietta, GA 30060-2004; (404) 528-2327; fax (404) 528-2349.

**Hawaii Library Association, Technical and General Services Section (TAGS),** Sandra Sakamoto, McCully-Moiliili Public Library, 2211 S. King St., Honolulu, HI 96826; (808) 946-1408; fax (808) 942-2237.

**Illinois Library Association, Forum of Library Assistants,** Tom Rich, Warren-Newport Public Library, 224 N. O'Plaine Rd., Gurnee, IL 60031; (708) 244-5150; fax (708) 872-8578.

**Indiana Library Federation, Support Staff Division,** Merrillyn Smith, Vigo County Public Library, One Library Square, Terre Haute, IN 47807; (812) 232-1113.

**Iowa Support Personnel Forum,** Kathryn Bly, Kirkwood Community College, Box 2068, Cedar Rapids, IA 52406; (319) 398-5553; fax (319) 398-4908.

**Kansas Library Operation Associates (KLOA),** Kay Kennedy, Sterling College Library, P.O. Box 98, Sterling, KS 67579; (316) 278-4209; fax (316) 278-2775.

**Louisiana Library Association, Support Staff Interest Group,** Pat Litz, Louisiana State University, 126 Middleton Library, Baton Rouge, LA 70803; (504) 388-4013; fax (504) 388-6992.

**Maine Library Support Staff Association,** Susan B. Raudin, Bowdoin College Library, Brunswick, ME 04011; (207) 725-3288.

**Maryland Library Association, Associates, Paraprofessionals and Library Support Staff (APLSS),** Paula Drnec-Thompson, Baltimore County Public Library, Catonsville Branch, 1100 Frederick Rd., Baltimore, MD 21228-0951; (410) 887-9051; fax (410) 887-8166.

**Minnesota Library Association, Library Support Staff Round Table,** Kathleen Martin, Gustavus Adolphus College, Folke Bernadotte Memorial Library, St. Peter, MN 56082; (507) 933-7562; fax (507) 933-6292.

**Missouri Library Association, Support Staff/Paraprofessional Council,** Connie Ury, Northwest Missouri State University, Owens Library, Maryville, MO 64468; (816) 562-1662; fax (816) 562-2153.

**Nebraska Library Association, Paraprofessional Section,** Susan Taylor, 306 Love Library, University of Nebraska, Lincoln, NE 68588-0410; (402) 472-2547; fax (402) 472-5131.

**Nevada Library Association, Action Interest Group,** Laura Oki, Elko County Library, 720 Court St., Elko, NV 89801; (702) 738-3066; fax (702) 738-8262.

**New Jersey Association of Library Assistants,** Barbara Sullivan, Woodbridge Public Library, George Frederick Plaza, Woodbridge, NJ 07095; (908) 634-4450; fax (908) 634-7610.

**[New York] Capital Area Library Assistants (CALA),** Jean Guyon, University Library ULB 34, State University of New York, 1400 Washington St., Albany, NY 12222; (518) 442-3625; e-mail: userbsew@mts.rpiedu.

**[New York] Central New York Library Assistants,** Victoria DeFrancisco, LeMoyne College Library, LeMoyne Heights, Syracuse, NY 13214; (315) 445-4328.

**[New York] North Country Library Assistants Committee,** Karen Smith, Paul Smiths College, Cubley Library, Paul Smiths, NY 12979; (518) 327-6313; fax (518) 327-6350.

**[New York] Rochester Region Library Assistants,** Joseph Valenti, Appellate

Division Law Library, New York State Judicial Department, 525 Hall of Justice, Rochester, NY 14614; (716) 428-1077.

[New York] South Central Research Library Council, Library Assistants Advisory Committee, Barbara Taylor, Olin Library, Cornell University, Ithaca, NY 14850; (607) 255-4247; e-mail: bwt1@cornell.edu.

New York State Library Assistants' Association (NYSLAA), Vida Bellisario, Rensselear Polytechnical Institute, Folsom Library, Troy, NY 12181; (518) 276-8300.

[New York] Western New York Library Assistants Discussion Group, Ruth Johnson, Lockwood Memorial Library, SUNY Buffalo, Buffalo, NY 14260; (716) 645-2785.

North Carolina Library Paraprofessional Association, Renee Pridgen, Cumberland County Public Library & Information Center, 300 Maiden Lane, Fayetteville, NC 28301; (910) 483-1580; fax (910) 483-8644.

[Ohio] Academic Library Association of Ohio, Support Staff Interest Group, Peggy Rector, William Howard Doane Library, Denison University, Granville, OH 43023; (614) 587-6479; fax (614) 587-6431; e-mail: rector@cc.denison.edu.

Ohio Library Association, Supportive Staff Division, Mary Beth Gratop, Toledo-Lucas County Public Library, South Branch, 1638 Broadway, Toledo, OH 43609; (419) 259-5395; fax (419) 243-4217.

Oregon Library Association, Library Support Staff Roundtable (LSSRT), Deborah Cook, Southern Oregon State College Library, 1250 Siskiyou Blvd., Ashland, OR 97520-5076; (503) 552-6825; fax (503) 552-6429.

Pennsylvania Library Association, Library Support Staff Roundtable, Mary Ann Gierradowicz, York County Library System, 118 Pleasant Acres Rd., York, PA 17402; (717) 759-9685; fax (717) 751-0741.

South Carolina Library Association, Paraprofessional Round Table, Tracy Thomas, Miller Whittaker Library, South Carolina State University, Orangeburg, SC 29117; (803) 536-8643.

Tennessee Library Association, Paraprofessional Roundtable, Donna K. Hawk, Chattanooga State Technical College Library, 4501 Amnicola Highway, Chattanooga, TN 37406; (615) 697-2572; fax (615) 697-4409; e-mail: hawk@cstcc.cc.tn.us.

Texas Library Association, Library Support Staff Interest Group, Laura Peterson, Map Collection/Government Documents, Texas Tech University Library, Lubbock, TX 79409-0002.

Utah Library Association, Library Paraprofessional and Support Staff (LPSS) Roundtable, Rebecca A. Gleason, Brigham Young University, 6380 HBLL, Provo, UT 84602; (801) 378-5938; e-mail: rebecca_gleason@byu.edu.

Virginia Library Association, Paraprofessional Forum, Sue Parham, University of Richmond, Boatwright Memorial Library, Richmond, VA 23173; (804) 289-8939; fax (804) 289-8757.

Washington Library Association, Association of Library Employees, Karen Blatman-Byers, Washington State Library, McNeil Island Correctional Center Branch Library, P.O. Box 88900, Steilacoom, WA 98388-0900; (206) 588-5281, x1509; fax (206) 589-4458.

Wisconsin Library Association, Support Staff Section, Paulette Feld, Libraries & Learning Resources Technical Services, Polk Library, University of Wisconsin-Oshkosh, Oshkosh, WI 54901; (414) 424-7369; fax (414) 424-2175; e-mail: feld@vaxa.cis.uwosh.edu.

Wyoming Library Association, Kathy Carlson, State Law Library, Supreme Court Bldg., Cheyenne, WY 82002; (307) 777-7509; fax (307) 777-7240; e-mail: kcarlson@teal.csn.org.

*Source:* Meralyn Meadows, *National Directory: Library Paraprofessional Associations* (Chicago: American Library Association, June 1994). 16p.

# Orienting new employees

*by Katherine Branch*

MANY SUPERVISORS BREATHE a sigh of relief once they have made a hiring decision; however, even greater time and effort should be devoted to orienting the new employee. New employees often lack a sense of belonging, which results in high turnover in the early weeks of employment. The new employee needs to be recognized as a person and feel that the job is important. The first day on the job can influence the way the new employee feels about the library throughout his or her employment. In addition, an organized plan for orientation that ensures that employees know where to go for help can increase morale and productivity.

## Before the employee arrives

Find out whether there are standard orientation procedures within the library. If there are not, consider asking that procedures be developed. Volunteer to work on a draft of procedures; form a committee to address the issue; or discuss the issue with your personnel librarian. Also, see what your parent institution provides as orientation information. Many universities, government agencies, and corporations provide in-depth orientation sessions or packets.

Preparation for the employee's first day at work is essential. First, ask other employees about their orientation experiences and needs. Listen for gaps in their orientation and determine how those gaps affected their performance.

Second, sit down with the job description for the new employee and analyze the job duties. Decide how the employee should be oriented so that she or he has an understanding of how her or his duties fit into the library's mission and relate to the duties of others in the library.

Third, decide who in the library is best suited to orient the new employee  to specific types of information. As the supervisor, you should not do the entire orientation yourself. It is important that the new employee get to know his or her coworkers and their areas of expertise. However, you should retain responsibility for the orientation because you have a vested interest in being sure that the employee is well oriented. In addition, the employee is motivated to learn from you since you will be evaluating his or her performance. Because you want to transmit the codes of conduct important to you, you should not delegate discussions of conduct or behavior to others.

Fourth, try to schedule a variety of orientation activities, because people have different methods of learning. Some alternatives to one-on-one discussions include written exercises, workbooks, audiovisual "tours," computer-assisted instruction, small group sessions, and written orientation, policy, and procedure materials.

Fifth, determine the time frame for the orientation period. A part-time shelving job may require a shorter orientation period than a professional reference or cataloging job. When deciding on the length of the orientation period, be sure to allow time for independent exploration by the employee, for formation of on-the-job friendships, and for beginning actual job duties. If new employees do not begin to do some work shortly after their first day, they can feel as though they are not making a contribution to the library. They may feel as though others are judging them and wondering why they are not beginning to do "real work." Remember that new employees are anxious and eager to begin work. Capitalize on this enthusiasm!

After completing the orientation plan, you should arrange for the new employee's desk or office space so that it is ready before she or he arrives.

Another essential step in making the new employee feel welcome is to prepare other staff members prior to the new employee's first day. This can help prevent unintentional (or intentional) "hazing." Hazing can occur when current employees feel threatened by the eagerness and enthusiasm of a new employee. Occasionally a new employee unwittingly encourages hazing by referring to how things were done in other libraries where she or he worked. To current employees, these references can imply a negative judgment about their library. To minimize or preclude this, be sure to define the role of the new employee, being clear about the authority and autonomy the new employee will have.

2

---

### Employee orientation in libraries

What do libraries do about employee orientation? Are formal orientation programs common, or do libraries throw new employees in to sink or swim? *LPN* took an informal survey of selected *LPN* readers. Sixty libraries responded to our questionnaire. Of the sixty respondents, a large majority, 58 (96.6%) conduct formal orientation sessions for new employees. Eighteen of the libraries (31% of those libraries that offer orientation) hold just one orientation session for their new employees. Another eighteen libraries have two-session orientation programs. Twenty libraries (34%) have orientation programs that consist of more than two sessions.

Orientation is a shared responsibility for library managers. Forty-three libraries (74%) report that two or more staff members share the responsibility for new employee orientation. Among libraries that assign joint responsibility for new employee orientation, twenty-six (44.8%) have more than two staff members involved in orientation. These libraries often divide the responsibility between the employee's supervisor, department heads, and sometimes, the new employee's peers.

Seventeen (29%) of the libraries that have shared responsibility for new employee orientation divide the responsibility between two staff members. The most likely division of responsibility is between the employee's immediate supervisor and a human resources staff member. Ten of the seventeen libraries that assign orientation duties to two people reported this arrangement.

Fifteen (25.8%) of the libraries that conducted orientation sessions assigned responsibility to one staff member. Twelve of the fifteen libraries assign employee orientation to a staff member in the human resources department. Two libraries that have only one person conduct the orientation session assign this responsibility to the employee's immediate supervisor, and one library assigns this responsibility to the library director.

Topics that are covered in library orientation programs include:

- job descriptions;
- work rules;
- library policies;
- benefits;
- organization of the library and parent institution;
- mission, philosophy, and customer service.

*Source: Library Personnel News* 8 (March/April 1994): 7.

## New Employee Orientation Checklist

### Before the employee arrives

Send a letter to the new employee specifying conditions of employment, such as salary, hours of work, and job title.

Equip the employee's desk or work area with basic supplies:

| | | |
|---|---|---|
| stapler | ruler | staff directory |
| cellophane tape | pens, pencils | phone books |
| stationery | paper | keys |
| scissors | note pads | procedure manuals |

Prepare an orientation packet including the following:

history and philosophy of the library
organization chart
descriptions of the functions of each library department
library staff directory
library or institution's newsletter
library's annual report
map of the institution, campus, or agency
information on the local area (if the employee is from out of town)

Order a nameplate (pin, badge, etc.) and business cards.
Update the staff directory to include the new employee.
Put the new employee on the mailing list for library and institutional newsletters.
Notify coworkers of the new employee's name, duties, and start date.
Provide the employee with parking information.

### First day

Introduce the employee to coworkers.
Conduct a library tour, focusing on rest rooms, cafeteria or lounge, and the location of supplies, photocopy machines, and telephones.
Cover safety and security issues, such as emergency procedures and personal safety.
Discuss hours, breaks, payday, and procedures for reporting absences.
Make lunch arrangements for the new employee with yourself, the new employee's guide, or a group of coworkers.
Tell the employee how you, the coworkers, and the administrators prefer to be addressed (e.g., by your first name, last name, or title).
Discuss the philosophy of the library and its commitment to service.
Discuss standards of conduct and any formal or informal dress code.
Be sure all personnel paperwork is completed.

### Second day

Discuss telephone procedures and policies.
Tour the entire institution or agency, pointing out the credit union, cafeteria(s), and post office.
Explain timekeeping procedures, including overtime and compensatory time.

### First week

Review the library's organizational chart and reporting structure.
Arrange for the employee to get ID and library cards.
Explain library policies on office collections, soliciting, confidentiality of library records, smoking, alcohol, and drugs.
Arrange for an explanation of benefits, such as insurance, vacation, leave policies, retirement, disability, credit union, tuition coverage, holidays, jury duty, bereavement leave, and travel policy.
Explain procedures for communicating problems or concerns.
Cover department-specific plans, policies, and procedures.
Cover housekeeping responsibilities.
Explain the operation of the employee's union (if applicable).

**2**

---

**Second week**

Discuss any probationary period.
Discuss performance standards and appraisal.
Discuss the library's tenure or salary review program.
Cover the long-range plans of the library.
Cover grievance procedures.

**First month**

Set an appointment with the library director and your supervisor.
Arrange for orientation to other departments with whom the employee frequently interacts.
Ask for the employee's feedback on the orientation.
Discuss opportunities for advancement.

---

Another step is to assign a "buddy" or guide to the new employee—someone from a different department who is friendly and knowledgeable about the library. A staff member from a different department can become a source of information for the new employee about how things are done outside his or her department. The guide might undergo training so that she or he knows what is expected in orienting the new employee.

## The first day

The first day is crucial and can have a significant impact on reducing the new employee's anxiety and encouraging a positive attitude. Perhaps the most important aspect of the first day's orientation is becoming aware of and attending to the new employee's social needs.

First, you should tell the new employee how you and others in the library prefer to be addressed. (Be sure the new employee knows how to pronounce difficult names correctly. There is nothing more embarrassing for a new employee than mispronouncing a name!)

Second, she or he should be introduced to her or his coworkers and others with whom she or he will have frequent contact. Schedule time so that the new employee can get to know coworkers. Stress teamwork in your discussions.

Third, the employee should have an introduction to the layout of the building so she or he feels comfortable about being there. Safety and security information should be covered, particularly in a library where theft or personal threats are a potential problem.

Fourth, give the employee a general outline of the job so that she or he is fully aware of, and comfortable with, her or his duties. Provide an orientation packet and discuss particularly important information in the packet.

Orientation duties on the first day might be divided in the following manner: The supervisor welcomes the new employee as the new employee arrives and briefly discusses general issues, such as the employee's hours, breaks, conduct, library philosophy, and procedures for reporting absences. The supervisor then introduces the new employee to coworkers. A coworker within the department gives the new employee a tour of the department. Depending on the size of the library, the coworker (or an assigned buddy or guide from another area of the library) gives the new employee a tour of the entire library. Be sure that lunch arrangements are made in advance with yourself, the new employee's guide, or a group of coworkers. The library's administrator or personnel librarian should discuss benefits, safety, and grievance procedures. Time should be scheduled so that the employee can read policies, get accustomed to his or her work area, and think about what has been learned so far.

## The first two weeks

By the end of the first two weeks, the new employee should understand the functions of other departments within the library and how the employee and his or her department interact with other departments. The new employee should be familiar with the library's organization chart and how the library fits into its parent institution's goals and plans. He or she should know how performance will be evaluated and be aware of acceptable and unacceptable behavior. He or she should know where to go for help and how to contact resource people within the library and institution. Other important topics for the first two weeks are included in the checklist.

## The first month

In the first month, discuss opportunities for advancement and career development with the new employee. By the end of the first month, schedule time for formal feedback about the new employee's orientation period. This meeting will provide an opportunity for you to fill any gaps in the orientation and can help you in planning for the next new employee.

In general, be nonthreatening and observant during the orientation period. Communicate your concerns and be open to the concerns, however trivial sounding, of your new employee. Small concerns, if neglected, can be blown out of proportion. By thoroughly preparing for the orientation period, you can do much to guarantee that your new employee adjusts easily to his or her new environment and becomes a productive employee.

*Source:* Joan Giesecke, ed., *Practical Help for New Supervisors* (Chicago: American Library Association, 1992). 69p.

# Telephone training

### *by Morell D. Boone, Sandra G. Yee, and Rita Bullard*

THE TELEPHONE CAN BE BOTH A BLESSING and a curse; some days it seems the phone will never stop ringing. Student assistants answering the phone must realize that it is also a part of the service component. Audiovisual materials are available that can be used to demonstrate proper telephone etiquette. Practice with telephones (simulation and role playing) is another excellent way to demonstrate and teach students how to handle telephone calls.

The following list is a sample of those items that student assistants need to know and practice.

1. The telephone is an important business tool. Therefore, it is to be used for business purposes only. Do not make or receive personal calls while working. (Staff, as an example, shouldn't either.)
2. When it is your responsibility to answer the phone, try to answer it promptly, not later than the fourth ring. If necessary, indicate to the caller that you are busy and ask if he or she can please hold.

3. When answering the phone, identify the exact location (media, circulation, etc.) and offer to be of service. Example: "Library circulation, How may I help you?" Provide lists of office phone numbers near the phone so that students can quickly redirect a call. Teach students how to transfer calls.

4. Always have paper and pencil close; preferably the pencil will already be in hand. You may need to jot down items to remember, or take a message. A pen or pencil permanently affixed near the phone will help. Also provide message forms so that all important information will be included.

5. Remember that your voice gives the patron a mental image of both you and the library. Try to put a smile in your voice. Sound alert. Speak actively.

6. Use good grammar and diction. Do not use slang or "library-type" abbreviations.

7. Hold the telephone receiver correctly, about one-half inch from your mouth. Do not carry on another conversation while talking with a patron. Never put the phone down without putting the call on hold.

8. Be of service; initiate offers of help. However, do not give information or refer callers to other areas unless you are absolutely sure you are correct. If there is any question about the best possible place to refer the call, take a name and number and tell the caller a staff member will call back with the proper information. Be certain to give the message to the staff member who can answer the question. Designate a staff member to handle telephone questions if it is not obvious to the student assistant where the message would go.

9. Never indicate that a staff member is on a break or at lunch if he or she is not in the office. Simply indicate that the staff member is "out of the office," and offer to take a message. Confirm the name and number. Promptly put the message in the staff member's designated message location. Vacations and absences should be clearly noted each day. If an absent staff member is requested by a caller, the student should ask if someone else can help.

10. Some staff members will want their calls "screened." You will be informed of those who prefer this service. This means that you should ask the callers' name, "May I ask who is calling?", put the caller on hold, call the staff member on the intercom, and give the callers' name. This allows the staff member the opportunity to mentally prepare for the call.

11. Always finish the conversation. Say good-bye and thank the caller, but always let the caller hang up first.

12. Do not leave messages on a desk or in a pile. Distribute them promptly. Write clearly on the standard message form. Include: to whom the message is directed; the date and time the call was received; the name of the caller (correctly spelled); the message; a return telephone number; and your initials. Provide message forms for the students to use. If there are any questions about the message the staff member will know whom to ask. All staff members should have a designated location for messages to be placed.

Telephone etiquette is something that must be continually monitored with frequent retraining. Short group sessions held throughout the semester will keep the telephone from becoming a difficult situation to handle.

Source: Morell D. Boone, Sandra G. Yee, and Rita Bullard, *Training Student Library Assistants* (Chicago: American Library Association, 1991). 110p.

# Managing your support staff: An insider's view

*by Shirley Rais*

WHY WOULD A PERFECTLY HAPPY library paraprofessional with 10 years of increasingly responsible experience want to become a "real" librarian when most people think anyone who works in a library is already a librarian anyway? When I entered a community college a decade ago to acquire certification as a Library Media Technical Assistant—whatever that is—I was told that I was being trained to assist librarians in their technical tasks so they could be free to be administrators. They would be the planners, policy makers, and decision makers while I would execute their administrative musings. Imagine my surprise to learn that out in the "real world" librarians were actually performing the technical and clerical tasks from which I was supposed to free them.

Well, I've done my best to "save" my librarian supervisors from themselves, and somewhere along the way I've decided to join them and propelled myself (slowly) into library school. As an aspiring professional librarian, I want to learn how to be an effective manager and make efficient use of my technical support staff so I can be free for administrative duties.

But when librarians are still doing nonprofessional tasks, how can a library technician making the transition to professional librarian let go of the technical tasks and move forward into managerial duties? And how can professionals free themselves from jobs they shouldn't be doing? The answer is to build an efficient team by developing an effective managerial style and philosophy so that everyone's role in the organization is properly understood and utilized.

For some of us in library school who are concurrently working in a library: first, our classes expose us to a vast amount of literature on our professional responsibilities as librarians, how successful libraries are managed, the challenges of the information age, the history of libraries, how to acquire, organize, and retrieve information, and so forth. Then we begin to look critically (even hypercritically) at the environment in which we work, and we discover that our managers have a lot to learn about librarianship and running a library.

Those of us who are tactful find ways to share our new knowledge with our supportive supervisors. Those with less tact may begin to openly criticize their management or complain to their coworkers. A supportive and effective supervisor tries to channel our new energy and enthusiasm for the library profession into constructive effort on behalf of the library; an exasperated supervisor gets tired of hearing about what we've been learning and fails to appreciate our new insights. I know of one aspiring librarian who was told by her supervisor to "Cut the library school crap."

## The voice of experience

Support staff employees who are motivated to attend library school and those who are content to stay where they are both need special handling by their managers. I would like to suggest some principles on how to manage your support staff, from one who has been there.

One of my classes in library school began with a brainstorming session on the qualities of good managers. Our list could be summarized into the following qualities we felt managers should have: competent and thorough knowledge of their position and its responsibilities; decisiveness; authority to reward or discipline; a supportive attitude toward their employees; approachability; willingness to share success with everyone; ambition; consistency; ability to delegate; ability to motivate; good communication skills; and being in tune with the organization's environment. Any manager would want to have these skills, and there is nothing mysterious about the meaning of any of them; so why are they so scarce? Three of these traits are the keys to mastering the rest: ability to motivate, utilization of authority to reward or discipline, and ability to delegate.

**2**

## Means of motivation

First, motivation. We will be more effective members of your team if you can motivate us. In my experience, most of us work in libraries because we like them; we often could earn more money elsewhere. Many of us are only one degree short of our supervisors. We often do some of the same things as the professionals, differing only in degree. The best way to motivate us is to avoid insulting our intelligence and make us a part of the team—not merely to *feel* a part of it, but to *know* we are part of it.

There are some practical ways to show us that you value our worth to you. For example, when you set goals for us, let us determine as much as possible how we're going to meet those goals; better yet, let us be a part of the goal-setting process. Back us up to your boss if there are questions about our performance. Do you insist that all memos originating from your department must have your signature? If we're composing it for you and it relates to an aspect of our responsibilities, let the memo go out under our names. This way of sharing success lets others in your organization know who your team players are.

Do you do all the planning and decision making yourself? Make us a part of your team by including us in problem-solving committees. Better yet, create teams of support staff as subcommittees who can give the main body input for their decisions. It could be intimidating if you put a "token" support person on a committee entirely of professionals or only include us if we are to act as recording secretaries. Ask yourself who will be ultimately responsible for implementing and performing a new service. If the answer is a support staff member, include us in the early stages of the planning teams. We're often more knowledgeable about the work flow and can provide valuable input.

## Exercise authority

Next, exercise your authority. You will be a more effective manager if you exercise any authority you have been given to reward or discipline your employees. Knowing when to discipline creates an atmosphere of fairness and equity. Why should employees who are productive have to carry the weight of those who are not? If you are in tune with the office atmosphere you'll know where to crack down and where to reward.

There are other ways to reward an employee who earns it, if you are not in a position to increase salaries. Make a sincere effort to look for ego rewards. Give public credit for our performance. Notice and recognize good work spontaneously, not just as part of an employee appreciation campaign. Such programs can be effective, but they are more forced than spontaneous recognition; why have an employee of the month if no one stands out?

Give opportunities to learn and grow to those who want them. Send us to some of the professional development programs available through local library consortia. These learning opportunities—seminars, workshops, classes—tell us you are willing to invest in us.

## The rewards of delegation

Finally, practice effective delegation. The best way to show that you are willing to invest in your support staff and to accomplish most of the suggestions I've given is to learn how to delegate. No one likes working for bosses who can't seem to get anything done because they cannot or will not let go of tasks that someone else can do.

Delegation offers a twofold reward: It lets you operate more efficiently and it shows your confidence in us by allowing us the opportunity to stretch our abilities. If we've reached the top of our classification, delegating new tasks to us may be our only chance for job enrichment. This is even more effective if you can provide the opportunity for us to exercise our delegation skills so we'll have time to do our new tasks! There is really no other way for you to show your confidence in our abilities.

Failure to delegate seems to be the main problem librarians have with letting go of clerical or other nonprofessional tasks that the paraprofessional should be doing. But beware of two pitfalls in delegation. First, don't delegate a task to an employee who does not have the skills to handle it; this breeds failure and loss of confidence. And please don't delegate tasks everyone knows you dislike doing while you hold onto those things you enjoy doing. We can tell what you're up to and instead of being encouraged by your confidence in us, we'll recognize we're being dumped on.

## Endorse the profession

These suggestions are useful for librarians who want to get the most out of their support staff. However, there is one final thing you can do for us: encourage us to take the steps toward becoming professionals and provide the means for us to go to library school if possible. Others did that for me and now here I am, presuming to tell professionals how to be better managers. I can think of no better way to endorse your profession than to recognize people who have talent and encourage them to embrace that profession.

To answer the question I started off with, there are probably many reasons why I'm in library school today. I could say that I've gone as far as I can as a paraprofessional, or that library school was the next logical step in my education, or that it was the opportunity for better pay, or the opportunity to be a manager, or the desire for professional status. But actually, I could have gotten a job as a "librarian"—many paraprofessionals have that title.

But I think I finally realized that I wanted to earn a master's degree when the library managers I worked for thought they recognized talent in me and encouraged me to stay in school, gave me added responsibilities to affirm their confidence in me, valued my contributions to the library, supported me in salary negotiations, supported me when I felt the need to look for a new job, and finally provided the means for me to go to school while still working (by accommodating schedule changes, for example, or buying items for the library that I happened to need for school).

These good managers, who have many of the qualities I've discussed here, have set a positive example for the profession. And I hope that I will get the chance to give back what I've been given, and apply what I've learned so that I will be able to motivate others to join this profession. I've seen what is desirable in an effective manager, and I think I can apply the suggestions I've made here in the real world. I am positive about one thing: after being a paraprofessional for 10 years, delegating paraprofessional tasks to any support staff working for me is going to be no problem at all!

*Source:* Shirley Rais, "Managing Your Support Staff: An Insider's View,"
*American Libraries* 24 (October 1993): 819–20.

# The professional/paraprofessional gap: Are there any solutions?

*by Diane J. Turner*

2

AFTER WORKING IN THREE VARIED LIBRARIES and learning the ropes in areas from circulation to reserve to interlibrary loan to reference, I have come to the conclusion that the library profession is determinedly overlooking or pushing under the rug a problem of enormous proportion. We won't admit that it happens and yet it can be seen in most academic and public libraries if we care enough to open our eyes. What is this cancer that spreads when budget cuts appear, longer hours are instituted, and staffing is minimal? The professional/paraprofessional schism.

In libraries, we are all working for the common goal of providing information to our patrons. Why is it, when we have such a clearcut objective, we too often fail to give the service that we are capable of giving? Why can a library have all the right people and still not function effectively? When there are divisions between the employees, between professional and paraprofessional, the job is not going to be done effectively. The costs add up very quickly, ranging from low morale to high absenteeism to costly employee turnover. With minimal staffing, low pay scales, and decreasing budgets, this spells trouble.

Management sets the tone in libraries as it does in corporations. Unfortunately, some directors try to run libraries like profit-making corporations, producing all of the stresses with none of the positive perks. Why? Because the management classes they took normally covered how to manage a business, not a unique system that offers very little money to employees and very few perks to balance stresses which are out of the realm of usual management situations. Rewards and benefits for library employees are not the same as in many corporations. Upward mobility hardly exists if one balances the added stress of those positions against the minimal pay increase. Profit sharing, not to mention the little perks like tickets to sporting events or the annual company picnic, is nonexistent in public and academic libraries. When managers try to run their libraries like businesses that offer such perks they are doomed to failure.

What are some of the other problems adding to the professional/paraprofessional schism? With the publish or perish trend infecting the library profession, causing increasing pressure to be put on the professionals, directors are trying their best to support them and provide the time to do research, attend conferences, and build contacts. The idea has merit, but we fail to consider the backlash. After all, who are the people left running the library when the professionals are at conferences or behind closed doors trying to write an article few will have time to read? The overburdened paraprofessionals and a few unrewarded professionals who feel that public service to their clientele and doing their jobs are more important than promoting their careers. Paraprofessionals make valuable contributions to the library profession and have as much right to go to conferences to enhance their skills as professionals do. This is also in the interest of the library; paraprofessionals are the ones that added continuity to their libraries because many stay in their positions long after the professionals have moved on.

Ironically, those people who run the library during all the times professionals are absent are the ones least likely to get positive recognition. I have actually heard some professionals say that they feel that a paraprofessional's job is anything the professional doesn't want to do. With logic like this it is no wonder that animosity and resentment exist. This same type of logic prevailed when I served in the military where I learned that it was the enlisted, for the most part, who held down the fort while the officers were off at their meetings.

Paraprofessionals deserve to be treated with the same respect as any other human being, and since managers in libraries don't have the same type of perks to offer as corporations they must employ an extra effort to treat all employees fairly and set the atmosphere of equal respect for all. Flex-time should be a privilege to all employees who have proven themselves on the job; not just a select few.

All employees want to feel that they are making a contribution to their job, and yet so many in libraries feel they are on a treadmill getting nowhere. Management must make an effort to bring professionals and paraprofessionals together for the common goal of providing the best service possible. A buddy system to conferences, collaborating with a professional on a project, or serving on committees where the paraprofessional's opinion is given more than lip service could provide the paraprofessionals with greater self-esteem and more pride in their incredible value to the library. I think we would find, as many corporations have, that the best ideas can come from the front line employees themselves. In my opinion, fairness is of utmost importance if we are to narrow the gap between professionals and paraprofessionals. Equitable treatment is a concern to people from infancy through adulthood and yet it seems to be a concept that is ignored by most managers. Divisions exist in almost any organization, but how we approach those divisions is the test of good management. Libraries need to concentrate more time on their human resources or they will turn into musty book depositories run by unhappy, burnt-out people with no creative desire and even less public service attitude.

I wish there were a magic pill to improve employee morale but since one has yet to be invented, we must put our heads together to start a trend of treating our professionals and paraprofessionals as the valuable resources they are. Yes, purchasing the new CD-ROMs, increasing serials budgets, pleasing the faculty or the all important board member, instituting literacy programs, and publishing some needed research are all very important, but let's stop for a moment and consider our human element first. What libraries must do is bring their people together with just, equitable, and impartial treatment. In many cases, this will be a real break from the past, but our future, my friends, depends on it.

*Source:* Diane J. Turner, "The Professional/Paraprofessional Gap: Are There Any Solutions?" *Library Mosaics,* July/August 1992, p.13.

# School library staff

THE SUCCESS OF ANY school library media program, no matter how well designed, depends ultimately on the quality and number of the personnel responsible for the program. A well-educated and highly motivated professional staff, adequately supported by technical and clerical staff, is critical to the endeavor.

Although staffing patterns are developed to meet local needs, they must at a minimum reflect the following principles:

1. All students, teachers, and administrators in each school building at all grade levels must have access to a library media program provided by one or more certificated library media specialists working full-time in the school's library media center.
2. Both professional personnel and support staff are necessary for all library media programs at all grade levels. Each school must employ at least one full-time technical assistant or clerk for each library media specialist. Some programs, facilities, and levels of service will require more than one support staff member for each professional.
3. More than one library media professional is required in many schools. The specific number of additional professional staff is determined by the school's size, number of students and teachers, facilities, specific library media program components, and other features of the school's instructional program. A reasonable ratio of professional staff to teacher and student populations is required in order to provide adequate levels of service and library media program development.

All school systems must employ a district library media director to provide leadership and direction to the overall library media program. The district director is a member of the administrative staff and serves on committees that determine the criteria and policies for the district's curriculum and instructional programs. The director communicates the goals and needs of both the school and district library media programs to the superintendent, board of education, other district-level personnel, and the community. In this advocacy role, the district library media director advances the concept of the school library media specialist as a partner with teachers and promotes a staffing level that allows the partnership to flourish.

*Source: Position Statement on Appropriate Staffing for School Library Media Centers* (Chicago: ALA American Association of School Librarians, 1991). 1p.

# Praise for media specialists who . . .

*by Doug Johnson*

Only read the newspaper in the lounge.
Don't publish overdue lists.
Read with a pencil in hand.
Can always find a book "just like the last one."
Can rescue lost computer files.
Exemplify the tenets of intellectual freedom and copyright.
Keep learning.
Write and phone their legislators.
Lead the way in inclusive education.
Have mastered skills not yet invented when last in college.
Remember media centers are the only place some children feel comfortable in school.
Can help you make "hanging indents."
Serve on deadly dull curriculum meetings after school.
Volunteer at the public library.
Buy posters from personal funds.

Say "anything's possible," rather than "no."
Have found a way to somehow serve every teacher on staff.
Who use "voices" when they read, and let children act out *Three Billy Goats Gruff*.
Don't agree with everything they read in professional journals.
Have media centers open both the first and last days of school.
Don't hesitate to confront the principal about bad policy.
Attend professional conferences, in and out of the field.
Recommend Roald Dahl and have kept books about ghosts and witches.
Make the world richer for nearly everyone with whom they work.

*Source:* Doug Johnson, "Editorial," Minnesota Educational Media Organization, *MEMOrandom*, May 1993, p.4.

# Alternative Careers

## Alternative careers: Information broker

In an information brokering business, there are no bureaucracies, no mindless meetings, no bosses to placate, no library committees to satisfy. If this makes information brokering sound like a utopian occupation, consider some of the negatives. Clients have bureaucracies, meetings, and bosses that information brokers must accommodate. It is not unusual for clients to say they need approval before contracting for services. Often that is the final thing heard from the client. Or, after a hiatus of several months, the client calls and demands the project be completed within hours.—*Marydee Ojala.*

## Alternative careers: Marketing management services firm

Marketing management can be an especially good alternative career if you are accustomed to managing your library as a business. In fact, if you have successfully switched your library to a fee-based information service, your operation is making money, and the only reason your services haven't grown more is because your organization won't let them, then you might very well be ready to leap into a marketing position where the "global village" is your oyster.—*Christine A. Olson.*

## Alternative careers: Freelance indexer

Client satisfaction is of utmost importance to the freelancer. Even with the best of intentions, the indexer and the client may have different perceptions of how the finished index should look. Be honest and let the client know if you believe he or she is asking for something that seems inadvisable. But remember that most indexes are works for hire and you are generally producing a product that will belong to someone else. Most publishers view freelancers as professionals and will respect your opinion once it is explained. In the end, by paying for your services, the publisher expects to receive the product he or she considers most valuable.—*Eileen Mackesy.*

## Alternative careers: Educator in library science

For those not put off by the nature of academic institutions, a career as a faculty member is extremely rewarding. It provides the opportunity to work with future colleagues and help them learn and grow. Academia also provides a structure for collaborative research and the communication of research results, with peer review and evaluation. A teaching career encourages you to keep abreast of the newest developments in the discipline, while remaining involved in the practice of your profession. The university community is a learning environment within a culturally diverse and exciting broader community.—*Toni Carbo Bearman.*

## Alternative careers: Library network manager

Salaries are generally higher for positions in library networks than for comparable positions in libraries and information centers. In a sense, however, this fact can also be a disadvantage, since higher salaries tend to make it difficult to move from a network position back into a library. Instead,

---

### Using information in non-library settings

A great deal of interest has been shown in using information skills in a variety of ways in non-library settings. These jobs are not usually found through the regular library placement sources, although many library schools are trying to generate such listings for their students and alumni. Job listings that do exist may not call specifically for "librarians" by that title so that ingenuity may be needed to search out jobs where information management skills are needed.

Some librarians are working on a freelance basis by offering services to businesses, alternative schools, community agencies, or legislators; these opportunities are usually not found in advertisements but created by developing contacts and publicity over a period of time. A number of information brokering business firms have developed from individual freelance experiences. Small companies or other organizations often need "one-time" service for organizing files or collections, bibliographic research for special projects, indexing or abstracting, compilation of directories, and consulting services. Bibliographic networks and online database companies are using librarians as information managers, trainers, researchers, systems and database analysts, and online services managers. Jobs in this area are sometimes found in library network newsletters or data-processing journals.

Librarians can be found working in law firms as litigation supervisors (organizing and analyzing records needed for specific legal cases); with publishers as sales representatives, marketing directors, editors, and computer services experts; with community agencies as adult education coordinators, volunteer administrators, grants writers, etc.

A listing of job titles is found in a 3-page handout on "Alternative Career Directions for Librarians," available from OLPR/ALA, 50 E. Huron St., Chicago, IL 60611.

*Source:* ALA Office for Library Personnel Resources, 1994.

network staff generally move to other corporate environments, such as automation vendors, database producers, corporate information centers, and their own consulting businesses.—*James E. Rush, Meryl Cinnamon, and Jeanne-Elizabeth Combs.*

## Alternative careers: Archivist/curator

While a certain amount of mystery has its place, and in fact may be part of the allure of the profession for some, the retiring personality usually is not happy with this professional choice. Archives are often active, busy places and especially in the case of one- or two-person operations, can sometimes seem like three-ring circuses. Aside from a love of history or a special subject or area of study, you must like people and papers, order and chaos, solitude and public speaking, the visual and the written, and pencils and computers. As the world progresses, so too does the nature of historical record; an archivist must handle change well.—*Megan Sniffin-Marinoff.*

*Source:* Ellis Mount, ed., *Opening New Doors: Alternative Careers for Librarians* (Washington, D.C.: Special Libraries Association, 1993). Reprinted with permission.

# THE PROFESSION 3

# Calendar to 1998

## 1995

### January

| | | |
|---|---|---|
| 25–29 | Assoc. for Educational Comm. & Tech. | Atlanta, Ga. |

### February

| | | |
|---|---|---|
| 3–9 | American Library Assoc. (Midwinter) | Philadelphia, Pa. |
| 8–12 | Music Library Assoc. | Atlanta, Ga. |
| 22–24 | South Carolina Library Assoc. | Myrtle Beach, S.C. |

### March

| | | |
|---|---|---|
| 3–5 | Michigan Assoc. for Media in Education | Traverse City, Mich. |
| 8–10 | Louisiana Library Assoc. | Lafayette, La. |
| 9–16 | Art Libraries Soc. of North America | Montreal, P.Q. |
| 10–14 | Alaska Library Assoc. | Juneau, Alaska |
| 15–18 | Utah Library Assoc. | Salt Lake City, Utah |
| 16–18 | Assoc. for Indiana Media Educators | Indianapolis, Ind. |
| 22–24 | Kansas Library Assoc. | Topeka, Kan. |
| 23–25 | ALA Public Libraries Assoc. Cluster | Chicago, Ill. |
| 24–25 | Hawaii Library Assoc. | Oahu, Hawaii |
| 27–30 | Catholic Library Assoc. | Cincinnati, O. |
| 29–April 1 | ALA Assoc. of College & Research Libraries | Pittsburgh, Pa. |
| 29–April 1 | Tennessee Library Assoc. | Nashville, Tenn. |
| 30–April 1 | ALA/LHRT-LC Library History Seminar IX | Tuscaloosa, Ala. |

### April

| | | |
|---|---|---|
| 4–8 | Texas Library Assoc. | Dallas, Tex. |
| 5–8 | Idaho Library Assoc. | Sun Valley, Id. |
| 5–8 | Washington Library Assoc. | Spokane, Wash. |
| 9–15 | National Library Week | |
| 11 | Legislative Day | |
| 11–12 | Connecticut Library Assoc. | Cromwell, Conn. |
| 25–28 | Indiana Library Federation | Indianapolis, Ind. |
| 26–28 | Alabama Library Assoc. | Auburn, Ala. |
| 26–29 | Montana Library Assoc. | Billings, Mont. |
| 26–29 | New Mexico Library Assoc. | Ruidoso, N.Mex. |
| 26–29 | Oklahoma Library Assoc. | Tulsa, Okla. |
| 26–29 | Oregon Library Assoc. | Portland, Ore. |

### May

| | | |
|---|---|---|
| 1–2 | Massachusetts Library Assoc. | Sturbridge, Mass. |
| 2–4 | New Jersey Library Assoc. | Atlantic City, N.J. |
| 3–6 | Illinois Library Assoc. | Peoria, Ill. |
| 3–6 | Maryland Library Assoc. | Ocean City, Md. |

| 4–5 | SOLINET (Annual meeting) | Atlanta, Ga. |
| 5–11 | Medical Library Assoc. | Washington, D.C. |
| 9–13 | Florida Library Assoc. | Ft. Lauderdale, Fla. |
| 17–18 | Vermont Library Assoc. | Burlington, Vt. |
| 21–23 | Maine Library Assoc. | Orono, Me. |

## June

| 3–6 | American Booksellers Assoc. | Chicago, Ill. |
| 10–15 | Special Libraries Assoc. | Calgary, Alb. |
| 14–18 | Canadian Library Assoc. | Calgary, Alb. |
| 22–29 | American Library Assoc. (Annual) | Chicago, Ill. |
| 26 | Theatre Library Assoc. | Chicago, Ill. |

## July

| 15–20 | American Assoc. of Law Libraries | Pittsburgh, Pa. |

## August

| 9–12 | Pacific Northwest Library Assoc. | Whistler, B.C. |
| 30–Sept. 3 | International Federation of Library Associations and Institutions | Istanbul, Turkey |
| 30–Sept. 3 | Society of American Archivists | Washington, D.C. |

## September

| 6–8 | Ohio Library Council | Dayton, O. |
| 29–Oct. 2 | Colorado Library Assoc. | Aspen, Colo. |

## October

| 1–3 | New England Library Assoc. | Providence, R.I. |
| 3–6 | North Carolina Library Assoc. | Greensboro, N.C. |
| 3–7 | Pennsylvania Library Assoc. | Pittsburgh, Pa. |
| 4–6 | Missouri Library Assoc. | Kansas City, Mo. |
| 4–7 | Mountain Plains Library Assoc. | Sioux Falls, S.Dak. |
| 4–7 | North Dakota Library Assoc. | Sioux Falls, S.Dak. |
| 4–7 | South Dakota Library Assoc. | Sioux Falls, S.Dak. |
| 11–13 | Minnesota Library Assoc. | Mankato, Minn. |
| 13–16 | Arkansas Library Assoc. | Fort Smith, Ark. |
| 18–20 | Iowa Library Assoc. | Des Moines, Ia. |
| 18–20 | Michigan Library Assoc. | Lansing, Mich. |
| 18–21 | Assoc. of Research Libraries | Washington, D.C. |
| 18–22 | Oral History Assoc. | Milwaukee, Wisc. |
| 19–21 | Literacy Volunteers of America | Buffalo, N.Y. |
| 19–21 | West Virginia Library Assoc. | Davis, W.Va. |
| 25–27 | Mississippi Library Assoc. | Jackson, Miss. |
| 25–27 | Nebraska Library Assoc. | Kentucky, Nebr. |
| 25–27 | Wisconsin Library Assoc. | Appleton, Wisc. |
| 25–29 | New York Library Assoc. | Rochester, N.Y. |
| 26–28 | Georgia Library Assoc. | Jekyll Island, Ga. |

## November

| 7–13 | Midwest Federation of Library Assocs. | Chicago, Ill. |
| 11–14 | California Library Assoc. | Santa Clara, Calif. |
| 17–19 | Theatre Library Assoc. | St. Louis, Mo. |

# 1996

## January

| | | |
|---|---|---|
| 16–19 | Assoc. for Library & Info. Sci. Education | San Antonio, Tex. |
| 19–25 | American Library Assoc. (Midwinter) | San Antonio, Tex. |
| 31–Feb. 4 | Assoc. for Educ. Comm. & Tech. | San Antonio, Tex. |

## February

| | | |
|---|---|---|
| 14–17 | Music Library Assoc. | Seattle, Wash. |

## March

| | | |
|---|---|---|
| 19–22 | Louisiana Library Assoc. | Alexandria, La. |
| 24–27 | Oregon Library Assoc. | Seaside, Ore. |
| 26–30 | ALA Public Library Assoc. | Portland, Ore. |

## April

| | | |
|---|---|---|
| 10–12 | Kansas Library Assoc. | Wichita, Kan. |
| 10–12 | Mountain Plains Library Assoc. | Wichita, Kan. |
| 14–20 | National Library Week | |
| 16 | Legislative Day | |
| 16–18 | Florida Library Assoc. | Tampa, Fla. |
| 21–24 | Montana Library Assoc. | Helena, Mont. |
| 23–27 | Texas Library Assoc. | Houston, Tex. |

## May

| | | |
|---|---|---|
| 2–3 | SOLINET (Annual meeting) | Atlanta, Ga. |
| 13–17 | Illinois Library Assoc. | Chicago, Ill. |
| 25–28 | American Booksellers Assoc. | Los Angeles, Calif. |
| 31–June 6 | Medical Library Assoc. | Kansas City, Mo. |

## June

| | | |
|---|---|---|
| 6–9 | Canadian Library Assoc. | Halifax, N.S. |
| 8–13 | Special Libraries Assoc. | Boston, Mass. |

## July

| | | |
|---|---|---|
| 4–10 | American Library Assoc. (Annual) | New York, N.Y. |
| 6–11 | American Assoc. of Law Libraries | Indianapolis, Ind. |

## August

| | | |
|---|---|---|
| 7–10 | Alaska Library Assoc. | Fairbanks, Alaska |
| 7–10 | Pacific Northwest Library Assoc. | Fairbanks, Alaska |
| 16–18 | Colorado Library Assoc. | Denver, Colo. |
| 19–24 | International Federation of Library Associations and Institutions | Beijing, China |
| 28–Sept. 1 | Society of American Archivists | San Diego, Calif. |

## October

| | | |
|---|---|---|
| 2–4 | Minnesota Library Assoc. | St. Cloud, Minn. |
| 2–5 | Idaho Library Assoc. | Nampa, Id. |
| 6–9 | Pennsylvania Library Assoc. | Lancaster, Pa. |
| 8–10 | Iowa Library Assoc. | Waterloo, Ia. |
| 9–11 | Missouri Library Assoc. | St. Louis, Mo. |

| 9–12 | South Dakota Library Assoc. | Spearfish, S.Dak. |
| 16–18 | Michigan Library Assoc. | Dearborn, Mich. |
| 22–26 | Kentucky Library Assoc. | Lexington, Ky. |
| 22–26 | Southeastern Library Assoc. | Lexington, Ky. |
| 22–27 | New York Library Assoc. | Saratoga Springs, N.Y. |
| 23–25 | Nebraska Library Assoc. | Lincoln, Nebr. |

## November

| 11–14 | Wisconsin Library Assoc. | Middleton, Wisc. |

## 1997

## January

| 7–10 | Assoc. for Library & Info. Sci. Education | New Orleans, La. |
| 30–Feb. 3 | Assoc. for Educ. Comm. & Tech. | Atlantic City, N.J. |

## February

| 14–20 | American Library Assoc. (Midwinter) | Washington, D.C. |

## March

| 19–22 | ALA Public Library Assoc. | Chicago, Ill. |

## April

| 8–11 | Kansas Library Assoc. | Topeka, Kan. |
| 8–12 | Texas Library Assoc. | Fort Worth, Tex. |
| 11–14 | ALA Assoc. of College & Research Libraries | Nashville, Tenn. |
| 13–19 | National Library Week | |
| 15 | Legislative Day | |
| 23–27 | Oregon Library Assoc. | Portland, Ore. |
| 30–May 3 | Mountain Plains Library Assoc. | Shangri La, Okla. |
| 30–May 3 | Oklahoma Library Assoc. | Shangri La, Okla. |

## May

| 31–June 3 | American Booksellers Assoc. | Chicago, Ill. |

## June

| 7–12 | Special Libraries Assoc. | Seattle, Wash. |
| 19–22 | Canadian Library Assoc. | Ottawa, Ont. |
| 26–July 3 | American Library Assoc. (Annual) | San Francisco, Calif. |

## July

| 19–24 | American Assoc. of Law Libraries | Baltimore, Md. |

## September

| 3–7 | Society of American Archivists | Chicago, Ill. |
| 25–28 | Pennsylvania Library Assoc. | Philadelphia, Pa. |

## October

| 1–4 | Idaho Library Assoc. | Boise, Id. |
| 22–24 | Nebraska Library Assoc. | S. Sioux City, Nebr. |
| 23–25 | Michigan Library Assoc. | Lansing, Mich. |

| 25–29 | Illinois Library Assoc. | Springfield, Ill. |

## November

| 4–7 | Wisconsin Library Assoc. | Milwaukee, Wisc. |

## 1998

## January

| 9–15 | American Library Assoc. (Midwinter) | New Orleans, La. |
| 20–23 | Assoc. for Library & Info. Sci. Education | Denver, Colo. |

## February

| 5–9 | Assoc. for Educ. Comm. & Tech. | St. Louis, Mo. |

## March

| 9–14 | Texas Library Assoc. | San Antonio, Tex. |

## April

| 19–25 | National Library Week | |
| 21 | Legislative Day | |

## May

| 23–26 | American Booksellers Assoc. | Orlando, Fla. |

## June

| 18–21 | Canadian Library Assoc. | Vancouver, B.C. |
| 25–July 2 | American Library Assoc. (Annual) | Washington, D.C. |

## October

| 7–10 | South Dakota Library Assoc. | Rapid City, S.Dak. |
| 21–23 | Michigan Library Assoc. | Grand Rapids, Mich. |
| 28–30 | Nebraska Library Assoc. | Grand Island, Nebr. |

## November

| 3–6 | Wisconsin Library Assoc. | Green Bay, Wisc. |
| 8–11 | Pennsylvania Library Assoc. | Hershey, Pa. |

# Past ALA annual conferences

A LIST OF ALL ALA annual conference dates and locations, with attendance figures, contrasted with total ALA membership (from 1900).

| Date | Place | Attendance | Membership |
| --- | --- | --- | --- |
| 1876, Oct. 4–6 | Philadelphia | 103 | [not available |
| 1877, Sept. 4–6 | New York | 66 | for 1876–1899] |
| 1877, Oct. 2–5 | London, England | 21* | |

*U.S. attendance

| Date | Place | Attendance | Membership |
|------|-------|-----------:|-----------:|
| 1878 | [No meeting] | | |
| 1879, June 30–July 2 | Boston | 162 | |
| 1880 | [No meeting] | | |
| 1881, Feb. 9–12 | Washington, D.C. | 70 | |
| 1882, May 24–27 | Cincinnati | 47 | |
| 1883, Aug. 14–17 | Buffalo, N.Y. | 72 | |
| 1884 | [No meeting] | | |
| 1885, Sept. 8–11 | Lake George, N.Y. | 87 | |
| 1886, July 7–10 | Milwaukee, Wisc. | 133 | |
| 1887, Aug. 30–Sept. 2 | Thousand Island, N.Y. | 186 | |
| 1888, Sept. 25–28 | Catskill Mountains, N.Y. | 32 | |
| 1889, May 8–11 | St. Louis, Mo. | 106 | |
| 1890, Sept. 9–13 | Fabyans (White Mts.), N.H. | 242 | |
| 1891, Oct. 12–16 | San Francisco | 83 | |
| 1892, May 6–21 | Lakewood, N.Y., Baltimore, Washington | 260 | |
| 1893, July 13–22 | Chicago | 311 | |
| 1894, Sept. 17–22 | Lake Placid, N.Y. | 205 | |
| 1895, Aug. 13–21 | Denver & Colorado Springs | 147 | |
| 1896, Sept. 1–8 | Cleveland | 363 | |
| 1897, June 21–25 | Philadelphia | 315 | |
| 1897, July 13–16 | London, England | 94* | |
| 1898, July 5–9 | Lakewood, N.Y. | 494 | |
| 1899, May 9–13 | Atlanta | 215 | |
| 1900, June 6–12 | Montreal, Quebec | 452 | 874 |
| 1901, July 3–10 | Waukesha, Wisc. | 460 | 980 |
| 1902, June 14–20 | Boston & Magnolia, Mass. | 1,018 | 1,152 |
| 1903, June 22–27 | Niagara Falls, N.Y. | 684 | 1,200 |
| 1904, Oct. 17–22 | St. Louis, Mo. | 577 | 1,228 |
| 1905, July 4–8 | Portland, Me. | 359 | 1,253 |
| 1906, June 29–July 6 | Narragansett Pier, R.I. | 891 | 1,844 |
| 1907, May 23–29 | Asheville, N.C. | 478 | 1,808 |
| 1908, June 22–27 | Lake Minnetonka, Minn. | 658 | 1,907 |
| 1909, June 28–July 3 | Bretton Woods, N.H. | 620 | 1,835 |
| 1910, June 20–July 6 | Mackinac Island, Mich. | 533 | 2,005 |
| 1910, Aug. 28–31 | Brussels, Belgium | 46* | |
| 1911, May 18–24 | Pasadena, Calif. | 582 | 2,046 |
| 1912, June 26–July 2 | Ottawa, Ontario | 704 | 2,365 |
| 1913, June 23–28 | Kaaterskill, N.Y. | 892 | 2,563 |
| 1914, May 25–29 | Washington, D.C. | 1,366 | 2,905 |
| 1915, June 3–9 | Berkeley, Calif. | 779 | 3,024 |
| 1916, June 26–July 1 | Asbury Park, N.J. | 1,386 | 3,188 |
| 1917, June 21–27 | Louisville, Ky. | 824 | 3,346 |
| 1918, July 1–6 | Saratoga Springs, N.Y. | 620 | 3,380 |
| 1919, June 23–27 | Asbury Park, N.J. | 1,168 | 4,178 |
| 1920, June 2–7 | Colorado Springs | 553 | 4,464 |
| 1921, June 20–25 | Swampscott, Mass. | 1,899 | 5,307 |
| 1922, June 26–July 1 | Detroit | 1,839 | 5,684 |
| 1923, April 23–28 | Hot Springs, Ark. | 693 | 5,669 |
| 1924, June 30–July 5 | Saratoga Springs, N.Y. | 1,188 | 6,055 |
| 1925, July 6–11 | Seattle, Wash. | 1,066 | 6,745 |
| 1926, Oct. 4–9 | Atlantic City, N.J. | 2,224 | 8,848 |
| 1927, June 20–27 | Toronto, Ontario | 1,964 | 10,056 |
| 1927, Sept. 26–Oct. 1 | Edinburgh, Scotland | 82* | |

*U.S. attendance

3

| Date | Place | Attendance | Membership |
|------|-------|------------|------------|
| 1928, May 28–June 2 | West Baden, Ind. | 1,204 | 10,526 |
| 1929, May 13–18 | Washington, D.C. | 2,743 | 11,833 |
| 1929, June 15–30 | Rome and Venice, Italy | 70* | |
| 1930, June 23–28 | Los Angeles | 2,023 | 12,713 |
| 1931, June 22–27 | New Haven, Conn. | 3,241 | 14,815 |
| 1932, April 25–30 | New Orleans | 1,306 | 13,021 |
| 1933, Oct. 16–21 | Chicago | 2,986 | 11,880 |
| 1934, June 25–30 | Montreal, Quebec | 1,904 | 11,731 |
| 1935, May 20–30 | Madrid, Seville & | | |
| | Barcelona, Spain | 42* | |
| 1935, June 24–29 | Denver | 1,503 | 12,241 |
| 1936, May 11–16 | Richmond, Va. | 2,834 | 13,057 |
| 1937, June 21–26 | New York | 5,312 | 14,204 |
| 1938, June 13–18 | Kansas City, Mo. | 1,900 | 14,626 |
| 1939, June 18–24 | San Francisco | 2,869 | 15,568 |
| 1940, May 26–June 1 | Cincinnati | 3,056 | 15,808 |
| 1941, June 19–25 | Boston | 4,266 | 16,015 |
| 1942, June 22–27 | Milwaukee | 2,342 | 15,328 |
| 1943 | [No meeting] | | 14,546 |
| 1944 | [No meeting] | | 14,799 |
| 1945 | [No meeting] | | 15,118 |
| 1946, June 16–22 | Buffalo, N.Y. | 2,327 | 15,800 |
| 1947, June 29–July 5 | San Francisco | 2,534 | 17,107 |
| 1948, June 13–19 | Atlantic City, N.J. | 3,752 | 18,283 |
| 1949: | Regional conferences [not recorded] | | 19,324 |
| Aug. 22–25 | (Far West) Vancouver, B.C. | | |
| Sept. 2–5 | (Trans-Miss.) Fort Collins, Colo. | | |
| Oct. 3–6 | (Middle Atlantic) Atlantic City, N.J. | | |
| Oct. 12–15 | (New England) Swampscott, Mass. | | |
| Oct. 26–29 | (Southeastern) Miami Beach, Fla. | | |
| Nov. 9–12 | (Midwest) Grand Rapids, Mich. | | |
| Nov. 20–23 | (Southwestern) Fort Worth, Tex. | | |
| 1950, July 16–22 | Cleveland | 3,436 | 19,689 |
| 1951, July 8–14 | Chicago | 3,612 | 19,701 |
| 1952, June 29–July 5 | New York | 5,212 | 18,925 |
| 1953, June 21–27 | Los Angeles | 3,258 | 19,551 |
| 1954, June 20–26 | Minneapolis | 3,230 | 20,177 |
| 1955, July 3–9 | Philadelphia | 4,412 | 20,293 |
| 1956, June 17–23 | Miami Beach, Fla. | 2,866 | 20,285 |
| 1957, June 23–30 | Kansas City, Mo. | 2,953 | 20,326 |
| 1958, July 13–19 | San Francisco | 4,400 | 21,716 |
| 1959, June 21–27 | Washington, D.C. | 5,346 | 23,230 |
| 1960, June 19–24 | Montreal, Quebec | 4,648 | 24,690 |
| 1961, July 9–15 | Cleveland | 4,757 | 25,860 |
| 1962, June 17–23 | Miami Beach, Fla. | 3,527 | 24,879 |
| 1963, July 14–20 | Chicago | 5,753 | 25,502 |
| 1964, June 28–July 4 | St. Louis | 4,623 | 26,015 |
| 1965, July 3–10 | Detroit | 5,818 | 27,526 |
| 1966, July 10–16 | New York | 9,342 | 31,885 |
| 1967, June 25–July 1 | San Francisco | 8,116 | 35,289 |
| 1968, June 23–29 | Kansas City, Mo. | 6,849 | 35,666 |
| 1969, June 22–28 | Atlantic City, N.J. | 10,399 | 36,865 |
| 1970, June 28–July 4 | Detroit | 8,965 | 30,394 |

*U.S. attendance

| Date | Place | Attendance | Membership |
|------|-------|-----------:|-----------:|
| 1971, June 20–26 | Dallas | 8,087 | 29,740 |
| 1972, June 24–30 | Chicago | 9,700 | 29,610 |
| 1973, June 24–30 | Las Vegas | 8,539 | 30,172 |
| 1974, July 5–13 | New York | 14,382 | 34,010 |
| 1975, June 29–July 5 | San Francisco | 11,606 | 33,208 |
| 1976, July 18–24 | Chicago (Centennial) | 12,015 | 33,560 |
| 1977, June 17–23 | Detroit | 9,667 | 33,767 |
| 1978, June 25–30 | Chicago | 11,768 | 35,096 |
| 1979, June 24–30 | Dallas | 10,650 | 35,524 |
| 1980, June 29–July 4 | New York | 14,566 | 35,257 |
| 1981, June 26–July 2 | San Francisco | 12,555 | 37,954 |
| 1982, July 10–15 | Philadelphia | 12,819 | 38,050 |
| 1983, June 25–30 | Los Angeles | 11,005 | 38,862 |
| 1984, June 23–28 | Dallas | 11,443 | 39,290 |
| 1985, July 6–11 | Chicago | 14,160 | 40,761 |
| 1986, June 26–July 3 | New York | 16,530 | 42,361 |
| 1987, June 27–July 2 | San Francisco | 17,844 | 45,145 |
| 1988, July 9–14 | New Orleans | 16,530 | 47,249 |
| 1989, June 24–29 | Dallas | 17,592 | 49,483 |
| 1990, June 23–28 | Chicago | 19,982 | 50,509 |
| 1991, June 29–July 4 | Atlanta | 17,764 | 52,893 |
| 1992, June 25–July 2 | San Francisco | 19,261 | 54,735 |
| 1993, June 24–July 1 | New Orleans | 17,165 | 55,836 |
| 1994, June 23–30 | Miami Beach | 12,627 | 55,356 |

# What to do if you are a conference speaker

### by Will Manley

I HAVE DEVOTED A GOOD PART of my professional career to researching the habits, interests, and traits of librarians, and I have come to one conclusion: Above all else, we librarians love to congregate. Despite our shy and retiring stereotype, there's nothing we like more than creating organizations. What profession could possibly have more consortia, councils, or committees? The American Library Association in fact has so many task forces, roundtables, and divisions that it actually created something called the Committee on Committees to keep track of them all.

This all helps to stimulate the global economy, because library associations are major consumers of such world-wide commodities as coffee, pastry, overhead projectors, identification badges, ribbons, sticky buttons, and program speakers. To be a program speaker you must meet one of the following criteria:

1. Have expertise in a particular subject area (right now something called the "virtual library" is your best bet).
2. Hold a recognizable office or position within the profession (i.e., president of ALA, editor of a major publication, director of a prestigious library, or dean of a defunct library school).
3. Be a successful author (but not too successful because people like Stephen King and Howard Stern are too expensive for most library associations).

4. Be a good friend of the program chair.
5. Get fired from your position as columnist for the *Wilson Library Bulletin* for running a survey on the subject of librarians and sex.

Number 5, of course, has been my qualifier, and over the years it has carried me to dozens of state, regional, and local conferences. In fact, I have so much experience in this area (which means that I've made every mistake a library speaker could possibly make) that I've decided to share a few tips that might be useful if you ever get the urge to hit the circuit. This is the advice I wish somebody had given me several years ago:

1. Stay humble, stupid. You may think that what you have to say is important, valuable, and even eloquent. But it is not. Conference-goers remember only two things: the food and the weather. "I remember you from the last time you were here," an Ohio librarian told me in Cleveland. "You were great," she continued. "I don't recall a single thing you said but the stir fry was delicious and the weather was fantastic."
2. Always know where you're speaking. You'll lose your audience for good if you begin your speech by saying "I'm really happy to be here in Virginia" when you're speaking to the West Virginia Library Association. Take it from me—I committed this faux pas several years ago. I've also gotten on the wrong plane and ended up in the wrong city. There's a big difference, for instance, between Columbus, Ohio, and Columbia, Missouri. Each place has its charms, but if you're scheduled to speak in Columbia, Columbus is the last place you want to be.
3. Do not use the terms "empowerment," "downsizing," and "visioning" in the title of your speech if you want anyone to attend. Overused buzzwords are conference program-killers, so try to stay fresh and provocative. The words "sex," "psycho," and "neo-Nazi," on the other hand, are sure to draw a crowd.
4. The later the better. When it comes to library conferences, the term "morning person" is an oxymoron; so if possible always try to speak later in the day unless you're into hostile audiences and you thrive on conflict. If you do humor, try for the post-banquet crowd. My jokes, for instance, are a lot funnier after everyone's had a few cocktails and a bottle of wine with their dinner.
5. Handouts help. Although they will never read them, librarians appreciate handouts with your speech. That's because librarians often have to account for the time and money they have spent on a conference. It's convenient for them to go back home to their boards and directors and say, "My total conference expenses were $578, but it was worth it because I got this great bibliography on Boolean searching."
6. Keep an open mind about planned social events. It's true that at most conference receptions and hospitality suites you'll end up getting trapped with a bunch of catalogers chitchatting about their latest retrospective conversions, but every once in a while you'll be rewarded with something wonderfully strange. At the 1993 Ohio Library Association banquet reception, for instance, I was treated to the delightful spectacle of watching librarians dancing with cornstalks. "It's the ultimate in safe sex," is the way one participant explained it to me; that may be true, because the next morning I saw pieces of cornstalks scattered all over the elevators and hallways of the conference hotel!

*Source:* Will Manley, "Dancing with Cornstalks in Cleveland,"
*American Libraries* 25 (February 1994): 186.

# Getting the most out of your exhibit hall time

*by Pat Ensor and Paul Nicholls*

- Don't forget your business cards, and have plenty of them. Many exhibitors have staplers you can use to attach your card to whatever form it is they have for you to fill out, and it is much easier than filling out form after form. If you did forget your cards, consider using one of those instant business card machines in the airport.
- Wear comfortable shoes. Many exhibitors, although dressed to kill, are also wearing sneakers. Emulate the pros and think ergonomics—you can hardly be effective if you are feeling miserable all day.
- Write down your current hardware and software specifications in comprehensive detail and take them with you.
- Have a good idea in advance about what exhibitors you want to see. There are many sources for preliminary exhibitor lists—preliminary programs and advertisements, preconference planning guides in major library periodicals, such as *American Libraries* and *Library Journal*, and conference sections in the journals of the companies that put on the conferences. Mecklermedia publications, such as *Computers in Libraries*, of course, feature information about the Computers in Libraries conference, and *CD-ROM Professional* has information about the ONLINE/CD-ROM conference.
- When you arrive at the conference, use the exhibit hall map given you with your registration materials to find the exhibitors that you want to visit.
- Visit the exhibitors you want to see in a natural and sequential order, so that you don't miss anyone, you don't get overwhelmed and you can go in and out of the exhibit hall efficiently when you have a spare half hour.
- Don't be afraid to go in and look around even if you have a comparatively small amount of time available. You should have at least a half hour, since it will probably take you that long to get to where you want to look, but you don't need hours free at a time.
- Don't allow yourself to be collared by enterprising salespeople who are showing a product you are not at all interested in. This is usually a major waste of your time.
- Don't hesitate to dive in, ask questions and try products that are on display. If you really are interested in a particular product, make sure that you get a chance to try it on your own; don't settle for just viewing a demonstration performed by an exhibitor.
- Many exhibitors have user group meetings, focused presentations and/or hospitality suites. Silver-Platter has all of these, for example, at ALA conferences. The user group meetings and the focused presentations are very good sources

of the most recent news about SilverPlatter, and hospitality suites can be a good chance to try a product in a quiet setting with more time to concentrate. (Food is often involved with these—a significant consideration for the frugal conference goer.) You may receive invitations to some of these things in advance, and sometimes invitations and/or notices are available at booths.

- Minimize the amount of paper you pick up and carry around. Only take with you what you are really interested in keeping, and then only if you can't get them to mail it to you. Often exhibitors have forms that allow you to specify what information you want, so it can be mailed to you. Be aware, though, that now they have your name and address, so they can put you on their mailing lists and call you.
- If you do (unwisely) encumber yourself with half a ton of the literature explosion, then consider mailing most of it home to yourself in a large padded envelope. Bringing a self-addressed envelope with you would be a convenience in this case.
- Watch for drawings and contests. It has not been unknown for a conference attender to go home with a free piece of hardware or subscription to a valuable CD-ROM title. The odds may be slim, but if you don't have a ticket, you haven't got a chance (as they say). And this is another reason to remember your business cards. However, be aware that you are probably going onto a mailing list.

*Source:* Pat Ensor and Paul Nicholls, *CD-ROM Collection Development: A Practical Guide* (London, Ontario: Pelican Island, 1992). Reprinted with permission.

Grants, Scholarships, Awards

MANY OPPORTUNITIES EXIST in the field of library and information science for its practitioners to obtain assistance for their research and to gain recognition for their achievements. The following list provides information on grants, scholarships, and awards given by ALA and other national associations. While 1995 deadlines are given, most of these programs are ongoing.

The list could be expanded substantially, especially in the grant area, by taking into consideration the offerings of state and regional library associations, private companies, and the public sector—e.g., OCLC, the Council on Library Resources, HEA and LSCA government grants, and many commercial organizations provide funds for research. The arrangement is topical under two major headings: **grants and scholarships** (money awarded for things you are going to do); and **awards** (honors and honoraria awarded for things you have already done).

Considered topically, this list can also be viewed as a measure of what we value most in our profession. Under grants and scholarships the subheads are: **for education; for programs;** and **for publications, research, and travel.** Under awards the subheads are: **for intellectual freedom; for professional achievement; for publications and research; for service in general; for service to children and young adults; for service to special populations; for social responsibility; for special libraries;** and **for technology.**—*GME.*

# Grants and Scholarships

## For education

**AALL Scholarships and Grants.** A number of scholarships in support of library degrees for both law school graduates and non-law school graduates, minority stipends, and law degrees for library school graduates. Administered by the American Association of Law Libraries. *For more information:* American Association of Law Libraries, 53 W. Jackson Blvd., Suite 940, Chicago, IL 60604. *Donated by:* West Publishing Company, Matthew Bender & Company, Thomson Professional Publishing, Columbia University Law School Library, Information America, AALL, and the Private Law Libraries Special Interest Section. *Deadline for applications:* March 1, 1995.

**AJL May K. Simon Scholarship.** A $500 award for a student who intends to become a Judaica librarian. Administered by the Association of Jewish Libraries. *For more information:* AJL, 15 E. 26th St., Room 1034, New York, NY 10010. *Deadline for applications:* February 28, 1995. *1994 winner:* Raphael I. Panitz.

**ALA David H. Clift Scholarship.** Scholarship in the amount of $3,000 given annually to a worthy student to begin a program of library education at the graduate level. Funded by interest from the ALA Scholarship Endowment, two awards are given annually. Administered by the ALA Awards Committee and the ALA Office for Library Personnel Resources. *For more information:* ALA Office for Library Personnel Resources, 50 E. Huron St., Chicago, IL 60611-2795. *Deadline for applications:* January 14, 1995. *1994 winner:* Zoe Butler.

**ALA Louise Giles Minority Scholarship.** Cash award in the amount of $3,000 made to a worthy student who is a U.S. or Canadian citizen and is also a member of a principal minority group. Funded by interest from the ALA Scholarship Endowment, two awards are given annually. Administered by the ALA Awards Committee and the ALA Office for Library Personnel Resources. *For more information:* ALA Office for Library Personnel Resources, 50 E. Huron St., Chicago, IL 60611-2795. *Deadline for applications:* January 14, 1995. *1994 winner:* Sherry Luna.

**ALA Miriam Hornback Scholarship.** A $3,000 award to assist an ALA or library support staff person who wishes to attain a master's degree in librarianship at a program accredited by ALA. Not presented every year. Administered by the ALA Awards Committee and the Office for Library Personnel Resources. *For more information:* ALA Office for Library Personnel Resources, 50 E. Huron St., Chicago, IL 60611-2795. *1994 winner:* Nina Lindsay.

**ALA NMRT EBSCO Scholarship.** A cash award of $1,000 for the following academic year. Applicants must enroll at a library school accredited by ALA and plan to begin graduate studies the following fall. Administered by the New Members Round Table. *For more information:* Judy Hambrick, ALA, 50 E. Huron St., Chicago, IL 60611-2795. *Donated by:* EBSCO Subscription Services. *Deadline for applications:* December 16, 1995. *1994 winner:* Patricia Curry.

**ALA Tom and Roberta Drewes Scholarship.** Scholarship in the amount of $3,000 to assist a library support staff person to begin a master's degree in library and information studies. Not presented every year. Administered by the ALA Awards Committee and the Office of Library Personnel Resources. *For more information:* ALA Office for Library Personnel Resources, 50 E. Huron St., Chicago, IL 60611-2795. *1994 winner:* June M. Rutkowski.

**ALA Tony Leisner Scholarship.** Scholarship in the amount of $3,000 to assist an ALA or library support staff person who wishes to attain a master's degree in librarianship at a program accredited by ALA. Not presented every year. Administered by the ALA Awards Committee and the Office for Library Personnel Resources. *For more information:* ALA Office for Library Personnel Resources, 50 E. Huron St., Chicago, IL 60611-2795. *1993 winner:* Patricia Anne Scott.

**ALA/AASL Information Plus Continuing Education Scholarship.** This scholarship provides financial assistance for the continuing education and professional development of a school library media specialist, supervisor, or educator. The $500 grant will enable an AASL member to attend an ALA or AASL pre- or postconference or an ALA- or AASL-sponsored regional workshop. Administered by the ALA American Association of School Librarians. *For more information:* ALA/AASL, 50 E. Huron St., Chicago, IL 60611-2795. *Donated by:* Information Plus. *Deadline for applications:* February 1, 1995. *1994 winner:* Linda de Lyon Friel.

**ALA/AASL School Librarian's Workshop Award.** An annual grant of $2,500 to provide financial assistance for the professional education of persons who plan to become school library media specialists working at the preschool, elementary, or secondary levels in public or private educational settings. Administered by the ALA American Association of School Librarians. *For more information:* ALA/AASL, 50 E. Huron St., Chicago, IL 60611-2795. *Donated by:* Library Learning Resources Co. *Deadline for applications:* February 1, 1995. *1994 winner:* Ginger Baird Fearey.

**ALA/ACRL Doctoral Dissertation Fellowship.** An annual award of $1,000 presented to a doctoral student in the field of academic librarianship whose research is significant and demonstrates originality and creativity. Administered by the ALA Association of College and Research Libraries. *For more information:* ALA/ACRL, 50 E. Huron St., Chicago, IL 60611-2795. *Donated by:* Institute for Scientific Information. *Deadline for applications:* December 1, 1995. *1993 winner:* Weijan Yuan.

**ALA/ALSC Book Wholesalers Summer Reading Program Grant.** An annual award of $3,000 and thematic materials for 100 children to encourage an ALSC member to develop an imaginative public library reading program based on the ALA National Reading Program theme. Administered by the ALA Association for Library Service to Children. *For more information:* ALA/ALSC, 50 E. Huron St., Chicago, IL 60611-2795. *Donated by:* Book Wholesalers, Inc. *Deadline for applications:* December 1, 1995. *1994 winner:* Emily Fowler PL, Denton, Tex.

**ALA/ALSC Bound to Stay Bound Books Scholarship.** Two annual $5,000 scholarships established to assist individuals who wish to work in the field of library service to children. Administered by the ALA Association for Library Service to Children. *For more information:* ALA/ALSC, 50 E. Huron St., Chicago, IL 60611-2795. *Donated by:* Bound to Stay Bound Books, Inc. *Deadline for applications:* March 1, 1995. *1994 winners:* Roberta Lee Pierce, Martin Juan Rivera Sr.

**ALA/ALSC Frederic G. Melcher Scholarship.** Two annual $5,000 scholarships established to encourage and assist people who wish to enter the field of library service to children. Administered by the ALA Association for Library Service to Children. *For more information:* ALA/ALSC, 50 E. Huron St., Chicago, IL 60611-2795. *Deadline for applications:* March 1, 1995. *1994 winners:* Andrea Michelle Chambers, Evi Klett.

**ALA/LITA GEAC-CLSI Scholarship in Library and Information Technology.** A cash award of $2,500 to a beginning student at the master's degree level in an ALA-accredited program in library and information science with an emphasis on library automation. Administered by the ALA Library and Information Technology Association. *For more information:* ALA/LITA, 50 E. Huron St., Chicago, IL 60611-2795. *Donated by:* GEAC and CLSI, Inc. *Deadline for applications:* April 1, 1995. *1994 winner:* Lydia Levins.

**ALA/LITA Library Systems and Services Minority Scholarship in Library and Information Technology.** Administered by the ALA Library and Information Technology Association. *For more information:* ALA/LITA, 50 E. Huron St., Chicago, IL 60611-2795. *Deadline for applications:* April 1, 1995.

**ALA/LITA OCLC Minority Scholarship in Library and Information Technology.** A cash award of $2,500 to a student to begin or continue a master's level ALA-accredited program in library automation and the information sciences. Its purpose is to encourage a qualified member of a principal minority group with a strong commitment to the use of automation in libraries to follow a career in that field. Administered by the ALA Library and Information Technology Association. *For more information:* ALA/LITA, 50 E. Huron St., Chicago, IL 60611-2795. *Donated by:* OCLC, Inc. *Deadline for applications:* April 1, 1995. *1994 winner:* Joy M. Barron.

**ALISE Doctoral Students Dissertation Awards.** Awards in the amount of $400 to promote the exchange of research ideas between doctoral students and established researchers. Administered by the Association for Library and Information Science Education. *For more information:* ALISE, 4101 Lake Boone Trail, Suite 201, Raleigh, NC 27607. *Deadline for applications:* October 1, 1995. *1994 winners:* Rose Albritton, Françoise Hébert.

**ASIS ISI Information Science Doctoral Dissertation Scholarship.** To support dissertation research in information science. Administered by the American Society for Information Science. *For more information:* ASIS, 8720 Georgia Ave., Suite 501, Silver Spring, MD 20910. *Deadline for applications:* July 1, 1995.

**BCALA E.J. Josey Scholarship Award.** An unrestricted grant of $1,500 awarded annually to an African American student enrolled in or accepted by an ALA-accredited program. Administered by the Black Caucus of the American Library Association. *For more information:* Stanton F. Biddle, Box 317, Baruch College, 17 Lexington Avenue, New York, NY 10010. *Deadline for applications:* January 15, 1995. *1994 winner:* Veberly Huda Abdus-Sabur.

**Beta Phi Mu Frank B. Sessa Scholarship.** Award in the amount of $750 for continuing education for a Beta Phi Mu member. Administered by the Beta Phi Mu International Library Science Honor

Society. *For more information:* Beta Phi Mu, School of Library and Information Science, University of Pittsburgh, Pittsburgh, PA 15260. *Deadline for applications:* March 1, 1995. *1994 winners:* Maureen Delaney-Lehman, Deborah Pawlik.

**Beta Phi Mu Harold Lancour Scholarship.** An award of $1,000 for graduate study in a foreign country related to the applicant's work or schooling. Administered by Beta Phi Mu International Library Science Honor Society. *For more information:* Beta Phi Mu, University of Pittsburgh SLIS, Pittsburgh, PA 15260. *Deadline for applications:* March 1, 1995. *1994 winner:* Mary Graham.

**Beta Phi Mu Sarah Rebecca Reed Scholarship.** Award in the amount of $1,500 for study at an ALA-accredited library school. Administered by the Beta Phi Mu International Library Science Honor Society. *For more information:* Beta Phi Mu, School of Library and Information Science, University of Pittsburgh, Pittsburgh, PA 15260. *Deadline for applications:* March 1, 1995. *1994 winners:* Andrea M. Chambers, Amy Melissa McAbee.

**CALA Sheila Suen Lai Scholarship of Library and Information Science.** An award of $500 for students of Chinese heritage to promote graduate studies in library and information science. Administered by the Chinese-American Librarians Association. *For more information:* CALA, c/o Sheila Lai, CSU Sacramento, 2000 Jed Smith Drive, Sacramento, CA 95819. *Deadline for applications:* March 1, 1995. *1994 winners:* Angela Giannousis, Hua Yi.

**CLA Defoe Scholarship.** An award of $1,750 (Can.) for a Canadian citizen or landed immigrant to attend an accredited Canadian library school. Administered by the Canadian Library Association. *For more information:* CLA, 200 Elgin St., Ottawa, Ontario K2P 1L5, Canada. *Deadline for applications:* May 1, 1995. *1994 winner:* Darlene Holowachuk.

**CLA H.W. Wilson Company Scholarship.** An award in the amount of $2,000 (Can.) available to a Canadian citizen or landed immigrant for pursuit of studies at an accredited Canadian library school. Administered by the Canadian Library Association. *For more information:* CLA, 200 Elgin St., Ottawa, Ontario K2P 1L5, Canada. *Donated by:* H.W. Wilson Co. *Deadline for applications:* May 1, 1995. *1994 winner:* Janis McKenzie.

**CLA Howard V. Phalin-World Book Graduate Scholarship in Library Science.** A scholarship in the amount of $2,500 (Can.) for a Canadian citizen or landed immigrant to attend an accredited library school in Canada or the United States. Administered by the Canadian Library Association. *For more information:* CLA, 200 Elgin St., Ottawa, Ontario K2P 1L5, Canada. *Donated by:* World Book, Inc. *Deadline for applications:* May 1, 1995. *1994 winner:* Heidi Julien.

**CLA Rev. Andrew L. Bouwhuis Scholarship.** A cash award of $1,500 for a student with a B.A. degree who has been accepted in an accredited library school. The award is granted on a basis of financial need. Administered by the Catholic Library Association. *For more information:* CLA, c/o Jean R. Bostley, S.S.J., St. Joseph Central High School, 22 Maplewood Ave., Pittsfield, MA 01201.

**CLA World Book, Inc. Grant.** An award of $1,500 for added proficiency in school or children's librarianship through a workshop or seminar, distributed among no more than four members of the Catholic Library Association. Administered by the Catholic Library Association. *For more information:* CLA, c/o Jean R. Bostley, S.S.J., St. Joseph Central High School, 22 Maplewood Ave., Pittsfield, MA 01201. *Donated by:* World Book, Inc. *Deadline for applications:* March 15, 1995. *1993 winner:* Sr. Lauretta McCusker, O.P.

**MLA Continuing Education Awards.** Awards of $100–$500 for MLA members to develop a knowledge of the theoretical, administrative, or technical aspects of librarianship. More than one may be offered in a year, and they may be used either for MLA courses or for other CE activities. Administered by the Medical Library Association. *For more information:* MLA, 6 N. Michigan Ave., Suite 300, Chicago, IL 60602. *Deadline for applications:* February 1, 1995. *1994 winners:* Karyn Pomerantz, Joan Stoddart.

**MLA Doctoral Fellowship.** A fellowship in the amount of $1,000 to foster and encourage superior students to conduct doctoral work in an area of medical librarianship and to provide support to individuals who have been admitted to a candidacy. The award may not be used for tuition. Administered by the Medical Library Association. *For more information:* MLA, 6 N. Michigan Ave., Suite 300, Chicago, IL 60602. *Donated by:* Institute for Scientific Information. *Deadline for applications:* February 1, 1995. *1994 winner:* Mary Moore.

**MLA Scholarship.** A $2,000 award for graduate study in medical librarianship. Administered by the Medical Library Association. *For more information:* MLA, 6 N. Michigan Ave., Suite 300, Chicago, IL 60602. *Deadline for applications:* February 1, 1995. *1994 winner:* Ronald Bank.

**MLA Scholarship for Minority Students.** A $2,000 award for a minority student intending to study medical librarianship and who is entering an ALA-accredited library school. Administered by the Medical Library Association. *For more information:* MLA, 6 N. Michigan Ave., Suite 300, Chicago, IL

60602. *Deadline for applications:* February 1, 1995. *1994 winner:* Hua Yi.

**SLA Affirmative Action Scholarship.** A $6,000 scholarship for a member of a minority group pursuing graduate study leading to an MLS in the United States or Canada. Administered by the Special Libraries Association. *For more information:* SLA, 1700 18th St., N.W., Washington, DC 20009. *Deadline for applications:* October 31, 1995. *1994 winner:* Alicia Randolph.

**SLA ISI Scholarship.** A $1,000 award for beginning doctoral candidates in library or information science. Administered by the Special Libraries Association. *For more information:* SLA, 1700 18th St., N.W., Washington, DC 20009. *Donated by:* Institute for Scientific Information. *Deadline for applications:* October 31, 1995.

**SLA Mary Adeline Connor Professional Development Scholarship.** One or more awards, not to exceed $6,000, for mid-career special librarians to assist with a post-MLS certificate or degree programs in any subject area, technological skills, or managerial expertise relevant to the applicant's career needs and goals in special librarianship. May include travel assistance. *For more information:* SLA, 1700 18th St., N.W., Washington, DC 20009. *Donated by:* Mary Adeline Connor. *Deadline for applications:* October 31, 1995. *1994 winner:* April Schwartz.

**SLA Plenum Scholarship.** An award in the amount of $1,000 for graduate study leading to a doctorate in library and information science. Administered by the Special Libraries Association. *For more information:* SLA, 1700 18th St., N.W., Washington, DC 20009. *Donated by:* Plenum Publishing Corp. *Deadline for applications:* October 31, 1995.

**SLA Scholarships.** Up to three $6,000 scholarships for students with financial need who show potential for special librarianship. Administered by the Special Libraries Association. *For more information:* SLA, 1700 18th St., N.W., Washington, DC 20009. *Deadline for applications:* October 31, 1995. *1994 winners:* Julia Overstreet, Vinita Singh, Gaylene Sloane.

## For programs

**ALA Grolier National Library Week Grant.** An annual $2,000 cash award for a promotional program supporting the goals of National Library Week to be conducted in the year in which the grant is presented. Administered by the ALA National Library Week Committee. *For more information:* ALA Public Information Office, 50 E. Huron St., Chicago, IL 60611-2795. *Donated by:* Grolier Educational Corporation. *Deadline for applications:* December 1, 1995. *1994 winner:* Dauphin County (Pa.) Library System.

**ALA H.W. Wilson Library Staff Development Grant.** A cash grant of $2,500 awarded to a library organization to assist it in a current or proposed program designed to further the goals and objectives of the library organization. The criteria for selection of a grant winner include: clearly defined documentation of need in relation to staff development, a well-defined program to meet the organization's needs, and the commitment and demonstrated ability to implement the program. Administered by the American Library Association Awards Committee. *For more information:* Mary Jo Lynch, ALA, 50 E. Huron St., Chicago, IL 60611-2795. *Donated by:* H.W. Wilson Co. *Deadline for applications:* December 1, 1995. *1994 winner:* Newport News (Va.) PL System.

**ALA Loleta D. Fyan Grant.** An annual grant of up to $10,000 to a library, library school, unit or chapter of ALA, or an individual for the development and improvement of public libraries. Administered by the ALA Awards Committee. *For more information:* Mary Jo Lynch, ALA, 50 E. Huron St., Chicago, IL 60611-2795. *Donated by:* An estate bequest. *Deadline for applications:* January 2, 1995. *1994 winners:* Middle County (N.Y.) PL and Onondaga (N.Y.) PL.

**ALA World Book-ALA Goal Grant.** An annual grant of up to $10,000 or two smaller grants totaling up to $10,000 made to a unit or chapter of the American Library Association. The proposals are judged by a jury of the American Library Association Awards Committee. *For more information:* Mary Jo Lynch, ALA, 50 E. Huron St., Chicago, IL 60611-2795. *Donated by:* World Book, Inc. *Deadline for applications:* March 3, 1995. *1994 winners:* ALA President-Elect Arthur Curley/ALA Special Committee on Public Awareness/ALA Chapter Relations Office/ALA Public Information Office/ALA Washington Office, for "Library Advocacy Now."

**ALA/AASL ABC-CLIO Leadership Development Award.** Annual grants of up to $1,750 to enable AASL Affiliate Organizations to plan and implement leadership development programs. Administered by the ALA American Association of School Librarians. *For more information:* ALA/AASL, 50 E. Huron St., Chicago, IL 60611-2795. *Donated by:* ABC-CLIO, Inc. *Deadline for applications:* February 1, 1995. *1994 winner:* Alaska Association of School Librarians.

**ALA/ALSC May Hill Arbuthnot Lecture.** An honorarium of $750 plus travel expenses to a distinguished individual to present a paper that will be a significant contribution to the field of children's literature. *For more information:* ALA/ALSC, 50 E. Huron St., Chicago, IL 60611-2795. *1994 winner:* Leonard Everett Fisher.

**ALA/RASD Facts on File Grant.** A cash grant of up to $2,000 awarded to a library for imaginative programming that would make current affairs more meaningful to an adult audience. The grant will be awarded for projects to be conducted in an informal setting and will emphasize quality rather than the magnitude of the project. Programs, bibliographies, pamphlets, and innovative approaches of all types and in all media qualify. Administered by the ALA Reference and Adult Services Division. *For more information:* ALA/RASD, 50 E. Huron St., Chicago, IL 60611-2795. *Donated by:* Facts on File, Inc. *Deadline for applications:* December 15, 1995. *1994 winner:* Eastern Montana College.

**ALA/YALSA Frances Henne Voice of Youth Advocates Research Grant.** An annual grant of $500 to provide seed money for small-scale projects encouraging significant research that will have an influence on library service to young adults. Applicants must be a member of YALSA. Grants will not be given for research leading to a degree. Administered by the ALA Young Adult Library Services Association. *For more information:* ALA/YALSA, 50 E. Huron St., Chicago, IL 60611-2795. *Donated by: Voice of Youth Advocates (VOYA). Deadline for applications:* December 14, 1995. *1994 winners:* Kathy Latrobe, Michael Havener.

**ARLIS/NA Chadwyck-Healey Professional Development Award.** A grant of $500 for session moderators, speakers, and panelists at the ARLIS/NA annual conference. Administered by the Art Libraries Society of North America. *For more information:* ARLIS/NA, 4101 Lake Boone Trail, Suite 201, Raleigh, NC 27607. *Donated by:* Chadwyck-Healey. *Deadline for applications:* December 15, 1995.

**MLA Janet Doe Lectureship.** An award of $250 to support a lecture in either the history or the philosophy of medical librarianship presented at the MLA annual meeting. Administered by the Medical Library Association. *For more information:* MLA, 6 N. Michigan Ave., Suite 300, Chicago, IL 60602. *1994 winner:* Nina Woo Matheson, "The Idea of the Library."

**MLA John P. McGovern Award Lectureship.** For a significant national or international figure to speak on a topic of importance to health sciences librarianship at the MLA annual meeting. Administered by the Medical Library Association. *For more information:* MLA, 6 N. Michigan Ave., Suite 300, Chicago, IL 60602. *1994 winner:* June Osborn, "AIDS Education and Public Policy."

**MLA NLM Joseph Leiter Lectureship.** For a lecture on biomedical communications presented every other year at the MLA annual meeting and in alternate years at the National Library of Medicine. Administered by the Medical Library Association. *For more information:* MLA, 6 N. Michigan Ave., Suite 300, Chicago, IL 60602. *1994 winner:* Marcie Greenwood, "21st Century Science."

**Viburnum Foundation/ALA Rural Family Literacy Project Grants.** Cash grants in the amount of $3,000 to enable several rural libraries within one public library system to initiate library-based family literacy programs in their communities. *For more information:* Office for Library Outreach Services, ALA, 50 E. Huron St., Chicago, IL 60611-2795. *Donated by:* Viburnum Foundation. *1994 winners:* Cameron Parish (La.) Library; Shreve Memorial Library, Shreveport; Terrebonne Parish (La.) Library; Assumption Parish (La.) Library; Beauregard Parish (La.) Library; Lafourche Parish (La.) Library..

## For publications, research, and travel

**AJL Doris Orenstein Memorial Fund.** For first-time attendees at the AJL conference. Administered by the Association of Jewish Libraries. *For more information:* AJL, 15 E. 26th St., Room 1034, New York, NY 10010. *Deadline for applications:* February 1, 1995. *1994 winner:* Joel Tuckman.

**AJL Travel Subsidy.** A $250 subsidy to encourage attendance at the annual convention by long-standing AJL members who have been active in the organization and newer members who would like to participate more fully. *For more information:* AJL, 15 E. 26th St., Room 1034, New York, NY 10010. *Deadline for applications:* March 1, 1995.

**ALA 3M/NMRT Professional Development Grant.** This grant is intended to encourage professional development and participation by new librarians in national ALA and NMRT activities. Cash awards are presented to librarians to attend an ALA Annual Conference. The recipients must be current members of ALA and the New Members Round Table. Administered by the ALA New Members Round Table. *For more information:* Judy Hambrick, 50 E. Huron St., Chicago, IL 60611-2795. *Deadline for applications:* November 15, 1995. *1994 winners:* Pamela Moffett Padley, Nancy Louise Cummings, David C.D. Gausv.

**ALA Bogle International Library Travel Fund.** A $500 award to assist ALA members to attend their first international library conference. Administered by the ALA International Relations Committee. *For more information:* Robert P. Doyle, ALA, 50 E. Huron St., Chicago, IL 60611-2795. *Deadline for applications:* January 1, 1995. *1994 winner:* Dona J. Helmer.

**ALA Carnegie Reading List Awards.** These awards are granted to official units of the American Library Association, such as divisions, committees, or round tables. They are based on a special fund established by Andrew Carnegie in 1902 and are "to be applied to the preparation and publication of such reading lists, indexes, and other bibliographical and library aids as will be especially useful in the circulating libraries of this country." Administered by the ALA Publications Committee. *Deadline for applications:* Accepted throughout the year. *Send nominations to:* ALA Publishing, 50 E. Huron St., Chicago, IL 60611-2795. *1994 winners:* ALSC Task Force for *Book Some Time Together;* ALTA Task Force for *Reading List for Public Library Board.*

**ALA Carroll Preston Baber Research Grant.** An annual cash reward of up to $7,500 and a citation presented to one or more librarians or library educators who will conduct innovative research that could lead to an improvement in services to any specified group(s) of people. Administered by a jury of the American Library Association Awards Committee. *For more information:* Mary Jo Lynch, ALA Office for Research, 50 E. Huron St., Chicago, IL 60611-2795. *Donated by:* Eric R. Baber. *Deadline for applications:* January 2, 1995. *1993 winner:* Debra Wilcox Johnson.

**ALA EBSCO Conference Sponsorship.** An award to help librarians attend ALA's Midwinter Meetings and Annual Conferences. Applicants must be ALA members and must submit an essay of no more than 200 words on the question, "How does attending an ALA Conference contribute to your professional development?" Five Midwinter Meeting Awards are for ALA members who have been assigned or appointed for the first time to any committee of ALA or any of its units, to attend a Midwinter Meeting. Five Annual Conference Awards are for ALA members who do not supervise another professional librarian to attend an Annual Conference. The winners will be reimbursed up to $1,000 in actual expenses. *For more information:* Judy Hambrick, ALA, 50 E. Huron St., Chicago, IL 60611-2795. *Donated by:* EBSCO Subscription Services. *Deadlines for applications:* December 1, 1995 (Annual); May 1, 1995 (Midwinter). *1994 winners:* Teresa Day, Linda Horiuchi, Loretta O. Lafferty, Beth Ann Zambella, Fannette Thomas, Eva Poole.

**ALA Herbert W. Putnam Honor Award.** An award of $500 presented as a grant-in-aid to an American librarian of outstanding ability for travel, writing, or any other use that might improve his or her service to the library profession or to society. Administered by a jury of the American Library Association Awards Committee. *Made possible by:* Herbert W. Putnam Honor Fund. *Send nominations to:* Peggy Barber, ALA, 50 E. Huron St., Chicago, IL 60611-2795.

**ALA Readex/GODORT Catharine J. Reynolds Grant.** An annual award of $2,000 for grants to documents librarians to travel and/or study in the field of documents librarianship or in an area of study that will directly benefit their performance as a documents librarian. Administered by the ALA Government Documents Round Table. *For more information:* ALA, 50 E. Huron St., Chicago, IL 60611-2795. *Donated by:* Readex Corporation. *Deadline for applications:* December 1, 1995. *1994 winner:* Irene Herold.

**ALA Shirley Olofson Memorial Award.** An annual cash award made to individuals to attend their second ALA Annual Conference. Recipients must be members of ALA and be potential or current members of NMRT. Administered by the ALA New Members Round Table. *For more information:* Judy Hambrick, 50 E. Huron St., Chicago, IL 60611-2795. *Deadline for applications:* December 1, 1995. *1994 winner:* Cathy Nelson Hartman.

**ALA Whitney-Carnegie Awards.** These awards are granted to individuals for preparation of guides to research resources. The aids must be aimed at a scholarly audience but have general applicability. $5,000 is the maximum amount awarded. The amounts and number of awards are at the discretion of the ALA Publishing Committee and vary from year to year. Preference is given to projects for which the American Library Association can serve as publisher. Administered by the ALA Publishing Committee. *Deadline for applications:* Accepted throughout the year. *Send nominations to:* ALA Publishing, 50 E. Huron St., Chicago, IL 60611-2795. *1994 winner:* Chestalene Pintozzi, for "Researching Social Change."

**ALA/AASL Frances Henne Award.** An annual grant of $1,250 to enable a school library media specialist with five or fewer years in the profession to attend an AASL regional conference or ALA Annual Conference. Administered by the ALA American Association of School Librarians. *For more information:* ALA/AASL, 50 E. Huron St., Chicago, IL 60611-2795. *Donated by:* R.R. Bowker Co. *Deadline for applications:* February 1, 1995. *1994 winner:* Robert Craig Bunch.

**ALA/AASL Highsmith Co. Research Grant.** An annual grant of $2,500 (up to $5,000 may be awarded to two or more researchers for a joint or group project) presented to one or more AASL members who are school library media specialists, library educators, or library information science/ education professors to conduct innovative research aimed at measuring and evaluating the impact of school library media programs on learning and education. Sponsored by the ALA American Association of School Librarians and The Highsmith Co., Inc. *For more information:* ALA/AASL, 50 E. Huron St., Chicago, IL 60611-2795. *Donated by:* The Highsmith Company, Inc. *Deadline for applications:* February 1, 1995. *1994 winners:* Kathleen Garland, for "The Information Search Process"; Roberta Ponis, Dian Walster, and Lynda Welborn, for "Information Literacy Standards."

**ALA/ACRL Martinus Nijhoff International West European Specialist Study Grant.** An annual grant for an ALA member to study some aspect of Western European studies, librarianship, or the book trade. The grant covers air travel to and from Europe, transportation in Europe, and lodging and board for no more than fourteen consecutive days. A maximum amount of 10,000 Dutch guilders is awarded per year. Administered by the Western European Specialists Section of the ALA Association of College and Research Libraries. *For more information:* ALA/ACRL, 50 E. Huron St., Chicago, IL 60611- 2795. *Donated by:* Martinus Nijhoff International. *Deadline for applications:* December 1, 1995. *1994 winner:* Stephen Lehmann.

**ALA/ACRL Samuel Lazerow Fellowship for Research in Acquisitions or Technical Services.** An annual award of $1,000 established to foster advances in acquisitions or technical services by providing librarians in those fields a fellowship. Administered by the ALA Association of College and Research Libraries. *For more information:* ALA/ACRL, 50 E. Huron St., Chicago, IL 60611-2795. *Donated by:* Institute for Scientific Information. *Deadline for applications:* December 1, 1995. *1994 winner:* Kuang-Hwei (Janet) Lee-Smeltzer.

**ALA/ALCTS Serials Section First Step Award/Wiley Professional Development Grant.** A $1,500 grant that provides librarians new to the serials field with the opportunity to broaden their perspective and participate in ALA Conference and Serials Section activities. All ALA members with five or fewer years' professional experience in the serials field, who have not previously attended an ALA Annual Conference, are eligible. *For more information:* ALA/AASL, 50 E. Huron St., Chicago, IL 60611- 2795. *Donated by:* John Wiley & Co. *Deadline for applications:* December 1, 1995. *1994 winner:* H. Charlene Chou.

**ALA/ALSC Louise Seaman Bechtel Fellowship Award.** A grant of $3,750 for ALSC members with at least twelve years of work at a professional level in a children's library collection, to read and study at the Baldwin Library of the George A. Smathers Libraries, University of Florida. *For more information:* ALA/ALSC, 50 E. Huron St., Chicago, IL 60611-2795. *Donated by:* Bechtel Fund. *Deadline for applications:* December 1, 1995. *1994 winner:* Cathy Toon.

**ALA/ALSC Putnam & Grosset Book Group Awards.** Four annual $600 awards presented to four children's librarians to enable them to attend ALA Annual Conference. The recipients must be members of ALSC, work directly with children, have one to ten years of library experience, and never have attended an ALA Annual Conference. Administered by the ALA Association for Library Service to Children. *For more information:* ALA/ALSC, 50 E. Huron St., Chicago, IL 60611-2795. *Donated by:* Putnam & Grosset Book Group. *Deadline for applications:* December 1, 1995. *1994 winners:* Abbey-jo Rehling, Leslie A. Page, Cecilia Swanson, Vera Florea.

**ALA/ALTA/Gale Outstanding Trustee Conference Grant.** A grant of $750 each to two trustees, enabling their first-time attendance at the ALA Annual Conference. The grant is awarded to two public library trustees who have demonstrated qualitative interests and efforts in supportive service to the local public library. Administered by the ALA American Library Trustee Association. *For more information:* ALA/ALTA, 50 E. Huron St., Chicago, IL 60611-2795. *Donated by:* Gale Research Co. *Deadline for applications:* December 1, 1995. *1994 winners:* Marina Gagic and Kenneth R. Perez.

**ALA/PLA New Leaders Travel Grant.** An award of up to $1,500 per applicant for PLA members new to the profession who have not had the opportunity to attend a major PLA continuing education event in the last five years. The grant is designed to enhance the professional development and improve the expertise of public librarians new to the field by making their attendance at professional development activities possible. Administered by the ALA Public Library Association. *For more information:* ALA/PLA, 50 E. Huron St., Chicago, IL 60611-2795. *Donated by:* GEAC/CLSI, Inc. *Deadline for applications:* December 1, 1995. *1994 winners:* Karen E. Brown, Eileen Papile, Mary E. Harper.

**ALA/RASD Disclosure Student Travel Award.** An annual travel award of $1,000 that will enable a student enrolled in an ALA-accredited master's degree program to attend ALA Annual Conference. The applicant must have a demonstrated interest in pursuing a career as a business reference librarian and the potential to be a leader in the profession. Administered by the ALA Reference and Adult

Services Division's Business Reference and Services Section. *For more information:* ALA/RASD, 50 E. Huron St., Chicago, IL 60611-2795. *Donated by:* Disclosure Incorporated. *Deadline for applications:* December 15, 1995. *1994 winner:* Lisa J. McClain.

**ALA/YALSA Baker & Taylor Conference Grants.** Two annual grants of $1,000 each awarded to young adult librarians who work directly with young adults in either a public library or a school library, to enable them to attend the ALA Annual Conference. Candidates must be members of YALSA, have 1–10 years of library experience, and never have attended an ALA Annual Conference. Administered by the ALA Young Adult Library Services Association. *For more information:* ALA/YALSA, 50 E. Huron St., Chicago, IL 60611-2795. *Donated by:* Baker & Taylor Books. *Deadline for applications:* December 14, 1995. *1994 winners:* Susan Wickenden Hunter, Myrna Kinkle.

**ALISE Jane Anne Hannigan Research Award.** An award of $500 for research on any aspect of library or information science, including children's literature or work with children and youth. Only untenured faculty or students in doctoral programs are eligible. Administered by the Association for Library and Information Science Education. *For more information:* ALISE, 4101 Lake Boone Trail, Suite 201, Raleigh, NC 27607. *Donated by:* Sheila Intner and Kaye Vandergrift from royalties on their festschrift, *Library Education and Leadership: Essays in Honor of Jane Anne Hannigan* (Scarecrow). *Deadline for applications:* October 1, 1995. *1994 winner:* Louise S. Robbins.

**ALISE Research Awards.** A cash award of up to $2,500 for a project that reflects ALISE goals and objectives. Administered by the Association for Library and Information Science Education. *For more information:* ALISE, 4101 Lake Boone Trail, Suite 201, Raleigh, NC 27607. *Deadline for applications:* October 1, 1995. *1994 winners:* Norman Howden, Thomas Kochtanek, Nancy Zimmerman.

**ARLIS/NA G.K. Hall Conference Attendance Award.** A grant of $400 for committee members, group moderators, and chapter officers at the ARLIS/NA annual conference to help finance conference expenses. Administered by the Art Libraries Society of North America. *For more information:* ARLIS/NA, 4101 Lake Boone Trail, Suite 201, Raleigh, NC 27607. *Donated by:* G.K. Hall Co. *Deadline for applications:* December 15, 1995.

**ARLIS/NA Léonce Laget Award.** An award of $1,000 to help finance expenses associated with traveling to the ARLIS/NA Conference. All art information professionals who reside outside North America are eligible. Administered by the Art Libraries Society of North America. *For more information:* ARLIS/NA, 4101 Lake Boone Trail, Suite 201, Raleigh, NC 27607. *Donated by:* Librairie Léonce Laget. *Deadline for applications:* December 15, 1995.

**ARLIS/NA Norman Ross Travel Award.** A travel award of $500 to an ARLIS/NA member who has never attended an ARLIS/NA conference. Administered by the Art Libraries Society of North America. *For more information:* ARLIS/NA, 4101 Lake Boone Trail, Suite 201, Raleigh, NC 27607. *Donated by:* Norman Ross Publishing Co. *Deadline for applications:* December 15, 1995.

**MLA Cunningham Memorial International Fellowship.** A six-month grant of $3,500 and travel expenses in the United States and Canada for a foreign librarian. Administered by the Medical Library Association. *For more information:* MLA, 6 N. Michigan Ave., Suite 300, Chicago, IL 60602. *Deadline for applications:* February 1, 1995. *1994 winner:* Elena Korotkova.

**MLA Research, Development and Demonstration Projects Grants.** Awards of $100-$500 to support projects that will promote excellence in the field of health sciences librarianship. Grants will not be given to support an activity that is operational in nature or has only local usefulness. Administered by the Medical Library Association. *For more information:* MLA, 6 N. Michigan Ave., Suite 300, Chicago, IL 60602. *Deadline for applications:* February 1, 1995. *1993 winners:* Jennifer Bayne, Joan Leishman.

**MLA Walter Gerboth Award.** A cash award of $500 to support research in the first five years as a music librarian. Administered by the Music Library Association. *For more information:* MLA, Box 487, Canton, MA 02021. *Deadline for applications:* October 31, 1995. *1993 winner:* Harriette Hemmasi.

**SAA Colonial Dames Scholarship.** Covers travel for two archivists to attend two meetings of the Modern Archives Institute. Administered by the Society of American Archivists. *For more information:* SAA, 600 S. Federal St., Suite 504, Chicago, IL 60605. *Donated by:* Colonial Dames of America. *Deadline for applications:* March 1 and November 1, 1995. *1994 winners:* Maricel Cruz, Wayne Coleman.

**SAA Minority Student Award.** Provides complimentary registration to the SAA Annual Meeting to a minority student enrolled in a postsecondary institution. *For more information:* SAA, 600 S. Federal St., Suite 504, Chicago, IL 60605. *Deadline for applications:* April 1995. *1994 winner:* Kathryn M. Neal.

**SAA Oliver Wendell Holmes Award.** This award allows overseas archivists, already in the United States or Canada for training, to augment their visit by traveling to other archival institutions, national or regional archival meetings, or archival institutes. Administered by the Society of American Archivists. *For* *more information:* SAA, 600 S. Federal St., Suite 504, Chicago, IL 60605. *Deadline for applications:* April 1995.

## Awards

### For intellectual freedom

**ALA John Phillip Immroth Memorial Award for Intellectual Freedom.** An annual award consisting of $500 and a citation presented to an intellectual freedom fighter who has made a notable contribution to intellectual freedom and demonstrated remarkable personal courage. Administered by the ALA Intellectual Freedom Round Table. *For more information:* ALA Office for Intellectual Freedom, 50 E. Huron St., Chicago, IL 60611-2795. *Deadline for applications:* December 1, 1995. *1994 winner:* John Swan.

**ALA State and Regional Achievement Award.** An annual award consisting of $1,000 and a citation presented to the state intellectual freedom committee that has implemented the most successful and creative state IFC project during the calendar year. Administered by the ALA Intellectual Freedom Round Table. *For more information:* ALA Office for Intellectual Freedom, 50 E. Huron St., Chicago, IL 60611-2795. *Donated by:* Social Issues Resources Series, Inc. *Deadline for applications:* December 1, 1995. *1994 winner:* Freedom to Read Foundation.

**ALA/AASL/SIRS Intellectual Freedom Award.** An annual award consisting of $2,000 and an engraved plaque presented to a school library media specialist at any level who has upheld the principles of intellectual freedom. The award also provides a grant of $1,000 and a framed certificate to a school library media center designated by the recipient. Administered by the ALA American Association of School Librarians. *For more information:* ALA/AASL, 50 E. Huron St., Chicago, IL 60611-2795. *Donated by:* Social Issues Resources Series, Inc. *Deadline for applications:* February 1, 1995. *1994 winner:* Ruth E. Dishnow.

**CLA Award for the Advancement of Intellectual Freedom in Canada.** Administered by the Canadian Library Association. *For more information:* CLA, 200 Elgin Street, Suite 602, Ottawa, Ontario, Canada K2P 1L5. *1994 winner:* Halifax City Regional Library Board.

**Coalition on Government Information James Madison Award.** An annual award honoring those who have championed, protected and promoted freedom of information and the public's right to know. Administered by the Coalition on Government Information. *For more information:* ALA Washington Office, 110 Maryland Ave., N.E., Washington, DC 20002. *1994 winner:* Secretary of Energy Hazel R. O'Leary.

**Freedom to Read Foundation Roll of Honor Awards.** Annual awards established in 1988 to honor those who have taken a courageous personal stand against censorship and have contributed substantially to the Freedom to Read Foundation's mission. *For more information:* ALA Office of Intellectual Freedom, 50 E. Huron St., Chicago, IL 60611-2795. *Deadline for applications:* December 1, 1995. *1994 winners:* Frank Zappa; the Juneau (Alaska) school board, superintendent, and school library media specialists.

### For professional achievement

**ALA CIS/GODORT "Documents to the People" Award.** An annual award, consisting of a citation of achievement and a cash stipend of $2,000 to be used to promote professional advancement in the field of librarianship. The award is presented to the individual and/or library, organization, or other appropriate noncommercial group that has most effectively encouraged the use of government documents and information in support of library services. Administered by the ALA Government Documents Round Table. *For more information:* ALA, 50 E. Huron St., Chicago, IL 60611-2795. *Donated by:* Congressional Information Service, Inc. *Deadline for applications:* December 1, 1995. *1994 winner:* Gary Cornwell.

**ALA Federal Librarians Achievement Award.** An annual citation and gift for leadership or achievement in the promotion of library and information science in the federal community. Administered by the ALA Federal Librarians Round Table. *For more information:* ALA Washington Office, 110 Maryland Ave., N.E., Washington, DC 20002. *Deadline for applications:* December 31, 1995. *1994 winner:* Louise Nyce.

**ALA Gale Research Company Financial Development Award.** An annual award of $2,500 and a certificate presented to a library organization that exhibited meritorious achievement in carrying out a library financial development project to secure new funding resources for a public or academic library entity. Administered by the American Library Association Awards Committee. *For more information:* Peggy Barber, ALA, 50 E. Huron St., Chicago, IL 60611-2795. *Donated by:* Gale Research Company. *Deadline for applications:* December 1, 1995. *1994 winner:* Staunton (Va.) PL.

**ALA Hugh C. Atkinson Memorial Award.** An annual award consisting of an unrestricted cash prize and a plaque established to honor the life and accomplishments of Hugh C. Atkinson, one of the major innovators in modern librarianship, and to recognize outstanding achievement (including risk-taking) by academic librarians that has contributed significantly to improvements in the area of library automation, library management, and/or library development or research. Nominees must be librarians employed in a university, college, or community college library in the year prior to application for the award and must have a minimum of five years of professional experience in an academic library. The award is jointly sponsored by the ALA Association of College and Research Libraries, the Library Administration and Management Association, the Library Information Technology Association, and the Association for Library Collections and Technical Services. It is funded by an endowment created by divisional, individual, and vendor contributions given in memory of Hugh C. Atkinson. *For more information:* ALA/ACRL, 50 E. Huron St., Chicago, IL 60611-2795. *Deadline for applications:* December 1, 1995. *1994 winner:* Dorothy Gregor.

**ALA James Bennett Childs Award.** An annual award, consisting of an engraved plaque, presented to a librarian or other individual for distinguished contributions to documents librarianship. Administered by the ALA Government Documents Round Table. *For more information:* ALA, 50 E. Huron St., Chicago, IL 60611-2795. *Deadline for applications:* December 1, 1995. *1994 winner:* Sandra Peterson.

**ALA John Ames Humphry/OCLC/Forest Press Award.** The $1,000 award is made to a librarian or other person who has made significant contributions to international librarianship. Primary consideration will be given to contributions in the field of classification and subject analysis, and to work in Third World countries, but the award is not limited to these areas. Administered by the ALA International Relations Committee. *For more information:* Robert P. Doyle, ALA, 50 E. Huron St., Chicago, IL 60611-2795. *Donated by:* OCLC/Forest Press, Inc. *Deadline for applications.* January 1, 1995. *1994 winner:* Robert D. Stueart.

**ALA Kohlstedt Exhibit Award.** An annual citation recognizing the best single, multiple, and island booth displays at ALA Annual Conference. The award is named after Donald W. Kohlstedt in recognition of his hard work for better library conference exhibits. Six librarians judge the exhibits on the first day they are open. Administered by a committee of the ALA Exhibits Round Table. *For more information:* ALA Conference Services, 50 E. Huron St., Chicago, IL 60611-2795. *1994 winners:* John Muir Publications; Grolier Educational Corp.; Demco, Inc.

**ALA MAGERT Honors Award.** A citation and cash award of $25 to recognize outstanding contributions by a MAGERT member to map librarianship, MAGERT, or a specific MAGERT project. Administered by the ALA Map and Geography Round Table. *For more information:* ALA, 50 E. Huron St., Chicago, IL 60611-2795. *Deadline for applications:* December 1, 1995. *1994 winner:* Philip Hoehn.

**ALA Melvil Dewey Medal.** An engraved medal and a citation presented annually to an individual or a group for recent creative professional achievement of a high order, particularly in those fields in which Melvil Dewey was actively interested, notably: library management, library training, cataloging and classification, and the tools and techniques of librarianship. Administered by the American Library Association Awards Committee. *For more information:* Peggy Barber, ALA, 50 E. Huron St., Chicago, IL 60611-2795. *Donated by:* OCLC/Forest Press, Inc. *Deadline for applications:* December 1, 1995. *1994 winner:* Frank Phillips Grisham.

**ALA/ACRL Academic or Research Librarian of the Year Award.** An annual award of $3,000 presented to the individual who has made an outstanding national or international contribution to academic and research librarianship and library development. Administered by a committee of the ALA Association of College and Research Libraries. *For more information:* ALA/ACRL, 50 E. Huron St., Chicago, IL 60611-2795. *Donated by:* Baker & Taylor Books. *Deadline for applications:* December 1, 1995. *1994 winner:* Irene B. Hoadley.

**ALA/ACRL BIS Innovation in Bibliographic Instruction Award.** This award of a citation honors librarians who have developed and implemented innovative approaches to bibliographic instruction in an academic or research library within the last two years. The emphasis is on creativity and innovation. *For more information:* ALA/ACRL, 50 E. Huron St., Chicago, IL 60611-2795.

**ALA/ACRL Distinguished Education and Behavioral Sciences Librarian Award.** This award honors a distinguished academic librarian who has made an outstanding contribution as an education and/or behavioral sciences librarian through accomplishments and service to the profession. *For more information:* ALA/ACRL, 50 E. Huron St., Chicago, IL 60611-2795. *Deadline for applications:* December 1, 1995. *1994 winner:* Mary Ellen Collins.

**ALA/ACRL EBSCO Community College Learning Resources Library Achievement Awards.** Two annual awards to recognize significant achievement in the areas of program development and leadership. Individuals or groups from two-year institutions, as well as the two-year institutions themselves, are eligible to receive the awards, which are printed citations. Administered by the Community and Junior College Libraries Section of the ALA Association of College and Research Libraries. *For more information:* ALA/ACRL, 50 E. Huron St., Chicago, IL 60611-2795. *Deadline for applications:* December 1, 1995. *1994 winners:* Imogene L. Book, Ed Rivenburgh.

**ALA/ACRL Miriam Dudley Bibliographic Instruction Librarian of the Year Award.** An annual award of $1,000 presented to a librarian who has made an especially significant contribution to the advancement of bibliographic instruction. Administered by the Bibliographic Instruction Section of the ALA Association of College and Research Libraries. *For more information:* ALA/ACRL, 50 E. Huron St., Chicago, IL 60611-2795. *Donated by:* Mountainside Publishing Co., on behalf of *Research Strategies. Deadline for applications:* December 1, 1995. *1994 winner:* Cerise Oberman.

**ALA/ALCTS Esther J. Piercy Award.** An annual citation and cash award of $1,500 presented in recognition of a contribution to librarianship in the field of library collections and technical services by a librarian with not more than ten years of professional experience who has shown outstanding promise for continuing contributions and leadership in any of the fields comprising technical services through leadership, methodology, publication, or research. Administered by the ALA Association for Library Collections and Technical Services. *For more information:* ALA/ALCTS, 50 E. Huron St., Chicago, IL 60611-2795. *Deadline for applications:* December 1, 1995. *1994 winner:* Nancy E. Elkington.

**ALA/ALCTS Margaret Mann Citation.** An annual citation made to a cataloger or classifier, not necessarily an American, for outstanding professional achievement in cataloging or classification, either through publication of significant professional literature, participation in professional cataloging associations, introduction of new techniques of recognized importance, or outstanding work in the area of teaching within the past five years. Administered by the Cataloging and Classification Section of the ALA Association for Library Collections and Technical Services. *For more information:* ALA/ALCTS, 50 E. Huron St., Chicago, IL 60611-2795. *Deadline for applications:* December 1, 1995. *1994 winner:* Carol Ann Mandel.

**ALA/ALCTS/Bowker/Ulrich's Serials Librarianship Award.** An annual award consisting of a citation and a $1,500 cash award for distinguished contributions to serials librarianship, including but not limited to the previous three years, demonstrated by such activities as leadership in serials-related activities through participation in professional associations and/or library education programs, contributions to the body of serials literature, conducting research in the area of serials, development of tools or methods to enhance access to or management of serials, or other advances leading to a better understanding of the field of serials. Administered by the Serials Section of the ALA Association for Library Collections and Technical Services. *For more information:* ALA/ALCTS, 50 E. Huron St., Chicago, IL 60611-2795. *Donated by:* R.R. Bowker Co. *Deadline for applications:* December 1, 1995. *1994 winner:* Christina Feick.

**ALA/ASCLA Leadership Achievement Award.** A citation presented to recognize leadership and achievement in the following areas of activity: consulting, multitype library cooperation, and state library development. The award recognizes sustained activity that has been characterized by professional growth and effectiveness, and has enhanced the status of these areas of activity. Administered by the ALA Association of Specialized and Cooperative Library Agencies. *For more information:* ALA/ASCLA, 50 E. Huron St., Chicago, IL 60611-2795. *Deadline for applications:* December 1, 1995. *1994 winner:* Clarence Walters.

**ALA/ASCLA Professional Achievement Award.** A citation presented to one or more ASCLA members for professional achievement within the areas of consulting, networking, statewide services, and programs. *For more information:* ALA/ASCLA, 50 E. Huron St., Chicago, IL 60611-2795. *Deadline for applications:* December 1, 1995. *1994 winner:* Sandra M. Cooper.

**ALA/LAMA AIA Library Buildings Award Program.** A biennial award presented by the American Institute of Architects and the ALA Library Administration and Management Association to encourage excellence in the architectural design and planning of libraries. Awards are made to all types of libraries. Citations are presented to the winning architectural firms and to libraries. *For more information:* ALA/LAMA, 50 E. Huron St., Chicago, IL 60611-2795. *Deadline for applications:* October 1, 1996. *1993 winners:* Hope (Alas.) Library; Parlin Memorial Library, Everett, Mass.; Howell (Mich.) Carnegie District

Library; Library of Art, Architecture and Planning, MIT; Harvey Firestone Library, Princeton; Science Library, UC-Santa Cruz; Albuquerque (N.M.) Academy; Powell Library Staging Facility, UCLA.

**ALA/LAMA John Cotton Dana Public Relations Awards.** An annual citation made to libraries or library organizations of all types submitting materials representing the year's public relations program or a special project. Sponsored jointly by the H.W. Wilson Company and the Public Relations Section of the ALA Library Administration and Management Association. *For more information:* H.W. Wilson Company, 950 University Ave., Bronx, NY 10452-9978. *Deadline for applications:* February 13, 1995. *1994 winners:* First United Methodist Church Library, Huntsville, Tex.; Minneapolis (Minn.) PL; Atlanta (Ga.)-Fulton PL System; Brown County PL, Green Bay, Wis.; Cuyahoga County PL, Parma, O.; Newark (N.J.) PL; Richland County PL, Columbia, S.C.; Signal Mountain (Tenn.) PL; California State Library; Florida Division of Library Information Services, Bureau of Library Development, Tallahassee; Earl Gregg Swem Library, College of William and Mary; Gustavus Library Associates, Gustavus Adolphus College.

**ALA/RASD Gale Research Award for Excellence in Business Librarianship.** An annual award of $1,000 and a citation made to an individual in the field of business librarianship. Administered by the Business Reference and Services Section of the ALA Reference and Adult Services Division. *For more information:* ALA/RASD, 50 E. Huron St., Chicago, IL 60611-2795. *Donated by:* Gale Research, Inc. *Deadline for applications:* December 15, 1995. *1994 winner:* Judith May Nixon.

**ALA/RASD Isadore Gilbert Mudge-R.R. Bowker Award.** An annual award of $1,500 and a citation to be given at ALA Annual Conference to a person who has made a distinguished contribution to reference librarianship. The contribution may take the form of an imaginative and constructive program in a particular library; the writing of a significant book or articles in the reference field; creative and inspirational teaching of reference service; active participation in professional associations; or other noteworthy activities that stimulate reference librarians to more distinguished performance. Administered by the ALA Reference and Adult Services Division. *For more information:* ALA/RASD, 50 E. Huron St., Chicago, IL 60611-2795. *Deadline for applications:* December 15, 1995. *1994 winner:* Anne Grodzins Lipow.

**ALISE Award for Outstanding Professional Contributions to Library and Information Science Education.** Administered by the Association for Library and Information Science Education. *For more information:* ALISE, 4101 Lake Boone Trail, Suite 201, Raleigh, NC 27607. *Deadline for applications:* June 1, 1995.

**ASIS Award of Merit.** For an outstanding contribution to the field of information science. Administered by the American Society for Information Science. *For more information:* ASIS, 8720 Georgia Ave., Suite 601, Silver Spring, MD 20910. *Deadline for applications:* June 1, 1995.

**BCALA Leadership in the Profession Awards.** To recognize continuing service and leadership in the library profession. Administered by the Black Caucus of the American Library Association. *For more information:* Stanton F. Biddle, Box 317, Baruch College, 17 Lexington Avenue, New York, NY 10010.

**BCALA Professional Achievement Awards.** For extraordinary achievement in professional activities. Administered by the Black Caucus of the American Library Association. *For more information:* Stanton F. Biddle, Box 317, Baruch College, 17 Lexington Avenue, New York, NY 10010.

**BCALA/DEMCO Award for Excellence in Librarianship.** An annual award of $500 presented to the librarian who has made significant contributions to promoting the status of African Americans in the library profession. Administered by the Black Caucus of the American Library Association. *Donated by:* DEMCO, Inc. *Deadline for applications:* May 1, 1995. *1994 winner:* E. J. Josey.

**CLA Award for Achievement in Technical Services.** To recognize achievement in technical services by any unit whose library has an institutional membership in CLA. Administered by the Technical Services Interest Group of the Canadian Library Association. *For more information:* CLA, 200 Elgin St., Ottawa, Ontario K2P 1L5, Canada. *Deadline for applications:* March 31, 1995. *1994 winner:* Computer Operations Unit, Regina Public Library.

**CLA/CACUL Innovation Achievement Award.** An award of a $1,500 gift certificate for the vendor of the institution's choice, to recognize academic libraries which, through innovation in ongoing programs and services or in a special event or project, have contributed to academic librarianship and library development. Administered by the Canadian Association of College and University Libraries of the Canadian Library Association. *For more information:* CLA, 200 Elgin St., Ottawa, Ontario K2P 1L5, Canada. *Deadline for applications:* March 31, 1995. *1994 winners:* University of Alberta, Edmonton, and Queen's University, Kingston.

**CLA/CACUL Outstanding Academic Librarian Award.** Administered by the Canadian

Association of College and University Libraries of the Canadian Library Association. *For more information:* CLA, 200 Elgin St., Ottawa, Ontario K2P 1L5, Canada. *Donated by:* Blackwell/North America. *Deadline for applications:* January 31, 1995. *1994 winner:* Ernie Ingles.

**CLA/CAPL Public Relations Award.** For a public library in Canada with a successful public relations program, project or campaign. Administered by the Canadian Association of Public Libraries of the Canadian Library Association. *For more information:* CLA, 200 Elgin St., Ottawa, Ontario K2P 1L5, Canada. *Deadline for applications:* March 31, 1995. *1994 winner:* Red Deer PL, Alberta.

**CLA/CASLIS Award for Special Librarianship in Canada.** Administered by the Canadian Association of Special Libraries and Information Services of the Canadian Library Association. *For more information:* CLA, 200 Elgin St., Ottawa, Ontario K2P 1L5, Canada. *Deadline for applications:* January 21, 1995. *1994 winner:* Marilyn Rennick.

**FOLUSA Baker & Taylor Awards for Outstanding Friends of the Library.** Awards of $1,000 each and a citation for outstanding activities by Friends groups in five categories: small public libraries, academic libraries, state libraries, large public libraries, and school libraries/media centers. *For more information:* Friends of Libraries U.S.A., 1326 Spruce St., #1105, Philadelphia, PA 19107. *Donated by:* Baker & Taylor Books. *1994 winners:* Friends of the Mazomanie (Wis.) Free Library; Friends of Indiana Libraries; Friends of the Library of Denton (Tex.) High School West; Friends of the Richland Public Library, Columbia, S.C.; Denver Public Library Friends Foundation.

**MLA Award for Excellence and Achievement in Hospital Librarianship.** Awarded to an MLA member who has contributed significantly to overall distinction or leadership in hospital library administration or service, production of a definitive publication, teaching, research, advocacy, or the development or application of innovative technology related to hospital librarianship. Administered by the Medical Library Association. *For more information:* MLA, 6 N. Michigan Ave., Chicago, IL 60602. *Deadline for applications:* September 1, 1995. *1994 winner:* Linda Garr Markwell.

**MLA Estelle Brodman Award.** A cash award of $500 and a certificate presented to honor both significant achievement and the potential for leadership and continuing excellence at midcareer in the area of academic health sciences librarianship. Administered by the Medical Library Association. *For more information:* MLA, 6 N. Michigan Ave., Chicago, IL 60602. *Donated by:* Irwin H. Pizer. *Deadline for applications:* September 1, 1995. *1993 winner:* Julia Sollenberger.

**MLA Louise Darling Medal.** Presented to individuals, institutions, or groups of individuals who have made significant contributions to collection development in health sciences librarianship. Administered by the Medical Library Association. *For more information:* MLA, 6 N. Michigan Ave., Suite 300, Chicago, IL 60602. *Donated by:* Ballen Booksellers International. *Deadline for applications:* September 1, 1995. *1994 winner:* Nancy Witten Zinn.

**MLA Marcia C. Noyes Award.** The award, an engraved 8-inch sterling silver Revere bowl, recognizes a career that has resulted in lasting, outstanding contributions to medical librarianship. Administered by the Medical Library Association. *For more information:* MLA, 6 N. Michigan Ave., Suite 300, Chicago, IL 60602. *Deadline for applications:* September 1, 1995. *1994 winner:* Erica Love.

**SLA John Cotton Dana Award.** For exceptional support and encouragement of special librarianship. Administered by the Special Libraries Association. *For more information:* SLA, 1700 18th St., N.W., Washington, DC 20009. *Deadline for applications:* December 2, 1995. *1994 winners:* Joan Gervino, Julia Peterson.

**SLA Professional Award.** Given to an individual or group in recognition of a specific major achievement in librarianship or information science, which advances the objectives of the SLA. Administered by the Special Libraries Association. *For more information:* SLA, 1700 18th St., N.W., Washington, DC 20009. *Deadline for applications:* December 2, 1995. *1994 winners:* Christine Wells and the Freedom Forum Foundation.

## For publications and research

**AALL Call for Papers Awards Program.** To promote scholarship, provide an outlet for creativity, and to draw attention to newer members of the Association. Papers may be submitted on any subject relevant to law librarianship. Administered by the American Association of Law Libraries. *For more information:* AALL, 53 W. Jackson Blvd., Chicago, IL 60604. *Deadline for applications:* March 1, 1995. *1994 winners:* Marcia Koslov, Nazareth A. M. Pantaloni, Jonathan Adlai Franklin.

**AALL Joseph L. Andrews Bibliographical Award.** For significant contribution to legal bibliographical literature. Administered by the American Association of Law Libraries. *For more information:*

AALL, 53 W. Jackson Blvd., Chicago, IL 60604. *Deadline for applications:* March 1, 1995. *1994 winner:* Fred Shapiro, *The Oxford Dictionary of American Legal Quotations* (Oxford, 1993).

**AALL Law Library Journal Article of the Year.** For the best article appearing in the *Law Library Journal* for the previous year. Selected by the *Law Library Journal* Advisory Committee and administered by the American Association of Law Libraries. *For more information:* AALL, 53 W. Jackson Blvd., Chicago, IL 60604. *1994 winner:* Donald Jack Dunn, "Why Research Skills Declined: Or, When Two Rights Make a Wrong," *Law Library Journal,* Winter 1993.

**AALL Law Library Publications Award.** For achievements in in-house, user-oriented library materials that are outstanding in quality and significance. Administered by the American Association of Law Libraries. *For more information:* AALL, 53 W. Jackson Blvd., Chicago, IL 60604. *Deadline for applications:* March 1, 1995. *1994 winner:* Cadwalader Wickersham & Taft, for *Check It Out* (library newsletter).

**AJL Bibliography Award.** Award of $500 for an outstanding book-length Judaica bibliography. Administered by the Association of Jewish Libraries. *For more information:* AJL, 15 E. 26th St., Room 1034, New York, NY 10010. *Deadline for applications:* March 1995. *1993 winner:* Robert Singerman, *Spanish and Portuguese Jewry: A Classified Bibliography* (Greenwood, 1993).

**AJL Reference Book Award.** Award of $500 for an outstanding general reference book in Judaica. Administered by the Association of Jewish Libraries. *For more information:* AJL, 15 E. 26th St., Room 1034, New York, NY 10010. *Deadline for applications:* March 1995. *1993 winners:* Charles Cutter and Micha Falk Oppenheim, *Judaica Reference Sources* (Denali Press, 1993), and Macy Nulman, *The Encyclopedia of Jewish Prayer* (Jason Aronson, 1993).

**AJL Sydney Taylor Body of Work Award.** An award of $1,000 for a lifetime of publications in the field of Jewish children's books. Administered by the Association of Jewish Libraries. *For more information:* AJL, 15 E. 26th St., Room 1034, New York, NY 10010. *1990 winner:* Yassa Ganz.

**AJL Sydney Taylor Children's Book Awards.** Awards of $500 each for the best Jewish children's books for older and younger children. Administered by the Association of Jewish Libraries. *For more information:* AJL, 15 E. 26th St., Room 1034, New York, NY 10010. *Deadline for applications:* January 31, 1995. *1993 winners:* Nina Jaffe, *The Uninvited Guest and Other Jewish Holiday Tales* (Scholastic, 1993); Carol Matas, *Sworn Enemies* (Bantam, 1993).

**AJL Sydney Taylor Manuscript Award.** An award of $1,000 for a Jewish children's book (either fiction or nonfiction) by a first-time author. Administered by the Association of Jewish Libraries. *For more information:* AJL, 15 E. 26th St., Room 1034, New York, NY 10010. *Deadline for applications:* January 31, 1995. *1994 winner:* Faye Silton, for her manuscript "Of Heroes, Hooks and Heirlooms."

**ALA Coretta Scott King Award.** Award(s) given to an African-American author and to an African-American illustrator for an outstandingly inspirational and educational contribution. They are designed to commemorate the life and work of Martin Luther King, Jr., and to honor Coretta Scott King for her courage and determination in continuing to work for peace and world brotherhood. Book(s) must be published one year prior to the year of the award presentation. The award consists of a plaque and a cash award of $250 to the author and $250 to the illustrator. Sets of encyclopedias are also donated: *Encyclopaedia Britannica* to the author and *World Book* to the illustrator. Administered by the ALA Social Responsibilities Round Table. *For more information:* Office for Library Outreach Services, ALA, 50 E. Huron St., Chicago, IL 60611-2795. *Donated by:* Johnson Publications. *1994 winners:* Angela Johnson, for *Toning the Sweep* (Orchard Books, 1993); Tom Feelings, for *Soul Looks Back in Wonder,* edited by Phyllis Fogelman (Dial Books, 1993).

**ALA Coretta Scott King Genesis Award.** The award, given to an African-American author and to an African-American illustrator for an outstanding book, is designed to bring visibility to a writer or artist at the beginning of his or her career as a published book creator. The winner's published works cannot exceed three in number. *For more information:* ALA, 50 E. Huron St., Chicago, IL 60611-2795.

**ALA Eli M. Oboler Memorial Award.** A biennial award of $1,500 presented to the author(s) of an article (including a review article), a series of thematically connected articles, a book, or a manual, published on the local, state, or national level, in English or in English translation. The works to be considered must have as their central concern one or more issues, events, questions, or controversies in the area of intellectual freedom. Administered by the ALA Intellectual Freedom Round Table. *For more information:* ALA Office for Intellectual Freedom, 50 E. Huron St., Chicago, IL 60611-2795. *Donated by:* HBW Associates, Inc. *Deadline for applications:* December 1, 1995. *1994 winner:* Joan DelFattore, "What Johnny Shouldn't Read: Textbook Censorship in America."

**ALA G.K. Hall Award for Library Literature.** An award, consisting of $500 and a citation, presented to an individual who makes an outstanding contribution to library literature issued during the three years preceding the presentation. Administered by the American Library Association Awards Committee. *For more information:* Peggy Barber, ALA, 50 E. Huron St., Chicago, IL 60611-2795. *Donated by:* G.K. Hall & Co., Inc. *Deadline for applications:* October 1, 1995. *1994 winner:* Hazel Rochman, *Against Borders: Promoting Books for a Multicultural World.*

**ALA Gay/Lesbian/Bisexual Book Award.** An annual award honoring a book or books of exceptional merit relating to the gay/lesbian/bisexual experience. The form of the award is not fixed but is designated by the ALA Gay Book Award Committee each year as appropriate. Literature and nonfiction titles, including book-length bibliographies, are eligible. Nominations must be made by any individual not affiliated with the publisher. Administered by the Gay and Lesbian Task Force of the ALA Social Responsibilities Round Table. *For more information:* Office for Library Outreach Services, ALA, 50 E. Huron St., Chicago, IL 60611-2795. *Deadline for applications:* December 31, 1995. *1994 winners:* Leslie Feinberg, Phyllis Burke.

**ALA H.W. Wilson Library Periodical Award.** An annual award consisting of $1,000 and a certificate, presented to a periodical published by a local, state, or regional library, library group, or library association in the United States or Canada that has made an outstanding contribution to librarianship. (This excludes publications of ALA, CLA, and their divisions.) Administered by the American Library Association Awards Committee. *For more information:* Peggy Barber, ALA, 50 E. Huron St., Chicago, IL 60611-2795. *Donated by:* H.W. Wilson Co. *Deadline for applications:* December 1, 1995. *1994 winner:* Colorado Library Association, for *Colorado Libraries.*

**ALA Jesse H. Shera Award for Research.** A $500 award presented annually to the person submitting the best completed library research paper. Submitted papers must not exceed 50 pages. The winner of the competition presents the research at one of the LRRT Research Forums at ALA Annual Conference. Administered by the ALA Library Research Round Table. *For more information:* ALA Office for Research, 50 E. Huron St., Chicago, IL 60611-2795. *Deadline for applications:* February 1, 1995. *1994 winners:* Judith Serebnick and Frank Quinn.

**ALA Justin Winsor Prize Essay.** An award of $500 established to encourage excellence in research in library history. The winner will be offered the privilege of being invited to submit the essay for publication in a future issue of *Libraries and Culture.* Essays should embody original historical research on a significant subject of library history, should be based on source materials and manuscripts if possible, and should use good English composition and superior style. Administered by the ALA Library History Round Table. *For more information:* Charles Harmon, ALA, 50 E. Huron St., Chicago, IL 60611-2795. *Deadline for applications:* February 15, 1995.

**ALA Phyllis Dain Library History Dissertation Award.** An award of $500 and a certificate given every two years to recognize outstanding dissertations treating the history of books, libraries, librarianship, or information science. Dissertations are eligible if they are completed during the designated period and have been submitted by the author along with a letter of support from the doctoral advisor or another faculty member at the institution where the degree was granted. Administered by the ALA Library History Round Table. *For more information:* Charles Harmon, ALA, 50 E. Huron St., Chicago, IL 60611-2795. *Deadline for applications:* February 1, 1995. *1993 winner:* Plummer Alston Jones, Jr., for "American Public Library Service to the Immigrant Community, 1876–1948."

**ALA/AASL Emergency Librarian Publication Award.** An annual grant of $500 presented to a school library media association that is an affiliate of AASL in recognition of an outstanding publication in the field of school librarianship. The award celebrates the efforts of AASL affiliates to promote excellence in school library media programs through publications for members. Administered by the ALA American Association of School Librarians. *For more information:* ALA/AASL, 50 E. Huron St., Chicago, IL 60611-2795. *Donated by:* The publishers of *Emergency Librarian. Deadline for applications:* February 1, 1995. *1994 winner: Medium,* the journal of the Washington Library Media Association.

**ALA/ACRL BIS Bibliographic Instruction Publication of the Year Award.** An annual award of an appropriate citation to recognize an outstanding publication related to bibliographic instruction. Eligible publications include journal articles, books, and book chapters. Publication year is defined as September through August of the preceding year. Administered by a subcommittee of the ALA Association of College and Research Libraries. *For more information:* ALA/ACRL, 50 E. Huron St., Chicago, IL 60611-2795. *Deadline for applications:* December 1, 1995. *1993 winner:* Terrence F. Mech and Donald W. Farmer, for *Information Literacy* (Jossey-Bass, 1992).

**ALA/ACRL K.G. Saur Award for Best C&RL Article.** An annual award of $500 presented to the author(s) to recognize the most outstanding article published in *College & Research Libraries* during the preceding volume year. The winning article will be selected on the basis of originality, timeliness, relevance to ACRL areas of interest and concern, and quality of writing. Administered by the ALA Association of College and Research Libraries. *For more information:* ALA/ACRL, 50 E. Huron St., Chicago, IL 60611-2795. *Donated by:* K.G. Saur. *1994 winner:* Ross Atkinson, "Networks, Hypertext, and Academic Information Services: Some Longer-Range Implications," *College & Research Libraries,* May 1993.

**ALA/ACRL Katharine Kyes Leab and Daniel J. Leab American Book Prices Current Exhibition Catalogue Awards.** Three annual awards for the best catalogue published by American or Canadian institutions in conjunction with exhibitions of books and/or manuscripts. Entries are divided into three budget categories: expensive, moderately expensive, and inexpensive, based on production costs of the catalogues. The awards take the form of printed citations to the institutions organizing the exhibitions. Administered by the Rare Books and Manuscripts Section of the ALA Association of College and Research Libraries. *For more information:* ALA/ACRL, 50 E. Huron St., Chicago, IL 60611-2795. *Donated by:* Katharine Kyes Leab and Daniel J. Leab. *Deadline for applications:* September 30, 1995. *1994 winners:* Beinecke Rare Book and Manuscript Library, Yale University; Van Pelt-Dietrich Library, University of Pennsylvania; University of Chicago Library; Houghton Library, Harvard University.

**ALA/ACRL Oberly Award for Bibliography in the Agricultural Sciences.** A biennial award given in odd-numbered years, consisting of a citation and a cash award, presented to an American citizen who compiles the best bibliography in the field of agriculture or one of the related sciences in the two-year period preceding the year in which the award is made. Administered by the Science and Technology Section of the ALA Association of College and Research Libraries. *For more information:* ALA/ACRL, 50 E. Huron St., Chicago, IL 60611-2795. *Donated by:* Oberly Memorial Fund. *Deadline for applications:* December 1, 1995. *1993 winner:* Albert H. Joy, *Acid Rain* (Meckler, 1991).

**ALA/ACRL Rare Books & Manuscripts Librarianship Award.** A biennial cash award of $1,000 to stimulate and increase the contribution of articles of superior quality to *Rare Books & Manuscripts Librarianship.* Any article published in the journal during the two preceding volume years is eligible. *For more information:* ALA/ACRL, 50 E. Huron St., Chicago, IL 60611-2795. *Deadline for applications:* December 1, 1995. *Donated by:* Christie, Mason & Woods, Inc. *1993 winner:* Hope Mayo, for "Medieval Manuscript Cataloguing and the MARC Format," vol.6, no.1.

**ALA/ALCTS Best of LRTS Award.** Annual citation to be given to the author(s) of the best paper published each year in the division's official journal, *Library Resources and Technical Services.* Each of the papers published in the volume for the preceding calendar year is eligible for consideration, with the exception of official reports and documents, obituaries, letters to the editor, and biographies of award winners. Administered by the ALA Association for Library Collections and Technical Services. *For more information:* ALA/ALCTS, 50 E. Huron St., Chicago, IL 60611-2795. *Deadline for applications:* December 1, 1995. *1994 winner:* Angela Giral and Arlene Taylor, "Indexing Overlap and Consistency between the Avery Index to Architectural Periodicals and the Architectural Periodicals Index."

**ALA/ALCTS Blackwell/North America Scholarship Award.** An annual award consisting of a citation given to the winner and a $2,000 scholarship to the library school of the winner's choice. The citation is presented to the author(s) of an outstanding monograph, published article, or original paper in the field of acquisitions, collection development, or related areas of resources development in libraries. Administered by the Resources Section of the ALA Association for Library Collections and Technical Services. *For more information:* ALA/ALCTS, 50 E. Huron St., Chicago, IL 60611-2795. *Donated by:* Blackwell/North America. *Deadline for applications:* December 1, 1995. *1994 winners:* Joel S. Rutstein, Anna L. DeMiller, Elizabeth A. Fuseler.

**ALA/ALSC Andrew Carnegie Medal.** A medal presented annually to an American producer for the outstanding video production for children released in the United States in the previous calendar year. Administered by the ALA Association for Library Service to Children. *For more information:* ALA/ALSC, 50 E. Huron St., Chicago, IL 60611-2795. *Endowed by:* Carnegie Corporation of New York. *1994 winner:* Rawn Fulton, "Eric Carle: Picture Writer" (Philomel Books, 1993).

**ALA/ALSC John Newbery Medal.** A medal presented annually to the author of the most distinguished contribution to American literature for children published in the United States in the preceding year. The recipient must be a citizen or resident of the United States. Administered by the ALA Association for Library Service to Children. *For more information:* ALA/ALSC, 50 E. Huron St., Chicago, IL 60611-2795. *Donated by:* Daniel Melcher. *1994 winner:* Lois Lowry, *The Giver* (Houghton Mifflin, 1993).

**ALA/ALSC Laura Ingalls Wilder Medal.** A medal presented to an author or illustrator whose books, published in the United States, have over a period of years made a substantial and lasting contribution to children's literature. Presented every three years. Administered by the ALA Association for Library Service to Children. *For more information:* ALA/ALSC, 50 E. Huron St., Chicago, IL 60611-2795.

*Deadline for nominations:* December 1, 1995. *1992 winner:* Marcia Brown.

**ALA/ALSC Mildred L. Batchelder Award.** A citation presented to an American publisher for a children's book considered to be the most outstanding of those books originally published in a foreign language in a foreign country and subsequently published in English in the United States during the preceding year. Administered by the ALA Association for Library Service to Children. For *more information:* ALA/ALSC, 50 E. Huron St., Chicago, IL 60611-2795. *1994 winner:* Farrar, Straus and Giroux, for *The Apprentice,* by Pilar Molina Llorente.

**ALA/ALSC Randolph Caldecott Medal.** A medal presented annually to the illustrator of the most distinguished American picture book for children published in the United States in the preceding year. Administered by the ALA Association for Library Service to Children. *For more information:* ALA/ALSC, 50 E. Huron St., Chicago, IL 60611-2795. *Donated by:* Daniel Melcher. *1994 winner:* Allen Say, for *Grandfather's Journey,* edited by Walter Lorraine (Houghton Mifflin, 1993).

**ALA/RASD Dartmouth Medal.** A medal presented to honor achievement in creating reference works outstanding in quality and significance. Creating reference works may include, but not be limited to, writing, compiling, editing, or publishing books or the provision of information in other forms for reference use, e.g., a database. Administered by the ALA Reference and Adult Services Division. *For more information:* ALA/RASD, 50 E. Huron St., Chicago, IL 60611-2795. *Donated by:* Dartmouth College. *Deadline for applications:* December 15, 1995. *1994 winner:* Darlene Clark Hine, *Black Women in America: An Historical Encyclopedia* (Carlson, 1993).

**ALA/RASD Denali Press Award.** An annual award of $500 and a citation to recognize achievement in creating reference works, outstanding in quality and significance, that provide information specifically about ethnic and minority groups in the United States. Administered by the ALA Reference and Adult Services Division. *For more information:* ALA/RASD, 50 E. Huron St., Chicago, IL 60611-2795. *Donated by:* Denali Press. *Deadline for applications:* December 15, 1995. *1994 winner:* Darlene Clark Hine, for *Black Women in America* (Carlson, 1993).

**ALA/RASD Genealogical Publishing Company Award.** An annual $1,000 cash award and a citation to recognize professional achievement in historical reference and research librarianship. The recipient will be selected for exceptional accomplishment related to bibliography, book reviewing, indexing, professional association leadership, programs, and training that has furthered the quality of librarianship in history and the related subject interests of librarians, archivists, bibliographers, genealogists, and others engaged in historical reference or research. Administered by the ALA Reference and Adult Services History Section. *For more information:* ALA/RASD, 50 E. Huron St., Chicago, IL 60611-2795. *Donated by:* Genealogical Publishing Company. *Deadline for applications:* December 15, 1995. *1994 winner:* J. Carlyle Parker.

**ALA/RASD Louis Shores-Oryx Press Award.** An annual award of $1,000 presented to an individual, a team of individuals, or an organization to recognize excellence in reviewing of books and other materials for libraries. The award may be given to reviewers, review editors, review media, teachers, or organizations that through their activities have furthered the quality and professionalism of reviews and the reviewing process. Administered by the ALA Reference and Adult Services Division. *For more information:* ALA/RASD, 50 E. Huron St., Chicago, IL 60611-2795. *Donated by:* Oryx Press. *Deadline for applications:* December 15, 1995. *1994 winner:* H. Robert Malinowsky.

**ALA/RASD Reference Service Press Award.** An annual award of $1,000 presented to recognize the most outstanding article published in *RQ* during the preceding two volume years. Administered by the ALA Reference and Adult Services Division. *For more information:* ALA/RASD, 50 E. Huron St., Chicago, IL 60611-2795. *Donated by:* Reference Service Press, Inc. *1994 winner:* Sally W. Kalin, "Support Services for Remote Users of Online Public Access Catalogs," *RQ* 31 (Winter 1991): 197-213.

**ALA/YALSA Margaret A. Edwards Award.** An award given to an author or co-author whose book(s) over a period of time have been accepted by young adults as an authentic voice that continues to illuminate their experiences and emotions, giving insight into their lives. The award consists of $1,000 cash and a citation. Administered by the ALA Young Adult Library Services Association. *For more information:* ALA/YALSA, 50 E. Huron St., Chicago, IL 60611-2795. *Donated by: School Library Journal. 1994 winner:* Walter Dean Myers.

**ALISE Research Paper Competition.** An award of $500 for a previously unpublished research paper concerning any aspect of librarianship or information studies by a member of ALISE. Administered by the Association for Library and Information Science Education. *For more information:* ALISE, 4101 Lake Boone Trail, Suite 201, Raleigh, NC 27607. *Deadline for applications:* October 1, 1995. *1994 winners:*

Patricia Dewdney and Catherine Sheldrick Ross, for "Flying a Light Aircraft, or What Really Happens to People Who Ask Reference Questions."

**ARLIS/NA George Wittenborn Memorial Award.** Awarded to publishers for excellence in art publications produced or distributed in North America during the previous calendar year. Administered by the Art Libraries Society of North America. *For more information:* ARLIS/NA, 4101 Lake Boone Trail, Suite 201, Raleigh, NC 27607. *Deadline for applications:* December 31, 1995.

**ARLIS/NA Gerd Muehsam Memorial Award.** A $200 cash award, one-year membership in ARLIS/NA, and $300 in travel funds for the best paper by a graduate student on a subject related to art or visual resources librarianship. Administered by the Art Libraries Society of North America. *For more information:* ARLIS/NA, 4101 Lake Boone Trail, Suite 201, Raleigh, NC 27607. *Deadline for applications:* October 15, 1995.

**ASI H.W. Wilson Company Indexing Award.** A cash award of $500 and a citation for excellence in indexing of an English-language monograph or other nonserial publication published in the United States during the previous calendar year. The publisher of the index also receives a citation. Administered by the American Society of Indexers. *For more information:* ASI, P.O. Box 386, 502 S. 12th St., Port Aransas, TX 78383. *Donated by:* H.W. Wilson Co. *Deadline for applications:* April 1, 1995. *1994 winner:* Patricia Deminna.

**ASIS Best Information Science Book.** For the best book published in the field of information science during the preceding year. Administered by the American Society for Information Science. *For more information:* ASIS, 8720 Georgia Ave., Suite 501, Silver Spring, MD 20910. *Deadline for applications:* June 1, 1995.

**ASIS Best JASIS Paper Award.** For the outstanding paper published in the *Journal of the American Society for Information Science.* Administered by the American Society for Information Science. *For more information:* ASIS, 8720 Georgia Ave., Suite 501, Silver Spring, MD 20910. *Deadline for applications:* June 1, 1995.

**ASIS Doctoral Forum.** For outstanding achievements by information scientists in the completion of dissertation projects. Administered by the American Society for Information Science. *For more information:* ASIS, 8720 Georgia Ave., Suite 501, Silver Spring, MD 20910. *Deadline for applications:* June 1, 1995.

**ASIS Research Award.** For a systematic program of research or outstanding research contributions in the field of information science. Administered by the American Society for Information Science. *For more information:* ASIS, 8720 Georgia Ave., Suite 501, Silver Spring, MD 20910. *Deadline for applications:* June 1, 1995.

**ASIS Student Paper Award.** For an outstanding student paper in information science. Administered by the American Society for Information Science. *For more information:* ASIS, 8720 Georgia Ave., Suite 501, Silver Spring, MD 20910. *Deadline for applications:* June 15, 1995.

**BCALA Literary Awards.** Two annual awards of $500 that recognize outstanding works by African American authors depicting the cultural, historical, or sociopolitical aspects of the Black Diaspora. One award is in the fiction category, the other in the nonfiction category. Administered by the Black Caucus of the American Library Association. *For more information:* Stanton F. Biddle, Box 317, Baruch College, 17 Lexington Avenue, New York, NY 10010. *Deadline for applications:* December 19, 1995. *1994 winners:* Ernest J. Gaines, *A Lesson Before Dying;* David Levering Lewis, *W.E.B. DuBois: Biography of a Race, 1868–1919.*

**CLA Student Article Award.** For an article written by a student registered in or recently graduated from a Canadian library school, a library techniques program, or faculty of education library program. Administered by the Canadian Library Association. *For more information:* CLA, 200 Elgin Street, Suite 602, Ottawa, Ontario, Canada K2P 1L5. *Deadline for applications:* March 15, 1995. *1994 winner:* Susan R. Fisher.

**CLA John Brubaker Memorial Award.** For the best article in *Catholic Library World* in the previous year. Administered by the *Catholic Library World* Committee of the Catholic Library Association. *For more information:* CLA, c/o Jean R. Bostley, S.S.J., St. Joseph Central High School, 22 Maplewood Ave., Pittsfield, MA 01201.

**CLA Regina Medal.** A silver medal awarded to an author or illustrator for a lifetime contribution to children's books. Administered by the Catholic Library Association. *For more information:* CLA, c/o Jean R. Bostley, S.S.J., St. Joseph Central High School, 22 Maplewood Ave., Pittsfield, MA 01201. *1994 winner:* Lois Lowry.

**CLA/ALS Jerome Award.** Presented annually for excellence in Catholic scholarship. Administered by the Academic Libraries Section of the Catholic Library Association. *For more information:* CLA, c/o Jean R. Bostley, S.S.J., St. Joseph Central High School, 22 Maplewood Ave., Pittsfield, MA 01201. *1994 winner:* Fr. Don Senior, C.P.

**CLA/CACL Amelia Frances Howard-Gibbon Award.** Presented annually to the illustrator of an outstanding children's book published in Canada. Administered by the Canadian Association of Childrens Librarians of the Canadian Library Association. *For more information:* CLA, 200 Elgin St., Ottawa, Ontario K2P 1L5, Canada. *Deadline for applications:* January 1, 1995. *1994 winner:* Leo Yerxa, *Last Leaf First Snowflake to Fall.*

**CLA/CACL Book of the Year for Children Award.** Presented annually to the author of an outstanding children's book published in Canada. Administered by the Canadian Association of Childrens' Librarians of the Canadian Library Association. *For more information:* CLA, 200 Elgin St., Ottawa, Ontario K2P 1L5, Canada. *Deadline for applications:* January 1, 1995. *1994 winner:* Tim Wynne-Jones, *Some of the Kinder Planets.*

**CLA/CSLA CANEBSCO School Library Media Periodical Award.** Recognizes a school library media periodical as a vehicle for the professional development of school library media personnel. Administered by the Canadian School Library Association of the Canadian Library Association. *For more information:* CLA, 200 Elgin St., Ottawa, Ontario K2P 1L5, Canada. *Donated by:* CANEBSCO, Inc. *Deadline for applications:* December 31, 1995. *1994 winner: School Library News* (School Curriculum Consultant, Manitoba Education & Training).

**CLA/CSLA Grolier Award for Research in School Librarianship in Canada.** A $1,000 award for theoretical or applied research that advances the field of school librarianship. Administered by the Canadian School Library Association of the Canadian Library Association. *For more information:* CLA, 200 Elgin St., Ottawa, Ontario K2P 1L5, Canada. *Donated by:* Grolier Education Associates. *Deadline for applications:* December 31, 1995. *1994 winner:* Roy Doiron.

**CLA/YASIG Young Adult Canadian Book Award.** Recognizes an author of an outstanding English-language Canadian book appealing to young adults. Administered by the Young Adult Services Interest Group of the Canadian Library Association. *For more information:* CLA, 200 Elgin St., Ottawa, Ontario K2P 1L5, Canada. *Deadline for applications:* January 1, 1995. *1994 winner:* Sean Stewart, *Nobody's Son.*

**CSLA Helen Keating Ott Award for Outstanding Contribution to Children's Literature.** Given to a person or organization that has made a significant contribution to promoting high moral and ethical values through children's literature. Administered by the Church and Synagogue Library Association. *For more information:* CSLA, Box 19357, Portland, OR 97219. *1994 winner:* David Adler.

**MLA Ida and George Eliot Prize.** An award of $200 for an essay published in any journal in the preceding calendar year that has been judged most effective in furthering medical librarianship. Administered by the Medical Library Association. *For more information:* MLA, 6 N. Michigan Ave., Suite 300, Chicago, IL 60602. *Donated by:* Login Brothers Book Co. *Deadline for applications:* September 1, 1995. *1994 winner:* Joceyln Rankin, for "Problem-Based Medical Education: Effect on Library Use."

**MLA Murray Gottlieb Prize.** An award of $100 for the best unpublished essay written by a medical librarian on the history of medicine and allied sciences. Administered by the Medical Library Association. *For more information:* MLA, 6 N. Michigan Ave., Suite 300, Chicago, IL 60602. *Donated by:* Ralph and Jo Grimes. *Deadline for applications:* September 1, 1995. *1994 winner:* Thomas Horrocks, for "A Poor Man's Riches, A Rich Man's Bliss."

**MLA Rittenhouse Award.** Given for the best unpublished paper on medical librarianship submitted by a student enrolled in a course for credit in an ALA-accredited library school, or a trainee in an internship in medical librarianship. Administered by the Medical Library Association. *For more information:* MLA, 6 N. Michigan Ave., Suite 300, Chicago, IL 60602. *Donated by:* Rittenhouse Medical Book Store. *Deadline for applications:* September 1, 1995. *1994 winner:* Mary Moore, for "The Economics of Health Care Information."

**MLA Eva Judd O'Meara Award.** A $250 award for the best book or score review published in the MLA journal, *Notes.* Administered by the Music Library Association. *For more information:* MLA, Box 487, Canton, MA 02021. *Deadline for applications:* November 15, 1995. *1993 winner:* Karl Kroeger, review of *American Sacred Music Imprints, 1698–1810,* in *Notes* 48 (Sept.1991):54–58.

**MLA Richard S. Hill Award.** A $250 award for the best article-length bibliography and article on music librarianship. Administered by the Music Library Association. *For more information:* MLA, Box 487, Canton, MA 02021. *Deadline for applications:* November 15, 1995. *1993 winner:* John Graziano, "Music in William Randolph Hearst's *New York Journal,*" *Notes* 48 (Dec.1991):383–424.

**MLA Vincent H. Duckles Award.** An award of $500 for the best book-length bibliography or music reference work. Administered by the Music Library Association. *For more information:* MLA, Box 487, Canton, MA 02021. *Deadline for applications:* November 15, 1995. *1993 winner:* Richard Kitson, *Dwight's Journal of Music (1852–1881)* (UMI, 1991).

**SAA C.F.W. Coker Prize.** For finding aids or finding aid systems that have a substantial impact on archival descriptive practices. Administered by the Society of American Archivists. *For more information:* SAA, 600 S. Federal St., Suite 504, Chicago, IL 60605. *Deadline for applications:* April 1995. *1993 winner:* Diane Vogt-O'Connor, for *Guide to Photographic Collections at the Smithsonian Institutions.*

**SAA Fellows' Posner Prize.** For the best article in the *American Archivist.* Administered by the Society of American Archivists. *For more information:* SAA, 600 S. Federal St., Suite 504, Chicago, IL 60605. *Deadline for applications:* April 1995. *1993 winners:* Avra S. Michelson and Jeff Rothenberg, for "Scholarly Communication and Information Technology."

**SAA Philip M. Hamer-Elizabeth Hamer Kegan Award.** For institutions that have increased public awareness of a specific body of documents. Administered by the Society of American Archivists. *For more information:* SAA, 600 S. Federal St., Suite 504, Chicago, IL 60605. *Deadline for applications:* April 1995. *1994 winner:* American Heritage Center at the University of Wyoming.

**SAA Preservation Publication Award.** Recognizes the author(s) or editor(s) of an outstanding work, published in North America, that advances the theory or the practice of preservation in archival institutions. *For more information:* SAA, 600 S. Federal St., Suite 504, Chicago, IL 60605. *Deadline for applications:* April 1995. *1994 winner:* Mary Lynn Ritzenthaler, for *Preserving Archives and Manuscripts.*

**SAA Theodore Calvin Pease Award.** For superior writing achievement by a student of archival administration. Administered by the Society of American Archivists. *For more information:* SAA, 600 S. Federal St., Suite 504, Chicago, IL 60605. *Deadline for applications:* April 1995. *1994 winner:* Anke Voss-Hubbard, "No Documents—No History: Mary Ritter Beard and the Early History of Women's Archives."

**SAA Waldo Gifford Leland Prize.** For writing of superior excellence and usefulness in the field of archival history, theory, or practice published as a monograph in North America. Administered by the Society of American Archivists. *For more information:* SAA, 600 S. Federal St., Suite 504, Chicago, IL 60605. *Deadline for applications:* April 1995. *1994 winner:* F. Gerald Ham.

**SLA H. W. Wilson Company Award.** An honorarium and certificate for the best paper published in *Special Libraries* during the previous calendar year. Administered by the Special Libraries Association. *For more information:* SLA, 1700 18th St., N.W., Washington, DC 20009. *Donated by:* H. W. Wilson Company. *1993 winner:* Sharyn Ladner, "Resource Sharing by Sci-Tech and Business Libraries: Formal Networking Practices," *SL,* Spring 1992.

**SLA Media Award.** Presented to a journalist who writes the most outstanding article on special librarianship published in a general circulation publication or radio or television production. Administered by the Special Libraries Association. *For more information:* SLA, 1700 18th St., N.W., Washington, DC 20009. *Deadline for applications:* December 4, 1995. *1994 winner:* Cara S. Trager, "Databases put librarians on line," *Crain's New York Business,* Dec. 13, 1993.

**TLA Award.** For excellence in writing books about film, TV, or radio. Reference books excluded. *For more information:* Stephen Vallillo, Betty Rose Theatre Collection, New York Public Library, 111 Amsterdam Ave., New York, NY 10023. *Deadline for applications:* February 15, 1995. *1994 winner:* David Bordwell, *The Cinema of Eisenstein.*

**TLA George Freedley Award.** A cash award of $250 for excellence in writing books about the theatre. Reference books excluded. Administered by the Theatre Library Association. *For more information:* Stephen Vallillo, Betty Rose Theatre Collection, New York Public Library, 111 Amsterdam Ave., New York, NY 10023. *Deadline for applications:* February 15, 1995. *1994 winner:* Rachel M. Brownstein, *Tragic Muse: Rachel of the Comedie française.*

## For service in general

**AALL Marian Gould Gallagher Distinguished Service Award.** To recognize extended and sustained service to law librarianship, for exemplary service to the Association, or for contributions to the professional literature. Administered by the American Association of Law Libraries. *For more information:* AALL, 53 W. Jackson, Chicago, IL 60604. *Deadline for applications:* February 1, 1995. *1994 winners:* Jack Ellenberger, Elizabeth Finley, Diana Vincent-Daviss.

**AALL/TS-SIS Renee D. Chapman Memorial Award for Outstanding Contributions in Technical Services Law Librarianship.** Administered by the Technical Services Special Interest

Section of the American Association of Law Libraries. *For more information:* AALL, 53 W. Jackson, Chicago, IL 60604. *Deadline for applications:* February 1, 1995. *1994 winner:* Margaret Maes Axtmann.

**AJL Fanny Goldstein Merit Award.** A certificate recognizing an outstanding contribution on behalf of AJL or in Judaica librarianship. Administered by the Association for Jewish Libraries. *For more information:* AJL, 15 E. 26th St., Room 1034, New York, NY 10010. *1994 winner:* Adaire Klein.

**AJL Life Membership Achievement Award.** Administered by the Association for Jewish Libraries. *For more information:* AJL, 15 E. 26th St., Room 1034, New York, NY 10010. *1994 winners:* Hazel Karp, Barbara Leff.

**ALA Beta Phi Mu Award.** An annual award consisting of $500 and a citation of achievement, presented to a library school faculty member or to an individual for distinguished service to education for librarianship. Administered by the ALA Awards Committee. *For more information:* Peggy Barber, ALA, 50 E. Huron St., Chicago, IL 60611-2795. *Donated by:* Beta Phi Mu International Library Science Honorary Society. *Deadline for applications:* December 1, 1995. *1994 winner:* Jane B. Robbins.

**ALA Joseph W. Lippincott Award.** An award consisting of $1,000 and a citation of achievement, presented annually to a librarian for distinguished service to the profession of librarianship, such service to include outstanding participation in the activities of professional library associations, notable published professional writing, or other significant activity on behalf of the profession and its aims. Administered by the ALA Awards Committee. *For more information:* Peggy Barber, ALA, 50 E. Huron St., Chicago, IL 60611-2795. *Donated by:* Joseph W. Lippincott, Jr. *Deadline for applications:* December 1, 1995. *1994 winner:* Frank Kurt Cylke.

**ALA "Sign Me Up" Contest.** Gift certificates from World Book awarded annually in school and public library divisions to libraries signing up the most users. *For more information:* ALA, 50 E. Huron St., Chicago, IL 60611-2795. *Donated by:* World Book Educational Products. *Deadline for applications:* June 15, 1995. *1994 winners:* Deschutes County (Ore.) Library System; Scotsdale Elementary School, El Paso, Texas.

**ALA/ALTA Major Benefactors Honor Award.** An annual award consisting of a citation to recognize benefactors to public libraries. The recipient may be any person(s), institution, agency, or organization. The significance of the gift will be measured from the point of view of the recipient library. Administered by the ALA American Library Trustee Association. *For more information:* ALA/ALTA, 50 E. Huron St., Chicago, IL 60611-2795. *Deadline for applications:* December 1, 1995. *1993 winners:* Charles and Philip Bosserman.

**ALA/ALTA Trustee Citations.** A citation presented to each of two outstanding trustees, in actual service during part of the calendar year preceding the presentation, for distinguished service to library development, whether on the local, state, or national level. Equal consideration is to be given to trustees of small and large public libraries. Administered by the ALA American Library Trustee Association. *For more information:* ALA/ALTA, 50 E. Huron St., Chicago, IL 60611-2795. *Deadline for applications:* December 1, 1995. *1994 winners:* Gloria Twine Chisum, Herbert A. Davis.

**ALA/ASCLA Service Award.** A citation presented to recognize an ASCLA personal member for outstanding service and leadership to the division. The award recognizes sustained leadership and exceptional service through participation in activities that have enhanced the stature, reputation, and overall strength of ASCLA. *For more information:* ALA/ASCLA, 50 E. Huron St., Chicago, IL 60611-2795. *Deadline for applications:* December 1, 1995. *1994 winner:* Stephen Prine.

**ALA/LAMA Recognition of Achievement Awards.** Presented annually to encourage, recognize, and command excellence in service to LAMA and its sections. The awards are a certificate of appreciation for a significant contribution to the goals of LAMA over a period of several years, and a certificate of special thanks for a single, specific, significant contribution to the goals of LAMA. Administered by the ALA Library Administration and Management Association. *For more information:* ALA/LAMA, 50 E. Huron St., Chicago, IL 60611-2795. *Deadline for applications:* December 1, 1995. *1994 winners:* Anders C. Dahlgren, Robert A. Daugherty, Carolyn A. Snyder, Robert A. Almony Jr., Dwight Burlingame.

**ALA/PLA Allie Beth Martin Award.** An award of $3,000 and a citation presented to a librarian who, in a public library setting, has demonstrated an extraordinary range and depth of knowledge about books or other library materials and has exhibited a distinguished ability to share that knowledge. Administered by the ALA Public Library Association. *For more information:* ALA/PLA, 50 E. Huron St., Chicago, IL 60611-2795. *Donated by:* Baker and Taylor Books. *Deadline for applications:* December 1, 1995. *1994 winner:* Carol G. Walters.

**ALA/PLA Excellence in Small and/or Rural Public Library Service Award.** An award to provide recognition and a $1,000 honorarium to a public library serving a population of 10,000 or less that demonstrates excellence of service to its community as exemplified by an overall service program or a special program of significant accomplishment. Administered by the ALA Public Library Association. *For more information:* ALA/PLA, 50 E. Huron St., Chicago, IL 60611-2795. *Donated by:* EBSCO Subscription Services. *Deadline for applications:* December 1, 1995. *1994 winner:* Decorah (Iowa) PL.

**ALA/PLA National Achievement Citations.** A citation presented to a public library for significant, innovative activities that improve the organization, management, or services of public libraries. Any public library may apply; the chief officer of the library must authorize the application. There is a $30 application fee. *For more information:* ALA/PLA, 50 E. Huron St., Chicago, IL 60611-2795. *Deadline for applications:* December 1, 1995. *1994 winners:* Allen County (Ind.) PL, Carroll County (Md.) PL, Clinton (Iowa) PL, Columbus (O.) Metropolitan Library, Davenport (Iowa) PL, Monterey County (Calif.) Free Libraries, Osceola County (Fla.) Library System, Pikes Peak (Colo.) Library District, San Antonio (Tex.) PL.

**ALA/RASD Gale Research Award for Excellence in Reference and Adult Services.** An annual award of $1,000 and a citation presented to a library or library system for developing an imaginative and unique library resource to meet the patrons' reference needs. Administered by the ALA Reference and Adult Services Division. *For more information:* ALA/RASD, 50 E. Huron St., Chicago, IL 60611-2795. *Donated by:* Gale Research, Inc. *Deadline for applications:* December 15, 1995. *1994 winner:* Wichita (Kan.) PL.

**ALA/RASD Margaret E. Monroe Library Adult Services Award.** A citation to be given to a librarian who has made significant contributions to and an impact on library adult services. The person may be a practicing librarian, a library and information science researcher or educator, or a retired librarian who has brought distinction to the profession's understanding and practice of services to adults. Administered by the ALA Reference and Adult Services Division. *For more information:* ALA/RASD, 50 E. Huron St., Chicago, IL 60611-2795. *Deadline for applications:* December 15, 1995. *1994 winner:* Elizabeth Ann Funk.

**ALISE Service Award.** For regular and sustained service to ALISE. Administered by the Association for Library and Information Science Education. *For more information:* ALISE, 4101 Lake Boone Trail, Suite 201, Raleigh, NC 27607. *Deadline for applications:* June 1, 1995.

**ASIS Outstanding Information Science Teacher Award.** A cash award of $500 acknowledging sustained excellence in the teaching of information science. Administered by the American Society for Information Science. *For more information:* ASIS, 8720 Georgia Ave., Suite 501, Silver Spring, MD 20910. *Donated by:* Institute for Scientific Information. *Deadline for applications:* June 15, 1995.

**ASIS Watson Davis Award.** For a significant long-term contribution to ASIS. Administered by the American Society for Information Science. *For more information:* ASIS, 8720 Georgia Ave., Suite 501, Silver Spring, MD 20910. *Deadline for applications:* July 15, 1995.

**BCALA Distinguished Service to the Profession Award.** Administered by the Black Caucus of the American Library Association. Administered by the Black Caucus of the American Library Association. *For more information:* Stanton F. Biddle, Box 317, Baruch College, 17 Lexington Avenue, New York, NY 10010.

**BCALA Library Advocacy Awards.** For exceptional service in support of libraries and library services. Administered by the Black Caucus of the American Library Association. *For more information:* Stanton F. Biddle, Box 317, Baruch College, 17 Lexington Avenue, New York, NY 10010.

**CLA Outstanding Service to Librarianship.** An award for distinguished service in the field of Canadian librarianship. Administered by the Canadian Library Association. *For more information:* CLA, 200 Elgin St., Ottawa, Ontario K2P 1L5, Canada. *Donated by:* R.R. Bowker. *Deadline for applications:* December 31, 1995. *1994 winner:* Erik J. Spicer.

**CLA/CAPL Outstanding Public Library Service Award.** An award for outstanding service in the field of Canadian public librarianship. Administered by the Canadian Association of Public Libraries of the Canadian Library Association. *For more information:* CLA, 200 Elgin St., Ottawa, Ontario K2P 1L5, Canada. *Deadline for applications:* January 31, 1995. *1994 winner:* Judith McAnanama.

**CLA/CLTA Merit Award for Distinguished Service as a Library Trustee.** For exceptional service as a trustee in the library field at local, provincial, and national levels. Administered by the Canadian Library Trustees Association of the Canadian Library Association. *For more information:* CLA, 200 Elgin St., Ottawa, Ontario K2P 1L5, Canada. *Deadline for applications:* March 1, 1995.

**FOLUSA Award.** *For more information:* Friends of Libraries U.S.A., 1326 Spruce St., Suite 1105, Philadelphia, PA 19107. *Deadline for applications:* April 7, 1995. *1994 winner:* John F. Cooke.

**MLA Distinguished Public Service Award.** Presented to honor persons whose exemplary actions have served to advance the health, welfare, and intellectual freedom of the public. Awardees are selected only on occasions when the merits of a nominee clearly recommend recognition by the MLA. Administered by the Medical Library Association. *For more information:* MLA, 6 N. Michigan Ave., Suite 300, Chicago, IL 60602. *1994 winner:* Sen. Edward Kennedy.

**MLA President's Award.** For a notable or important contribution to medical librarianship made during the past association year. Administered by the Medical Library Association. *For more information:* MLA, 6 N. Michigan Ave., Suite 300, Chicago, IL 60602. *1992 winner:* Susan Crawford.

**SAA Distinguished Service Award.** To recognize an archival institution for outstanding public service and an exemplary contribution to the archival profession. Administered by the Society of American Archivists. *For more information:* SAA, 600 S. Federal St., Suite 504, Chicago, IL 60605. *Deadline for applications:* April 1995. *1994 winner:* Research Libraries Group.

**SAA J. Franklin Jameson Archival Advocacy Award.** To recognize an individual, institution, or organization not directly involved in archival work, that promotes greater public awareness of archival activities or programs. Administered by the Society of American Archivists. *For more information:* SAA, 600 S. Federal St., Suite 504, Chicago, IL 60605. *Deadline for applications:* April 1995. *1994 winner:* Hudson's Bay Company.

**SLA Fellows.** Given to SLA members in recognition of their leadership in the field of special librarianship and for their outstanding contributions and expected future service to the Association. Administered by the Special Libraries Association. *For more information:* SLA, 1700 18th St., N.W., Washington, DC 20009. *Deadline for applications:* December 2, 1995. *1994 winners:* Judith J. Field, Ellen Steininger Kuner, Dorothy McGarry.

**SLA Hall of Fame Award.** Granted to a member of SLA at or near the end of an active professional career for an extended period of distinguished service to the association in all spheres. Administered by the Special Libraries Association. *For more information:* SLA, 1700 18th St., N.W., Washington, DC 20009. *Deadline for applications:* December 2, 1995. *1994 winners:* Judith Genesen, Herbert S. White.

**SLA Honorary Member.** Presented to an individual (not a member of SLA). Administered by the Special Libraries Association. *For more information:* SLA, 1700 18th St., N.W., Washington, DC 20009. *Deadline for applications:* December 2, 1995. *1994 winner:* Rodney L. Everhart.

**SLA President's Award.** Given to an SLA member or group of members for a notable or important contribution to SLA during the past association year. Administered by the Special Libraries Association. *For more information:* SLA, 1700 18th St., N.W., Washington, DC 20009. *Deadline for applications:* December 2, 1995. *1993 winner:* John Ganly.

**SLA Public Relations Member Achievement Award.** Awards in three categories for outstanding contributions by an SLA member to the association's public relations goals during the previous year. Administered by the Special Libraries Association. *For more information:* SLA, 1700 18th St., N.W., Washington, DC 20009. *Deadline for applications:* December 2, 1995. *1994 winner:* SLA Wisconsin Chapter Public Relations Committee.

## For service to children and young adults

**ALA Grolier Foundation Award.** An annual award, consisting of $1,000 and a citation of achievement presented to a librarian who has made an unusual contribution to the stimulation and guidance of reading by children and young people. The award is given for outstanding work with children and young people through high school age, for continuing service, or in recognition of one particular contribution of lasting value. Administered by the ALA Awards Committee. *For more information:* Peggy Barber, ALA, 50 E. Huron St., Chicago, IL 60611-2795. *Donated by:* Grolier Foundation. *Deadline for applications:* December 1, 1995. *1994 winner:* Jane Botham.

**ALA/AASL Baker & Taylor Distinguished Service Award.** An annual award of $3,000 presented to the individual who has demonstrated excellence and provided an outstanding national or international contribution to school librarianship and school library media development. Administered by the ALA American Association of School Librarians. *For more information:* ALA/AASL, 50 E. Huron St., Chicago, IL 60611-2795. *Donated by:* Baker and Taylor Books. *Deadline for applications:* February 1, 1995. *1994 winner:* Lucille C. Thomas.

**ALA/AASL National School Library Media Program of the Year Award.** Cash awards presented annually to school districts that display outstanding achievement in exemplary library media programs. Schools or districts representing elementary schools, secondary schools, or a combination of both may apply. Administered by the ALA American Association of School Librarians. *For more information:* ALA/AASL, 50 E. Huron St., Chicago, IL 60611-2795. *Donated by:* Encyclopaedia Brittanica Educational

Corporation. *Deadline for applications:* February 1, 1995. *1994 winners:* Duneland School Corporation, Chesterton, Ind.; Lakeview Elementary School, Neenah, Wisc.; Providence Senior High School, Charlotte, N.C.

**ALA/AASL SIRS Distinguished School Administrators Award.** An annual grant of $2,000 presented to a person directly responsible for the administration of a school or group of schools who has made an outstanding and sustained contribution toward furthering the role of the library and its development in elementary and/or secondary education. Administered by the ALA American Association of School Librarians. *For more information:* ALA/AASL, 50 E. Huron St., Chicago, IL 60611-2795. *Donated by:* Social Issues Resources Series, Inc. *Deadline for applications:* February 1, 1995. *1994 winner:* James C. Enochs.

**ALA/ALSC Distinguished Service Award.** A $1,000 award plus service pin to honor an ALSC member who has made significant contributions to library service to children and/or ALSC. Administered by the ALA Association for Library Service to Children. *For more information:* ALA/ALSC, 50 E. Huron St., Chicago, IL 60611-2795. *Deadline for applications:* December 1, 1995. *1994 winner:* Carolyn W. Field.

**ALA/ALSC Econo-Clad Literature Program Award.** One annual $1,000 award to help defray the cost of ALA conference attendance, presented to a member of ALSC who has developed and implemented a unique and outstanding library program for children involving reading and the use of literature with children. The recipient must be a librarian who works directly with children and whose program, targeted at and designed for children, has taken place within the past 12 months in a public library or school library media center. Administered by the ALA Association for Library Service to Children. *For more information:* ALA/ALSC, 50 E. Huron St., Chicago, IL 60611-2795. *Donated by:* Econo-Clad Literature Program. *Deadline for applications:* December 1, 1995. *1994 winner:* Vaunda M. Nelson.

**ALA/YALSA Econo-Clad Reading or Literature Program Award.** An annual award given to a member of YALSA who has developed and implemented a unique and outstanding library program for young adults involving reading and the use of literature. The $1,000 award is to be used to help defray the cost of ALA conference attendance by the winner. Administered by the ALA Young Adult Library Services Association. *For more information:* ALA/YALSA, 50 E. Huron St., Chicago, IL 60611-2795. *Donated by:* Econo-Clad Literature Program. *Deadline for applications:* December 1, 1995. *1994 winner:* Barbara Blosveren.

**CLA/CSLA Canadian School Executive Award.** To a Canadian school executive for distinguished service to school libraries. Administered by the Canadian School Libraries Association of the Canadian Library Association. *For more information:* CLA, 200 Elgin St., Ottawa, Ontario K2P 1L5, Canada. *Deadline for applications:* December 31, 1995. *1994 winners:* E. A. Hodgson, Gary Parkinson.

**CLA/CSLA Margaret B. Scott Award of Merit.** For the development of school libraries at the national level in Canada. Administered by the Canadian School Libraries Association of the Canadian Library Association and the Ontario Library Association. *For more information:* CLA, 200 Elgin St., Ottawa, Ontario K2P 1L5, Canada. *Deadline for applications:* December 31, 1995. *1994 winner:* Dianne Oberg.

**CLA/CSLA National Book Service Teacher-Librarian of the Year Award.** To a school-based teacher librarian who has made an outstanding contribution to school librarianship in Canada. The award consists of a plaque and registration and travel costs to the CLA Annual Conference. Administered by the Canadian School Library Association of the Canadian Library Association. *For more information:* CLA, 200 Elgin St., Ottawa, Ontario K2P 1L5, Canada. *Donated by:* National Book Service. *1994 winner:* Marilynne Earl.

**CLA/HSLS Certificate of Merit.** For an outstanding contribution to high school librarianship. Administered by the High School Library Section of the Catholic Library Association. *For more information:* CLA, c/o Jean R. Bostley, S.S.J., St. Joseph Central High School, 22 Maplewood Ave., Pittsfield, MA 02101. *1994 winner:* Follett Books and Software.

**DeWitt Wallace-Reader's Digest Fund National Library Power Program Grants.** A collaborative effort of the DeWitt Wallace-Reader's Digest Fund, local education funds, and public school districts to develop plans for making school library media centers a focal point for educational activities in their elementary and/or middle schools. The Fund supports programs that help American youth fulfill their educational and career aspirations. Planning grant recipients are eligible for three-year implementation grants of up to $1.2 million pending successful completion of a comprehensive community-supported plan. Implementation grants are to be used for staff development, to match city and state funds for school library materials, to refurbish school library media centers, and to hire Library Power project staff who will be based at the local education fund. *For more information:* National Library Power Program, ALA, 50 E.

Huron St., Chicago, IL 60611-2795; or DeWitt Wallace-Reader's Digest Fund, (212) 953-1208. *1994 winners:* APPLE Corps, Atlanta; Forward in the Fifth, Berea, Ky.; New Haven (Conn.) Public Education Fund, Inc.; San Francisco (Calif.) Education Fund.

## For service to special populations

**ALA Bessie Boehm Moore Award.** An annual award consisting of $1,000 and a citation of achievement, presented to a library organization that has developed an outstanding and creative program for public library service to the aging. Administered by the ALA Awards Committee. *For more information:* Peggy Barber, ALA, 50 E. Huron St., Chicago, IL 60611-2795. *Donated by:* Bessie Boehm Moore. *Deadline for applications:* December 1, 1995. *1994 winner:* Decorah (Iowa) PL.

**ALA EMIERT/Gale Research Multicultural Award.** An annual award of $1,000 and citation given to persons in the library world in recognition of outstanding achievement and leadership in serving the multicultural/multiethnic community with significant collection building, public and outreach services to culturally diverse populations and creative multicultural materials and programs. Administered by the ALA Ethnic Materials Information Exchange Round Table. *For more information:* ALA Office for Library Outreach Services, ALA, 50 E. Huron St., Chicago, IL 60611-2795. *Donated by:* Gale Research. *Deadline for applications:* December 1, 1995.

**ALA/ASCLA Exceptional Service Award.** A citation presented to recognize exceptional service to patients, to the homebound, to medical, nursing, and other professional staff in hospitals, and to inmates, as well as to recognize professional leadership, effective interpretation of programs, pioneering activity, and significant research of experimental projects. Administered by the ALA Association of Specialized and Cooperative Library Agencies. *For more information:* ALA/ASCLA, 50 E. Huron St., Chicago, IL 60611-2795. *Deadline for applications:* December 1, 1995. *1994 winner:* Joanne Crispen.

**ALA/ASCLA Francis Joseph Campbell Citation.** An annual award consisting of a citation and a medal, presented to a person who has made an outstanding contribution to the advancement of library service for the blind and physically handicapped. Administered by the Libraries Serving Special Populations Section of the ALA Association of Specialized and Cooperative Library Agencies. *For more information:* ALA/ASCLA, 50 E. Huron St., Chicago, IL 60611-2795. *Deadline for applications:* December 1, 1995. *1994 winner:* Richard C. Peel.

**ALA/ASCLA National Organization on Disability Award.** An annual award of $1,000 and a certificate are given to a library organization in recognition of either a specific innovative, creative, and well-organized program of services for persons who are disabled or for a library that has made its total services more accessible through changing physical and/or attitudinal barriers. Administered by the ALA Association of Specialized and Cooperative Library Agencies. *For more information:* ALA/ASCLA, 50 E. Huron St., Chicago, IL 60611-2795. *Donated by:* J.C. Penney Co., through the National Organization on Disability. *Deadline for applications:* December 1, 1995. *1994 winner:* Broward County (Fla.) Library.

**ALA/PLA Leonard Wertheimer Multilingual Award.** An award presented to a person, group, or organization in recognition of work that enhances and promotes multilingual public library service. Administered by the ALA Public Library Association. *For more information:* ALA/PLA, 50 E. Huron St., Chicago, IL 60611-2795. *Donated by:* National Textbook Co. Publishing Group. *Deadline for applications:* December 1, 1995. *1994 winners:* Dina Abramowicz, Sylva Manoogian.

**ALA/RASD John Sessions Memorial Award.** A plaque to be presented to a library or a library system in recognition of significant efforts to work with the labor community. Such efforts may include outreach projects to local labor unions; the establishment of, or significant expansion of, special labor collections; or other library activities that serve the labor community. Administered by the ALA Reference and Adult Services Division. *For more information:* ALA/RASD, 50 E. Huron St., Chicago, IL 60611-2795. *Donated by:* AFL/CIO. *Deadline for applications:* December 15, 1995. *1994 winner:* Archives of Labor and Urban Affairs, Walter P. Reuther Library, Wayne State University.

**APALA Distinguished Service Award.** For significant contributions to Asian/Pacific society in the field of library and information science. Administered by the Asian/Pacific American Library Association. *For more information:* Erlinda Regner, Chicago Public Library, 400 S. State St., Chicago, IL 60605.

**CALA Distinguished Service Award.** To a member of CALA. Administered by the Chinese-American Librarians Association. *For more information:* CALA, c/o Sheila Lai, CSU Sacramento, 2000 Jed Smith Drive, Sacramento, CA 95819. *1994 winner:* Julie Tung.

## For social responsibility

**ALA Equality Award.** A certificate and a cash award of $500 given to an individual or group for an outstanding contribution towards promoting equality between women and men in the library profession. The contribution may be either a sustained one or a single outstanding accomplishment. The award may be given for an activist or scholarly contribution in such areas as pay equity, affirmative action, legislative work, and nonsexist education. Administered by the ALA Awards Committee. *For more information:* Peggy Barber, ALA, 50 E. Huron St., Chicago, IL 60611-2795. *Donated by:* Scarecrow Press, Inc. *Deadline for applications:* December 1, 1995. *1994 winner:* Lotsee Patterson.

**ALA Social Issues Resources Series, Inc., Peace Award.** An annual award given to a library, which in the course of its educational and social mission, or to a librarian, who in the course of professional activities, has contributed significantly to the advancement of knowledge related to issues of international peace and security. The contribution may be in the form of, but not limited to, a bibliographical compilation, research and publication of an original historical nature, or a nonprint media creation, display, or distribution. Administered by the ALA Social Responsibilities Round Table. *For more information:* ALA, 50 E. Huron St., Chicago, IL 60611-2795. *Donated by:* Social Issues Resources Series, Inc. *Deadline for applications:* January 6, 1995.

**ALA/ALTA Literacy Award.** An annual award given to that individual who has done an outstanding job in making contributions toward the extirpation of illiteracy. Administered by the ALA American Library Trustee Association. *For more information:* ALA/ALTA, 50 E. Huron St., Chicago, IL 60611-2795. *Deadline for applications:* December 1, 1995. *1994 winner:* Phyllis Kline.

**ALA/PLA Advancement of Literacy Award.** An award presented to an American publisher, bookseller, hardware and/or software dealer, foundation or similar group (not an individual) that has made a significant contribution to the advancement of adult literacy. Administered by the Adult Lifelong Learning Section of the ALA Public Library Association. *For more information:* ALA/PLA, 50 E. Huron St., Chicago, IL 60611-2795. *Donated by:* Library Journal. *Deadline for applications:* December 1, 1995. *1994 winner:* California State Library Foundation.

**CLA/CLTA Achievement in Literacy Award.** To recognize a public library board that has initiated an innovative program which has made a significant contribution to the advancement of literacy in its community. Administered by the Canadian Library Trustee Association of the Canadian Library Association. *For more information:* CLA, 200 Elgin St., Ottawa, Ontario K2P 1L5, Canada. *Deadline for applications:* March 1, 1995.

## For specialized military and congregational libraries

**ALA Armed Forces Library Achievement Citation.** An annual citation presented to members of the Armed Forces Library Round Table who have made significant contributions to the development of armed forces library service, and to organizations encouraging an interest in libraries and reading. Administered by the Armed Forces Library Round Table. *For more information:* ALA Washington Office, 110 Maryland Ave., N.E., Washington, DC 20002-5626. *Deadline for applications:* December 1, 1995. *1994 winner:* Nellie B. Stricklan.

**ALA Armed Forces Library Certificate of Merit.** This award is presented in recognition of special contributions to Armed Forces Libraries. Recipients need not be librarians or members of ALA. Administered by the Armed Forces Library Round Table. *For more information:* ALA Washington Office, 110 Maryland Ave., N.E., Washington, DC 20002-5626. *Deadline for applications:* December 1, 1995. *1994 winner:* Daniel S. Jones.

**ALA Armed Forces Library Newsbank Scholarship Award.** This award recognizes members of the Armed Forces Library Round Table who have given exemplary service in the area of library support for off-duty education programs in the armed forces. Administered by the ALA Armed Forces Library Round Table. *For more information:* ALA Washington Office, 110 Maryland Ave., N.E., Washington, DC 20002-5626. *Deadline for applications:* December 1, 1995. *1994 winner:* Nova C. Maddox.

**CLA/PLS Aggiornamento Award.** For an outstanding contribution to the growth of parish librarianship. Administered by the Parish Library Section of the Catholic Library Association. *For more information:* CLA, c/o Jean R. Bostley, S.S.J., St. Joseph Central High School, 22 Maplewood Ave., Pittsfield, MA 01201. *1994 winner:* Resource Publications, Inc.

**CSLA Award for Outstanding Congregational Librarian.** For distinguished service to the congregation and/or community through devotion to the congregational library. Administered by the

Church and Synagogue Library Association. *For more information:* CSLA, Box 19357, Portland, OR 92719. *1994 winner:* Ruth Ridgeway.

**CSLA Award for Outstanding Congregational Library.** For responding in creative and innovative ways to the library's mission of reaching and serving the congregation and/or the wider community. Administered by the Church and Synagogue Library Association. *For more information:* CSLA, Box 19357, Portland, OR 92719. *1994 winner:* Steven Hill.

**CSLA Award for Outstanding Contribution to Congregational Libraries.** For providing inspiration, guidance, leadership, or resources to enrich the field of church or synagogue librarianship. Administered by the Church and Synagogue Library Association. *For more information:* CSLA, Box 19357, Portland, OR 92719. *1994 winner:* Charles C. Brown.

**CSLA Pat Tabler Memorial Scholarship Award.** Presented to a librarian who has shown initiative and creativity in starting a new, or renewing, a congregational library. Administered by the Church and Synagogue Library Association. *For more information:* CSLA, Box 19357, Portland, OR 97219.

**SAA Sister M. Claude Lane Award.** For significant contribution to the field of religious archives. Administered by the Society of American Archivists. *For more information:* SAA, 600 S. Federal St., Suite 504, Chicago, IL 60605. *Deadline for applications:* April 1995. *Donated by:* Society of Southwest Archivists. *1994 winner:* Sr. Emma Busam, O.S.U.

## For technology

**ALA Mecklermedia Library of the Future Award.** An annual award of $2,000 and a free-standing piece of Tiffany crystal to an individual library, library consortium, group of librarians, or support organization for innovative planning for applications of or development of patron training programs about information technology in a library setting. Administered by the ALA Awards Committee. *For more information:* Peggy Barber, ALA, 50 E. Huron St., Chicago, IL 60611-2795. *Donated by:* Mecklermedia Corporation. *Deadline for applications:* December 1, 1995. *1994 winner:* University of Iowa Libraries.

**ALA/AASL Follett Software Company Microcomputer in the Media Center Award.** This award is designed to recognize and honor library media specialists who have demonstrated innovative approaches to microcomputer applications in their respective libraries or media centers. There are two award categories: 1) for the innovative use of the microcomputer in the school library media center in an elementary (K–6) setting; 2) for the innovative use of the microcomputer in the school library media center in a secondary (7–12) setting. Two national winners may be recommended, one in each category. Each recipient librarian will receive a $1,000 cash award and travel to the award ceremony; and each recipient library will receive a $500 cash award. Administered by the ALA American Association of School Librarians. *For more information:* ALA/AASL, 50 E. Huron St., Chicago, IL 60611-2795. *Donated by:* Follett Software Co. *Deadline for applications:* February 1, 1995. *1994 winner:* Becky Mather.

**ALA/LITA Gaylord Award for Achievement in Library and Information Technology.** An annual award of $1,000 presented to recognize distinguished leadership, notable development or application of technology, superior accomplishments in research or education, or original contributions to the literature of the field. Administered by the ALA Library and Information Technology Association. *For more information:* ALA/LITA, 50 E. Huron St., Chicago, IL 60611-2795. *Donated by:* Gaylord Bros., Inc. *Deadline for applications:* December 15, 1995. *1994 winner:* Davis B. McCarn.

**ALA/LITA Library Hi Tech Award.** An award of $1,000 presented to a single individual or institution for a single seminal work or body of work taking place within or continuing into the five years preceding the award, that shows outstanding achievement in communicating to educate practitioners within the library field in library and information technology. *For more information:* ALA/LITA, 50 E. Huron St., Chicago, IL 60611-2795. *Donated by:* Pierian Press. *Deadline for applications:* December 15, 1995. *1994 winner:* Ching-chih Chen.

**ALA/PLA Library Video Award.** Recognition and a $1,000 honorarium to a public library demonstrating excellence and innovation in library programming with video and the ability to market and promote the use of these services to library users. Administered by the ALA Public Library Association. *For more information:* ALA/PLA, 50 E. Huron St., Chicago, IL 60611-2795. *Donated by:* Baker and Taylor Video. *Deadline for applications:* December 1, 1995. *1994 winner:* Wichita (Kan.) PL.

**CLA/Meckler Award for Innovative Technology.** An annual award of $500 and a plaque to honor a CLA member or members for innovative use and application of technology in a Canadian library setting. Administered by the Canadian Library Association. *For more information:* CLA, 200 Elgin St., Suite 602, Ottawa, Ontario, Canada K2P 1L5. *Donated by:* Meckler Corporation. *Deadline for applications:*

March 1, 1995. *1994 winners:* National Library of Canada and the Canadian Institute for Scientific and Technical Information.

**MLA Frank Bradway Rogers Information Advancement Award.** A cash award of $500 for an outstanding contribution to the application of technology to the delivery of health sciences information, to the science of information, or to the facilitation of information delivery. Administered by the Medical Library Association. *For more information:* MLA, 6 N. Michigan Ave., Suite 300, Chicago, IL 60602. *Donated by:* Institute for Scientific Information. *Deadline for applications:* September 1, 1995. *1994 winner:* Nancy Start.

**SLA Meckler Award for Innovations in Technology.** An honorarium to honor an SLA member for innovative uses and applications in technology in a special library setting. Administered by the Special Libraries Association. *For more information:* SLA, 1700 18th St., N.W., Washington, DC 20009. *Donated by:* Meckler Corporation. *Deadline for applications:* March 1995. *1993 winner:* Karen Bleakley.

---

## Librarians on leadership

**Robert H. Rohlf, director, Hennepin County (Minn.) Library:**
Last year I went into a budget meeting, and I brought in a whole bunch of books, and I piled up two stacks of books, and I had another item in a sack, and they didn't know what it was. I said, "This number of books is what the average citizen in the county took out of our libraries last year, and this is the number they used in the library." I reached in the bag, and I brought out half a book, and I said, "This is the number of books we bought last year. Now you've got to do something about that." An administrator came up to me afterwards and said, "That was the most effective audiovisual presentation I've ever seen." And I said, "Why? It's just a fact."

**Gary Strong, state librarian of California:**
I enjoy the hell out of what I do. I really enjoy it. I frequently on weekends may be out playing tennis with some other guys, and they will begin moaning about the "Monday syndrome," and they look upon me as a weirdo because I'm excited to be getting back to the work at the library and the opportunities at hand. That has rarely waned.

**Eric Moon, former president of Scarecrow Press:**
I'm terribly nervous about speaking always . . . and I don't like doing it, but you have to overcome that fear.

*[Moon reminisced about the Library Association when he was extremely active, speaking all over England.]* I couldn't get over this nervousness, and they had a speaker there who was one of the senior ministers in the government who was the most fluid, articulate speaker I had ever heard in my life, hardly used a note, so cool. And I went up to him afterwards and said, "God, that was incredible. Would you tell me how you can do that sort of stuff without being nervous?" And he said, "My boy, if ever you get up there and you are not nervous, you won't be worth a damn." So that encouraged me a bit.

*[Moon also described chairing a meeting in New York when John Lindsay then Mayor of the city, was the speaker.]* I was sitting next to him when he was at the lectern, and his hands were visibly shaking. . . . they said the same thing about Kennedy at his inauguration, his hands were shaking at the podium. The only thing you learn through experience is how to hide it completely so that people won't know . . . and I think I've learned to do that.

*Source:* Brooke E. Sheldon, *Leaders in Libraries: Styles and Strategies for Success* (Chicago: American Library Association, 1991). 93pp.

# The master's degree

**LIBRARIES IN THE UNITED STATES** contribute fundamentally to the processes of democracy, public education, research and development, and industrial competitiveness. They are critically important agencies and institutions in our society.

Librarians are professionals who organize and preserve recordable information and knowledge, provide library and information services, and deliver information products. Librarians contribute fundamentally to excellence in library and information services by managing library resources prudently, by exercising sound professional judgment in fulfilling their duties and public responsibilities, and by promoting unrestricted access to information.

Within the profession, librarians have consistently evaluated the demands associated with their responsibilities and have developed academic programs appropriate to these requirements. Professional education occurs at the graduate level with curricula that provide a focus for the theoretical and philosophical issues relevant to library and information services. The academic courses provide managerial and technical education, preparing graduates to create, manage, and use information resources in a wide variety of settings. Successful completion of a program of this type, resulting in the master's degree for library and information professionals, provides the requisite education for professional entry into positions in all types of libraries, information agencies, and information services.

## An effective educational path

The need for and value of professional education have long been recognized. Professional education is generally explicitly connected with a program of substantial length in an institution of higher education. In the United States, the Council on Postsecondary Accreditation recognizes approximately forty associations that accredit schools or programs for specialized professional study. Among these, the American Library Association (ALA) is recognized as the accrediting agency for graduate programs in library and information studies (see pp. 165–69). The National Council for the Accreditation of Teacher Education (NCATE) is recognized as the accrediting agency for education units (schools or departments) in which a specialty in school library media may be offered. The ALA cooperates with NCATE in preparing and reviewing curriculum guidelines for those programs.

The master's programs are reviewed to verify that their content is appropriate for professional education, their approach is sufficiently theoretical, their faculty are capable, and their offerings are responsive to constituencies and changing demands in the information environment. These programs concentrate on recordable information and knowledge and the services and technologies to facilitate their management and use. The curriculum of library and information studies encompasses information and knowledge creation, communication, identification, selection, acquisition, organization and description, storage and retrieval, preservation, analysis, interpretation, evaluation, synthesis, dissemination, and management. In addition, the curriculum:

- fosters development of library and information professionals who will assume an assertive role in providing services;
- emphasizes an evolving body of knowledge that reflects the findings of basic and applied research from relevant fields;
- integrates the theory, application, and use of technology;
- responds to the needs of a rapidly changing multicultural, multiethnic, multilingual society including the needs of underserved groups;
- responds to the needs of a rapidly changing technological and global society;
- provides direction for future development of the field; and
- promotes commitment to continuous professional growth.

The curriculum encompasses elements of professional practice including knowledge, skills, and attitudes required for such functions as reference services, cataloging, resource selection, automation, and library administration. In addition, the curriculum provides students with exposure to professional issues and competencies, including a systematic body of theory and knowledge, basic social values, a sense of common identity, a code of ethics, and a commitment to intellectual freedom which will underlie their professional careers. For school library media specialists, the curriculum also provides content needed to meet state certification requirements. The curriculum links professional practice with academic study and research to develop understanding and knowledge of:

- the libraries' responsibilities as educational and information organizations;
- the theoretical aspects of collecting, organizing, preserving, presenting and providing access to information;
- information sources and the competencies required to assist users by locating and interpreting library materials, and retrieving and analyzing required information;
- the principles of administration required to organize information programs and provide information services;
- the principles of intellectual freedom embodied in the ALA Library Bill of Rights;
- the ethical responsibilities of librarians and information professionals as embodied in the ALA Code of Ethics; and
- the librarian's responsibility to help people of all ages to become information literate and effective users of ideas and information.

The contemporary field of study recognizes the interdisciplinary demands of professional work, and therefore includes components related to communications, the research process, media and technology, and information science. Specific conceptual and methodological concerns which are essential components include:

- relationships of libraries and librarians with other institutions, education agencies, professions, and occupations that provide information services;
- identification of information user needs and behaviors and the roles and responsibilities of librarians in identifying and responding to them;

- introduction to existing and emerging information technologies and their impact on the access, storage, and delivery of information;
- knowledge of the content and process of library and information studies research; and
- recognition and respect for society's cultural, ethnic, and linguistic diversity and the attendant responsibilities to serve the community and to show sensitivity to the needs of special groups.

## Foundation for the professional's career

The curricula of these programs encompass substantial elements of professional practice and prepare graduates to assume public services, technical services, technology-related, and managerial positions in public libraries, academic institutions, school library media centers, special libraries, government agencies, and industry. The commitment to service which these programs inspire is unique among the educational tracks that prepare individuals for information-related work. Employers choosing program graduates are able to offer their communities and organizations assurance that they have hired personnel qualified for their positions, and administrators have considerable flexibility in staffing decisions given the versatility of program graduates. In the majority of settings, graduates are able to contribute immediately, both in their specific positions and to the goals of their organizations.

It is the breadth, as well as the theoretical nature of the curricula in these programs, that aims graduates towards the achievement of the highest level of competence—the professional, managerial and research level. Education for professional practice in the field of library and information studies provides the foundation for the ultimate realization of the practitioner's career goals.

*Source: The Master's Degree for Library and Information Professionals*
(Chicago: American Library Association, 1993). 3p.

# Accredited library programs

THE FOLLOWING GRADUATE LIBRARY and information studies programs are accredited (as of fall 1994) by the American Library Association under its *Standards for Accreditation*. All programs offer a master's-level degree; those marked with an asterisk(*) offer a doctorate or post-master's specialist or certificate program.

**\*Catholic University of America,** School of Library and Information Science, Washington, DC 20064; (202) 319-5085. Elizabeth S. Aversa, dean.

**\*Clarion University of Pennsylvania,** College of Communication, Computer Information Science and Library Science, Clarion, PA 16214; (814) 226-2328. Rita Rice Flaningam, dean.

**\*Clark Atlanta University,** School of Library and Information Studies, Atlanta, GA 30314; (404) 880-8697. Charles D. Churchwell, dean.

**Dalhousie University,** School of Library and Information Studies, Halifax, Nova Scotia, Canada B3H 4H8; (902) 494-3656. Louis Vagianos, interim director.

**\*Drexel University,** College of Information Studies, Philadelphia, PA 19104; (215) 895-2474. Richard H. Lytle, dean.

**\*Emporia State University,** School of Library and Information Management, Emporia, KS 66801; (316) 341-5203. Martha L. Hale, dean.

**\*Florida State University,** School of Library and Information Studies, Tallahassee, FL 32306-2048; (904) 644-5775. F. William Summers, dean.

**\*Indiana University,** School of Library and Information Science, Library 011, Bloomington, IN 47405-1801; (812) 855-2018. Blaise Cronin, dean.

**\*Kent State University,** School of Library and Information Science, Kent, OH 44242; (216) 672-2782. Rosemary R. DuMont, dean.

**\*Long Island University,** Palmer School of Library and Information Science, Brookville, NY 11548; (516) 299-2855. Anne Woodsworth, dean.

**\*Louisiana State University,** School of Library and Information Science, Baton Rouge, LA 70803; (504) 388-3158. Bert R. Boyce, dean.

**McGill University,** Graduate School of Library and Information Studies, Montreal, Québec, Canada H3A 1Y1; (514) 398-4204. J. Andrew Large, director.

**North Carolina Central University,** School of Library and Information Sciences, P.O. Box 19586, Durham, NC 27707; (919) 560-6485. Benjamin F. Speller, Jr., dean.

**\*Pratt Institute,** School of Information and Library Science, Brooklyn, NY 11205; (718) 636-3702. S. M. Matta, dean.

**\*Queens College, City University of New York,** Graduate School of Library and Information Studies, 254 Rosenthal Library, Flushing, NY 11367; (718) 997-3790. Marianne Cooper, director.

**\*Rosary College,** Graduate School of Library and Information Science, River Forest, IL 60305; (708) 524-6844. Michael E. D. Koenig, dean.

**\*Rutgers University,** School of Communication, Information and Library Studies, 4 Huntington St., New Brunswick, NJ 08903; (908) 932-7917. Betty J. Turock, chair and program director.

**\*St. John's University,** Division of Library and Information Science, 800 Utopia Parkway, Jamaica, NY 11439; (718) 990-6200. James A. Benson, director.

**San Jose State University,** School of Library and Information Science, San Jose, CA 95192-0029; (408) 924-2492. Stuart A. Sutton, director.

**\*Simmons College,** Graduate School of Library and Information Science, Boston, MA 02115-5898; (617) 521-2805. James M. Matarazzo, dean.

**\*Southern Connecticut State University,** School of Library Science and Instructional Technology, New Haven, CT 06515; (203) 392-5781. Edward C. Harris, dean.

**\*Syracuse University,** School of Information Studies, 4-206 Center for Science and Technology, Syracuse, NY 13244-4100; (315) 443-2911. Jeffrey Katzer, interim dean.

**\*Texas Woman's University,** School of Library and Information Studies, Denton, TX 76204-0905; (817) 898-2602. Keith Swigger, dean.

**Université de Montréal,** Ecole de bibliothéconomie et des sciences de l'information, Montréal, Québec, Canada H3C 3J7; (514) 343-6044. Gilles Deschatelets, director.

**\*University at Albany, State University of New York,** School of Information Science and Policy, Albany, NY 12222; (518) 442-5115. Vincent Aceto, interim dean.

**\*University at Buffalo, State University of New York,** School of Information and Library Studies, Buffalo, NY 14260. George S. Bobinski, dean.

**\*University of Alabama,** School of Library and Information Studies, Tuscaloosa, AL 35487-0252; (205) 348-4610. Philip M. Turner, dean.

**University of Alberta,** School of Library and Information Studies, Edmonton, Alberta, Canada T6G 2J4; (403) 492-4578. Sheila Bertram, director.

**\*University of Arizona,** School of Library Science, Tucson, AZ 85719; (602) 621-3565. Charlie D. Hurt, director.

**University of British Columbia,** School of Library, Archival and Information Studies, Vancouver, British Columbia, Canada V6T 1Z1; (604) 822-2404. Ken Haycock, director.

**\*University of California, Los Angeles,** Graduate School of Library and Information Science, Los Angeles, CA 90024-1520; (310) 825-8799. Beverly P. Lynch, dean.

*University of Hawaii, School of Library and Information Studies, Honolulu, HI 96822; (808) 956-7321. Miles M. Jackson, dean.

*University of Illinois, Graduate School of Library and Information Science, 501 E. Daniel, Champaign, IL 61820; (217) 333-3281. Leigh Estabrook, dean.

University of Iowa, School of Library and Information Science, Iowa City, IA 52242-1420; (319) 335-5707. Carl F. Orgren, director.

University of Kentucky, School of Library and Information Science, Lexington, KY 40506-0039; (606) 257-8876. Donald O. Case, director.

*University of Maryland, College of Library and Information Science, College Park, MD 20742; (301) 405-2033. Ann E. Prentice, dean.

*University of Michigan, School of Information and Library Studies, Ann Arbor, MI 48109-1092; (313) 764-9376. Daniel E. Atkins, dean.

University of Missouri, Columbia, School of Library and Informational Science, Columbia, MO 65211; (314) 882-4546. Thomas R. Kochtanek, acting dean.

*University of North Carolina, School of Information and Library Science, Chapel Hill, NC 27599-3360; (919) 962-8366. Barbara B. Moran, dean.

University of North Carolina at Greensboro, Department of Library and Information Studies, Greensboro, NC 27412; (910) 334-3477. Marilyn L. Miller, chair.

*University of North Texas, School of Library and Information Sciences, Denton, TX 76203; (817) 565-2445. Raymond F. von Dran, dean.

*University of Oklahoma, School of Library and Information Studies, Norman, OK 73019-0528; (405) 325-3921. June Lester, dean.

*University of Pittsburgh, School of Library and Information Science, Pittsburgh, PA 15260; (412) 624-5230. Toni Carbo Bearman, dean.

University of Puerto Rico, Escuela Graduada de Bibliotecología y Ciencia de la Información, P.O. Box 21906, San Juan, PR 00931-1906; (809) 763-6199. Mariano A. Maura, director.

---

### Closings of ALA-accredited programs since 1978

| | |
|---|---|
| 1978 | University of Oregon |
| 1981 | Alabama A&M |
| 1983 | Western Michigan University |
| 1984 | SUNY Geneseo |
| 1984 | University of Mississippi |
| 1985 | University of Minnesota |
| 1985 | University of Denver |
| 1985 | Ball State University |
| 1986 | Case Western Reserve University |
| 1986 | University of Southern California |
| 1988 | Emory University |
| 1988 | Vanderbilt University |
| 1990 | University of Chicago |
| 1992 | Columbia University |
| 1993 | Brigham Young University |
| 1994 | Northern Illinois University |

In 1970 there were 50 accredited programs; in 1980 there were 69, and in 1994 there are 57. The highest number was 70 programs, in March 1982. Since 1978 there has been a 17% reduction in the number of accredited programs.

Since 1980, three programs have been accredited for the first time: University of Southern Mississippi, 1980; University of North Carolina at Greensboro, 1982; and University of Puerto Rico, 1990.

*Source:* ALA Office of Accreditation.

**University of Rhode Island,** Graduate School of Library and Information Studies, Rodman Hall, Kingston, RI 02881-0815; (401) 792-2947. Elizabeth Futas, director.

**\*University of South Carolina,** College of Library and Information Science, Columbia, SC 29208; (803) 777-3858. Fred W. Roper, dean.

**University of South Florida,** Division of Library and Information Science, Tampa, FL 33620-7800; (813) 974-3520. Kathleen de la Peña McCook, director.

**University of Southern Mississippi,** School of Library and Information Science, Hattiesburg, MS 39406; (601) 266-4228. Joy Greiner, director.

**University of Tennessee, Knoxville,** Graduate School of Library and Information Science, Knoxville, TN 37996-4330; (615) 974-2148. José-Marie Griffiths, director.

**University of Texas at Austin,** Graduate School of Library and Information Science, Austin, TX 78712-1276; (512) 471-3821. Brooke E. Sheldon, dean.

**\*University of Toronto,** Faculty of Information Studies, Toronto, Ontario, Canada M5S 1A1; (416) 978-3202. Adele M. Fasick, dean.

**University of Washington,** Graduate School of Library and Information Science, 133 Suzzallo, FM-30, Seattle, WA 98195; (206) 543-1794. Phyllis Van Orden, director.

**\*University of Western Ontario,** Graduate School of Library and Information Science, London, Ontario, Canada N6G 1H1; (519) 661-3542. Jean Tague-Sutcliffe, dean.

**\*University of Wisconsin-Madison,** School of Library and Information Studies, Helen C. White Hall 4217, 600 North Park St., Madison, WI 53706; (608) 263-2900. James Krikelas, interim director.

**\*University of Wisconsin-Milwaukee,** School of Library and Information Science, 2400 E. Hartford Ave., Enderis Hall 1110, Milwaukee, WI 53211; (414) 229-4707. Mohammed M. Aman, dean.

**\*Wayne State University,** Library and Information Science Program, 106 Kresge Library, Detroit, MI 48202; (313) 577-1825. Robert P. Holley, director.

*Source: Library & Information Studies Accredited Master's Programs*
(Chicago: ALA Committee on Accreditation, October 1994).

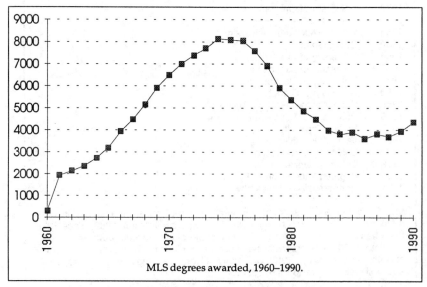

MLS degrees awarded, 1960–1990.

*Source:* National Center for Education Statistics, *120 Years of American Education: A Statistical Portrait* (Washington, D.C.: U.S. Department of Education, January 1993). 107p.

# Standards for accreditation of master's programs in library and information studies

THE ALA COMMITTEE ON ACCREDITATION is the official accrediting agency for master's programs in library and information studies. Accreditation ensures that these programs meet appropriate standards of quality and integrity.

A school seeking initial accreditation of its program must file a letter of intent with the director of the ALA Office for Accreditation at least two years prior to the date of the anticipated review. An initial accreditation requires an on-site review. When a program is granted initial accreditation, the accreditation status is retroactive to cover the academic year prior to on-site review.

These standards describe the essential features of programs of education that prepare library and information professionals. Within the context of the school's rights and obligations regarding initiative, experimentation, innovation, and individual programmatic differences, these standards identify the indispensable components of such programs. The standards are based on qualitative rather than quantitative measures. Evaluation based on qualitative measures ultimately depends on the observation and judgment of experienced and capable evaluators. The programs are granted accreditation when the evaluators determine that they meet these standards.

## Mission, goals, and objectives

A school's mission and program goals are pursued, and its program objectives achieved, through implementation of a broad-based planning process that involves the constituency that a program seeks to serve. Consistent with the values of the parent institution and the culture and mission of the school, program goals and objectives foster quality education.

Program objectives are stated in terms of educational results to be achieved and reflect:

- the essential character of the field of library and information studies; that is, recordable information and knowledge, and the services and technologies to facilitate their management and use, encompassing information and knowledge creation, communication, identification, selection, acquisition, organization and description, storage and retrieval, preservation, analysis, interpretation, evaluation, synthesis, dissemination, and management;
- the philosophy, principles, and ethics of the field;
- appropriate principles of specialization identified in applicable policy statements and documents of relevant professional organizations;
- the value of teaching and service to the advancement of the field;
- the importance of research to the advancement of the field's knowledge base;
- the importance of contributions of library and information studies to other fields of knowledge;
- the importance of contributions of other fields of knowledge to library and information studies;
- the role of library and information services in a rapidly changing multicultural, multiethnic, multilingual society, including the role of serving the needs of underserved groups;

- the role of library and information services in a rapidly changing technological and global society;
- the needs of the constituencies that a program seeks to serve.

Within the context of these standards each program is judged on the degree to which it attains its objectives. In accord with the mission of the school, clearly defined, publicly stated, and regularly reviewed program goals and objectives form the essential frame of reference for meaningful external and internal evaluation. The evaluation of program goals and objectives involves those served: students, faculty, employers, alumni, and other constituents.

## Curriculum

The curriculum is based on goals and objectives and evolves in response to a systematic planning process. Within this general framework, the curriculum provides, through a variety of educational experiences, for the study of theory, principles, practice, and values necessary for the provision of service in libraries and information agencies and in other contexts.

The curriculum is concerned with recordable information and knowledge, and the services and technologies to facilitate their management and use. The curriculum of library and information studies encompasses information and knowledge creation, communication, identification, selection, acquisition, organization and description, storage and retrieval, preservation, analysis, interpretation, evaluation, synthesis, dissemination, and management.

The curriculum:

- fosters development of library and information professionals who will assume an assertive role in providing services;
- emphasizes an evolving body of knowledge that reflects the findings of basic and applied research from relevant fields;
- integrates the theory, application, and use of technology;
- responds to the needs of a rapidly changing multicultural, multiethnic, multilingual society including the needs of underserved groups;
- responds to the needs of a rapidly changing technological and global society;
- provides direction for future development of the field; and
- promotes commitment to continuous professional growth.

The curriculum provides the opportunity for students to construct coherent programs of study that allow individual needs, goals, and aspirations to be met within the context of program requirements established by the school and that will foster development of the competencies necessary for productive careers. The curriculum includes as appropriate cooperative degree programs, interdisciplinary coursework and research, experiential opportunities, and other similar activities. Course content and sequence relationships within the curriculum are evident.

When a program includes study of services and activities in specialized fields, these specialized learning experiences are built upon a general foundation of library and information studies. The design of specialized learning experiences takes into account the statements of knowledge and competencies developed by relevant professional organizations.

The curriculum, regardless of forms or locations of delivery selected by the school, conforms to the requirements of these standards.

The curriculum is continually reviewed and receptive to innovation; its evaluation is used for ongoing appraisal, to make improvements, and to plan for the future. Evaluation of the curriculum includes assessment of students' achievements and their subsequent accomplishments. Evaluation involves those served by the program: students, faculty, employers, alumni, and other constituents.

## Faculty

The school has a faculty capable of accomplishing program objectives. Full-time faculty members are qualified for appointment to the graduate faculty within the parent institution and are sufficient in number and in diversity of specialties to carry out the major share of the teaching, research, and service activities required for a program, wherever and however delivered. Part-time faculty, when appointed, balance and complement the teaching competencies of the full-time faculty. Particularly in the teaching of specialties that are not represented in the expertise of the full-time faculty, part-time faculty enrich the quality and diversity of a program.

The school demonstrates the high priority it attaches to teaching, research, and service by its appointments and promotions; by encouragement of innovation in teaching, research, and service; and through provision of a stimulating learning and research environment.

The school has policies to recruit and retain faculty from multicultural, multiethnic, and multilingual backgrounds. Explicit and equitable faculty personnel policies and procedures are published, accessible, and implemented.

The qualifications of each faculty member include competence in designated teaching areas, technological awareness, effectiveness in teaching, and active participation in appropriate organizations.

For each full-time faculty member the qualifications include a sustained record of accomplishment in research or other appropriate scholarship.

The faculty hold advanced degrees from a variety of academic institutions. The faculty evidence diversity of backgrounds, ability to conduct research in the field, and specialized knowledge covering program content. In addition, they demonstrate skill in academic planning and evaluation, have a substantial and pertinent body of relevant experience, interact with faculty of other disciplines, and maintain close and continuing liaison with the field. The faculty nurture an intellectual environment that enhances the accomplishment of program objectives. These characteristics apply to faculty regardless of forms or locations of delivery of programs.

Faculty assignments relate to the needs of a program and to the competencies and interests of individual faculty members. These assignments assure that the quality of instruction is maintained throughout the year and take into account the time needed by the faculty for teaching, student counseling, research, professional development, and institutional and professional service.

Procedures are established for systematic evaluation of faculty; evaluation considers accomplishment and innovation in the areas of teaching, research, and service. Within applicable institutional policies, faculty, students, and others are involved in the evaluation process.

## Students

The school formulates recruitment, admission, financial aid, placement, and other academic and administrative policies for students that are consistent with the school's mission and program goals and objectives; the policies reflect the needs and values of the constituencies served by a program. The school has policies to recruit and retain a multicultural, multiethnic, and multilingual student body from a variety of backgrounds. The composition of the student body is such that it fosters a learning environment consistent with the school's mission and program goals and objectives.

Current, accurate, and easily accessible information on the school and its program is available to students and the general public. This information includes announcements of program goals and objectives, descriptions of curricula, information on faculty, admission requirements, availability of financial aid, criteria for evaluating student performance, assistance with placement, and other policies and procedures. The school demonstrates that it has procedures to support these policies.

Standards for admission are applied consistently. Students admitted to a program have earned a bachelor's degree from an accredited institution; the policies and procedures for waiving any admission standard or academic prerequisite are stated clearly and applied consistently. Assessment of an application is based on a combined evaluation of academic, intellectual, and other qualifications as they relate to the constituencies served by a program, a program's goals and objectives, and the career objectives of the individual. Within the framework of institutional policy and programs, the admission policy for a program ensures that applicants possess sufficient interest, aptitude, and qualifications to enable successful completion of a program and subsequent contribution to the field.

Students construct coherent programs of study that allow individual needs, goals, and aspirations to be met within the context of program requirements established by the school. Students receive systematic, multi-faceted evaluation of their achievements. Students have access to continuing opportunities for guidance, counseling, and placement assistance.

The school provides an environment that fosters student participation in the definition and determination of the total learning experience. Students are provided with opportunities to form student organizations and to participate in the formulation, modification, and implementation of policies affecting academic and student affairs.

The school applies the results of evaluation of student achievement to program development. Procedures are established for systematic evaluation of the degree to which a program's academic and administrative policies and activities regarding students are accomplishing its objectives. Within applicable institutional policies, faculty, students, staff, and others are involved in the evaluation process.

## Administration and financial support

The school is an integral yet distinctive academic unit within the institution. Its autonomy is sufficient to assure that the intellectual content of its program, the selection and promotion of its faculty, and the selection of its students are determined by the school within the general guidelines of the institution. The parent institution provides the resources and administrative support needed for the attainment of program objectives.

The school's faculty, staff, and students have the same opportunity for representation on the institution's advisory or policy-making bodies as do those of comparable units throughout the institution. The school's adminis-trative relationships with other academic units enhance the intellectual envi-ronment and support interdisciplinary interaction; further, these administra-tive relationships encourage participation in the life of the parent institution.

The executive officer of a program has title, salary, status, and authority comparable to heads of similar units in the parent institution. In addition to academic qualifications comparable to those required of the faculty, the executive officer has leadership skills, administrative ability, experience, and understanding of developments in the field and in the academic environment needed to fulfill the responsibilities of the position. The school's executive officer nurtures an intellectual environment that enhances the pursuit of the school's mission and program goals and the accomplishment of its program objectives; that environment also encourages faculty and student interaction with other academic units and promotes the socialization of students into the field.

The school's administrative and other staff are adequate to support the executive officer and faculty in the performance of their responsibilities. The staff contributes to the fulfillment of the school's mission and program goals and objectives. Within its institutional framework the school uses effective decision-making processes that are determined mutually by the executive officer and the faculty, who regularly evaluate these processes and use the results.

The parent institution provides continuing financial support sufficient to develop and maintain library and information studies education in accordance with the general principles set forth in these standards. The level of support provides a reasonable expectation of financial viability and is related to the number of faculty, administrative and support staff, instructional resources, and facilities needed to carry out the school's program of teaching, research, and service.

Compensation for a program's executive officer, faculty, and other staff is equitably established according to their education, experience, responsibilities, and accomplishments and is sufficient to attract, support, and retain personnel needed to attain program goals and objectives.

Institutional funds for research projects, professional development, travel, and leaves with pay are available on the same basis as in comparable units of the institution. Student financial aid from the parent institution is available on the same basis as in comparable units of the institution.

The school's planning and evaluation process includes review of both its administrative policies and its fiscal policies and financial support. Within applicable institutional policies, faculty, staff, students, and others are involved in the evaluation process. Evaluation is used for ongoing appraisal to make improvements and to plan for the future.

## Physical resources and facilities

A program has access to physical resources and facilities that are sufficient to the accomplishment of its objectives.

Physical facilities provide a functional learning environment for students and faculty; enhance the opportunities for research, teaching, service, consultation, and communication; and promote efficient and effective administration of the school's program, regardless of the forms or locations of delivery.

Instructional and research facilities and services for meeting the needs of students and faculty include access to library and multimedia resources and services, computer and other information technologies, accommodations for independent study, and media production facilities.

The staff and the services provided for a program by libraries, media centers, and information technology facilities, as well as all other support facilities, are sufficient for the level of use required and specialized to the degree needed. These facilities are appropriately staffed, convenient, accessible to the disabled, and available when needed, regardless of forms or locations of delivery of the school's program.

The school's planning and evaluation process includes review of the adequacy of access to physical resources and facilities for the delivery of a program. Within applicable institutional policies, faculty, staff, students, and others are involved in the evaluation process.

*Sources: Standards for Accreditation of Master's Programs in Library & Information Studies* (Chicago: ALA Office for Accreditation, 1992). 29p.; *Accreditation Under the 1992 Standards for Accreditation of Master's Programs in Library and Information Studies: An Overview* (Chicago: ALA Office for Accreditation, 1993). 19p.

# Requirements for school library media specialists

SCHOOL LIBRARY MEDIA SPECIALISTS have a broad undergraduate education with a liberal arts background and hold a master's degree or equivalent from a program that combines academic and professional preparation in library and information science, education, management, media, communications theory, and technology. The academic program of study includes some directed field experience in a library media program, coordinated by a faculty member in cooperation with an experienced library media specialist. Library media specialists meet state certification requirements for both the library media specialist and professional educator classifications. While there may be many practicing library media specialists who have only an undergraduate degree and whose job performance is outstanding, the master's degree is considered the entry-level degree for the profession.

The graduate degree is earned at colleges and universities whose programs are accredited by appropriate bodies such as the American Library Association (ALA), the National Council for the Accreditation of Teacher Education (NCATE), or state education agencies.

*Source: Position Statement on Preparation of School Library Media Specialists* (Chicago: ALA American Association of School Librarians, 1992). 1p.

# Competencies for librarians serving children in public libraries

EFFECTIVE LIBRARY SERVICE for children entails a broad range of expertise and professional skills. The librarian serving children is first of all fully knowledgeable in the theories, practices, and emerging trends of librarianship and has, as well, specialized knowledge of the particular needs of children as library users.

In developing the following list of recommended competencies, definitions have been drawn from numerous sets of standards for children's services and lists of competencies developed by state agencies and library associations. The intent of this document is to define the role of the librarian serving children in the public library. The competencies will apply in varying degrees according to the professional responsibilities of the librarian serving children. The assignment of responsibilities for planning, managing, and delivering library services to children will vary in relation to the size and staffing pattern of the public library. In many libraries there is only one professional children's librarian, who serves as both manager and principal provider of services. In larger libraries there may be a coordinator of children's services who oversees the delivery of services.

The philosophical basis for children's services in public libraries is full access for children to library materials and services. Other philosophical underpinnings for these competencies are the American Library Association's (ALA) Library Bill of Rights and the ALA-endorsed Freedom to View Statement adopted by the Educational Film Library Association (now the American Film and Video Association). Related ALA statements also include the Library Education and Personnel Utilization Policy and the policy that the master's degree from a program accredited by the ALA is the appropriate professional degree for librarians. It is recommended that the policy manuals of local libraries include copies of these statements in conjunction with relevant state standards or guidelines.

The competencies that follow represent a systematic process. In order to plan and administer an effective program, one must first have knowledge of the community and client group. Planning and management are then based on valid data. Communication is essential in order to articulate goals and objectives. Collection development provides the resources for services and programming. The future of children's services depends upon advocacy and professional development.

Competencies are not static but evolve throughout one's professional career. Librarians must be alert to the changes in society which may necessitate changes in library services and the acquisition of additional competencies. Thus it is understood that professional growth and development are a lifelong process.

## Knowledge of client group

1. Understands theories of infant, child, and adolescent learning and development and their implications for library service.
2. Recognizes the effects of societal developments on the needs of children.
3. Assesses the community regularly and systematically to identify community needs, tastes, and resources.
4. Identifies clients with special needs as a basis for designing and implementing services.
5. Recognizes the needs of an ethnically diverse community.
6. Understands and responds to the needs of parents, care givers, and other adults who use the resources of the children's department.
7. Maintains regular communication with other agencies, institutions, and organizations serving children in the community.

## Administrative and management skills

1. Participates in all aspects of the library's planning process to represent and support children's services.
2. Sets long- and short-range goals, objectives and priorities.
3. Analyzes the costs of library services to children in order to develop, justify, administer, and evaluate a budget.
4. Writes job descriptions, and interviews, trains, and evaluates staff who work with children, consulting with other library administrators as indicated in library personnel policy.
5. Demonstrates problem-solving, decision-making, and mediation techniques.
6. Delegates responsibility appropriately and supervises staff constructively.
7. Documents and evaluates services.
8. Identifies outside sources of funding and writes effective grant applications.

## Communication skills

1. Defines and communicates the needs of children so that administrators, other library staff, and members of the larger community understand the basis for children's services.
2. Demonstrates interpersonal skills in meeting with children, parents, staff, and community.

3. Adjusts to the varying demands of writing planning documents, procedures, guidelines, press releases, memoranda, reports, grant applications, annotations, and reviews.
4. Speaks effectively when addressing individuals as well as small and large groups.
5. Applies active listening skills.
6. Conducts productive formal and informal reference interviews.
7. Communicates constructively with "problem patrons."

## Materials and collection development

*Knowledge of materials*
1. Demonstrates a knowledge and appreciation of children's literature, audiovisual materials, computer resources, pamphlet file materials, and other materials that constitute a balanced, relevant children's collection.
2. Keeps abreast of new materials and those for retrospective purchase by consulting a wide variety of reviewing sources and publishers' catalogs, including those of small presses; by attending professional meetings; and by reading, viewing, and listening.
3. Is aware of adult reference materials and other library resources that may serve the needs of children and their care givers.

*Ability to select appropriate materials and develop a children's collection*
1. Establishes collection development, selection, and weeding policies for children's materials consistent with the policies of the parent library and the ALA Library Bill of Rights, and applies these policies in acquiring materials for the children's collection.
2. Acquires materials that reflect the ethnic diversity of the community as well as the need of children to become familiar with other ethnic groups and cultures.
3. Understands and applies criteria for evaluating the content and artistic merit of children's materials in all genres and formats.
4. Keeps abreast of current issues in children's materials collections and formulates a professional philosophy with regard to these issues.
5. Cooperates with library technical services to ensure that desired materials are added to the collection as expeditiously as possible.

*Ability to provide patrons with appropriate materials and instruction*
1. Inspires children to become lifelong library users by introducing them to the wealth of library resources and enabling them to use libraries effectively.
2. Creates an environment in the children's department which provides for enjoyable and convenient use of library resources.
3. Matches patrons with materials appropriate to their interest and abilities.
4. Provides help where needed and respects children's rights to browse.
5. Instructs children in information gathering and research skills as appropriate.
6. Understands and applies search strategies to give children access to information from the widest possible range of sources—children's and adult reference works, indexes, catalogs, computerized databases, information and referral files, and interlibrary loan networks.
7. Maintains direct contact with community resource people so that children and adults working with children can be referred to appropriate sources of assistance.
8. Consults with library technical services to guarantee that the children's

collection is organized for the easiest possible access by its users.
9. Composes bibliographies, booktalks, displays, and other special tools to increase access to library resources and motivate their use.

## Programming skills

1. Designs, promotes, executes, and evaluates programs for children of all ages, based on their developmental needs and interests and the goals of the library.
2. Presents a variety of programs or brings in skilled resource people to present these programs, including storytelling, booktalking, book discussions, puppet programs, and other appropriate activities.
3. Provides outreach programs commensurate with community needs and library goals and objectives.
4. Establishes programs and services for parents, individuals and agencies providing child care, and other professionals in the community who work with children.

## Advocacy, public relations, and networking skills

1. Promotes an awareness of and support for meeting children's library and information needs.
2. Considers the opinions and requests of children in the development and evaluation of library services.
3. Ensures that children have full access to library materials and services as prescribed by the Library Bill of Rights.
4. Acts as liaison with other agencies in the community serving children.
5. Develops cooperative programs between the public library, schools, and other community agencies.
6. Extends library services to individuals and groups presently unserved.
7. Utilizes effective public relations techniques and media to publicize library activities.
8. Understands state, county, and local legal statutes applying to children.
9. Monitors legislation affecting libraries, understands the political process, and lobbies on behalf of children's services.

## Professionalism and professional development

1. Acknowledges the legacy of children's librarianship and past contributions to the development of the field.
2. Keeps abreast of current trends and emerging technologies, issues, and research in librarianship, child development, and education.
3. Practices self-evaluation.
4. Conveys a nonjudgmental attitude toward patrons and their requests.
5. Demonstrates an understanding of and respect for diversity in cultural and ethnic values.
6. Adheres to the American Library Association's Code of Ethics.
7. Preserves confidentiality in interchanges with patrons.
8. Works with library educators to meet field information needs of students, welcome interns, and promote professional association scholarships.
9. Participates in professional organizations to strengthen skills and contribute to the profession.
10. Understands that professional development and continuing education are activities to be pursued throughout one's career.

*Source: Competencies for Librarians Serving Children in Public Libraries*
(Chicago: ALA Association for Library Service to Children, 1989).

# Useful addresses

YOUR UNANSWERED QUESTIONS on library matters might be directed to one of the following organizations. See also other lists of addresses and telephone numbers on **pages 63–65** (job placement sources), **101–3** (support staff networks), **161–64** (accredited library school programs), **195–201**(federal libraries and archives), and **438–39** (theft protection and recovery).

**African Library Association of South Africa,** c/o Library, University of the North, Private Bag X1106, Sovenga 0727, South Africa; 01522-4310.

**American Association for Higher Education,** 1 Dupont Circle, N.W., Suite 360, Washington, DC 20036; (202) 293-6440.

**American Association of Law Libraries,** 53 W. Jackson Blvd., Suite 940, Chicago, IL 60604; (312) 939-4764; e-mail: lawchq@orion.depaul.edu.

**American Association for State and Local History,** 530 Church St., Suite 600, Nashville, TN 37219; (615) 255-2971.

**American Booksellers Association,** 828 S. Broadway, Tarrytown, NY 10591; (914) 591-2665; e-mail: amer.bk@aol.con.

**American Council of Learned Societies,** 228 E. 45th St., 16th Floor, New York, NY 10017; (212) 697-1505.

**American Council on Education,** 1 Dupont Circle, N.W., Suite 800, Washington, DC 20036; (202) 939-9300; e-mail: jill_bogard@ace.nche.edu.

**American Film and Video Association,** c/o Kevin Conner, Allegheny Intermediate Unit, Film/Video Library, 17 Terminal Way, Pittsburgh, PA 15219; (416) 736-5508 (Kathy Elder).

**American Indian Library Association,** c/o Lisa A. Mitten, 207 Hillman Library, University of Pittsburgh, Pittsburgh, PA 15260; (412) 648-7723; e-mail: lmitten@vms.cis.pitt.edu.

**American Library Association,** 50 E. Huron St., Chicago, IL 60611-2795; (800) 545-2433.

**American Library Association, Washington Office,** 110 Maryland Ave., N.E., Washington, DC 20002; (202) 547-4440; e-mail: alawash@alawash.org.

**American Merchant Marine Library Association,** 1 World Trade Center, Suite 2161, New York, NY 10048; (212) 775-1038.

**American National Standards Institute,** 11 W. 42nd St., 13th Floor, New York, NY 10036; (212) 642-4900.

**American Society for Information Science,** 8720 Georgia Ave., Suite 501, Silver Spring, MD 20910-3602; (301) 495-0900; e-mail: asis@cni.org.

**American Society of Indexers,** P.O. Box 386, 502 S. 12th St., Port Aransas, TX 78373; (512) 749-4052.

**American Theological Library Association,** 820 Church St., Suite 300, Evanston, IL 60201-5603; (708) 869-7788.

**AMIGOS Bibliographic Council,** 12200 Park Central Dr., Suite 500, Dallas, TX 75251; (214) 851-8000; e-mail: amigos@utdallas.edu.

**Antiquarian Booksellers Association of America,** 50 Rockefeller Plaza, New York, NY 10020; (212) 757-9395.

**Art Libraries Society of North America,** 4101 Lake Boone Trail, Suite 201, Raleigh, NC 27607; (919) 787-5181.

**Asian/Pacific American Librarians Association,** c/o Erlinda J. Regner, Chicago Public Library, 400 S. State St., Chicago, IL 60605; (312) 747-4414.

**Asociacion Mexicana de Bibliotecarios,** Apartado Postal 27-651, Administracion de Correos 27, 06760 Mexico City, D.F., Mexico; (05) 5751135.

**Association for Educational Communications and Technology,** 1025 Vermont Ave., N.W., Suite 820, Washington, DC 20005; (202) 347-7834.

**Association for Information and Image Management,** 1100 Wayne Ave., Suite 1100, Silver Spring, MD 20910-5603; (301) 587-8202.

**Association for Library and Information Science Education,** 4101 Lake Boone Trail, Suite 201, Raleigh, NC 27607; (919) 787-5181; e-mail: omg@ruby.ils.unc.edu.

**Association for Recorded Sound Collections,** P.O. Box 10162, Silver Spring, MD 20914; (301) 593-6552.

**Association of American Colleges and Universities,** 1818 R St., N.W., Washington, DC 20009; (202) 387-3760.

**Association of Architectural Librarians,** 1735 New York Ave., N.W., Washington, DC 20006; (202) 626-7490.

**Association of Assistant Librarians,** British Library Science Reference and Information Service, 25 Southampton Bldgs., London WC2A 1AW, England; (71) 3237959.

**Association of Canadian Archivists,** P.O. Box 2596, Station D, Ottawa, Ontario, Canada K1P 5W6; (613) 443-0251.

**Association of Canadian Map Libraries and Archives,** National Archives of Canada, 344 Wellington, Room 1016, Ottawa, Canada K1A 0N3; (613) 992-8188.

**Association of Christian Librarians,** P.O. Box 4, Cedarville, OH 45314; (513) 766-7842.

**Association of Jewish Libraries,** 15 E. 26th Street, Room 1034, New York, NY 10010; (212) 678-8092.

**Association of Mental Health Librarians,** c/o Lenore W. Freehling, Research Library, Reiss-Davis Child Study Center, 3200 Motor Ave., Los Angeles, CA 90034; (310) 204-1666.

**Association of Records Managers and Administrators International,** 4200 Somerset Dr., Suite 215, Prairie Village, KS 66208; (913) 341-3808, (800) 422-2762.

**Association of Research Libraries,** 21 Dupont Circle, N.W., Washington, DC 20036; (202) 296-2296; e-mail: arlhq@cni.org.

**Association of Research Libraries, Office of Management Services,** 21 Dupont Circle, N.W., Washington, DC 20036; (202) 296-8656.

**Australian Library and Information Association,** Box E441, Queen Victoria Terrace, Canberra, ACT, Australia 2600; (062) 2851877.

**Beta Phi Mu International Library Science Honor Society,** School of Library and Information Science, University of Pittsburgh, Pittsburgh, PA 15260; (412) 624-9439.

**Bibliographical Society of America,** Box 397, Grand Central Station, New York, NY 10163; (212) 647-9171.

**Black Caucus of the American Library Association,** c/o Stanton F. Biddle, Baruch College, CUNY, 17 Lexington Ave., Box 317, New York, NY 10010; (212) 447-3881; e-mail: sfbbb@cunyvm.cuny.edu.

**British-Irish Association of Law Libraries,** University of Wales Law Library, College of Cardiff, Box 430, Cardiff, Wales CF1 3XT; (021) 200-1050.

**Brother's Brother Foundation,** 824 Grandview Ave., Pittsburgh, PA 15211; (412) 431-1600.

**Canadian Health Libraries Association,** P.O. Box 94038, 3332 Yonge St., Toronto, Ontario, Canada M4N 3R1; (416) 485-0377; e-mail: Envoy 100, CHLA.

**Canadian Library Association,** 200 Elgin St., Suite 602, Ottawa, Ontario, Canada K2P 1L5; (613) 232-9625; e-mail: ai077@freenet.carleton.ca.

**Catholic Library Association,** c/o Jean R. Bostley, S.S.J., St. Joseph Central High School, 22 Maplewood Ave., Pittsfield, MA 01201; (413) 447-9121.

**Chief Officers of State Library Agencies,** c/o Maurice Travillian, Maryland Department of Education, Division of Library Development and Services, 200 W. Baltimore, Baltimore, MD 21201-2500; (410) 333-2115.

**Chinese-American Librarians Association,** c/o Sheila Lai, CSU Sacramento, 2000 Jed Smith Drive, Sacramento, CA 95819-6039; (916) 278-6201; sheilalai@csus.edu.

*Choice,* 100 Riverview Center, Middletown, CT 06457; (203) 347-6933.

**Church and Synagogue Library Association,** P.O. Box 19357, Portland, OR 97280; (503) 244-6919.

**Coalition for Networked Information,** 21 Dupont Circle, N.W., Suite 600, Washington, DC 20036; (202) 296-5098; e-mail: joan@cni.org.

**College and University Personnel Association,** 1233 Twentieth St., N.W., Suite 301, Washington, DC 20036; (202) 429-0311.

**Commission on Preservation and Access,** 1400 16th Street, N.W., Suite 740, Washington, DC 20036-2217; (202) 939-3400; e-mail: msitts@cni.org.

**Copyright Royalty Tribunal,** 1825 Connecticut Ave., N.W., Suite 918, Washington, DC 20009; (202) 606-4400.

**Council of National Library and Information Associations,** 1700 18 St., N.W., Suite B-1, Washington, DC 20009.

**Council on Botanical and Horticultural Libraries,** c/o John F. Reed, New York Botanical Garden, 200th St. and Southern Blvd., Bronx, NY 10458; (718) 817-8705, ext. 8729; e-mail: jfreed@nybg.org.

**Council on Library/Media Technical Assistants,** c/o Margaret Barron, Cuyahoga Community College, Library Media/Technology Department, SSC 201, 2900 Community College Ave., Cleveland, OH 44115; (216) 987-4296.

**Council on Library Resources,** 1400 16th St., N.W., Suite 510, Washington, DC 20036; (202) 483-7474; e-mail: clr@cni.org.

**Equal Employment Opportunity Commission,** 1801 L. St., N.W., Washington, DC 20507; (202) 663-4900.

**Federal Library and Information Center Committee,** Library of Congress, Washington, DC 20540; (202) 707-4800; e-mail: flicc@mail.loc.gov.

**Friends of Libraries USA,** 1326 Spruce St., #1105, Philadelphia, PA 19107; (215) 790-1674.

**Indian Library Association,** A/40-41, Flat 201, Ansal Bldg., Mukherjee Nagar, New Delhi 110-009, Delhi, India; (11) 7117743.

**Interagency Council on Library Resources for Nursing,** c/o The Library, *American Journal of Nursing,* 555 W. 57th St., New York, NY 10011; (212) 582-8820.

**International Association of Aquatic and Marine Science Libraries and Information Centers,** Harbor Branch Oceanographic Institute Library, 5600 U.S. 1 North, Fort Pierce, FL 34946; (407) 465-2400, ext. 201; e-mail: harbomet@class.org.

**International Association of Law Libraries,** c/o Roberta Shaffer, Library Director, Covington & Burling, 1201 Pennsylvania Ave., N.W., P.O. Box 7566, Washington, DC 20044; (202) 662-6152.

**International Association of School Librarianship,** P.O. Box 1486, Kalamazoo, MI 49005; (616) 343-5728.

**International Book Bank,** 608-L Folcroft St., Baltimore, MD 21224; (410) 633-2929, (800) US-GRANT.

**The International Book Project,** 1440 Delaware Ave., Lexington, KY 40505; (606) 254-6771.

**International Council of Library Association Executives,** c/o Ann Hanning, Ohio Educational Library Media Association, 1631 Northwest Professional Plaza, Columbus, OH 43220; (614) 326-1460.

**International Federation of Library Associations and Institutions,** Postbus 95312, NL-2509 CH The Hague, Netherlands; (070) 3140884.

**Laubach Literacy,** Box 131, 1320 Jamesville Ave., Syracuse, NY 13210; (315) 422-9121; e-mail: laubach1@transit.nyser.net.

**Library Association,** 7 Ridgmount St., London, England WC1E 7AE; (071) 6367543.

**Library Association of Ireland,** 53 Upper Mount St., Dublin 2, Ireland; (1) 619000.

**Library of Congress,** First Street & Independence Ave., S.E., Washington, DC 20540; (202) 707-5000; copyright application forms, (202) 707-9100.

**Library Public Relations Council,** 2 Jean Walling Civic Center, East Brunswick, NJ 08816; (908) 390-6761.

**Library Users of America,** c/o American Council of the Blind, 1155 15th St., N.W., Suite 720, Washington, DC 20005; (202) 467-5081.

**Literacy Volunteers of America,** 5795 Widewaters Parkway, Syracuse, NY 13214; (315) 445-8000; e-mail: lvanat@aol.com.

**Medical Library Association,** 6 N. Michigan Ave., Suite 300, Chicago, IL 60602; (312) 419-9094; e-mail: cfunk@life.jsc.nasa.gov.

**Modern Language Association of America,** 10 Astor Place, 5th Floor, New York, NY 10003; (212) 475-9500; e-mail: mlaod@cuvmb.columbia.edu.

**Music Library Association,** P.O. Box 487, Canton, MA 02021-0487; (617) 828-8450.

**National Association for the Education of Young Children,** 1509 16th Street, N.W., Washington, DC 20036-1426; (202) 232-8777, (800) 424-2460.

**National Association of Government Archives and Records Administrators,** New York State Archives and Records Administration, Room 10A46, Cultural Education Center, Albany, NY 12230; (518) 473-8037.

**National Center for Education Statistics,** 555 New Jersey Ave., N.W., Washington, DC 20208-5650; (202) 219-1839.

**National Coalition Against Censorship,** 275 7th Ave., 20th Floor, New York, NY 10001; (212) 807-6222; e-mail: jsamncac@panix.com.

**National Commission on Libraries and Information Science,** 1111 18th St., N.W., Washington, DC 20036; (202) 254-3100.

**National Committee on Pay Equity,** 1126 16th St., N.W., Room 411, Washington, DC 20036; (202) 331-7343.

**National Council for History Education,** 26915 Westwood Rd., Suite B2, Westlake, OH 44145-4657; (216) 835-1776; e-mail: ae515@cleveland.freenet.edu.

**National Council for the Accreditation of Teacher Education,** 2010 Massachusetts Ave., N.W., Suite 200, Washington, DC 20036-1023; (202) 466-7496.

**National Council of Teachers of English,** 1111 Kenyon Rd., Urbana, IL 61801; (217) 328-3870.

**National Council of Teachers of Mathematics,** 1906 Association Dr., Reston, VA 22091-1593; (703) 620-9840; e-mail: nctmath@tmn.com.

**National Endowment for the Arts,** 1100 Pennsylvania Ave., N.W., Washington, DC 20506; (202) 682-5400.

**National Endowment for the Humanities,** 1100 Pennsylvania Ave., N.W., Washington, DC 20506; (202) 686-8438.

**National Historical Publications and Records Commission,** National Archives Building, Washington, DC 20408; (202) 501-5603.

**National Information Standards Organization,** P.O. Box 1056, Bethesda, MD 20827; (301) 975-2814; e-mail: niso@enh.nist.gov.

**National Librarians Association,** P.O. Box 486, Alma, MI 48801; (517) 463-7227.

**National Science Teachers Association,** 1840 Wilson Blvd., Arlington, VA 22201; (703) 243-7100.

**National Technical Information Service,** 5285 Port Royal Rd., Springfield, VA 22161; (703) 487-4650.

**New Zealand Library Association,** Level 8, Petecorp House, 86 Lambton Quay, Wellington North, New Zealand; (04) 4735834.

**North American Cartographic Information Society,** American Geographic Society Collection, P.O. Box 399, Milwaukee, WI 53201; (414) 229-6282; e-mail: cmb@alpha1.csd.uwm.edu.

**North American Serials Interest Group,** 2103 N. Decatur Rd., #214, Decatur, GA 30033.

**Northeast Document Conservation Center,** 100 Brickstone Square, Andover, MA 01810; (508) 470-1010.

**OCLC, Inc.,** 6565 Frantz Road, Dublin, OH 43017-3395; (800) 848-5878, (614) 764-6000.

**Online Audiovisual Catalogers,** University of North Florida, Carpenter Library, P.O. Box 17605, Jacksonville, FL 32245-7605; (904) 646-2550.

**Popular Culture Association,** Bowling Green State University, Popular Culture Center, Bowling Green, OH 43403; (419) 372-7861; e-mail: rbrown@andy.bgsu.edu.

**Public Record Office,** Ruskin Avenue, Kew, Richmond, London, England TW9 4DU; (081) 8763444.

**Reforma: National Association to Promote Library Services to the Spanish-Speaking,** c/o Mario M. Gonzalez, New York Public Library, Office of Special Services, 455 Fifth Ave., New York, NY 10016; (212) 340-0952.

**Research Libraries Group,** 1200 Villa St., Mountain View, CA 94041-1100; (415) 691-2207, (800) 537-RLIN; e-mail: bl.jlh@rlg.stanford.edu.

**Scottish Library Association,** Motherwell Business Centre, Coursington Road, Motherwell, Strathclyde, Scotland ML1 1PW; 698-252526.

**Seminar on the Acquisition of Latin American Library Materials,** General Library, University of New Mexico, Albuquerque, NM 87131-1466; (505) 277-5102.

**Sociedad de Bibliotecarios de Puerto Rico,** University of Puerto Rico Station, P.O. Box 22898, Rio Piedras, PR 00931; (809) 758-1125.

**Society of American Archivists,** 600 S. Federal St., Suite 504, Chicago, IL 60605; (312) 922-0140; e-mail: info@saa.mhs.compuserve.com.

**Society of School Librarians International,** 620 W. Roosevelt Rd., Suite B2, Wheaton, IL 60187; (708) 665-7977.

**Special Libraries Association,** 1700 18th St., N.W., Washington, DC 20009; (202) 234-4700; e-mail: sla1@capcon.net.

**Substance Abuse Librarians and Information Specialists,** P.O. Box 9513, Berkeley, CA 94709-0513; (510) 642-5208.

**Theatre Library Association,** 111 Amsterdam Ave., Room 513, New York, NY 10023; (212) 870-1670.

**Ukrainian Library Association of America,** P.O. Box 455, New City, NY 10956; (201) 684-5895.

**Universal Serials and Book Exchange,** 2969 W. 25th St., Cleveland, OH 44113; (216) 241-6960.

**Urban Libraries Council,** 1800 Ridge Ave., Suite 208, Evanston, IL 60201; (708) 866-9999.

**Utlas International Canada,** 3300 Bloor St. West, 16th Floor, West Tower, Etobicoke, Ontario, Canada M8X 2X2; (416) 923-0890.

**Welsh Library Association,** c/o Publications Office, Public Library, Dew St., Haverford West, Dyfed, Wales SA62 1SU; 0437-764591, ext. 5245.

**Western Association of Map Libraries,** c/o Herb Fox, 1883 Ashcroft, Clovis, CA 93611; (209) 294-0177.

**WLN,** 4224 6th Ave., S.E., Building 3, P.O. Box 3888, Lacey, WA 98503-0888; (800) 342-5956; e-mail: info@wln.com.

# Losing the foundation of understanding

*by Donald E. Riggs*

THE MATURITY OF LIBRARIANSHIP DEPENDS largely on the research conducted by its practicing librarians. This maturity has been slowed in recent years due to the diminishing amount of research performed by librarians, especially by academic librarians, who do the bulk of this work. What has caused this "drifting from research" phenomenon?

In recent years, librarians have had less time to engage in research and publish its results. Due to widespread financial constraints, the number of library positions has been shrinking; we frequently hear that library staffs are doing more with less. New technologies have actually placed pressure on librarians to do more work for patrons, and the more we offer them, the more they want. In short, there is less time for thought and reflection on why we are doing what we are doing.

## Tenure review a factor?

There has been no recent sea change in the number of academic institutions requiring research and publication for their librarians to achieve promotion and/or tenure. Actually, the number of institutions granting full faculty rank and status to their librarians is rather small; for example, only about 15% of the Association of Research Libraries' university members provide full faculty rank and status for their librarians. In most of the institutions requiring some research and publications from their librarians, the librarians' promotion/tenure portfolio does not go to the institution's faculty review committee, but to the library's promotion/tenure group. Thus, the requirement for promotion or tenure for librarians may be less stringent than that for faculty. The perception of a "less stringent" process may help to reduce the amount of research being done by librarians.

## The proof is in the publications

The de-emphasis on both qualitative and quantitative research is clearly indicated in the literature now being published by librarians. There are fewer intellectual and theoretically based library science monographs being published and fewer provocative thought pieces in the literature. Due to increasing job demands placed on librarians, we have come to depend more on "how-to" and recipe-type publications and journal articles to help us do our jobs better. The irony is that now we have more areas than ever before in the history of librarianship that require systematic investigation.

Library schools are producing more Ph.Ds each year, yet the number of empirical and fundamental research publications continues to decline. Should we be examining why these freshly minted Ph.Ds are not participating more in research endeavors? Are library schools taking the necessary time to sufficiently educate their doctoral students on the fundamentals of research? Are the schools encouraging their graduate students to understand and appreciate that contribution of research findings to the scholarly process is required if the profession is to have a theoretical base? These questions deserve thoughtful answers.

Library conference proceedings contain fewer research pieces. For example, 30.3% of papers presented at the first Association of College and

Research Libraries conference in 1978 had a research focus; however, the percentage of papers with a research focus given at the subsequent five ACRL conferences never reached that level again. Librarians at public and school library conferences present even fewer research papers. One could assume that these conferences are geared to help librarians do their jobs better back home.

## Changing the climate

What can be done to turn this situation around? Library administrators should make release time and financial support available for librarians wanting to engage in research. Without encouragement and incentives from top administrators such as in-house grants, secretarial support, and microcomputers, there is likely to be little change. Librarians who are interested in doing research should negotiate support for this activity in their employment conditions. Library schools and libraries can do a better job in co-sponsoring research opportunities. And library schools can assume more responsibility in preparing their graduates to conduct research. A greater emphasis should be placed on ideas and creativity, and less on things.

What will happen if further slippage occurs in our research activities? Perhaps the perception by some that library work is more like a trade than a profession will be reinforced. Without a theoretical base, we may win the battle in providing day-to-day services for our patrons, but lose the war in saving the profession. The profession will suffer a major tragedy if it loses its foundation of understanding. This is serious stuff to ponder.

*Source:* Donald E. Riggs, "Losing the Foundation of Understanding,"
*American Libraries* 25 (May 1994): 449.

# How to convert a dissertation or thesis into a book

A MANUSCRIPT DESIGNED to communicate mastery of the research process to an examining committee frequently fails to satisfy the requirements of a publisher. Authors submitting theses and dissertations to a publisher may anticipate requests for extensive modifications of their manuscript if it is accepted for publication. Indeed, some effort at revision prior to submission will enhance the likelihood of acceptance.

A book is addressed to an audience that is very different from the audience to whom a thesis, dissertation, or other research report is addressed. These differences include level of interest, prior knowledge of the subject, and objectives in reading the work. Major revisions are usually necessary, even to the most effective works.

Revisions that are often required include deletions, reorganization, and the writing of additional material. Some examples:

- The style of a dissertation frequently requires the repetition of material from section to section. In many cases this redundancy can be eliminated. Tables often should be deleted or converted into an explanatory narrative.
- Many of the fine points concerning prior research or methodology on the subject should be placed in appendices or footnotes.
- Abstractions must be carefully related to the concrete world through more extensive interpretation than would be necessary in a dissertation or thesis.

*Source: College & Research Libraries News,* April 1986, p. 277.

# MATERIALS 4

# How to identify a first edition

*by Bill McBride*

### Editing, printing, impression

AN EDITION IS the number of books printed before a certain percentage of the contents is revised. A printing is the number of copies produced when the printing plates or type are on the press. An impression is the same thing as a printing.

To the book collector, a **first edition** means a copy from the first printing of the first edition. To the publisher, a first edition may mean any copy of a title before it was substantially revised.

When a book says on the copyright page, "First and second printings before publication," it means that before the book was actually released for sale (publication), orders from booksellers exceeded the quantity of the first printing and the book had to be reprinted. Such a copy is not a book collector's first edition.

For a publisher-by-publisher guide to identifying first editions, see my *Pocket Guide to the Identification of First Editions* (5th ed., 1994), available from McBride/Publisher, 585 Prospect Ave., West Hartford, CT 06105.

### Numbers and letters

Since the late 1940s, some publishers have adopted a new method of identifying their first editions. A series of letters (abcde . . . ) or numbers (123456 789 or 987654321 or 135798642) appears somewhere on the copyright page. If the "a" or the "1" is present, the copy in hand is from the first printing of the first edition. If this method were used by all publishers, there would be few identification problems.

Some questions have been raised about numbers and letters when they are used in conjunction with "first edition" or "first printing." A copyright page might show "FIRST EDITION B C D E" or "FIRST PRINTING 23456789." These are usually first editions because on second printings, the words "first edition" or "first printing" are removed, leaving the letters or numbers only.

Unfortunately, some publishers have used the system of numbers and letters in conjunction with FIRST EDITION, but leave the FIRST EDITION on the copyright page and remove the number "1" or letter "a" to indicate the second printing.

### Issue, state and point

To the book collector, **issue** means an intermediary copy within the first printing of a first edition. **State** is synonymous with issue. A **point of issue** occurs when an error is discovered before the first printing is complete.

Typically the error is corrected, but the identification method used on the copyright page is not, resulting in a copy of the book which, at first glance, seems to be a correct first edition. Thus, the first edition is divided into two issues or states—those copies with the error and those with the error corrected. In the case of multiple errors, three or more issues may exist as some errors are corrected and others are not. This state of affairs is much more common in books of the 19th century.

Points of issue may consist of errors in punctuation, spelling, location of illustrations, presence or absence of specific material in the text or in inserted advertisements, colors of printing ink or binding cloths, size of book or page, or the imprint of the publisher. Many important books in the last 150 years contain points of issue. For more information, see McBride/Publisher's *Points of Issue: A Compendium of Points of Issue of Books by 19th and 20th Century Authors.*

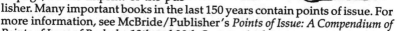

## Sleuthing first editions

Dustjackets and author biographies, publisher's ads, and copyright information all may contain clues. If a biographical sketch of the author printed on the dustjacket mentions other works, check to see when they were published. If they followed the work in hand, then the book isn't likely a first. A dustjacket may say "second printing" when the copyright page may not. Ads for books by other authors can also help pinpoint a date. The address of a publisher may be a significant thing in itself—if a zip code is included in the address, the book must have been published no earlier than July 1, 1963, the date the codes were introduced to the public.

## Identifying Book Club editions

Many titles of 20th-century fiction and nonfiction were published in Book Club editions. These editions often resemble the true first trade editions. Here are some ways to identify Book Club editions:

1. **No price** on the dust jacket. In the last few years some publishers, notably Vanguard, have taken to printing dust jackets without prices so that individual retail booksellers can affix their own price stickers. This is confounding to the collector, but typically the Book Club versions are lighter, smaller, and do not carry the standard first edition identifier on the copyright page. In addition, university publishers usually do not print prices on their dust jackets.

2. **Book Club Edition** printed on the dust jacket's lower inner front flap. If this portion of the jacket is cut off, be wary and look further.

3. **Back cover debossing** at the bottom near the spine. A debossed (indented) star, circle, dot, crown, or other geometric device, colored or uncolored, indicates a Book Club edition, even when all other first edition indicators check out. This practice began about 1947, primarily by the Book-of-the-Month Club. Occasionally, the debossed symbol is found at the top of the back cover or somewhere in between the bottom and top edges of the back cover along the spine.

4. **"A Selection of the Book-of-the-Month Club"** printed on the dust jacket where the price is usually printed (upper front dust jacket flap). This practice was common in the 1960s and early 1970s. In the later 1970s and up, the same phrase was used as a promotional line on the jacket, and you may need to compare Book Club editions side by side with trade editions to determine firsts from Book Club editions, especially if there is no debossing on the back cover.

5. **Reprints from original plates.** Many books printed by such publishers as A. L. Burt, Grosset & Dunlap, Tower Books, The Book League, The Literary Guild, and others, often used the printing plates of the true first edition and neglected to alter the copyright page. Thus, some books may appear to be first editions, when in fact they are actually reprints by another company.

6. **Switched dust jackets: a caution.** Some Book Club editions so closely resemble true first editions that the mere substitution of a second trade edition dust jacket for the Book Club jacket can fool even veteran collectors and dealers. It is therefore wise to check all points of Book Club identification before purchase or sale. Many of these books are termed *false firsts*, Book Club editions that masquerade as true firsts.

## British Commonwealth countries

Before the adoption of the International Copyright Convention of 1957, many British Commonwealth publishers were notoriously inconsistent in identifying their firsts. Since then, most have adopted the form "First published in (year)" or simply list only second and later printings, not first printings.

## First paperback editions

In recent years, considerable interest has arisen in first paperback editions of 20th-century literature. First paperbacks sometimes contain new prefatory material by the author, a noted editor, annotator or bibliographer. In some cases, a title appears in paperback before it does in hardback (early Kurt Vonnegut and Louis L'Amour titles are good examples). Special movie or stage editions are often printed when a book is made into a movie or play. These editions are frequently illustrated inside or on the covers with scenes from the production. Additional material by the author may also be included. First and special paperback editions are as much a part of an author's bibliography as are true firsts.

*Source:* Bill McBride, comp., *A Pocket Guide to the Identification of First Editions* (Hartford, Ct.: The author, 5th ed., 1994). Reprinted with permission.

# Book sizes

**THERE IS MUCH CONFUSION** about the definition of book sizes and little consistency in usage. The common book trade designation of sizes was based originally on the relation to a sheet of paper measuring approximately 19 by 25 inches. When folded once to make two leaves (4 pages), it was a **folio;** when folded twice to make four leaves (8 pages), it was a **quarto;** when folded to eight leaves (16 pages), an **octavo;** when folded to 12 leaves (24 pages), a **duodecimo** or **twelvemo;** when folded to 16 leaves (32 pages), a **sixteenmo,** etc.

This is the historical background of book sizes and is the basis for terms still used in the rare book trade. In exact bibliographical descriptions, as in describing rare books, the historical definition applies.

However, present trade practice almost invariably refers to a measurement of the height of the binding, not the size of the leaf. Usual library practice calls for the use of centimeters, the measurement again referring to the height of the binding.

With the present variety of paper sizes, all dimensions are approximate:

**Folio,** F or 2o, over 30 cm (approx. 15 inches) high.
**Quarto,** 4to, 30 cm (approx. 12 inches) high.

**Octavo,** 8vo, 25 cm (approx. 9 ¾ inches) high.
**Duodecimo** or **twelvemo,** 12mo, 20 cm (approx. 7 ¾ inches) high.
**Sixteenmo,** 16mo, 17 ½ cm (approx. 6 ¾ inches) high.
**Twentyfourmo,** 24mo, 15 cm (approx. 5 ¾ inches) high.
**Thirtytwomo,** 32mo, approx. 5 inches high.
**Fortyeightmo,** 48mo, approx. 4 inches high.
**Sixtyfourmo,** 64mo, approx. 3 inches high.

Other sizes include:

**Double elephant folio,** approx. 50 inches high.
**Atlas folio,** approx. 25 inches high.
**Elephant folio,** approx. 23 inches high.

Any book wider than it is high is designated as oblong and such descriptive note is abbreviated "obl." or "ob." and precedes such terms as quarto, octavo, etc. If the width of the book is less than three-fifths of its height, it is designated narrow, abbreviated "nar." If the width of a book exceeds three-fourths of its height, but is no greater than its height, it is designated square.

*Source:* Heartsill Young, ed., *The ALA Glossary of Library and Information Science* (Chicago: American Library Association, 1983).

# Bookbinding in modern times

*by Leila Avrin*

LIKE MUCH OF 19th-CENTURY ROMANTIC ART and architecture, fine leather binding styles were eclectic. Architectural bindings either were Neo-Classical or Gothic, in cathedral style. Although craftsmanship in forwarding was still high, there were few original cover designs. Nineteenth-century innovation can be found in new binding materials, seen first in England. Mass-produced books demanded faster and cheaper binding methods. For the convenience of the retail bookseller or publisher of the late 18th and early 19th centuries, entire editions, especially of textbooks, were bound in paper boards with leather sometimes stuck over them. These came to be known as *edition bindings.*

From the 1820s, cases were manufactured separately from their books, with identical covers made in quantity. Sometimes books were bound in canvas or in cheap leather, especially in roan, sheepskin that imitated morocco. The English publisher William Pickering, always conscious of book design, introduced cloth bindings on some of his books in the 1820s, although not for entire editions. By 1823, glazed calico was used, or other cloth pressed with dyed starch that was impervious to adhesive. By the 1830s cloth could be grained, and embossed or stamped with titles. These cloth bindings displayed striped, floral, and pictorial designs. Most innovations were accomplished by binder Archibald Leighton (1784–1841).

Cloth casings became more popular in England and in the United States in the 1830s and 1840s for large editions, although the publisher often bound one batch at a time as the edition was sold, sometimes with different casings. Blind and gilt pictorial dies were popular for cover designs in the 1840s, with the book's endpapers painted or printed with publishers' ads until the 1890s. Many Victorian stamped bindings of cloth and leather that were charming monuments to the age are still gracing library stacks of England and America, displaying their bird, animal, vegetal, abstract, and floral motifs, with cathedrals for prayerbooks, and arabesques in all colors, including gold, silver, and black, against colored cloth. Even when they have darkened, they render today's cloth and imitation-cloth bindings pale by comparison. Printed paper covers were more popular than cloth in continental Europe, and this tradition has continued to the present for scholarly works.

Throughout the 19th century there was little change in the method of manufacturing the case binding of the cloth-covered book. Manual labor was gradually replaced by the machine, first for trimming (the guillotine) in the 1850s, then for sewing in the 1880s. By the early 20th century, all aspects of bookbinding were mechanized: folding, gathering, cutting, rounding and backing, trimming, case making, and casing-in. Today larger printing firms take the responsibility for casing the book, providing complete book-manufacturing services to the publisher.

As 20th-century readership made even heavier demands on publishers for more and cheaper books, paperbacks filled the need. One might say that there is nothing new in paperbacks—there were always books that the printer or bookseller never bothered to bind. Printed paper covers can be traced back to Augsburg, where a woodcut decoration appeared on the wrapper of a book printed by Erhard Ratdolt, dated 1494. Woodcuts on pasteboard covers also

served as bindings of some books from Venice and Ferara in the early 16th century. By the mid-17th century, paper covers were pasted to the spine or the endpapers, especially on pamphlets. Later in the century these often were printed. In the late 18th century, paperboard covers with typographic ornament and lettering became more common. Some mid-19th-century novels had colored paper wrappers with pictorial designs. Popular in England were cheap works of fiction bound in glazed yellow paper boards, called yellowbacks, which disappeared by the early 20th century.

Another paperback tradition began in Germany in 1841, when Leipzig publisher Christian Bernhard Tauchnitz inaugurated a reprint series of English and American authors to be sold in Europe only. The popular Tauchnitz books are often considered the true forerunners of the modern paperback. In 1932 they inspired the Albatross library series in Hamburg (later managed by Tauchnitz), whose covers were designed by Giovanni Mardersteig, the 20th century's finest handprinter. In 1935 there appeared the first Penguin books, created by Allen Lane, all fiction titles. Their success begat the Pelican nonfiction series in 1937, to be followed by other flying triumphs.

American paperbacks have their own traditions, beginning in 1842, with their ups and downs until the turn of the 20th century, when the low hardcover price of $2 drove them from the market. They were revived again in the 1920s, first with the Reynolds Publishing Company's fiction reprints at 10 cents a copy, then with the shabby squarish-format Little Blue Books at 5 cents a book. Of much higher quality were Paper Books, in the format of today's paperbacks, the creation of Charles Boni. These were distributed by the Boni brothers' Book Club beginning in 1929, with twelve books a year for $5. The best typography was sought and skilled printers were employed; Rockwell Kent was commissioned to design the covers. Ten years later, Pocket Books entered the field, with multicolored cover designs.

World War II and its aftermath made paperbacks a permanent and essential part of the book market. American mass market paperback publishers have eschewed British Penguin subtlety in cover design in an attempt to catch the eye of the supermarket and drugstore shopper. (Penguin has since become more colorful.) Fifteen years ago a sensational, sexy illustration was the norm, even if it belied the book's content. Of late, titles in fat, metallic letters printed in relief have all but replaced pictures in an attempt to draw the reader's attention. Ironically, unsewn and pasted-on paper covers are called *perfect bindings* by their manufacturers. The books are almost guaranteed to shed their pages after a few readings. Trade paperbacks, larger and more costly, usually are bound to last longer.

Hand binding in fine leather never ceased completely during the time cloth and separately manufactured case binding became popular. The art of fine binding was revitalized in the late 19th century, especially by a Parisian craftsman, Henri Marius-Michel, son of a *doreur* who worked in traditional styles. Henri went on to create leather covers of Art Nouveau inspiration, with swirling floral and vegetal patterns created by onlays in brown, red, purple, gray-green, and white on citron morocco, often outlined. Marius-Michel's suggestion that a binding should reflect the contents of the book was not necessarily fulfilled in all of his own work, but it did inspire many 20th-century binders of fine books and even ordinary paperbacks to disprove the adage, "you can't tell a book by its cover." The binders of England's Private Press Movement often preferred plain limp vellum, as they looked back to late medieval and Renaissance books for inspiration. Yet a Basilisk Press facsimile of William Morris's Kelmscott Chaucer (1975) used a Morris fabric design for its cover, manufactured by Liberty of London. Other printers of the Private Press Movement had their books leather-bound and gold-tooled in extremely fine taste. T. J. Cobden-Sanderson, who later founded the Doves Press, started his craft career as a bookbinder. He designed his own tools, which were relatively simple. "I charge as much for my restraint as I do for my elaboration," he once told a customer. The opposite end of the London binding spectrum at the turn of the 20th century was represented by Sangorski and Sutcliffe's overbejeweled and gilded creations. This firm is still in existence, binding books with simpler covers of fine workmanship.

The 20th century's prominent binders are persons of international reputation: Douglas Cockerell (1870–1929); his son Sydney Cockerell (1906–1987), famous for his decorated papers; Pierre Le Grain (1888–1929); Paul Bonet (1889–1971, a designer rather than a *doreur*); Rose Adler (1890–1959); and Michael Wilcox (b. 1939). At times their work reflects their personal interpretation of the art movements of the day. At other times they are inspired by the book's subject. From the 18th century, binders have more consistently stamped or printed their names onto their creations, usually on an inside cover, near the tail. At times they pasted in tickets—labels with their names.

The potential for variety in materials used for binding the book today is limited only by the imagination of the designer-binder. Just as there has been a Renaissance in hand-papermaking and calligraphy, the last few decades have seen a rise in the quality of design and workmanship in the art and craft of bookbinding. All materials are possible, from fabrics of all kinds to plastics to fur—even electronic parts and growing grass have been set into book covers. One of the most imaginative of today's designer-bookbinders working in leather is Philip Smith in England, who utilizes sophisticated colored leather inlays in a unique way. In addition to striking bindings on individual books, he has created a "book wall," a series of twenty-one covers of *The Lord of the Rings*, which, mounted together, form a picture of Tolkien's fantasy world.

*Source:* Leila Avrin, *Scribes, Script and Books: The Book Arts from Antiquity to the Renaissance* (Chicago and London: American Library Association/British Library, 1991). 356p.

# Rising costs of monographs and serials, 1986–1993

BY 1993, RESEARCH LIBRARIES acquired 5% fewer serials but spent nearly twice as much for those serials as they did in 1986. The median price of a serial subscription may reach $440 by the year 2000.

By 1993, research libraries bought 23% fewer monographs than they did in 1986 while paying 16% more. By the year 2000, research libraries may be purchasing only half the number of new books they acquired in 1986.

## Monograph and Serial Costs in ARL Libraries, 1986-1993

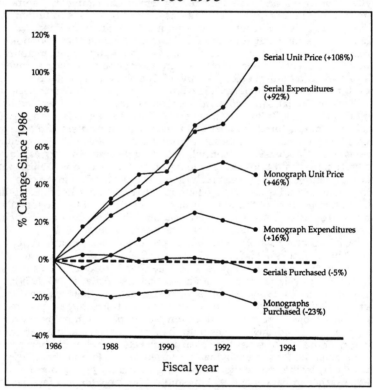

*Source:* Kendon Stubbs, *1992–93 ARL Statistics* (Washington, D.C.: Association of Research Libraries, 1994). 120p. Reprinted with permission.

## U.S. Periodical Price Index for 1994

The 1994 U.S. Periodical Price Index (USPPI) represents the 34th annual study of this type sponsored by the Library Materials Price Index Committee (LMPIC) of the Association of Library Collections and Technical Services (ALCTS), a division of the American Library Association. For the 10th consecutive year, the price index is based on subscription price information supplied, compiled, and analyzed by the Faxon Company, which shares the committee's concern for and interest in serials pricing trends. This annual study follows guidelines, definitions, and criteria established in the ANSI standard (Z39.20-1983) for price indexes.

The accompanying table provides a ranking of average periodical prices for each of 25 subject categories included in this survey and the average annual subscription price percent increase since 1985. For more details on the U.S. Periodical Price Index, see *American Libraries* for May 1994.

| Category | Average 1994 Price | Average Annual Increase Since 1985 |
|---|---|---|
| Russian translations | $964.13 | — |
| Chemistry and physics | 678.03 | 11.5% |
| Medicine | 321.39 | 9.9% |
| Math, botany, geology, general science | 271.68 | 9.9% |
| Zoology | 243.38 | 12.0% |
| Engineering | 195.62 | 9.8% |
| Psychology | 171.80 | 9.5% |
| Sociology and anthropology | 106.28 | 9.4% |
| Business and economics | 88.10 | 8.6% |
| Home economics | 82.23 | 8.4% |
| Journalism and communications | 80.14 | 7.5% |
| Industrial arts | 78.78 | 10.1% |
| Labor and industrial relations | 78.42 | 10.2% |
| Law | 76.06 | 9.4% |
| Education | 74.76 | 8.2% |
| Political science | 70.50 | 8.1% |
| Library and information sciences | 63.04 | 5.0% |
| Agriculture | 57.06 | 9.1% |
| History | 44.99 | 6.7% |
| Fine and applied arts | 44.92 | 5.3% |
| Philosophy and religion | 40.25 | 6.3% |
| Literature and language | 39.72 | 5.6% |
| Physical education and recreation | 39.47 | 6.8% |
| General interest periodicals | 37.39 | 3.0% |
| Children's periodicals | 20.43 | 5.3% |
| | | |
| USPPI excluding Russian translations | $135.37 | |
| USPPI including Russian translations | $179.53 | |
| Average USPPI increase since 1985 | | 9.5% |

*Source:* Kathryn Hammell Carpenter and Adrian W. Alexander, "U.S. Periodical Price Index for 1994," *American Libraries* 25 (May 1994): 450–59.

# Outstanding reference sources

EACH YEAR THE ALA's Reference and Adult Services Division's References Sources Committee examines hundreds of reference works to identify those that are essential for small and medium-sized public or academic libraries. The following are their picks for 1993 and 1994, incorporating reference sources published between 1991 and 1993.

*Academic Press Dictionary of Science and Technology,* ed. Christopher Morris (Academic Press, 1992).

*The Activist's Almanac,* by David Walls (Simon & Schuster, 1993).

*American Golfer's Guide,* by Herbert Pedroli (Turner, 1992).

*The American Horticultural Society Encyclopedia of Gardening,* ed. Christopher Brickell (Dorling Kindersley, 1993).

*The Anchor Bible Dictionary,* ed. David Noel Freedman (Doubleday, 1992).

*Black Literature Criticism,* ed. James P. Draper (Gale, 1992).

*Black Women in America: An Historical Encyclopedia,* ed. Darlene Clark Hine (Carlson, 1993).

*The Cambridge Encyclopedia of Human Evolution,* ed. Steve Jones, Robert Martin, and David Pilbeam (Cambridge, 1992).

*The Cambridge World History of Human Disease,* ed. Kenneth F. Kiple (Cambridge, 1993).

*The Cancer Dictionary,* by Roberta Altman and Michael Sarg (Facts on File, 1992).

*The Columbia Guide to Standard American English,* by Kenneth G. Wilson (Columbia, 1993).

*Contemporary Composers,* ed. Brian Morton and Pamela Collins (St. James, 1992).

*Contemporary Lesbian Writers of the United States,* ed. Sandra Pollack and Denise D. Knight (Greenwood, 1993).

*A Dictionary of American Proverbs,* ed. Wolfgang Mieder, Stewart A. Kingsbury, and Kelsie B. Harder (Oxford, 1992).

*Dictionary of Symbols,* by Carl G. Liungman (ABC-Clio, 1992).

*DISCovering Authors* [CD-ROM] (Gale, 1993).

*Encyclopedia of African American Religions,* ed. Larry G. Murphy, J. Gordon Melton, and Gary L. Ward (Garland, 1993).

*Encyclopedia of American Social History,* ed. Mary Kupiec Cayton, Elliot J. Gorn, and Peter W. Williams (Scribner's, 1993).

*Encyclopedia of Arms Control and Disarmament,* ed. Richard Dean Burns (Scribner's, 1993).

*Encyclopedia of Career Change and Work Issues,* ed. Lawrence K. Jones (Oryx, 1992).

*Encyclopedia of Child Bearing,* ed. Barbara Katz Rothman (Oryx, 1993).

*Encyclopedia of Ghosts and Spirits,* by Rosemary Guiley (Facts on File, 1992).

*Encyclopedia of Sleep and Dreaming,* ed. Mary A. Carskadon (Macmillan, 1993).

*Encyclopedia of Sociology,* ed. Edgar F. Borgatta and Marie L. Borgatta (Macmillan, 1992).

*Encyclopedia of the Confederacy,* ed. Richard N. Current (Simon & Schuster, 1993).

*Endangered Wildlife of the World* (Marshall Cavendish, 1993).

*The Evolving Constitution: How the Supreme Court Has Ruled on Issues from Abortion to Zoning,* by Jethro K. Lieberman (1992).

*The Facts on File Dictionary of Environmental Science,* by Harold Stevenson and Bruce Wyman (Facts on File, 1991).

*Guide to the Gods: A Dictionary of the Functions and Aspects of Deities,* by Marjorie Leach (ABC-Clio, 1992).

*Guinness Encyclopedia of Popular Music,* ed. Colin Larkin (Guinness, 1992).

*Have a Nice Day—No Problem! A Dictionary of Clichés,* by Christine Ammer (Dutton, 1992).

*Hazardous Substances Resource Guide,* ed. Richard P. Pohanish and Stanley A. Greene (Gale, 1993).

*The Henry Holt Handbook of Current Science and Technology,* by Bryan Bunch (Holt, 1992).

*Hispanic-American Almanac,* ed. Nicolas Kanellos (Gale, 1993).

*Historic U.S. Court Cases, 1690–1990,* ed. John W. Johnson (Garland, 1992).

*The Illustrated Encyclopedia of Fly-Fishing,* by Silvio Calabi (Holt, 1993).

*Information Please Environmental Almanac, 1992,* comp. World Resources Institute (Houghton Mifflin, 1992).

*International Dictionary of Ballet,* ed. Martha Bremser (St. James, 1993).

*Japan: An Illustrated Encyclopedia* (Kodansha, 1993).

*Japanese American History,* ed. Brian Niiya (Facts on File, 1993).

*Jewish-American History and Culture: An Encyclopedia,* ed. Jack Fischel and Sanford Pinsker (Garland, 1992).

*The McGraw-Hill Recycling Handbook,* ed. Herbert F. Lund (McGraw-Hill, 1993).

*Macmillan Encyclopedia of Computers,* ed. Gary G. Bitter (Macmillan, 1992).

*The Mark Twain Encyclopedia,* ed. J. R. LeMaster, James D. Wilson (Garland, 1993).

*The Multicultural Student's Guide to Colleges,* by Robert Mitchell (Farrar/ Noonday, 1993).

*The New Palgrave Dictionary of Money and Finance,* ed. Peter Newman, Murray Milgate, and John Eatwell (Stockton, 1992).

*The New Shorter Oxford English Dictionary, on Historical Principles,* ed. Lesley Brown (Oxford, 1993).

*Notable Black American Women,* ed. Jessie Carney Smith (Gale, 1992).

*Nuclear Power Plants Worldwide,* ed. Peter D. Dresser (Gale, 1993).

*The Oxford Companion to the Bible,* ed. Bruce M. Metzger and Michael D. Coogan (Oxford, 1993).

*The Oxford Companion to the English Language,* ed. Tom McArthur (Oxford, 1992).

*The Oxford Companion to the Supreme Court of the United States,* ed. Kermit L. Hall, et al. (Oxford, 1992).

*The Oxford Dictionary of American Legal Quotations,* comp. Fred R. Shapiro (Oxford, 1993).

*The Oxford Guide to Classical Mythology in the Arts, 1300–1990s,* by Jane Davidson Reid (Oxford, 1993).

*Professional and Occupational Licensing Directory* (Gale, 1993).

*Pronouncing Dictionary of Proper Names,* ed. John K. Bollard (Omnigraphics, 1993).

*Random House Word Menu,* by Stephen Glazier (Random House, 1992).

*Reference Guide to Science Fiction, Fantasy, and Horror,* by Michael Burgess (Libraries Unlimited, 1992).

*Roget's Thesaurus of the Bible,* by A. Colin Day (HarperCollins, 1992).

*Smithsonian Timelines of the Ancient World,* ed. Chris Scarre (Dorling Kindersley, 1993).

*The Supreme Court A to Z,* ed. Elder Witt (Congressional Quarterly, 1993).

*The Supreme Court Justices,* ed. Clare Cushman (Congressional Quarterly, 1993).

*Toxics A to Z: A Guide to Everyday Pollution Hazards,* by John Harte, et al. (University of California, 1991).

*Two Hundred Years of the American Circus,* by Tom Ogden (Facts on File, 1993).

*Venomous Reptiles of North America,* by Carl H. Ernst (Smithsonian, 1992).

*What You Need to Know about Psychiatric Drugs,* by Stuart C. Yudofsky, Robert E. Hales, and Tom Ferguson (American Psychiatric Press, 1991).

*World Explorers and Discoverers,* ed. Richard Bohlander (Macmillan, 1992).

*Source:* Reference Sources Committee, ALA Reference and Adult Services Division.

# Notable books, 1993–1994

THE FOLLOWING BOOKS, all published in 1992 or 1993, have been chosen for their significant contribution to the expansion of knowledge or for the pleasure they can provide to adult readers. Each year the Notable Books Council of the ALA Reference and Adult Services Division makes the selections, based on the criteria of wide general appeal and literary merit. More information on the books can be found by consulting *Booklist, Choice,* or other review journals.

## Fiction

Austin, Paul. *Leviathan* (Viking, 1992).

Brown, Rosellen. *Before and After* (Farrar, 1992).

Butler, Robert Olen. *A Good Scent from a Strange Mountain* (Holt, 1992).

Coyle, Beverly. *In Troubled Waters* (Ticknor & Fields/Houghton Mifflin, 1993).

Duncan, David James. *The Brothers K* (Doubleday, 1992).

Eugenides, Jeffrey. *The Virgin Suicides* (Farrar, 1993).

Gaines, Ernest. *A Lesson Before Dying* (Knopf, 1993).

Hoffman, Alice. *Turtle Moon* (Putnam, 1992).

Jones, Thom. *The Pugilist at Rest* (Little, Brown, 1993).

Kenan, Randall. *Let the Dead Bury Their Dead and Other Stories* (HBJ, 1992).

Klima, Ivan. *Judge on Trial* (Knopf, 1993).

McCarthy, Cormac. *All the Pretty Horses* (Knopf, 1992).

McCracken, Elizabeth. *Here's Your Hat, What's Your Hurry?* (Random House, 1993).

Malouf, David. *Remembering Babylon* (Pantheon, 1993).

Maxwell, William. *Billie Dyer and Other Stories* (Knopf, 1992).

Moore, Alison. *Small Spaces Between Emergencies* (Mercury House, 1992).

Morrison, Toni. *Jazz* (Knopf, 1992).

Naylor, Gloria. *Bailey's Cafe* (HBJ, 1992).

Nordan, Lewis. *Wolf Whistle* (Algonquin, 1993).

Ondaatje, Michael. *The English Patient* (Knopf, 1992).

Patchett, Ann. *The Patron Saint of Liars* (Houghton, 1992).

Proulx, E. Annie. *The Shipping News* (Scribner, 1993).

Russo, Richard. *Nobody's Fool* (Random House, 1993).

Smiley, Jane. *A Thousand Acres* (Knopf, 1992).

Watson, Larry. *Montana, 1948* (Milkweed Editions, 1993).

## Poetry

Budbill, David. *Judevine: The Complete Poems, 1970-1990* (Chelsea Green, 1991).

Fiser, Karen. *Words Like Fate and Pain* (Zoland, 1992).

Gallagher, Tess. *Moon Crossing Bridge* (Graywolf, 1992).

Van Duyn, Mona. *If It Be Not I* (Knopf, 1993).

## Nonfiction

Arenas, Reinaldo. *Before Night Falls* (Viking, 1993).

Chernow, Ron. *The Warburgs: The Twentieth-Century Odyssey of a Remarkable Jewish Family* (Random House, 1993).

Cook, Blanche Wiesen. *Eleanor Roosevelt: A Life, v.1, 1884-1933* (Viking, 1992).

Delany, Sarah Louise, and A. Elizabeth Delany. *Having Our Say: The Delany Sisters' First 100 Years* (Kodansha, 1993).

Drakulic, Slavenka. *Balkan Express: Fragments from the Other Side of War* (Norton, 1993).

Galvin, James. *The Meadow* (Holt, 1992).

Greider, William B. *Who Will Tell the People: The Betrayal of American Democracy* (Simon & Schuster, 1992).

Kaplan, Robert D. *Balkan Ghosts: A Journey through History* (St. Martin's, 1993).

Kaysen, Susanna. *Girl, Interrupted* (Turtle Bay, 1993).

Kelly, Michael. *Martyrs' Day: Chronicle of a Small War* (Random House, 1993).

Kennedy, Paul M. *Preparing for the Twenty-first Century* (Random House, 1993).

Maclean, Norman. *Young Men and Fire* (University of Chicago, 1992).

McCullough, David G. *Truman* (Simon & Schuster, 1992).

Mills, Kay. *This Little Light of Mine: The Life of Fannie Lou Hamer* (Dutton, 1993).

Minatoya, Lydia Yuri. *Talking to High Monks in the Snow: An Asian American Odyssey* (HarperCollins, 1992).

Monette, Paul. *Becoming a Man: Half a Life Story* (HBJ, 1992).

Postman, Neil. *Technopoly: The Surrender of Culture to Technology* (Knopf, 1992).

Prejean, Helen. *Dead Man Walking: An Eyewitness Account of the Death Penalty in the United States* (Random House, 1993).

Remnick, David. *Lenin's Tomb: The Last Days of the Soviet Empire* (Random House, 1993).

Schaller, George B. *The Last Panda* (University of Chicago, 1993).

Selzer, Richard. *Down from Troy: A Doctor Comes of Age* (Morrow, 1992).

Shelton, Richard. *Going Back to Bisbee* (University of Arizona, 1992).

Vidal, Gore. *United States: Essays, 1952-1992* (Random House, 1993).

Wills, Garry. *Lincoln at Gettysburg: The Words That Remade America* (Simon & Schuster, 1992).

*Source:* Notable Books Council, ALA Reference and Adult Services Division.

# Coretta Scott King Awards

THE CORETTA SCOTT KING AWARD is presented annually by the Coretta Scott King Task Force of the ALA's Social Responsibilities Round Table. Recipients are African-American authors and illustrators whose distinguished books promote an understanding and appreciation of the culture and contribution of all people to the realization of the "American dream." The award commemorates the life and work of Martin Luther King, Jr., and honors his widow, Coretta Scott King, for her courage and determination in continuing the work for peace and world brotherhood.

The award was founded in 1969 by the late Glyndon Flynt Greer, a distinguished African American school librarian, and it became an official ALA unit award in 1982. The following are the award-winning authors and illustrators since 1970.

## Authors

1994—Angela Johnson, *Toning the Sweep* (Orchard Books, 1993).

1993—Patricia C. McKissack, *The Dark-Thirty: Southern Tales of the Supernatural* (Knopf, 1992).

1992—Walter Dean Myers, *Now Is Your Time* (HarperCollins, 1991).

1991—Mildred D. Taylor, *The Road to Memphis* (Dial, 1990).

1990—Patricia and Frederick McKissack, *A Long Hard Journey: The Story of the Pullman Porter* (Walker, 1989).

1989—Walter Dean Myers, *Fallen Angels* (Scholastic, 1988).

1988—Mildred D. Taylor, *The Friendship* (Dial, 1987).

1987—Mildred Pitts Walter, *Justin and the Best Biscuits in the World* (Lothrop, 1986).

1986—Virginia Hamilton, *The People Could Fly: American Black Folktales* (Knopf, 1985).

1985—Walter Dean Myers, *Motown and Didi* (Viking, 1984).

1984—Lucille Clifton, *Everett Anderson's Goodbye* (Holt, 1983).

1983—Virginia Hamilton, *Sweet Whispers, Brother Rush* (Philomel, 1982).

1982—Mildred D. Taylor, *Let the Circle Be Unbroken* (Dial, 1981).

1981—Sidney Poitier, *This Life* (Knopf, 1980).

1980—Walter Dean Myers, *The Young Landlords* (Viking, 1979).

1979—Ossie Davis, *Escape to Freedom: A Play about Young Frederick Douglass* (Viking, 1977).

1978—Eloise Greenfield, *Africa Dream* (Crowell, 1977).

1977—James Haskins, *The Story of Stevie Wonder* (Lothrop, 1976).

1976—Pearl Bailey, *Duey's Tale* (Harcourt, 1975).

1975—Dorothy Robinson, *The Legend of Africania* (Johnson, 1974).

1974—Sharon Bell Mathis, *Ray Charles* (Crowell, 1973).

1973—Alfred Duckett, *I Never Had It Made: The Autobiography of Jackie Robinson* (Putnam, 1972).

1972—Elton C. Fax, *17 Black Artists* (Dodd, 1971).

1971—Charlemae Rollins, *Black Troubadour: Langston Hughes* (Rand McNally, 1970).

1970—Lillie Patterson, *Dr. Martin Luther King, Jr., Man of Peace* (Garrard, 1969).

## Illustrators

1994—Tom Feelings, for *Soul Looks Back in Wonder*, edited by Phyllis Fogelman (Dial Books, 1993).

1993—Kathleen Atkins Wilson, for *The Origin of Life on Earth: An African Creation Myth*, retold by David A. Anderson/SANKOFA (Sight Productions, 1992).

1992—Faith Ringgold, for *Tar Beach* (Crown, 1991).

1991—Leo and Diane Dillon, for *Aida*, by Leontyne Price (HBJ, 1990).

1990—Jan Spivey Gilchrist, for *Nathaniel Talking*, by Eloise Greenfield (Black Butterfly, 1988).

1989—Jerry Pinkney, for *Mirandy and Brother Wind*, by Patricia C. McKissack (Knopf, 1988).

1988—John Steptoe, for *Mufaro's Beautiful Daughters* (Lothrop, 1987).

1987—Jerry Pinkney, for *Half a Moon and One Whole Star*, by Crescent Dragonwagon (Macmillan, 1986).

1986—Jerry Pinkney, for *The Patchwork Quilt*, by Valerie Flournoy (Dial, 1985).

1984—Pat Cummings, for *My Mama Needs Me*, by Mildred Pitts Walter (Lothrop, 1983).

1983—Peter Magubane, for *Black Child* (Knopf, 1982).

1982—John Steptoe, for *Mother Crocodile: An Uncle Amadou Tale from Senegal*, translated by Rosa Guy (Delacorte, 1981).

1981—Ashley Bryan, for *Beat the Story Drum Pum-Pum* (Atheneum, 1980).

1980—Carole Byard, for *Cornrows*, by Camille Yarbrough (Coward-McCann, 1979).

1979—Tom Feelings, for *Something on My Mind*, by Nikki Grimes (Dial, 1978).

1974—George Ford, for *Ray Charles*, by Sharon Bell Mathis (Crowell, 1973).

*Source:* ALA Social Responsibilities Round Table and ALA Office for Library Outreach Services.

---

### Best-selling recorded books, 1993

1. John Grisham, *The Client* (1993)
2. John Grisham, *The Pelican Brief* (1992)
3. William Manchester, *A World Lit Only by Fire* (1992)
4. John Grisham, *A Time to Kill* (1989)
5. Patricia D. Cornwell, *All That Remains* (1992)
6. Robert Ludlum, *The Scorpio Illusion* (1993)
7. Clive Cussler, *Sahara* (1992)
8. Peter Mayle, *A Year in Provence* (1989)
9. James B. Stewart, *Den of Thieves* (1991)
10. Terry McMillan, *Waiting to Exhale* (1992)
11. Patricia D. Cornwell, *Cruel & Unusual* (1993)
12. Tom Clancy, *Without Remorse* (1993)
13. Patricia D. Cornwell, *Body of Evidence* (1991)
14. Jonathan Kellerman, *Devil's Waltz* (1993)
15. Clive Cussler, *Treasure* (1988)

*Source:* Books on Tape®, Inc.

**4**

# Documents

# Federal regional depository libraries

THE FEDERAL DEPOSITORY LIBRARY PROGRAM was established by Congress to provide free public access to government publications. Nearly 1,400 public, academic, state, and law libraries maintain collections of government publications. These collections, which are tailored to local needs, are open to the public. Fifty-three of these libraries are designated as regional depository libraries. They are responsible for retaining material permanently and providing interlibrary loan and reference services in their regions.

A complete listing of regional depositories follows. To obtain a complete listing of all depository libraries, write to: Federal Depository Library Program, U.S. Government Printing Office, Superintendent of Documents, Stop: SM, Washington, DC 20402.

**Alabama:** Auburn University at Montgomery Library, 7300 University Drive, Montgomery, AL 36117-3596; (205) 244-3650.

University of Alabama Libraries, Documents Department—Box 870266, Tuscaloosa, AL 35487-0266; (205) 348-6046.

**Alaska:** Served by Washington State Library.

**American Samoa:** Served by the University of Hawaii.

**Arizona:** Department of Library, Archives and Public Records, Third Floor, State Capitol, 1700 West Washington, Phoenix, AZ 85007; (602) 542-4444.

**Arkansas:** Arkansas State Library, One Capitol Mall, Little Rock, AR 72201; (501) 682-2326.

**California:** California State Library, Government Publications Section, P.O. Box 942837, Sacramento, CA 94237-0001; (916) 653-0085.

**Colorado:** University of Colorado Libraries, Government Publications Division, Campus Box 184, Boulder, CO 80309-0184; (303) 492-8834.

Denver Public Library, Government Publications Department, 1357 Broadway, Denver, CO 80203-2165; (303) 640-8876.

**Connecticut:** Connecticut State Library, Government Documents Unit, 231 Capitol Avenue, Hartford, CT 06106; (203) 566-4971.

**Delaware:** Served by the University of Maryland.

**District of Columbia:** Served by the University of Maryland.

**Florida:** University of Florida Libraries, Library West, Documents Department, Gainesville, FL 32611; (904) 392-0367.

**Georgia:** University of Georgia Libraries, Government Reference Department, Athens, GA 30602-1645; (706) 542-8949.

**Guam:** Served by the University of Hawaii.

**Hawaii:** University of Hawaii Library, Government Documents Collections, 2550 The Mall, Honolulu, HI 96822; (808) 956-8230.

**Idaho:** University of Idaho Library, Documents Section, Moscow, ID 83844-2353; (208) 885-6344.

**Illinois:** Illinois State Library, 300 South Second Street, Springfield, IL 62701-1796; (217) 782-4887.

**Indiana:** Indiana State Library, Serials Documents Section, 140 North Senate Avenue, Indianapolis, IN 46204-2296; (317) 232-3686.

**Iowa:** University of Iowa Libraries, Government Documents Department, Iowa City, IA 52242; (319) 335-5925.

**Kansas:** University of Kansas, 6001 Malott Hall, Lawrence, KS 66045-2800; (913) 864-4660.

**Kentucky:** University of Kentucky Libraries, Government Publications Department, Lexington, KY 40506-0039; (606) 257-8400.

**Louisiana:** Louisiana State University, Middletown Library, Government Documents Department, Baton Rouge, LA 70803-3312; (504) 388-2570.

Louisiana Technical University Library, Prescott Memorial Library, Ruston, LA 71272-0046; (318) 257-4962.

**Maine:** University of Maine, Raymond H. Fogler Library, Tri-State Regional Documents Deposits, Orono, ME 04469-5729; (207) 581-1680.

**Maryland:** University of Maryland, McKeldin Library, Documents Division, College Park, MD 20742; (301) 405-9165.

**Massachusetts:** Boston Public Library, Government Documents Department, 666 Boylston Street, Boston, MA 02117; (617) 536-5400, ext. 227.

**Michigan:** Detroit Public Library, 5201 Woodward Ave., Detroit, MI 48202-4093; (313) 833-1025.

Michigan State Library, Library of Michigan, 717 West Allegan Street, P.O. Box 30007, Lansing, MI 48909; (517) 373-1307.

**Micronesia:** Served by the University of Hawaii.

**Minnesota:** University of Minnesota, Government Publications Division, 409 Wilson Library, 309 South 19th Street, Minneapolis, MN 55455; (612) 626-7520.

**Mississippi:** University of Mississippi Library, Williams Library, University, MS 38677; (601) 232-5857.

**Missouri:** University of Missouri at Columbia, Ellis Library, Government Documents, Columbia, MO 65201; (314) 882-6733.

**Montana:** University of Montana, Mansfield Library, Documents Division, Missoula, MT 59812-1195; (406) 243-6700.

**Nebraska:** University of Nebraska-Lincoln, Love Library, Documents Department, Lincoln, NE 68588-0410; (402) 472-2562.

**Nevada:** University of Nevada Library, Government Publications Department, Reno, NV 89557-0044; (702) 784-6579.

**New Hampshire:** Served by the University of Maine.

**New Jersey:** Newark Public Library, 5 Washington Street, Newark, NJ 07101-0630; (201) 733-7812.

**New Mexico:** University of New Mexico, General Library, Government Publications Department, Albuquerque, NM 87131-1466; (505) 277-5441.

New Mexico State Library, Reference Department, 325 Don Caspar Avenue, Santa Fe, NM 87503; (505) 827-3852.

**New York:** New York State Library, Cultural Education Center, Albany, NY 12230-0001; (518) 474-3940.

**North Carolina:** University of North Carolina at Chapel Hill, Davis Library, CB #3912, BA/SS Division, Chapel Hill, NC 27599; (919) 962-1151.

**North Dakota:** North Dakota State University Library, P.O. Box 5599, Fargo, ND 58105-5599; (701) 237-8863.

University of North Dakota, Chester Fritz Library, Documents Department, Grand Forks, ND 58202; (701) 777-3316.

**Northern Marianas:** Served by the University of Hawaii.

**Ohio:** State Library of Ohio, Documents Department, 65 South Front Street, Columbus, OH 43266-0334; (614) 644-1971.

**Oklahoma:** Oklahoma Department of Libraries, Government Documents, 200 N.E. 18th Street, Oklahoma City, OK 73105; (405) 521-2502, ext. 252.

Oklahoma State University Library, Documents Department, Stillwater, OK 74078; (405) 744-6546.

**Oregon:** Portland State University Library, Documents Department, P.O. Box 1151, Portland, OR 97207; (503) 725-4123.

**Pennsylvania:** State Library of Pennsylvania, Government Publications Section, P.O. Box 1601, Harrisburg, PA 17105; (717) 787-3752.

**Puerto Rico:** Served by the University of Florida.

**Rhode Island:** Served by the Connecticut State Library.

**South Carolina:** Clemson University, Cooper Library, Box 343001, Documents Department, Clemson, SC 29634-3001; (803) 656-5174.

University of South Carolina, Thomas Cooper Library, Documents/Microform Department, Green & Sumter Street, Columbia, SC 29208; (803) 777-4841.

**South Dakota:** Served by the University of Minnesota.

**Tennessee:** Memphis State University Library, Government Documents Department, Memphis, TN 38152; (901) 678-2206.

**Texas:** Texas State Library, Public Services Department, P.O. Box 12927, Capital Station, Austin, TX 78711; (512) 463-5455.

Texas Tech University Library, Government Documents Department, Lubbock, TX 79409-0002; (806) 742-2236.

**Utah:** Utah State University, Merrill Library, U.M.C. 30, Logan, UT 84322; (801) 750-1000, ext. 2683.

**Vermont:** Served by the University of Maine.

**Virgin Islands:** Served by the University of Florida.

**Virginia:** University of Virginia, Alderman Library, Public Documents, Charlottesville, VA 22093-2498; (804) 924-3133.

**Washington:** Washington State Library, Documents Section, Olympia, WA 98504; (206) 753-4027.

**West Virginia:** West Virginia University Library, Documents Department, Morgantown, WV 26506-6069; (304) 293-3640.

**Wisconsin:** State Historical Library of Wisconsin, Government Publications

Section, 816 State Street, Madison, WI 53706; (608) 264-6525.

Milwaukee Public Library, 814 West Wisconsin Ave., Milwaukee, WI 53233; (414) 278-2167.

**Wyoming:** Served by Utah State University.

*Source: Monthly Catalog of U.S. Government Publications.*

# Federal archives and records

THE NATIONAL ARCHIVES AND RECORDS ADMINISTRATION (NARA) establishes policies and procedures for managing the records of the U.S. government. It was established in 1985 as an independent agency to replace the National Archives and Records Service, which was an office of the General Services Administration. The NARA makes original documents and records available for use by researchers, answers requests for information, and provides copies of documents for a fee. The office also publishes the daily *Federal Register, the Code of Federal Regulations,* the *U.S. Government Manual,* and many other public documents.

## How to locate an unpublished government record

First, contact the Records Officer for the Federal agency in question. They should be able to tell you the location and accessibility of the document. If it is available at a Federal Records Center or the National Archives, they can give you the reference and box numbers you will need when you contact the appropriate records center or archive.

Second, if the agency cannot provide satisfactory information, contact the Federal Records Center or archives office directly.

Third, if the document is classified or otherwise unfindable, you have the option of issuing a Freedom of Information Act request to the appropriate Federal agency.

## National archives offices

The National Archives in Washington receives records from cabinet offices, the Supreme Court, and agency headquarters offices in the District of Columbia. The National Archives regional offices receive the records of all federal agencies and courts in the regions they serve. Roughly 3% of all Federal records are eventually retained in the National Archives offices. The other 97% are destroyed after 10–75 years, according to schedules set by statute. When documents are transferred to the National Archives, they become public property and are usually accessible to researchers, although they are subject to certain restrictions to protect the privacy of individuals or for national security reasons.

In January 1994 a new National Archives facility opened to researchers and the general public in College Park, Maryland. The new building, known as Archives II, represents six years of planning and construction and is the largest and most technologically advanced archives facility in the world.

The main National Archives building, which was completed in 1937, reached its records storage capacity of approximately 900,000 cubic feet in the late 1960s. To alleviate the space shortage, more than 500,000 cubic feet of archival records were stored in leased or government-owned space in the Washington area since 1970.

Archives II was designed to consolidate all of these scattered sites and to serve as an archives for the 21st century, protecting and preserving historical materials for future generations. It has the most advanced pollution and environmental controls; 520 miles of high-density mobile shelving for storing records; nine sophisticated preservation and conservation laboratories; and extensive research facilities. The total record storage capacity is approximately 2 million cubic feet, and the building is designed so that additional storage units can be added on as needed.

**National Archives,** Pennsylvania Ave. and 7th Street, N.W., Washington, DC 20408; (202) 501-5403.

**National Archives II,** 8601 Adelphi Rd., College Park, MD 20740-6001.

**National Archives—Suitland Reference Branch,** 4205 Suitland Rd., Suitland, MD 20409; (301) 763-7410.

**National Archives—New England Region,** 380 Trapelo Road, Waltham, MA 02154; (617) 647-8100; fax (617) 647-8460.

**National Archives—Pittsfield Region,** 100 Dan Fox Dr., Pittsfield, MA 01201; (413) 445-6885; fax (413) 445-7596.

**National Archives—Northeast Region,** 201 Varick Street, New York, NY 10014-4811; (212) 337-1303; fax (212) 337-1306.

**National Archives—Mid-Atlantic Region,** 9th and Market Streets, Room 1350, Philadelphia, PA 19107; (215) 597-3000; fax (215) 597-2303.

**National Archives—Southeast Region,** 1557 St. Joseph Ave., East Point, GA 30344; (404) 763-7477; fax (404) 763-7033.

**National Archives—Great Lakes Region,** 7358 S. Pulaski Rd., Chicago, IL 60629; (312) 581-7816; fax (312) 353-1294.

**National Archives—Central Plains Region,** 2312 E. Bannister Road, Kansas City, MO 64131; (816) 926-6272; fax (816) 926-6235.

**National Archives—Southwest Region,** 501 W. Felix St., P.O. Box 6216, Fort Worth, TX 76115, (817) 334-5525; fax (817) 334-5621.

**National Archives—Rocky Mountain Region,** Building 48, Denver Federal Center, P.O. Box 25307, Denver, CO 80225; (303) 236-0818; fax (303) 236-9354.

**National Archives—Pacific Southwest Region,** 24000 Avila Road, P.O. Box 6719, Laguna Niguel, CA 92677-6719; (714) 643-4241; fax (714) 643-4832.

**National Archives—Pacific Sierra Region,** 1000 Commodore Drive, San Bruno, CA 94066; (415) 876-9009; fax (415) 876-9233.

**National Archives—Pacific Northwest Region,** 6125 Sand Point Way, NE, Seattle, WA 98115; (206) 526-6507; fax (206) 526-4344.

**National Archives—Alaska Region,** 654 W. Third Ave., Room 012, Anchorage, AK 99501; (907) 271-2441; fax (907) 271-2442.

## Federal records centers

The National Archives and Records Administration also manages sixteen Federal Records Centers. Federal agencies retire certain noncurrent public records to these centers in accordance with established disposition schedules. These records are still controlled by the originating agencies, but stored at the centers until they are either destroyed or sent to the National Archives. The Federal Records Centers provide reference services and furnish information from the records they hold.

**Federal Records Center—Atlanta,** 1557 St. Joseph Ave., East Point, GA 30344; (404) 763-7476; fax (404) 763-7815.

**Federal Records Center—Boston,** 380 Trapelo Rd., Waltham, MA 02154; (617) 647-8745; fax (617) 647-8088.

**Federal Records Center—Chicago,** 7358 S. Pulaski Rd., Chicago, IL 60629; (312) 581-7816; fax (312) 886-7883.

**Federal Records Center—Dayton,** 3150 Springboro Rd., Dayton, OH 45439;

(513) 225-2878; fax (513) 225-7236.

**Federal Records Center—Denver,** Building 48, Denver Federal Center, P.O. Box 25307, Denver, CO 80225; (303) 236-0804; fax (303) 236-9297.

**Federal Records Center—Fort Worth,** Box 6216, Fort Worth, TX 76115; (817) 334-5515; fax (817) 334-5511.

**Federal Records Center—Kansas City,** 2312 E. Bannister Rd., Kansas City, MO 64131; (816) 926-7271; fax (816) 926-6235.

**Federal Records Center—Los Angeles,** 24000 Avila Rd., Laguna Niguel, CA 92677; (714) 643-4220; fax (714) 643-4500.

**Federal Records Center—New York,** Building 22, Military Ocean Terminal, Bayonne, NJ 07002; (201) 823-7161; fax (201) 823-5432.

**Federal Records Center—Philadelphia,** 5000 Wissahickon Ave., Philadelphia, PA 19144; (215) 951-5588; fax (215) 951-7808.

**Federal Records Center—Pittsfield,** 100 Dan Fox Dr., Pittsfield, MA 01201; (413) 445-6885; fax (413) 445-7305.

**Federal Records Center—San Francisco,** 1000 Commodore Dr., San Bruno, CA 94066; (415) 876-9003; fax (415) 876-0920.

**Federal Records Center—Seattle,** 6125 Sand Point Way, NE, Seattle, WA 98115; (206) 526-6501; fax (206) 526-6575.

**National Personnel Records Center,** Civilian Personnel Records, 111 Winnebago St., St. Louis, MO 63118; (314) 425-5722; fax (314) 538-4005.

**National Personnel Records Center,** Military Personnel Records, 9700 Page Blvd., St. Louis, MO 63132-5100; (314) 263-7201; fax (314) 425-5719.

## Presidential libraries

Through the Presidential libraries, which are located at sites selected by the Presidents and built with private funds, the National Archives and Records Administration preserves and makes available the records and personal papers of a particular President's administration. In addition to providing reference services on Presidential documents, each library prepares documentary and descriptive publications and operates a museum to exhibit documents, historic objects, and other memorabilia of interest to the public.

The records of each President since Herbert Hoover are administered by the agency. Once considered personal papers, all Presidential records created on or after January 20, 1981, are declared by law to be owned and controlled by the United States and are required to be transferred to the National Archives at the end of the administration.

**Herbert Hoover Library,** Parkside Drive, P.O. Box 488, West Branch, IA 52358; (319) 643-5301.

**Franklin D. Roosevelt Library,** 259 Albany Post Road, Hyde Park, NY 12538; (914) 229-8114.

**Harry S. Truman Library,** 1200 N. McKoy Street, Independence, MO 64050; (816) 833-1400.

**Dwight D. Eisenhower Library,** Southeast Fourth St., Abilene, KS 67410; (913) 263-4751.

**John Fitzgerald Kennedy Library,** Columbia Point, Boston, MA 02125; (617) 929-4500.

**Lyndon Baines Johnson Library,** 2313 Red River St., Austin, TX 78705; (512) 482-5137.

**Richard Nixon Presidential Materials Project,** National Archives, 8601 Adelphi Rd., College Park, MD 20740-6001; (301) 713-6950.

**Gerald R. Ford Library,** 1000 Beal Ave., Ann Arbor, MI 48109-2114; (313) 668-2218.

**Gerald R. Ford Museum,** 303 Pearl Street N.W., Grand Rapids, MI 49504-5353; (616) 456-2259.

**Jimmy Carter Library,** 1 Coppenhill Ave., Atlanta, GA 30307-1498; (404) 331-3942.

**Ronald Reagan Library,** 40 Presidential Dr., Simi Valley, CA 93065; (805) 522-8444.

**George Bush Presidential Materials Project,** 701 University Drive East, Suite 300, College Station, TX 77840-1987; (409) 260-9552.

**Office of Presidential Libraries,** Washington, D.C.; (202) 501-5700.

*Source:* National Archives—Great Lakes Region; Federal Records Center—Chicago.

# The Government Printing Office

*by Ridley Kessler and Jack Sulzer*

4

SINCE ITS INCEPTION IN JUNE OF 1860 by Joint Resolution 25, the Government Printing Office has been "authorized and directed to have executed the printing and binding authorized by the Senate and House of Representatives, the executive and judicial departments." The mission of the GPO has changed little over the last 132 years. It is still responsible for the printing and binding for Congress, the Executive Office, and the executive departments and independent agencies. Title 44, section 501, of the U.S. Code, the statute now governing public printing, states that the only exceptions to printing outside the GPO must be granted specially by the Joint Committee on Printing (JCP). The JCP decides whether government printing should be done by another federal agency or by private contract.

The Public Printer, who heads the GPO, oversees a huge printing and distribution operation with a workforce of approximately 5,000 people. According to the 1990 Government Printing Office *Annual Report,* the GPO printed 1.9 billion publications for the government. This is too large a job for the GPO to do in-house, and in 1990 only 24% of the publishing revenue received came from the Central Printing Plant or from the six regional printing plants the GPO operates. Seventy-six percent of the GPO's printing revenue is contracted out to private commercial printers, who now do the bulk of all government printing.

Printing and production of government information are just one part of the Government Printing Office's mission. More important to librarians are its document dissemination activities. The first law concerning public access was passed on December 27, 1813, during the Thirteenth Congress. Joint Resolution 1 empowered Congress to distribute the *Journals* of both houses to colleges and universities in each state. This law stated that distribution would begin with the Thirteenth Congress and continue with all future congresses. This resolution was the first recognition of government's obligation to provide public access to the information it produced. Subsequent resolutions and laws passed in the 1840s, 1850s, and 1860s increased the numbers of documents to be disseminated, authorized congressional designation of depositories, and created the Office of Superintendent of Public Documents.

On January 12, 1895, the Richardson Bill was passed into law. Generally known as the "Printing Act of 1895," this major statute codified all of the laws dealing with the printing and distribution of public documents. It is now the heart and soul of Title 44. It gathered all functions of government printing, distribution, and sale of information under the bureaucratic umbrella of the

Government Printing Office. The Superintendent of Documents was put under the authority of the Public Printer and placed in charge of all distribution, including the depository system and sales. The Printing Act of 1895 also mandated the establishment of the first official bibliographic sources for government information, later known as the *Monthly Catalog*, the *Documents Catalog*, and the *Documents Index*.

Today the Public Printer is appointed by the president and confirmed by the Senate. The Deputy Public Printer is the chief administrative officer of the GPO, and the operational units of Customer Services, Production Services, and Procurement Services report directly to this office. The Chief Financial Officer is in charge of budget, accounting, and financial planning, and oversees all personnel and labor matters. The Superintendent of Documents, who reports directly to the Public Printer, is most directly concerned with the Depository Library Program (DLP) and government documents librarians.

*Source:* Ridley Kessler and Jack Sulzer, "The Politics of Documents Librarianship," in Diane H. Smith, ed., *Management of Government Information Resources in Libraries* (Englewood, Colo.: Libraries Unlimited, 1993), pp.183–212. Reprinted with permission.

# Using historical documents

*by Ann D. Gordon*

RESEARCHERS TURN TO THE HISTORICAL RECORD not for the sake of using it but to answer questions. The distinction is an important one in defining the relationship between archivists and researchers. The former speak of archives as "underused," while researchers want solutions. The 1,394 researchers who responded to the Historical Documents Study, conducted by the National Historical Publications and Records Commission in 1991, were all members of national historical and genealogical societies. The intent of the survey was to understand current demand for historical sources and the extent to which researchers avail themselves of services provided to enhance their use.

Most of the researchers turned to a common core of sources long recognized as the basic material of historical research: records and manuscripts in the private sector, government records and documents, and newspapers.

| Table 1. Usefulness of sources—all respondents | | |
| --- | --- | --- |
| **Types of sources** | **% rating indispensable** | **% not using** |
| Government records | 61 | 10 |
| Records/manuscripts | 61 | 9 |
| Newspapers | 41 | 11 |
| Institutional records | 35 | 24 |
| Maps | 26 | 23 |
| Personal interviews | 24 | 35 |
| Photographs/still images | 23 | 25 |
| Machine-readable data | 20 | 52 |
| Oral histories | 19 | 40 |
| Pamphlets/published ephemera | 18 | 30 |
| Artifacts | 8 | 60 |
| Moving images | 3 | 77 |
| Audio materials | 3 | 74 |

Historians and genealogists selected their repositories in different proportions. Not only do historians alone have a different order of preference, they also concentrate more than genealogists in the more popular types of repositories.

### Table 2. Repositories used to obtain sources—genealogists and historians

| Repository | % using |
|------------|---------|
| Local or state historical society | 67 |
| College or university library | 60 |
| National Archives | 53 |
| State archives | 51 |
| Branches of local government | 37 |
| Library of Congress | 33 |
| Independent research library | 32 |
| Museum collection or archives | 29 |

### Table 3. Repositories used to obtain sources—historians only

| Repository | % using |
|------------|---------|
| College or university library | 80 |
| Local or state historical society | 56 |
| State archives | 36 |
| Museum collections or archives | 36 |
| National Archives | 35 |
| Library of Congress | 32 |
| Independent research library | 27 |
| Branches of local government | 22 |

4

*Source:* Ann D. Gordon, *Using the Nation's Documentary Heritage: The Report of the Historical Documents Study* (Washington, D.C.: National Historical Publications and Records Commission/American Council of Learned Societies, 1992). 112p.

# Tips for libraries distributing IRS tax forms

*by Irene M. Padilla*

MANY PUBLIC LIBRARIES JUMPED into tax form distribution with both feet when tax forms were first offered for distribution through libraries. Since then, many problems have arisen and countless hours have been spent reviewing the requirements necessary to enable public libraries to provide a quality service. While a number of solutions have been offered by the Internal Revenue Service (IRS), and some progress has been made in service delivery and follow-through, many problems remain.

Providing IRS tax forms to the public continues to be a frustrating and time-consuming experience. As a result, many libraries have elected to either limit the types of forms offered or to discontinue the service altogether. Those libraries that still continue to provide tax forms to the public indicated an ongoing need for help in establishing an efficient and effective tax distribution center.

## Define your library's role in tax form distribution

Your library is volunteering to take on the IRS task of tax form distribution. You are not expected to be an IRS service center.

Think of tax form distribution as a service that you choose to provide in cooperation with the IRS. This is not necessarily an essential library service in every community.

Decide what level of service your community needs and what your library can reasonably offer. The IRS offers more than 300 forms, instructions, and publications. Some libraries offer only the basic forms and reproducibles, while others offer every item that the IRS makes available to them. Some libraries enlist volunteers to help elderly patrons prepare their tax forms. In other communities, however, this service is taken care of very effectively through other public service agencies.

Consider the potential benefits of offering the program in terms of drawing people into the library who would not otherwise have come to the library and increasing the library's visibility by providing a public service not easily available elsewhere.

Consider the costs of offering the program in terms of the staff time, effort, and space requirements necessary to support the level of service your library has chosen to offer.

## Develop a relationship with your local IRS office

Identify the local IRS agent assigned to your library by contacting your local IRS office or by calling the IRS Library Hotline.

Make a list of previous or current problems and questions and ask your IRS agent for answers and clarification.

You can expect your local IRS agent to help you deal with unusual circumstances and idiosyncrasies, solve problems with forms orders, and guide you through the bureaucracy by finding the appropriate person or agency to help you solve your particular problem.

Invite the local agent to come into your facility and assist with either setting up a new center or rearranging an existing area.

Know who to call when you have a problem and be persistent! Don't take no for an answer.

Severe problems should be brought to the attention of your local congressional representative.

## Streamline ordering procedures

Order early and anticipate demand.

IRS staff can help you decide which package plan for forms and publications would work best for your size library.

Don't hesitate to ask for additional copies of reproducible forms or other materials that you feel will help satisfy the demand.

Designate sufficient storage space for extra forms to keep them out of the way of regular library operations.

Keep accurate records to streamline the ordering process in subsequent years. At the end of the tax season, take note of what forms and publications are left over to adjust the order for the following year.

## Staff allocation and training

Assign a particular staff member or volunteer the responsibility for ordering forms, receiving and recording shipments, and filling displays.

Acquaint all staff with required procedures, including the location of extra forms and procedures for display.

Provide staff with a refresher course on tax services and available reference sources.

Make sure staff understand and feel comfortable with the concept of making the forms available without having to give advice. Some libraries display a sign saying "Tax Forms Yes, Tax Advice NO!" near the service desk.

## Effective display of tax materials

Request tax form display racks from the IRS or be creative. Tax forms can be displayed on most of the space-saving racks currently available. Milk crates with hanging files and adjustable pamphlet racks work just as well as more formal displays. Temporarily assign forms to a prominent display area.

Locate forms so that they are convenient to the public but keep them as far from library staff as possible to disassociate them from library reference services.

Keep your backstock of forms out of sight to discourage the public from taking more forms than they need.

Place several notebooks of reproducible forms near photocopiers and let patrons serve themselves. This will help to prevent overburdening staff in an already busy season. The staff time and energy saved are more important than any forms that may be lost.

## Photocopiers: Technical considerations

Have photocopiers serviced prior to the beginning of the tax season.

Increase the amount of change obtained from the bank. Stocking up on extra change reduces stress for both staff and public.

Order adequate supplies of paper for the photocopier to meet the demand. A review of the past year's usage records can provide valuable ordering information.

## Marketing of services

Stress the tax services you do provide rather than highlighting those you don't offer.

Display related library materials such as Lasser's tax guides, Prentice-Hall tax forms, bookmarks, and brochures near the tax forms.

Provide a printed list of additional outlets in the area for both federal and state forms.

Advertise IRS telephone numbers (including local and toll-free) on posters, fliers, and bookmarks. Include information on when, where, and how to file. Eye-catching graphics and bright colors are recommended.

Consider working with other community resources such as local financial-service providers to publicize requested tax-referral information.

## Participation in volunteer tax-assistance programs

Providing space for volunteer tax-assistance programs in your library can be a service that your community will find beneficial.

Work with volunteer organizations such as Volunteer Income Tax Assistance (VITA), the American Association of Retired Persons (AARP), and Tax Counseling for the Elderly (TCE) to schedule a consistent time and place for providing assistance to the elderly and others in need of advice. Your local

IRS taxpayer education coordinator can help you contact these organizations.
Refer patrons with tax questions to these volunteers when possible.

Setting up appointments for people is time consuming. A system of "first come, first served" may work best for your library.

Remember, tax volunteers are there to help you. Do not hesitate to schedule meetings with them at your convenience and when you need them.

## Provide feedback to the IRS

Contact the IRS through your local taxpayer education coordinator or write the IRS (with a copy to your local office) at either of the following addresses:

IRS, BPOL Program Manager, Taxpayer Services, T:T:VE, Room 2714, 1111 Constitution Ave., N.W., Washington, DC 20224.

IRS, BPOL Program Manager, Publishing Services, HR:F:P, Room 1523, 1111 Constitution Ave., N.W., Washington, DC 20224.

*Note:* Taxpayer Services routinely deal with issues concerning volunteers, education, and service, while Publishing Services deal with issues related to forms, publication, and service.

Mention problems along with suggestions for enhancements that will help to prevent the problems in the future.

Compliments on features that worked well are helpful in guiding future efforts.

When offering thanks for help, mention specific individuals by name if possible.

## Withdrawal from the program

It is possible to withdraw from the program if the service no longer meets your library's defined role or needs. Withdrawal can be accomplished by indicating your intentions in a letter to the IRS, by calling the taxpayer education coordinator assigned to your state or region, or by not completing the annual survey of forms needed for the coming tax year (however, this last tactic doesn't always work unless you submit a more formal notice).

Accompany your decision to withdraw with a publicity campaign designed to let the taxpayer know where to turn. Successful strategies often involve identifying other local tax form distribution centers by issuing press releases and fliers. Signs displayed prominently on the outside doors of the library are a method of publicizing the library's decision. Whatever the method chosen, it is important to start the process of notifying the public long before the new tax season begins.

*Source:* Irene M. Padilla, "Establishing an Efficient and Effective Tax Distribution Center,"
*Public Libraries* 31 (November/December 1992): 344–46.

# Technical reports

*by Ellen Calhoun*

THE THREE MAJOR SOURCES OF TECHNICAL REPORTS—corporations, government agencies, and their contractors—produce a great variety of material in the conduct of their research. Some types of reports are more readily available than others, so it may help to know what kind of report your patron is looking for.

The Committee on Scientific and Technical Information (COSATI) identified eight major kinds of technical reports in 1967. Beginning in order with the least formal type, these are:

*Preprints.* Generally manuscripts designed to be circulated among colleagues for review, though they may end up being more formally printed or reviewed by an institution or even indexed and distributed by a clearinghouse.

*Corporate proposal report.* For example, a corporate proposal to an agency when applying for a grant. These are usually proprietary and not available.

*Institutional reports.* Such as the annual or progress reports of government agencies, foundations, corporations, societies, and laboratories. These reports generally give a good overview and include bibliographies.

*Contract progress report.* The largest class of technical reports in circulation, produced either monthly or quarterly or as required by the terms of the research contract. The information reported in the progress report may or may not be contained in the final report of the contract.

*Contract final report.* Probably the most valuable technical reports, for they generally give a good overview of the research performed under contract, and have some editorial review before release. There is a great variety in the format, distribution, and indexing of these contract final reports.

*Separate, topical technical report.* Closest to the journal article in terms of style and type. Many originate with either the sponsor or staff working on a project, and may be released as research memoranda, research notes, or technical memoranda. These reports often appear later in journals in an abbreviated form. At times, the corporation or government laboratory may take the resulting journal article and put the cover of the organization on it, creating a confusing hybrid.

*Book in report form.* Survey materials, such as reviews and state-of-the-art reports. These appear earlier than the commercial book at lower cost.

*Committee reports.* The findings and conclusions of research by scientific advisory groups. Most of these reports include bibliographic annotations, but their style varies greatly. They often have poor distribution and are usually not adequately described in references. Series designations, for example, are often ignored in descriptions of these reports.

The COSATI list is still a valid assessment of the various kinds of technical reports, but in recent years other agencies have identified additional kinds of reports. The Department of Energy includes among its list of 36 types of technical reports such formats as magnetic tapes, computer codes, video tapes, and floppy disks. Design reports, incident reports, trip reports, and backup reports are also listed, along with more formal types such as dockets, hearings, and environmental impact statements. With so many types of technical reports produced by so many sources, it's not surprising that technical reports are sometimes difficult to recognize.

## Elements of a technical report

A complete citation for a technical report normally contains the following seven elements: personal author, title, date of report, issuing agency or corporation, report series number, clearinghouse accession number, and contract or grant number. Rarely does a patron approach the reference desk with all of this information. If all is known is the author, title, and date, you will not be able to distinguish the technical report from any other type of publication. If the issuing agency is known, you have a clue that this might be a government document. Technical reports are most frequently cited and requested, however, by a report number.

**Report numbers** are assigned by the originating agency or agencies, and represent the origin and status of the document. This report number may contain any or all of the following: the initial letters of the name of the issuing agency, such as MIT for Massachusetts Institute of Technology or AERE for Atomic Energy Research Establishment; an indication of the form of the document, such as TN for technical note or PR for progress report; an indication of the status of the document, such as C for classified or S for secret; the date of the report, such as 78/7 for July 1978; the name of the project which is reported; an indication of the subject content of the report, such as H for health or LS for literature search; and a number indicating the series placement of the report. Examples of report codes are:

> **NACA-WR-A-6**—6th Wartime Report issued by the Ames Laboratory of the National Advisory Committee for Aeronautics.
> **CONF-8410131**—the 131st conference report sponsored by this agency in October of 1984.
> **EPA 600/2-84-036**—the 36th report done in 1984 for the Environmental Protection Agency's environmental protection technology series.

Sources for identifying report series codes include: *Corporate Author Authority List, 1983* (Springfield, Va.: NTIS, 1983); Lois E. Godfrey and Helen F. Redman, *Dictionary of Report Series Codes* (Washington, D.C.: Special Libraries Association, 1973); U.S. Defense Technical Information Center, *How to Get It: A Guide to Defense-Related Information Resources* (Springfield, Va.: NTIS, 1988); U.S. Defense Documentation Center, *Government Acronyms and Alphabetic Designations Used in DDC* (Springfield, Va.: NTIS, 1972).

**Contract numbers** are not as useful for identifying technical reports because they are not unique to one item. Several reports may have been generated from one contract. Also, not every index includes contract numbers. Contract numbers are easy to confuse with report series numbers, for they sometimes include the acronym for the agency awarding the contract. The sequence and format of contract numbers serve as an internal identification code to the contracting agency. Examples of contract numbers are AT(29-2)-2831; DACW 72-74-C-0012; NAS2-9410; AC09-76SR00001.

**Clearinghouse accession numbers** can be extremely useful for verifying technical reports. These numbers are either assigned by the sponsoring agency, in cases where the agency produces its own index, or assigned by the National Technical Information Service to the items it procures for sale. NTIS does not reassign accession numbers to reports it acquires from the federal agencies that have previously assigned their own. The major clearinghouse accession numbers are:

> **AD** — stands for ASTIA Document. ASTIA (Armed Services Technical Information Agency) is the former name of the Defense Technical Information Center (DTIC). Examples are AD 473920, and for more recent reports, AD-A 694219.
> **DE** — numbers are assigned by the Department of Energy (DOE). Examples are DE81016863 or DE84004926 where the first two digits indicate the year of the report.
> **N** — numbers are assigned by the National Aeronautics and Space Administration (NASA). Examples are N64-02345 or N88-238641 where the first two digits indicate the year of the report.
> **PB** — stands for Publications Board. These are assigned by NTIS, and were in one numerical sequence until 1980, when the indexing year was added to the number. Examples are PB239580 and PB80381264.

These four accession numbers are the ones most frequently encountered, but there are others. At times, these clearinghouses use the report series code as an accession number instead of assigning a separate accession number.

The most useful indexes and abstracts that list technical reports are: the biweekly *Technical Abstract Bulletin (TAB)* published by the Defense Technical Information Center since 1953 (AD numbers); the semi-monthly *Energy Research Abstracts (ERA)* published by the Department of Energy since 1976 (DE numbers); the semi-monthly *Scientific and Technical Aerospace Reports (STAR)*, published by NASA since 1963 (N numbers); the biweekly *Government Reports Announcements and Index (GRAI)*, published by the National Technical Information Service since 1946 (AD and PB numbers); and the *Monthly Catalog of U.S. Government Publications*.

*Source:* Ellen Calhoun, "Technical Reports De-Mystified," in Robin Kinder, ed., *Government Documents and Reference Services* (New York: Haworth Press, 1991). pp. 163–75.
Reprinted with permission.

# Genealogical collections

PUBLIC LIBRARIES HAVE A RESPONSIBILITY to serve the needs of patrons interested in genealogical research by providing basic genealogical reference materials and how-to-do-it books in the library and by providing access to additional genealogical research materials through interlibrary loan or referral. Other libraries that wish to develop a genealogical collection and provide services may find these guidelines useful as well.

These guidelines address collection development, personnel, access, and fiscal considerations for genealogical services. They are intended to assist those who need to create a beginning genealogical collection and services in order to meet the above-mentioned responsibilities, the American Library Association's Library Bill of Rights, and the markedly increased public interest in genealogical research.

## Services

Genealogical reference service should include, but may not be limited to, assisting and instructing genealogical patrons to determine what research materials may help them, locating research materials through interlibrary loan, and referring genealogical patrons to other known libraries, institutions, agencies, and archives that have particular genealogical research materials that may be able to help them.

When necessary, genealogical patrons or their questions should be referred to system or network resource centers, or to archives, government agencies, or libraries where the referring librarian knows that the needed research material that cannot be provided by the library through its own collection or interlibrary loan is available.

If a specific genealogical reference service cannot be provided, the library's general reference service should include assistance for genealogical patrons.

## Collection development

Genealogical collections should include, but may not be limited to, manuals and handbooks of how to do genealogical research; family histories; pedigrees, originals or copies thereof, and published compilations of family group sheets; vital records; census schedules; probates and wills; land records; local history materials and indexes to the above materials of communities, states, and countries other than the community in which the library is located or the area it serves.

A genealogical collection should be developed and maintained to support the basic research needs of the community served by the library. An assessment should be made concerning the ethnic background and countries of origin of the members of the community served by the library in order to determine the scope of the genealogical collection. The scope of the collection should represent, at least, the majority of the community but not be limited to it. The collection should include basic materials on genealogical research procedures. These materials should include the widest possible range of nationalities and ethnic groups represented in the community.

In communities where private genealogical collections that are accessible, without charge, to the general public exist, libraries may wish to consider cooperative collection development.

Basic bibliographies of genealogical sources and reviews in library and genealogical journals should be utilized in materials selection.

## Personnel

In order to provide reference service for genealogical patrons, all reference librarians serving genealogical patrons should be trained and periodically updated in genealogical research, which may include, but not be limited to, attendance at local, state, regional, and national genealogical and/or library conferences, seminars, or meetings where genealogical research procedures are presented, or through home study courses.

The responsibility of referring genealogical patrons to archives, government agencies, and libraries requires that the trained reference librarian also know about the centers where genealogical resources are maintained.

Knowledgeable genealogical research volunteers may be utilized to supplement reference service provided to genealogical patrons by the reference staff but should not replace it.

## Access

Genealogical materials should circulate, including on interlibrary loan, unless the materials are rare, are considered to be reference, or are in great local daily demand.

Bibliographies or guides to both reference and circulating genealogical materials should be provided to enhance ease of access.

The acquisition and cataloging of genealogical materials should receive the same priority as other library materials.

*Source: Guidelines for Developing Beginning Genealogical Collections and Services* (Chicago: ALA Reference and Adult Services Division, 1992). 2p.

| Top 20 academic libraries in cartographic holdings, 1989 | | | |
|---|---|---|---|
| U.C. Santa Barbara | 4,075,000 | University of Minnesota | 487,929 |
| UCLA | 839,471 | University of Hawaii | 478,259 |
| U.C. Berkeley | 660,437 | Louisiana State University | 472,225 |
| University of Oregon | 628,000 | Yale University | 385,503 |
| Cornell University | 595,400 | University of Kansas | 376,698 |
| University of Illinois, Urbana | 592,614 | University of Tennessee | 359,199 |
| University of Florida | 548,716 | Univ. of Wisconsin, Madison | 344,324 |
| University of Georgia | 547,250 | Washington Univ. (St. Louis) | 339,112 |
| Indiana University | 521,425 | University of Chicago | 339,100 |
| Harvard University | 520,000 | Pennsylvania State University | 337,336 |

Survey of map collections of Association of Research Libraries member institutions.

*Source:* Charles A. Seavey, "Ranking and Evaluating the ARL Library Map Collections," *College & Research Libraries* 53 (January 1992): 31–43.

# Special Collections

# Pricing scarce and rare books and manuscripts

*by Allen and Patricia Ahearn*

**4**

HOW ARE RARE OR SCARCE ITEMS PRICED? Not easily.

There was a comedian back in the 1950s named Brother Dave Gardner. When someone would say, "Let's do that again," Brother Dave would say: "You can't do anything again. You can do something similar." Well, if a book or manuscript is truly rare or unique, you will not be able to find anything exactly comparable to base your price on, so you must find something similar.

In order to provide a complete picture of the process of pricing, we must consult all the sources, though some of these may not be helpful in many cases. It is relatively easy to arrive at a price or, at least, a price range for most collected books because copies are bought and sold fairly regularly throughout the year. It does, however, become much more difficult to arrive at a price as one explores the pricing of the unique item, such as a great association copy of a book, a unique manuscript, or even a perfect copy of a relatively common book.

The prices paid by dealers and, in turn, the new prices they set on the books or manuscripts they sell are a factor of the individual dealer's sense of the real market price based on his or her own knowledge and readings of the auction records, other dealers' catalogs, and price guides.

To show how a price is set for a modern first edition, for example, let us look at Larry McMurtry's *Lonesome Dove* (New York: Simon and Schuster, 1985), a title published in a fairly large first printing of 42,000 copies at the publication price of $18.95. A nice copy started out on the market in 1985 at $25. It sold easily. The price moved to $40, then to $50, $75, $100, $125, $150, and finally to $175. We had continued to sell the book at $150, but at $175 we had no orders. Now this is a snapshot of a period of a few years. We eventually sold the $175 copy and now the book may sell for more if in mint condition, but the point is that the marketplace set the price. The dealers, of course, could not continue buying *Lonesome Dove* at $10 or $15, but paid more for each successive copy. The scouts or other sellers demanded a higher price at the wholesale level as time went on, which also had a great deal to do with the higher prices charged at the retail level.

The foregoing is a relatively common process in the marketplace and is easy to understand and follow; however, there is a tendency in some cases in recent years to jump straight to the higher value. In other words, a book which was in high demand, such as Tom Clancy's *The Hunt for Red October*, moved from $50 to $100 to $650 to $750, almost overnight. A dealer (or dealers) decided the book was truly scarce and would sell at the higher level. In this case they appear to have been right, even though the first printing was 30,000 copies, of which 15,000 copies went to libraries. The book continues to sell at the higher level. Whether it will continue to sell at this level in future years is anyone's guess. But now let us consider the uncorrected proof of *The Hunt for Red October*. The proof in paper wrappers had a proof dust jacket which was different from the dust jacket used on the first edition. A copy in dust jacket was offered for $3,500. A Clancy collector who wanted the proof but was not willing to pay more than $2,000, had asked us to find him one. Eventually, we purchased the copy that had been priced at $3,500 at a lower price and sold it to our collector for $1,850. This is not to say that the $3,500 price was too high. We have heard of only three copies being offered on the market, so it is a rare item. We do not know what the others sold for, but we believe the price we sold our copy for influenced the asking price of the other two copies.

So it is clear that the buyers—the market—really set the prices in these three examples. In the last example, the seller could have held out for the $3,500, and perhaps our customer would have eventually paid it; or someone else may have come along and bought it for $3,500. We will never know.

There are three types of published value guides that are used to determine prices.

1. **Price guides based on dealer catalog entries.** The most common price guides are those that report the prices asked for books in dealer catalogs. The oldest and largest of these is the *Bookman's Price Index*, which is published twice a year and is up to 46 volumes (and does include a section on association copies). There are others, including Zempel and Verkler's *Book Prices Used and Rare*; the series edited by Michael Cole under the title *International Rare Book Prices*; and many others that are general or specific, such as Shelly and Richard Morrison's annual price guides to *Western Americana* and *Texiana*.

These are the most useful for finding the relatively common collected books. Occasionally, one may be lucky and find an item very close to the one being priced or being offered. Although it is not certain whether an item actually sold for the price asked (more on that below), if one finds multiple entries by different dealers year after year, it can be assumed that the prices are in the ballpark.

The problems with these guides are that:

a. It is not at all certain a book sold for the price asked. This can be overcome if one calls the dealer and asks if the item was sold, which may not always be possible.
b. The price may be so out of date that it really is not relevant to today's market, even if it did sell. And the market on certain types of books and manuscripts changes rapidly.
c. The guides can report only on books that have appeared on the market; rare books either do not show up often (we *are* talking about *rare* books) or, more realistically, they are sold without ever being cataloged.

So it is recommended that you start with one of these guides because it is just possible that something similar has been cataloged recently; but keep in mind that they may not prove very useful.

**2. Auction records.** In the United States the *American Book Prices Current* is published annually (with index volumes published every four years). There are comparable publications in Europe and elsewhere. The chances of finding a price for a comparable rare book, association copy, or manuscript in the auction records would be greater than in the dealer catalog price guides, but in the auction records the prices for the same title will vary greatly, which may reflect condition of each book, or, more likely, who showed up to bid that day. It should be understood that auctions are where many dealers buy books for stock. Therefore, many of the auction prices may represent wholesale rather than retail prices. In some cases, the auction prices may represent forced sales and resulting low prices, while in some cases, when the auction has received high visibility, the prices paid may be significantly higher than retail. A recent example of a price that was highly inflated was Henry James's *The Ambassadors*, which sold for $5,000 at auction, yet the buyer could have found five or more copies in comparable condition on dealers' shelves for $500 to $750.

The point is that auction prices require the knowledge of a dealer, a rare book librarian, or a collector of the particular author to be interpreted properly.

Another point worth noting is that the index volumes provide little or no description of condition; and the annual volumes are not much better. When using the auction records, it is always best to check the index first and then go back to the annual volumes, and then to the actual auction catalog (if it is available) and read the complete description.

The problems with the auction records are similar to the price guide problems in that they can report only what is put at auction; the prices may be out of date. Their advantage over price guides based on dealer catalog entries is that you know the auction prices that were actually paid. Remember, auction houses charge a premium to the buyer and the seller, so find out if the price included the premium(s).

**3. Price guides prepared by individuals.** These are price guides that express the opinion (we hope an informed one) of the compiler(s) of the guides. The prices are based on their experience buying and selling books, as well as their own abilities to interpret auction prices and other dealer catalog prices.

The most commonly used guide at present is our *Collected Books: The Guide to Values*, which lists estimated prices for about 15,000 books. We have also compiled *Book Collecting: A Comprehensive Guide*, which lists values for authors' first books; and individual *Author Price Guides* which include all the American and English first editions by a particular author, with points for identification of first editions and values.

One of the reasons for the popularity of these guides is that they contain bibliographical information useful in determining if a particular book in hand is a first edition (or a first state or issue within a first edition).

There are similar works such as Joseph Connolly's *Modern First Editions* and Tom Broadfoot's *Civil War Books: A Priced Checklist with Advice*. These books represent their authors' opinions of what they would price a copy of the individual book if they were cataloging it the day the guide was prepared.

The problem with these guides is that the

DEMONOMANIE
DES SORCIERS

*A MONSEIGNEVR M. CHRE-*
*stofle de Thou Chevalier Seigneur de Cæli, premier Pre-*
*sident en la Cour de Parlement, & Conseiller*
*du Roy en son privé Conseil.*

**PAR I. BODIN ANGEVIN.**

A PARIS,
Chez Iacques du Puys Libraire Iuré, à la Samaritaine.

M. D. LXXX.

AVEC PRIVILEGE DV ROY.

prices are only as good as the knowledge of their authors. The tendency is to price relatively common books high and scarce or rare books low. This is reasonable: the common books are cataloged often and the expense of the cataloging makes it difficult to price a book under $25. Also, if the book was published at $25, it is hard to value it at, say, $5, which in fact is the price you might find it at in your local bookstore. On the other hand, if one is attempting to come up with a price for a rare copy of Faulkner's *Soldier's Pay* in a dust jacket, and no copy in this condition has been on the market in ten years—at least none that the author is aware of—what price do you put into the guide? You list a price based on the last price, perhaps ten years old, which you can find, tempered by the prices you know a few inferior copies have brought on the market in recent years. This may or may not be a reasonable price estimate, but the odds are that it will be low, particularly if there is a pent-up demand for the book.

A standard comment on price guides is that they are out of date as soon as they are published. Actually, we do not find this to be true. Most collected books tend to stay at a certain level for a year or two; and most prices do not get really out of date until three or four years go by. What people are commenting on are the "hot" authors or books that they have heard so much about and find the price guides very low compared to current prices. Did anyone project Cormac McCarthy's *The Orchard Keeper* as a $2,000 book before *All the Pretty Horses*? Was it obvious in 1990 that Hemingway's *For Whom the Bell Tolls* and *The Old Man and the Sea* would be selling for $500 to $600 in 1994?

First, on McCarthy, no one could have known *The Orchard Keeper* would reach such heights. Of course, the $2,000 was in a catalog and will eventually appear in a price guide; and we will have to ask if it actually sold—although, in the case of McCarthy, it probably did. Now, as to Hemingway, if one were astute enough in 1990 to realize that after the October 1987 stock market crash (perhaps coincidentally), the price of "high spots" of collected books would go up faster than the prices of other collected books, then you could have foreseen that *For Whom the Bell Tolls* and *The Old Man and the Sea* would go up from about $100 to $150 in 1990 to $500 to $600 in 1994, while *Across the River and Into the Trees* would go up from $100 to only $150. Incidentally, the other Hemingway titles after 1930 have followed the latter trend and not the former, and the price guide prices in our 1991 book are, although a little low, not bad.

"High spots" are hot and if you are trying to set a price for a beautiful copy of one that has not appeared in dealer catalogs or at auction in years, you are not going to get any help anywhere, because there are new record prices being set every time one appears, and most copies sold are not recorded.

As a final note on price guides and auction records it should be said that users of these reference works have their own way of interpreting the prices. A number of people have told us they always use our guides: some use half our values; some use three-quarters of them; some double our prices; and some believe that our prices are for very good copies and that fine copies would be twice as much and mint copies would be three times as much.

A local bookstore owner who buys our guides told us he got a copy of a certain book and, if it had not been for our guides, he would have priced it at $10. As it was, he found the book listed in our guide for $150 so he priced it at $60. We bought it.

For auction records, one can usually assume that the retail price for a comparable copy of a book would be 50% to 100% higher than the auction price, but as we mentioned above, there are many instances where this rule of thumb would be way off the mark.

## Other considerations

**Prices paid.** Obviously the amount the dealer paid for an item will influence the price he or she asks. This comes up quite often when dealers are handling unusual if not unique items; and it can cause concern on the part of the buyers when it is obvious that a book priced at $x appears in another dealer's catalog or is offered to the buyer at $2x or $3x. In this case, the buyer is aware of the cost to the dealer and may believe the "profit" is too high, but it must be that the dealer bought the book because he or she believed the first dealer underpriced it. The price may be "high," but time will tell if it is too high. One of our esteemed colleagues, when asked if a book is really worth the price he has on it, always responds, "Not yet." This means a buyer must legitimize the price. If no buyer comes along, the dealer has two choices: maintain the price or lower it. Although small, the antiquarian book field is a marketplace, and supply and demand factors do apply.

**Consignor's desired price.** It is not uncommon for an unusual or unique item to be on consignment with a dealer. In this case, the price being asked may simply be the price the consignor has set plus a nominal profit for the dealer. The dealer may believe the price is high but is aware that the consignor will not sell the item for less; therefore, the price is set.

We recall a case in which a library that had a comprehensive collection of a certain author's works, including manuscripts and letters, was offered an important collection of letters for a high five-figure amount. The librarian felt the price was too high. The dealer had the letters on consignment. Eventually, the letters were offered to another university at the same price and the second university purchased them. Again, if no other buyer had been willing to buy the letters, the price would have been lowered or the letters would have been taken off the market.

**Individual dealer "experience."** It seems that a book becomes more attractive and thus more valuable once it is owned. There is clearly a psychological aspect to pricing books. If Dealer A has a book and Dealer B is interested in it, Dealer B will often exclaim about the high price Dealer A wants, how common the book is, the obvious defects that make it only a marginally collectible book, and so on. But having gotten Dealer A down as low as he possibly can and purchased the book, Dealer B becomes transfixed with the beauty and rarity of the volume. A price is not set immediately as time is needed for Dealer B to absorb the aura of the volume and determine a "fair" price for this now "priceless" tome.

I remember a knowledgeable dealer seeing a second edition, albeit the first illustrated edition, of a very famous book. He told the dealer who owned it that it was nicely bound but only a second edition, after all, and perhaps worth as much as $300. The other dealer, who had not priced the book yet, listened to the sage advice of the first dealer and priced it $750. The first dealer bought the book immediately and returned to his shop. After some deliberation, he priced it at $1,250. A third dealer came in and asked how anyone could price a second edition of this book at over $1,000! After much discussion, the third dealer bought the book. This dealer went to some lengths to check on previous prices and came up with nothing of any use from any of the price guides available. He then checked all the major libraries in the United States, England, and France, and he discovered that none of them had a copy. He priced the book at $10,000, and he ultimately sold it at something approaching this amount. As a footnote, the second dealer proclaimed that the third dealer and his customer were both fools.

There is another story about how dealers' prices are set which might also prove educational. One day a dealer on a trip spied a book he believed was truly rare. The book was priced at $17,500 and was included in a catalog just mailed by the shop. The dealer asked for and received a dealer discount and

GIRO
DEL MONDO
DEL DOTTOR
D. GIO: FRANCESCO
GEMELLI CARERI.
Nuova edizione accresciuta, ricorretta, e divi-
fa in nove volumi. Con un Indice de'
viaggiatori, e loro Opere.
Dedicata all' Illustrissimo Signor
STEFANO MESSA
CAVALIERE DEL S. R. I.
E Comissario dell' Armata di S. M. C. C.
TOMO PRIMO
Contenente le cose più ragguardevoli
vedute
NELLA TURCHIA.

VENEZIA, MDCCXIX.
Presso Giovanni Malachin.
A spese di GIULIO MAFFEI.
Con Licenza de' Superiori, e Privilegio.

left the shop with the book. He was aware that the local university did not have a copy of the book and decided to go over and offer the book to the librarian. He offered it at $24,000. The librarian had just received the catalog from the shop where the book had been purchased and realized that this was the same copy offered in the catalog at $17,500. The librarian mentioned that she had seen the book for $17,500. The dealer responded that he had bought the book and believed it was much scarcer than the catalog price would indicate and had repriced it at $24,000, which he believed was a much more realistic price. The librarian told him that she thought $17,500 was a fair price and she would be willing to pay that amount for it. The dealer said he owned the book now and felt his price was fair, and then left. He went home and did more research. He learned that the Library of Congress did not have a copy and decided that it was even scarcer than he had originally thought. He made an appointment with the rare book librarian at the Library of Congress and at their meeting offered the book for $28,000. The LC librarian had also seen the catalog and stated the price was much too high, implying that the dealer was price gouging and making too high a profit. No deal was made. The dealer was upset that the librarian believed the book was overpriced, but he was becoming more convinced that it was scarcer than he had thought. He decided to offer it to a midwestern university on his way to California the next week. He did offer it, at $34,000, and he sold it.

We must admit we are not sure that all the details of these stories are accurate, but we know that these scenarios have played out before and will play out again.

## Summary

Most dealers do not want to sell a customer an item at a very high price when another copy may turn up on the market at a much lower price within a few years. However, when a dealer is faced with placing a price on a unique item, there is no possibility that another copy will come on the market. The problem is, what is comparable to the item? If it is a great association copy inscribed by Ernest Hemingway, what have other Hemingway association copies brought? If it is a manuscript by a prominent author, what have other manuscripts by that author brought? If none has been sold, what have the manuscripts of authors with comparable reputations sold for? There is always some comparison that can be made, but many times the comparisons may be tenuous.

Another approach is to have an independent appraisal of the item but this presents a problem if the appraisal is very high or very low. We were called in once to reappraise a collection because the owners refused to sell the material at the original appraised value. We did our own appraisal of the material and honestly thought the original appraisal had been ludicrously low. The owner and university were able to work out a price, probably somewhere between the two appraisals, although we were never told the final result. It must be added, though, that there are different kinds of, and reasons for, appraisals—for insurance purposes, for tax or estate purposes, to help the owner know what to ask for the collection if she or he were to sell it, to inform a potential buyer of the value of an item or a collection, and so on—these factors will influence the appraisal's final figures. It would seem reasonable when contemplating the purchase of an expensive collection or item to have one, or perhaps even two, independent appraisals of the value to assure that the price is within reason.

The truly rare or unique item, if demand is high, can be priced as high as the seller wants, but the seller must find a buyer in order to legitimize the price. Even the fact that a book sells for a certain amount does not necessarily mean that another copy will sell for the same amount. The first book may have found the only buyer in the marketplace willing to pay that much. Also, a high price on one copy may bring other copies into the market, thus increasing the supply and lowering the value. The market is constantly changing with new hyper-modern authors coming into fashion and record prices being set every week or so, it seems. All the materials and expertise available should be used in making a purchasing decision.

*Source:* Allen and Patricia Ahearn, "Pricing Scarce and Rare Books and Manuscripts," *Rare Books & Manuscripts Librarianship* 9, no.1 (1994): 31–38.

**4**

# Local history collections

MUCH HAS BEEN WRITTEN ABOUT the organization and care of local materials. Items of particular usefulness are: James H. Conrad, *Developing Local History Programs in Community Libraries* (Chicago: ALA, 1989); Sam A. Suhler, *Local History Collection and Services in a Small Public Library* (Chicago: ALA, 1970); Technical Leaflets, various authors and dates, American Association for State and Local History; and Enid T. Thompson, *Local History Collections: A Manual for Librarians* (Nashville, Tenn.: American Association for State and Local History, 1978).

These guidelines are intended to assist those beginning local history collections. In surveying the literature about the collecting of local materials it is apparent that many have already written about the use and the maintenance of the various media employed in local history. Therefore, these guidelines exist to:

1. Identify factors which need to be resolved before the institution is committed to action.
2. Assist those interested in the creation of local history programs.

## Before making a commitment

A local history program should be developed only after a careful assessment has been made of the services currently or potentially being provided by other institutions and libraries within the community. The institution seeking to develop a local history collection must determine what is presently being collected and what is not being collected; what services are needed and what services are not; and to what depth such collections will be developed.

Institutions developing a local history collection should make certain that such materials are placed in the most suitable collection for their best use, dissemination, and preservation.

## Identification of collection limits

A major factor in the successful development of the collection is to identify its emphasis. By definition this could be geography, format, or whatever the institution desires. Identify those materials which are to be acquired and maintained exclusively by the institution and those to be acquired cooperatively.

## Acquisitions

Write an acquisitions policy for collecting local history materials.

   a. State the intended geographic collection area.
   b. Describe those materials desired by the institution and the extent to which they will be collected.
   c. Identify the types of materials which will definitely *not* be collected by the institution. Bear in mind that there may be other institutions which are better equipped to handle a given type of material.
   d. Identify those subject areas which will be acquired only on a cooperative basis.

The institution should process promptly and make available all materials collected.

## Collection location and security

Local history collections should be established in an identifiable place, separate from the other collections of the library. The space so designated for local history collections should be an area secure from theft with proper provisions for monitoring the materials. An environment which is conducive to the preservation of the materials should be provided.

### Fiscal considerations

The local history collection should be processed and maintained by trained staff. Professionals can be assisted by properly trained volunteers to provide service to the patrons. A budget sufficient to acquire, process, and maintain the basic collection must be provided.

Consideration must be given for the cost of reproducing local history materials. Rare and fragile items must be protected from constant use by the patrons; copies will usually suffice to make the information available.

*Source: Guidelines for Establishing Local History Collections (Chicago: ALA Reference and Adult Services Division, 1993).*

# The status of comic books in society

### by Randall W. Scott

SOON AFTER THE FIRST REGULARLY PUBLISHED newsstand comic book went on sale in 1934, and especially by 1938 with the arrival of *Superman in Action Comics,* no. 1, comic books were established as a distinctly separate medium from newspaper strips. Early publishers were not subject to many restrictions, and some began to take chances by introducing violence and sex in order to improve their circulation. This caught the eyes of parents, teachers, librarians, and a psychiatrist named Dr. Fredric Wertham. Wertham's 1954 book, *Seduction of the Innocent,* helped to crystallize a feeling that comic books were responsible for juvenile delinquency. Hearings in the United States Senate, extensive media coverage, and the beginnings of industry-wide self-

regulation through the Comics Code (1954) caused profound changes in the comic book during the middle 1950s. Creators and publishers fled the industry, and the superhero, horror, and crime genres all but disappeared. With the adoption of the Code, comic books seemed to have admitted guilt, and any school or public library actively collecting them would have had angry parents to deal with.

General and serious disapproval of comic books seems to have declined since the 1950s, but the image of comic books in the public eye still bears the scars. In the 1960s, college students discovered the Marvel Comics of Stan Lee. Together the students and Lee tried to convince the world that comic books had grown up, but despite their efforts what really set the tone of the decade was the "Batman" television show. The television Batman was a silly, self-lampooning comedy with lots of mindless action and drawn-in sound effects. "Bam!" "Pow!" A "comic-book" plot, as the term is sometimes seen in movie reviews, is thus likely to be not only violent but also stupid.

## Academic libraries

Results of society's general disapproval of and low esteem for comic books are easy to see in the bibliographic world. *New Serial Titles* (1953) and *Ulrich's International Periodicals Directory* (1932) excluded comic books by policy from the beginning. Until the late 1970s, no librarian anywhere on earth would have been able to prove, using any standard library catalogs, whether such titles as *Wonder Woman, Superman,* or *The Amazing Spider-Man* even existed as bibliographic entities.

Several substantial general research collections of comic books, and a few dozen more specialized research collections, have begun in academic libraries since about 1970. Most have been taken seriously by the sponsoring institutions, and are growing to some degree, but comic books in research libraries are still viewed as something exceptional by most of the world. If daily broadcast and print reporters can be trusted to know how interested and informed the public is on any given subject, it can probably be proven that news of comic books in a library is about on an equivalent level to news of a new elephant in the zoo. Journalists are perpetually willing to exploit the image of the weird librarian surrounded by the colorful pages of Spider-Man and (Bam! Pow!) Batman comic books. Even among college librarians and in library literature, the idea of deliberately collecting comic books and strips is in some circles a novelty.

Part of the reason that comics are not collected must be the inconvenience of the format. They are fragile, they are printed on bad paper, and if you want to read newspaper strips efficiently you have to clip them out or photocopy them. Thus comics are easy to exclude from a collection, as are videocassettes or phonograph records, because they are a different physical medium and require different kinds of care and storage. Currently there seems to be a willingness in the library profession to tackle new formats, which is lucky because there are so many new formats. Comic books are over fifty years old, however. Job listings for media librarians are becoming common, but so far few have included comic books in the list of responsibilities advertised. Maybe it seems silly to think about comic books and strips as communications media so different from the usual content of a library as to prevent their being collected. But, just as the possibility that it takes separate skills to read and understand comics is worth consideration, the possibility that it takes separate skills to properly acquire, organize, store and preserve comics must be raised.

Although the comics medium may not always have been seen as valuable, there is a tradition of recognition that it is separate and different. As a good case in point, a review of the translation of a Japanese nonfiction comic book, called *Japan Inc.: An Introduction to Japanese Economics,* appeared in the *Library Journal* for March 15, 1989. The reviewer never gets around to commenting on the quality or value of the book, but instead calls it "unusual" and concentrates on the fact that it is a comic book. The heart of the review is that, "given the title and publisher, one could assume it is a scholarly work. But, golly gee, Batman, it's a comic book!" An explanation follows, correctly stating that "the Japanese see nothing incongruous in presenting serious topics in what we consider comic book format." The intent of the review seems not to be to evaluate the book, but to entertain the reader with an invitation to shared condescension toward comic books. The review of *Japan Inc.* was not written with the intent to be malicious in any way. It is presented in good humor and the book is actually given more positive ink than the rest of the books reviewed in the column. But the medium comes off badly, and thus in the final analysis so does the book. The librarian reading the review is hardly likely to notice how pointed are the remarks about comic books. It is precisely such matter-of-fact put-downs that come from the heart of a culture and a profession, and not just from the whim of an individual writer. The Japanese people are correct. There is nothing incongruous about being serious in the comics medium.

Perhaps the general lack of positive attention given to comics by academic librarians can be explained simply by saying that comics are a subliterature for kids, appropriately beneath the notice of the general library profession. On the other hand, perhaps librarians just need to be introduced to the idea of comics librarianship as a specialty involving both some substantial knowledge and some reasonable payoffs in terms of the usual goals of library service. Comics carry unique messages to a mass readership who, at least as comics readers, can expect little or no help from the library profession in choosing, finding, or understanding those messages. The situation does not seem healthy.

In the future most libraries, it seems safe to predict, will represent the comic book and comic strip in their collections. Research library users will be able to examine firsthand the trends and landmarks of comics history. Public library readers will find the current best-sellers and enough old favorites to introduce their kids to the joys of comics reading. When that millennium arrives, most of the current special collections of comics will seem like normal parts of a research library. Seen from this perspective, most of today's research collections of comics are remedial collections that bring the level of preservation of these cultural artifacts up to a point that might be considered normal if certain social pressures were relieved.

## The public library sector

Most public libraries, unless they are also research libraries, are not going to be able to keep retrospective collections of comic books. Comic books are so fragile that it doesn't usually pay for a public library to even catalog them. The typical public library collection has a revolving stock, frequently kept going by trading with readers or by adding new comic books periodically. The flimsy physical nature of the medium, plus the presumption that kids can easily get comics elsewhere because they're cheap, probably accounts for the major fraction of public libraries that do not carry current comic books. The percentage of public libraries that don't provide comic books is unknown, but some do, and some don't. Whether a public library circulates its comic books to death, trades them indiscriminately, confines them to a laundry basket near the 8-piece jigsaw puzzles, or refuses to let them in at all, a public library is not ordinarily the place to learn respect for the comic book medium.

These problems with the comic book format are real and operative in public libraries, but social pressures against the comic book medium operate on public librarians as well. Unlike research librarians, public librarians don't have the same arguments about historical value and the encouragement of research to back them up. Attitudes about comic books vary when they are admitted to the public or school libraries. Sometimes comics are presented to the readers in open recognition that they have their own unique and appropriate entertainment value, or in other words, without apologies to anyone. Probably as often, comic books are part of a "bait and switch" scheme. The comic books are used as a way of attracting young readers to the library, with the hope of sooner or later diverting their attention to "real" books. Although this practice tends to perpetuate the idea that comics are a subliterature, it can be used to get around parents, library administrators, and others who are against comic books.

The "comics are valuable" and the "bait and switch" attitudes can coexist in the same library, with one staff member being able to name all the X-Men, and another staff member trying to turn kids on to C. S. Lewis. It's not even unreasonable for one person to do both.

Public and school library workers who believe in the value of any particular kinds of comic books can best spread the attitude by being able to talk intelligently about them to readers and fellow staff members.

There are plenty of reprint volumes and graphic novels appearing currently that are more durable physically, and it is logical to expect that public libraries will begin to routinely buy them. Most of the reprints of older strips are not being marketed to libraries yet, however. Current favorites like "Garfield" and "Calvin and Hobbes" are easy enough to get in book form, but the "Krazy Kat" and "Li'l Abner" volumes have less visibility. Public librarians can do their readers a favor by looking at the ads in the *Comics Buyer's Guide* or *The Comics Journal,* and sampling the reprints for sale there.

Source: Randall W. Scott, *Comics Librarianship: A Handbook*
(Jefferson, N.C.: McFarland, 1990). 188p.
Reprinted with permission.

## Nonbook Materials

# Media bookings

**FOR A TIME, THE SHIFT** from film to video appeared to spell the end of media booking modules in integrated, multifunction library systems, but new signs of interest are emerging. Many libraries are now booking videos months ahead of time much as they did formerly with films. To accommodate this service, a library system needs a calendar and several other special features. This felt need is causing libraries to dust off old media booking specifications and local library system vendors are renewing development efforts. We are pleased to furnish the following "boiler plate" specifications for an online media booking module as part of an integrated automated library system:

## Media booking

The system shall include an online media booking module which is fully integrated with the other modules. (If vendor has no integrated module, it shall offer and interface a standalone PC-based system.)

The fields to be included in media records are: title; identification number; producer; distributor; series title; date of production; format; number of reels, cassettes, etc.; color/b & w; sound/silent; audience level; subject fields; ISBN/ISSN; depositor; duplication rights; broadcast rights; number of authorized copies; lease expiration date; date added to collection; original cost; date of last inspection; date of last cleaning; physical condition.

Media shall be searchable through the online patron access catalog.

It shall be possible to circulate any type of material the library wishes to handle by advance reservation, and also the use of AV equipment and listening and viewing rooms, using the related circulation module.

The system must be able to book up to 365 days in advance.

The system must have the capacity to input booking requests by keying and by scanning barcodes on patron cards and materials.

The system must book the material first from the location where the request originates, then from any other location.

The system shall make it possible to enter not only a specific date, but a span of dates during which a booking is sought.

The system should attempt to book the title sought sequentially from the first requested date to the last desired date.

The system should have the capacity to allow staff to specify a maximum number of bookings for a patron.

The system shall have the capacity to limit the number of bookings of the same title to a single patron.

The system shall provide for the booking of alternate titles in case the preferred title is not available.

It should be possible to book an item to a circuit.

It must be possible to alter a booking online, but with retention of the previous booking.

The system shall display on command a calendar indicating all open dates when any particular title is available for booking.

The system must have the capacity to restrict circulation on selected titles.

The system should be capable of storing a preferred delivery method indicator in the patron file.

The system should support pick-up, staff delivery, and mailings of booked material.

It shall be possible to override the preferred delivery method indicator.

The system shall have the capacity to schedule materials for inspection or cleaning after a set number of bookings.

The system must retain lease expiration dates for film and video copies.

The system must be able to record the number of copies which can be legally made, and keep track of how many have been made.

The system must be able to display or print a booking schedule by title, patron, or course.

The system shall be able to print a list of all media by title, subject, format, producer, distributor, or holding location.

The system should be able to print mailing labels.

The system must print booking confirmations.

Information on the most recent booking must be available until the next booking has been discharged.

Statistics on use must be available by title, subject, patron type, or length of use.

*Source:* "Media Booking Interest Revives," *Library Systems Newsletter* 12 (June 1993): 43–45.

# Notable nonbook materials for children, 1994

THE NOTABLE CHILDREN'S Films/Videos, Recordings and Computer Software list is compiled annually by three committees of the ALA Association for Library Service to Children to highlight nonbook materials. These are their selections of material released in 1993.

## Films/Videos

**Dog and His Boy** (Pyramid Film & Video). This dramatic, wordless video tells of a small boy who wanders empty streets, along with the dog who adopts him, looking for adventure. He uses his imagination to create his own play world of swashbuckling heroes. Primary.

**Dollhouse Murders** (Aims Media). Amy and her developmentally challenged sister, Lou Anne, discover the truth about their great-grandparents' death in this absorbing, live-action psychological mystery. Based on the popular book by Better Ren Wright. Upper elementary and up.

**Eric Carle: Picture Writer** (Searchlight Films/Putnam). Fat brushes, bright paints and large sheets of paper have always been the springboard for Eric Carle's artistic works. Carle also discusses his life and writings in which themes of hope and love are strongly portrayed. Primary and up.

**Hailstones and Halibut Bones** (Aims Media). In this video based on Mary O'Neill's timeless poems about color, brilliant explosions fire the imagination, heightening our awareness of the hues that surround us. Primary and up.

**Musical Max** (Weston Woods). Max, a musically inclined hippo, drives his father and the neighbors to distraction practicing various musical instruments.

The soundtrack of the video adds another dimension to the animated retelling of this well-known picture book by Robert Kraus. Primary.

**Song of Sacajawea** (Rabbit Ears Prods). The true story of the young Shoshoni woman's experiences guiding the Lewis and Clark expedition through the Rocky Mountains to the Pacific Ocean. Strong woodcut illustrations and an outstanding musical accompaniment bring this iconographically filmed biography to life. Upper elementary.

**Squanto and the First Thanksgiving** (Rabbit Ears Prods). Unusual and powerful graphic images by Michale A. Donato and expressive narration by actor Graham Greene contribute to this moving iconographic presentation of the life of the Pawtuxet Indian who helped the Plymouth settlers celebrate the first Thanksgiving. Upper elementary.

**Sylvester and the Magic Pebble** (Weston Woods). Sylvester Duncan finds a red pebble that can fulfill wishes until he meets a menacing lion and accidentally turns himself into a rock. Primary.

**Tall Ship: High Sea Adventure** (ABC/Kane). For their first voyage at sea, Danish Merchant Marine cadets spend six months training on a tall ship. Striking photography and continuous adventure. Middle school to adult.

## Recordings

**Animal Tales.** Performed by Bill Schontz (Lightyear Entertainment, 1993). 39 min. cassette; CD.

**Brer Rabbit and Boss Lion.** Read by Danny Glover (Rabbit Ears/BMG Kidz, 1993). 50 min. cassette; CD.

**Comin' Round the Mountain.** Performed by Phil Rosenthal, et al. (American Melody, 1993). 40 min. cassette.

**Family Garden.** Performed by John McCutcheon (Rounder Records, 1993). 53 min. cassette; CD.

**From Generation to Generation: A Legacy of Lullabies.** Performed by Tanja Solnik (Dreamsong, 1993). 36 min. cassette.

**i will hold your tiny hand.** Performed by Steve Rashid (Woodside Avenue, 1993). 38 min. cassette; CD.

**Intrepid Birdmen.** Performed by Syd Lieberman (Syd Lieberman, 1993). 45 min. cassette.

**Jim Gill Sings the Sneezing Songs and Other Contagious Tunes.** Performed by Jim Gill (Jim Gill, 1993). 32 min. cassette.

**Johnny Whistletrigger: Civil War Songs from the Western Border.** Performed by Cathy Baron, Dave Para and Bob Dyer (Big Canoe, 1993). 70 min. cassette; CD.

**Julie of the Wolves.** Read by Christina Moore (Recorded Books, 1993). 270 min. cassettes.

**Maynard Moose: Sleeping Beastly and Other Tales.** Performed by Willy Claflin (Old Coyote, 1993). 53 min. cassette.

**Morning, Noon and Nighttime Tales.** Performed by Bill Gordh (Lingonberry, 1993). 46 min. cassette.

**Mrs. Katz and Tush.** Read by Patricia Polacco and Omar Sharif Scroggins (Bantam, 1993). 12 min. book/cassette.

**Mystery! Mystery!** Performed by Jim Weiss (Greathall, 1993). 60 min. cassette.

**Not for Kids Only.** Performed by Jerry Garcia and David Grisman (Acoustic Disc, 1993). 48 min. cassette; CD.

**Nightjohn.** Read by Michele Denise Woods (Recorded Books, 1993). 120 min. cassettes.

**Peter, Paul and Mommy, Too.** Performed by Peter, Paul and Mary (Warner Brothers, 1993). 52 min. cassette; CD.

**Rhythm of the Rocks.** Performed by Marylee and Nancy (Friends Street,

1993). 33 min. cassette.

**The Savior Is Born.** Read by Morgan Freeman (Simon and Schuster, 1993). 27 min. book/cassette.

**Starfishing.** Performed by the Green Chili Jam Band (Green Chili Jam Band, 1993). 45 min. cassette.

**A Storytelling Treasury.** Compiled by Carol Birch (National Storytelling Press, 1993). 300 min. cassettes.

**Tchaikovsky Discovers America.** Performed by Classical Kids (Children's Group, 1993). 50 min. cassette; CD.

**Treasure Island.** Read by Michael Page (Brilliance, 1993). 420 min. cassettes.

**Voices on the Wind.** Performed by Barbara G. Schutz-Gruber (Barbara G. Schutz-Gruber, 1993). 57 min. cassette.

## Computer software

**Super Solvers: Gizmos and Gadgets!** Fremont, Calif.: The Learning Company, 1993. PC. Young scientists thwart the Master of Mischief using thinking skills to solve more than 200 physical science puzzles.

**Thinkin' Things.** Redmond, Wash.: Edmark Corporation, 1993. Mac or PC. Children from 4 to 8 can explore and deepen their musical, rhythmic, visual, spatial, logical, and mathematical abilities.

*Source:* ALA Association for Library Service to Children.

# Selected films for young adults, 1994

**THESE FILMS FOR** young adults were chosen by a committee of the Young Adult Library Services Association on the basis of young adult appeal, technical quality, subject content, and use for different age levels.

**Blind Geronimo and His Brother** (Carousel). A traveler's evil lie that he has given Carlo a gold coin angers Carlo's brother Geronimo, a blind musician. Based on a short story by Arthur Schnitzler.

**Boy Soldiers** (Direct Cinema). From the More Winners Series, this film shows a young teen in pre-World War I Australia who stands up for his beliefs despite the harsh consequences.

**Clean Water** (Schlessinger Video). Former MTV host Kevin Seal presents this look at water pollution problems and their solutions.

**Etiquette: Fundamental Restaurant Etiquette** (Creative Educational Video). Practical scenes illustrate proper teen behavior for various situations in restaurants.

**Gay Youth** (Filmmakers Library). The emotional challenges of being gay and lesbian are explored through interviews with gay and lesbian teens. A prominent feature of the film is a portrait of Gina Gutierrez, a recipient of the Bobby Griffith Memorial Scholarship sponsored by the family of a 20-year-old gay man who committed suicide.

**He's So Fine** (Media Inc.). This look at a reversed sexual harassment makes its points with humor.

**Just for Fun** (Direct Cinema). When Justin realizes that his friends' idea of fun is gay bashing in the park, he faces the difficult choice of turning his friends into the police or losing his gay brother's trust.

**Marilyn Hotchkiss' Ballroom Dancing and Charm School** (Carousel Film and Video). Within the nostalgic backdrop of the early 1960s, the universal coming-of-age story of boy likes girl is played out in fact and fantasy.

**Model Perfect** (Direct Cinema). Amanda's best friend helps her realize that good eating habits and a healthy body image are more important than starving herself to look like a model.

**Out of Bounds: Teenage Sexual Harassment** (Coronet/MIT Film and Video). Factual advice on how to deal with harassment is presented throughout this story of harassment of high school girls by a rock band.

**Punk** (Carousel Film and Video). Nine-year-old Dominic struggles to grow up in a dysfunctional inner-city family. His life is complicated by an ex-con who talks about what being a punk is and the sexual advances of an older man.

**Real People: Teens Who Choose Abstinence** (Sunburst Communications). Through group discussions, role-playing and class presentations, teens who have chosen abstinence show how this choice has affected their lives.

**Sour Death Balls** (Carousel Film and Video). A group of adults and children are presented experiencing their first taste of sour death ball candy in this witty nonverbal short.

**Troubled Waters: Plastic in the Marine Environment** (Bullfrog Films). This video provides an education for teens on the effects of plastic waste pollution on marine life.

**Withstanding Ovation** (Fanlight Productions). A high school senior and a college freshman both born with severe congenital limb deformities face their physical challenges with courage and confidence.

*Source:* ALA Selected Films and Videos for Young Adults Committee,
Young Adult Library Services Association.

## How to raise a reader

SHARING BOOKS WITH CHILDREN is a gift you can give infants from the time they are born. Chanting nursery rhymes, singing songs, and reading stories can comfort and entertain even the youngest child. Parents, child-care providers, teachers, and other adults interested in the development of young children have a wealth of good books to choose from. Here is a list of some of the best with easy-to-do tips developed by members of the ALA Association for Library Service to Children.

### Sharing books . . .

- Helps create a special bond between parents and children.
- Introduces children to art through the illustrations.
- Enhances children's listening skills and develops language skills.
- Introduces children to a wide variety of experiences.
- Helps prepare children to learn to read.
- Improves and enriches the quality of children's lives.

- Provides fun and enjoyment for children and adults.

## When to share books

- Begin when your child is born.
- Set aside a special time each day, such as nap time, bedtime, or after meals.
- Share books when you and your child are in a relaxed mood.
- Limit sharing time if your child becomes fussy or restless.
- Take advantage of "waiting" times to share books—on trips, at the doctor's office, in line at the grocery store.
- Soothe your child when sick or cranky.

## How to share books

- Find a comfortable place to sit (a rocking chair is wonderful).
- Recite or sing rhymes from your favorite books.
- Turn off other distractions—television, radio, or stereo.
- Hold the book so your child can see the pages clearly.
- Involve your child by having him or her point out objects, talk about the pictures, or repeat common words.
- Read with expression.
- Vary the pace of your reading—slow or fast.
- Have your child select books to read.
- Reread your child's favorite books whenever asked.

## And remember . . .

- Be enthusiastic about books.
- Be an example for your child— let her or him see you read books, too.
- Keep a wide selection of reading materials at home.
- Be aware of your child's reading interests.
- Give books as presents.
- Begin to build a child's home library.
- Use your local library regularly and register your child for a library card.

## Some good books to share

**Bang, Molly.** *Ten, Nine, Eight* (Greenwillow, 1983).

**Barton, Byron.** *Trucks* (Harper, 1986).

**Brown, Marc.** *Play Rhymes* (Dutton, 1985).

**Brown, Margaret Wise.** *Goodnight, Moon* (Harper, 1947).

**Burningham, John.** *The Blanket* (Harper, 1976).

**Campbell, Rod.** *Buster's Bedtime* (Bedrick Books, 1987).

**Carle, Eric.** *The Very Hungry Caterpillar* (Putnam, 1981).

**Chorao, Kay.** *The Baby's Lap Book* (Dutton, 1977).

**Crews, Donald.** *Freight Train* (Greenwillow, 1978).

**dePaola, Tomie.** *Tomie dePaola's Mother Goose* (Putnam, 1985).

Hill, Eric. *Where's Spot?* (Putnam, 1987).
Isadora, Rachel. *I See* (Greenwillow, 1985).
Jonas, Ann. *Holes & Peeks* (Greenwillow, 1984).
Keats, Ezra Jack. *Peter's Chair* (Harper, 1967).
Martin, Bill, Jr. *Brown Bear, Brown Bear, What Do You See?* (Holt, 1985).
Ormerod, Jan. *Reading* (Lothrop, 1985).
Oxenbury, Helen. *Clap Hands* (Macmillan, 1987).
Pooley, Sarah. *A Day of Rhymes* (Knopf, 1988).
*Songs from Dreamland* (Random, 1989).
Steptoe, John. *Baby Says* (Lothrop, 1988).
Tafuri, Nancy. *Have You Seen My Duckling?* (Greenwillow, 1984).
Watanabe, Shigeo. *How Do I Put It On?* (Putnam, 1984).
Wells, Rosemary. *Max's Bath* (Dial, 1985).
Yolen, Jane. *Lap-Time Song and Play Book* (Harcourt, 1989).

*Source:* ALA Association for Library Service to Children, *How to Raise a Reader*
(Chicago: American Library Association, 1992).

---

## Characteristics of good readers

Good readers:
1. Possess positive habits and attitudes about reading;
2. Read with enough fluency so that they can focus on the meaning of what they read;
3. Use what they already know to understand what they read;
4. Form an understanding of what they read and extend, elaborate, and critically judge its meaning;
5. Use a variety of effective strategies to aid their understanding and to plan, manage, and check the progress of their reading;
6. Can read a wide variety of texts and can read for different purposes.

*Source:* NAEP Reading Consensus Project, *Reading Framework for the 1992 National Assessment of Educational Progress* (Washington, D.C.: US Gov't Printing Office, 1992). 62p.

---

# Teaching and learning to read

*by Anne P. Sweet*

THE FOLLOWING TEN IDEAS to transform instruction in reading and heighten literacy learning for all students are based both on solid research in cognition and on practical experience. They represent a shift away from well-known reading instruction practices in place for half a century. Each concept is explained more fully in *State of the Art: Transforming Ideas for Teaching and Learning,* a booklet published by the Department of Education's Office of Research.

1. Children, when reading, construct their own meaning.
2. Effective reading instruction can develop engaged readers who are knowledgeable, strategic, motivated, and socially interactive.
3. Phenomic awareness, a precursor to competency in identifying words, is one of the best predictors of later success in reading.
4. Modeling is an important form of classroom support for literacy learning.
5. Storybook reading, done in the context of sharing experiences, ideas,

and opinions, is a highly demanding mental activity for children.

6. Responding to literature helps students construct their own meaning which may not always be the same for all readers.
7. Children who engage in daily discussions about what they read are more likely to become critical readers and learners.
8. Expert readers have strategies that they use to construct meaning before, during, and after reading.
9. Children's reading and writing abilities develop together.
10. The most valuable form of reading assessment reflects our current understanding about the reading process and simulates authentic reading tasks.

Source: Anne P. Sweet, *State of the Art: Transforming Ideas for Teaching and Learning to Read* (Washington, D.C.: Office of Research, November 1993). 17p.

# Books to match children's developmental stages

**4**

*by Maralita L. Freeny*

## Infants

PUBLISHERS HAVE BEEN SLOW to realize that babies constitute an audience for books. For example, the excellent Brimax series of books is appropriate for infants, but according to the covers of the books, its publisher is promoting it for two- to four-year-olds.

**Developing a sense of hearing.** In the earliest months, read anything aloud—newspapers, your favorite magazines, a professional journal.

In the earliest months, the sound of a voice is more important than the sense of what is being read. Therefore, Mother Goose books are among the best first books for babies. The rhymes are melodic and easily memorized, and they can be used anywhere by parents who want to amuse their children. Later, as children learn to talk, they will be able to memorize and recite the rhymes easily, giving themselves a sense of accomplishment. Raymond Briggs' *Mother Goose Treasury* (Putnam, 1966) is a good collection of rhymes and a good first book.

Song books, poetry, and the so-called sound or noise books are also appropriate for infants. Aliki, *Hush Little Baby* (Prentice-Hall, 1968); Sally Kilroy, *Animal Noises* (Four Winds, 1983); and Peter Spier, *Crash! Bang! Boom!* (Doubleday, 1972), present interesting songs and sounds for babies.

*Sharon, Lois and Bram's Mother Goose* (Atlantic Monthly, 1986) includes both rhymes and songs and makes an excellent gift for a new baby.

**Developing a sense of touch.** Board books lend themselves to use by babies. They are nearly indestructible. Babies can pull or chew on them. Good choices among the many board books available are Patricia Wynne, *Animal ABC* (Random, 1977); Ethel and Len Kessler, *Are There Hippos on the Farm?* (Simon & Schuster, 1987); and Helen Oxenbury, *All Fall Down* (Macmillan, 1987).

Texture or "touch and feel" books are appropriate when children are developing their sense of touch. Dorothy Kunhardt's *Pat the Bunny* (Western, 1942), now a classic, provides a variety of textures for baby to experience.

**Developing clearer vision when the eyes begin to focus.** Books with large, clear, uncluttered illustrations in bright, primary colors provide the best visual experience when baby's eyes first begin to focus. Naming books, alphabet books, and color and number books, such as Brian Wildsmith's *ABC* (Watts, 1962) and Lucille Ogle's *I Spy* (American Heritage, 1970), are examples.

**Identifying objects.** In their earliest experiences with books, children especially delight in finding objects on a page. *Baby's Catalogue*, by Janet and Allan Ahlberg (Little, 1983), is a naming book that is appropriate.

Number, alphabet, and color books also lend themselves to point and name activities with a parent. *Colors* by Jan Pienkowski (Simon & Schuster,

| General attitudes of public librarians toward programs for children under 18 months | | | |
|---|---|---|---|
| | Do program and agree | Do not program and agree | Total agreeing |
| *Positive statements* | | | |
| Sets an early pattern of library use by parents | 97% | 63% | 72% |
| Provides ideas for appropriate first books and related activities | 93% | 60% | 70% |
| Helps to establish an early appreciation for books and reading | 87% | 54% | 63% |
| Offers a valuable source of language development during the crucial early learning period | 97% | 49% | 62% |
| Is a pleasant, positive way to begin socializing the child | 87% | 48% | 55% |
| Provides role models of adults who read | 71% | 48% | 55% |
| Offers a "head start" for the child who is not read to at home | 55% | 43% | 46% |
| Provides a valuable aid to day-care centers with increasingly large numbers of very young children | 22% | 23% | 23% |
| *Negative statements* | | | |
| Should only be attempted by staff knowledgeable in child development | 13% | 32% | 27% |
| Needs more research and development before implementation | 0% | 27% | 20% |
| Is an example of society's overemphasis on achievement | 3% | 18% | 14% |
| Is of benefit only to the adults attending | 0% | 18% | 13% |
| Attempts to introduce activities too advanced for the age level | 3% | 13% | 11% |
| Is a misuse of library funds and staff time | 0% | 7% | 5% |

*N* = do program, 31; do not program, 81; total, 112.

*Source:* "Should Public Libraries Program for Babies? A National Survey of Children's Coordinators," *Public Libraries* 32 (January/February 1993): 29–36.

1981) and Helen Oxenbury's *Numbers of Things* (Watts, 1968) are good choices to use.

**Naming objects.** In order to enhance language development, use the books cited earlier, but instead of having the child point to the object and the parent name it, the parent should point and have the child do the naming. Feodor Rojankovsky, *Great Big Animal Book* (Golden, 1950); Richard Scarry, *Early Words* (Random House, 1976); and John Burningham, *Mr. Gumpy's Outing* (Holt, 1971), are illustrated with pictures of items children can easily learn to identify.

## Toddlers

The books you use during these years will depend on whether or not you read to the child during her infancy. It is not necessary to limit books to those with vocabularies within the immediate experience of the child.

**Developing manual dexterity.** Use books that are small, "little books for little hands." Small board books, such as *You Do It Too*; Sesame Street, *Muppets in My Neighborhood* (Random, 1977); and Rosemary Wells, *Max's New Suit* (Dial, 1979), are appropriate for toddlers to handle even without supervision.

Little books with paper pages, such as Jan Ormerod, *Young Joe* (Lothrop, 1985), and John Burningham, *The Rabbit* (Harper, 1975), are also easily handled by toddlers, but adults must supervise their use more closely.

**More advanced language usage.** More complicated alphabet, naming, sound, and number books can be used to enhance the toddler's rapidly developing language. Try Brian Wildsmith, *Wild Animals* (Oxford University, 1976), and Janet Beller, *A-B-Cing* (Crown, 1985).

Descriptive books, such as Chiyoko Nakatani, *My Day on the Farm* (Crowell, 1976); Ruth Brown, *Our Cat Flossie* (Dutton, 1986); and Douglas Florian, *A Winter Day* (Greenwillow, 1987), are excellent books to use for language development while a child's attention span is too short to use picture stories effectively.

**Negativism.** Books which ask questions, especially when the appropriate answers are negative, are ideal for a stage when the toddler's favorite word is "no."

Shigeo Watanabe, *How Do I Put It On?* (Putnam, 1980); and Eric Hill, *Where's Spot?* (Putnam, 1987), are two favorite books with questions answered in the negative.

**Sense of accomplishment.** Flap books, such as Rod Campbell's *Dear Zoo* (Macmillan, 1984), and the Spot series, provide a sense of accomplishment to toddlers, who quickly learn how and when to lift the flap.

When children can independently know when to turn the page, they feel a sense of accomplishment. Simple stories are good to use as is a good collection of Mother Goose rhymes, for example, Tomie dePaola's *Mother Goose* (Putnam, 1985).

**Learning simple concepts, such as numbers, letters, colors, and days of the week.** Simple concepts can be taught through a good book. Donald Crews, *Freight Train* (Greenwillow, 1978); Bill Martin, Jr., *Brown Bear, Brown Bear, What Do You See?* (Holt, 1983); and Robert Kalan, *Rain* (Greenwillow, 1978), introduce colors within a lively and appealing context.

Good books to use to teach counting and number recognition are Pat Hutchins, *One Hunter* (Greenwillow, 1982), and Nancy Tafuri, *Who's Counting?* (Greenwillow, 1986).

**Increased attention spans.** Simple descriptive books can be followed by short, simple stories with believable situations. The story is all important; the text must be good. Look for books by Eve Rice, Pat Hutchins, Ann Jonas, and Eric Carle. *Benny Bakes a Cake* by Rice (Greenwillow, 1981), *Titch* by

Hutchins (Macmillan, 1971), *Two Bear Cubs* by Jonas (Greenwillow, 1982), and *The Very Hungry Caterpillar* by Carle (Putnam, 1981), are among my favorites.

It's okay for animals to act like children in these stories. *Wide-Awake Timothy,* by Joyce Wakefield (Childrens Press, 1981), is a good example of a short, simple story in which an animal, in this case a koala bear, is very childlike.

## Three-year-olds

I can't emphasize enough how important it is to remember that children develop at different rates. Some three-year-olds will be ready for the books listed in this section; some will have devoured them during their toddler years. The following are merely loose guidelines to help you in your selections.

**Increased interest in the use of words.** Poetry provides richness of language and rhythm which enhances a child's interest in language. Frank Josette, ed., *Poems to Read to the Very Young* (Random, 1982); Jack Prelutsky, ed., *Read-Aloud Rhymes for the Very Young* (Knopf, 1986); and David McCord, *Every Time I Climb a Tree* (Little, 1967), are collections that are personal favorites of mine. "Mary Had a Little Lamb" and "Three Little Kittens" are examples of single rhymes that are often illustrated and published as whole books.

Nonsense books present new words to youngsters who are becoming really interested in language. These same books also demonstrate rhythm and cadence. In addition to books by the well-known Dr. Seuss, Bruce Degen's *Jamberry* (Harper, 1983) is a good choice.

The repetition in cumulative stories also provides a rich experience for the preschooler who has an increased interest in language. Good cumulative stories are Audrey Woods, *Napping House* (Harcourt, 1984); Kaj Beckman, *Lisa Cannot Sleep* (Watts, 1969); and Rose Robart, *The Cake That Mack Ate* (Little, 1987).

**Growing independence and sense of accomplishment.** Books that allow the child to participate in the telling are ideal for three-year-olds. Children respond to the hidden pictures and shapes in Janet and Allan Ahlberg, *Each Peach Pear Plum* (Viking, 1979), and Charles G. Shaw, *It Looked Like Spilt Milk* (Harper, 1988). Robert Crowther's *The Most Amazing Hide-and-Seek Alphabet Book* (Viking, 1978) is an unusually fine tab book which also invites participation by the child.

Singing is another way to involve children in books. Songs illustrated and published as whole books can be used to accomplish this. Raffi, *Wheels on the Bus* (Crown, 1988); Merle Peek, *Mary Wore Her Red Dress* (Ticknor & Fields, 1985); Nadine Westcott, *The Lady with the Alligator Purse* (Little, 1988); and Paul Galdone, *The Cat Goes Fiddle-i-fee* (Ticknor & Fields, 1985), are always popular.

**Development of self-esteem.** As children develop personality and accept themselves, they respond to books with characters with whom they can identify.

Ezra Jack Keats, *Whistle for Willie* (Viking, 1964); Shirley Hughes, *Alfie's Feet* (Lothrop, 1983); and Rosemary Wells, *Noisy Nora* (Dial, 1973), are some good authors to use. While Wells' characters are usually animals, children will have no trouble identifying with them.

**Comfort with familiar things.** Preschoolers are curious about the world around them, but they are most comfortable with the familiar. Read books about their everyday life, about their pets, their toys, their experiences in the community. Try Gene Zion, *Harry the Dirty Dog* (Harper, 1956), or Keiki Kanao, *Kitten up a Tree* (Knopf, 1987), excellent stories about pets; or try *My*

*Barber* (Macmillan, 1981) and *The Supermarket* (Macmillan, 1979), both by Anne and Harlow Rockwell, who have written about a variety of everyday experiences.

**Advanced concept-learning.** Books can encourage a child's understanding of concepts. Shapes, spatial relationships, and time are within the grasp of a three-year-old.

Leonard Everett Fisher, *Look Around!* (Viking, 1987); Betsy Maestro, *Where Is My Friend?* (Crown, 1976); and Robert Kalan, *Blue Sea* (Greenwillow, 1979), introduce shapes, spatial relationships, and contrasting sizes respectively.

**Developing imagination.** Read books that appeal to the child's imagination. Books that personify animals, toys, and other things are well-liked by three-year-olds.

Look for books by Don Freeman; his *Corduroy* (Viking, 1968) and *Dandelion* (Viking, 1964) are sure-fire hits.

Virginia Lee Burton's *Mike Mulligan and His Steam Shovel* (Houghton, 1939), in which a steam shovel has a personality, has become a classic.

**Need for parental love and security.** Mood books, or books that help children settle down are appropriate for this age. Books like Molly Bang, *Ten, Nine, Eight* (Greenwillow, 1983); Robert Kraus, *Whose Mouse Are You?* (Macmillan, 1970); Nancy Carlstrom, *The Moon Came Too* (Macmillan, 1987); and Margaret Wise Brown, *Goodnight, Moon* (Harper, 1949), are perfect for sharing at nap time or bedtime.

Read books that reflect parental love, for instance, Ann Herbert Scott, *On Mother's Lap* (McGraw, 1972); and Dick Gackenback, *Claude and Pepper* (Houghton, 1976).

## Four- and five-year-olds

**Desire for fairness.** Older preschoolers have a strong feeling about what is and isn't fair. They like and want poetic justice of the kind that is present in Beatrix Potter's *The Tale of Peter Rabbit* (Warne, 1987). They also like happy endings in books in which a character has been in danger. Wilhelmina Harper, *Gunniwolf* (Dutton, 1967), and Leo Lionni, *Swimmy* (Pantheon, 1966), are prime examples.

Beast fairy tales are appropriate at this stage. Preread fairy tales so that you are not disappointed with unfamiliar variations. For example, in some versions of "The Three Little Pigs," the pigs are eaten by the wolf; in others, all three escape unharmed. Determine which version you have before reading it aloud to the child. Many versions of traditional fairy tales are nicely illustrated. Paul Galdone's *The Three Bears* (Houghton, 1972) comes to mind, as does *Red Riding Hood* by James Marshall (Dial, 1987).

Modern nontraditional fairy tales are popular with four- and five-year-olds. Anita Lobel, *The Straw Maid* (Greenwillow, 1983), and Joanna Galdone, *The Little Girl and the Big Bear* (Houghton, 1980), are personal favorites of my family.

**Curiosity about the world at large.** Older preschoolers become interested in the world outside their own everyday experiences. They yearn to find out about science, religion, history, famous people, other lands, and more. Factual picture books are now in plentiful supply on this level. Gail Gibbons is a prolific author to remember. Her nonfiction books are brief, precise, and quite interesting. *Boat Book* (Holiday, 1983) is just one example.

The world of science is widely represented in preschool books. Kate Petty, *Snakes* (Watts, 1985); Helen and Kelly Oechsli, *In My Garden* (Macmillan, 1985); and Franklyn M. Branley, *The Sky Is Full of Stars* (Harper, 1983), are just three examples of the many excellent books available.

To introduce history, you can read stories based on truth as well as traditional nonfiction books. Riki Levinson, *Watch the Stars Come Out* (Dutton,

1985), is an appealing historical picture story; Betsy Maestro, *The Story of the Statue of Liberty* (Lothrop, 1986), is an example of a factual historical picture book.

**Advanced verbal skills.** Wordless books encourage children to be creative and expressive by allowing them to tell stories in their own words. Nonny Hogrogian, *Apples* (Macmillan, 1972), and John S. Goodall, *Creepy Castle* (Atheneum, 1975), are two such wordless picture books.

Panorama books, such as those made popular by Richard Scarry, provide detailed illustrations just waiting for children with advanced verbal skills to describe. *Richard Scarry's Best Word Book Ever* (Western, 1963) is one of the author's best.

**Increased attention span.** There is less need for illustrations in the stories you share with four- and five-year-olds. You will now be able to read the many excellent, longer picture book stories, especially folk stories. Try Arlene Mosel, *Tikki Tikki Tembo* (Holt, 1968), and Jakob Grimm's *Snow White and the Seven Dwarfs* (Farrar, 1972).

Collections of stories are suitable for this age. Anne Rockwell's *Three Bears and Fifteen Other Stories* (Harper, 1975) is a good choice, as is *Tomie dePaola's Favorite Nursery Tales* (Putnam, 1986).

**Adventurous nature.** Four- and five-year-olds love adventure and suspense in their books; many children this age enjoy being scared.

Adventure books to read are Chris Van Allsburg, *Jumanji* (Houghton, 1981); Tomi Ungerer, *Crictor* (Harper, 1958); David McPhail, *Pig Pig Grows Up* (Dutton, 1980); and Tan Koide, *May We Sleep Here Tonight?* (Macmillan, 1983).

**Advanced sense of humor.** Children at this stage begin to understand the humor in many situations. Jack Kent writes wonderfully funny books for this age. *Round Robin* (Prentice-Hall, 1982) and *The Once-upon-a-Time Dragon* (Harcourt, 1982) are examples of his best work.

You will laugh along with your child when you read Raymond Briggs, *Jim and the Beanstalk* (Putnam 1980), and Marc Brown, *Pickle Things* (Parents, 1980).

*Source:* Nell Colburn and Maralita L. Freeny, *First Steps to Literacy*
(Chicago: American Library Association, 1989). 108p.

# Reading achievement: One state's scorecard

**Research shows that:**

Normal development in reading over the summer requires reading for about one hour a day.

Of all the ways children spend their time away from school, reading books is the best predictor of several measures of reading achievement, including gains in reading achievement between second and fifth grade.

Students with higher reading achievement scores read more books, and parents of advanced students read more often to them and provide them with more books.

Reading at the library is a truly positive experience especially for the slowest readers.

Among the factors influencing children to become avid readers, the way books are arranged, displayed, and made accessible is second only to the role played by teachers.

**During 1991 in Colorado:**

Summer reading programs were responsible for almost 50,000 elementary
school pupils completing approximately 180,000 hours of reading.
More than 18,000 public library programs for children (mostly story hours)
logged attendance of almost 450,000.
Young Coloradans participating in summer reading programs read almost
500,000 books.
More than 3,000 summer reading programs logged attendance of almost
180,000.
Loans of children's books by public libraries topped 8.4 million.

*Source: Fast Facts: Recent Statistics from the Library Research Service*
(Library Research Service, Colorado State Library), May 26, 1992. Reprinted with permission.

# Evaluating picture books

4

*by Barbara Kiefer*

## Design choices

The *elements* of design (line, shape, color, value, and texture) are chosen for
their expressive qualities.
Lines and shapes convey action, rhythm; they can be strong and solid or
diminutive and quick.

- Colors convey mood, emotions.
- Value creates contrast, highly dramatic or soothing effects.
- Texture conveys tension, adds interest or movement.

The *principles* of design or composition (balance, rhythm, repetition,
variety in unity, eye movement) are chosen to tie individual pages into a
complete whole that reinforces the overall meaning of the book.

- Layout and size of pictures carry the eye from page to page and
  create a rhythm in keeping with the meaning of the book.
- Pictures and printed text are well balanced and create a pleasing
  pattern.
- Elements of design are used to create variety in unity.

## Technical choices

Original media, end papers, paper stock, and typography are chosen to
strengthen ideas or story.

- Choice of watercolor, acrylics, pencil, or print is in keeping with
  the mood of the story or concept.
- Typeface appropriate to type of book or story.
- End papers prepare the reader by setting the mood, giving a
  preview, or complementing the illustrations.
- The paper itself is in keeping with original media (acrylic on shiny
  paper, watercolor or pencil on a matte finish).

Pictorial content and the artist's point of view extend and enhance the
story or concept.

- Choice of what to include in the picture is appropriate to the story

and adds new dimensions, new or additional meanings.
- Pictures add information and help us see ideas in new ways.
- Close-ups, traditional perspective, worm's-eye view, or bird's-eye view are chosen to lend excitement, drama, and interest to the story.

## Choices of historical or cultural conventions

Pictorial conventions are borrowed from styles of art throughout history to enhance and extend the meaning of the story or concept.

- Aspects of early Christian art, Renaissance painting, French impressionism, etc., are used to convey mood and meaning.

Pictorial conventions are borrowed from particular cultural groups to enhance meaning.

- Folk motifs or styles lend authenticity to tales, poems, or concepts related to particular cultures.

*Source:* Barbara Kiefer, "Visual Criticism and Children's Literature," in Betsy Hearne and Roger Sutton, eds., *Evaluating Children's Books: A Critical Look* (Urbana: University of Illinois at Urbana-Champaign Graduate School of Library and Information Science, 1993), pp. 73–91. Reprinted with permission.

# Reading and writing programs in ancient Greece

*by Leila Avrin*

WE KNOW THAT THERE WERE elementary schools in 5th-century Athens, and we even know something of how students were taught to read. Even if the average Athenian citizen could not read well, he at least knew the alphabet. The richer the citizen, the better the education. Slaves were at times taught to read and write. At school, reading and writing were taught together; the instructor wrote out the letters for students to copy and learn. Syllables were taught after the individual letters were mastered: two-, three-, then four-letter syllables. Lines of poetry came next.

Students were taught to read aloud, and learned music and gymnastics as well as literature. The real purpose of Athenian education was to train the sons of citizens, from age 6 to 14, to have a sound mind and sound body, so that at age 18 they would in turn become good citizens. From sculpture and vase paintings we know that girls were taught to read and write. They undoubtedly were taught at home by tutors and not in the schools attended by boys. The woman who could read was exceptional; seldom was she encouraged to learn more than she would need for operating her household.

After a young man's military service, at about age 20, higher education was undertaken by the Sophists, paid professors of wisdom. At times Sophists came from foreign countries and were much in demand. They trained Athenians in public speaking (rhetoric—the art of persuasion through oratory) for success in political life. The Sophists and their students were responsible for creating a need for literary works to be copied.

Whether there was training for scribehood in Athens, either for the purpose of reproducing literary texts or for government service, is unknown. Was there a separate training program in calligraphy for students of a certain age group or for students with a fine hand? Were all boys taught the Greek equivalent of the Palmer method and only those whose handwriting did not deteriorate grew up to be literary copyists? Were favored slaves singled out to be future scribes? Did a student learning with a Sophist do scribal work to earn his own tuition when his parents couldn't afford it? Were scribes apprenticed to master scribes? Was a scribe merely an educated drudge who couldn't make it as politician? As yet, nothing is known or can be reconstructed of the careers of classical Greek and Hellenistic literary scribes.

In Hellenistic times they undoubtedly worked for authors, teachers, publishers or booksellers, and libraries. Argument still rages among those scholars who care, and the issue may never be resolved, whether Hellenistic scribes in Alexandria wrote from dictation or copied from an exemplar, as did medieval scribes. Some historians have imagined a large scriptorium with a master dictating to the assembled scribes so that a multiple-copy edition could be published. This debate centers around the plethora of mistakes made by Alexandrian scribes. Were they mistakes of the eye, and therefore the scribe copied a text, or mistakes of the ear, and therefore many scribes wrote from dictation to produce multiple copies?

*Source:* Leila Avrin, *Scribes, Script and Books: The Book Arts from Antiquity to the Renaissance* (Chicago and London: American Library Association/British Library, 1991). 356p.

# Homeschoolers and the public library

*by Susan G. Scheps, Janice Hedin, Susan Richman, and Susan Madden*

ESTIMATES OF THE ACTUAL NUMBER OF CHILDREN who are taught at home currently range from ten or twenty thousand to over a million. This wide variation in figures stems from the impossibility of obtaining statistics from one (or even a few) sources. A large percentage of homeschoolers do not belong to a national organization. Local groups are often small, with mailing addresses and member families changing frequently. While many homeschooling families have regular contact with their local school districts, benefiting from the use of school-owned equipment, curricula, and counseling, many others must do their own footwork. They must seek out a curriculum that meets both their personal needs and those of the state in which they reside, track down specialists in various fields who can provide enrichment materials or private tutelage for their children, and become familiar with laws regarding educational requirements.

To public librarians, the recent surge in homeschooled children represents a new challenge for service excellence. The homeschooled child gains wisdom as a result of his own curiosity. As more and more libraries begin to recognize homeschooled children within their communities, an understanding of their parents' philosophies and their learning methods can help us to provide the materials, programs, educational opportunities and support that will satisfy their needs.

## What homeschoolers want from public libraries

A file, regularly updated, that includes the following:

- the laws of your state regarding homeschooling;
- a directory of homeschoolers in the area;
- names and addresses of national and state (if they exist) homeschool organizations that they can contact for information;
- addresses of local schools and their contact persons; also the name and address of the state superintendent;
- addresses and information on suppliers of materials for homeschooling (publishers/distributors).

Workshops on how to use the library.

Involvement with state-level home organizations. (For example, by setting up a booth at the state homeschool conference, staffed by personnel from one or more libraries, at which library brochures are handed out.)

A bulletin board in the library on which homeschoolers can display such things as:

- state and area meeting calendars, including library programs and other area programs that are open to the public;
- information on contests (writing, poetry, essay, art) for young people; science fairs, humanities programs, etc.;
- reviews of new books for homeschooled children and their parents (keeping an organized home, reading aloud to children);
- monthly pages from Chase's calendar;
- dates of book sales (library and others).

Regular displays of homeschool projects, art, hobbies, etc., in the library. Curriculum guides of local schools.

Workshops on topics such as materials available in the library in various subject areas, new books, reference books, videos and other materials, including quality children's magazine.

Tours of the library, including information on interlibrary loans and other information sources (DIALOG, INFOTRAC, and others).

Special programs: a reading program during the school year for homeschoolers; special bibliographic instruction; programs offered by a specialist in some subject area during the day.

A volunteer program (volunteers in various libraries around the country have helped with fundraising, for example, at book sales) and lobbying, tutoring, reviewing books and audiovisual materials. They have also presented children's programs on topics that they have studied or put on plays for children at the library. They are especially interested in intergenerational volunteer opportunities (children working alongside older community members).

Access to publishers' catalogs and book review journals. A good collection of audiotapes.

Use of the library's meeting room for group meetings, plays and other activities.

Use of personal computers and (occasional) use of AV equipment (film projectors, overhead projectors) for programs.

A library column in the local home newsletter, highlighting programs, services, book reviews, books of special interest, new books.

Attentiveness from their librarian. (Help in finding materials, knowledgeable information regarding materials, an interest in their needs).

Special borrowing privileges (like those extended to teachers). Longer loans, use of AV equipment, books on reserve, filmstrips, videos, VCRs reserved for their use.

A good collection of children's books and materials (the public library should provide a core curriculum for people of all ages).

*Source:* Susan G. Scheps, ed., *Homeschoolers and the Public Library: A Resource Guide for Libraries Serving Homeschoolers* (Chicago: ALA Public Library Association, 1993).

# Newbery Medal awards

**THE NEWBERY MEDAL,** named for 18th-century British bookseller John Newbery, is awarded annually by the ALA Association for Library Service to Children to the author of the most distinguished contribution to American literature for children. Here are the award winners since the award's inception in 1922.

4

1994—Lois Lowry, *The Giver* (Houghton Mifflin, 1993).

1993—Cynthia Rylant, *Missing May* (Orchard, 1992).

1992—Phyllis Reynolds Naylor, *Shiloh* (Atheneum, 1991).

1991—Jerry Spinelli, *Maniac Magee* (Little, Brown, 1990).

1990—Lois Lowry, *Number the Stars* (Houghton, 1989).

1989—Paul Fleischman, *Joyful Noise: Poems for Two Voices* (Harper, 1988).

1988—Russell Freedman, *Lincoln: A Photobiography* (Houghton, 1987).

1987—Sid Fleischman, *The Whipping Boy* (Greenwillow, 1986).

1986—Patricia MacLachlan, *Sarah, Plain and Tall* (Harper, 1985).

1985—Robin McKinley, *The Hero and the Crown* (Greenwillow, 1984).

1984—Beverly Cleary, *Dear Mr. Henshaw* (Morrow, 1983).

1983—Cynthia Voigt, *Dicey's Song* (Atheneum, 1982).

1982—Nancy Willard, *A Visit to William Blake's Inn: Poems for Innocent and Experienced Travelers* (Harcourt, 1981).

1981—Katherine Paterson, *Jacob Have I Loved* (Crowell, 1980).

1980—Joan W. Blos, *A Gathering of Days* (Scribner, 1979).

1979—Ellen Raskin, *The Westing Game* (Dutton, 1978).

1978—Katherine Paterson, *Bridge to Treblinka* (Crowell, 1977).

1977—Mildred D. Taylor, *Roll of Thunder, Hear My Cry* (Dial, 1976).

1976—Susan Cooper, *The Grey King* (Atheneum, 1975).

1975—Virginia Hamilton, *M.C. Higgins, the Great* (Macmillan, 1974).

1974—Paula Fox, *The Slave Dancer* (Bradbury, 1973).

1973—Jean Craighead George, *Julie of the Wolves* (Harper, 1972).

1972—Robert C. O'Brien, *Mrs. Frisby and the Rats of NIMH* (Atheneum, 1971).

1971—Betsy Byars, *Summer of the Swans* (Viking, 1970).

1970—William H. Armstrong, *Sounder* (Harper, 1969).

1969—Lloyd Alexander, *The High King* (Holt, 1968).

1968—E. L. Konigsburg, *From the Mixed-Up Files of Mrs. Basil E. Frankweiler* (Atheneum, 1967).

1967—Irene Hunt, *Up a Road Slowly* (Follett, 1966).

1966—Elizabeth Borton de Trevino, *I, Juan de Pareja* (Farrar, 1965).

1965—Maia Wojciechowska, *Shadow of a Bull* (Atheneum, 1964).

1964—Emily Neville, *It's Like This, Cat* (Harper, 1963).

1963—Madeleine L'Engle, *A Wrinkle in Time* (Farrar, 1962).

**1962**—Elizabeth George Speare, *The Bronze Bow* (Houghton, 1961).
**1961**—Scott O'Dell, *Island of the Blue Dolphins* (Houghton, 1960).
**1960**—Joseph Krumgold, *Onion John* (Crowell, 1959).
**1959**—Elizabeth George Speare, *The Witch of Blackbird Pond* (Houghton, 1958).
**1958**—Harold Keith, *Rifles for Watie* (Crowell, 1957).
**1957**—Virginia Sorensen, *Miracles on Maple Hill* (Harcourt, 1956).
**1956**—Jean Lee Latham, *Carry On, Mr. Bowditch* (Houghton, 1955).
**1955**—Meindert DeJong, *The Wheel of the School* (Harper, 1954).
**1954**—Joseph Krumgold, *. . . And Now Miguel* (Crowell, 1953).
**1953**—Ann Nolan Clark, *Secret of the Andes* (Viking, 1952).
**1952**—Eleanor Estes, *Ginger Pye* (Harcourt, 1951).
**1951**—Elizabeth Yates, *Amos Fortune, Free Man* (Dutton, 1950).
**1950**—Marguerite de Angeli, *The Door in the Wall* (Doubleday, 1949).
**1949**—Marguerite Henry, *King of the Wind* (Rand McNally, 1948).
**1948**—William Pène du Bois, *The Twenty-One Balloons* (Viking, 1947).
**1947**—Carolyn Bailey, *Miss Hickory* (Viking, 1946).
**1946**—Lois Lenski, *Strawberry Girl* (Lippincott, 1945).
**1945**—Robert Lawson, *Rabbit Hill* (Viking, 1944).
**1944**—Esther Forbes, *Johnny Tremain* (Houghton, 1943).
**1943**—Elizabeth Gray, *Adam of the Road* (Viking, 1942).
**1942**—Walter Edmonds, *The Matchlock Gun* (Dodd, 1941).
**1941**—Armstrong Sperry, *Call It Courage* (Macmillan, 1940).
**1940**—James Daugherty, *Daniel Boone* (Viking, 1939).
**1939**—Elizabeth Enright, *Thimble Summer* (Rinehart, 1938).
**1938**—Kate Seredy, *The White Stag* (Viking, 1937).
**1937**—Ruth Sawyer, *Roller Skates* (Viking, 1936).
**1936**—Carol Brink, *Caddie Woodlawn* (Macmillan, 1935).
**1935**—Monica Shannon, *Dobry* (Viking, 1934).
**1934**—Cornelia Meigs, *Invincible Louisa* (Little, Brown, 1933).
**1933**—Elizabeth Lewis, *Young Fu of the Upper Yangtze* (Winston, 1932).
**1932**—Laura Armer, *Waterless Mountain* (Longmans, 1931).
**1931**—Elizabeth Coatsworth, *The Cat Who Went to Heaven* (Macmillan, 1930).
**1930**—Rachel Field, *Hitty, Her First Hundred Years* (Macmillan, 1929).
**1929**—Eric P. Kelly, *The Trumpeter of Krakow* (Macmillan, 1928).
**1928**—Dhan Mukerji, *Gay Neck, the Story of a Pigeon* (Dutton, 1927).
**1927**—Will James, *Smoky, the Cowhorse* (Scribner, 1926).
**1926**—Arthur Chrisman, *Shen of the Sea* (Dutton, 1925).
**1925**—Charles Finger, *Tales from Silver Lands* (Doubleday, 1924).
**1924**—Charles Hawes, *The Dark Frigate* (Atlantic/Little, 1923).
**1923**—Hugh Lofting, *The Voyages of Doctor Dolittle* (Lippincott, 1922).
**1922**—Henrik Van Loon, *The Story of Mankind* (Liveright, 1921).

*Source:* ALA Association for Library Service to Children.

# Caldecott Medal winners

**THE CALDECOTT MEDAL,** named in honor of 19th-century English illustrator Randolph Caldecott, is awarded annually by the ALA Association for Library Service to Children to the artist of the most distinguished American picture book for children. Here are the award winners since the award's inception in 1938.

1994—Allen Say, *Grandfather's Journey* (Houghton Mifflin, 1993).

1993—Emily Arnold McCully, *Mirette on the High Wire* (Putnam, 1992).

1992—David Wiesner, *Tuesday* (Clarion, 1991).

1991—David Macaulay, *Black and White* (Houghton, 1990).

1990—Ed Young, *Lon Po Po* (Philomel, 1989).

1989—Karen Ackerman, *Song and Dance Man* (Knopf, 1988); illustrated by Stephen Gammell.

1988—Jane Yolen, *Owl Moon* (Philomel, 1987); illustrated by John Schoenherr.

1987—Arthur Yorinks, *Hey, Al* (Farrar, 1986); illustrated by Richard Egielski.

1986—Chris Van Allsburg, *The Polar Express* (Houghton, 1985).

1985—Margaret Hodges, *Saint George and the Dragon* (Little, Brown, 1984); illustrated by Trina Schart Hyman.

1984—Alice and Martin Provensen, *The Glorious Flight: Across the Channel with Louis Blériot* (Viking, 1983).

1983—Blaise Cendrars, *Shadow* (Scribner, 1982); illustrated by Marcia Brown.

1982—Chris Van Allsburg, *Jumanji* (Houghton, 1981).

1981—Arnold Lobel, *Fables* (Harper, 1980).

1980—Donald Hall, *Ox-Cart Man* (Viking, 1979); illustrated by Barbara Cooney.

1979—Paul Goble, *The Girl Who Loved Wild Horses* (Bradbury, 1978).

1978—Peter Spier, *Noah's Ark* (Doubleday, 1977).

1977—Margaret Musgrove, *Ashanti to Zulu* (Dial, 1976); illustrated by Leo and Diane Dillon.

1976—Verna Aardema, *Why Mosquitoes Buzz in People's Ears* (Dial, 1975); illustrated by Leo and Diane Dillon.

1975—Gerald McDermott, *Arrow to the Sun* (Viking, 1974).

1974—Harve Zemach, *Duffy and the Devil* (Farrar, 1973); illustrated by Margot Zemach.

1973—Lafcadio Hearn, retold by Arlene Mosel, *The Funny Little Woman* (Dutton, 1972); illustrated by Blair Lent.

1972—Nonny Hogrogian, *One Fine Day* (Macmillan, 1971).

1971—Gail E. Haley, *A Story A Story* (Atheneum, 1970).

1970—William Steig, *Sylvester and the Magic Pebble* (Windmill, 1969).

1969—Arthur Ransome, *The Fool of the World and the Flying Ship* (Farrar, 1968); illustrated by Uri Shulevitz.

1968—Barbara Emberley, *Drummer Hoff* (Prentice-Hall, 1967); illustrated by Ed Emberley.

1967—Evaline Ness, *Sam, Bangs & Moonshine* (Holt, 1966).

1966—Sorche Nic Leodhas, *Always Room for One More* (Holt, 1965); illustrated by Nonny Hogrogian.

1965—Beatrice Schenk de Regniers, *May I Bring a Friend?* (Atheneum, 1964); illustrated by Beni Montresor.

1964—Maurice Sendak, *Where the Wild Things Are* (Harper, 1963).

1963—Ezra Jack Keats, *The Snowy Day* (Viking, 1962).

1962—Marcia Brown, *Once a Mouse* (Scribner, 1961).

1961—Ruth Robbins, *Baboushka and the Three Kings* (Parnassus, 1960); illustrated by Nicolas Sidjakov.

1960—Marie Hall Ets and Aurora Labastida, *Nine Days to Christmas* (Viking, 1959).

1959—Barbara Clooney, *Chanticleer and the Fox* (Crowell, 1958).

1958—Robert McCloskey, *Time of Wonder* (Viking, 1957).

1957—Janice Udry, *A Tree Is Nice* (Harper, 1956); illustrated by Marc Simont.

**1956**—John Langstaff, *Frog Went A-Courtin'* (Harcourt, 1955); illustrated by Feodor Rojankovsky.

**1955**—Marcia Brown, *Cinderella* (Scribner, 1954).

**1954**—Ludwig Bemelmans, *Madeline's Rescue* (Viking, 1953).

**1953**—Lynd Ward, *The Biggest Bear* (Houghton, 1952).

**1952**—Will Lipkind, *Finders Keepers* (Harcourt, 1951); illustrated by Nicolas Mordvinoff.

**1951**—Katherine Milhous, *The Egg Tree* (Scribner, 1950).

**1950**—Leo Politi, *Song of the Swallows* (Scribner, 1949).

**1949**—Berta and Elmer Hader, *The Big Snow* (Macmillan, 1948).

**1948**—Alvin Tresselt, *Mite Snow, Bright Snow* (Lothrop, 1947); illustrated by Roger Duvoisin.

**1947**—Golden McDonald, *The Little Island* (Doubleday, 1946); illustrated by Leonard Weisgard.

**1946**—Maude and Miska Petersham, *The Rooster Crows* (Macmillan, 1945).

**1945**—Rachel Field,*Prayer for a Child*(Macmillan,1944); illustrated by Elizabeth Orton Jones.

**1944**—James Thurber, *Many Moons* (Harcourt, 1943); illustrated by Louis Slobodkin.

**1943**—Virginia Lee Burton, *The Little House* (Houghton, 1942).

**1942**—Robert McCloskey, *Make Way for Ducklings* (Viking, 1941).

**1941**—Robert Lawson, *They Were Strong and Good* (Viking, 1940).

**1940**—Ingri and Edgar Parin d'Aulaire, *Abraham Lincoln* (Doubleday, 1939).

**1939**—Thomas Handforth, *Mei Li* (Doubleday, 1938).

**1938**—Helen Dean Fish, *Animals of the Bible* (Lippincott, 1937); illustrated by Dorothy P. Lathrop.

*Source:* ALA Association for Library Service to Children.

# Batchelder Award winners

**THE MILDRED L. BATCHELDER AWARD** is given each year to an American publisher for the most outstanding children's book originally published in a foreign language or in another country. The ALA Association for Library Service to Children gives the award to encourage American publishers to seek out superior children's books abroad and to promote communication between the peoples of the world. The award is named for Mildred L. Batchelder, a children's librarian whose work over three decades has had an international influence. Here are the award winners since the award's inception in 1968.

**1994**—Pilar Molina Llorente, *The Apprentice* (Farrar, Straus and Giroux, 1993); translated by Robin Longshaw.

**1993**—no award presented

**1992**—Uri Orlev, *The Man from the Other Side* (Houghton Mifflin, 1991); translated from the Hebrew by Hillel Halkin.

**1991**—Rafik Schami, *A Hand Full of Stars* (Dutton, 1990); translated from the German by Rika Lesser.

**1990**—Bjarne Reuter, *Buster's World* (Dutton, 1989); translated from the Danish by Anthea Bell.

**1989**—Peter Härtling,*Crutches* (Lothrop, 1988); translated from the German by Elizabeth D. Crawford.

**1988**—Ulf Nilsson, *If You Didn't Have Me* (Macmillan, 1987); translated from the Swedish by George Blecher and Lone Thygesen-Blecher.

**1987**—Rudolph Frank, *No Hero for the Kaiser* (Lothrop, 1986); translated from the German by Patricia Crampton.

**1986**—Christophe Gallaz and Roberto Innocenti, *Rose Blanche* (Creative Education, 1986); translated from the French by Martha Coventry and Richard Graglia.

**1985**—Uri Orlev, *The Island on Bird Street* (Houghton, 1984); translated from the Hebrew by Hillel Halkin.

**1984**—Astrid Lindgren, *Ronia, the Robber's Daughter* (Viking, 1983); translated from the Swedish by Patricia Crampton.

**1983**—Toshi Maruki, *Hiroshima No Pika* (Lothrop, 1982); translated from the Japanese through the Kurita-Bando Literary Agency.

**1982**—Harry Kullman, Jr., *The Battle Horse* (Bradbury, 1981); translated from the Swedish by George Blecher and Lone Thygesen-Blecher.

**1981**—Els Pelgrom, *The Winter When Time Was Frozen* (Morrow, 1980); translated from Dutch by Maryka and Raphael Rudnik.

**1980**—Aliki Zei, *The Sound of the Dragon's Feet* (Dutton, 1979); translated from the Greek by Edward Fenton.

**1979**—Jörg Steiner, *Rabbit Island* (Harcourt, 1978); translated from the German by Ann Conrad Lammers.

**1978**—Christine Nöstlinger, *Konrad* (Watts, 1977); translated from the German by Anthea Bell.

**1977**—Cecil Bødker, *The Leopard* (Atheneum, 1977); translated from the Danish by Gunnar Poulsen.

**1976**—Ruth Hürlimann, *The Cat and the Mouse Who Shared a House* (Walck, 1974); translated from the German by Anthea Bell.

**1975**—Aleksandr Linevskii, *An Old Tale Carved out of Stone* (Crown, 1973); translated from the Russian by Maria Polushkin.

**1974**—Aliki Zei, *Petros' War* (Dutton, 1972); translated from the Greek by Edward Fenton.

**1973**—S. R. van Iterson, *Pulga* (Morrow, 1971); translated from the Dutch by Alexander and Alison Gode.

**1972**—Hans Peter Richter, *Friedrich* (Holt, 1970); translated from the German by Edite Kroll.

**1971**—Hans Baumann, *In the Land of Ur: The Discovery of Ancient Mesopotamia* (Pantheon, 1969); translated from the German by Stella Humphries.

**1970**—Aliki Zei, *Wildcat under Glass* (Holt, 1968); translated from the Greek by Edward Fenton.

**1969**—Babbis Friis-Baastad, *Don't Take Teddy* (Scribner, 1967); translated from the Norwegian by Lise Sømme McKinnon.

**1968**—Erich Kästner, *The Little Man* (Knopf, 1966); translated from the German by James Kirkup.

*Source:* ALA Association for Library Service to Children.

# Canadian Library Association books of the year for children

**THE BOOK OF THE YEAR FOR CHILDREN,** sponsored by the Canadian Library Association, is given to the Canadian author of the best book published in Canada for children or young adults. Here are the award winners since the award's inception in 1947.

**1994**—Tim Wynne-Jones, *Some of the Kinder Planets* (Groundwood/Douglas & McIntyre, 1993).

**1993**—Celia Barker Lottridge, *Ticket to Curlew* (Groundwood/Douglas & McIntyre, 1992).

**1992**—Kevin Major, *Eating Between the Lines* (Doubleday, 1991).

**1991**—Michael Bedard, *Redwork* (Lester & OrpenDennys, 1990).

**1990**—Kit Pearson, *The Sky Is Falling* (Penguin, 1989).

**1989**—Brian Doyle, *Easy Avenue* (Groundwood, 1988).

**1988**—Kit Pearson, *A Handful of Time* (Viking Kestrel, 1987),

**1987**—Janet Lunn, *Shadow of Hawthorn Bay* (Lester & Orpen Dennys, 1986).

**1986**—Cora Taylor, *Julie* (Western Producer Prairie Books, 1985).

**1985**—Jean Little, *Mama's Going to Buy You a Mockingbird* (Penguin, 1984).

**1984**—Jan Hudson, *Sweetgrass* (Tree Frog, 1984).

**1983**—Brian Doyle, *Up to Low* (Douglas & McIntyre, 1982).

**1982**—Janet Lunn, *The Root Cellar* (Lester & Orpen Dennys, 1981).

**1981**—Donn Kushner, *The Violin Maker's Gift* (Macmillan, 1980).

**1980**—James Houston, *River Runners* (McClelland & Stewart, 1979).

**1979**—Kevin Major, *Hold Fast* (Clarke, Irwin, 1978).

**1978**—Dennis Lee, *Garbage Delight* (Macmillan, 1977).

**1977**—Christine Harris, *Mouse Woman and the Vanished Princesses* (McClelland & Stewart, 1976).

**1976**—Mordecai Richler, *Jacob Two-Two Meets the Hooded Fang* (McClelland & Stewart, 1975).

**1975**—Dennis Lee, *Alligator Pie* (Macmillan, 1974).

**1974**—Elizabeth Cleaver, *The Miraculous Hind* (Holt, 1973).

**1973**—Ruth Nichols, *The Marrow of the World* (Macmillan, 1972).

**1972**—Ann Blades, *Mary of Mile 18* (Tundra, 1971).

**1971**—William Toye, *Cartier Discovers the St. Lawrence* (Oxford, 1970).

**1970**—Edith Fowke, *Sally Go Round the Sun* (McClelland & Stewart, 1969).

**1969**—Kay Hill, *And Tomorrow the Stars* (Dodd, 1968).

**1968**—James Houston, *The White Archer* (Longmans, 1967).

**1967**—Christine Harris, *Raven's Cry* (McClelland & Stewart, 1966).

**1966**—James Houston,*Tikta'liktak*(Longmans, 1965); James McNeill,*The Double Knights* (Oxford, 1965).

**1965**—Dorothy Reid, *Tales of Nanabozho* (Oxford, 1964).

**1964**—Roderick Haig-Brown, *The Whale People* (Collins, 1962).

**1963**—Sheila Every Burnford, *The Incredible Journey* (Little, 1961).

**1961**—William Toye, *The St. Lawrence* (Oxford, 1959).

**1960**—Marius Barbeau and Michael Hornyansky, *The Golden Phoenix and Other French Canadian Fairy Tales* (Oxford, 1958).

**1959**—John Hayes, *The Dangerous Cove* (Copp, Clark, 1957).

**1958**—Farley Mowat, *Lost in the Barrens* (Little, 1956).

**1957**—Cyrus Macmillan, *Glooscap's Country* (Oxford, 1955).

**1956**—Louise Riley, *Train for Tiger Lily* (Macmillan, 1954).

**1952**—Catherine Anthony Clark, *The Sun Horse* (Macmillan, 1951).

**1950**—Richard Lambert, *Franklin in the Arctic* (McClelland & Stewart, 1949).

**1949**—Mabel Dunham, *Kristli's Trees* (McClelland & Stewart, 1948).

**1947**—Roderick Haig-Brown, *Starbuck Winter Valley* (Morrow, 1943).

*Source:* Canadian Library Association.

# Young Adult Materials

# Best books for young adults, 1993

EACH YEAR THE ALA Young Adult Library Services Association compiles a list of fiction and nonfiction titles that have potential appeal to young adults and exhibit either high literary standards or technical accuracy. The following 1993 list encompasses 60 fiction and 18 nonfiction titles.

## Fiction

Alcock, Vivien. *Singer to the Sea God* (Delacorte, 1993).
Anderson, Rachel. *The Bus People* (Holt, 1992).
Berg, Elizabeth. *Durable Goods* (Random House, 1993).
Block, Francesca Lia. *Missing Angel Juan* (HarperCollins, 1993).
Blume, Judy. *Here's to You Rachel Robinson* (Orchard, 1993).
Bruchac, Joseph. *Dawn Land* (Fulcrum, 1993).
Conly, Jane Leslie. *Crazy Lady!* (HarperCollins, 1993).
Cooney, Caroline B. *Whatever Happened to Janie?* (Delacorte, 1993).
Crutcher, Chris. *Staying Fat for Sarah Byrnes* (Greenwillow, 1993).
Deuker, Carl. *Heart of a Champion* (Joy Street, 1993).
Dickinson, Peter. *A Bone from a Dry Sea* (Delacorte, 1993).
Esquivel, Laura. *Like Water for Chocolate* (Doubleday, 1992).
Fleischman, Paul. *Bull Run* (HarperCollins, 1993).
Gaines, Ernest J. *A Lesson Before Dying* (Knopf, 1993).
Garland, Sherry. *Shadow of the Dragon* (Harcourt Brace, 1993).
Gee, Maurice. *The Champion* (Simon & Schuster, 1993).
Gibbons, Kaye. *Charms for the Easy Life* (Putnam, 1993).
Grant, Cynthia D. *Shadow Man* (Atheneum, 1992).
Grant, Cynthia D. *Uncle Vampire* (Atheneum, 1993).
Hahn, Mary Downing. *The Wind Blows Backward* (Clarion, 1993).
Haynes, David. *Right by My Side* (New Rivers, 1993).
Hobbs, Will. *Beardance* (Atheneum, 1993).
Hodge, Merle. *For the Life of Laetitia* (Farrar, Straus, Giroux, 1993).
Johnson, Angela. *Toning the Sweep* (Orchard, 1993).
Jordan, Sherryl. *Winter of Fire* (Scholastic, 1993).
LeMieux, Anne Connelly. *The TV Guidance Counselor* (Tambourine, 1993).
Lowry, Lois. *The Giver* (Houghton Mifflin, 1993).
Lynch, Chris. *Shadow Boxer* (HarperCollins, 1993).
McKinley, Robin. *Deerskin* (Ace, 1993).
MacLachlan, Patricia. *Baby* (Delacorte, 1993).
Mazer, Harry. *Who Is Eddie Leonard?* (Delacorte, 1993).
Mazer, Norma Fox. *Out of Control* (Morrow, 1993).
Merrick, Monte. *Shelter* (Hyperion, 1993).
Meyer, Carolyn. *White Lilacs* (Gulliver/Harcourt Brace, 1993).
Mori, Kyoko. *Shizuko's Daughter* (Holt, 1993).
Napoli, Donna Jo. *The Magic Circle* (Dutton, 1993).
Paulsen, Gary. *Harris and Me: A Summer Remembered* (Harcourt Brace, 1993).

Paulsen, Gary. *Nightjohn* (Delacorte, 1993).

Philbrick, Rodman. *Freak the Mighty* (Blue Sky/Scholastic, 1993).

Qualey, Marsha. *Revolutions of the Heart* (Houghton Mifflin, 1993).

Rendell, Ruth. *The Crocodile Bird* (Crown, 1993).

Reynolds, Marilyn. *Detour for Emmy* (Morning Glory, 1993).

Rinaldi, Ann. *In My Father's House* (Scholastic, 1993).

Roberson, Jennifer. *Lady of the Forest: A Novel of Sherwood* (Zebra, 1992).

Rochman, Hazel, and Darlene Z. McCampbell, eds. *Who Do You Think You Are? Stories of Friends and Enemies* (Joy Street/Little Brown, 1993).

Ruby, Lois. *Miriam's Well* (Scholastic, 1993).

Sleator, William. *Oddballs* (Dutton, 1993).

Smith, Wayne. *Thor* (St. Martin's, 1992).

Staples, Suzanne Fisher. *Haveli* (Knopf, 1993).

Sweeney, Joyce. *The Tiger Orchid* (Delacorte, 1993).

Tamar, Erika. *Fair Game* (Harcourt Brace, 1993).

Taylor, Theodore. *Timothy of the Cay* (Harcourt Brace, 1993).

Temple, Frances. *Grab Hands and Run* (Orchard, 1993).

Vick, Helen Hughes. *Walker of Time* (Harbinger House, 1993).

Walker, Kate. *Peter* (Houghton Mifflin, 1993).

Watson, Larry. *Montana 1948* (Milkweed, 1993).

Weaver, Will. *Striking Out* (HarperCollins, 1993).

Wittinger, Ellen. *Lombardo's Law* (Houghton Mifflin, 1993).

Wolff, Virginia Euwer. *Make Lemonade* (Holt, 1993).

Yep, Lawrence, ed. *American Dragons: Twenty-Five Asian American Voices* (HarperCollins, 1993).

## Nonfiction

Ashe, Arthur. *Days of Grace* (Random House, 1993).

Atkin, S. Beth. *Voices from the Fields: Children of Migrant Farmworkers Tell Their Stories* (Joy Street, 1993).

Brandenburg, Jim. *To the Top of the World: Adventures with Arctic Wolves* (Walker, 1993).

Delany, Sarah Louise, and A. Elizabeth Delany. *Having Our Say: The Delany Sisters' First 100 Years* (Kodansha, 1993).

Drucker, Olga Levy. *Kindertransport* (Holt, 1992).

Feelings, Tom. *Soul Looks Back in Wonder* (Dial, 1993).

Freedman, Russell. *Eleanor Roosevelt: A Life of Discovery* (Clarion, 1993).

Isaacson, Philip M. *A Short Walk Around the Pyramids and Through the World of Art* (Knopf, 1993).

Janeczko, Paul B. *Stardust Otel* (Orchard, 1993).

Janeczko, Paul B. *Looking for Your Name* (Orchard, 1993).

Kaysen, Susanna. *Girl, Interrupted* (Turtle Bay, 1993).

Levine, Ellen. *Freedom's Children: Young Civil Rights Activists Tell Their Own Stories* (Putnam, 1993).

Littlefield, Bill. *Champions: Stories of Ten Remarkable Athletes* (Little, Brown, 1993).

Macy, Sue. *A Whole New Ball Game* (Holt, 1993).

Myers, Walter Dean. *Malcolm X: By Any Means Necessary* (Scholastic, 1993).

Sutcliff, Rosemary. *Black Ships Before Troy* (Delacorte, 1993).

van der Rol, Ruud, and Rian Verhoeven. *Anne Frank: Beyond the Diary* (Viking, 1993).

Volavkova, Hana, ed. *. . . I Never Saw Another Butterfly . . . Children's Drawings and Poems from Terezin Concentration Camp, 1942–1944* (Schocken, 1993).

*Source:* ALA Young Adult Library Services Association.

# Quick picks: books for young adults

WHAT BOOKS MAKE GREAT READING? Books with exciting stories and interesting characters—books about real-life heroes and fantastic adventures— books that tell you how to fix up your car and help you deal with day-to-day problems. The following recent books are recommended by the ALA Young Adult Library Services Association's Recommended Books for the Reluctant Young Adult Reader Committee for young adults who, for whatever reason, do not like to read. The books chosen demonstrate high appeal in terms of content, format, and artwork. All titles are sixth-grade reading level or below, demonstrate simplicity of plot or organization of information, contain short sentences and short paragraphs, and have uncomplicated dialogue and vocabulary.

**4**

**Angelou, Maya.** *Life Doesn't Frighten Me* (Stewart, Tabori & Chang, 1993).

**Bauer, Marion Dane.** *Taste of Smoke* (Clarion, 1993).

**Bernotas, Bob.** *Spike Lee, Filmmaker* (Enslow, 1993).

**Biesty, Stephen.** *Stephen Biesty's Incredible Cross-Sections* (Knopf, 1992).

**Block, Francesca Lia.** *Missing Angel Juan* (HarperCollins, 1993).

**Bode, Janet.** *Death Is Hard to Live With: Teenagers and How They Cope with Loss* (Delacorte, 1993).

**Brandenburg, Jim.** *To the Top of the World: Adventures with Arctic Wolves* (Walker, 1993).

**Coman, Carolyn.** *Tell Me Everything* (FSG, 1993).

**Cooney, Caroline B.** *The Stranger* (Scholastic, 1993).

**Deuker, Carl.** *Heart of a Champion* (Joy Street, 1993).

**Dolan, Ellen M.** *Susan Butcher and the Iditarod Trail* (Walker, 1993).

**Feelings, Tom.** *Soul Looks Back in Wonder* (Dial, 1993).

**Fleischman, Paul.** *Copier Creations: Using Copy Machines to Make Decals, Silhouettes, Flip Books, Films, and Much More!* (HarperCollins, 1993).

**Godfrey, Martyn.** *Please Remove Your Elbow from My Ear* (Avon, 1993).

**Gordon, John.** *The Burning Baby and Other Ghosts* (Candlewick, 1993).

**Grant, Cynthia D.** *Uncle Vampire* (Atheneum, 1993).

**Groening, Matt.** *Bart Simpson's Guide to Life* (Harper Perennial, 1993).

**Hoffius, Stephen.** *Winners and Losers* (Simon & Schuster, 1993).

**Janeczko, Paul B.** *Stardust Otel* (Orchard, 1993).

**Jennings, Paul.** *Unmentionable! More Amazing Stories* (Viking, 1993).

**Kindl, Patrice.** *Owl in Love* (Houghton Mifflin, 1993).

**Klass, Sheila Solomon.** *Rhino* (Scholastic, 1993).

**Kuklin, Susan.** *Speaking Out: Teenagers Take on Race, Sex and Identity* (Putnam, 1993).

**Lance, Kathryn.** *Going to See Grassy Ella* (Lothrop, 1993).

**Lavies, Bianca.** *A Gathering of Garter Snakes* (Dutton, 1993).

**Levitin, Sonia.** *The Golem and the Dragon Girl* (Dial, 1993).

**Levy, Barrie.** *In Love and in Danger: A Teen's Guide to Breaking Free of Abusive Relationships* (Seal Press, 1993).

**Lewin, Ted.** *I Was a Teenage Professional Wrestler* (Orchard, 1993).

**Lindsay, Jeanne Warren.** *Teen Dads: Rights, Responsibilities and Joys* (Morning Glory, 1993).

**Lynch, Chris.** *Shadow Boxer* (HarperCollins, 1993).

**Matas, Carol.** *Sworn Enemies* (Bantam, 1993).

**Mattera, Joanne.** *Glamour Do's and Don'ts Hall of Fame* (Villard, 1992).

**McFann, Jane.** *Free the Conroy Seven* (Avon, 1993).

**Miklowitz, Gloria D.** *The Killing Boy* (Bantam Starfire, 1993).
**Mullins, Hilary.** *The Cat Came Back* (Naiad, 1993).
**Murphy, Jim.** *Night Terrors* (Scholastic, 1993).
**Murrow, Liza Ketchum.** *Twelve Days in August* (Holiday House, 1993).
**Napoli, Donna Jo.** *The Magic Circle* (Dutton, 1993).
**Nasaw, Jonathan.** *Shakedown Street* (Delacorte, 1993).
**Naylor, Phyllis Reynolds.** *Alice in April* (Atheneum, 1993).
**Nottridge, Rhoda.** *Care for Your Body* (Crestwood House, 1993).
**Paulsen, Gary.** *Harris and Me: A Summer Remembered* (Harcourt, 1993).
**Perkins, Mitali.** *The Sunita Experiment* (Little, Brown, 1993).
**Philbrick, Rodman.** *Freak the Mighty* (Scholastic/Blue Sky, 1993).
**Pilkey, Dav.** *Dogzilla* (Harcourt, 1993).
**Pilkey, Dav.** *Kat Kong* (Harcourt, 1993).
**Putnam, James.** *Mummy* (Knopf, 1993).
**Qualey, Marsha.** *Revolutions of the Heart* (Houghton Mifflin, 1993).
**Simon, Seymour.** *Wolves* (HarperCollins, 1993).
**Sleator, William.** *Oddballs* (Dutton, 1993).
**Sleator, William.** *Others See Us* (Dutton, 1993).
**Staples, Donna.** *Arena Beach* (Houghton Mifflin, 1993).
**Stearns, Michael.** *A Wizard's Dozen* (Harcourt, 1993).
**Tanaka, Shelley.** *The Disaster of The Hindenburg* (Scholastic, 1993).
  **Tennyson, Jeffrey.** *Hamburger Heaven: The Illustrated History of the Hamburger* (Hyperion, 1993).
  **van der Rol, Ruud, and Rian Verhoeven.** *Anne Frank: Beyond the Diary* (Viking, 1993).
**Vande Velde, Vivian.** *Dragon's Bait* (Harcourt, 1993).
**Walker, Kate.** *Peter* (Houghton Mifflin, 1993).
**Wesley, Valerie Wilson.** *Where Do I Go from Here?* (Scholastic, 1993).
**Westall, Robert.** *The Stones of Muncaster Cathedral* (FSG, 1993).
**Wilkinson, Brenda.** *Definitely Cool* (Scholastic, 1993).
**Wittlinger, Ellen.** *Lombardo's Law* (Houghton Mifflin, 1993).
**Wolff, Virginia Euwer.** *Make Lemonade* (Holt, 1993).

*Source:* ALA Young Adult Library Services Association.

# What should youth know? Some observations

*by Mary K. Chelton*

WITHIN THE SOCIAL, ECONOMIC, and demographic forces shaping late 20th-century American society, it is important to reflect on exactly what knowledge we are advocating for youth to have. It is equally important to make a distinction between information and knowledge. Information is external to the individual. Information only becomes knowledge when it is understood and internalized by the individual. The library community frequently falls into the semantic trap of discussing the two as if they were synonymous. Dictionary definitions concerning the terms are also circular, referring one to the other and vice versa. The necessity of two words implies different meanings for each, however, if only because of their different etymological histories. That difference is crucial both to the advocacy of youth's right to know as well as to library programs delivering it.

Knowledge is a developmentally determined combination of voluntary and compulsory exposure to, and understanding of, information (recorded, spoken, demonstrated, or modeled), skills and abilities (natural or acquired), and experience (good and bad, reinforcing or inhibiting). Knowledge is acquired on a continuum that may or may not be synchronized within any particular individual and within specific social and individual contexts. The presence or absence of key developmental, personal, and social variables can be crucial in turning information into individual knowledge. Merely providing information is at best a predisposing factor for either knowledge or for any behavioral change that may result from it.

A library should promote knowledge that allows individuals to grow up as healthy, functioning, moral, productive, and socially competent individuals, with the greatest amount of privacy and personal freedom possible. The following elements encapsulate what youth should know.

## That one is valued

The experience of success, of being needed and recognized by others creates not only the knowledge of self-worth and potential, but also provides the necessary psychosocial underpinning to all other knowledge.

## How to communicate

Knowledge of how to identify concepts, feelings and things, and to communicate them in words to others is basic to the human condition. Equally basic is the need, not only to listen, but also to be heard when one communicates. One also has to be able to hear communication from others. In a sophisticated, technological, media-rich society such as the United States, knowledge of aural, written, visual, digital, as well as spoken communication is vital.

## How to be part of a community

Knowledge of community involves understanding oneself in relation to others, regardless of whether they are family, friends, enemies, other ages, or coworkers. Being part of a community demands knowledge of and respect for human interdependence, reciprocity, culture, history, values, and differences. How to make friends and resolve conflicts are important here, as is the knowledge that the rights and privileges granted by community membership demand particular responsibilities. How to take, counter, defend, and gain support for a political position is also part of being engaged in a democratic community.

## How to learn

Knowledge of how to learn involves knowing that additional information is needed, what it is, where and how to find it, how to understand and evaluate it, and how to remember it. Knowing how and when to study in order to acquire new information is important. This knowledge also demands the time and ability to reflect on experience in relation to prior assumptions, as well as intellectual curiosity. Equally vital in terms of youth is the knowledge that adults can help in this process.

## How to work

Knowledge of how to work is obviously related to knowledge of how to be part of a community. The ways in which work can be a conscious choice that gives meaning to one's life is not well understood by many young people, nor is the way in which one chooses a career, prepares for employment, or closes off career options early in life through bad academic choices. Another aspect is the knowledge that one may be called upon to have several successive careers because of the nature of the human life cycle and the pace of social and technological change in American culture.

## How to make choices

The ability to make choices involves understanding cause and effect, that both decisions and nondecisions have consequences, and that there is a logical sequence to all events from which one is not immune. Decision-making knowledge also involves understanding alternatives and being able to weigh them critically against known or hypothetical outcomes for oneself and others.

## How to protect oneself

One might sum up this elusive knowledge as knowing "when to hold 'em and when to fold 'em," but it also includes how to recognize and avoid a threat, how to get help, how to stay healthy, how to cope with stress, how and when to relax, and the most elusive of all survival skills—when to laugh or cry.

## How to be a moral person

This knowledge covers those values against which one measures and decides whether behavior is good or bad beyond mere self-interest or what is dictated by others, a belief in possible goodness, honor and self-sacrifice, and acknowledgment of the spiritual dimensions of human existence, whether personal or historical. Like the knowledge of being valued, this knowledge underpins all others.

*Source:* Mary K. Chelton, "Youth's Right to Know: Societal Necessity or National Oxymoron?"
in *Your Right to Know: Librarians Make It Happen*
(Chicago: American Library Association, June 1992), pp. 35–44.

# Teen behavior

*by Mary K. Chelton and James M. Rosinia*

SINCE FEW LIBRARIES ARE SET UP with young adults primarily in mind, their normal behavior can often lead frustrated or frightened librarians to consider them troublemakers. A disruptive teenager can be unnerving, but most perceptions of young adults as troublemakers in libraries stem from unrealistic library regulations, frightened staff, or community attitudes toward youth. A few rules of thumb for coping with young adult behavior include: (1) understand exactly what constitutes normal adolescent behavior; (2) make sure that you and your library's policies are fairly administered toward all ages so that young adults do not perceive that they are being discriminated against; (3) threaten nothing that you cannot actually deliver; (4) involve young adults themselves in solutions; and (5) maintain good relations with local law enforcement personnel so that they understand that when you call them, you really need them. The worst thing many librarians do is call the police the minute they think they have a problem with teenagers, and the police in general consider their complaints trivial. If you or your administrator overreacts constantly, you run the risk that the police will ignore you or delay their response when you really need them.

Normal healthy teenagers travel in herds. Young adults can be disruptive just because they are in a group and talking. Usually they are so involved with each other that they do not realize that they are disturbing other people. Also, adolescent culture is much more tolerant of noise than are those over thirty (which includes many librarians). Most of the time if teenagers are asked to quiet down, they will cooperate. The noise level will go down for a while, but it will rise again because the teens are still talking and still oblivious. As long as they are not destructive or disruptive to others, another reminder to quiet down will usually be sufficient. It is important for you to realize that this behavior is normal; the kids are not doing it deliberately to annoy you.

Another normal characteristic of adolescence, however, is to test the limits of imposed authority, so it is possible that, after several warnings to quiet down, the young adults will begin to take delight in seeing how far they can push you. This is the time to ask them to step outside for a couple of minutes to get it out of their system, or to break up the group and ask them to sit at separate tables, or to "pick a victim" whose parents will be called. The victim will no doubt be very aggrieved that he or she has been singled out for what everybody was doing, but you may point out that he or she did nothing to stop it, and is therefore equally guilty. The "pick-a-victim" routine only works when you know how to get the parent's name, but you can also ask for a library card, assuming the young adult has one, and work from there. The other technique is to take the loudest mouth in the group into a back room for a private discussion. This is usually intimidating enough to have a group effect, at least temporarily. Depending on the personality of the young adult, the discussion can include either a further warning or a request for help. It is wise not to make any discussions too private in case there is subsequent misunderstanding about what took place. Perhaps one additional neutral witness should be present.

Another aspect of teenage herd behavior is congregating near the front door or in the parking lot. Usually the teens are just talking, flirting, and acting out for each other, oblivious to the fact that their very presence is frightening to little kids and senior citizens alike. Again, a simple reminder or request to move on will usually be honored, but this could become a real problem if there

is no place else in the community for teenagers to hang out together, or if the teens themselves decide that it is fun to intimidate people coming to the library. If there is good reason to believe that drug dealing is going on, the problem must be referred to the library administration for negotiation with community authorities.

Whether the herding problem is a group making noise inside the library, or a group congregating outside the library, it is important to remember that an unfounded but real fear of minority kids sometimes plays a large role in both staff perceptions and those of other library users. Do not jump to prejudicial conclusions if the young adults in question are ethnic or racial minorities.

There is increasing evidence of overwhelming resentment on the part of well-behaved minority kids for being accused of doing things that they neither did nor intended, solely because they are minorities. Try not to jump to

4

any conclusions about *possible* behavior by anyone. Deal only with actual behavior.

Problems of theft, graffiti, and vandalism are not unique to adolescents, but are ubiquitous enough to be considered here. Since it is impossible to watch young adults (or, for that matter, anyone) every minute they are in the library, removing the sources of temptation is important. Mediated access to audiovisual materials is generally recommended. Some libraries have locked audiotape, videotape, and compact disc holders; others display only empty sleeves that have to be taken to the desk for checkout. Other libraries depend on formal security systems either alone or in combination with locked displays. If your library has a security system, it is important that it be taken seriously, even when false alarms are given. If the staff is casual about security, you may rest assured that the public will be, too.

While it is important that merchandising displays of popular materials for young adults be in highly visible areas, they can be immediately visible from the front door without being so close to the door that there is little to deter someone from grabbing something and walking out with it. The problem with much "front-end" space in libraries is that the circulation desk is set too far back, thus creating not only prime display space, but also prime theft space.

Another source of temptation stems from overly strict library card and overdue fine rules that encourage young adults to steal materials, because stealing is easier than getting a library card or negotiating a fine.

Graffiti can be an expensive nuisance. Since most places cannot start from scratch with graffiti-proof fabrics, tabletops, or wall paint, most libraries wash off, reupholster, refinish, or paint over the graffiti at regular intervals, unless the culprit is caught in the act. While there is no foolproof solution, some libraries have tried chalkboards in the rest rooms, using dark brown paint, or placing note pads near phone booths, and offering doors or tables covered with brown paper at regular intervals.

Unfortunately, despite your best public relations, staff training, and preventive efforts, there will inevitably be the smart mouth or destructive young adult that causes real problems. Make sure you know the policy in place to cover any action you must take. If there is not one, suggest that the library administrator draft one, and suggest possibilities for inclusion. If you know that, for whatever reason, you have an exceptionally low tolerance for normal, let alone abnormal, adolescent behavior, try to get some training or at least some help and perspective from coworkers. Never threaten anything beyond library policy nor anything illegal in a heated verbal exchange. Try to keep all discussions calm under all circumstances.

*Source:* Mary K. Chelton and James M. Rosinia, *Bare Bones: Young Adult Services Tips for Public Library Generalists* (Chicago: ALA Public Library Association and Young Adult Library Services Association, 1993). 73p.

# Tips for successful young adult programming

### by Mildred G. Wallace

**PROGRAMS FOR YOUNG ADULTS** have received short shrift in the allocation of library resources. Librarians have traditionally provided story hours for young children, summer reading programs for young children, and various programs for adults. Young adults have been sadly neglected. It is time to change this pattern and make young adult programming an important element of total library service. These are some tips, based on the author's experience with young adult programming to help librarians break out of the traditional mold and plan effective programs for young adults.

**Study the literature.**
- Gather statistics about the rising rate of crime and violence among adolescents; the high incidence of teenage pregnancy; the accelerating rate of teenage prostitution, teenage suicide, and drug abuse; the numbers of young people at risk of dropping out of school; and other social problems.
- Search the literature for discussions of young adult programs that have worked in other libraries.
- Compile a list of ideas for young adult programs that sound worthwhile and feasible.
- Do not focus solely on library literature; the literature of all professions in service to youth is a useful source of information and ideas.

**Talk to every library staff member.**
- Talk with all members of the staff—from student assistants to principals, from pages to department heads.
- Explain the rationale for young adult programming, ask for suggestions, and listen. These conversations result in an expanded list of ideas and also indicate which staff members are genuinely interested in being a part of young adult programming.

**Conduct a needs assessment.**
- Use a short questionnaire or use focus groups to conduct a needs assessment of the targeted audience.
- Find out what types of library programs the young people want and when they want them. Young adults will support only what *they* want.
- Remember to include parents, teachers, and other youth workers in the survey.
- Save time and money by keeping the needs assessment simple and by collecting only information relevant to young adult programming. Refrain from asking useless questions simply out of curiosity.
- Where information already exists, use it.
- Work with and through established groups to collect data.
- Involve the young adults themselves in the needs assessment process. Young people are experts at getting answers from their peers.

**Secure administrative support.**
- Armed with statistics and ideas gleaned from a review of the literature, from discussions with staff, and from the needs assessment, talk with those who are responsible for making decisions about the allocation of resources. This would include community leaders, the library director, school officials, parents, school-based council members, and library board members.
- Discuss the importance of young adult programs, cite statistics, be practical, outline several possible approaches, and be prepared to answer questions.
- Note questions that arise for which no immediate answers are available, and offer to research the questions and provide answers at a later time.

**Involve the participants.**
- Appoint a youth advisory committee composed of both genders and with several representatives from each ethnic, cultural, racial, and socioeconomic group (representatives are more likely to express their opinions when there is more than one on an advisory committee).
- Involve young people in the planning, conducting, and evaluation of the programs.
- *Listen* to the young people, incorporate their ideas, *always* respect their opinions, and give them something meaningful to do.

**Seek community support.**
- Involve as many community people as possible.
- Keep a current file of community resource people, their areas of expertise, and the types of resources they are willing or might be willing to contribute.
- Keep a record of past contributions from community resource people and the date to prevent calling on the same people for help or donations every time something is needed.
- Remember that the community is more likely to endorse a program in which it has a stake, and many community members and businesses are willing to assist. For example, as advertising, managers of fast food restaurants and theaters will often donate free food coupons or movie passes. These make good prizes.
- *Always* send a prompt note of thanks to all who provide assistance.

**Coordinate library programs with other social agencies.**
- Contact key personnel in every social agency serving young people, find out what they are doing, what has worked for them, and decide which agency will do what. Collaboration not only saves time and energy, it widens the talent pool and results in better programs. Jointly sponsored programs can also be effective.

- Where there is collaboration of any kind, let the public know about it. Taxpayers like to feel that their money is not being wasted through needless duplication.

**Solicit outside funding.**
- Do not hesitate to explore the possibility of receiving a private or government grant to

fund a special program or series of programs for young people.
- Become familiar with grant writing. This can be accomplished by attending grant writing workshops and/or by reading books on grant writing.
- External funds are available for both small and large programs for young adults. It is a matter of learning about these possible sources of funding and being willing to give grant writing a try.

### Start with something simple.
- Start with a program that takes a minimum of effort.
- Pick a program that cannot fail. There is much truth in the adage "Nothing succeeds like success": everyone likes to be involved with a winner, and several successful programs provide a sound foundation for tackling something more ambitious.
- Never consider an initial program with even a slight element of risk.

### Remember the importance of public relations.
- Advertise the program. It is important to let the entire community know what is being planned.
- Instead of relying on one or two sources, try an advertising blitz.
- Use flyers, posters, radio, television, and personal contacts.
- Brag a little when a program is successful. Be certain that the entire community hears the success story.

### Practice imaging.
- Imaging—mentally walking through every step of a process—is a useful technique in preparing young adult programs. Visualize every detail of every stage of the program. Jot down every possible thing that could go wrong, and devise alternate ways to cover these contingencies. Chances are, most of the time things will go very much as planned, but unanticipated flukes can cause disruptions that may destroy a program.

### Evaluate every program.
- Keep careful records of staff time involved, cost of supplies, numbers in attendance, donations, public relations techniques, things that went especially well, and things that need to be done differently. Good records help not only in evaluating the effectiveness of a particular program but in making decisions about future programs. Records of past programs are also extremely useful when personnel changes occur.

The suggestions offered here carry no absolute guarantee. They are, however, basic ideas that have facilitated work with young adults in several libraries where young adult programming is emphasized. Programs for young adults do not just happen. They take time, effort, and commitment.

Programming for young adults is a vital component within all libraries open to this age group. Librarians who whine about insufficient resources and offer excuses for not providing young adult programs are missing a richly rewarding experience. Even worse, they are failing in their responsibility to help young adults become happy, healthy, self-actualizing, productive adults.

*Source:* Mildred G. Wallace, "Tips for Successful Young Adult Programming,"
*Journal of Youth Services in Libraries* 6 (Summer 1993): 387–90.

# OPERATIONS

5

# International Standard Book Numbers (ISBNs)

ISBNs ARE SPECIALLY DESIGNED and computed ten-digit numbers that are supposed to be printed on the back cover and the reverse side of the title page of every book published in the world. The ISBN numbering system was designed in the late 1960s and is followed by essentially all publishers in the industrialized, wealthy nations, but is largely ignored by publishers in poorer countries. Each publisher is assigned special ISBN numbers by its nation's ISBN agency. To begin to understand the intricacies of the ISBN, let's look at the example below—the number for Anthony Browne's book, *Willy the Wimp*, published by Knopf.

> This last number is the "secret" **check digit**, to make sure this is an authentic ISBN.

## ISBN 0–394–87061–1

| This first number tells the **place of publication**; books published in the United States and the United Kingdom begin with either 0 or 1; books published in France, 2; Germany, 3; Japan, 4; Russia, 5; and so on. | This group of numbers, which can be up to 7 digits long, is the **publisher's number.** For example, all books published by Random House are 394; all books published by Scholastic Books are printed with the numbers 590. | This group of numbers identifies each specific book **title and binding**; a different binding for the same book receives a different number; for example, the library (heavy duty) binding of *Willy the Wimp* is 97061. |
|---|---|---|

The last number, the **check digit,** is computed by taking the first nine numbers of the ISBN and multiplying, adding, dividing, and then subtracting. See the sidebar on the next page for instructions on computing the check digit; it's fun—try it! The check digit is designed to identify any ISBNs that might be incorrectly printed. The fact is that an average of only one of every eleven ten-digit numbers qualifies as an authentic ISBN.

## What needs an ISBN?

**General.** A separate ISBN must be assigned to every different edition of a book, but *not* to an unchanged impression or unchanged reprint of the same book in the same format and by the same publisher. Price changes do not need a new ISBN.

**Facsimile reprints.** A separate ISBN must be assigned to a facsimile reprint produced by a different publisher.

**Books in different formats.** A separate ISBN must be assigned to the

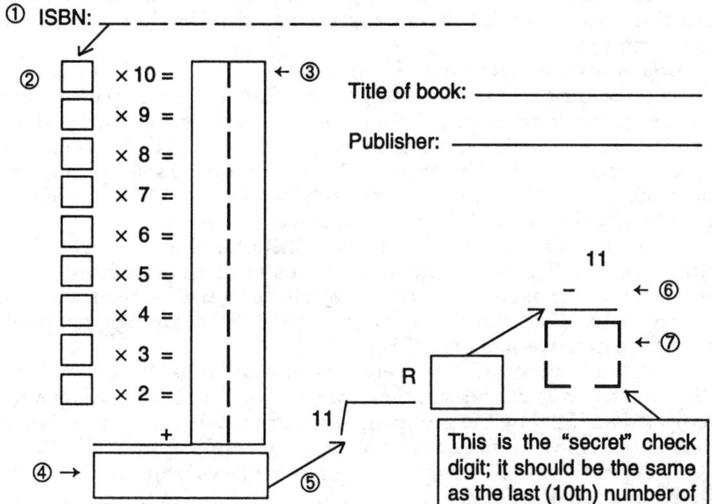
① ISBN:
② × 10 =
× 9 =
× 8 =
× 7 =
× 6 =
× 5 =
× 4 =
× 3 =
× 2 =
+
← ③
④ →
⑤
11
R
11
–
← ⑥
← ⑦
Title of book:
Publisher:

This is the "secret" check digit; it should be the same as the last (10th) number of the ISBN. If your check digit is 11, it will be shown as a 0 in the ISBN; if your check digit is 10, it will be printed as an X in the ISBN.

*Directions:*

1. Write the ten numbers of the ISBN on the lines.
2. Then write the first nine of the ten numbers of the ISBN inside the boxes, with the first number going in the top box, and so on.
3. Multiply each of the first nine numbers of the ISBN by the number indicated and write the answer inside the tall box with the dotted line dividing the tens and the ones, for example:

   4 × 10 = 4 ¦ 0
4. Add all nine numbers you got in step 3 and write your answer in ☐
5. Divide the total you got in step 4 by 11 and write the remainder in R ☐
6. Subtract that remainder from 11.
7. Check to see if your answer in [ ] is the same as the last, or tenth, number of the ISBN. If the numbers are the same, hooray! You solved the incredible ISBN.

different formats in which a particular title is published. For example, a hardback edition and a paperback edition each receives a separate ISBN. On the same principle, a microform edition receives a separate ISBN.

**Looseleaf publications.** If a publication appears in looseleaf form, an ISBN is allocated to identify an edition at a given time. Individual issues of additions or replacement sheets will likewise be given an ISBN.

**Multivolume works.** An ISBN must be assigned to the whole set of volumes of a multivolume work as well as to each individual volume in the set.

**Back stock.** Publishers are required to number their back stocks and publish the ISBN in their catalogs. They must also print the ISBN in the first available reprint of an item from back stock.

5

**Collaborative publications.** A publication issued as a co-edition or joint imprint with other publishers is assigned an ISBN by the publisher in charge of distribution.

**Books sold or distributed by agents.**

a. According to the principles of the ISBN system, a particular edition, published by a particular publisher, receives only one ISBN. This ISBN must be retained no matter where or by whom the book is distributed or sold.

b. A book imported by an exclusive distributor or sole agent from an area not yet in the ISBN system and for which therefore no ISBN has been assigned, may be assigned an ISBN by the exclusive distributor.

c. Books imported by an exclusive distributor or sole agent to which a new title page, bearing the imprint of the exclusive distributor, has been added in place of the title page of the original publisher, are to be given a new ISBN by the exclusive distributor or sole agent. The ISBN of the original publisher is also to be given as a related ISBN.

d. A book imported by several distributors from an area not yet in the ISBN system and for which, therefore, no ISBN has been assigned, may be assigned an ISBN by the group agency responsible for these distributors.

**Publishers with more than one place of publication.**

a. A publisher operating in a number of places, which are listed together in the imprint of a book, will assign only one ISBN to the book.

b. A publisher operating separate and distinct offices or branches in different places may have a publisher identifier for each office or branch. Nevertheless, each book published is to be assigned only one ISBN, the assignment being made by the office or branch responsible for publication.

**Register of ISBN.** Every publisher must keep a register of ISBN numbers that have been assigned to published and forthcoming books. The register is to be kept in numerical sequence giving ISBN, author, title and edition (where appropriate).

**ISBN not to be re-used under any circumstances.** An ISBN once allocated must, under no circumstances, be re-used. This is of the utmost importance to avoid confusion. It is recognized that, owing to clerical errors, numbers will be incorrectly assigned. If this happens, the number must be deleted from the list of usable numbers and must not be assigned to another title. Every publisher will have sufficient numbers in his range for the loss of these numbers to be insignificant. Publishers should advise the group agency of the numbers thus deleted and of the titles to which they were erroneously assigned.

**For more information** about ISBNs, contact the R. R. Bowker Company, 121 Chanlon Road, New Providence, NJ 07974; (908) 464-6800.

## What about ISBNs for software?

An ISBN is used to identify a specific software product. If there is more than one version (perhaps versions adapted for different machines, carrier media, or language version), each version must have a different ISBN.

When a software product is updated, revised, or otherwise amended and the changes are sufficiently substantial for the product to be called a new edition (and thus probably the subject of a new launch, or marketing push), then a new ISBN must be allocated.

A relaunch of an existing product, even in new packaging where there is no basic difference in the performance of the new and the old product, does *not* justify a new ISBN, and the original ISBN must be used.

When software is accompanied by a manual, useful only as an adjunct to the software, and the software needs the manual before it can be operated, and the two items are always sold as a package, one ISBN must be used to cover both items.

When two or more items in a software package (as above) can be used separately, or are sold separately as well as together, then:

    a.  The package as a whole must have an ISBN.

    b.  Each item in the package must have its own ISBN.

ISBNs should be allocated to a software product independent of its physical form, e.g., if software is only available from a remote database whence it is downloaded to the customer.

As well as identifying the product itself, an ISBN identifies the publisher or manufacturer; it should not be used to identify a distributor or wholesaler.

# International Standard Serial Numbers (ISSNs)

IF YOU PUBLISH A SERIAL you will want to obtain an ISSN (International Standard Serial Number) for your publication. The ISSN is the essential element in an international system designed to improve bibliographic control over serial publications.

The ISSN should be displayed prominently on every issue, preferably in the top right corner of the cover. It is acceptable, however, for the number to appear elsewhere on the publication, usually in the masthead area. If the serial has an ISBN for the individual volumes within a series, in addition to the ISSN

**5**

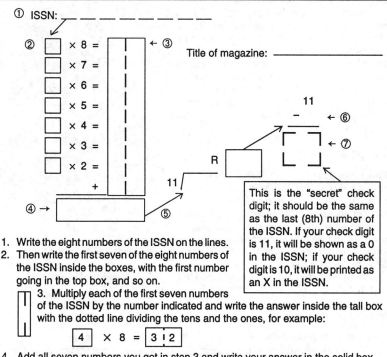

① ISSN: _ _ _ _ _ _ _ _

② × 8 =  ← ③

    × 7 =

    × 6 =

    × 5 =

    × 4 =

    × 3 =

    × 2 =

    +

④ →

Title of magazine: _____

11

− ← ⑥

← ⑦

R

This is the "secret" check digit; it should be the same as the last (8th) number of the ISSN. If your check digit is 11, it will be shown as a 0 in the ISSN; if your check digit is 10, it will be printed as an X in the ISSN.

11

⑤

1. Write the eight numbers of the ISSN on the lines.
2. Then write the first seven of the eight numbers of the ISSN inside the boxes, with the first number going in the top box, and so on.

    3. Multiply each of the first seven numbers of the ISSN by the number indicated and write the answer inside the tall box with the dotted line dividing the tens and the ones, for example:

        4   × 8 =   3 ¦ 2

4. Add all seven numbers you got in step 3 and write your answer in the solid box.
5. Divide the total you got in step 4 by 11 and write the remainder in the dashed box.
6. Subtract that remainder from 11.
7. Check to see if your answer is the same as the last.

for the series as a whole, the two numbers should appear together, each with its own prefix. The ISSN should be printed right after the title of the series, both in books and in advertisements.

The last number, the **check digit,** can be computed by the following method. No special meaning is attached to the first seven digits of the ISSN.

The ISSN is suitable to many management functions applied to serials—from invoicing and inventory control to checking in issues and citing articles. Acknowledged as an invaluable identification number for serials, particularly in a computer environment, the ISSN is being used by groups such as the Copyright Clearance Center, Inc., and the U.S. Postal Service.

For further information and ISSN assignments, write to the Library of Congress, National Serials Data Program, Washington, DC 20540; (202) 707-6452. The assignment of ISSNs is a free service.

*Sources:* Warren A. Hatch, "An Explanation of the ISSN System," *Arithmetic Teacher,* April 1989, pp. 2–3 (text and diagrams reprinted with permission from *Arithmetic Teacher* © 1989 by the National Council on Teachers of Mathematics); *The ISBN System Users' Manual* (Berlin: International ISBN Agency, 1986);The Library of Congress.

# How to prepare a bibliography

**THE BIBLIOGRAPHY COMMITTEE** of the ALA Reference and Adult Services Division (RASD) has prepared these guidelines intended for bibliographers, publishers, and evaluators. They are concerned with the quality and character of the elements included in a bibliography; the purpose and place of a given bibliography vis-a-vis other available resources; and its accessibility, its availability, its durability, and its readability. The elements of a good bibliography are the same whether they are produced online or printed on paper.

## Purpose

The bibliography should fill a significant need in order to justify its compilation. The subject should fit into the general scheme of available bibliographical sources, without unnecessary duplication. If similar bibliographies exist, they should be reviewed and the unique contribution of this new one should be stated explicitly.

The subject should be clearly stated in the title and defined in a preliminary statement.

## Scope

Scope should be clearly defined.

The work should strive for completeness within its stated limitations (period, geographical area, form, language, library holdings, best books only, intended audience, etc.).

Formats, where different, should be identified and each described appropriately.

# Methodology

Sources consulted and information on the method of compilation should be provided.

The compiler should work with the bibliographic units. A bibliographic unit is any entity in a bibliography: book; chapters of a book; journal articles; reports; manuscripts; sound and video recordings; computer programs or printouts; films; charts; etc. All items not personally examined by the compiler should be so identified.

# Organization

**Principles of organization.** The organization of material should be suitable for the subject. The main arrangement should make it possible to use the bibliography from at least one approach without consulting the index. Multiple means of access should be provided. Means of access include both the meaningful arrangement of materials and the indexes to those materials. The scheme for a classified bibliography should be logical and easy for users to understand.

**Necessary components.** Every bibliography should have a statement of scope and purpose. An explanation of how to use the bibliography should be given. Every bibliography should have a key to all abbreviations used. A table of contents should be provided.

An index or indexes should be provided. Indexes should be sufficiently detailed to provide acceptable levels of recall and precision. Terminology should be appropriate to both subject and intended users. Cross-references should be adequate for normal reference purposes. Multiple indexes should be provided if required for complete access to the materials.

**Desirable features.** Entry numbers for bibliographic units should be considered. Location of copies of bibliographical units, if not readily available, is helpful.

# Annotations and notes

These may be at one of three levels:

1. Informative notes, used chiefly when the nature or reason for inclusion of a title is not clear. Use of this minimal level of description should be limited to those bibliographies that approach comprehensiveness for the area they are covering.
2. Descriptive annotations should give enough of the contents to enable users to decide whether they want to read the original. Any bibliography designated as *annotated* should have annotations at least at this level.
3. Critical evaluations should be discriminating and should be written by someone knowledgeable in the field. They should assess the value of each item in its relationship to other works in the area. Any bibliography designated *critical* or *evaluative* should have annotations at this level.

In each case the annotations or notes should be succinct, informative, and on a suitable level for the intended users. If the author has drawn upon another source for the annotation, that source should be appropriately acknowledged.

# Bibliographic form

There should be sufficient information to identify the bibliographic unit easily for the purpose of the bibliography and needs of the intended user.

The bibliographic form should follow a recognized standard. Examples of these standards include, but are not limited to, those described in *The Chicago Manual of Style*, *The MLA Style Manual*, and the *Publication Manual of the American Psychological Association*.

The bibliographic form should be followed consistently.

## Timeliness

Retrospective bibliographies should keep the time lag between closing the bibliography and its publication to a minimum. Introductory material should make it clear at what point the bibliography was closed.

Those bibliographies intended to be current should be issued as closely as possible after the publication of the bibliographical units listed.

## Accuracy

Citations should be correct and free from typographical errors. Information provided in annotations and elsewhere should be factually accurate and grammatically correct. Provision for corrections after publication should be considered.

## Format

Format and typeface should be clear and appropriate. The volume should be sturdy enough to withstand anticipated use. The bibliography should be designed to keep its price within the means of potential users without sacrificing important features that facilitate its use.

Cumulation of ongoing bibliographies is strongly recommended.

## Distribution

Published bibliographies should be properly advertised and distributed. Notice of the bibliography should be sent to a standard national bibliography.

*Source:* "Guidelines for the Preparation of a Bibliography," *RQ* 32 (Winter 1992): 194–96.

# How to evaluate an index

THIS CHECKLIST WAS PREPARED by the American Society of Indexers chiefly for publishers and editors who are about to hire an indexer and wish to examine an applicant's previous work. However, it is also very useful to librarians or book reviewers for rating the usefulness of an index in a reference or nonfiction book.—*GME.*

## Indexing scheme

Is it appropriate to the material indexed?

Does it permit easy and quick scanning and ready pinpointing of the desired references?

Are the main entries easily differentiated from subentries?

Is the arrangement of subentries self-evident?

Do subentries bear a logical and grammatical relationship to main entries?

If any explanations are required, are they easily spotted and lucid?

Are page references clear? When a reference covers several consecutive pages, has the indexer indicated clearly the beginning and the end of the reference, e.g., 35-43, not 35ff?

Do page references differentiate between principal discussion and cursory mention of the topic?

If there are deviations from the normal alphabetical order, or if some other order (e.g., chronological) is employed, is this necessary and is it obvious to the user?

## Depth of indexing

Are all important topics (concepts, subjects, proper names) and pertinent statements represented in the index? Check several.

Are entries sufficiently specific to permit ready access to the desired material yet sufficiently comprehensive to prevent the scattering of related items? Headings chosen should be concise, each referring to one particular subject.

Are there adequate cross-references to guide the user to main entries or other entries offering additional information?

Are there duplicate entries instead of cross-references where space permits?

Test the index for depth in two ways:

1. Choose a few passages from the work and check in the index the terms representing the major topics discussed. If the index fails to locate the selected passages through the terms chosen in more than 5% of the attempts, something is wrong. A further test should be made: Attempt to locate the selected passages through more general or broader terms than those originally chosen; if this succeeds, then the terms in the index are not sufficiently specific.

2. Scan the index for terms having a noticeably large number of page references. Good indexers try to give no more than 10–12 references for any one term, avoiding strings of page numbers.

## Accuracy

Are the index terms used accurate?

Are the spelling, capitalization, italicization, and punctuation used in the book followed? Is the alphabetizing accurate, either word-by-word or letter-by-letter?

Check a sample of references to be sure the material indexed is actually on the page cited. (The indexer is responsible for the original compilation of the page references, though the publisher's proofreader must catch typographical errors.)

Accuracy in the choice of index terms may be tested by checking some technical and some ambiguous terms in the index against the passages they refer to in order to make sure the terms chosen are appropriate. (In one such check, "meteors" was found to be the term used to index a passage on meteorological research!)

## Consistency

Are terms used consistently in the index? (If "sodium chloride" is used, "table salt" cannot also be used.)

Is a topic indexed by a specific term in one passage indexed by the same term (not a broader or narrower one) in another passage? (If a recipe on lamb stew is indexed in a cookbook under "lamb," then a recipe on leg of lamb must also be indexed under "lamb," not under "meat.")

*Source: Guidelines for Publishers & Editors on Index Evaluation* (American Society of Indexers).

# RLIN facts and figures

**THE RESEARCH LIBRARIES INFORMATION NETWORK (RLIN)** is an international information management and retrieval system, owned and operated by the Research Libraries Group (RLG). It consists of an online catalog of more than 64 million items held by more than 200 of the world's leading research institutions.

RLIN® was created in 1977 to support the online cataloging of RLG's four founding members (New York Public Library, Columbia, Harvard, and Yale). The organization made an agreement with Stanford University to acquire and operate the computerized library system Stanford had already developed for local and regional use. The Stanford system (BALLOTS) was rechristened RLIN, transformed, and networked nationwide. As its use expanded to dozens of other research libraries, RLIN evolved to accommodate the requirements of different libraries. Online cataloging led to shared cataloging, which led to its present status as an online union catalog.

Besides searching and library processing in all Roman-alphabet languages, RLIN supports this work in Chinese, Japanese, Korean, Arabic, Hebrew, and Cyrillic. In addition to this library support interface, users can access the RLIN databases by two other paths: Eureka™, an end-user search service in use for campuswide access at many colleges and universities; and Zephyr™, RLG's Z39.50 service, which lets users of other online systems search RLIN files using the same commands they use to search their own local catalogs or utility services. Eureka and Zephyr also provide access to CitaDel®, RLG's citations and document-delivery service. Ariel®, document transmission software developed by RLG for the Internet, serves as the delivery mechanism of choice for documents requested through CitaDel. It is faster and more reliable than fax transmission, and sends documents of greater resolution and quality than Group 3 fax.

The RLIN database contains bibliographic records in more than 365 languages. Most are in English (57.6%), followed by German (7.8%), French (6.7%), Spanish (4.7%), Russian (2.8%), Italian (2.4%), Chinese (2.3%), Japanese (1.8%), Latin (1.1%), Portuguese (1.1%), Hebrew (0.8%), Dutch (0.7%), and Polish (0.6%). In 1994 the RLIN bibliographic files increased at a rate of 16,871 records per day. Interlibrary loan requests in 1993 totaled 269,009.

The RLG main office is in Mountain View, California, close to Stanford University, where the RLIN mainframe computer is housed. As of January 1994, the RLIN system consisted of an Amdahl 5990-700 mainframe with 384 MB of memory, 64 mips, and 32 channels; a private X.25 network of approximately 1,100 terminals, with dial-up through a commercial carrier and Internet connection through stanford.edu.

*Source:* Research Libraries Group.

---

## Librarians on leadership

**Kathleen de la Peña McCook, dean of the Graduate School at Louisiana State University:**
Have a very clear sense of what you want to accomplish, and always have it so big that you can never accomplish it. . . . I always keep in mind why I'm doing something and try to make a clear goal and that's to get information to people better. And I try now to only do things that fit in with that, and to turn down things that don't.

*Source:* Brooke E. Sheldon, *Leaders in Libraries: Styles and Strategies for Success* (Chicago: American Library Association, 1991). 93p.

# Serials librarian lingo

**Berne Convention.** The common name of a copyright agreement signed in 1886 and its revisions establishing the International Union for the Protection of Literary and Artistic Works. To receive protection under this convention, first publication of a work must occur in a signatory country. The United States signed the agreement September 9, 1986.

**Bind with lacks.** The decision by a library to bind the issues of a volume on hand even though one or more issues are missing and the resultant bound volume will be incomplete.

**Dumb bar codes.** In automated library systems, bar codes not linked to a unique title in a database.

**Greenaway plan.** A type of blanket order plan, originated at the Philadelphia Free Library by Emerson Greenaway, whereby libraries arrange with publishers to receive at a nominal price one advance copy of all trade titles so that titles selected for acquisition can be ordered in advance of publication.

**Macroform.** Any medium, transparent or opaque, bearing images large enough to be easily read or viewed without magnification.

**Rolling-year subscription.** A subscription supplied on a consecutive 12-month basis beginning in whichever month the order is entered.

**'Til forbid.** A type of standing order usually given to a serials agent or publisher specifying that the supplier should renew the order for a particular title or group of titles until notified to the contrary.

*Source:* Serials Section of the ALCTS Acquisitions Committee, *Serials Acquisitions Glossary* (Chicago: ALA Association for Library Collections and Technical Services, 1993). 33p.

# How to negotiate with subscription agencies

### by Judy McQueen and N. Bernard Basch

LIBRARIANS CAN MAXIMIZE their returns on serials expenditures by negotiating services and fees with subscription agencies. Effective negotiation requires that both parties have an understanding of each other's needs, priorities, and constraints. In this regard, subscription agents are well prepared; they cannot succeed in business unless they understand library service requirements. In their everyday activities, librarians have little need to know about the details of subscription agency operations; but such knowledge becomes significant when they are preparing to negotiate with agencies.

Librarians can put this knowledge to work by examining the characteristics of a library's serials collection from the perspective of a supplier; clarifying the library's service requirements; establishing the priorities to be pursued in a negotiation; and identifying strategies for negotiating. The following checklists outline basic approaches from which librarians can develop strategies appropriate to their specific library situations.

## Preparing for negotiations

1. **Profile the collection.** Review your serials collection and the patterns of change within it. Also examine the mix of titles and group items according to publisher discounting policies. Agencies use a similar approach when deciding the service charges they assign to an account. You will be better prepared to identify appropriate vendors and to negotiate with them if you are aware of publication characteristics that are significant in pricing and the relative representation of each group of materials in your collection. Identify:

- *Mass-market and trade publications.* Publishers often provide high discounts to agencies on these titles.
- *Popular consumer titles.* Some agencies process orders for these titles as subscriptions for individuals to obtain maximum publisher discounts.
- *Commercial scientific, technical, and medical publications.* Publisher discounts to agencies can be significant on these materials.
- *Foreign commercial titles.* Publishers of such titles may offer higher discounts to non-U.S. agencies than to domestic vendors. Thus, a foreign agency may be able to service this material at a lower cost than a domestic vendor.
- *Association publications.* Many associations offer discounts to members. Some require that members order direct, others will allow membership subscriptions to be processed through an agency.
- *Nonperiodical serials, such as annuals and monographs-in-series.* Publishers may provide higher discounts to book jobbers than to serial vendors, which may enable a library to buy its nonperiodical serials for less from a book vendor.
- *Expensive individual titles.* If you are aware that your collection includes such titles, you may be able to exclude them from your vendor's percentage service fee calculations and instead negotiate a dollar cap on service charges for expensive items.
- *Newspapers, government publications, and university press titles.* Publishers rarely provide discounts on these materials. Consequently, agencies generally levy full service fees against them.

Also identify any publishers from which the library orders many titles. Increasingly, publishers who support a large number of titles will offer libraries consolidated invoices and discounts for orders placed directly.

Examine the patterns of change in the collection. A stable collection (with little change in variables such as the number of titles and copies ordered, ship-to addresses, and cost assignment codes) is less expensive to service than a collection that is subject to frequent change. On the other hand, an account with a continual increase in the number of titles to be serviced is also attractive to vendors.

2. **Emergency services and pricing practices.** Develop an awareness of the pricing and service options offered by different vendors. Survey the professional literature, query agency representatives, and talk to colleagues in other libraries.

Explore the services offered by different vendors. Which vendors provide machine-readable invoicing data that a library can load into its spreadsheet software for analysis? Which vendors support interfaces from their internal automated systems to the automated systems used by libraries? Do agencies with these capabilities price them as part of their basic services or do they levy additional charges for their use? This information is as useful to librarians who have no interest in spreadsheets or automated systems as to those who do; the former can seek reductions in service charges as a credit for nonuse of services covered by the basic fee.

Determine how different agencies price their services. What services are covered by basic service charges and which attract additional fees? Expect variations in the ways in which different agencies apply fees. For instance, an agency may calculate the service charge on periodical serials as a percentage of the subscription price and apply different percentages to domestic and foreign titles. Within this structure, there may be a limit to the charge that accrues to any individual title. Nonperiodical serials, gratis materials, and government publications may be excluded from the percentage charge and instead carry a fixed dollar-per-item (per-line) service fee. Or, the percentage approach may apply to these items and be supplemented by a line charge; the line charge may be included in the price on which the percentage charge is based, or it may be added after the percentage charge is calculated. Shipping and handling fees for nonperiodical serials reshipped by an agency may be excluded from service fee calculations or they may attract charges at the standard percentage rate. No one approach is inherently right or wrong. What is important is an awareness of the range of industry practices.

When negotiating with an agency that levies an additional fee for a service

**5**

---

## Ten commandments for dealing with a subscription agency: A vendor's recommendations

### by Ray Reinalda

1. Remember—it's a business relationship. Agency cocktail parties, tours, and lunches are fun and it is nice to be included. However, you need to select an agency that provides the services you require at as low a price as possible.

2. Understand what you are buying. Identify your needs and priorities. Don't be swayed into paying for services that are nice but not essential.

3. Get your requirements down in writing. Be specific about your expectations, such as how you wish to have invoices sent, renewal lists sorted, and claims followed up.

4. Get a good understanding of the limitations of both the agency and the library. This keeps expectations of both organizations in line with the capacities of each.

5. Evaluate an agency by both its technical capacity *and* its inclination. Technical capacity is important, but no more so than willingness to work hard for you.

6. Learn about the alternatives. You need to understand the capabilities of other agencies. This requires you to listen to the competition and provide enough information about your library to elicit realistic proposals.

7. Develop a problem-solving partnership with your agency. No relationship will be perfect. Mistakes and problems will arise on both sides. It is more fruitful, and ultimately less frustrating, if both parties expend their efforts resolving problems.

8. Don't buy a brand name. There are several excellent agencies currently providing services to the U.S. marketplace. Don't fall into the trap of restricting your selection to only one or two agencies because of their "name" recognition.

9. Remember where your loyalties lie. Being loyal to your agency is nice, but that should not get in the way of your first loyalty to the library that employs you.

10. Make a decision. Don't live with indifferent service or high rates simply because it's too hard to change. It isn't as hard as the prevailing perception, and signals management that you continue to search for better alternatives on your library's behalf.

*Source:* "Helpful Hints from Friendly Vendors," *American Libraries* 22 (July/August 1991): 645.

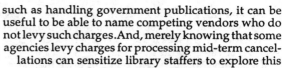

such as handling government publications, it can be useful to be able to name competing vendors who do not levy such charges. And, merely knowing that some agencies levy charges for processing mid-term cancellations can sensitize library staffers to explore this aspect of pricing with other vendors.

More variables operate in agency management of foreign titles. Agencies differ in how they apply and calculate foreign exchange: One may use the exchange rate in force when the agency pays the publisher, another the rate at the time the library's invoice is prepared, and yet another the rate in effect on the day payment is received from the library. Agencies also vary in how they assess charges for foreign currency drafts: Some levy the full cost of a draft against every title even though they submit most subscription renewals in batches and are likely to incur the full cost of a draft only for new orders.

3. **Review current service charges.** Whether negotiating with an existing vendor or considering an alternate supplier, it is essential to have a clear picture of what the library is currently paying for subscription services.

It may not be easy to determine the service charges levied on an account. Even when an agency is able to provide an apparently coherent explanation, it is prudent to review the agency's invoices to confirm the assessment.

Although most U.S. agencies issue a consolidated annual invoice showing all charges accruing to a library's account, it is almost inevitable that some changes will occur during the year. These are billed on supplemental invoices. Unless a library and its supplier have a specific agreement about the fees applied to supplemental billings, there can be significant variations between these charges and those on the consolidated invoice. Inspect all invoices when reviewing the service charges on an account.

4. **Determine service needs.** Libraries share many common characteristics, but each library is unique and has unique service needs. Clear definition of a library's service requirements is essential for effective vendor selection and/or negotiation. It is equally important that these requirements be communicated to vendors so they can present informed service and pricing proposals.

Identify and evaluate *all* assumptions. What works for most libraries will not necessarily be relevant for a specific library. For example, agency support for claiming missing issues can be a valuable service, particularly since it is usually covered by the basic service fee. However, claiming support will be of little use in a library that lacks the staff or automated system support to prepare claims. Likewise, traditional claiming support may be too slow for a special library with a corporate intelligence mission. Similarly, standard claim services may not be appropriate for a public library that needs to replace missing issues of popular magazines—publishers rarely retain back issues of such titles. Distinguish between symptoms and diseases. A library that generates a large number of claims may be suffering from the effects of inexperienced check-in personnel or a vendor that does not process renewal subscriptions in a timely manner, rather than from a missing issue problem.

As well as identifying specific service requirements, also note which of the services commonly offered by agencies will *not* be used by your library. Vendors need this information to realistically estimate the cost of servicing an account. However, they do not necessarily use these data in allocating costs among clients. Library negotiators can parley nonuse of a service covered by an agency's standard fee into a useful bargaining point.

5. **Establish priorities.** To negotiate effectively, library representatives must have clear objectives and priorities. Consider a negotiation in which cost

is the primary concern. How "primary"? Is the library prepared to accept the lowest cost option regardless of all other factors? If not, what services *must* be provided? What is the library prepared to pay for such services? If cost is secondary to service, what level of service is the library seeking? (And how can the library define service requirements in a way that allows vendor performance to be monitored and evaluated?) Is service the primary concern only up to a specific cost ceiling? What ceiling?

6. **Communicate with the agency.** Effective negotiation requires that *both* parties be prepared. Give vendors advance warning of your interest in negotiation. Proceedings will be facilitated if you also indicate the concerns of most significance in the negotiation. Negotiators should schedule a mutually convenient time for a face-to-face meeting or a telephone conference.

## Negotiating strategies

1. **Segment the collection.** Use the information developed during collection profiling. If your collection is dominated by high-discount titles, you may be able to negotiate significantly reduced service charges. With more varied collections that include substantial numbers of high-discount titles, you may be able to achieve reductions in service charges on the high-discount segments of the collection. Even if you cannot agree on service charge reductions, segmentation can provide you with valuable insight into agency costs, services, and pricing philosophies.

2. **Consider multiple vendors, but maximize the size of each account.** Different agencies have different interests and specialties. Libraries can benefit from mirroring the segmentation of their collections in the choice of vendors selected to service their lists. European agencies may provide lower cost service for European titles and materials from commercial publishers who operate on a global scale; book jobbers or agencies with close ties to the book trade may enjoy an advantage over generalist agencies in servicing nonperiodical serials; and agencies that process large numbers of orders for mass-market publications may use subscription management techniques that attract higher publisher discounts for individual subscribers. The specialization reflected in pricing may also apply to the services that vendors offer to support different types of serial materials.

Bear in mind, though, that negotiation is a two-way street. The objective is to arrive at an agreement acceptable to both a library and its vendors. In most situations, a vendor is interested in maximizing the size of each account. When a vendor offers an attractive service and pricing proposal, consider strategies that will enhance the vendor's return on the account. Such strategies include:

- *Establishing a multiyear contract.* Vendors incur most of their expenses establishing service on an initial order. Once the order is operating smoothly, ongoing renewal and maintenance require a lower investment of vendor resources.
- *Consolidating* as many orders as possible with a single vendor.
- *Increasing* the number of orders by including materials previously handled by branches or the purchasing department of the parent organization.

3. **Negotiate credits and ceilings.** This is the area in which you will find information about the practices of other libraries most rewarding. Such knowledge can alert you to a range of opportunities for limiting or reducing service charges. These opportunities include:

- *Discounts for early payment of invoices.* If your library can settle the bulk of its invoices in advance of the normal renewal cycle, you can negotiate service charge discounts for early payment.

- *Caps on service charges for expensive titles.* You may be able to negotiate a "not-to-exceed" ceiling on the charge levied against any individual title.
- *Fixed fees for multiyear contracts.* Multiyear contracts are attractive to vendors, particularly so on stable lists or lists with little change other than an increase in titles. If your library can enter into a multiyear contract, you should seek recognition of the value of this arrangement from your vendors. An agency may be willing to offer both a low service charge and a guarantee of no increase in service fees for the life of the contract.
- *Credits for limited use/nonuse of a service that an agency includes in its standard service fee.* A library that does not use a service covered by an agency's basic fee should seek a credit, either in the form of a service fee reduction or substitution of a service that normally attracts additional charges. For example, a library that claims direct from publishers (limiting its use of agency claiming support to requesting proof of payment as needed) may be able to apply part of the basic service fee to a separately priced service such as the provision of machine-readable invoices or access to the agency's online database. To negotiate effective credits or substitutions, you need to be knowledgeable about your vendors' service and pricing schedules and those of competing agencies.

## Bid situations

Formal bid situations can limit negotiation opportunities. However, you can enhance your library's chances of obtaining favorable responses to bids by:

- *Providing sufficient information* on the characteristics of the collection and the library's service requirements and patterns of service use—and nonuse. This enables a prospective bidder to realistically estimate the likely cost of servicing the account.
- *Identifying mandatory service requirements* as well as common support services that are *not* required.
- *Indicating the selection criteria* and priorities to be applied in awarding the contract.
- When a collection contains distinct groups of materials with different pricing and service characteristics, *structuring the bid to permit awards to multiple vendors and specifying that all materials in a defined class will be awarded to a single vendor.* Vendors are wary of undefined multiple vendor bids as some libraries use them to "pick the eyes" from each vendor's response. Such clients place orders with multiple vendors but order from each only those titles offered at a discount from list price and/or at no service charge.
- *Critically evaluating bid specifications from other sources.* It can be helpful to review specifications from other libraries or from vendors, but do not adopt them without carefully assessing the extent to which they meet your library's unique needs.
- *Guarding against unintentionally disqualifying vendors.* Librarians are justifiably anxious to ensure that bidders have the capabilities and experience to provide reliable service. They seek to qualify bidders by defining basic levels of corporate capability and service provision that must be met for a vendor to secure an award. The objective of such qualification should be to weed out unreliable or incompetent vendors, not to reduce the number of eligible vendors to only one or two.

## Two-way street

The relationship between libraries and subscription agencies is one of inter-dependence, not dependence. Libraries need a pool of viable vendors; agencies need clients. Sensitive and responsive communication is essential if both groups are to get what they need.

Negotiation is a communications tool. To be effective in negotiations, librarians must define and prioritize their service requirements, including the price they are prepared to pay for specific services and levels of service. Similarly, agencies must articulate their pricing structures and the factors that influence their allocation of service charges among libraries. In negotiations, the mutual exchange of information acts as a catalyst, enabling libraries and agencies to develop service and pricing packages that reflect the needs of both parties.

*Source:* "Negotiations with Subscription Agencies," *American Libraries* 22 (July/August 1991): 644–47.

5

# Cataloging in Publication (CIP)

CATALOGING IN PUBLICATION (CIP) is a free international cooperative venture between publishers and librarians that enables books to be cataloged before they are published. This prepublication cataloging information is then distributed widely to booksellers and librarians, giving them advance infor-mation so that they can select, buy, and process new books. The service benefits publishers in the United States because the cataloging records for CIP titles are entered onto Library of Congress MARC computer tapes, which alert librarians to forthcoming publications and enable them to select and order new publications promptly and accurately. CIP programs exist in a number of countries, including the United States, Canada, Great Britain, Australia, Germany, Brazil, and the Netherlands.

Under this program, publishers submit nonreturnable galleys or manu-scripts of forthcoming books to the CIP Division. Soon after this material is received, CIP cataloging data are returned to the publisher to be printed on the copyright page. Since the data include an LC catalog card number, it is not necessary for publishers to request a preassigned card number in addition to requesting CIP data.

There is no charge for this service, but the publisher is obliged to send the CIP Division one advance complimentary copy of each publication contain-ing CIP information so that a final cataloging record can be produced. This record is supplied to libraries who use LC cataloging records in card form or from the computer tapes. The advance copy, which is in addition to any copies necessary for copyright compliance, should be sent to the address below.

More information about the CIP program is available from the Library of Congress, Cataloging in Publication Division, Washington, DC 20540; (202) 707-6372. In Canada, contact the CIP Office, Acquisitions and Bibliographic Services, National Library of Canada, 395 Wellington St., Ottawa, Ontario, Canada K1A 0N4; (819) 994-6881.

## LC catalog card numbers

A unique Library of Congress catalog card number is assigned to each individual catalog record prepared by the Library of Congress. Librarians use this number to order printed catalog cards and to locate specific catalog records in automated databases. The card number is also often cited when placing book orders with dealers or publishers. Each number consists of two digits, a hyphen, and one to six digits; for example, 78-1 or 78-123456. The first two digits indicate the year that the number is issued, not the publication date of the title to which it has been assigned.

LC catalog card numbers are assigned in one of two ways:

1. A card number is routinely assigned to each published book that has been selected for the Library's collections and for which full cataloging will be done. To obtain a number for a published book, the publisher should donate a copy to the Library so that it can be considered for LC's collections. Complimentary copies should be addressed to the Library of Congress, Gift Section, Exchange and Gift Division, Washington, DC 20540. A letter should be enclosed, asking to be informed of the selection decision and of the card number assigned if the book is selected for Library cataloging.

2. A card number may also be preassigned to a title in advance of publication, for the purpose of printing it on the copyright page, as an aid to librarians. To request a preassigned LC catalog card number for a forthcoming title, publishers should submit an application form to the CIP Division, as early as possible in the publication cycle. Application forms and printed instructions may be obtained from the address on page 273. There is no charge for this service, but the publisher is obliged to send LC one advance complimentary copy of each finished publication to which a card number has been preassigned. This copy, which is additional to any copies required by the Copyright Office for copyright compliance, should be sent to the address on page 273. If, after a final review, it is determined that the title is needed for the Library's collections, catalog cards are prepared.

Publications being submitted for Cataloging in Publication (CIP) data need not be submitted separately for a preassigned LC card number. The number will be assigned automatically when the CIP data are created.

Certain types of material are not eligible to receive a preassigned card number; for example, publications under fifty pages, periodicals and other serial publications, foreign publications, and workbooks.

*Source:* The Library of Congress and the National Library of Canada.

# Cataloging myths debunked

*by Sheila S. Intner*

EVERY NOW AND THEN WE NEED to look our myths in the face and see which ones cause us to nod sagaciously and say, "There is a grain of truth in that," and which ones cause us to shrink back in horror, gasping, "For heaven's sake, can't we ever erase that piece of stupidity?"

During a Midwinter Meeting of the American Library Association a few years ago, I heard some of the myths about catalogers and cataloging that anger me the most repeated by people who should know better. I'd like to mount a campaign to debunk them, even though I know success in these endeavors is elusive. (After all, Americans still respond positively to the myth about George Washington and the cherry tree, even though we have long been aware that evidence doesn't support it.)

## Myth 1: Catalogers have no people skills

One of the worst myths is that catalogers are shy and retiring people who cannot interact effectively with other people. It belongs with the image of librarians as single, old, bespectacled, bun-wearing females. Go ask one hundred ordinary people on the street about librarians and you might be surprised to hear—still—about mean old maids wearing glasses and buns who go around the library hushing everyone. Even worse, however, is the probability that if you went up to one hundred ordinary librarians—say, in the busiest aisle of an ALA conference exhibit area—and asked them about catalogers' interpersonal skills, they would—still—mumble replies about timid souls lacking people skills.

If you are a cataloger, for pity's sake give vent to your aggressions, push ahead in the cafeteria lines, and keep a list of snappy retorts to requests for more work without extra pay or added responsibilities without more pay, more authority, and extra staff thrown in for good measure. And don't you dare agree to take your turn at the reference desk unless a reference librarian takes a turn at the cataloging terminal.

## Myth 2: Cataloging is badly taught in library school

Certainly the catalogers at that ALA conference who were attending a session on recruiting and educating catalogers were anything but shy and retiring. I would have used the adjectives strident and angry to describe them. I was among them, to be sure. I was annoyed by the myth expressed by members of the speakers' panel and the audience that cataloging is poorly taught in library schools. I think I teach it quite well and I number quite a few excellent cataloging teachers among my close friends. I defy anyone to treat the subject better than we do.

Most cataloging professors are forced by the educational systems in which they operate to teach descriptive cataloging, subject cataloging, classification, and MARC content designation in a single term. I challenge everyone in the world of library education to try to teach a complete novice everything there is to know about AACR2-revised in five weeks (which is the amount of time I devote to description and access—and it is more than I should, since it means each of the other topics gets less than that in a fourteen-week semester). It can be even harder to teach standard methods to students who already work as paraprofessional catalogers in small libraries and believe that the nonstandard "rules" they follow are correct. These students have to unlearn what they know before they can make room for an objective learning experience. It is very hard for them, since they spend much more time at work doing things the other way. But at least currently employed nonprofessionals do not have to learn a whole new language, full of strange and terrible acronyms that whirl

5

around in their heads like dervishes, failing to broadcast their individual significance until the poor students are well past the initial required course.

We cataloging professors try, and usually succeed, in balancing theory and practical skills, but a corollary myth is that we *only* teach theory or that we *only* teach rules. There ought to be library encounters patterned after marriage encounters in which the participants are forbidden to say "You *always*..." or "You *never*. ..."

## Myth 3: "Real" catalogers teach cataloging better than professors

Another myth about cataloging courses, perpetrated mostly by practitioners, is that they could do a better job than the ivy-covered professors if they only had the time. Some of us full-time cataloging faculty who face anywhere from fifty to more than two hundred beginning cataloging students every year might point out that there are library schools where beginning cataloging is taught by practitioners who moonlight as educators. Any blame for poor teaching in these programs should be laid at the door of these sometime-educators and the administrators who believe that courses as important as beginning cataloging do not need to be taught by full-time faculty.

Many adjunct faculty are fine teachers. I can vouch for that because I was taught cataloging by one and I have served as an adjunct myself more than once. But adjuncts are not committed to teaching as a career, nor are they accountable to the same degree as full-time faculty, nor are they directly involved with curriculum development, faculty-led program development, or service to the rest of the university community. They can't be faulted if they don't teach their hearts out (although some do) after working all day and arriving for class only to be greeted by the graveyard shift maintenance crew, which raises a ruckus in the halls with floor polishers and heavy equipment until classes are over. Adjuncts usually find the offices dark and all the administrative facilities locked up for the night, so they have to prepare their teaching materials elsewhere. They may share an office with all of the other adjuncts and have no private place in which to counsel students. They simply do not have the roots, links, and time in the library school to do what full-time faculty are expected to do as a bare minimum.

Part of the bare minimum expected of full-time faculty is the obligation to conduct research. Part-time faculty are not hired or retained on the basis of their research or publications, while it is a time-honored practice among university professors that they must publish or perish. The research done by cataloging faculty, especially when it is significant and well-executed, triggers widespread reaction in the field, building on the findings of these studies. This leadership function—an integral part of the job description of full-time faculty—sometimes goes unrecognized by the practitioners who benefit from it.

## Myth 4: Students hate cataloging

Another myth that really annoys me is that students hate cataloging, some even before they take it. Mine don't. If yours do, then you should look to improving your teaching methods and style, assignments, curriculum, etc. After each semester a number of students tell me they liked cataloging. Many admit that they were frightened of it because it is touted as difficult (I won't argue with that) and a great deal of work (that is true, too). There are, however, other courses with equally intimidating reputations (beginning reference, for example). Students who come to graduate school expecting to breeze through with minimal effort are dilettantes who should be drummed out of the corps before we get stuck with them as colleagues.

Many of my students, taught by their practitioner-bosses to do copy cataloging, tell me they never knew cataloging was so intellectually demanding and that it could be so much fun—like doing puzzles. (I hear this even from students who don't do copy cataloging in their jobs. Perhaps a generation brought up on *Trivial Pursuit* is perfectly prepared to become the new crop of original catalogers.) The way paraprofessionals are taught to work obviously bears no relation to the process of cataloging. They seem to be given a mess of unrelated and uncoordinated rules to apply by rote. They learn little or nothing about the principles that underlie the rules or the development process by which the rules are formulated and amended, about the investigative work that cataloging requires, about access and user behavior, and about library cataloging policies and how they affect access. In short, copy catalogers seem to get none of the good stuff—the intellectually challenging theory and its relation to practice.

## Myth 5: Learning cataloging means memorizing the rules

It is a myth that all it takes to learn cataloging is memorizing gobs of rules. A corollary to this myth is that cataloging teachers only have to assign the rules to be memorized and give tests at the end of the semester to ensure that the assignments were done. Nothing could be further from the truth. The rules and tools of cataloging are dynamic—they change all the time. If students just memorize the rules at any given moment, what will they do when they get out into the world and find the questions have changed and the answers they learned are obsolete? To function in the real world, they need to learn how to solve problems and what ideas drive the rules and are embodied in the tools they use so they can make decisions and handle real-life cataloging.

## Myth 6: New catalogers don't need on-the-job training

Another big myth that isn't limited to catalogers is that a graduate professional librarian shouldn't need extensive on-the-job training. This goes hand in hand with a similar myth about turnkey computer systems, e.g., you just turn it on and use it. As any owner of a turnkey system can tell you, it takes months of incredibly hard work consuming many staff hours to use a turnkey system. It also takes months of hard work to train a graduate professional librarian to do the particular job for which she or he was hired, provided, of course, that the job is truly a professional one. The only way to avoid a training period is to hire someone who is already employed at the institution, who knows all of the local practices and idiosyncrasies, and who is doing the job now without the benefit of the title.

I suspect that institutions who hire new professionals as catalogers expecting not to train them think they are saving money. To be sure, they are hiring the least expensive professional—the person without any experience—a person whose professional confidence is not yet established and who probably will not negotiate effectively for a higher salary. The directors and middle managers in these places are naive or stupid if they think they can just walk off and have this newly hired person do a good job all alone. One former student told me that after being hired as an entry-level cataloger she was given a nice tour of the library, including being shown where the OCLC terminal and the card catalog were, and then was told to get to work, which included supervising several support staff. These libraries will get what they pay for. As soon as their new catalogers get their bearings and accumulate some experience, they will leave.

## Myth 7: Beginning cataloging teaches you everything you ever needed to know about cataloging

I hear practitioners say that they don't feel it is their job to teach someone with a professional degree how to use OCLC or catalog a rare book, a government document, or a video. It is definitely a myth that library schools teach students everything there is to know about cataloging in one semester (or even in two, if students opt to take an advanced course). How many of these employers found out whether the prospective employee had more than one cataloging course? Did they ask if the courses included OCLC experience—particularly the more "professional" tasks of profiling, making editing decisions, and setting up procedures for searching, inputting, and training nonprofessional personnel? Did they find out if the person was familiar with rare books, government documents, or special media? If these questions weren't asked or evidence produced to document competency, how can it be expected?

Teaching students the basics of cataloging monographic books (the curriculum in beginning cataloging courses in the six library schools in which I taught) can't prepare them to do original cataloging for other things—serials, nonbook materials, and so forth. It can't prepare them for the trickiest and most difficult materials, even if it includes an introduction to everything covered in AACR2, LCSH, and Dewey and LC classifications.

## Myth 8: We don't have to hire inexperienced catalogers

Another big myth held by personnel directors—especially in some large and prestigious libraries—is that they can acquire "turnkey catalogers" (see Myth 6) by hiring only experienced catalogers. Thus, they figure, someone else has done the training. This disregards everything common sense tells us about new jobs, new environments, and new situations. The larger the library and institutional setting, the more complex it is and the longer it takes a new employee to learn the ropes and adjust to it. This philosophy fails to take into account other factors that affect job performance: The person may still be getting used to a new neighborhood and new home or apartment—things psychologists tell us consume a great deal of a person's energy—as well as learning to live without the familiar places and people on whom he or she relied for companionship and support. One's family, friends, doctor, lawyer, hair stylist, druggist, and local librarian may be far away, and replacements or substitutes are needed before the person is 100 percent effective at work. It also ignores the need for every employee, experienced or not, to absorb local priorities, local politics, and local methods of getting things done.

Furthermore, it ignores a more pertinent issue, namely, that smaller, less research-oriented collections usually contain a far smaller proportion of esoteric materials requiring original cataloging. Experience with large numbers of difficult materials is hard to get in smaller libraries. Whether they like it or not, large, prestigious, research libraries have to spend a great deal of time, effort, *and* money training new catalogers until they achieve enough experience with the materials to feel confident confronting decisions that would discomfort a Solomon.

## Myth 9: Copy catalogers don't need cataloging education

The last notion I want to challenge is not a myth but a reality. It is the perception that paraprofessional copy catalogers don't need any preparation outside of what is provided by their supervisors. In truth, they need as much library school cataloging coursework as anyone else doing cataloging. I believe if they had it libraries might dispense with some costly revision processes and our network databases would be cleaner, contain higher quality information, and function more efficiently.

The problem with copy cataloging is that it requires high-level knowledge of certain kinds of detail that can be understood only in the context of theory. While copy catalogers don't need an MLS to do most of the work in run-of-the-mill public or college libraries, they always encounter a residue of material requiring professional decisions. Copy cataloging really can't be learned by imitating the entries found in network databases. Some entries are too old to be consistent with current standards while others suffer from lack of data or inaccuracies of various kinds.

So what can we do? That's easy. Send the cataloging clerk to library school for the one or two courses that will make him or her more effective on the job. In the long run the tuition for a course or two will not break the library budget, the trustees can boast about their generous staff development program, and, in the still longer run, the libraries and the networks to which they belong will reap the rewards in greater productivity and efficiency.

Another option, one that OCLC's PACNET experimented with in 1986, is for the networks to hold cataloging training sessions at the most basic level for nonprofessionals and professionals needing to upgrade their cataloging knowledge and skills. Library school faculty should teach such sessions, because what needs to be taught is not the latest change to the 007 field but the theories underlying AACR2, MARC, LCSH, and classification systems.

*Source:* Sheila S. Intner, *Interfaces: Relationships Between Library Technical and Public Services* (Englewood, Colo.: Libraries Unlimited, 1993). 231p. Reprinted with permission.

**5**

# Subject headings for fiction

*by Steven Olderr*

*OLDERR'S FICTION SUBJECT HEADINGS* was developed to allow consistent subject cataloging for fiction using the basic structure of the *Library of Congress Subject Headings* (LCSH). He accomplishes this by explaining confusing LC terms, adding cross references where needed, and adding new terms where LC has not provided them. Catalogers should use LCSH first, then turn to the thesaurus when there is a problem. Here are a few tantalizing categories from the Olderr thesaurus that will make you wonder which novels would fit these parameters.—*GME.*

**Celibacy** [Here are entered works dealing with not marrying.]

**Cheerful fiction** [Here are entered lighthearted works characterized by the absence of explicit sex, violence, or language.]

**Galloglasses** [Here are entered works dealing with the mercenary troops maintained in former times by Irish chieftains.]

**Impersonating an officer** [Here are entered works that deal with imposture of a public official as a legal charge. Works that deal with the trial of someone accused of this charge are entered under *Trials (Impostors and imposture).*]

**Swearing** [Here are entered works dealing with profane language. Works characterized by the frequent use of foul or obscene language are entered under *Linguistically profane fiction.* Works about the use of abuse to expose or discredit human vice or folly are entered under *Invective.*]

**Ver sacrum** [Here are entered works dealing with the Greek and Italian custom of sacrificing animals born in the spring and of sending away 20-year-old humans in times of distress or overpopulation.]

**Worry** [Here are entered works dealing with the mental activity of fretting or stewing over a problem. Works dealing with apprehensive uneasiness of mind, often involving self-doubt, and with doubt concerning the nature and reality of the uneasiness are entered under *Anxiety*. (Anxiety involves the anguish of fear with the anticipation or uncertainty of failure and may have physiological symptoms.) Works dealing with a loss of courage that may amount to cowardice are entered under *Fear*.]

**Yezidis** [Here are entered works dealing with a Middle Eastern sect that worships an angel believed to have formerly been the author of evil but who now is the chief angel of good.]

*Source:* Steven Olderr, *Olderr's Fiction Subject Headings*
(Chicago: American Library Association, 1991). 147p.

# Understanding MARC

*by Betty Furrie*

**WHAT IS A MARC RECORD?** A MARC record is a **MA**chine-**R**eadable **C**ataloging record.

**Machine-readable:** "Machine-readable" means that one particular type of machine, a computer, can read and interpret the data in the cataloging record.

**Cataloging record:** "Cataloging record" means a bibliographic record, or the information shown on a catalog card. The record includes (not necessarily in this order): 1) a description of the item; 2) main entry and added entries; 3) subject headings; and 4) the classification or call number. (MARC records often contain much additional information.)

## MARC terms and their definitions

To recognize what people are talking about when they discuss MARC records, you need to know what is meant by these terms: fields, tags, subfields, subfield codes, indicators, and content designators.

**Why can't a computer just read a catalog card?** The information from a catalog card cannot simply be typed into a computer to produce an automated catalog. The computer needs a means of interpreting the information found on a cataloging record. The MARC record contains a guide to its data, or "signposts," before each piece of bibliographic information.

This section covers how to read, understand, and use a USMARC record. It deals with what librarians using a library automation system will see and need to understand on their computer screens when adding, editing, or examining records.

1. **Fields are marked by tags.**

**A field:** Each bibliographic record is divided logically into fields. There is a field for the author, a field for title information, and so on. These fields are subdivided into one or more "subfields."

**A tag:** Each field is associated with a 3-digit number called a "tag." A tag identifies the field—the kind of data—that follows. Even though a printout or screen display may show the tag immediately followed by indicators (making it appear to be a 4- or 5-digit number), the tag is always the first 3 digits.

The tags used most frequently are:

010 tag marks the **Library of Congress Control Number** (LCCN)
020 tag marks the **International Standard Book Number** (ISBN)
100 tag marks a **personal name main entry** (author)

| Main Entry, personal name with a single surname: | |
|---|---|
| *The name:* | Arnosky, Jim. |
| Title and statement of responsibility area, pick up title for a title added entry, file under "Ra . . ." | |
| *Title proper:* | Raccoons and ripe corn / |
| *Statement of responsibility:* | Jim Arnosky. |
| Edition area: | |
| *Edition statement:* | 1st ed. |
| Publication, distribution, etc., area: | |
| *Place of publication:* | New York : |
| *Name of publisher:* | Lothrop, Lee & Shepard Books, |
| *Date of publication:* | c1987. |
| Physical description area: | |
| *Pagination:* | 25 p. : |
| *Illustrative matter:* | col. ill. ; |
| *Size:* | 26 cm. |
| Note area: | |
| *Summary:* | Hungry raccoons feast at night in a field of ripe corn. |
| Subject added entries, from Library of Congress subject heading list for children: | |
| *Topical subject:* | Raccoons. |
| Local call number: | 599.74 ARN |
| Local barcode number: | 8009 |
| Local price: | $15.00 |

Record with textual "signposts"

| 100 1 | ǂa | Arnosky, Jim. |
|---|---|---|
| 245 10 | ǂa | Raccoons and ripe corn / |
| | ǂc | Jim Arnosky. |
| 250 | ǂa | 1st ed. |
| 260 0 | ǂa | New York : |
| | ǂb | Lothrop, Lee & Shepard Books, |
| | ǂc | 1987. |
| 300 | ǂa | 25 p. : |
| | ǂb | col. ill. ; |
| | ǂc | 26 cm. |
| 520 | ǂa | Hungry raccoons feast at night in a field of ripe corn. |
| 650 1 | ǂa | Raccoons. |
| 900 | ǂa | 599.74 ARN |
| 901 | ǂa | 8009 |
| 903 | ǂa | $15.00 |

Same record with MARC tags

5

245  tag marks the **title information** (which includes the title, other title information, and the statement of responsibility)
250  tag marks the **edition**
260  tag marks the **publication information**
300  tag marks the **physical description** (often referred to as the "collation" when describing books)
440  tag marks the **series statement/added entry**
520  tag marks the **annotation or summary note**
650  tag marks a **topical subject heading**
700  tag marks a **personal name added entry** (joint author, editor, or illustrator)

Here is an example of a field. The number 100 is the tag, defining it as a personal name main entry (author) field.

> 1001Ɓ ‡a Pirsig, Robert M.

The Cataloging Distribution Service of the Library of Congress distributes a detailed listing of all tags in both the 2-volume publication *USMARC Format for Bibliographic Data* and a summarized single-volume work entitled *USMARC Concise Formats.* For continued work with USMARC records, these sets are highly recommended. They are detailed documents containing many examples.

In the USMARC record, 10% of the tags are used over and over, and the other 90% are seen only occasionally or rarely. After even a short exposure to the USMARC format, it is not unusual to hear librarians speaking in "MARCese." Librarians who work with MARC records soon memorize the numbers for the fields common to the materials they catalog.

2.  **Some fields are further defined by indicators.**

**Indicators:** Two character positions follow each tag (with the exception of Fields 001 through 009). One or both of these character positions may be used for indicators. In some fields, only the first or second position is used; in some fields, both are used; and in some fields, like the 020 and 300 fields, neither is used. When an indicator position is not used, that indicator is referred to as "undefined" and the position is left blank. It is the convention to represent a blank, or undefined, indicator position by the character "Ɓ."

**Each indicator value is a number from 0 to 9.** (Although the rules say it can be a letter, letters are uncommon.) Even though two indicators together may look like a 2-digit number, they really are two single-digit numbers. The allowable indicator values and their meanings are spelled out in the USMARC documentation. In the example that follows, the first 3 digits are the tag (245 defines this as a title field) and the next 2 digits (1 and 4) are indicator values.

> 24515 ‡a  The emperor's new clothes / ‡c adapted from Hans Christian Andersen and illustrated by Janet Stevens.

A *first indicator* value of 1 in the title field indicates that there should be a separate title entry in the catalog. In the card catalog environment, this means that a title card should be printed for this item and an entry for "Title" added to the tracings. A first indicator value of 0 would mean that a title main entry is involved; the card would be printed with the traditional hanging indention, and no additional tracing for the title would be required (since it is the main entry).

*Nonfiling characters:* One of the most interesting indicators is the second indicator for the title field. It displays the number of characters at the beginning of the field (including spaces) to be disregarded by the computer in the sorting and filing process. For the title *The emperor's new clothes,* the second indicator is set to "4" so that the first four characters (the "T," the "h," the "e," and the space) will be skipped and the title will be filed under "emperor's."

3. **Subfields are marked by subfield codes and delimiters.**

A subfield: Most fields contain several related pieces of data. Each type of data within the field is called a subfield, and each subfield is preceded by a subfield code. Fields 001 through 009 have no subfields.

For example, the field for the book's physical description (defined by the tag 300) includes a subfield for the extent (number of pages), a subfield for other physical details (illustration information), and a subfield for dimensions (centimeters):

> 300ᵦᵦ ǂa 675 p. : ǂb ill. ; ǂc 24 cm.

A subfield code: Subfield codes are one lowercase letter (occasionally a number) preceded by a delimiter. A delimiter is a character used to separate subfields. Each subfield code indicates what type of data follows it.

A delimiter: Different software programs use different characters to represent the delimiter on the screen or on printouts. Examples are a double dagger (ǂ), an "at" sign (@), a dollar sign ($), an underline (_), or the graphic symbol "ǂ".

In this example, the subfield codes are ǂa for the extent, ǂb for other physical details, and ǂc for dimensions.

4. **Content designators is an inclusive term used to refer to tags, indicators, and subfield codes.**

The three kinds of content designators—tags, indicators, and subfield codes—are the keys to the USMARC notation system. In his book, *MARC for Library Use: Understanding the USMARC Formats*, 2d ed. (Boston: G.K. Hall & Co., 1989), Walt Crawford calls the MARC system a "shorthand notation" system. The three types of content designators are the shorthand symbols that label and explain the bibliographic record.

*Source:* Betty Furrie, *Understanding MARC: Bibliographic* (Washington, D.C.: Library of Congress Cataloging Distribution Service, in collaboration with the Follett Software Co., 1994). ©1994 The Library of Congress, except within the U.S.A. Reprinted with permission.

# USMARC format integration

IN 1994, THE LIBRARY COMMUNITY has seen implementation of a proposal approved by MARBI (the ALA/ALCTS/LITA/RASD Machine-Readable Bibliographic Information Committee). This proposal (MARBI 88-1) is informally called USMARC Format Integration.

The purpose of this proposal is to identify the inconsistencies among existing USMARC formats and to remove as many inconsistencies as possible.

Format integration involves "the elimination, insofar as possible, of restrictions on data elements that currently make them valid only for specific forms of material. The USMARC bibliographic format would become chiefly a list of data elements and data definitions along with MARC structural specifications" (from MARBI *Proposal 88-1*, prepared by the Network Development and MARC Standards Office of the Library of Congress, 1988).

According to Susan Oros's article "A Format Integration Primer" (*ALCTS Newsletter* 3, no.4 (1992): 41-42), with format integration, fields, subfields, and indicators will be defined across all formats and can be used as appropriate. "This universal application of fields across all formats will be beneficial for systems, since only one validation table will be needed instead of one for each format. . . . It will also be beneficial for USMARC users, who will not have to remember format-dependent inputting rules for the same type of information. For example, *frequency* is recorded in field 315 for maps and computer files, while for serials it is recorded in fields 310 and 321. With format integration, field 315 will no longer be used, and fields 310 and 321 will be valid for all formats. Many specialized 5XX note fields have also been made obsolete based on new criteria that were developed to determine the need for a separate note field."

Complete information on format implementation is available in *Format Integration and Its Effect on the USMARC Bibliographic Format*. Copies are available from the Library of Congress's Cataloging Distribution Service (800) 255-3666.

*Source:* ALA Library and Information Center.

# Format integration and multimedia

*by Glenn Patton*

FORMAT INTEGRATION WILL BE PARTICULARLY USEFUL for cataloging mixed-media items. Some of the hard-to-catalog items have grown out of technology introduced since the original development of the USMARC formats. Other items are the result of new options for reproducing or preserving materials.

Some classic examples of mixed media that have posed problems in the current formats include the following:

- a map that is a puzzle
- a computer file that is a game
- a computer file with a user's manual
- a kit containing a videorecording, computer files, a sound cassette, and several maps
- microscope slides reproduced on videodisc

The problem for each of these mixed-media examples is that current USMARC structure and coding practice require that the cataloger choose only one format for a record. One then is locked into that format for coded values in the 008 field and for the selection of variable fields available in that format. The only exception is in coding for kits. Since any of the existing types of 007 fields was valid for that format type, at least some aspects of the formats can be coded.

Because the Type of Record code in the Leader and the 008 field are linked closely together, and because the 008 field is not repeatable, choosing the primary format usually also means that one cannot code any other characteristics, no matter how important those characteristics might be.

Under Format Integration, however, the new, repeatable 006 field lets one code multiple kinds of materials within a single bibliographic record. In addition, field 007 now can be used with any format type. Together, these fields will ensure that one can code any aspect of a mixed-media item. Although one still will need to choose a primary format, this task for multimedia materials should be simpler, thanks to the model laid out in *Format Integration and Its Effect on the USMARC Bibliographic Format*. This model should become a prominent part of USMARC documentation as well as the bibliographic utility's documentation:

- If an item is basically textual, then the primary format will be coded for Language Material (Type of Material: a), Manuscript Language Material (Type of Material: t), or Mixed Material (Type of Material: p). The 008 field would be coded for book, serials, or archival and manuscript control.
- If an item is *not* basically textual, then the primary format will be chosen from among one of the Type of Material codes appropriate for music, maps, sound recordings, computer files, or visual materials, and the matching 008 field will be used.

One must keep in mind that, in the second case, the general AACR2 rule (rule 0.24) points to the physical form of the item in hand as the starting point of the cataloging process. Multiple 006 and 007 fields then can be used to cover any other aspects of the item. In addition, any variable field that is appropriate to the form or control of the item is available for use.

*Source:* Glenn Patton, "Multimedia Materials," in Karen Coyle, ed., *Format Integration and Its Effect on Cataloging, Training, and Systems* (Chicago: American Library Association, 1993). 110p.

# Making your MARC

### *by Patrick Collins and Deborah Mekeel*

**5**

**THERE'S USMARC, UKMARC, OCLC/MARC, RLIN/MARC**... the possibilities are perhaps endless, but we hope the following will put a stop to this once and for all.

- AfterDarkMARC—saves on telecommunications costs after prime time;
- ArchMARC—archival materials;
- ArkMARC—two (count 'em, two) of everything;
- BenchMARC—cartographic materials;
- BirthMARC—genealogy materials;
- CzechMARC—without Slovakia, it's only half a database;
- DenMARC—more than enough on Hamlet;
- DeutschMARC—the "wurst" of German literature;
- GrouchoMARC—collections of dirty old jokes;
- HallMARC—overpriced greetings from your database;
- KarlMARC—Soviet archives;
- LandMARC—geology materials;
- Mark & ParkMARC—the LC shelflist;
- ScratchMARC—violence in cataloging;
- WaterMARC—rain-damaged materials.

Of course, there's also BarkMARC, BookMARC, TradeMARC and so on, but enough already.

*Except for NarcMARC—materials on substance abuse, and TwainMARC—Mississippi River anecdotes and facetiae.—GME.*

*Source:* "AL Aside—List: Making Your Mark," *American Libraries* 23 (December 1992): 912.

# Dewey Decimal Classification: The hundred divisions

MOST LIBRARY USERS KNOW the general structure of Melvil Dewey's decimal classification. First published in 1876, the Dewey Decimal Classification divides knowledge into ten main classes, with further subdivisions. Here is an outline of its 100 major subdivisions.

## 000 (Generalities)

010 Bibliography
020 Library and information sciences
030 General encyclopedic works
040 [not assigned]
050 General serials and their indexes
060 General organizations and museology
070 News media, journalism, publishing
080 General collections
090 Manuscripts and rare books

## 100 (Philosophy and psychology)

110 Metaphysics
120 Epistemology, causation, humankind
130 Paranormal phenomena
140 Specific philosophical schools
150 Psychology
160 Logic
170 Ethics (Moral philosophy)
180 Ancient, medieval, Oriental philosophy
190 Modern Western philosophy

## 200 (Religion)

210 Natural theology
220 Bible
230 Christian theology
240 Christian moral and devotional theology
250 Christian orders and local church
260 Christian social theology
270 Christian church history
280 Christian denominations and sects
290 Other and comparative religions

## 300 (Social sciences)

310 General statistics
320 Political science
330 Economics

340 Law
350 Public administration
360 Social services; association
370 Education
380 Commerce, communications, transport
390 Customs, etiquette, folklore

# 400 (Language)

410 Linguistics
420 English and Old English
430 Germanic languages
440 Romance languages; French
450 Italian, Rumanian, Rhaeto-Romanic
460 Spanish and Portuguese languages
470 Italic languages; Latin
480 Hellenic languages; classical Greek
490 Other languages

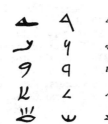

# 500 (Natural sciences and mathematics)

510 Mathematics
520 Astronomy and allied sciences
530 Physics
540 Chemistry and allied sciences
550 Earth sciences
560 Paleontology, paleozoology
570 Life sciences
580 Botanical sciences
590 Zoological sciences

5

# 600 (Technology and applied sciences)

610 Medical sciences; medicine
620 Engineering and allied operations
630 Agriculture
640 Home economics and family living
650 Management and auxiliary services
660 Chemical engineering
670 Manufacturing
680 Manufacture for specific uses
690 Buildings

# 700 (The arts)

710 Civic and landscape art
720 Architecture
730 Plastic arts, sculpture
740 Drawing and decorative arts
750 Painting and paintings
760 Graphic arts; printmaking and prints
770 Photography and photographs
780 Music
790 Recreational and performing arts

# 800 (Literature and rhetoric)

810 American literature in English
820 English and Old English literature
830 Literatures of Germanic languages
840 Literatures of Romance languages

850  Italian, Rumanian, Rhaeto-Romanic
860  Spanish and Portuguese literatures
870  Italic literatures; Latin
880  Hellenic literatures; classical Greek
890  Literatures of other languages

## 900 (Geography and history)

910  Geography and travel
920  Biography, genealogy, insignia
930  History of the ancient world
940  General history of Europe
950  General history of Asia
960  General history of Africa
970  General history of North America
980  General history of South America
990  General history of other areas

*Source: Dewey Decimal Classification Summaries, DDC 20 (Albany, N.Y.: Forest Press, 1989).*

# LC classification outline

THE LC CLASSIFICATION was developed and used at the Library of Congress beginning in 1899. It has become the system of choice for many large research libraries. This list gives the scope for most one- or two-letter designators, which may serve as an aid in learning the classification schedules in more detail.

## A (General works)

AC  Collections, series, collected works
AE  Encyclopedias (general)
AG  Dictionaries and other general reference books
AI  Indexes (general)
AM  Museums (general), collectors and collecting
AN  Newspapers
AP  Periodicals (general)
AS  Academies and learned societies (general)
AY  Yearbooks, almanacs, directories
AZ  History of scholarship and learning

## B (Philosophy, psychology, religion)

B    Philosophy (general)
BC   Logic
BD   Speculative philosophy
BF   Psychology, parapsychology, occult sciences
BH   Aesthetics
BJ   Ethics, social usages, etiquette
BL   Religions, mythology, rationalism
BM   Judaism
BP   Islam, Bahaism, theosophy
BQ   Buddhism
BR   Christianity
BS   The Bible
BT   Doctrinal theology
BV   Practical theology
BX   Christian denominations

## C (Auxiliary sciences of history)

C    Auxiliary sciences of history (general)
CB    History of civilization
CC    Archaeology (general)
CD    Diplomatics, archives, seals
CE    Technical chronology, calendars
CJ    Numismatics
CN    Inscriptions, epigraphy
CR    Heraldry
CS    Genealogy
CT    Biography (general)

## D (History, general and Old World)

D    History (general)
DA    Great Britain
DAW Central Europe
DB    Austria, Liechtenstein, Hungary, Czechoslovakia
DC    France
DD    Germany
DE    The Mediterranean region, the Greco-Roman world
DF    Greece
DG    Italy
DH    The Low Countries
DJ    Holland
DJK    Eastern Europe
DK    Soviet Union, Poland
DL    Scandinavia
DP    Spain, Portugal
DQ    Switzerland
DR    Balkan Peninsula
DS    Asia
DT    Africa
DU    Australia, Oceania
DX    Gypsies

POMPEIUS MAGNUS.

**5**

## E-F (History, America)

E    Indians, United States (general)
F    U.S. local history, Canada, Mexico, Central and South America

## G (Geography, anthropology, recreation)

G    Geography (general), atlases, maps
GA    Mathematical geography, cartography
GB    Physical geography
GC    Oceanography
GF    Human ecology, anthropogeography
GN    Anthropology
GR    Folklore
GT    Manners and customs
GV    Recreation, sports, leisure

## H (Social sciences)

H    Social sciences (general)
HA    Statistics
HB    Economic theory, demography
HC    Economic history and conditions (by region or country)

HD   Production, land use, agriculture, industry, labor
HE   Transportation, communications
HF   Commerce, accounting
HG   Finance
HJ   Public finance
HM   Sociology (general and theoretical)
HN   Social history, social problems, social reform
HQ   Sex, the family, marriage, women's studies
HS   Societies (secret, benevolent), clubs
HT   Communities, classes, races
HV   Social pathology, social and public welfare, criminology
HX   Socialism, communism, anarchism

## J (Political science)

J    General legislative and executive papers
JA   Collections and general works
JC   Political theory, theory of the state
JF   Constitutional history and administration
     (general and comparative)
JK   United States government
     (federal and state)
JL   British America, Latin America
JN   Europe
JQ   Asia, Africa, Australia, Oceania
JS   Local government
JV   Colonies and colonization, emigration and immigration
JX   International law and international relations

## K (Law)

K          Law (general)
KD-KDK     United Kingdom and Ireland
KDZ        America, North America
KE-KEZ     Canada
KF-KFZ     United States
KG-KGZ     Mexico, Central America, West Indies
KH-KHW     South America
KJ-KKZ     Europe

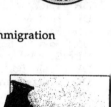

## L (Education)

L    Education (general)
LA   History of education
LB   Theory and practice of education
LC   Special aspects of education
LD   United States
LE   America, except United States
LF   Europe
LG   Asia, Africa, Oceania
LH   College and school magazines and papers
LJ   Student fraternities and societies, U.S.
LT   Textbooks

## M (Music and books on music)

M    Music
ML   Literature of music
MT   Musical instruction and study

# N (Fine arts)

| | |
|---|---|
| **N** | Visual arts (general) |
| **NA** | Architecture |
| **NB** | Sculpture |
| **NC** | Drawing, design, illustration |
| **ND** | Painting |
| **NE** | Print media |
| **NK** | Decorative arts, applied arts, antiques, other arts |
| **NX** | Arts in general |

# P (Language and literature)

| | |
|---|---|
| **P** | Philology and linguistics (general) |
| **PA** | Classical languages and literature |
| **PB** | General European languages, Celtic |
| **PC** | Romance languages |
| **PD** | Old Germanic, Scandinavian |
| **PE** | English |
| **PF** | Dutch, Flemish, Friesian, German |
| **PG** | Slavic, Baltic, Albanian |
| **PH** | Finno-Ugrian, Basque |
| **PJ** | Egyptian, Libyan, Berber, Cushitic, Semitic languages |
| **PK** | Indo-Iranian, Armenian, Caucasian |
| **PL** | East Asian, African, Oceanic languages |
| **PM** | Inuit, Native American, and artificial languages |
| **PN** | Literary history and collections, drama, journalism, collections |
| **PQ** | Romance literatures |
| **PR** | English literature |
| **PT** | Germanic literatures |
| **PZ** | Juvenile belles lettres, miscellaneous literature |

5

# Q (Science)

| | |
|---|---|
| **Q** | Science (general), information theory |
| **QA** | Mathematics |
| **QB** | Astronomy |
| **QC** | Physics |
| **QD** | Chemistry |
| **QE** | Geology |
| **QH** | Natural history, biology |
| **QK** | Botany |
| **QL** | Zoology |
| **QM** | Human anatomy |
| **QP** | Physiology |
| **QR** | Microbiology |

# R (Medicine)

| | |
|---|---|
| **R** | Medicine (general) |
| **RA** | Public aspects of medicine |
| **RB** | Pathology |
| **RC** | Internal medicine, medical practice |
| **RD** | Surgery |
| **RE** | Ophthalmology |
| **RF** | Otorhinolaryngology |
| **RG** | Gynecology and obstetrics |
| **RJ** | Pediatrics |
| **RK** | Dentistry |

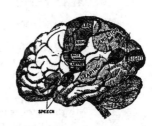

| | |
|---|---|
| **RL** | Dermatology |
| **RM** | Therapeutics, pharmacology |
| **RS** | Pharmacy and materia medica |
| **RT** | Nursing |
| **RV** | Eclectic medicine |
| **RX** | Homeopathy |
| **RZ** | Other systems of medicine |

## S (Agriculture)

| | |
|---|---|
| **S** | Agriculture (general) |
| **SB** | Plant culture |
| **SD** | Forestry |
| **SF** | Animal culture |
| **SH** | Aquaculture, fisheries, angling |
| **SK** | Hunting, wildlife management |

## T (Technology)

| | |
|---|---|
| **T** | Technology (general) |
| **TA** | Engineering (general), civil engineering (general) |
| **TC** | Hydraulic engineering |
| **TD** | Environmental technology, sanitary engineering |
| **TE** | Highway engineering, roads and pavements |
| **TF** | Railroad engineering and operation |
| **TG** | Bridge engineering |
| **TH** | Building construction |
| **TJ** | Mechanical engineering and machinery |
| **TK** | Electrical engineering, electronics, nuclear power |
| **TL** | Motor vehicles, aeronautics, UFOs |
| **TN** | Mining engineering, metallurgy |
| **TP** | Chemical technology |
| **TR** | Photography |
| **TS** | Manufactures |
| **TT** | Handicrafts, arts and crafts |
| **TX** | Home economics |

## U (Military science)

| | |
|---|---|
| **U** | Military science (general) |
| **UA** | Armies |
| **UB** | Military administration |
| **UC** | Maintenance and transportation |
| **UD** | Infantry |
| **UE** | Cavalry, armored and mechanized cavalry |
| **UF** | Artillery |
| **UG** | Military engineering, air forces, air warfare |
| **UH** | Other services |

## V (Naval science)

| | |
|---|---|
| **V** | Naval science (general) |
| **VA** | Navies |
| **VB** | Naval administration |
| **VC** | Naval maintenance |
| **VD** | Naval seamen |
| **VE** | Marines |
| **VF** | Naval ordnance |
| **VG** | Minor services of navies |
| **VK** | Navigation, merchant marine |

**VM** Naval architecture, shipbuilding, diving

# Z (Bibliography, library science)

| | |
|---|---|
| Z | Books in general |
| Z 4-8 | History of books and bookmaking |
| Z 40-115.5 | Writing |
| Z 116-659 | Book industries, the booktrade |
| Z 662-1000.5 | Libraries and library science |
| Z 1001-8999 | Bibliography |

*Source: LC Classification Outline* (Washington: Library of Congress, 1990).

---

### Thomas Jefferson the librarian

Long believed lost, the classification system devised by the third president of the United States for his own library was published on April 13, 1989, by the Library of Congress, on the 246th anniversary of Jefferson's birth. The lost manuscript, discovered by James Gilreath of LC and Douglas L. Wilson of Knox College, Galesburg, Ill., was bound with a printed 1815 catalog of the Jefferson collection. According to LC sources, the discovery "restores to the world the intellectual order Jefferson imposed on his library and throws light on the way one of the country's leading intellectuals organized knowledge."

*Source: Thomas Jefferson's Library: A Catalog with the Entries in His Own Order*
(Washington, D.C.: Library of Congress, 1989).

**5**

---

## Reference

# Mistakes of the information age

*by Thomas Mann*

- **IT IS A MISTAKE TO THINK** that a vocabulary-controlled system of subject category terms can be replaced (rather than supplemented) by key word searching.
- It is a mistake to think that *LCSH* headings are merely a carryover from a manual system to an online age, and that precoordinated, multiword strings of terms can be replaced (rather than supplemented) by postcoordinate computer manipulations of single terms.
- It is a mistake to think that browsing access to printed full-texts arranged in subject groups is no longer necessary for scholars in research libraries, or that scholars of the 21st century won't need it.
- It is an equally bad, and related, mistake to think that the ability to search superficial catalog records grouped by class number in an online catalog renders unnecessary the practice of making full texts themselves searchable in classified subject groupings.
- It is a mistake to think that information that cannot be searched for directly and immediately by computer therefore cannot be retrieved systematically, or worse, that it cannot be searched for, or found, *at all*.

- It is a mistake to think that access can replace (rather than merely supplement) acquisition.
- It is a mistake to think that the mere acquisition of books without proper cataloging renders them accessible (the false assumption is that software enhancements such as word proximity or Boolean search capabilities can replace rather than supplement the intellectual work of categorization and standardization).
- It is a mistake for librarians to believe that the work of cataloging can be abandoned in the expectation of the imminent arrival of expert-system or artificial intelligence programs, which will probably never be successful when applied outside very narrow disciplinary bounds, and which will also not work outside the confines of one language. (Do librarians need to be reminded that their catalogs must cover all disciplines and also a wide variety of languages?)
- It is a mistake to believe that the mere *existence* of information ensures *access* to it. While the Documentation movement provided a major advance for information science by insisting that the content of a knowledge record could be freed from its original physical container, the movement also made a correspondingly large mistake in failing to attach sufficient weight to the fact that changing the *format* of a knowledge record also radically changes *access* to it. If access to a high-quality record becomes more difficult (e.g., a microfilm capture of the contents of a large card catalog), then the Principle of Least Effort will bring about a marked drop-off in actual use. Similarly, if a notably superficial index is presented in an attractive CD-ROM format, the same principle will ensure an increase in its use, in spite of its low quality, with users "satisficing" with any results they get from it and disregarding better sources in less attractive formats.
- It is a mistake to think that the copyright law will magically change in a radical way to make everything freely available online.
- It is a mistake to think that the "transportability of digitized data" is sufficient to transform electronic formats into preservation media.
- It is a mistake for librarians themselves to think that their own traditional model is reducible to a classification scheme plus controlled vocabulary catalog *alone*. This view overlooks the existence, and the function, of bibliographies and indexes in providing the very same kind of access that overzealous Workstation advocates are now claiming to have invented afresh, ex nihilo.

As a reference librarian myself, I think that the most important of the distinctive contributions that librarians make lies in creating, maintaining, extending, and stocking the standardized intellectual gridwork that makes the literature of the world—in all subject areas and in all languages—identifiable and retrievable in a systematic manner even by people who are not already experts in the subject they wish to research. Part of this gridwork is created by the intellectual work of cataloging (categorizing and standardizing, as opposed to merely transcribing existing natural language words), which is done to make research more predictable, to increase the serendipity of the search, and to improve the depth of access to knowledge records.

*Source:* Thomas Mann, *Library Research Models: A Guide to Classification, Cataloging, and Computers* (New York: Oxford University Press, 1993). 248pp. Copyright © 1993 by Thomas Mann. Reprinted by permission of Oxford University Press, Inc.

# Behaviors that contribute to correct reference answers

*by Lillie Seward Dyson*

"THE VARIABLES THAT CONTRIBUTE to good reference performance are within the control of the individual librarian." This statement was again confirmed by an unobtrusive statewide survey taken in Maryland in 1990 that investigated what librarians did as they attempted to answer reference questions. The survey found that the following librarian behaviors were positively associated with the correctness of the answers received:

Approachability
    Smiles
    Makes eye contact
    Gives friendly greeting
    Is at same level as patron

Comfort
    Speaks in relaxed tone
    Is mobile, goes with patron

Interest
    Maintains eye contact
    Makes attentive comments
      ("I see," "Uh-huh")
✔ Gives patron full attention

Listening
    Does not interrupt patron
✔ Paraphrases or repeats to demonstrate an understanding
✔ Asks clarifying questions if not sure of patron's question

Inquiring
✔ Asks open questions to probe
✔ Verifies specific question before searching

Searching
✔ Finds answer in first source
    Searches in more than one source (if not found in first)
    Keeps patron informed of progress of search

Informing
    Speaks clearly and distinctly
    Checks with patrons to be sure answer is understood
    Cites the source

Follow-up
✔ Asks, "Does this completely answer your question?"

The most important behaviors are checked (✔).

*Source:* Lillie Seward Dyson, "Improving Reference Services: A Maryland Training Program Brings Positive Results," *Public Libraries*, September/October 1992, pp. 284–89.

### Why do reference librarians use the online catalog or a bibliographic database?

A recent study of catalog use patterns in three research libraries (Rutgers, New York University, and SUNY at Stony Brook) showed that reference staff members consulted only a limited number of elements in their bibliographic searches—titles (53.1%), authors (22.9%), author-title combinations (6.6%), and subject headings (9.2%). The same study provided data on why the searches were performed:

| | |
|---|---|
| Patron working on course paper | 25.9% |
| Patron interested in finding something to read for enjoyment or edification | 25.0% |
| Interlibrary loan transaction | 13.2% |
| Collection development by staff member | 8.5% |
| Patron with classroom reading assignment | 7.2% |
| Information needed by patron for thesis | 5.2% |
| Catalog maintenance by staff member | 3.0% |
| Patron needing information for work to be published | 2.6% |
| Professional curiosity on the part of the staff member | 1.9% |
| Patron seeking job-related information | 1.9% |
| Professor preparing for teaching | 1.8% |
| Staff member compiling bibliography | 1.2% |
| Teaching done by staff member | 0.6% |
| Preparation for oral presentation | 0.5% |
| Collection maintenance by staff member | 0.5% |
| Staff member seeking information for work to be published | 0.3% |
| Patron with class film project | 0.3% |
| Compiling bibliography for patron | 0.2% |
| Information needed by patron to fill out form (not job-related) | 0.1% |
| Legal research provided to patron | 0.1% |
| Preparation for sermon | 0.1% |

*Source:* Jon R. Hufford, "Elements of the Bibliographic Record Used by Reference Staff Members at Three ARL Academic Libraries," *College & Research Libraries* 52 (January 1991): 54–64.

# The art of answering quotation questions

*by Susan Coburn*

ONE OF THE MOST CHALLENGING AREAS of reference work for librarians is verifying or identifying the source of quotations for patrons. Beyond Bartlett's (*Familiar Quotations*) and Stevenson's (*Home Book of Quotations*), where to look next? As an experienced librarian once told a trainee, "It isn't whether you find the quotation or not that will make you a better librarian, it's all of the interesting little things you learn along the way." That is certainly true. However, to improve the chances for a successful search, there are several important guidelines the librarian should follow.

**Avoid mindset.** Be open and flexible. Allow no communication blocks. Maintain a fresh approach, and keep a clear head. Is the "quotation" really a quotation? Or is it a familiar phrase or the first or last line of a poem? Perhaps a song title? A patron called in knowing only two pieces of her quotation, "The Three Trees" and "there, there, there." Or would that be "there, their, they're"? A quotation and poem search in the Literature Department turned up nothing, but an enterprising librarian in the Fine Arts Division found a 1927 song titled "The Three Trees" with a spoken introduction containing the words "there—there—and there." It was just what the patron wanted. Another patron asked us to find the word "gizmo" or "gismo" that he read once in a science fiction story. Keyword searches in quotation books yielded no results. A librarian had to remember that the *Oxford English Dictionary* is a quotation book; under "gismo" it gives a 1949 citation to Robert Heinlein and "Red Planet." Again, it was just what the patron wanted.

**Remember that the patron is sincere, but may be inaccurate.** A new librarian was reading and rereading the "Rime of the Ancient Mariner" and commented that it was a lot longer than he remembered it. It seems that a patron had asked for a particular quotation from that work, using the words "gift" and "giver." A veteran librarian immediately produced the desired quotation from "The Vision of Sir Launfal" by James Russell Lowell. The first librarian was shocked. "The patron was so sure." Then there was the patron who said he needed the quote by Albert Einstein that says, "God is complicated but not tricky." After a long and fruitless search, the librarian contacted him to say that Bartlett's had only phrases from Einstein like "The Lord God is subtle, but malicious he is not," to which the patron replied, "That's it!" Most librarians realize that a patron's version may only remotely resemble the actual quotation. When people ask for "Those who ignore the mistakes of history are doomed to repeat them," what they really want is George Santayana's "Those who cannot remember the past are condemned to repeat it."

**Keep your search orderly.** Document it, track it. List the sources you have checked; abbreviate them. Make sure that when you list a source, your quotation wasn't there. If your search is interrupted, or if you want to turn it over to someone else, there will be a full record of where you have been.

**Know your limits.** How much time can you spend on one quotation question? Often it cannot be until you find the answer. Your library may have a policy about time limitations for questions. Your department or division may have a policy. Do fill-rate statistics require an answer within the same day? Know from the start that you will have to draw a line somewhere. Inform the patron of the results of your search, whether you found what she or he wanted or not. It is much better to say "I have been unable to locate" than to say "We don't have."

**Use special local available resources.** Is there a Fact File or other similar resource for hard-to-find questions? Some quotation questions are asked over and over. Patrons never know the speaker, Martin Niemoeller, and they may or may not remember "Catholics" or "Jews" or "Communists," but they always know "No one was left to speak up (for me)." A Fact File card under "Communists" (or any other word you choose to train people to use) with the reference from *Bartlett's* saves repeated search time for this quotation. Over the years special files or indexes may have been compiled as timesavers; be aware of such treasures in your library and use them. Perusing a needlework/sampler catalog or telephoning a religious bookstore for a plaque wording or contacting a local fire museum for "A Fireman's Prayer" are alternative methods of finding quotations.

**Build a collection of adequate resources.** The Ohio Library Association's *Standards for the Public Libraries of Ohio* recommends having at least one quotation book published within the last five years. These will be the sources that help with modem quotations. There are several older standard works. Never throw away a copy of *Granger's Index to Poetry* if you can avoid it; editions are unique, not cumulative, and there is often occasion to search the old editions. Those fortunate enough to have *Notes and Queries* and the index to the "Reference Exchange" column from *RQ* should keep them. Online searching, especially using Quotations Database from DIALOG, is the newest technique for quotation reference.

**Keep a "Did Not Find" File.** If you do not find a quotation, chances are that some day you will find it while looking for something else! It is amazing that people called as much as six months later are still grateful to have their question answered. Sometimes patrons write or call the library back with answers or additional information they have found. Quotations can be elusive, and a new search with a different strategy, perhaps shared with colleagues, could produce results.

**Expand your knowledge; increase your expertise.** Pay attention to skill building in this area of reference service. Read the "Reference Exchange" column edited by Charles Anderson in *RQ* each month. Read the "Author Author" quotation game each week in the *Times Literary Supplement*. If your library carries an Arco Civil Service test series for Librarian, try the quotation section. Borrow or purchase *The Quote Sleuth: A Manual for the Tracer of Lost Quotations*, published by Anthony W. Shipps in 1990. This noted practitioner, who does research for the *New York Times Book Review*, *RQ*, *Harvard Magazine*, and the *Times Literary Supplement*, among others, has written a delightful

---

### How to grade your reference performance

In an unobtrusive study of the ability of reference librarians to deal with factual questions at Illinois State University, a scoring system was developed to rate the degree of correctness provided to the walk-in reference questioner. Points of 10 or above were given to answers that at least led to a complete and correct answer, while partial or incorrect answers were graded 9 or less. The librarians in the study obtained scores of 10 or higher 58.3% of the time. Here is the scoring system the study used:

| Performance | Points |
| --- | --- |
| Student *provided* with complete and correct answer | 15 |
| Student *led to a single source* which provided complete and correct answer | 14 |
| Student *led to several sources*, at least one of which provided complete and correct answer | 13 |
| Student *directed to a single source*, which provided complete and correct answer | 12 |
| Student *directed to several sources*, at least one of which provided complete and correct answer | 11 |
| Student *given an appropriate referral to a specific person or source*, which provided complete and correct answer | 10 |
| Student *provided* with partial answer | 9 |
| Student given an *appropriate referral to the card catalog or another floor* | 8 |
| Librarian *did not find an answer* or suggest an alternative source | 5 |
| Student given an *inappropriate referral to catalog, floor, or source*, or librarian unlikely to provide complete and correct answer | 3 |
| Student given *inappropriate sources* | 2 |
| Student given *incorrect answer* | 0 |

*Source:* Cheryl Elzy, Alan Nourie, F. W. Lancaster, and Kurt M. Joseph, "Evaluating Reference Service in a Large Academic Library," *College & Research Libraries* 52 (September 1991): 454–65.

guidebook for reference librarians, including maxims such as "Time spent looking for quotations is never wasted."

An unexpected quotation experience illustrates the challenge and frustration of working with the quoted word. At the close of a library convention program, the speaker tossed in a favorite quotation clipped from an issue of *NRTA Journal,* September–October 1976. The clipping is titled "Recipe for Success" and reads:

> To laugh often and much; to win the respect of intelligent people and the affection of children; to earn the appreciation of honest critics and endure the betrayal of false friends; to appreciate beauty, to find the best in others; to leave the world a bit better, whether by a healthy child, a garden patch or redeemed social condition; to know even one life has breathed easier because you have lived. This is to have succeeded.
>
> *Ralph Waldo Emerson*

At that point a member of the audience stood up to say that her library had that quotation attributed to a woman, but she couldn't remember her name. It was a surprise to hold an Emerson quotation dear for 14 years, then to learn that Emerson may not have said it at all. Further correspondence with Debbie Charvat of Cleveland Public Library resulted in copies of an Aids File reference under "Quotations—Success," written by a Mrs. A. J. Stanley of Lincoln, Kansas. She won a $250 prize from a Boston firm for the best answer to the question "What constitutes success?" According to *Notes and Queries,* the same lines were used on illuminated cards and motto cards sold in 1911, with text attributed to Mrs. A. J. Stanley. The version quoted is this:

> He has achieved success who has lived well, laughed often and loved much; who has gained the respect of intelligent men and the love of little children; who has filled his niche and accomplished his task; who left the world better than he found it, whether by an improved poppy, a perfect poem, or a rescued soul; who has never lacked appreciation of earth's beauty or failed to express it; who has always looked for the best in others and given the best he had; whose life was an inspiration; whose memory is a benediction.

A thorough review of Emerson's works, beginning with the obvious essay on "Success" and continuing through many volumes of essays, notes, and journals, has failed to find the passage attributed to him by the *NRTA Journal.* Research done by Anthony W. Shipps in *Notes and Queries,* July 1976, including reading two different versions printed by local newspapers in 1905 and corresponding with Mrs. Stanley's son, mentions that the definition is "still quoted from time to time in American magazines and newspapers, but it is now often attributed to Emerson."

Answering quotation questions is an art. It requires a blend of skill and imagination, knowledge and recall. For the patient and the persistent, the regards are great. Bear it in mind the next time you hear the words, "Who said that?"

*Source:* Susan Coburn, "'Who Said That?' The Art of Answering Quotation Questions," *Ohio Libraries,* May/June 1992, pp. 24–25. Reprinted with permission.

# How to handle medical, legal, and business questions

LIBRARY USERS NEED INFORMATION in order to make decisions. They have a right to gain access to any published information available in library collections. Staff are responsible for providing complete and accurate responses to users' questions when possible and for guiding patrons to the most appropriate resources for their needs. (The terms *user* and *patron* are used interchangeably.)

The following guidelines are designed to assist staff at general reference desks in responding to users requesting medical, legal, or business information. To ensure that malpractice claims will not follow, librarians need to keep current in their subject areas, refer questions beyond their level of competency to others, document search strategies and sources, and explain to the user the librarians' responsibility to provide sources rather than interpretation. Although these guidelines are written for medical, legal, and business reference service, they may be applied to any reference transaction.

Each library's reference collection should contain current, accurate, and accessible medical, legal, and business information appropriate to the needs of the community served. The reference transaction should fully satisfy the user's need for information, either by providing accurate sources in hand, or clear and concise referrals to obtainable sources located elsewhere.

## The role of librarians

When asked legal, medical, or business reference questions, librarians should make clear their role as information providers. Librarians can provide information but should not interpret that information. They should provide instruction in the use of resources, enabling users to pursue information independently and effectively, if so desired. Libraries should develop written disclaimers stating a position on providing specialized reference service.

**Interpretation.** The reference librarian provides the library user with information but does not evaluate that information. If the patron has trouble understanding the source, an alternative source should be sought. If no appropriate sources can be located, the patron should be referred to the legal, medical, or financial community for interpretation of the information.

**Advice.** Libraries may advise patrons regarding the relative merits of sources and make recommendations regarding library materials when appropriate. Materials recommended should be the most comprehensive and the most current available.

**Confidentiality.** Confidentiality of user requests must be respected at all times. Questions should not be discussed outside the library, and names should never be mentioned without the user's permission.

**Tact.** As in all situations, reference librarians should use discretion when interviewing users regarding medical, legal, and business questions. While it is important to conduct a thorough reference interview, this should be done in such a way as to minimize discomfort to the user. The librarian should try to identify the issue in question without intruding on the user's privacy. Librarians should be impartial and nonjudgmental in handling users' queries.

## Sources

The library should acquire appropriate materials in medical, legal, and business subject areas that meet the needs of the community served. The reference librarian should direct the user to possible sources, both in and out of the library, where the information the user requires will be provided. These materials might include books, pamphlets, journals, electronic services, service agencies, and professionals in the appropriate field. When helping a user, librarians must be careful to avoid using technical terms. Under no circumstances should information be withheld from a user.

**Currency of sources.** The reference librarian should always point out publication dates to the user. Because information in medical, legal, and business areas changes rapidly, the user should be advised that there may be more current information available on the topic.

In subject areas where up-to-date information is essential, libraries should provide the most current information possible, consistent with the needs of the library's primary clientele and within the limitations of the library's materials budget and collection development policy.

Reference collections should be weeded periodically to remove dated materials in subject areas where up-to-date information is essential. If retention of older materials is required for historical purposes, distinctions in dates should be obvious.

**Referrals to other sources.** Referrals should be made only if the librarian expects that the agency, service, individual, or other source can and will provide the information needed. Librarians should be prepared to refer questions to human as well as to written sources. Awareness of community, state, and private services outside of the library proper is important. Reference librarians may provide access to biographical and other information that is available in directories and other sources. They may not make recommendations to specific lawyers, legal firms, doctors, other medical care providers, or financial professionals. Users should be referred to county or state professional associations for additional information.

## Telephone or mail reference

Special care must be taken with telephone, mail, electronic mail, and telefacsimile since it is easy to misinterpret phone messages, and written communications may need explanations or interpretation. Only factual information—such as dates, names and addresses, specific citations, or catalog checks—should be given out over the telephone. Brief information may be read verbatim without interpretation. The source should be given for all information provided. Users must come to the library, or be directed to a special library, for statutory or case law material, medical information beyond quoted definitions of terms from standard medical dictionaries, or financial information encompassing more than the above.

Telephone or mail requesters may have to be informed that the library does have information on the topic but that they will have to come into the library to use the material. Questions received through the mail should be answered with full citations for the source or with well-documented photocopies if such copies can be done within copyright requirements.

## Ethics

The American Library Association's current Code of Ethics (as stated in the ALA *Policy Manual* in the ALA *Handbook of Organization*) governs the conduct of all staff members providing information service.

*Source: Guidelines for Medical, Legal, and Business Responses at General Reference Desks* (Chicago: ALA Reference and Adult Services Division, 1992).

Circulation and Usage

# Evaluating public library collections

### by Sheila S. Intner and Elizabeth Futas

PUBLIC LIBRARIANS KNOW THE VALUE of building dynamic collections, and they spend considerable time and money selecting useful material. Although collection building is based on the concept of the public library as a public good, many librarians are still wrestling with the ramifications of that premise.

If an institution is a public good, we must be able to prove to the taxpaying public that it is. But how can we do this? One of the ways librarians can prove the worth of collections is by systematic evaluation against objective criteria.

## Evaluation, the process of the 1990s

If planning was the process of the 1980s, evaluation is the process of the 1990s. Three forces have prompted this need for evaluation: accountability, cooperation, and the economy.

**Accountability.** Public money supports public libraries. Members of the public are held accountable in their own lives for their actions, including spending money, so they expect the same from their institutions. And this is right and proper. As citizens we want to know where our money goes, how it gets there, and what it buys. We hold government officials accountable for how tax money is collected, contracted, and consumed. Libraries need to show how their expenditures of tax dollars benefit the public. Evaluation helps do that.

**Cooperation.** Networks cannot succeed unless each partner shares some portion of its holdings with the others. When two or more entities join together to form a larger group, each one must enter the agreement with knowledge of itself as well as of the other participants. In setting up cooperative organizations among libraries, participants must be aware of their capabilities and demonstrate their worth. It is hard to strike a bargain if you don't know the bottom line.

In recent years, resource sharing and networking have increased in importance. Public libraries that have not evaluated their collections and do not know their worth are in a poor position to coexist successfully in partnership with other libraries.

When the public service arms of libraries automate and network, the impact of evaluation will be even more critical. The determination of new groups to be formed by combining smaller units will be based chiefly on the knowledge gained through collection evaluation.

**The Economy.** The impetus toward greater accountability and more cooperation can be laid almost entirely at the doorstep of the economic environment of the 1990s.

When the economy expanded in the 1950s and 1960s, all institutions—including libraries—thought they, too, could expand indefinitely.

In the 1970s, when budget increases began to taper off and costs began rising more rapidly, libraries began suffering withdrawal symptoms as the years of largess ended. In the 1980s, budget restrictions intensified. The entire decade was spent gathering information to make better decisions in order to make the most of severely limited resources.

The time has come for implementation. A still-stringent economy is forcing us to be decisive and determined. Evaluation no longer is an option, but an essential part of decision-making processes.

## Evaluation options

Once public libraries decide to evaluate their collections, there are several possible ways to do the job. The evaluation can be an internal project, accomplished by the library's personnel; it can be contracted out to consultants who specialize in this kind of work; or it can combine in-house staff and consultants. Each option has advantages and disadvantages.

**Do-it-yourself, with a little help from your friends.** A public library can undertake its own evaluation either by assigning the task to one or a few staff members, or by involving larger numbers of people—staff members, administrators, and even members of the public.

A do-it-yourself evaluation does not require paying fees to consultants and avoids the necessity for public approval of such special expenditures. The cost of the evaluation can be hidden in the ordinary course of paying staff salaries. But no director or library board should think that sidestepping consulting fees means that the do-it-yourself evaluation is either cheap or free.

Internal evaluation costs are very difficult to control. Every minute spent on the project by each staff member involved is a twofold cost measured in salary-plus-benefits for the time plus the postponement of the work they would do if they weren't doing the evaluation. Depending on who does it and how long they take, a do-it-yourself evaluation could cost more or less than an equivalent job done by outside specialists.

Library staff members are familiar with their community and its information needs. They need not spend time, as consultants must, preparing for the evaluation by getting to know community demographics and speculating about their implications. Taking part in an evaluation is a means of getting staff to buy into desirable collection goals and objectives. But library personnel—who often live in the communities where they work—are more likely than outsiders to be defensive about local problems. They have a stake in upholding particular views. When the same people who selected materials are asked as evaluators to decide whether those selections were good or bad, they may find it hard to be dispassionate and objective.

Using library staff allows the evaluation to proceed slowly, in a part-time manner. An internal evaluation can be designed to suit the library's individual staff and budget situation. The person who is best suited for the job or who has the most training can be chosen to do the job or coordinate a team effort.

**Using consultants—Judgment Day.** Some advantages of contracting with outside specialists to perform the evaluation already are clear. Consultants usually do the job quickly, for a specified, controllable amount of money, and the regular work of the library does not suffer. Consultants are knowledgeable about systematic data collection and analysis. Because they are not involved in day-to-day selection and programming decisions, they have no particular bias. They will present library officials with a detailed report as well as suggestions or recommendations for the future.

Some disadvantages of hiring consultants are also clear. Consultants do not know the community the way members of the staff do. Once the job is done and consultants are paid, they leave, with no guarantee that a stake in improving the collections has been developed within the library staff.

**Combining staff with consultants.** Is it the best of both worlds? It sounds too good to say the best alternative is to hire consultants to work with staff, but it can be ideal. To succeed, however, the consultants must be able to engage the enthusiasm and good will of the staff. They cannot just issue orders, but must continually supervise progress. Consultants bring their special expertise and objectivity to evaluation. Using outsiders ensures that data interpretations are unbiased and that mismatches between collections and communities are not glossed over or ignored.

The downside of using consultants with staff is cost. It is also likely to take longer than using consultants alone. In an era of cost cutting it may be hard to justify the added expenditures without a perceived payoff in the long run.

## Problems uncovered by an evaluation

A proper evaluation should reveal any mismatch between currently held collections and the people they are supposed to serve. Communities change, and so do bodies of literature. Selections that might have served well 10 or 20 years ago may not be relevant today or represent a good cross section of materials available.

Other common collection problems that show up when evaluation is done include the following:

- peculiarities in placement of materials that cause problems for browsers—these peculiarities do not bother librarians, who are so used to dealing with these quirks they no longer see them;
- differences in the way individual librarians budget, allocate, select, and/or weed;
- gaps in the existing written documentation for collection policies and procedures;
- communication gaps among members of the staff, the administration, and the library's board.

An objective evaluation should expose these and other problems as well as document the adequacy of holdings in particular subject areas or for particular audiences. It is critical that librarians be ready to accept objective evidence that problems exist so they can get to work on solutions, and not jump to offer excuses or explanations in order to play down the importance of the problems and show that they aren't worth addressing. This raises a most important issue of follow-up to the collection evaluation: How to use the information it provides in making decisions.

## Preserve or pitch?

Evaluation data should be used wisely, because decisions with far-reaching implications have to be made. What is important in making collection development decisions? Four focuses are relevant: the community, material use, shelf allocations, and user views of individual items on the shelf.

**The community.** Enormous amounts of both anecdotal and statistical information on almost every community have been and continue to be collected. Census data, which reports population by age, gender, ethnic group, language, racial group, economic status, and educational level, should inform selectors' forecasts of which formats of material the public might prefer, which subjects might be of interest, and what quantities of materials—both numbers of titles and multiple copies—should be purchased. Using both census data and in-house surveys, librarians can better understand their community and use that knowledge to shape collections that increase use.

**Material use.** Statistics on the use of materials are important in collection decision making. Materials that circulated well in the immediate past are likely to circulate well in the near future, so more of that material might be purchased; materials that didn't circulate well in the immediate past are not likely to do better and should not be purchased.

Circulation reports from automated systems should provide this information easily; however, many librarians now realize they cannot automatically produce the statistics they want because they were not programmed into their libraries' systems.

**Shelf allocations.** General observations should be made about shelf space relationships, e.g., how much space is devoted to fiction and how much to nonfiction? Does it match the intent of local policies? How is space divided among various subject groups? If materials in a certain subject area always seem to be out, buying more is a good decision. How much space is given to magazines and journals? How big are the record, CD, or video collections? Are records always in, and should they be replaced by tapes or CDs? Decisions on formats are as important as decisions on subjects.

**User views of the shelves.** Librarians should look at the shelves regularly, trying to see them as patrons do when they come to the library. If the shelves are cluttered with tattered, torn, dirty, outdated, or unpleasant looking materials, they are offputting. These materials are candidates for weeding, binding, or repair. Preservation decisions can be made only through an item-by-item examination.

Patrons tend to look mainly at eye level and a little above and below, so items on higher and lower shelves are easily overlooked. Moving materials around on the shelves can be very beneficial to their circulation. Dark corners are uninviting and materials shelved there are at a disadvantage. Lighting can be improved or materials can be shifted.

## Universal rules of thumb

Here are three universal rules of thumb for deciding how to proceed with a collection evaluation:

1. If you want to energize the library staff and make them feel part of the whole process of collection development, then it would be wise to use the whole staff or as many of them as possible to do the evaluation. However, doing it this way risks objectivity, time, and hidden costs, and some current services to patrons will have to be sacrificed.

2. If you want the most objective, unbiased, and nonpartisan view of the collection and a tight rein on costs, then it is wise to contract with outside consultants for the evaluation. But in doing so you probably will sacrifice the potential knowledge gained from the evaluation process, which will leave with the consultants who have no ongoing ties to the library or its community.

---

### Public libraries express

According to a recent report, Federal Express delivered 1.7 million packages per day in 1993.

Based on recent National Center for Education Statistics reports, it may be estimated that U.S. public libraries circulated 4.4 million books and other materials per day in 1993. That is more than two and a half times the daily number of Federal Express deliveries.

*Source: Fast Facts: Recent Statistics from the Library Research Service*
(Library Research Service, Colorado State Library), no. 78 (March 14, 1994).
Reprinted with permission.

3. If you want to involve the staff and keep feedback in the collection development loop, yet insure more objectivity, the wisest choice (if you can afford the investment) is to have outside consultants supervise the library's staff in performing the evaluation.

The right decisions are the cement that ties a collection of materials together and turns it into a library. Information is the key to those decisions.

*Source:* Sheila S. Intner and Elizabeth Futas, "Evaluating Public Library Collections: Why Do It, and How to Use the Results," *American Libraries* 25 (May 1994): 410–12.

# No food, no drink, no noise

### by Elaine Clement and Patricia A. Scott

AS IS PROBABLY THE CASE with most other academic libraries, the University Libraries at the Pennsylvania State University are confronted with problems generated by food, drink, and noise. Patrons bring to the library many different behavior patterns. Students who have come from high schools where the library was also the cafeteria or the detention hall are often not in the habit of leaving food or drinks and conversations outside the building. Our expectations of what their behavior should be is often at odds with reality.

At the University Park Campus, concerns voiced by staff and faculty led to the formation of a group to investigate the problem and suggest solutions. The group was made up of faculty and staff from public service areas in rare books, documents/maps, general reference, periodicals, the science branch libraries, and the undergraduate library (a 24-hour facility).

## The campaign

In January of 1991 the group was convened by the assistant to the dean for public information. As participants traded stories about noise levels in quiet study areas and pizza deliveries made to study carrels, it became apparent that all libraries were plagued by the same problems in varying degrees. A discussion of how staff in each of the branch libraries at University Park dealt with these problems revealed a lack of consistency among all the areas. Many staff were reluctant to confront student offenders without a university-endorsed code of conduct for the libraries. Staff members also felt uncomfortable about approaching coworkers who carry food and drink through the library during breaks or lunch.

At the end of our first meeting we had reached two decisions: (1) we needed a written code of conduct for patrons and staff to follow, and (2) we needed to make an organized and concerted effort to publicize it. Thus was born our "campaign" to curb food, drink, and noise problems in the libraries.

Group opinion varied widely on what standards we should adopt and how they should be enforced. Despite this, during spring 1991 the group was able to reach consensus and drafted a food and noise policy. We began by searching library literature for articles about similar campaigns and examined the policies found in ARL/OMS's SPEC Kit Number 144, *Building Use Policies.* We incorporated parts of these policies into our recommendations, adapting them to suit the needs of our institution.

## Getting students involved

The group decided that eye-catching posters would be an effective way to educate students about the damage caused by the presence of food and drink and the disruptive effects of noise. We enlisted the help of a member of the graphic arts faculty, who allowed some of his students to use our campaign as a senior project. This idea of students designing for students appealed to the group because we felt it would have a greater impact on our primary audience.

The students designed posters, brochures, bookmarks, and buttons that used four graphics. Two graphics were aimed at noise control: one showed a picture of a lock and chain with the text "Laughing Learners Lock Your Lips!"; the other showed a clamp with the words "Clamorous Collegians Clamp Your Chops!" Both contained the tag line "Don't make noise in the library." Two graphics targeted food and drink problems. One showed a cockroach with the text "Ravenous Roaches Ravage Rootbeer and Rare Books!" The other showed a silverfish with the text "Salivating Silverfish Savor Sandwiches in the Stacks!" Each contained the line "Don't eat or drink in the library."

In summer 1991, after presenting mock-ups of the posters at a session for library faculty and staff, the final draft of the "Food, Drink and Noise Policy" was submitted to the Libraries Academic Council.

In August, group members distributed posters and brochures to public service areas. The brochure stated the University Libraries' mission; explained how food, drink, and noise hinder our efforts; and gave costs for replacing damaged materials in a way which would be meaningful to students. For example, the money needed to repair five damaged library books is equivalent to the cost of twelve issues of *Billboard*, or 45 issues of *Rolling Stone*, or 60 issues of the *Wall Street Journal*.

## Printed publicity

During fall 1991, the group conducted a publicity campaign to acquaint users and staff with the policy. Articles appeared in the student newspaper, the student orientation guide, and in the university faculty and staff newsletter.

Bookmarks and buttons were not distributed to public service desks until January 1992. An exhibit called "Trashing the Libraries: The Preservation Problem" was mounted from late August through November in display cases in the lobby of the main library. The exhibit showed trash collected from wastebaskets in public service areas. From October 17 to October 24 a modular panel exhibit from the Commission on Preservation and Access was installed in the public catalog room. By phasing in promotional materials we hoped to maintain interest in the campaign.

In spring 1993, the group reconvened to assess the campaign's impact. All agreed that the posters and other materials had helped to improve the situation, but in varying degrees. The undergraduate library had the most success in reducing food/drink/ noise incidents, largely due to the vigilance of its staff. All group members agreed that having a brochure to explain our policy made confronting offenders easier and more positive.

Some areas of the library reported little or no reduction in food, drink, and noise problems. As expected, student cooperation has been harder to achieve in areas with large study tables or where few staff members are visible.

Two years after its inception, the "University Libraries Code of Conduct" has been approved. Training for faculty and staff on what the code means and how staff will be expected to handle food, drink and noise problems was conducted in the summer of 1993.

The No Food, No Drink, No Noise Group mounted a campaign to heighten awareness of problems in the library. Our goal was to try to alleviate the problems through humor and nonconfrontational means. In general, the group feels that the campaign was a success. A policy containing many specific recommendations for behavior was written and some of the suggestions were incorporated into a broad "University Libraries Code of Conduct," which is now in place. A marketing plan was devised to phase in each aspect of the campaign at timed intervals. Some of our ideas for publicizing our policy had to be dropped due to lack of funds (i.e., plastic bags printed with our logo), while others could not be implemented until a written code of conduct was approved (i.e., asking librarians to talk to students about the policy in orientation meetings and bibliographic instruction sessions).

The graphic designs we used worked very well for brochures, bookmarks, and buttons, but were not effective for communicating our message on posters. The messages "Don't eat or drink in the library" and "Don't make noise in the library" appeared in small print at the bottom of the posters. The small print was intended to provoke interest and encourage the viewer to take a closer look. One reason that people were not drawn to read the small print may have been because of the height at which many posters had to be hung.

### Recommendations

The group recommends the following actions to others who want to institute a similar campaign in their library:

1. Have a code of conduct in place before you begin the campaign. Both patrons and employees must know what is expected of them.
2. Examine closely the kinds of problems most common in your library and where they occur.
3. Devise a plan to sell your campaign. Calculate your costs and explore free sources of assistance. Check to see if a class can help.
4. Time the campaign so that things are in place at the beginning of the fall semester.
5. Be prepared to rethink your position on food, drink, and noise issues. Achieving group consensus requires some compromise.
6. Gain administrative and staff commitment to the campaign. Signs alone won't change behavior.

*Source:* Elaine Clement and Patricia A. Scott, "No Food, No Drink, No Noise," *College & Research Libraries News* 55 (February 1994): 81–83. Bookmarks by Penn State Design Practicum.

Interlibrary Loan

# National interlibrary loan code for the United States

INTERLIBRARY LOAN IS ESSENTIAL to the vitality of libraries of all types and sizes and is a means by which a wider range of materials can be made available to users. In the interests of providing quality service, libraries have an obligation to obtain materials to meet the informational needs of users when local resources do not meet those needs.

Interlibrary Loan has been described as an adjunct to, not a substitute for, collection development in individual libraries. Changes in the last decade have brought increasing availability of materials in alternative formats, an abundance of verification and location information, and a shift in the very nature of interlibrary cooperation. Interlibrary borrowing is an integral element of collection development for all libraries, not an ancillary option.

The effectiveness of a national resource sharing system depends upon the responsible distribution of borrowing and lending. Libraries of all types and sizes should be willing to share their resources liberally so that a relatively few libraries are not overburdened. Libraries must be willing to lend if they wish to borrow.

This code is designed to regulate lending and borrowing relations between libraries. It is not the intent of this code to prescribe the nature of interlibrary cooperation within formally established networks and consortia, or to regulate the purchase of materials from document suppliers. However, this Code may be used as a model for development of state, regional, or local interlibrary loan codes.

This code provides general guidelines for the requesting and supplying of materials between libraries.

**Definition.** Interlibrary loan is the process by which a library requests materials from, or supplies materials to, another library.

**Purpose.** The purpose of interlibrary loan as defined by this code is to obtain, upon request of a library user, materials not available in the user's local library.

**Scope.** Interlibrary loan is a mutual relationship and libraries should be willing to supply materials as freely as they request materials. Any materials, regardless of format, may be requested from another library. The supplying library determines whether the material can be provided.

**Responsibilities of the requesting library.** The requesting library:

- should establish and maintain an interlibrary loan policy for its borrowers and make it available;
- should process requests in a timely fashion;
- should identify libraries that own and might provide the requested materials;
- should check the policies of potential suppliers for special instructions, restrictions, and information on charges prior to sending a request;
- is responsible for all authorized charges imposed by the supplying library;
- should send requests for materials for which locations cannot be identified to libraries that might provide the requested materials and be accompanied by the statement "cannot locate"—the original source of the reference should be cited or a copy of the citation provided;
- should avoid sending the burden of its requests to a few libraries. Major resource libraries should be used as a last resort;
- should transmit all interlibrary loan requests in standard bibliographic format in accordance with the protocols of the electronic network or transmission system used (in the absence of an electronically generated form, the American Library Association Interlibrary Loan request form should be used);
- must ensure compliance with U.S. copyright law and its accompanying guidelines; copyright compliance must be determined for each copy request before it is transmitted, and a copyright compliance statement must be included on each copy request; copyright files should be maintained as directed in the CONTU Guidelines;
- is responsible for borrowed materials from the time they leave the supplying library until they have been returned and received by the

supplying library; if damage or loss occurs, the requesting library is responsible for compensation or replacement, in accordance with the preference of the supplying library;

- is responsible for honoring due dates and enforcing all use restrictions specified by the supplying library;
- should request a renewal before the item is due; if the supplying library does not respond, the requesting library may assume that the renewal has been granted for the same length of time as the original loan;
- should return materials by the due date and respond immediately if the item has been recalled by the supplying library;
- should package materials to prevent damage in shipping, and comply with special instructions stated by the supplying library;
- is responsible for following the provisions of this code; continued disregard for any provision may be reason for suspension of borrowing privileges by a supplying library.

**Responsibilities of the supplying library.** The supplying library:

- should establish and maintain an interlibrary loan policy, make it available in paper and/or electronic format, and provide it upon request;
- should process requests within the timeline established by the electronic network; requests not transmitted electronically should be handled in a similar time frame;
- should include a copy of the original request, or information sufficient to identify the request, with each item;
- should state any conditions and/or restrictions on use of the materials lent and specify any special return packaging or shipping requirements;
- should state the due date or duration of the loan on the request form or on the material;
- should package the items to prevent damage in shipping;
- should notify the requesting library promptly when unable to fill a request, and if possible, state the reason the request cannot be filled;
- should respond promptly to requests for renewals; if the supplying library does not respond, the borrowing library may assume that the renewal has been granted for the same length as the original loan period;
- may recall materials at any time;
- may suspend service to any requesting library which fails to comply with the provisions of this code.

*Source:* "National Interlibrary Loan Code for the United States," *RQ* 33, no.4 (Summer 1994): 477–79.

---

### ILL costs

The major cost of interlibrary loan operations is for staff; less than one-fourth of the total goes to all other elements—communications, photocopying, supplies, equipment, delivery, etc.

More than half of all filled interlibrary loan transactions are done through photocopies rather than transmitting the original item.

The average cost for a completed interlibrary loan transaction (incurred by both the lender and the borrower) is close to $30—nearly $19 for the requester and $11 for the lender.

*Source:* Marilyn M. Roche, *ARL/RLG Interlibrary Loan Cost Study* (Washington, D.C.: Association of Research Libraries, 1993). 64p. Reprinted with permission.

# Loaning rare and unique materials

THESE GUIDELINES ARE INTENDED for use by libraries, museums, public archives, historical agencies, and other cultural repositories in order to facilitate the interinstitutional loan for research use of special collections, including books, manuscripts, archives, and graphics.

Basic assumptions underlying these guidelines are:

1. Interinstitutional loan from special collections for research use is strongly encouraged but must be conducted in a manner that ensures responsible care and effectively safeguards items from loss or damage.
2. The decision to lend an item rests with the individual exercising curatorial responsibility for that item. Such decisions should reflect an item-by-item consideration rather than broad categorical responses.
3. It is not expected that items of significant rarity or monetary value or items in fragile condition will normally be lent for research purposes.
4. Although personal familiarity and/or direct communications with curatorial staff at other institutions can facilitate the lending process, the loan of materials should not depend solely on personal contacts but should rest on well-defined interinstitutional commitments.
5. A borrowing institution must meet significant criteria in order to provide appropriate conditions for housing and use of rare and unique materials.

## Responsibilities of borrowing institutions

**Institutional prerequisites for borrowing.** The borrowing institution must: provide a secure reading room under constant surveillance to ensure the safety of the materials during use; have a special collections program, including staff assigned to and trained in the care and handling of special collections; provide secure storage for borrowed items during the loan period; provide storage under environmental conditions that meet accepted standards for housing special collections.

**Guidelines for initiating a loan request.** Requests for the loan of materials from noncirculating special collections must indicate that the borrowing institution meets the institutional criteria specified above and that the borrowing institution subscribes to the principles expressed in these guidelines.

Loan requests should normally be routed through the respective interlibrary lending (ILL) departments.

Every effort should be made to locate requested material in a general collection before submitting a request to a special collection of noncirculating materials. When a circulating copy cannot be located, that fact should be noted when requesting the item from a noncirculating collection.

Patrons should be encouraged to travel to other institutions for on-site access when their research involves long-term use or large quantities of material, or when distance presents no extraordinary hardship for them.

The borrowing institution should describe the requested material fully. Standard bibliographic sources should be used to verify each request. When a request cannot be verified in these sources, full information regarding the original source of citation should be submitted.

In addition to full bibliographic description, it is desirable that requests include RLIN, OCLC, or other bibliographic utility record identification number and the call number for each item, and, whenever possible, requests should include the name of the special collection or department from which the item is being requested.

The request should indicate whether or not another edition, version, or form of material (photocopy, microform, or photograph) can be substituted for the one specified.

**Guidelines for handling materials on loan.** No copies of borrowed materials should be made without the explicit permission of the lending institution.

If copying is permitted by the lending institution, it should be done by special collections staff at the borrowing institution and in compliance with U.S. copyright law. The borrowing institution may, however, decline to make copies in any case and refer the patron directly to the lending institution to negotiate arrangements for copying.

The borrowing institution must comply with the loan period established by the lending institution. Unless otherwise specified by the lending institution, the loan period will be thirty days. Renewal of a loan should only be requested under unusual circumstance, and renewal requests should be submitted in a timely fashion.

The borrowing institution must abide by and administer any special conditions governing the handling and use of borrowed materials as specified by the lending institution.

If a borrowing institution fails to comply with the conditions of a loan, including proper care and packaging of borrowed items, that institution can expect that future requests to borrow special collections materials will be denied.

## Responsibilities of lending institutions

Institutions receiving requests should be as generous as possible, consonant with their responsibilities both to preserve and to make accessible to their on-site user community the materials in their care.

Requests should be considered on a case-by-case basis by the individual with curatorial responsibility for the requested material.

Response to a request for the loan of special collections materials should be made within five working days.

It is the responsibility of the lending institution to indicate any special conditions governing the use of loaned materials, clearly stating any restrictions or limitations on research use, citation, publication, or other forms of dissemination.

Lending institutions reserve the right to limit the volume of material lent and the loan period. The normal loan period for special collections is thirty days.

If it is determined that a request can best be fulfilled by photocopying, lending institutions are expected to provide photocopies at a cost comparable to the standard rate within the lending institution.

Unless the lending institution so stipulates, it will not be necessary for the borrowing institution to return photocopies from special collections. If the lending institution does wish the return of photocopies, the copies should be clearly marked as loans.

Refusals either to lend or copy a requested item should include a specific reason (fragile paper, tight binding, too large to ship safely, etc.). That an item is part of a special collection is not a sufficient reason.

It is assumed that the lending institution will lend rare material at a cost comparable to the standard ILL fee charged by that institution for the loan of general library material. If the costs of shipping and insurance exceed the ILL fee, the lending institution may require additional payment. Before the material is sent, however, the lending institution must notify the borrowing institution of any additional charges and secure the borrowing institution's agreement to pay prior to sending the material.

## Liability and transport for borrowed materials

The safety of borrowed materials is the responsibility of the borrowing institution from the time the material leaves the lending institution until it is returned to the lending institution.

The lending institution is responsible for packing the borrowed material so as to ensure its return in the condition in which it was sent. The borrowing institution is responsible for returning the material in the same condition as received, using the same, or equivalent, packing material.

If damage or loss occurs at any time after the material leaves the lending institution, the borrowing institution must meet all costs of repair, replacement, or appropriate compensation, in accordance with the preference of the lending institution.

The lending institution has the option of specifying alternative methods of delivery. These methods may include a different system of transportation, insurance, and special wrapping instructions. The borrowing institution can specify that the material be delivered directly to its special collections department. The lending institution can specify that the material be returned directly to the special collections department.

If alternative methods are to be employed, delivery specifications must be communicated to the borrowing institution, which must agree to return the material in the manner specified.

Verification of transfer and delivery must be made through the respective ILL department, regardless of method of delivery.

The borrowing institution will normally assume the costs of all fees associated with the loan.

*Source: Guidelines for the Loan of Rare and Unique Materials*
(Chicago: ALA Association of College and Research Libraries, 1993).

# Selecting a preservation photocopy machine

*by Dorothy W. Wright*

IN-HOUSE PRESERVATION PHOTOCOPYING is a common feature of library preservation programs today. Increasingly, librarians are relying on preservation photocopies to replace brittle books in circulating collections, particularly those that are highly used or of local interest. Selecting copying equipment that insures the permanence and durability of photocopied images is a critical aspect of any in-house preservation photocopy operation. Suitability for production copying is another important consideration. A variety of photocopiers on the market today are capable of producing archival quality copies. Their widely varying features and costs can make a purchasing decision very difficult.

With funding from a U.S. Department of Education Title II-C grant, the A. R. Mann Library at Cornell University began a preservation photocopy program in 1991 to reformat brittle books in Cornell's Entomology Library collection. The process we undertook and the criteria we used to select a photocopy machine are described.

## Archival quality and image adherence

For archival quality photocopies it is important not only that the paper used for copying adhere to standards of permanence and durability but also that the stability of the toner, the carrier, and the fusing process of the photocopier be considered. A Government Printing Office report on archival xerographic copying summarized studies on the materials used in archival copying and factors that influence the fix quality of toner to paper (Sylvia S. Y. Subt and John G. Koloski, *Archival Xerographic Copying*, GPO Jacket no. 484-988 Final Report, August 25, 1987). Archivability was based upon the individual stabilities of the paper and toner and on the initial strength of the bond between these materials. Time, temperature, and pressure were identified as the important parameters in hot roll fusing.

The ability to evaluate the fusing property of toner to paper is essential to determining the suitability of a copier for preservation copying purposes. Numerous laboratory tests have been devised to evaluate the fix quality of toner to paper. A simple on-site pass or fail "Tape Pull Test" has been developed that correlates very well with the results of the laboratory abrasion test, ASTM D3458, part 24, "Retention of Print Contrast after Abrasion" for determining adhesion of the image onto the paper.

For this simple procedure, a 3–4" strip of 3M #240 drafting tape is placed on a photocopy of a test target (a black ring, a black rectangle, and a 1" black strip—the test target may be obtained from the Special Media Preservation Branch, National Archives, Washington, DC 20408) covering as much of the black ring as possible. The tape is rubbed 5–6 times with four fingers. The tape strip is peeled off the paper and the adhesive side of the tape examined. If the curved image of the test pattern is detected (i.e., black toner on the adhesive), the copier fails the test and cannot be considered for archival photocopying. This test was invaluable in determining the suitability of copiers for preservation purposes.

## Selection process

We designated a Photocopy Selection Committee (composed of the preservation librarian, preservation technician, and several other library staff members) to evaluate and select our preservation copier. We began by developing a list of required and desirable specifications for the copier. The primary requirement for all preservation copy machines was consistently passing the Tape Pull Test. Other required specifications included:

- minimum copying capacity of 50,000 copies per month;
- duplexing capability;
- a maximum five-second first copy speed (very important since all preservation photocopies are essentially first copies);
- accurate registration of the photocopied image on each side of a duplexed page (top to bottom and side to side);
- excellent contrast and clarity of photocopied images;
- excellent local service; and
- ease of use.

Other desirable features included:

- paper size to 11" x 17" (for copying oversized books and foldouts);
- photo or halftone mode; and
- edge copier for copying bound books.

In addition, we looked at warm-up time, copies per minute, maximum and minimum copy size, paper cassette capacity, toner type, reduction and enlargement range, margin shift, margin erase, and estimated drum, toner, and developer life and costs. Purchase price was also an important consideration since we had a limited amount of money budgeted for the copier.

We found it helpful to solicit advice from librarians managing in-house photocopy operations and from commercial preservation photocopy vendors to find out what machines were used and why. Although no consensus was expressed among those we spoke with as to the ideal preservation photocopier, it was useful to learn what type of copiers others were using, their level of satisfaction, and features deemed important. Consistently passing the tape pull test, copy quality, cost, service, first copy speed, volume of work, and features such as a photo mode were most frequently mentioned as important criteria to consider.

## Vendors

Local photocopy vendors supplied us with sales brochures for brands which met our initial list of specifications. We reviewed the sales literature and independent evaluations (e.g., *Library Technology Reports*) for copiers we were initially interested in. After a close evaluation of the literature and discussion with each vendor, we narrowed our search to seven models. We visited locations on campus that had these models and, either alone or with the salesperson, tested each copier's archival quality with the tape pull test, copied sample pages from a brittle book to determine copy quality and ease of use, and assessed the suitability of each machine for our purposes. In addition to testing the machines, we contacted the references supplied by each vendor. The references were important in determining the reliability of the machine and the vendor's service reputation.

## Testing the machines

We found it extremely useful to test the copiers we were considering under actual working conditions. We arranged to have three machines loaned to us for one-week trial periods. During each one-week trial, four members of the Preservation Unit staff copied brittle volumes on a daily basis. This allowed us to get an accurate sense of each machine's suitability for preservation photocopying. An evaluation form was developed to objectively compare each copier. We looked at the following factors:

1. **Tape pull test.** Each copier was tested daily and had to consistently pass the tape pull test.
2. **Photocopy set-up.** We were interested in comparing how easy it was to set up unique templates for each book copied (ease can vary depending on the platen's shape, size, and orientation); whether, when using a template, shadows appeared on the copies and copying workflow (again, dependent on the size, shape, and orientation of the copier and platen). We were also concerned about the weight of the copier lid which is opened and closed repeatedly during the copying process and could become fatiguing over time. We were interested in knowing whether it was possible to move the copier lid back 45° out of the way and to use a lightweight cardboard cover instead.
3. **Copy quality.** We wanted to compare the contrast and clarity of the

copies on the text, line drawings, illustrations, and photographs. Since we would be copying many scientific illustrations and drawings, this was a crucial consideration. The range of contrast settings is very important in ensuring the clearest copy possible, particularly with illustrated materials.

4. **Registration.** Registration is affected by the route the paper takes as it passes through the machine in the duplex mode. Consistently accurate registration is extremely important in producing exact facsimiles.

5. **Duplexing speed.** We were interested in how quickly the machine could copy both sides of the paper.

6. **Copier controls.** We wanted copier controls displayed in a clear, obvious, easy-to-use manner. In addition, placement of the controls was another important consideration. We found that the copier controls on some machines would inadvertently and repeatedly be hit in setting up the template and using the machine.

7. **Environmental variables.** This includes factors such as the heat and noise generated by the machine, and the height, size, and physical aspects that affect comfort in using the copier for prolonged periods.

8. **Warm-up time and speed.** How quickly the machine warmed up after turning it on and first copy speed were also considered.

9. **Any other comments.** Anything not covered by the above categories or additional notes were included at the end.

## Evaluating and choosing

Each factor was evaluated on a scale of 1–5 (1=lowest, 5=highest) with a total of 110 points possible. The four staff members testing the machines completed an evaluation form for each copier. At the end of the test period the results were averaged for each copier. In addition to the copier evaluations, we also considered price, service agreement, and references in our final decision. Of the three copiers we tested (Minolta 5400, Savin 9710, and Konica 4045), we chose the Konica copier with an average score of 96.6 out of 110 possible points. It should be noted, however, that given changing xerographic technology and newer copier models on the market, we might choose a different copier if we were to repeat this exercise today.

The copier met all our required and desirable features except that it did not have a photo mode. Having seen the photo mode on other machines, we did not consider this to be a serious drawback. The Konica does a satisfactory job of copying photographs and halftone illustrations. The cost of the machine and the service agreement were very reasonable. In addition to a five-year, one-million copy warranty, the dealer also agreed to put in writing as part of our service contract that the machine would be repaired or replaced if it ever failed to pass the tape pull test. Other vendors we spoke to would not agree to this added stipulation in the service contract. For archival copying, this is an extremely important consideration and every effort should be made to include this provision in your maintenance agreement.

## Conclusion

We have found that an excellent service agreement and reliable repair technicians are among the most important factors to a successful preservation photocopying program. To maintain optimal copy quality, the machine must be serviced more frequently than a regular office copier. In addition, preservation photocopying with repeated, individual, duplexed copies seems to cause more wear and tear on a copier than the single or multiple copies typically made in general office copying. When selecting a preservation copier, be sure to look carefully at the manufacturer's claim of minimum monthly copying capacity to accurately gauge the copier's durability over time for your projected volume of copying.

Although it is impossible to fully anticipate the dependability and durability of any copier you purchase, there are many important factors to consider when evaluating copiers for a preservation photocopy program. Once the archival quality of the copier is established, a careful evaluation (including an in-house trial period) of copy quality, registration, speed, cost, service, monthly copying capacity, and other features of several copiers can be undertaken using an evaluation form to compare each. Using references to ascertain the reliability of the product and service reputation of the dealer is also very important. This systematic, comparative approach to preservation photocopier selection was invaluable in determining the most suitable machine.

*Source:* Dorothy W. Wright, "Selecting a Preservation Photocopy Machine," *College & Research Libraries News* 55 (January 1994): 14–18.

# Choosing a mass deacidification process

*by Astrid-Christiane Brandt*

5

GREAT HOPES HAVE BEEN PLACED in finding an effective mass deacidification method because of the vast number of books and documents requiring treatment. However, there is no miracle solution that will wipe away the traces of time and prevent aging. The concept underlying Lucas Cranach's painting *The Fount of Eternal Youth* is purely mythical in nature.

Conservation is a very difficult task because of the complexity of the phenomena involved in the self-destruction of papers.

According to the criteria laid down by researchers and curators, a mass deacidification process—whether or not it is combined with a strengthening process—should ideally meet the following requirements that have been summarized by Peter Sparks, in *Technical Considerations in Choosing Mass Deacidification Processes* (Washington, D.C.: Commission on Preservation and Access, May 1990):

1. Unbinding the book should not be necessary.
2. The process must be applicable to all grades of paper.
3. The process must be compatible with all materials used in the book, and must not call for preselection.
4. The appearance of the book or document treated must not be changed.
5. All the acids in the paper must be neutralized completely and durably.
6. The alkaline reserve must be equivalent to the incorporation of 2% of calcium carbonate in the paper.
7. The distribution of pH and alkaline reserve must be homogeneous inside the book.
8. The pH of the paper must be between 7 and 8.5 to prevent acid and alkaline hydrolysis of the paper or inks.
9. The useful lifetime of the paper must be shown by accelerated aging tests to have increased by at least 5 times.
10. The chemicals used must not be dangerous for process operators, the future user of the book, or the environment.
11. The chemicals used must be and remain totally innocuous at all times for all constituents of the book.
12. The action of the chemicals used must be reversible and must remain so.

Unfortunately, none of the mass processes currently available meets all these criteria.

There are various unknowns relating to the long-term effectiveness of the treatment: it is feared that reacidification of the paper may occur. To prevent this, an alkaline reserve is deposited in most processes. The durability of the treatment essentially depends on the stability of the reserve in the long term. Perhaps there has been a failure to analyze in depth the acids and other harmful substances (peroxidable substances) in paper. If it is not possible to extract the acidity from paper totally, this would mean that it exists in macromolecular form; in other words, it is definitively fixed on the cellulose. This would explain why it is difficult to prevent the process of degradation.

As shown earlier in the report, the chemical degradation of paper is largely attributable to a synergy between the processes of hydrolysis and oxidation. The combined influence of the two processes complicates the analysis of the effect of deacidification treatment.

It is difficult to assess the various processes described, because there is a lack of significant and comparable data on the effect of each type of treatment. Test conditions for the same process are not always reproducible, as studies have often been carried out over a period of years on plant units that evolve from the prototype to the pilot stage.

Several comparative studies are now in progress to analyze the physico-chemical behavior of papers treated in the various pilot plants currently operating. Studies of this type are being conducted in Germany by the Battelle Institute (commissioned by the Deutsche Bibliothek). In the United States, the Library of Congress—which hopes to treat a significant proportion of its collections—has requested the Atlanta Institute of Paper Science and Technology to analyze papers treated in various pilot plants. In Canada, the Canadian Conservation Institute (CCI) is studying papers and books treated by the Wei T'o, Lithco-FMC and Akzo processes. Other analyses are in progress at the Institut Royal du Patrimoine Artistique (IRPA) in Belgium. In France, the Centre de Recherches sur la Conservation des Documents Graphiques is continuing to assess the impact of air pollution on deacidified papers.

Although the results of the studies will not be available for some time, a few observations may still be made.

1. **There is no treatment that can be applied to all types of paper and is compatible with all the constituents of the book.** Paper is in fact a heterogeneous and diversified material. As a result, paper behaves differently during treatment according to its nature and aging. This is particularly clear in the case of paper-strengthening treatment. The inventors of the Lithco and British Library processes plainly admit this fact.

Few studies have been made of the behavior of the other materials used in making books or documents (inks, leathers, textiles, adhesives), and most of the studies available go no further than a visual assessment. The inventors of the Wei T'o process (and its French variant) and of the British Library process, in fact indicate that some materials are incompatible with the treatment.

2. **Doubts remain about the homogeneity and effectiveness of some treatments.** Processes involving solvent-phase treatment often face problems relating to the penetration of reagents inside the book. This results in a heterogeneous distribution of pH and alkaline reserve, which can cause incomplete neutralization.

These problems are accentuated by the heterogeneous nature of paper and the other constituents of the book, and by the degree of aging of the materials.

The processes involving gas-phase treatment seem to promote treatment homogeneity. However there are doubts as to the effectiveness of such gas-phase treatments, and it is also thought they may make the paper more fragile. The Booksaver process, for example, does not seem to achieve its aims. The treated papers rapidly become acid again, as the alkaline reserve is not stable in the long term. In Akzo's DEZ process, the alkaline reserve is suspected of degrading the paper by promoting photochemical reactions.

3. **As for the solvent-phase processes, the problem of finding substitutes for chlorofluorocarbons (CFC) has not been solved.** Those responsible for developing the various processes promise that their plants will also operate with CFC substitutes when such substances are available. However the behavior of the substitutes will not be identical to that of the CFC currently used. As a result, studies aimed at adapting the process to the substitutes will be necessary at some later stage.

4. **A deacidification process combined with satisfactory strengthening of already fragile old papers is not yet available.** The Lithco process which combines paper deacidification and strengthening gives good results with recent papers. However, it is much less successful in improving the characteristics of aged papers. The electrostatic bonds ("hydrogen bridge") are probably not strong enough to effectively strengthen paper that is already fragile.

The process proposed by the British Library would seem to be more successful in strengthening fragile papers, as it forms a veritable composite between the polymer and the paper. The corollary of this is that the treatment is irreversible; but is there any point in reversibility if the paper is too fragile to withstand operations to make the treatment reversible? The bonds created are chemical, and cannot be broken without the use of a great deal of energy. However the British Library indicates that ease of treatment depends on the type of paper and the degree of alteration. Highly degraded papers made from mechanical pulp are the most difficult to treat.

5. **It is impossible to establish with any degree of precision the costs and capacities of a large-scale plant.** The proposed deacidification processes are still at the prototype or pilot stage. The annual treatment capacities planned vary considerably from one treatment to another (from a few dozen to several hundred thousand books). Some processes are only economically viable if their capacity is considerable, for example Akzo's DEZ process (for which a minimum of 1 million books/year is needed). In 1991, treatment cost quotations vary from 5 to 10 U.S. dollars per book, depending on services provided.

Clearly, therefore, the information currently available is not comprehensive enough to enable a rational choice to be made between the various processes available.

In the United States the Library of Congress has decided to delay a decision to subcontract the mass deacidification of its books and documents to Akzo, Lithco-FMC or Wei T'o. The report commissioned by the Library of Congress indicates that none of these three tested processes is satisfactory.

The current trend is towards developing a process combining paper deacidification and strengthening. Many books can no longer be handled at all without risking a loss of substance. The Battelle Institute is aiming ultimately at adding a strengthening action to the methoxy methyl magnesium carbonate process. The Bibliothèque de France is also pursuing the same path, and has entered into a joint research and development project with USSI-Ingénierie and Société Française Hoechst. The objective of the project is to develop a new book-impregnation process that deacidifies and strengthens the paper of a book or document in a single operation.

While awaiting more detailed data, or the development of new and more effective processes, libraries themselves must devote considerable thought to the ways in which the new technology can be applied.

1. **Libraries must precisely assess their deacidification needs.** The assessment must consist of the identification and quantification (by sampling) of those books and documents which can no longer be circulated and which must be treated as a matter of urgency.

Faced with the difficulties of effectively treating books which have already deteriorated considerably, some organizations are considering the preventive treatment of collections. In the United States, libraries tend to divide the problem into two parts: a preventive treatment (deacidification) is used for newly received publications which are not printed on permanent paper, and a remedial treatment (deacidification and strengthening) for old books and documents which have already become fragile to a greater or lesser extent.

2. **Libraries must find technical solutions appropriate to the diversity of books and documents to be treated.** Appropriate conservation measures must be found, taking into account the nature of the document and the degree of deterioration. Deacidification must form part of a set of conservation measures aimed at ensuring the upkeep of the collections, and extending their useful lifetime as much as possible.

3. **Libraries must assess the impact of mass treatment of books and documents on the day-to-day management of collections.** Experience gained from the operation of pilot plants over a number of years, such as the Public Archives in Canada and the Bibliothèque Nationale in France, has shown that the implementation of a major deacidification program has a significant effect on the day-to-day running of the library. Each curator must therefore assess the impact by analyzing the particular situation of the library. There can be marked differences between the situations faced by a national library, and those faced by a university or municipal library.

4. **Libraries must decide which treatment infrastructure best meets their particular needs.** Several types of infrastructure are suitable, depending on the case in hand: a centralized plant enabling a major library, or a group of libraries, to treat its collections; or a small or average-sized decentralized treatment unit in each library.

Another question is that of subcontracting treatment either within or outside the library. Some processes require the sending of collections to a unit outside the library (Akzo, Booksaver, British Library, Lithco). Others could be installed inside the library, provided that rooms are available (methoxy magnesium methyl carbonate, Bookkeeper).

5. **Libraries must assess their financial requirements in order to develop a long-term strategy.** The mass deacidification of all books and documents that need it will take a long time to implement, and will call for significant financial resources.

It is important to ensure that such conservation programs are coherent, not only from a scientific but also from a financial viewpoint. Curators bear a heavy responsibility in this area, and must ensure that these matters are conducted with great clearness of vision.

**Akzo Chemicals Inc.,** Performance Chemicals Department, 300 South Riverside Plaza, Chicago, IL 60606.

**Archival Aids Ltd.,** Unit 29, Trent Lane Industrial Estate, Castle Donington, Derby DE7 2NP, United Kingdom.

**Atlantis France,** 26 rue des Petits Champs, 75002 Paris, France.

**Battelle-Europe,** Battelle-Institut e.V., Am Römerhof 35, Postfach 900160, 6000 Frankfurt/Main 90, Germany.

**Book Preservation Associates (BPA),** 6 Self Boulevard, Carteret, NJ 07008.

**FMC Corporation,** Lithium Division, Highway 161, Box 795, Bessemer City, NC 28016.

**Mallet Ingénierie,** 2 rue Jean-Philippe Rameau, 91440 Bures-sur-Yvette, France.

**Preservation Technologies, Inc.,** Farmhill Road, Sewickley, PA 15143.

**Union Carbide Corporation,** Corporate Communications Department, 39 Old Ridgebury Road, Danbury, CT 06817-0001.

**Wei T'o Associates, Inc.,** P.O. Box 40, Matteson, IL 60443.

*Source:* Astrid-Christiane Brandt, *Mass Deacidification of Paper* (Paris: Bibliothèque Nationale, 1992). 92p. Reprinted with permission.

# The Emergency Response Plan

*by Dianne Lueder and Sally Webb*

PRIOR TO DEVELOPING A PLAN, the library should identify the types of emergencies that are most applicable to the specific geographic area and type of institution. The categories of emergency threat to the building include:

- fire damage;
- water damage;
- damage to the building superstructure caused by wind, hail, tornadoes, hurricanes, earthquakes, explosions, impacts from moving objects, or civil disorders;
- power failures and broken utility supply lines.

A different response system may be required by each type of emergency and for each institution. Keep in mind that no manual can answer every question. However, a calm review of the priorities for emergency response developed for the specific institution will aid tremendously in assuring an effective response in emergencies.

**Priority response analysis.** Which items should take priority when an emergency arises? The following questions will need to be answered as emergency procedures are outlined for each type of potential emergency:

5

- Is there threat to human life?
- Is there a threat to building and contents (building, collection, furnishings and equipment, legal and business records, the collection database, and vehicles housed in the building garage)? What is of most value in the institution? (Usually, human life comes first, but in some military or government applications this may not hold true.)
- What can be easily duplicated at minimum expense?
- What can be saved by prompt action to move it out of the building? Does the cost or importance of the item warrant the risk involved in moving it during a specific type of emergency?
- Is a duplicate copy of the item stored off-site?
- What can be saved by prompt and appropriate restoration efforts following the disaster?

Priority should be given to those items that are highly valued, those for which no duplicate is stored off-site and that cannot be duplicated easily, and those that cannot be moved off-site.

The following emergency action response plan outline contains five basic components that should be developed for each specific type of emergency threat.

1. Determine the type of emergency.
2. Decide which outside agency should be notified immediately.
3. Decide what immediate steps may be taken to minimize damage to the building and contents incorporating the established priority list.
4. Determine the source or cause of the emergency.
5. Determine the follow-up actions that should be implemented to protect the building and contents, to repair any areas or equipment that contributed to the emergency conditions, and to restore service.

An emergency plan is only useful if it is followed. Keep copies of the plan both at the library and at home. Remember, emergencies often occur when the building is unoccupied. In addition, certain emergency supplies should be kept on hand to facilitate quick action.

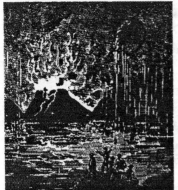

Different responses may be required depending on the type of emergency. Therefore, each type requires individual analysis.

## Fire damage

Fires in libraries can occur due to a number of causes including arson, poor housekeeping procedures, explosion, lightning strikes, faulty wiring, or ignition from a welder's torch during remodeling. Fire is particularly threatening because it often leaves only the charred remains of once cherished items, and efforts to put out the fire may have brought water damage.

When fire alarms sound it is essential to act promptly. Identify the location of the fire and notify the fire department immediately. Although automatic fire alarms connected to the sprinkler system will notify the fire department when a sprinkler is activated, call anyway in case the alarm malfunctions. Order the evacuation of the building. Try to extinguish the fire with a portable extinguisher if the fire is *localized and in the early stages*. Relinquish control to fire department personnel upon their arrival.

Disaster recovery following a fire can begin only after the building is declared safe to occupy. While waiting to initiate cleanup operations, the building should be made secure from vandals and damage by elements of the weather. Board up openings and lock doors before leaving the building unattended.

Contact the insurance agent to report the fire. Save any receipts for cleanup expenses and take photographs to document claims. An insurance inspector will be sent to estimate the extent of the damage.

Check the building for structural damage caused by the fire. The fire department may help with this assessment.

Before leaving the site, the fire department also will check to see that utilities are safe to use or are disconnected. If the fire department has disconnected the water, gas, or electricity, contact the utility company to check the building equipment and electric power, fuel, and water lines to make sure they are in proper working order, to make necessary repairs, and to reinstitute the utility service to the building.

Clear the building of extra moisture and smoke as quickly as possible. The insurance agent will recommend a fire-damage restoration firm for this process. Save any damaged goods until after an inventory is made because all damages are taken into account when developing the insurance claim. Do not contract for estimating, inventorying, or repair services without the knowledge of the insurance agent or adjuster. Gather eyewitness accounts, if any, and save these statements. File an incident report including staff descriptions of the emergency and steps taken to control its impact.

## Water damage

The overwhelming majority of all library disasters result in some water damage to the building, materials, and furnishings. Sometimes the water damage is the secondary result of another type of disaster. For example, in some geographic regions earthquakes can cause water pipes to strain and break, tornados and hurricanes bring strong winds and rain, and tidal waves accompany hurricanes. Fire-fighting efforts and in-house fire-suppression systems use water to put out fires, but this water also soaks the affected area of the building. Failure of building systems, such as water pipes, the roof, and drainage systems are often the causes of localized water damage. The recovery efforts required as the result of any water damage may be similar to those of flooding depending upon the amount of water involved.

**Plumbing emergencies.** A broken water pipe or a blocked drain can cause flooding. However, quick action can minimize the extent of flooding and prevent extensive damage.

If a leak is detected, shut off the water supply to the fixture or to the specific area of the building. The goal at this point is to quickly eliminate the water flowing through the system to the point of the leak. If in doubt as to where the leak originated, turn off the water main. Drain the remaining water already in the piping system by turning on the faucets on the main level of the building.

Try to find the source of the leak after the water is out of the system. If the leak is in the piping above a ceiling, water may have accumulated above ceiling tiles or plaster. Try to relieve the pressure from the accumulated water and control the release of the water so that it does not damage equipment and materials in the area of the leak by puncturing a small hole in the plaster or ceiling tile and draining the water into a bucket. Protect or move furnishings in the area before attempting this procedure and in the event the leak continues.

A frozen water pipe may be the source of flooding in colder climates. As soon as a break is detected, turn off the water main and make a temporary repair of the burst pipe to prevent any frozen water left in the pipe from flooding when it thaws. Call a plumber to make permanent repairs. Welding may be required.

**Roof leaks.** If evidence of a leak can be seen on the ceiling, first determine if it may be due to a broken water pipe. If there are no water pipes in the area, assume that it is due to a leak in the roofing system. Follow the procedure to relieve water accumulation as explained for plumbing emergencies, and install a temporary moisture barrier to prevent continued leaking. A plastic tarpaulin may be used for this purpose. A roofing consultant should be called in to determine the cause of the roof leak because the roofing system is complex, and the site where the leak is manifested may not be the source of the leak.

If water has covered any switches, wiring, outlets, or electrical components of equipment located in the flooded areas, turn off the power. Make sure that electrical elements are dry and clean of mud and debris before turning on the power again.

**Flooding.** Flooding due to weather or heavy runoff from melting snow or ice is usually preceded by some advance warning.

Use this time to move valuable papers, equipment, furnishings, and library materials to higher elevations and upper floors. Turn off all utilities at the main power switch and close the main gas valve in case an evacuation is necessary. If the flooding is the result of severe weather, board up windows or protect them with storm shutters or tape to prevent flying glass. Bring equipment or tools stored outside into the library or fasten them down securely (movable objects might be swept away in the flood waters).

After the flood, immediately

call the insurance agent who handles the flood insurance policy. If the library is in a flood prone area, investigate the purchase of flood insurance if it is not already in place.

Inspect the property. Prior to entering, check for structural damage to make sure the building is not in danger of collapsing. Turn off any outside gas lines at the meter. Then let the library air for several minutes to remove foul odors or escaping gas.

Upon entering the building, do not use open flame as a source of light since gas may be trapped inside the building; use a flashlight instead. Watch out for electrical shorts or live wires. Turn off the main power switch if this was not done before evacuation. Do not turn on any appliances or lights until an electrician has checked the system for shorts and until all wiring is clean and dry.

Cover any broken windows and holes in the roof or walls to prevent further water damage. Begin cleanup procedures immediately, if possible, to prevent any health hazards and to minimize the chance of permanent damage to furnishings and equipment. The insurance agent should be contacted promptly. A contractor who specializes in disaster cleanup and restoration may be called in at this point to ensure that proper procedures for salvaging equipment and furnishings are followed. Remember to document damage and to save all receipts relating to cleanup.

Flooded basements should be drained and cleaned as soon as possible. However, structural damage can occur if the water is pumped out too quickly. Water should be drained gradually over a period of several days if the depth of the flood water was more than several feet. Shovel out mud while it is still moist. Water heater and plumbing systems should be cleaned out and sterilized if water from the flood may have contaminated the water supply. Inspections and repair of the water heater and the heating system should be conducted by a trained heating service person. Air-intake systems, air ducts, the heat exchanger, and all components of the furnace or boiler system should be cleaned of any debris or mud deposited by the flood. Water for drinking should be tested for safety following a flood.

Stabilize the environment to prevent the growth of mold and the deterioration of carpeting and furnishings. In the first forty-eight hours, proper response is crucial in a water-damage scenario since this is the time it takes mold to grow if the temperature and humidity exceed recommended levels. Vent the building as promptly as possible by opening windows and circulating air with large fans. Try to maintain the internal building temperature at 65°F. and no more than 50 percent humidity to retard the growth of mold.

Clean mud and silt off furnishings using a stream of water from a hose. Towel dry them and then let them finish air-drying. Carpeting and tile left on flood-soaked floors may trap moisture on the underlying floor and cause damage and rotting. The carpet and tile will also rot if left in place on a wet floor. Attempts should be made to remove as much moisture as possible using a water vacuum. If the decision is made to remove the carpet or tile to allow the floor to dry, there is a chance that the carpeting will shrink or the tile will be damaged. Here again, an experienced disaster restoration professional may be able to avoid this type of damage during the cleanup process.

## Power-supply failures

Power failures are annoying and disruptive to library service. Furthermore, they often occur during the most intense heat waves or severe weather conditions. Planning in advance and taking some basic precautions in the event of a power failure can minimize the inconvenience and eliminate the potential for accidents.

When the power goes out, all appliances should be unplugged at the outlet. This will prevent possible damage or a blown fuse from a large power surge when the power resumes. Central heating systems and refrigerators can be left in the "on" position so that, when the power is restored, they begin to operate again. At least one light should be left on in each separate area of the building. That is, the switches that control lights left on when the building is closed should be in the "on" position. All other lights should be switched off.

If a power failure lasts longer than fifteen minutes, evacuation should be considered, especially if it occurs in the evening and it is dark outside. Emergency lights are designed to provide light only for fifteen minutes to a maximum of one hour. Power failure may also prevent HVAC systems from operating. Lack of heating, cooling, and ventilation for prolonged periods may lead to conditions unsuitable for human occupancy (for example, temperatures above 90°F. or below 55°F.).

Call the power company to report the power outage. When power is restored, remember to reset all timed controls for the lighting and HVAC systems.

## Gas leaks

A strong odor of gas will alert staff to a gas leak in or near the library. If a leak is suspected, call the gas company immediately to report it. Everyone should be alerted to the leak and evacuated from the building.

Anything with an open flame should be put out immediately if a gas leak is suspected, because a spark or open flame could cause an explosion. If gas can be smelled outside, follow the same precautions. A visual inspection that reveals dry soil or dead or wilting plants near the outdoor gas meter may signal a gas leak. Remember that an automobile ignition system could generate the spark to ignite gas. If parked near the leak, leave the car and walk to the nearest telephone to notify the gas company.

A sudden drop or rise in gas pressure may signal gas-supply problems. If the flames on a furnace or water heater become much smaller than usual or if they shoot up in larger bursts, turn off the gas. Call the gas company to request an emergency safety check.

The local fire department should also be alerted in the event an evacuation is necessary. It will want to be aware of any potential emergency conditions, such as fire or explosion, that could result from the leak or a burst gas main. Do not assume that the gas company will automatically notify the fire department. Stay out of the building until the gas smell has cleared and the equipment has been inspected and repaired by gas company personnel or a qualified contractor.

## Threats/damage to the superstructure

Strong winds, flying debris, falling objects, explosions of bombs or faulty equipment, and violent movement caused by earthquakes can cause damage to the superstructure, interrupt power sources, and break water lines. Such occurrences can result in multiple types of disasters including simultaneous fire and water damage. Be prepared for the common types of natural disasters prevalent in the area by developing a risk-management procedure for each.

Follow emergency board-up procedures recommended for areas predicted to have hurricane-force winds. Usually there is sufficient warning in advance to allow this.

Brace and reinforce shelving, hot water heaters, gas supply lines, and water pipes to withstand the violent movement of an earthquake. This should be a standard construction requirement in earthquake-prone areas.

Other threats to the superstructure may come with no or very little advance notice. The best that building personnel can do is to respond to the resulting damage. Analyzing the damage into fire, water, power failure, and structural

---

### Earthquake preparedness

After the 1989 Loma Prieta earthquake, the California Library Association published a 31-page *Earthquake Preparedness Manual for California,* funded by a grant from the American Library Association. The February 1994 issue of *California Libraries* extracted the following preparedness tips.

- Have a plan worked out with the library's parent organization.
- Be sure your library emergency plan is prepared in conjunction with your parent-body plan.
- If your parent body does not have a plan, prepare your own and point out the need for an overall one to your supervisor.
- Review and rehearse the plan at least twice a year. Include each employee.
- Be sure each employee understands he/she is required to fulfill a role in an emergency as part of the condition of employment.
- Assume no outside help will be available for some time.
- Be prepared to make decisions on your own and take risks.
- Have backup files for inventory and circulation, and at least one copy of the emergency plan stored outside the library.
- Document all damage with photographs. It is helpful if pre-disaster photos of the damaged area exist.
- Be prepared for long delays in dealing with the Federal Emergency Management Administration.
- After the next quake, evaluate the effectiveness of your library's emergency plan.
- Plan for the worst—anything better will be a gift.

*Source:* "Quick Takes from Quakes," *American Libraries* 25 (April 1994): 304.

---

damage components can aid in outlining the specific steps to be taken. (Refer to the fire, water, and power failure sections.) The object of building maintenance efforts is to restore the library to safe operating condition as quickly as possible. Depending on the severity of the damage, it may be advisable to request consulting reports from structural and mechanical engineers before beginning any major restoration.

## Points to remember in a building emergency

1. Contact fire or police and utility companies if appropriate.
2. Cooperate fully with emergency personnel.
3. Secure the site. Close openings in walls, windows, roof. Lock doors. Consider using security personnel if warranted.
4. Minimize damage from water. Work quickly to stabilize the environment.
5. Contact the insurance company as soon as possible. Enlist its cooperation for cleanup and restoration efforts.
6. Save receipts for any cleanup expenses.
7. Record damage with a camera or video recorder and a written report.
8. Save any damaged items until after the insurance inventory is completed.
9. Do not contract for estimating, inventory, or repair services without first contacting the insurance agent or adjuster.
10. File the insurance claim promptly.
11. Determine if the building is safe to reoccupy. Restore library service as quickly as possible.
12. Use all safety precautions for electric shock and/or natural gas leaks.
13. Seek professional assistance in restoring structural damage and dam-

age to electrical systems and equipment. (If extensive repairs are required, it may be necessary to relocate library services to a temporary site.)

14. Clean everything thoroughly before reoccupying the building and opening it to the public. Work with a professional fire and water damage-restoration firm.

*Source:* Dianne Lueder and Sally Webb, *Administrator's Guide to Library Building Maintenance* (Chicago: American Library Association, 1992). 202p.

# Basic budgeting practices

*by Richard S. Rounds*

**5**

MOST LIBRARIANS MUST DEAL WITH some aspects of the library budget at some time in their professional careers. A crucial point in budgeting is the written or oral presentation, whereby one must convince the administrators of funding that library programs and personnel are crucial to the existence of Western civilization. Here Richard Rounds recommends some strategies for successful in-person presentations.—*GME.*

## Organizing your presentation

Since your purpose is to inform and persuade, you need to master the deductive, inductive, and eliminative methods of organizing your presentation.

*Deductive reasoning* moves forward from a statement or premise that must be accepted as true by everyone you are talking with. This premise is used together with facts or other premises to develop particular arguments or plans of action.

Be careful in choosing a premise on which to base your presentation. Librarians often feel that the importance of education, reading, and libraries is self-evident. They may begin budget presentations by stating that "libraries are basic to one's happiness." Unfortunately, this premise does not have unanimous support. Indeed, library support may be in inverse relation to budgetary demands of life-sustaining institutions (i.e., police and fire departments).

Since deductive reasoning moves from generalization to specifics, the line-item, incremental budget is a good candidate for deductive presentation. Whether the budgetary guidelines limit you to a 10% increase or require a 3% decrease is a premise on which you should build your presentation. If you act on this premise, your argument will be persuasive. The line-item budget is easy to defend, as long as you stay within the guidelines, because tradition expects percentage adjustments.

As a school librarian, you might begin your deductive reasoning by stating: "The school library exists to support and supplement the school curriculum." It is hard to believe that anyone would disagree with that statement, but you may have to prove it before you gain concensus and can continue with your presentation. Once you are convinced that everyone agrees with that premise, you might explain that the curriculum expanded during the year to include creative writing, two foreign languages, and office management. "Therefore, we need $4,000 to buy materials to support these new curricula."

*Inductive reasoning* moves from specifics to create a generalization. Usually, this means building on a series of facts that result in a conclusion. Fact: "Circulation has increased 100% during this fiscal or school year." Fact: "Staff has decreased by 0.5 FTE during this fiscal or school year." Fact: "There is a two-week lag between the return of books to the library and their return to the shelves." Fact: "Accessibility of materials to users has decreased proportionately." Conclusion: "Pages must be hired to reshelve materials. This is the reason for a $700 increase in the circulation program."

Function budget formats are well suited to inductive presentations. By using function budgeting, you begin with a number of activities and services that create the entirety of the operations of the library. By gaining support for each component, you establish that these activities and services are worth supporting. From those specifics, you can accumulate support for the whole.

You can picture the shape of this argument as a pyramid: you make a series of statements which, together, provide the base for the apex or conclusion.

*Eliminative reasoning* allows you to identify a problem, then address the alternative solutions, eliminating each until only one remains. You can fall into traps with this method if you have not considered all the alternatives and if their rejection is not clearly conceived. Alternative solutions usually have advantages and disadvantages. Sometimes one clearly outweighs the other, but all too often they depend on opinion, and the opinions of board members may differ from yours.

## Visual presentation

The most common presentation is a lecture. But because audiences retain only about 20% of what they hear, and 50% of what they see and hear, you will want to prepare visual aids: slides or a slide/tape presentation, charts and graphs on chalkboard or flip chart, overhead transparencies, and/or a videotape. The room arrangement, equipment availability, and preparation time will determine which method(s) you use.

A slide/tape presentation requires the ability to darken and arrange the room for ease of viewing, requires equipment, and is time-consuming in preparation. It is, on the other hand, an effective way of bringing the library to life.

Charts and graphs require a wall or easel, and require less time to prepare. Moreover, you can focus your audience on the specifics you wish to highlight. If you use charts or graphs, be sure there is plenty of "white space." If you present a table, present no more than three or four columns per visual, and do not talk more than about one minute with any one visual.

Overhead transparencies require an overhead projector and screen, and no more time to prepare than charts and graphs. Your presentation can be drawn, printed, or typed onto a piece of paper that can be made into a transparency by a photocopier. When you present word visuals, highlight what you say by using key words. Never use complete sentences. Use no more than seven words per line and limit the visual to eight lines. By following these rules of thumb you will ensure the necessary "white space."

As videotapes have become common, they are used more and more often during budget presentations. They require a somewhat darkened room, a particular seating arrangement, and special equipment, and can be time-consuming to prepare. But this medium brings the library to life by providing action.

Remember: Any visuals used, including videotapes, are a supplement to your oral presentation, not a substitute for it. You are still presenting the library budget.

## Are there any questions?

You needn't flinch when you hear the moderator of the hearing board ask for questions. It's an opportunity, if you have done your homework.

"Yes, I have a question," says Mr. Brown. "I still don't see what will be gained from a deposit library at the rest home in the Heights."

Having done your homework, you know that Mr. Brown's mother-in-law lives in a different rest home, and you might respond this way:

"Our survey of library users showed a lower representation from that home than others. We plan to pilot a deposit library in that home. If it's successful, we may be able to accommodate other homes in town."

"How many of your program participants are residents of this city?" asks Mr. Smith.

"I'm happy to report that the proportion of residents to out-of-towners has doubled since last year, Mr. Smith."

Knowing that Mr. Smith does not want to support anyone outside his tax base, you have prepared for this question. (Be sure not to say too much.)

"What I want clarified," insists Mr. Jones, "is the meaning behind that flap I read about last month."

Don't assume you know what "that flap" refers to. Don't answer too quickly.

"What flap, Mr. Jones? Was it something you read in a magazine?"

"No, no, no. I saw something about a library conference in the newspaper. It was held in Chicago. Why weren't you there?"

What started as a challenge can suddenly be turned to your advantage.

"Yes, that *was* an excellent opportunity. I didn't attend because we didn't have sufficient travel funds. I've recommended a travel budget this year of $600. Luckily, the conference will be nearer home and I'll be able to attend and report back to you."

By restating the question and having it clarified, you gain better understanding of the motive behind the question, as well as time to formulate a response.

"How exactly do the circulation figures compare between the high school and the junior high school?" demands Ms. Gray, the newest member of the funding board—a question you hadn't anticipated. Moreover, the statistics are not readily available. What do you say?

"I don't have those statistics handy, Ms. Gray. I'll pull them together and get them to you tomorrow."

It is better to be straightforward (no apologies are necessary) than to respond uncertainly. A guess may mar credibility or raise more questions.

Why is Ms. Gray interested in those statistics? You might probe by asking: "Are you interested in any other data?"

"No. I'm thinking that one way to cut our costs would be to shorten the hours of whichever library is used least."

This gives you information. Now you know her motive, and you can give her information regarding the in-library use of material, the use of facilities, and the use of the reference staff, as well as the circulation figures. Your new board member needs to be oriented and educated about library uses and needs.

Besides identifying board members who need education, the question-and-answer period offers you a chance to witness an exchange of views among board members. You can learn a great deal about the individuals' values and assumptions through their group interaction. Every detail will make next year's presentation easier.

## The critique

You have made the best presentation that you knew how to make. There is always room for improvement. Whether it is the procedure of the board to act on requests immediately or take them under advisement until their entire budget is completed, you have had your input.

Therefore, as soon as possible after the end of the presentation, make notes to yourself:

What unanswered questions and requests for information do you need to provide? To whom? By when?

What do you feel were the strongest and the weakest parts of the presentation? Why? What changes could you have made? What issues arose that you hadn't anticipated?

Would alternative media have been more helpful at any point?

Make sure you follow up with preferred or requested information promptly. Then relax and wait for further budget negotiations with representatives of your parent organization and/or final approval of your library budget.

*Source:* Richard S. Rounds, *Basic Budgeting Practices for Librarians,* 2d ed. (Chicago: American Library Association, 1994). 159p.

# SPECIAL POPULATIONS

6

# Historically black colleges and universities

**HISTORICALLY BLACK COLLEGES AND UNIVERSITIES** have contributed significantly to the effort to attain equal opportunity through postsecondary education for black, low-income, and educationally disadvantaged Americans. In 1965, Congress introduced its institutional aid program for Historically Black Colleges and Universities (HBCUs). Since 1987, this Act has provided for additional funding to support a small cadre of institutions of higher education which have persevered through decades of segregation and neglect. They provide higher education to minority students who might not have been able to attend college otherwise, according to the report, *Historically Black Colleges and Universities, 1976–90,* published by the Department of Education's National Center for Education Statistics.

Highlights of the report include:

- Overall HBCU enrollment rose by 16% between 1976 and 1990, with 258,000 students attending the 105 HBCUs in 1990.
- Black enrollment at HBCUs between 1976 and 1990 lagged behind the 20% rise in black enrollment at other colleges, but between 1988 and 1990, the number of black students increased by 8% at both HBCUs and other colleges.
- Although the 105 2-year, 4-year, and professional school HBCUs constitute only 3% of the nation's 3,559 institutions of higher learning, they enroll over 17% of the black students in college.
- In 1990, the 86 HBCUs that award bachelor's degrees enrolled 28% of all black students enrolled in a 4-year college, and awarded 27% of all bachelor's degrees earned by blacks nationwide. Thus today, as in the past, HBCUs still assume a major share of the nation's responsibility for providing educational opportunities for blacks.
- About 15% of black master's degree recipients, 12% of black doctor's degree recipients, and 16% of black first-professional degree recipients received their degrees from HBCUs in 1989–90.
- Between 1976 and 1990, more students from other racial/ethnic groups attended HBCUs, and the student body has become slightly more diverse.
- Increases in faculty salaries generally kept pace with those at other colleges, though salaries at HBCUs remained somewhat lower. In 1989–90, female faculty earned 87% of the average for all female faculty compared to male HBCU faculty who earned 78% of the average for all male faculty. Within HBCUs, men's salaries averaged 12% higher than women's compared to a 26% difference for all institutions.

*Source: Historically Black Colleges and Universities, 1976–90 (Washington, D.C.: National Center for Education Statistics, 1992).*

Lincoln College, Lincoln, Pennsylvania, 1857

# Martin Luther King, Jr., Day activities

THE BIRTHDAY OF MARTIN LUTHER KING, JR. (January 15, but observed on the third Monday in January) and Black History Month (February) offer special opportunities to become involved with your community.

Your participation will:

- Highlight the key role played by libraries in preserving and sharing the record of African-American history.
- Show librarians as leaders in actively promoting community awareness of this heritage.
- Celebrate diversity and promote appreciation of all people and all cultures.
- Strengthen the library's relationships within a multicultural community.
- Attract new library users through innovative activities for all ages.
- Build partnerships with community organizations and individuals with special talents and knowledge to share.
- Focus attention on the principles of racial equality and nonviolent social change taught by Martin Luther King, Jr.

Libraries across the country have offered a vast array of programs to celebrate the Martin Luther King, Jr. holiday and Black History Month. Here's a sampling of activities:

**Celebrate**

6

*"I find, in being black, a thing of beauty, a joy; a strength;*
*a secret cup of gladness—a native land in neither time nor place*
*—a native land in every negro face!"*—Ossie Davis

- Host a concert of African-American music. The Chicago Public Library offered a series that combined readings and performances of gospel, blues, and jazz. Or, offer a tribute to a single composer— Scott Joplin, Duke Ellington, and W. C. Handy are only a few possibilities.
- Offer a program for families exploring African and African-American contributions to science, literature, and other aspects of our nation's culture. Set the mood by inviting all who attend to wear something from an African or African-American culture.
- Offer a taste of something special. The Metropolitan Library System in Oklahoma City sponsored a Soul Food Luncheon featuring African-American, Caribbean, and African food. Ask restaurants to donate their specialty. Hold a cooking demonstration.
- Celebrate the creativity of contemporary African Americans. Invite nationally or locally known writers, musicians, and other artists to participate in a series of programs. Famed actor Ossie Davis is among those who have made appearances as part of the St. Louis (Mo.) Public Library's Black History Month celebration.
- Work with a local school or drama group to commission a short play written and produced by African Americans. Present the play at the library.
- Organize a festival of African and African-American art, crafts, and collectibles. Set up tables where local artists, crafts people, and

collectors can demonstrate or display their special interests. Your local art guild, antiques club, or college may be able to assist.

## Spread the word

*"Truth is proper and beautiful in all times and in all places."*
—Frederick Douglass

- Work with a local TV or radio station to sponsor a "Black History Question of the Day" contest. Award books, videotapes, and recordings featuring African Americans.
- Promote the library as a central clearing house for information on events of interest to the African-American community. Set up a single location to highlight activities. Post notices of lectures, workshops, performances, radio and television programs of special interest.
- Extend a program experience by publishing a booklist. Encourage your audience to explore the library's resources with a listing printed conveniently on the back of a program flyer.
- Work with your local TV or radio station to produce a "read more about it" tag line to follow their Black History Month programs.
- Use visual impact to convey your message. Feature pictures of Dr. King in January library publications. Create bulletin board displays using relevant quotations during February.
- Send a black history fact sheet to local radio disc jockeys for use during Black History Month, compliments of your library.

## Remember

*"Know from whence you came. If you know whence you came, there is really no limit to where you can go."*—James Baldwin

- Organize a commemorative program to honor Dr. King's birthday.
- Host an open house and provide an opportunity for local residents to share their experiences in the Civil Rights Movement. These memories may be the beginning of a local oral history project.
- Work with a local genealogical society or archive to present a workshop on "Tracing Your Roots," such as the one sponsored by the L. S. Navarre Branch of the Monroe (Mich.) Public Library.
- Sponsor a community sing-along of traditional hymns and freedom songs used during the Civil Rights Movement. Provide copies of words and music for the audience. The New Orleans Public Library sponsors an annual Gospel festival.
- Offer a trip into the past using slides, photographs, and memorabilia from other eras. "The Black Experience in the West" was the theme for a Black History Month celebration featuring exhibits and programming at the Pikes Peak (Colo.) Library District.
- Stage a tribute to a famous African American. With poetry and music, the Harlem Branch of the New York Public Library sponsored a tribute to Malcolm X.

## Share

*"Education is our passport to the future, for tomorrow belongs to the people who prepare for it today."*—Malcolm X

- Hold a discussion of Dr. King's ideas, such as his philosophy of nonviolence and its significance in confronting contemporary problems. Show films depicting King's life and the history of the Civil Rights Movement.

- Offer a multimedia learning experience.
- The Harlem Renaissance is a rich source of inspiration. Contact your local college or speaker's bureau for a lecturer. Recordings or a performance of the music of the period, documentary films, and selections of readings can introduce the audience to this memorable era.
- Sponsor an African dance workshop. New York Public Library's Harlem Branch invited a dancer to instruct the audience in the dance movements of Africa, Haiti, and Brazil.
- Present a film festival. Feature African-American directors or a theme highlighting the contributions of African Americans. "Artistry in Black," presented by the Boston Public Library, focused on prominent black artists.
- Offer a hands-on exploration of African musical instruments and the American instruments they inspired. The Hamilton Grange Branch of the New York Public Library offered a lecture and live demonstration of African-American drum rhythms.
- Present a lecture/discussion series on African-American literature featuring local scholars or authors. The Flint (Mich.) Public Library received a grant from the Michigan Council for the Humanities for such a program. Or, launch a year-round Black Literature Discussion Group beginning in February.
- Use a special exhibit as the focal point for panel discussions, films, and other programming. "Ethnic Images in Comics and Advertising" was the theme for Black History Month activities offered at the St. Louis Public Library in cooperation with the Anti-Defamation League of B'nai B'rith, the Junior League, and other community groups.

## Recognize achievement

> *"Bring me all of your dreams / You dreamers /*
> *Bring me all of your / Heart melodies . . ."*—Langston Hughes

- Recognize local citizens who exemplify Dr. King's principles. Involve local civic groups in selecting honorees. Spotlight community heroes.
- Sponsor a contest honoring achievements by African Americans. Essays, short stories, art, and rapping are among the possibilities. Include local schools in your planning and promotion. Donations for prizes can come from local businesses. Hold an awards ceremony featuring readings, performances, or displays of the winning entries. The Ypsilanti (Mich.) District Library compiled a 16-page booklet featuring the winners of a creative writing contest.
- Encourage budding African-American poets by organizing a poetry recital. Send invitations to local writers' workshops, area schools, and colleges.
- Organize a competition among schools. African-American history can be turned into a fun and informative challenge with an interscholastic quiz. Arrange to have the final round of competition broadcast on radio or TV. Contact the Prince George's County (Md.) Memorial Library System for information on its "Black Pursuits" contest.
- Display Coretta Scott King Award-winning books. Sponsored annually by the Social Responsibilities Round Table of the American Library Association (ALA), the award honors outstanding African-American authors and illustrators of children's books.

**Special for kids**

> *"Our children may learn about heroes of the past*
> *Our task is to make ourselves architects of the future."*—Jomo Kenyatta

- Have an "unbirthday party" honoring a famous African American. Provide cake, ice cream, balloons and party favors, such as photographs or buttons featuring the person being honored. Appropriate songs can be sung, a story told. Have each child read aloud a fact about the honoree.
- Present a special story hour focusing on Dr. King's life and writing.
- Offer performances by folksingers, storytellers, dancers, and theater groups based on African folklore and music.
- Help children visualize the big picture. The Fairmount Heights Branch of Prince George's County Memorial Library System invited children to color in large drawings of people and events in African-American history. The colorful posters were displayed throughout the year. Children at the Newark (N.J.) Public Library created a mural in honor of Dr. King.
- Bring history to life with portrayals of African-American heroes. The Beta Gamma Xi sorority provided the performances at a "Positive Images for Black Youth in the 1990s" program at the Kent branch of the Toledo-Lucas County (Ohio) Public Library.

*Source: A Time to Celebrate!* (Chicago: ALA Public Information Office, 1990).

# Library services to Hispanics

PROVIDING LIBRARY SERVICES to Hispanics can be complex; nationality, regional differences, and culture provide myriad combinations for that single community. For example, there are significant linguistic and cultural differences reflected in the varieties of Spanish spoken by Mexicans, Puerto Ricans, Cubans, and other Hispanic groups. Recognizing these differences and responding correctly to them are major themes.

REFORMA, the National Association to Promote Library Services to the Spanish Speaking, has taken an active role in the production of these guidelines. They were written consciously for all librarians who may need to initiate service to this population. In that sense, they are a beginner's manual intended for a hypothetical librarian serving as an administrator of a medium-to-small institution newly aware of the needs of a Hispanic community within its service area.

## Collection and selection of materials

Persons in the Hispanic communities in the United States do not all speak and read only Spanish; they do not all speak and read only English; nor are they all bilingual. The members of these communities have diverse needs and are entitled to access to materials diverse enough to meet those needs.

**Relevancy.** The selection of library materials for Hispanics should meet the educational and recreational needs of the community by providing relevant and culturally sensitive materials. Stereotypes should be avoided.

**Language.** The collection should contain materials in Spanish, materials in English, and bilingual materials. Materials selected should reflect the particular linguistic characteristics of the community served. They should also include standard Spanish-language titles from Spain and other Hispanic cultures.

**Physical access.** If a separate collection of materials for Hispanics is maintained by the library, it should be visible and accessible to the community. In libraries that do not separate these materials, adherence to bibliographic access is strongly recommended.

**Bibliographic access** to the library's collection should include Spanish-language subject headings in the public catalog when appropriate for the population served. Locally produced access and identification aids, including lists, bibliographies, and point-of-use bibliographic instructional materials, should be in Spanish when appropriate.

**Formats.** Print and nonprint materials, whether educational or recreational, should be included.

## Programs, services, and community relations

Programming, both traditional and nontraditional, is an effective vehicle to attract and meet the needs of the members of the Hispanic community. This is particularly true for those who have recently immigrated and who are unfamiliar with the library services available in the United States. As a result of the potentially limited resources available for service to Hispanics within any given institution, cooperation among all libraries serving the target population is encouraged. Such cooperation may manifest itself in the sharing of program costs, cooperative acquisitions, or joint borrowing privileges, to name but a few.

**Diversity of culture.** Because the population served may comprise several different Hispanic cultures, each specific culture must be considered in the development of programming and should be accurately reflected in its content.

**Outreach services.** In order to aid in the planning and delivery of library services to meet community needs, there should be an ongoing process of community analysis and assessment. To further these aims:

1. the library should participate in the work of local community organizations of Hispanics; and
2. the library should work with such organizations in the development and presentation of library programs and services.

**Intercultural understanding.** As part of its activities in working with local populations in which a multiplicity of cultures is represented, the library should actively promote intercultural communication and cooperation among them.

**Service to nonusers.** Attention should be paid to the library nonuser. Programs, literature, and publicity should be used in nontraditional ways and in settings designed to attract those for whom libraries are not part of the experience of life.

**Bibliographic instruction.** Bibliographic instruction should be offered in Spanish when necessary.

**Language.** In keeping with the ALA policy in support of multilingual services, the language used for programming and services (Spanish or English, bilingual or monolingual) as well as vocabulary, accent, and nuance must be carefully selected. Choices should be based upon characteristics of the local community.

## Personnel

Librarians serving Hispanic communities should be actively recruited. Contact should be made with Hispanic graduates of library education programs accredited by the American Library Association, and extensive use should be made of hotlines, minority recruiting services, and services provided by Hispanic library organizations. Professional staff should be recruited from library education programs accredited by the American Library Association. Written personnel procedures and affirmative action programs should be established and fully implemented.

**Qualification—professional and support staff.** In addition to the required standards for librarians and support staff, bilingualism and biculturalism are qualities that should be sought; these qualities will ensure sensitivity to the library and information needs of the Hispanic community and enhance service delivery.

Bilingual and bicultural librarians and support staff should be adequately compensated in positions where job specifications or actual conditions require the knowledge of Spanish.

**Staff development.** Librarians and support staff should be provided opportunities to exchange information and ideas as well as to participate in continuing education programs that would enhance the services provided to libraries in Hispanic communities. Examples of programs that could be explored include training in teaching English as a second language, acquisition of Spanish-language materials, citizenship requirements, and community information services.

*Source:* Library Services to the Spanish Speaking Committee, *Guidelines for Library Services to Hispanics* (Chicago: ALA Reference and Adult Services Division, 1988). 4p.

---

### Six videos for diversity collections: Asian-Americans

*Becoming American: The Odyssey of a Refugee Family.* New Day Films, 1983. 58 min., study guide. A documentary portraying a Hmong family's saga of resettlement from war-ravaged Laos to Seattle.

*Carved In Silence.* National Asian-American Telecommunications Association/Cross Current Media, 1987. 45 min. The story of Angel Island, California, the "Ellis Island" of the West, focusing on Chinese immigrants.

*Mitsuye and Nellie: Asian American Poets.* Light-Saraf Films, 1981. 58 min. A chronicle of the immigration and adaptation of several generations of Chinese and Japanese Americans to life on the west coast of the United States.

*The New Puritans: The Sikhs of Yuba City.* National Asian-American Telecommunications Association/Cross Current Media, 1985. 27 min. The history of the Sikhs in Yuba City, California, from their first migrations in the 1900s to the 1980s.

*Pockets of Hate.* Films for the Humanities, 1988. 25 min. The film focuses on the murder of an Asian Indian in Jersey City and seeks to explain the post-civil rights resurgence of racism.

*Slaying the Dragon.* National Asian-American Telecommunications Association/Cross Current Media, 1988. 60 min. The history of stereotypical and one-dimensional portrayals of Asian and Asian-American women in Hollywood films.

*Source:* Gregory I. Stevens, *Videos for Understanding Diversity: A Core Selection and Evaluative Guide* (Chicago: American Library Association, 1993). 217p.

---

# Native American patrons

KNOW YOUR PATRONS. Know both the general tribal groups to which they belong (e.g., Plains Indians) and something about Indian Nations across the country.

Locate someone who can act as liaison between your library and the patrons you wish to serve.

If you are near a reservation, attempt to make a contact through your liaison with a member of the tribal council. Ask for an opportunity to explain library services.

Never promise anything you cannot deliver.

Ask the tribal council to appoint a consultant whose responsibility would be to advise on types of materials and services the tribe might need.

For Indian people away from their reservations, your first contact might be through an Indian center.

Build your collection to include items on American Indian history and culture.

Be prepared to furnish services of a nontraditional nature; for example, space for classes in arts and crafts, storytelling, cooking, languages, tutoring for high school equivalency exams.

Hire Native Americans.

Remember that it took a long time to alienate Indian people. It will take a long time to regain their trust.

American Indian cultures do not celebrate "holidays" in the usual sense. The ceremonies and rituals that mark their lives are closely tied to the rhythms of nature and are, as a consequence, highly regional. Each nation or tribe has different celebrations that cannot and should not be perceived as "universal" or "national" holidays. American Indians see themselves as dozens of individual peoples or nations, not as a monolithic group. Many American Indian celebrations do not have fixed calendar dates. In many ways, the modern calendar is antithetical to American Indian culture and its ties to natural cycles.

In October 1991, Congress authorized and requested the president to proclaim the month of November "National American Indian Heritage Month" (PL 102-123). This observance, however, is not consistent with the localized characteristics of most American Indian celebrations.

Seek out the Native American communities in your area to learn what days are most significant to them. Attend local powwows, which welcome everybody and are good family excursions, to learn about Native American people close to home. Powwow activities include dancing, drumming, singing and food and crafts vendors.

Giveaways also are important to most powwows. This custom originates from the tradition that the chief of a tribe was said to be the poorest man in the village. He was responsible for everyone's being provided for, even when that meant "giving away" his own possessions.

In honor of Native American cultures, plan programs that center on themes of environmental awareness and respect for the earth.

- Invite community people who plant organic gardens or run organic farms to share their experiences. What are your state's laws concerning labeling food "organic"?
- Sponsor a study group for children and young people to research the location and content of local toxic industries and their dumping sites. How is the term "toxic" defined and by whom? What are the long-term effects of pesticide buildup in the soil, in the water?
- Sponsor a study group for children and young people to research the benefits and obstacles to practices like recycling, gleaning (collecting and distributing crops left in fields by automated pickers) and matching restaurants, which always have extra food, with agencies that feed people.
- Hold a health fair and invite alternative health practitioners to participate, e.g., chiropractors, acupuncturists, herbalists, body workers.

*Sources: Factors in Serving American Indian Patrons* (Chicago: ALA Reference and Adult Services Division, 1976); *Celebrate America's Diversity* (Chicago: ALA Graphics, 1993).

# Products for the print-impaired

*by Tom McNulty and Dawn M. Suvino*

**WE ARE, AS A CIVILIZATION,** dominated by our visual perception. As librarians we can hardly conceive of information being stored and transmitted in any form other than print. Certainly, technological advances made in recent decades have familiarized us all with so-called machine-readable formats, but generally we think of information as existing in some form of print. How, then, are the blind or visually impaired to obtain this information which, by its very nature, seems unavailable to them?

Most of us assume that the primary method of information exchange available to the blind and visually impaired is braille, the well-known system of raised-dot configurations that transcribes the orthography and syntax of the language in question. While braille is still commonly used by many visually impaired individuals, it is no longer considered the primary method of information exchange despite the fact that for many print-impaired people it is still the most efficient means of storing information in written format. Taking notes in the classroom, writing down phone numbers or grocery lists, and labeling cans in the pantry are all tasks that are frequently best performed with a braille-writing device. However, such things as bank statements, telephone directories, and library card catalogs are not generally produced in braille; those who are print impaired must find alternative means to access the vast majority of information that is available in our society.

When we seek to make our library programs and facilities available to the print-impaired patron, we must be aware of the many methodological options that now exist. We must understand the value of each and plan accordingly.

Here is a partial list of adaptive devices in use today that allow print-impaired individuals to access information.

## Braille

### A. Soft Braille Systems

**ALVA Braille Terminal.** Humanware, Inc. Computer braille display which features 43 or 83 eight-dot braille cells. Displays vital information, such as location of system cursor and special screen attributes. Special touch cursor allows fast and accurate cursor routing.

**Braille 'n Speak.** Blazie Engineering. Converts braille input to synthetic speech. Weighing less than one pound, the Braille 'n Speak is used as a talking notetaker, clock, calendar, and telephone directory. Connects to PC via RS-232 serial port.

**BrailleMate.** Telesensory Systems, Inc. Handheld computer featuring a braille keyboard, one 8-dot braille cell, and a built-in speech synthesizer. Optional memory card extends storage capacity. Software includes word processing, calendar, and telephone directory.

**KeyBraille.** Humanware, Inc. Provides braille output from PCs on a refreshable display. Five braille cells devoted to display line information. Available in 25- or 45-cell options.

**Navigator.** TeleSensory Systems, Inc. Braille output computer system gives easy access to PCs. Many different configurations available. Display strip available with 20, 40, or 80 cells.

### B. Braille Translation Programs

**Braille Talk.** GW Micro. Braille translation software converts standard

ASCII text to grade-1 or grade-2 braille. Available for Apple and PC computers.

**Duxbury Braille Translator.** Duxbury Systems, Inc. Available for both Macintosh and PC computers, converts standard ASCII text into formatted grade-2 braille. Foreign languages, as well as Nemeth code translation tables available.

**Hot Dots.** Raised Dot Computing, Inc. PC braille translation program features grade-2 braille translation and back-translation, print formatter, and speech interface. Documentation provided in print, audio, or floppy disk.

**PC Braille.** Arts Computer Products, Inc. Translation program converts text files into grade-1, grade-2, or computer braille. PCs only.

*C. Braille Printers*

**Braille Blazer Personal Braille Printer.** Blazie Engineering. Braille printer equipped with speech output for setting parameters. Built-in sound muffler. Works with PCs.

**Braille BookMaker.** Enabling Technologies Co. Braille embosser available for PC or Macintosh computers. Embosses approximately 80 characters per second, and features interpointed, i.e., two-sided, braille printing.

**Braille 'n Print.** Humanware, Inc. Connects to a Perkins Brailler to produce braille and print copy of documents. A 22K memory allows file storage. Slimline version attaches directly to the bottom of a Perkins Brailler; MK 2MB version intended for multiuse settings.

**Braillo 90.** American Thermoform Corp. Personal braille printer features 90 character-per-second printing speed. Printing speed as well as pressure adjustable.

**Index Advance, Index Classic.** Humanware, Inc. Small, quiet, braille embossers. The Classic produces 25 characters per second; the Index Advance embosses at a rate of 50 characters per second. Available for Macintosh and PC computers.

**Ohtsuki BT-5000.** American Thermoform Corp. Braille printer has three modes of operation: braille embossing, ink print, or a combination of braille and print. Manufactured by Technol Eight Corporation.

**Versapoint.** TeleSensory Systems, Inc. Available for Macintosh and PC computers, this braille printer offers bidirectional line printing at 40 characters per second. Thirty thousand character buffer frees host computer for other work once file has been sent to the printer.

## Synthetic speech hardware and software

**Accent Speech Synthesizer.** Aicom Corp. Various models, including Accent PC (full-length PC plug-in card), Accent MC (microchannel), and a stand-alone version, the Accent SA.

**Artie Vision, Business Vision.** Attic Technologies, Inc. Artie Vision is a sophisticated screen-access system used with PCs. Business Vision incorporates a talking calculator and special spreadsheet functions with the standard Attic Vision software. Artic's software is designed to run only with the company's own Synphonix series of internal speech cards.

**ASAP (Automated Screen-Access Program).** MicroTalk. Synthetic speech screen-access system used with PCs. Supports a variety of internal and external synthesizers. MicroTalk maintains speech-friendly support electronic bulletin board.

**DECTalk Synthesizer.** Digital Equipment Corp. External device with remarkable sound quality. One of DECTalk's most popular features is its use of nine different voices. It should be noted, however, that this synthesizer's response time is notoriously slow.

**ECHO series synthesizers.** Street Electronics Corp. Variety of models, both internal and external, compatible with all PCs and Apple II series.

**Echo II with Textalker and Textalker-GS.** American Printing House for the Blind. Complete speech synthesis program for Apple computers. Hardware consists of Echo II synthesizer, interface, and external speaker with volume control.

**Flipper.** Omnichron. Used with PCs, this software supports a number of internal and external synthesizers. Reports indicate that Flipper helps compensate for DECTalk's sluggish response time so that institutions which already own one of these synthesizers may consider purchasing this software. One of the program's outstanding features is its ability to handle terminal emulation.

**IBM Screen-Reader.** IBM Educational Systems. Combination hardware/software screen-access system features programmable 18-key external keypad to navigate screen. External keypad can minimize confusion for novice users. Note that the system was originally designed to work with the company's PS/2 line of computers and, while the software will run with earlier versions of the PC, this requires an additional interface card. Screen-Reader does not, generally, support internal synthesizers.

**JAWS (Job Access with Speech).** Henter-Joyce, Inc. Screen-reading program features dual cursor design, built-in macros, logical speech pad, and help mode.

**MasterTouch.** Humanware, Inc. Screen-access system that combines software with external touch tablet which provides users with a tactile representation of the full video display. Foreign language capabilities including French, Spanish, and German.

**Outspoken,** Berkeley Systems, Inc. (BSI). Synthetic speech screen-access system used with the Macintosh. Note that the software takes advantage of the Mac's built-in speech synthesizer so no additional hardware is required with this system.

**Synphonix.** Attic Technologies, Inc. A series of internal synthesizers designed for use with PC systems including all ISA-bus desktop configurations, microchannel architecture, and Toshiba laptops. Note that running screen-access software other than Artic Business Vision with a Synphonix synthesizer requires the use of Artic's Sonix text to speech program (Sonixtts).

**VERT Plus.** TeleSensory Systems, Inc. (TSI) Screen-access software used with PCs. Supports a number of internal and external speech synthesizers including TSI's own products. Features include user-definable windows, recognition of video attributes, and bar-tracking.

**Vocal-eyes.** GW Micro. Speech-based, screen-access software used with PCs. The product was specifically designed for use with the Sounding Board (distributed by GW Micro as well) but supports several other synthesizers, both internal and external. Features include good interruptability and full review mode as well as secondary cursor.

## OCR Technologies

**Arkenstone Reader.** Arkenstone, Inc. The Arkenstone employs Calera TrueScan recognition software and a front-end user interface, EasyScan, to provide users with a high quality, speech-friendly recognition system. Includes a TrueScan Recognition Card, Hewlett-Packard scanner, and software.

**DocuRead Expert.** Adhoc Reading Systems, Inc. Optical character recognition device intended for use by print-impaired users. Friendly to standard synthetic speech, soft braille, and screen-enlarging access systems. Full package includes scanner, interface card, and recognition software.

**Kurzweil Personal Reader (KPR).** Xerox Imaging Systems, Inc. Portable reading system that converts text to high quality DecTalk speech. Options include flatbed and hand scanners. System can be used in standalone mode for immediate speech output or interfaced with a PC via serial port. Includes talking calculator.

**OsCaR.** TeleSensory Systems, Inc. Optical character recognition system uses Calera TrueScan-E Recognition software with Hewlett-Packard scanner. Menu-driven system is very user friendly, permitting independent use by visually impaired readers.

**PC/Kurzweil Personal Reader.** Xerox Imaging Systems, Inc. Unlike the KPR, this system is not a standalone unit but must be interfaced with a PC. The flatbed scanner converts printed documents quickly and accurately into ASCII text files for output in braille, large-print, or via synthetic-speech screen-access hardware and software.

## Reading aids for low vision

**Clear View.** Humanware, Inc. A 14-inch CCTV features windowing, underlining and overlining, contrast, and intensity and brightness controls. Zoom lens allows numerous magnification settings.

**Compu-Lenz.** Able-Tech Connection. The fresnel lens doubles the size of characters on computer display. Glare filter eliminates background glare. Requiring no power source or wiring, the Compu-Lenz is also lightweight and durable.

**DP-11 Plus Large Print Display Processor.** TeleSensory Systems, Inc. A hardware device that enlarges characters into solid, proportional characters. Magnification options from 2 to 16 times. Enlarges all ASCII characters but does not support graphics. Designed for use with special monitor and PCs.

**Fonts-on-the-Fly.** LaserTools Corp. A software package that supplies WordPerfect with supplementary printer drivers for a diversity of scalable typefaces. Useful in the preparation of large-print hard copy.

**InLarge.** Berkeley Systems, Inc. Large-print software for Macintosh computers. Magnifies anything on the screen, including graphics, by 2 to 16 times. Can magnify the entire screen or selected portions.

**Large Print DOS (LP DOS).** Optelec USA, Inc. Software-based screen-enlarging system. Uses standard system keyboard to invoke magnification options. Drawbacks include a tendency to conflict with running applications.

**Vantage CCD.** TeleSensory Systems, Inc. This CCTV device includes a 14-inch monitor. Magnification ranges from 3 to 45 times original size. May be used as a stand-alone CCTV device or with VISTA VGA for split-screen video display magnification.

**Viewpoint.** Humanware, Inc. This portable CCTV features a 14-inch monitor, which is detachable from the camera and electronics. Optional second monitor.

**Vista.** TeleSensory Systems, Inc. Large-print computer screen-access device for PCs. Uses a three-button mouse to control magnification as well as manual or automatic cursor. Enlarges graphics and text up to 16 times.

**Voyager CCD.** TeleSensory Systems, Inc. This closed-circuit television enlargement device features a 12-inch monitor and magnification up to 45 times. Electronic line markers isolate individual lines from rest of text. Features X/Y platform, fluorescent light source, monitor, and camera.

**Voyager XL CCD.** TeleSensory Systems, Inc. A 19-inch diagonal black-and-white monitor CCTV. Magnification ranges to 60 times, electronic line markers, fluorescent light source. Can be interfaced with a computer, or used as a standalone enlargement device.

**ZoomText Plus.** Telesensory Systems, Inc. Unobtrusive screen-enlarging TSR for PCs. Uses menustem invoked by unusual key combination unlikely to interfere with software applications.

6

## Vendors

**Able Tech Connection**
P.O. Box 898
Westerville, OH 43081
(614) 899-9989

**Ad Hoc Reading Systems**
28 Brunswick Woods Dr.
East Brunswick, NJ 08816
(201) 254-7300

**Aicom Corp.**
1590 Oakland Rd.
San Jose, CA 95131
(408) 453-8251

**American Thermoform Corp.**
2311 Travers Ave.
City of Commerce, CA 90040
(213) 723-9021

**Arkenstone, Inc.**
1185 Bordeaux Dr., Ste. D
Sunnyvale, CA 94089
(408) 752-2200

**Artic Technologies**
55 Park St., #2
Troy, MI 48083
(313) 588-7370

**Arts Computer Products, Inc.**
121 Beach St., Ste. 400
Boston, MA 02111
(800) 343-0095

**Berkeley Systems, Inc.**
2095 Rose St.
Berkeley, CA 94709
(510) 540-5535

**Blazie Engineering**
3660 Mill Green Rd.
Street, MD 21154
(301) 879-4944

**Boston Information and
Technology Corp.**
52 Roland St.
Boston, MA 02129-1122
(800) 333-2481

**Digital Equipment Corp.**
30 Forbes Rd.
Northboro, MA 01532
(508) 351-5205

**Duxbury Systems, Inc.**
435 King St., P.O. Box 1504
Littleton, MA 01460
(508) 486-9766

**Enabling Technologies Co.**
3102 S.E. Jay St.
Stuart, FL 34997
(407) 283-4817

**GW Micro**
310 Racquet Dr.
Fort Wayne, IA 46825
(219) 483-3625

**Henter-Joyce, Inc.**
816-75 Avenue N
St. Petersburg, FL 33716
(813) 576-5658
(800) 336-5658

**Humanware, Inc.**
6245 King Rd.
Loomis, CA 95650
(916) 652-7253

**IBM Special Needs Information
Referral Center**
c/o IBM Educational Systems
P.O. Box 2150
Atlanta, GA 30301-2150
(800) 426-2133
(800) 284-9482 (TDD)

**LaserTools Corp.**
1250 45th St., Ste. 100
Emeryville, CA 94608
(800) 767-8004

**MicroTalk**
3375 Peterson
Louisville, KY 40206
(502) 897-2705
(502) 893-2269 (modem)

**Omnichron**
6881 Sherwick Dr.
Berkeley, CA 94705
(415) 540-6455

**Optelec USA, Inc.**
4 Lyberty Way
Westford, MA 01886
(508) 392-0707

**Raised Dot Computing, Inc.**
408 S. Baldwin St.
Madison, WI 53703
(608) 257-9595

**Telesensory Systems, Inc.**
455 N. Bernardo Ave.
Mountain View, CA 94039-7455
(415) 960-0920

**Street Electronics Corp.**
6420 Via Real
Carpinteria, CA 93013
(805) 684-45493

**Xerox Imaging Systems, Inc.**
Centennial Dr.
Peabody, MA 01960
(508) 977-2000
(800) 343-0311

*Source:* Tom McNulty and Dawn M. Suvino, *Access to Information*
(Chicago: ALA Library and Information Technology Association, 1993). 162p.

# Service to older adults

THE IMPORTANCE OF LIBRARY SERVICES to meet the particular needs of older adults increases along with this group's numbers. These guidelines, developed by ALA's Library Services to an Aging Population Committee, suggest means whereby librarians can meet those needs.

1. **Exhibit and promote a positive attitude toward the aging process and older adults.**

Actively seek to improve communication skills with people of all ages.

Educate the administrators, librarians, and library staff regarding physiological, psychological, social, and cultural development of people throughout the lifespan.

Participate in continuing education which will enhance skills in working with older adults.

Avoid labeling and look beyond the stereotypes and mythologies of aging.

Exhibit the same level of interest, comfort, and respect with older adults as with any other patrons.

2. **Promote information and resources on aging and its implications** not only to older adults themselves but also to family members, professionals in the field of aging, and other persons interested in the aging process.

Assess the information needs of the older population in order to build a collection that meets the real needs of:
- people interested in understanding the aging process;
- people planning for a change in lifestyle or employment;
- individuals who act as advocates for the aging;
- service providers; and
- younger people learning about the potential for growth over the lifespan.

Assure that library selection and weeding policies lead to the acquisition of current and useful materials that reflect diverse formats and information needs. Collection development should include information on:
- lifelong learning;
- older adults as consumers of aging services;
- behavioral implications;
- cultural, ethnic, economic, and regional differences;
- leisure time activities; and
- issues raised by the rapid aging of our society.

Locate sources of appropriate materials including large-print books, pamphlets, and audiovisual materials (e.g., talking books, tapes, films, videotapes, etc.) that are available for purchase, for loan, or at no cost.

Survey the existing gerontological resources within the community and make available the materials or information about them.

Organize information on community agencies, activities, and resources for use by older adults and those who work with them.

Provide ready access to an information and referral service which includes current information on:

- human services agencies serving older adults;
- speakers, reviewers, and other resource people available for programming; and
- publications, reports, community population profiles, funding agencies, and other research sources.

Publicize the availability of resources by:

- providing reading lists, advertisements, and exhibits of interest to the publics identified above;
- introducing the materials, demonstrating their use or cosponsoring with other agencies and organizations, discussion series and programs at the library or in the community;
- mailing informative brochures to club presidents, committee chairpersons, interested individuals, and concerned agencies and organizations; and
- attending meetings, giving presentations, and working actively towards community involvement.

**3. Assure services for older adults that reflect cultural, ethnic, and economic differences.**

Become knowledgeable about the cultural, ethnic, and economic composition of the community.

Use this information to purchase materials and arrange service, to train staff, to conduct programs, and to develop and maintain interagency cooperation.

Actively participate with existing agencies to serve the literacy needs of the older population.

**4. Provide library service appropriate to the special needs of all older adults, including the minority who are geographically isolated, homebound, institutionalized, or disabled.**

Provide trained staff to serve older adults.

Provide special materials such as talking books or large-print books and periodicals.

Provide special equipment such as tape recorders, magnifying devices, page turners, reading machines, etc., to help in the reading process.

Provide personalized library service to meet the special needs of the individual within the institution (i.e., bed-to-bed, etc.) or the home.

Cooperate with the institutional administration in the planning and implementation of library services for the institutionalized.

Provide on-site service to the homebound and institutionalized, with training and transportation provided by the library.

**5. Utilize the potential of older adults (paid or volunteer) as liaisons to reach their peers and as a resource in intergenerational programming.**

Develop and implement well-organized training sessions for the individuals carrying out the library program.

Invite staff (including volunteers) to participate in library staff meetings so that they can be kept current about resources and policies.

Work closely with staff to solicit ideas, ensure a meaningful work experience, and provide as much autonomy as is desirable.

**6. Employ older adults at both professional and support levels for either general library work or for programs specifically targeted to older adults.**

Make certain that older adults are given serious consideration as candidates for either professional or support staff positions as available.

Request volunteer help only when funding is not available for paid positions.

**7. Involve older adults in the planning and design of library services and programs for the entire community and for older adults in particular.**

Identify representative older adults to participate in library planning.

Assure that adequate needs assessment is conducted to represent the needs and interests of the older adults of the community.

Actively plan and implement programming to meet the needs identified.

**8. Promote and develop working relationships with other agencies and groups connected with the needs of older adults.**

Identify agencies, organizations, and groups in the community that are interested in older adults. Confer with agency leadership about ways in which the library can contribute to the achievement of their goals and objectives through:

- providing resources, materials, and services for older adults and for professional and lay workers in the field;
- cooperating in programming, service delivery, and in-service training; and
- involving key persons in cooperative library and interagency planning.

Identify organizations of older adults in the community and involve them in the planning and delivery of services.

Enlist participation of area librarians in developing cooperative collection development, and in developing services, programs, continuing education, and staff training to improve library service to older adults.

Work toward comprehensive cooperative planning for older adults by:

- working with educational institutions to promote lifelong learning opportunities for older adults;
- locating and working with preretirement groups sponsored by business, industry, and other agencies;
- coordinating with other agencies to eliminate unnecessary duplication of services;
- making available a list of community resources for information and referral which would then be available to older adults and the agencies that serve them; and
- asking that professional staff and administration keep abreast of current developments in gerontology and geriatrics regionally and nationally so that informed interagency communication can be facilitated.

**9. Provide programs, services, and information for those preparing for retirement or later-life career alternatives.**

Develop a collection of materials and information on preretirement planning, retirement, and career alternatives, and provide bibliographies on these topics.

Cooperate with other community agencies to provide workshops, programs, and seminars on such topics as preretirement planning, retirement, and career alternatives.

Serve as a clearinghouse for information on retirement, alternate employment, and other career opportunities.

**10. Facilitate library use by older persons through improved library design and access to transportation.**

Make sure that both the collection and meeting rooms are physically accessible to older adults, with special regard for the impaired elderly, by providing as necessary ramps, hand bars, and other design features.

Provide or be knowledgeable about the availability of assistive devices such as audio loops, infrared listening systems, etc.

Provide furniture for use with wheelchairs.

Strategically locate large-print signage, including informational and safety guides.

Inform or assist older adults in securing transportation by utilizing public or volunteer transportation, new or existing van services, or dial-a-ride systems.

Seek and secure funding for any of the above.

**11. Incorporate as part of the library's planning and evaluation process the changing needs of an aging population.**

Conduct periodic needs assessments to determine whether library resources and programs are satisfying the changing needs of older adults.

Use the results of the needs assessments and continuing evaluation of current programs and services to assist with planning.

**12. Aggressively seek sources of funding, and commit a portion of the library budget to programs and services for older adults.**

Use these funds to acquire resources, assign or recruit staff, promote services, conduct staff development, and forge interagency cooperation.

Pursue sources of additional funds in order to provide for special or one-time-only projects.

*Source: Guidelines for Library Service to Older Adults*
(Chicago: ALA Reference and Adult Services Division, 1987). 4p.

# Serving the impaired elderly

*by Nancy Bolin, Sheila Carlson, Elliott Kanner, and Carol Rickert*

LIBRARIES PROVIDE PROGRAMMING for the impaired elderly in a wide variety of ways in order to meet the broad range of the needs of the individuals and the organizations that serve them.

The ideal program is one that takes into account the self-expressed needs and interests of the individuals involved appropriate to their age and life experience. Consider these examples:

**Homebound**

• Book discussion groups that link homebound individuals to one another to discuss books and topics of interest. Library service providers get individual permission and exchange participant numbers.

• Program packages which allow homebound persons, their family, neighbors and friends to share a group experience with ensuing discussion. Library staff furnish the audiovisual materials and equipment where needed for the patron, or for others to utilize at an appropriate time.

• Library program participation, when the client's condition and available transportation (e.g., volunteer, handicap van service, etc.) allow for a trip to the library. Coordination of the trip with other agencies is likely to be needed.

• Special interest visits from library volunteers who share a hobby, an interest, a career or a life experience with the homebound person. Related book materials should be sent at the time or shortly thereafter. An oral history project is an example of what can be developed for this shared experience.

**Care Facilities (long-term, intermediate, and hospice)**

• Discussion groups may include specific book titles, poetry, or topics of interest to provide for reminiscence, for reality orientation, needed information, or pure enjoyment. Books in large or regular print, multiple copy titles, audiovisual materials, realia, discussion leadership training or facilitation may be provided by a library.

• Audiovisual programs using films, slides, or multisensory kits may be provided to facilities or used by staff for interactive programs with participants. In using audiovisual materials for group programs, special attention should be given to the quality of the sound (speakers away from projection equipment, limited overlapping of music and narrative voices) and clarity of the projected image (avoid dissolved or diffused quality of images—crisp and sharp images are easier to see). Follow-up discussion is a must for active involvement of clients!

• Talking Book/Radio Readers Listening Service groups allow three or four clients to share a listening experience as well as discussion with or without formalized leadership.

• Book talks stimulate an interest in reading or remaining in touch with what is current. They can be used as a separate program or as a part of another activity.

• Library programs can be replicated on-site through the use of videotapes of the original programs. Handouts, displays, and refreshments might be duplicated as well.

• Therapy programs may involve library materials and personnel in a structured therapeutic program (i.e., activity, poetry, laugh, reminiscence, current events, death, and dying, validation, et al.). If a program is thus identified by a facility, the library staff involved in presenting the program or selecting materials should be familiar with the objectives of the program, what the therapy entails, and any necessary documentation, reporting, or credentialing involved.

## Locating clients

The most essential steps in the delivery of service to the frail or impaired older person may be the initial steps taken in identifying potential clients for library service. To identify clients for homebound and nursing home service, library staff may want to explore a variety of resources:

• Census tracts that give population densities may help in locating community organizations (i.e., churches) that would promote service availability or help in locating clients within a given area.

• State or local agencies responsible for services to the elderly receive as well as make referrals for services.

• Visiting nurses and Meals-on-Wheels organizations may assist in the initial identification of clients as well as in helping, through referral, with the continuity of service should a client be in need of long- or short-term residential care.

• Disability groups, Libraries for the Blind and Physically Handicapped, and groups dealing with the aging children of aging parents may serve as sources for referrals as well as continued publicity.

• Clients, family members, social workers, activity staff, nursing personnel, and direct service providers may be useful referral sources for themselves, their peers, or family of the clients.

## Delivering service

Whether homebound, in a care facility, or impaired enough to warrant support in accessing regular library services, the client needs a range of choice in meeting his or her library and information needs. Ideally, service delivery methods should be designed to give the broadest range of choice and accessibility possible.

### Homebound

• Personalized home visits by librarians or library volunteers can bring the range of choice and services the library offers into the home.

• Piggy-backed delivery with other services, such as Meals-on-Wheels, allows for the regular delivery of materials. However, a personal link between library staff and clients is necessary for the selection of materials.

• Van or bookmobile service, with portable shelving units or a lift, allows client accessibility to a variety of materials.

• Books by Mail offers the client both a choice of materials as well as delivery to the home.

• Technological access to the library is available where home computers can be used to generate requests or to gather information; TDDs connect the client to the library as well as a broader range of community services; and where programs featuring library resources are available on cable television.

### Care facilities

• Bed-to-bed delivery can personalize service and facilitate access to information and resources. Delivery is best when provided by librarians and scheduled at a time when the client is able to participate fully in the process of selection.

• The use of librarian surrogates (i.e., trained facility staff or volunteers) to provide for individual client needs allows for the delivery of the service at a time when the client may be better able to enjoy both the interaction as well as the resources (i.e., talking book service in the evening when there is little ambient or background noise).

• In-house library stations with rotating materials from the library should be staffed by the library, and might with library supervision use trained volunteers or clients to actively meet the needs of residents, including those confined to their beds.

• Vans or bookmobiles with portable shelving units or a lift allow client accessibility to a variety of materials.

### Don't forget

• Alternative transportation services may bring the impaired older adult into the library.

• Between visits or service delivery clients should be encouraged to use the phone to call the library to meet their information needs.

• Aids and appliances such as magnifiers and telecaption devices may be loaned as well.

• Library accessibility for those who can come in ramps, automatic doors, doors wide enough for wheelchairs and walkers, accessible fountains and toilets; visible signage, tactile signage, and large-print listings in large print, availability of aids and appliances, and handicapped parking need to be considered if service is to be fully accessible.

*Source: 101 Ideas for Serving the Impaired Elderly*
(Chicago: ALA Association of Specialized and Cooperative Library Agencies, 1989).

# Prison law librarianship

*by Karen Westwood*

I STRAP ON AN ALARM BELT and enter the library. From the room I'm in, I can see a bubble mirror high on the hallway wall. In it I see my next patron being searched with a handheld metal detector. As he walks in the door, I remind him that we have only 10 minutes to discuss his research, so we'd better be all business.

I'm in the law library of a maximum security prison, and if a patron has a pass that only allows him 10 minutes, he knows we won't be spending 15 together. If I run into any difficulties with any of my patrons, I'm to press the alarm belt button. I'm promised that the "Emergency Response Team" will arrive within 15 seconds to assist me. In nearly three years, I've never pressed the button but I know it's there. More importantly, my patrons know it's there.

My assumption that you had to be a big, burly male to work in a prison was the first stereotype I lost when I began work at Law Library Service to Prisoners (LLSP), a part of the Outreach Services Department of the Minnesota State Law Library (MSLL). LLSP began in 1984 as a six-month pilot project for the Minnesota Department of Correction.

The philosophy of the program was to emphasize legal-information services rather than to establish large prison law libraries. The program set up small, core legal collections in each state prison and regular visits from a circuit-riding law librarian to meet with inmates and discuss their research needs. Inmates are encouraged to make use of the core collections, but questions that are more complex are researched by LLSP staff at the state law library.

I am one of two circuit-riding law librarians; we each visit three institutions regularly and serve a handful of work farms, jails, and other sites by mail. Our program continues to grow—partly because more and more inmates know about us and have heard about the valuable service we provide and partly because there are simply more and more inmates.

My background in librarianship consists of reference work in public and academic libraries. When I moved back to my home state of Minnesota after a couple of years on the East Coast, I set my sights on one of the large public libraries in the greater Twin Cities area. It was while I was working part-time in academic and public libraries that I discovered the job announcement for LLSP. I applied mostly out of curiosity, knowing that since I couldn't find a statute if my life depended on it, my chances of actually landing the job were slim. As it turned out, knowing legal research wasn't the uppermost hiring criteria; my references were asked questions about how I handled manipulative people and how I dealt with stress. Now I find myself strapping on a body alarm each week, sitting down with inmates, and providing legal research assistance.

So, I have an interesting job. But what value does that have for the majority of librarians who will never have contact with prisons and prisoners? Law librarianship in prisons—a specialized area of librarianship in a specialized location—illustrates that a solid grounding in general principles of librarianship can enable you to serve professionally in an area you may never have previously considered. Those areas we studied in school, or learned on the job, turn out to be similar no matter where we practice. Let me illustrate with a few examples.

**The reference interview.** I visit three prisons—one weekly, one twice a month, and one monthly. When I'm at each institution, I conduct the best reference interview possible, since when I'm back at MSLL doing the research I can't call the inmate to clarify what he/she was talking about.

More than once I've looked with mortification at a request slip on which I've written something like "lawsuit—shoes." What could I have meant? In this case, the inmate's hightop tennis shoes were seized as evidence and presented as such at trial; now that the prisoner has been convicted, can he get them back, and does he have to file some kind of suit to accomplish that?

If only they were all that easy. I never did find an answer to satisfy the inmate who wanted a list of prisoners' rights amendments to the Constitution. He wouldn't believe me when I told him that the copy of the Constitution I'd given him included all of the amendments.

We hear a lot of sad stories in the course of a prison visit, and a solid grounding in reference-interview techniques allows me to get beyond the desperation of the tale to the library questions involved. Just as a public librarian doesn't ask the patron if she has the disease she's trying to find in a medical dictionary, I don't ask about the crime the inmate has committed. Many times an inmate's offense is a closely guarded secret, and, in most instances, it's simply irrelevant to the reference interview. Conducting an effective reference interview keeps my client encounters at a professional level and enables me to provide better reference service.

**Legal reference versus legal advice.** All law librarians, and many public and academic librarians, run into this problem (as well as requests concerning tax or medical advice) at one time or another. I encounter it nearly every day.

I have more ways to play off requests for legal advice than I can count. They range from "I don't have a law degree, so any advice I would give you would probably do you more harm than good, and *certainly* wouldn't carry any weight in a court of law," to "Beats me." I've often convinced myself that I know, without a doubt, where the line is drawn on legal advice, only to have an inmate phrase his/her request in such a way as to blur it again; inmates frequently have limited or no access to attorneys and are anxious to find someone who will confirm their interpretation of the law.

I give my patrons the information they're asking for, along with a reminder that they're in charge of their own research so they need to read the material I send and continue to ask for information based on what they're finding out. Having the inmates do their research through me throws a different wrinkle into the "advice" problem, but it's still an issue of providing legal reference, not legal advice.

**Confidentiality.** Here's an interesting prison dilemma. Minnesota has a state law that protects public libraries from having to release information that ties a patron with the subject matter of his/her requests. We are not unique in that respect, by the way. At least 40 states have statutes on the confidentiality of library records, and as far back as 1971, ALA adopted a policy on the confidentiality of library records.

What if a prison official asks me whether an inmate convicted of a ritual satanic murder has been asking for materials that describe satanic rituals? What if the attorney general's office calls to say the Department of Corrections is being sued over access to law library materials, and asks how much we sent this guy, and what it was about? What if a pretrial detainee's attorney calls and says she wants to use an insanity defense for her client but won't be able to if he's receiving information from our office about insanity defenses.

On the prison library circuit, we've had all of these situations arise. When we consider the law, we also consider our own policies, refer to professional policy, and make a decision. It is currently our policy to indicate whether or not we have provided law library service to an inmate and the dates of that service; we do not release information about the subject matter of an inquiry to anyone. As clear as that policy is, we have to look at it closely each time a new situation arises to make a decision consistent with both the law and the principles of librarianship.

**Public service.** One major reason I became a librarian was to help people find information. I like the feedback I get from locating something that makes a difference to a patron. I'm sure that's why many of us enjoy public service: the knowledge that the information we've helped provide is enabling someone to accomplish his or her goals.

Nowhere is this satisfaction greater than in prison librarianship. Even when an inmate never uses the information we provide or is nearly illiterate and doesn't understand what we do, we provide an adult, professional exchange and treat him or her with respect. In a prison setting, even such a simple thing as taking a reference request seriously and treating the questioner with respect is providing a service to the inmate. And sometimes it makes a larger difference. From a man to whom I sent information on the different degrees of theft, came a letter that said in part, "My charge was dropped to attempted theft thanks to your efforts. You are truly a holy of holies." How many jobs give you that kind of feedback?

Of course, there are elements to prison librarianship that you don't generally encounter in other library arenas:

6

- Many times I've felt like a bit player in a bad B-movie as the metal doors clang behind me and I walk down a cigarette-smoke-filled cell tier with shouts of "Hey, are you the law lady?" ringing out behind me.
- I haven't had any other job where I've had to rule out purchasing loose-leaf items because the metal binder is considered "contraband"; i.e., it could be fashioned into a weapon.
- I certainly didn't have general library principles to draw on when I was asked to oversee the "shakedown" of the law library. I simply stood to one side while correctional officers removed each book from the shelf and flipped through the pages, looking down the spine searching for drugs and other contraband.
- I've also learned a new vocabulary on this job: a "kite" is a prison memo form (and the way I receive many reference requests), a "shaw" is a homemade weapon, a "dirty UA" is a urinalysis test that reveals drug use, the "public pretender" is the public defender—and the list goes on.

So, I've learned a bit about prisons and prisoners, and I've learned more about the criminal justice system than I ever thought I would. But mostly I've learned, and continue to learn, more about professional librarianship. This specialized research for a very special population will help me be a better librarian in whatever setting I find myself in next. And after this job, I'm not ruling out anything.

*Source:* Karen Westwood, "Prison Law Librarianship: A Lesson in Service for All Librarians," *American Libraries* 25 (February 1994): 152–54.

# Services to adult correctional institutions

TECHNICAL SERVICES SHALL INCLUDE planned collection management to meet the identifiable needs of users, standardized organization of resources for the most effective use in the institution, and procedures designed for the maximum circulation of library materials.

The library shall provide resources and services to reflect stated inmates' needs based on an annually updated profile of the inmate population. User services shall include:

- Reader services with materials at the appropriate reading level (including those for adult new readers).
- Library orientation and instruction at appropriate levels offered on a regular basis to all inmates.
- Access to other library collections through state and regional library systems, networks, consortia, or other cooperative relationships.
- Advisory service to aid inmates in the meaningful use of library materials.
- Reference and information services to meet the inmates' needs for facts and data.
- Access to special need services (e.g., materials from the Regional Library for the Blind and Physically Handicapped).

The library shall offer programs that provide a variety of activities. These programs may be in accordance with the roles the library has selected.

The library shall regularly promote its programs and services.

Library service to individual inmates shall be restricted only for documented abuse of the library service itself.

The library shall provide services to inmates in limited access status comparable to those provided the general population, and shall include at least one of the following:

- Separate access to the main library facility at least once a week for a minimum of one hour.
- A deposit collection in the unit consisting of at least 100 books or other appropriate library materials, or 2 per inmate in the unit, whichever is greater. This collection shall be changed at least once every month.
- A book cart with at least 100 items. Each inmate shall be able to browse and select at least 2 titles from this cart at least once per week. These books should be changed at least once every month.
- A list of at least 300 current titles of books and other appropriate library materials. Inmates may select from this list at least 2 items per week. Deliveries of requested items or suitable substitutes shall be made within 7 working days. This list shall be revised at least annually.

Materials for limited access units shall be selected according to the same criteria as materials in the general collection. Services to inmates in limited access units shall include access to circulating materials in the general collection on request, interlibrary loan, and answers to reference questions. Inmates in limited access units shall have the opportunity to suggest acquisitions and services.

The annual reassessment of library and information needs shall include the limited access population(s). The periodic performance audit shall include services to inmates in limited access status.

*Source: Library Standards for Adult Correctional Institutions*
(Chicago: ALA Association of Specialized and Cooperative Library Agencies, 1992). 47p.

# PUBLIC RELATIONS 7

## National Library Week

*by Peggy Barber and Marcia Kuszmaul*

AMERICAN LIBRARIANS AND BOOK PUBLISHERS noted an alarming trend in the mid-1950s: people were spending more money for radios, television sets, and musical instruments and less for books. To encourage reading and keep books free and widely available, the American Library Association and the American Book Publishers Council summoned a group of concerned citizens and formed the nonprofit National Book Committee in 1954.

Before long, the committee dreamed up the idea of a National Library Week. The Junior Chamber of Commerce of Youngstown, Ohio, had originated a local observance of library week in 1937, and Jackson, Miss., had successfully celebrated a "Know your library week." California had celebrated several statewide library observances.

The National Book Committee organized America's first National Library Week (NLW), March 16–22, 1958, in cooperation with ALA through local and state committees. The United States and Canada were advised to "Wake Up and Read!" President Dwight D. Eisenhower kicked off the week by a proclamation that called for "the fullest participation" by the people of the United States. The Advertising Council approved NLW as a public service campaign, and more than 5,000 cities and towns joined in the celebration, setting library records in registration and circulation.

The following year, Canadian libraries and publishers formed the Canadian Library Week Council to celebrate the week simultaneously with the United States. The ALA Council voted to continue observing the library week annually in April.

Since the National Book Committee was formed to promote reading, its NLW campaign slogans often focused on that theme. After the National Book Committee disbanded in 1974, the American Library Association continued the tradition of National Library Week. In 1975, NLW became the framework for a Legislative Day in Washington, D.C., when librarians and trustees personally talk to their legislators about library needs.

An *American Libraries* reader spotted Elvis among the library workers in the 1950 yearbook of L.C. Humes High School, Memphis, Tenn. Since 1993 the photo has been used as one of ALA Graphics' "READ" posters.

As the first truly national program for library promotion, National Library Week gave ALA a leadership role in the previously neglected area of increasing public awareness. Using bold graphics and messages emphasizing libraries and library services, ALA won two top public relations awards with its 1975 "Information power" campaign. The Public Relations Society of America said, "Libraries no longer looked dull, they looked alive and exciting."

In addition to providing theme posters and other materials and ideas for local library celebrations, ALA publicizes National Library Week on network television and radio, national wire services, and in consumer magazines with feature stories and public service announcements.

National Library Week is a tool for getting librarians together to make the most of limited promotion resources. Whether it works depends on how realistically and enthusiastically the tool is put to work. NLW has inspired criticism as well as praise in its 36-year history.

*Source:* Peggy Barber and Marcia Kuszmaul, "Whither National Library Week—and Why?"
*American Libraries,* January 1983, p. 28.

---

### National Library Weeks to 2002

| | |
|---|---|
| 1995, April 9–15 | 1999, April 11–17 |
| 1996, April 14–21 | 2000, April 9–15 |
| 1997, April 13–19 | 2001, April 1–7 |
| 1998, April 19–25 | 2002, April 14–20 |

---

# National Library Week countdown

## August: Get organized

- Brainstorm with key staff. Discuss the national NLW theme, special events, and other promotion ideas. Come up with your own ideas. Come up with your own ideas to suit the needs and interests of your community.
- Outline a year-round plan with goals, target audiences, timeline, budget. Make program assignments.
- Make sure you're on the mailing list to receive ALA's Graphics Catalog, published in the fall. If you ordered ALA posters last year, you'll automatically receive the catalog. If not, see what you've been missing—write ALA Graphics, Public Information Office, for a free catalog.

## September: Plan the action

- Meet with the library board and/or Friends. Explain the NLW theme. Present your ideas and invite theirs. Ask for a commitment in time and money.
- Hold a staff meeting. Outline your ideas and invite input. Aim to inspire enthusiasm and a sense of involvement. Explain your purpose, whether it's to increase public awareness of the library and its varied services or raise badly needed funds. Offer a choice of assignments where possible.
- Work with the board to organize an honorary NLW committee. Send

letters of invitation to the
mayor, newspaper editor,
well-known figures whose
support will inspire cooperation from others. Make
follow-up calls. Commit-
tees should be asked to
participate in special
events.

## October: Follow through

- Contact local chapters of
NLW Partner organiza-
tions. Invite their participation in helping to organize, fund, and promote
library activities, espe-
cially those of special interest to their members.
- Hold a breakfast meeting to acquaint honorary committee members
and representatives with the library and your plans. Encourage suggestions on how they can best support you (also what you can do for
them).
- If you plan to invite celebrity participation—local or national—now is
the time to write letters inviting their cooperation.

## November: Spread the word

- Finalize your calendar of events.
- Outline a publicity plan, with a timeline for contacting all media. Be
sure to include newsletters—business, PTA, church, government, partner, other community organizations.
- Announce your committee and plans. Seek support from local media.
Will they create public service announcements? What kind of stories
can the library develop for the newspaper?

## December: Keep going

- Order posters and other publicity materials from ALA.
- Follow up unanswered letters.
- Monitor staff and volunteer progress. Send holiday greetings, an
activity update, and thank you for work performed so far.

## January: Full speed ahead

- Get commitments from speakers for NLW events. Collect bios and
other background for NLW news releases.
- Keep making those follow-up calls.
- Attend the NLW workshop at ALA's Midwinter Meeting.
- Mail releases and public service ads early to monthly newsletters and
other publications with a long lead time.

## February: The heat is on

- You should have a day-by-day listing of all your NLW activities. Meet
with staff. Who needs help?

- Write out drafts of news releases on NLW events. What are the photo possibilities? What would be good for television?
- Make sure your press lists are current. Start booking—or find out when you need to start trying to make placements on radio or TV talk shows.

## March: No turning back

- Do you have all your materials from ALA?
- Finalize your program plans. Send letters of confirmation to speakers, other cosponsors.

## April: Showtime!

- Distribute posters and flyers throughout the community.
- Distribute evaluations at programs.
- Clip all mentions of your activities for your scrapbook and reports.
- Send thank-you letters and/or certificates of appreciation to all involved.

*Source: The Card with a Charge* (Chicago: ALA Public Information Office, 1988).

# Library promotion ideas

*by Steve Sherman*

## For public libraries

OF ALL TYPES OF LIBRARIES, a public library serves the broadest clientele. Public-library users include the entire range of age and intellectual levels. However, service only to those who venture up the steps and into the chambers is not enough. Aggressive development of promotional projects that attract as many people as possible to a community library is necessary. Such projects are expressions of progress and justification of the existence of the library itself. Public librarians must not take for granted, because jobs have always been available in the past, that they will inevitably have jobs in the future.

Public libraries around the country that hum with activity and are used by the young and old, the stay-ins and drop-outs, are the libraries that look to the future by promoting the present. They are the ones that not only bloom with neighborhood energy but also prosper with increased budgets.

To meet the needs of current users of public libraries and to attract nonusers, librarians must be prepared to experiment with promotional ideas of all types. Some will fail, some succeed. Some are more difficult than others, but all of them will help place a perspective on the importance of public relations for the area you service.

Here are some suggestions:

1. *Sponsor a photographic contest.* Get in touch with local photo-supply shops for advice and support. One of the stores may donate prizes, and probably one of the judges. A newspaper editor and a teacher of photography could be the other judges. Divide the contest into juvenile, young adult, and adult sections. Display the top twenty or thirty photographs (or however many you choose) in the library before the final decisions. When the judges pick the first three winners of each group, publish their photos in the newspaper and exhibit them further in the library. Stretch the publicity for the library over a month with posters in the photo shops and announcements in

the newspapers. Distribute lists of the best books on photography in the library. Nearly everyone has a camera these days. Nearly everyone should be interested in the library as well. Join the two in such a contest.

2. *Invite a nearby university professor to conduct a short series of courses or lectures on the Great Books of the Western World.* The series could be a primer for the professor's own course at the university. He or she might find that a different type of person may be attracted to the series from your library, thereby bringing fresh viewpoints into the classroom. On the other hand, many members of your community may still consider the public library a storehouse of only mysteries and science fiction. Here's your chance to show them that your library is also concerned with promoting interest in the great works of literature and social commentary. The series may not attract as many people as a fitness group, but it would diversify your overall program and fulfill the needs of an important community minority.

3. *Have an area in your children's room set aside for artwork drawn by the children themselves.* Either formally or informally, have children draw their own version of illustrations inspired by books they have read in the library. A wall of children's drawings with their names, ages, home addresses, and schools is always attractive both to other children and to their parents. Photograph an especially fine drawing and publish it in a newspaper as a sample of what is being done in the children's section. Such a feature in the library could be continued indefinitely. Prizes might be awarded for the best drawings, or they might be used in displays in the adult area.

4. *Hold a lecture series on social security benefits.* Federal laws in this area change, and members of the older generation with little income often miss new opportunities simply because they do not have the chance to learn about these changes. Social security benefits now include many programs devoted to individuals of all ages. Many people are not aware of this and would be surprised to learn how they may be advantageously affected by a program that was once thought of as being entirely geared to people over sixty-five. People are interested in how to raise their income. Your library can help them.

5. *Draft a bibliography on how best to invest money.* Include books and magazine articles; refer to your pamphlet file if you have such material in it. Be sure that you annotate the list with at least one or two lines of information, as a good library should. Then distribute these bibliographies at banks and savings-and-loan companies around town or pass them out at your lecture series on social security benefits.

6. *Show films and videos of general interest.* Perhaps you'll find that the popularity of such a free program might be carried over from the summer months into the winter. A standard year-long program of movies on a weekly or monthly basis could attract widespread family interest. You might have two types run on two different days. One would appeal to a general audience, the second to more specialized interests. A large number of noncommercial movies are being made each year. Include selection of everything from travelogues of exotic islands of the world to analyses of the light spectrum, to the space program, to mountain climbing. Show some of the better Hollywood and foreign films of old. One staff member could coordinate the entire program. Print and distribute time-and-place schedules. The newspaper may print them on a regular basis. The popularity of movies helps popularize your library.

7. *Take a poll among readers of what they consider the best book they ever read.* Then publish the list as one from local users of the library rather than the "best books" often chosen by professional critics and librarians. The survey might enlighten you about local priorities. Even more, it would give readers an idea of the tastes of their neighbors. People like to read what friends are reading. This type of list provides this friendship. Place a simple form at the

chargeout desk. One title from each reader who wished to participate is enough. Later, post the results at the library entrance and in the newspaper. If one particular title has an overwhelming response, this could be used as an interesting item for radio and television newscasts. A lot of mileage may be had with little effort.

8. *Enter all parades.* Nearly every community has at one time or another during the year some sort of parade or civic celebration. The public library should be represented at every one. Let the public know that they have a free municipal library and that their library is front and center along with other civic agencies. Libraries with bookmobiles can easily decorate their wagons of reading with signs and ribbons appropriate to the celebration theme. Some of the library workers might enjoy walking in the appropriate theme costume and passing out bookmarks or library registration blanks to the people at curbside. Even if no more is possible than riding in an open car with a sign on the door, be sure to enter. It's effortless publicity.

9. *Sponsor a music group.* So much of the population is under twenty-five years of age that public librarians must make special efforts to attract this age group to the library. Your town may have many small amateur music groups that would appreciate an opportunity for a free stage. A concert of two or three local groups on a Saturday night, either inside the library or on the grounds, could attract an age group that might otherwise assume a library has nothing relevant to offer. A local concert at the public library would also undoubtedly make the local news media.

10. *Conduct a book fair.* You might work with a local bookstore and specialize in promoting children's books or local history or a combination of mysteries and science fiction. Set up tables on the front lawn or porch. If the weather is inclement, set aside an area inside the library. Have cookies and punch or coffee available. Paint big signs with red letters and run streamers from tree to tree, window to window, or bookshelf to bookshelf. Generate a festive atmosphere. Make the world of books what it is—enjoyable.

11. *Offer the library building or grounds for speeches of visiting dignitaries or prominent authors.* Check with city hall personnel periodically to see if a visit by political leaders or big-business officials is planned in the near future. Suggest the library as an ideal central, nonpartisan location for speeches and welcoming committees. Also, try to place your library on the list of city sights that visitors should see, including a quick but pleasant tour of your most prized possessions. This pride in your library sparks similar pride and interest on the part of other city officials and community residents. The association of prominent personages with your library can only upgrade your image of importance to the people of your town.

12. *Set up a library booth downtown every Saturday.* A small, colorful painted cubicle on the corner of the central shopping area is a reminder to harried shoppers that the library offers them a healthy breather in their lives. You must secure permission from the city for such a booth but should be able to do so without too much trouble. Station an attractive assistant inside to issue library cards to passersby and hand out book lists. The assistant might also take requests for books back to the library and then have them ready for pickup at the circulation desk when the patron goes to the library in the next two or three days.

13. *Drive the bookmobile to factories.* Some librarians use their bookmobiles only for schools and only during certain hours of the day. As a result, the bookmobile often stands idle and is not used to full potential. Experiment with your bookmobile during these unused times by peddling books to factory workers. Find out when coffee breaks are scheduled during mornings and afternoons at nearby factories or offices and meet this schedule at a few stops. Commercial lunch wagons do it all the time. A book wagon could offer appropriate reading refreshment to the workers at the same time. Make

bookmobile stops at shopping malls and supermarkets along the way. An expensive machine like a bookmobile cannot afford to be sitting idle in the parking lot.

14. *Insert library information in other cultural program material.* Place specialized book lists and library schedules and circulation procedures in art-show guides, museum brochures, stage-production notes, and program publications handed out at cultural presentations. With a professional-looking insert, you shouldn't have much difficulty in convincing the management of your plan. A pleasing one-pager is sufficient. Your audience is captive and appropriate besides. The library insert provides an attractive addition not usually found in such programs and represents the library at quality events.

15. *Stage open houses periodically to introduce newcomers to your library.* An exceptional exhibit deserves more than a casual glance by someone walking through the building. So announce a library open house in the newspaper, decorate a table with cookies and coffee, invite some appropriate special guests, and present a short explanation of the exhibit. Open houses and an informal, friendly atmosphere create an opportunity for you and your staff to meet members of your community and to establish a better rapport with them and their needs.

16. *Conduct a workshop on how to use the public library.* Such a workshop may be valuable to many casual visitors to your library. The average layperson knows little about good library use. A workshop in the morning or afternoon (or the evening to catch the day workers) might be met with enthusiasm. Cover the basics of what is on a catalog card, how the Dewey Decimal or Library of Congress classification systems are arranged, the most-used reference books. Have an ample supply of printed information distributed at the workshop for the participants to take home with them. By the initial response you can decide whether more one-day workshops would be valuable or whether you might move toward more detailed instruction.

17. *Distribute a list of home reference materials that may be purchased inexpensively.* Include in the list books available at your library so that patrons may check to see what they contain. Parents constantly ask public librarians their judgment of the best encyclopedia to purchase for their school children at home. When they discover the cost of encyclopedias their purchase is usually postponed and nothing takes its place. A home reference collection suggested by your library is a welcome replacement. The following list won't take the place of an encyclopedia, but it helps: *World Almanac, Columbia-Viking Desk Encyclopedia, Random House Dictionary of the English Language—College Edition,* (Dictionary of place names in your state), *Bartlett's Familiar Quotations, Guinness Book of World Records, Rand McNally World Atlas.*

Part of the cost may be spent for reference books in favorite subject areas. Here are only a few possibilities: *Benet's Reader Encyclopedia, Encyclopedia of World History, Webster's New Dictionary of Synonyms, Complete Guide to Everyday Law.*

18. *Begin a campaign to achieve 100% library registration of people or households in your community.* At the same time construct a tall "thermometer" of progress and station it on your front lawn or beside the entrance to the building. Indicate by red paint up the center of the thermometer the current registration percentage. Indicate on one side the number of people or households in your community (which you may easily secure at City Hall). Then keep a running tabulation of your actual number of registrants and of the number of possibilities. This giant thermometer gives you both an excuse to solicit new names and a publicity gimmick to exploit in the local newspaper.

19. *Have a remote radio broadcast periodically from your library.* Interview shows are the life-blood of many radio stations around the country. Perhaps no one at your nearest station ever suggested a show from the public library, where the array of fascinating people is virtually endless. Scholars,

drop-outs, members of women's-liberation groups, seers, writers, researchers: the entire gamut of daily library users whom you may take for granted may be a discovery for program managers. The response could be so successful that the radio station will wish to make a regular feature of remote broadcasts from your library.

20. *Supply the local newspaper with a question-and-answer quiz.* Your reference librarian should be able to come up with five easy questions and answers a day. If not, then perhaps a ten-question quiz for the Sunday edition would work. A quiz is one of those simple feature items in a newspaper that many people try their heads with daily. Be sure that the name of your library is assigned to the quiz, as a place to find answers to these and other more personal questions, a place to keep in mind.

## For school libraries

A school library is designed primarily to support the general curriculum of a school and to provide recreational reading as an enhancement of this curriculum. Materials in a school library must be kept relevant and up-to-date with an evolving instructional program. This way the library is integrated effectively into an overall education goal, that is, to activate each child's individual potential with the latest and fullest scope of materials possible.

More than any other type of library, with the possible exception of some special libraries, the school library has taken the lead in moving toward extensive use of other media as well as print materials. The trend toward instructional-materials centers at elementary, junior high school, and secondary levels is indicative of the vital role a school library plays in education. No longer is a library stocked only with books and pamphlets. Now, videotapes, slides, maps, audiotapes, individualized listening stations, charts, pictures, multimedia kits, television, computers, periodicals, microfilm, microfiche, and other materials are part and parcel of the modern instructional materials center, once known as a library.

The challenge to utilize the entire range of a school library is no small one. All these pieces of equipment and materials are of little focused use unless they are incorporated into the classroom curricula. School librarians must exert their professionalism by aggressively promoting their library. Otherwise, their programs will be directed by the relatively uninformed suggestions of others. Use of a school library does not depend nearly so much on the children in the classroom as it does on the teacher and other adults involved in the education of the young.

A combination, therefore, of making a school library attractive to students and adults alike is paramount. Here are some suggestions:

1. *Ask teachers what units they may be preparing for the near future.* If a unit on space exploration is planned, suggest to the teacher that you can prepare a short lesson in the library or in the classroom on reference books and supplementary material on space that may be helpful and interesting to students. Emphasize materials that have been published or acquired recently. Mention a new film or video relevant to the unit and suggest showing it in the library along with a short lesson on materials on the shelves that may be used immediately after and in conjunction with the movie. Keep yourself informed of the units teachers plan and then try to meet those units with materials they might find useful. Make good teachers of them and they'll come back for more.

2. *Prepare a videotape on the better use of the school library.* Many school districts are now producing their own tapes for instructional television programs as complements to the tapes they receive from the national network. Make certain the library is represented in your local series. A one-shot lesson is better than none. A series on: a) generating enthusiasm and introducing the library in general; b) the organization of the library; c) reference

and other nonfiction materials; d) fiction, and a brief review, would provide the opportunity to particularize the television lesson to your own school district. The first production demands work, but the tape may be used many times after this and reap long-lasting benefits.

3. *Develop a story hour.* Some school librarians schedule a regular time during the school day to tell stories with books. Other possibilities include a story hour right after the last bell rings or on Saturday afternoon. Often the school library is unused during summer months. If a local public library has no summer program, the school library could be used for such story activities. This opening of the library would be a solid preparation for the regular session, when students return to classes. Try to set aside a certain area in the library for the story hours. A rug to sit on, a few chairs, and a cozy corner make the storytelling a little more appealing.

4. *Give book talks periodically.* Select some of the finer books relevant to both the class unit and the types of children in the class. Then arrange with the teachers for you to take a few minutes to generate interest in new titles, as well as the classics that need to be introduced to new students each year. Be sure to emphasize to students that other good books are available if the ones you present are checked out, and that you will be more than pleased to help anyone find a book that appeals.

5. *Organize a library club.* Such a club not only develops better awareness of library use among its members but also establishes a relationship with the rest of the students by opening the library administration to young people. Library club members may give tours to younger students and parents during open houses, help with such daily work as keeping circulation records and shelving, and set up exhibits and displays. With some help they may also publish their own newsletter and suggest books for other students to read. They could also help you design library-aid materials, such as bookmarks and posters.

6. *Demonstrate the use of audiovisual equipment.* The school librarian in an instructional materials center must be familiar with the slide projectors, video cassettes, film projectors, record-tapes, film-loop machines, microfilm readers, and equipment needed to make audiovisual materials usable. The direction toward more individualized instruction, however, warrants student familiarity with these machines as well. Teachers, who in most states must take audiovisual courses for certification, also need refreshers on how to fix machines. Your demonstrations of these to a few students and teachers at a time may be extremely valuable and lead to more use of your expensive multimedia materials.

7. *Present a slide program to the school board.* A short, information-packed presentation that shows the goals of your library program in action may keep school-board members aware of library activities and predispose them to back your policies and proposals in the future. Take 35mm color slides of students and teachers using your materials. Have plenty of action in the pictures, no obvious poses. Prepare a short script with solid information and statistics. Then request a time slot in one of the board meetings for the presentation of ten minutes or less, no more. Stick to this ten minutes. Convince the board members with concrete evidence, not wishes and myths, that the library program they support is an active one and contributes substantially to the overall effectiveness of the schools they govern.

8. *Publish a newsletter for teachers and administrators.* The newsletter could have the effect of informing the school-board members, superintendent, principals, and classroom teachers of new material available while at the same time keeping the library program up front in public view. Working for the students is your primary responsibility. All the good programs you develop or hope to develop do little good, however, unless they have the support of the administrators. One effective way to develop this support is to

keep the administrators informed of your activities. Let them know once a month, in a photocopied one-sheet newsletter, of unusual displays, special programs at certain schools, library staff participation in other school activities, how much new sets of materials are being used, about any increases in the use of the library as a result of certain innovations, and about other activities.

9. *Develop an "Our Library Is . . . " display for the next PTA meeting.* Have some of the students from all grade levels write short lines about what they think a library is and why it is important. Either have the students themselves print the statement on large paper or copy them on a large-type typewriter. Then paste the words on a piece of cloth-covered backing and set up a display table. Statements in the students' own words (such as "Without libraries the whole world would be in a mess up") give parents and teachers alike not only a few smiles and chuckles but an indication that children do consider their library important.

10. *Alternate grades for library exhibits.* Set aside one particular display area to be used solely by the students themselves. Give each grade level or class, depending on the size of the school, a turn in the preparation and execution of a library display. Within bounds of taste, let the students display exactly what they wish. Let them take the initiative in producing ideas. Guide them perhaps in the use of materials but allow them complete freedom in the use of their showcase. Indicate which grade prepared the current display and give credit to the individuals involved. In a short time competition should develop to see which grade can come up with the best display. Such competition brings both notice and students to the library.

11. *Paint a long mural on incidents or information on one subject culled from various books.* You might suggest this as a project to one of the classroom teachers or you might have your library club members work on it. A fifteen- or twenty-foot piece of butcher paper and some watercolor paints are all the materials needed. Space travel, the history of your state, the water cycle, the Civil War—any number of subjects may be the focus. Students could illustrate the mural with scenes they have read in books on whatever subject they choose. The title, author, and call number could be painted next to the scene taken from the book. Afterward, hang the mural on a wall in the library or place it in the hall somewhere in public sight.

7

12. *Work toward flexible scheduling.* The trend toward a closer arrangement of student time and following more closely the student's immediate inclination of interest is appropriate to the use of a library also. The need to go to the library to research a subject the moment the need arises should not be blocked. Arrange with classroom teachers and principals to allow students to go to the library when students themselves are ready, not merely when you are ready. Flexible scheduling brings the library into the forefront of the student's learning process, a process that cannot be departmentalized into time slots or artificially created.

13. *Conduct tours of the library for new teachers.* Make a concerted effort to have a spot in the new-teacher orientation program for a brief in-person explanation of your library facilities and materials. No matter how brief, such a tour establishes the library as a central organ of the school program, familiarizes new teachers with the capability of the library, and allows you the opportunity to invite them to use your services so that they may become better teachers and in turn create better students.

14. *Prepare a photo spread for the local newspaper.* Let the community at large know that the library program is integral to the overall education of its children. Some school districts have their own public relations personnel; they should be notified to execute such a picture page. If not, then you may either get in touch with the editor of the paper and ask him to send one of his photographers or you will have to track down a photographer (such as

yourself) to take the photos. Don't forget you have an edge. Newspaper editors know that most people like to see photos of children. Make sure your pictures are full of action, that they tell a story, and that they have a professional quality equal to your professional interest in the library.

15. *Develop student library skills in multimedia.* Offer to teachers and principals to organize some small workshop sessions in which you would provide practice for students to research a subject in the wide variety of formats available in the library. With a teacher, prepare a plan to expose students to a broad range of information on, for example, personal hygiene. List the films, videos, books, pamphlets, listening-station material, pictures, charts, and other media available on this one subject. Concentrate on generating awareness in students that research information is available in many other forms than books and that using a variety of media in your library makes research projects more fun.

16. *Send classroom ideas to teachers.* At times some teachers become annoyed when outsiders seem to intrude into their classroom domains. However, most competent, enthusiastic teachers welcome new ways to present old ideas. Photocopy any unusual article, or photograph of a striking bulletin board, or list of effective learning steps in presenting mathematical concepts, and send them to appropriate teachers. Read nonprofessional magazines also, because many contain informative articles on education. Give a teacher the feeling that you are in the library to serve them, that they are really not alone in the classroom, and demonstrate your interest in how well they teach by periodically passing along tricks of the trade from other competent, enthusiastic teachers in the country.

17. *Experiment with paperbacks.* The amazing spread of paperbound books is symptomatic of their appeal to readers of all ages. Paperbacks may be displayed in a separate paperbound section, on a spin-rack as in drugstores, or incorporated within the main section of the book shelves. Suggest to teachers that students have their own paperbound dictionaries at their desks. The cost is minimal for the long-range benefits such a handy personal dictionary may bring. Every classroom should also have a couple of paperbound almanacs. Many suitable fiction books for school children are published in paperback and may be processed informally for library use. The affinity young people have for paperbound books outside the school building should be put to advantage inside the library.

18. *Have students prepare their own bibliographies.* Announce that the library is seeking students to make a list of the five best books they have ever read. With short annotations, the students can write the reasons that they enjoyed the books. Publish the list in some form and then distribute it in their classrooms. Students sometimes are more likely to read a book suggested by their peers than by a teacher or librarian. Student-produced bibliographies give them this suggestion. They also give students skills in preparing bibliographies in proper form and a concentrated interest in what a library has provided them.

19. *Show films or videos after school in your library.* Select movies that have been recently shown in classrooms by teachers as part of certain lessons. This will not detract from your potential audience, since children like to see movies a second or third time. In addition, the repeat showings help reinforce the learning process. You could select movies from each class level and show them on certain days of the week so that a pattern results: movies for lower grades on Monday, middle grades on Wednesday, upper grades on Friday. Keep the atmosphere relaxed and informal. Make the library a center of activity and as important as the playground.

20. *Attend all school meetings and functions.* Through you the library should be represented at PTA meetings, school-board meetings, principal meetings, faculty meetings, rallies, parties, assemblies, sports events, the

entire range of school activities. The library gains a certain stature through librarians who are attentive to the current needs of the school program and who exhibit a professional interest in how their own program relates to the overall educational goals. Volunteer for committee work—and produce. Make your opinions and aims for the school library known. Public exposure and the acquaintances you make by attendance at many school-related functions establish the image of your library as a dynamic and aggressive center of service.

*Source:* Steve Sherman, *ABC's of Library Promotion* (Metuchen, N.J.: Scarecrow Press, 1992). 251p. Reprinted with permission.

# How academic libraries can celebrate National Library Week

## *by Linda K. Wallace*

- Invite the college president to issue a "National Library Week" proclamation acknowledging the library's contributions.
- Recruit a journalism class to interview students, faculty, administrators, and visiting VIPs on "How Books and the Library Changed My Life." Have photography students take shots to accompany the interviews. Publish all this in a special National Library Week newsletter or in the library's (maybe even the college's) annual report.
- Do a "Changing Lives . . . Changing Libraries" exhibit. Pick a significant year in the life of the school and contrast library and information resources then and now using posters and other memorabilia. Include photos and lists such as "Bestsellers then—and now," "The card catalog then—and now," "The librarian then—and now," and "The library collection then—and now." Suggest this as a feature story to campus and community newspapers.
- Start a running notebook near the circulation desk asking those in line to jot down their thoughts on how the library changed their lives. Select a "quote of the week" for posting.
- Hold a National Library Week daily drawing. Have entrants write their thoughts on "How Books and the Library Changed My Life" on a postcard. Draw daily winners and be generous in awarding t-shirts, buttons, and gift certificates as prizes.
- Send a letter to distinguished faculty and alumni inviting them to share their thoughts. Create a special bulletin board display. Submit an article to the alumni magazine.
- Have student copywriters write commercials about the life-changing effect of the college library's books and libraries in general. Ask a local advertising or public relations association to select "winners" and recruit a local TV station or the Broadcast Communications Department to produce them. Submit them as public service advertising for campus and community stations. Suggest a story about the cooperative venture for the station—or local newspaper.

*Source:* Linda K. Wallace, "Ideas for Celebrating NLW," *College & Research Libraries News* 54 (February 1993): 65.

# How to photograph your library

*by Edith McCormick and Sharon M. Hill*

YES, LIBRARIANS CAN BECOME skilled photographers and place stories in national library publications or local media. At one time, it may have been enough to call the local newspapers before the arrival of a scheduled clown or ethnic dance troupe. Today, however, librarians also must learn how to make it easy, economical, and irresistible for editors to use their photographs. Whether it's advance or postprogram, publicity is good for libraries, and photographs can help to get it.

## Getting the right tools

"Just point and shoot," claim the ads for the $14.95 to $49.95 automatic fixed-focus cameras. Probably the only improvement that these "buys" actually offer over the old fixed-focus instamatics or Polaroids that have been serving well enough for the staff newsletter is that they require using 35mm film, which produces a larger negative than most old instamatics. The added value good photographic equipment brings to any public-relations effort cannot be exaggerated. To produce photographs that warrant publication, plan to invest anywhere from $300 to $450 on a good compact 35mm single-lens reflex (SLR) camera with an autofocus system. Cameras equipped with a basic 50mm SLR allow the user to add lenses and accessories and expand the photographic system indefinitely as needs change. You needn't buy everything at once. Just make sure the camera is adaptable and can accommodate special lenses or features that you may want to add later.

Move in close. Fill the frame with the subject. Crop the photo to eliminate unnecessary background.

Even ordinary events can make appealing pictures. Move in close and capture the facial expression.

A much more successful image than the unimaginative group shot: cutting the ribbon at a dedication service.

Two basic lenses that should be purchased are a 35mm lens for group shots, which gives a wider field of view in low light than the standard 50mm lens, and an 80mm and 85mm telephoto lens, which is useful for portraits, architectural details, or honing in on a single subject from an active scene. The more powerful the zoom, the more money the buyer will need to invest. What such lenses accomplish can be found in Raymond Bial's excellent paperback *Looking Good: A Guide to Photographing Your Library* (Chicago: ALA, 1991). Shop around, read recommendations and reviews in local newspaper photography columns, in magazines such as *Modern Photography* and in books such as *Looking Good*, then set out to a good camera store.

Sharon Hill, public relations director at Birmingham Public Library (Alabama) whose photographs are shown here, recommends a Minolta 5000I that sells for $399.90 plus $80 for a Minolta D316 flash unit. The camera, which has both a program and a manual mode, comes with a 35mm-80mm wide-angle zoom lens. Scan *Time, Newsweek,* and *People* magazines to see how often a wide-angle is used to exaggerate distances. A 24mm lens, for example, could show a group of people in the foreground wearing library t-shirts with the library in the background a football field away.

For daylight shooting and flash photography in either a small or cavernous library, consider the Nikon N5005. Hill says it compares favorably with the Nikon FG—a camera her library supplied her with when she arrived there four years ago. Usual prices are about $330 for the N5005 body and $173 for a 35mm-70mm wide-angle zoom lens. The camera has a powerful built-in flash and several easy-to-use creative options: for example, shutter-priority or aperture-priority automatic control modes. These allow the user to select the shutter speed while the camera selects the aperture, or vice versa. Once you become more skilled, you can use the manual exposure settings. Until then, however, keep the camera in the program mode, where both the shutter speed and the aperture are set automatically to control the amount of light reaching the film. Hill says that instead of merely a snap-on leather case to suspend the camera from her neck, she uses a waterproof $40 camera bag to stash her gear. In this she places her camera, extra lenses, film, filters, lens cleaner, batteries, note pads, and pencils.

7

## Read, practice, and look

Spend an afternoon paging through the easy-to-follow owner's instruction manual that comes with the new camera. Handheld camera techniques can be found in such general and useful guides as *The Joy of Photography* (Reading, Mass.:Addison-Wesley, 1991) by the editors at the Eastman Kodak Company. Hill advises: "The next time you read your favorite newspaper or magazine, stop when a photograph catches your eye and analyze what caught your attention. Was it subject, technique, composition, someone's expression? Learn from others and try the same techniques with your photographs."

Buy some print film; either ASA 100 or 200 Kodacolor "Gold," Fuji Reala ASA 100, or Agfa ASA 100 (which Hill swears by), and start photographing the library staff, keeping them within ten feet of the camera. Be ready to use up at least a thirty-six frame roll of film on each major scene. Film is cheap compared to a lost chance at a story in print.

## Be creative

The challenge now is how to make every event at your library look exciting. For example, a local magician is performing for the children's program. You might persuade the magician to produce his or her white rabbit one more time so you can photograph a child gently petting the creature in the performer's hand.

Place a visiting author in an unlikely context or with a disarming library prop. Envision vampire-story writer Anne Rice admiring the children's storytelling nook or Gothic novelist Stephen King laughing at a cartoon display.

Library magazines will give your photograph more immediate attention if the library context speaks loud and clear. Library magazines like to see librarians involved in the programming, especially if the program or event has a newsy edge to it—a centennial, an author award, or a celebration after winning a bond issue. Cab Calloway on a stage in the library auditorium is not as compelling as Cab Calloway performing in the library's main reading room. A dog show? Shoot the hounds jumping over five copies of *Books in Print*. Showing either a library interior or a recognizable library prop always makes a photograph more relevant. If you're tired of showing visiting writers inside, take them outdoors on a beautiful spring or summer day and add the luster and color of natural surroundings to the background. Ask the visitor to wear a library t-shirt, don a library hat, or hold a new library umbrella while talking with a library staffer or director.

Try to get into the action, especially when shooting children's programming. Shoot at child's eye level. The frenzy and excitement of the activity is more readily captured than it would be from the adult eye view from above or afar. Develop a story line when a major performer does a program at the library. Photograph the person entering the library, meeting staff and/or the public signing autographs, and talking to visitors. Then shoot the "performance" itself, leave taking, and/or tiredness at the conclusion.

To make people photography interesting, first put your subjects at ease. Relax the subjects while you're setting up, telling them how the compact shelves accidentally started closing while you were dusting the books—anything that will temper the natural stress they feel and make their body language more fluid. Use reverse psychology. Say, "I want you to look nervous and terrified when the shutter goes off." Tell them you'll be taking a great number of pictures to catch their most characteristic moods. Apologize for that but stay good-natured and build up rapport.

Find something for the subjects to do. Shoot from a different angle—from below or above—looking up from a position on the floor surrounded by books

This photo says it all: Composition, facial expressions, and action produce interest in what is taking place.

Capitalize on programs: The children enjoy an opportunity to say hello to the white rabbit.

or down from a scaffold while your subjects examine the new mosaics on the ceiling. Line up that city council or a group of honored guests in a row in the children's room and have each member cut the ribbon inaugurating a window display. Being "good sports," librarians also deserve highlighting if the circumstances magically combine for a "natural," such as a long-haired librarian being a model for a young-adult hair-braiding demonstration. If you are taking an action shot, for example, with a librarian walking rapidly in a businesswoman's briefcase relay, show her at a moment of intense psychic and physical pressure with her face contorted, or her jaw set as she forges onward: her expression determined, her briefcase tightly gripped at waist level, the muscles of her legs flexed at the extreme position of race walking. Show more space in front of her—where the action is received—and crop in close behind her when framing the photograph in your lens. Such a candid shot makes for a salable photograph. Newspapers, especially, find this appealing. So, barring a child tweaking a dog's ear or squeezing a fragile bird, if you can capture something off-the-record, go for it!

## Providing the right background

As Hill points out, "Keep it plain and simple. If the background or foreground is busy, it will detract from your main subject. If you are dissatisfied with the background, move your subjects to another location." Once you receive prints, ask the photograph processor to crop out undesirable elements such as telephone wires, parked automobiles, or any distracting background. Sidewalks in the foreground, a child mugging into the camera eye off to the side, and other distractions also can be cropped.

Areas in libraries a photographer should shun include dark paneling (unless all subjects are light-skinned, light-haired, and wearing white or yellow), busy drapery or wallpaper, reflective surfaces such as glass or enameled walls, and ugly monochromatic spaces. Watch out for backgrounds brighter than the subject, though, so the subject is not underexposed.

## A few lighting considerations

Flash fills a picture with more light and allows you to take a photograph in front of a window and still illuminate a face. Bounced flash (aiming the flash at a piece of cardboard or a bright nearby wall or ceiling) creates softer shadows than direct head-on front lighting. Natural or available light always creates a more interesting and textured result. Often, stark contrasts of light and dark are alleviated and a stronger sense of dimension is created.

Another technique called sidelighting can be achieved by placing subjects near a window and having the diffused light fall on their faces at an angle. Ask what you're doing wrong when photographs come back badly lit. The August 1991 *Consumer Reports* article "Best Film Processing" also offers some ways to improve print results.

## Compose the photographs in your camera

As Hill says, "Today's new semiautomatic cameras are simple to operate. The key is in conceiving the picture. Shoot what you want to see on a printed page." Hill puts it this way: "You become the artist as you compose the photograph through the rectangular frame of your camera—and remember, your camera can be used to create vertical formats as well as horizontal." Frame the picture in the viewfinder and get close enough in some shots so the real subject fills the whole frame. Get in close! Be brazen, if necessary. If there's a great shot there, you've got to get it. Try to maintain goodwill, but remember professionalism. You're not shooting for fun, you're trying to help the library gain the public eye—and support.

## Dos and don'ts

Here are several suggestions to consider while taking photographs for publication.

- Don't shoot in black and white exclusively. Doing so will only guarantee that the media you contact require color exclusively.
- Do shoot in color or at least as a backup to black and white. Color is fast becoming the norm in trade publishing. You'll also have a better chance of marketing your shots to *USA Today* and other general media if your photographs are in living color. Publishers usually can convert color photographs to decent black-and-white photographs, while the reverse is not true, even in this age of colorization of old films.
- Do write down names or initials before people break the pose. If your library owns a Polaroid, you can back up your 35mm photos with a quick duplicate shot for identification of major participants. Don't ever let go of a photograph without the subjects being correctly identified.
- Do develop the habit of jotting down on a 3-by-5-inch card the name, date, and major participants and/or sponsors of an event that you're about to shoot. Take a photograph of the card as frame number one on the roll you then use.
- Don't handwrite or even type captions on the backs of pictures. Ink transfers to the front of those photographs that follow; writing crushes the front surface. It is better to code each photograph on a

back corner with a crayon and enclose a corresponding sheet of captions—or prepare captions in pencil on stick-on-labels, then apply and cover with transparent tape.

- Do store negatives in glassine envelopes in a dry place, marked with the date and the event photographed. If you have a 35mm proof sheet, identify the event on the back with a crayon, china marker, or stick-on label.
- Above all, don't get caught without film or spare batteries for the flash attachment. As Hill reminds all potential photographers, "Always keep your camera loaded and ready for action!"

*Source:* Edith McCormick and Sharon M. Hill, "Putting Your Library in Print with Outstanding Photographs," *Public Libraries* 32 (May/June 1993): 148–53. Photos courtesy of Sharon Hill.

# The U.S. national library symbol

THE NATIONAL LIBRARY SYMBOL was launched at the 1982 ALA Annual Conference for use by libraries throughout the United States in promoting awareness of their services. Originally developed by the Western Maryland Public Libraries, this symbol was recommended for national use by an ALA presidential task force.

Its purpose is to increase public awareness of libraries through widespread use on library directional signs and promotional materials. The symbol was designed primarily for use on exterior library signs appearing on streets, highways, campuses, and buildings; but it can also be used by individual libraries on newsletters, posters, booklists, library cards, bookmarks, letterhead, and other promotional materials.

The impetus for adopting a national library symbol developed from a recommendation of the 1979 White House Conference on Library and Information Services, which suggested "adopting a library symbol for the Nation" as one way to increase public awareness.

The ALA task force chose the Western Maryland symbol because it was designed as part of a total, coordinated sign system and because it met the following criteria for a good library symbol:

- instantly understood by the average person without supporting text;
- easily reproduced for both large and small applications;
- universally recognized and associated with a library;
- suggestive of the active use of information by library patrons;
- aesthetically pleasing, clear, and simple in design, similar to the graphic style of international symbols already in widespread use;
- capable of modification if the nature of libraries should change significantly in the future.

The symbol triggers instant recognition of a library through a graphic representation that people instantly associate with libraries—the book and reader. It does not attempt to capture the essence of the modern library or represent the range of its resources. This would be impossible to do in a clean, easily recognized image. Once the public is cued to the presence of a library by the basic symbol, additional symbols, signs, and promotional materials can be used to further educate users about the full range of library resources.

A standard shade of blue (PMS 285) is generally used as the background color for exterior use of the symbol on directional and building signs.

*Source:* ALA Public Information Office.

# Down with slogans

*by Charles Curran*

SLOGANS ARE OKAY IF YOU BELIEVE "taxation without representation is tyranny" and you want to think up some catchy rewording of this complex notion that the masses could understand. Maybe someday someone will even think of a clever way to invite the Almighty's judgment on submarine projectiles while giving the order for high vessel velocity and forward direction. I'm joking, of course; that could never happen.

However, what *has* happened is that we have come up with some slogans and metaphors about libraries. We actually *use* these sayings, sometimes where it matters, in libraries; but also where it doesn't, in the literature, in the classroom, and in meetings of the cognoscenti.

So we've got:

- "The library is the heart of _____" (fill in the blank).
- "Support staff are the backbone of the library."
- "Service is our highest calling."
- "*Access* has replaced *ownership.*"

"The library is the heart of the *whatever*" is our favorite metaphor, despite massive empirical evidence that the library is more like the liver and considerable suspicion that it sometimes behaves like the appendix.

Fascination with comparing ourselves to body parts has also inspired us to scatter skeletal references among the organs; hence, the support-staff-as-backbone metaphor. In the army, NCOs are called the backbones. Of course, as a PFC infantry grunt, I selected a part directly south of the backbone to describe my bosses. This accounts for my discomfort with slogans that etch our profession into public consciousness through comparison with fleshy gristle or the spiny things we use to filter poisons, maintain posture, sit on, or in the case of the appendix, don't use at all.

The real crime in the support staff/backbone deal is that we say support staff are crucial, frontline ambassadors, but we:

- pay them minimum wage, plus carfare;
- exclude them from participation in decision making;
- contradict and embarrass them in the presence of clients;
- and ridicule them with a lower-caste term: *nonprofessional.*

"Service is our highest calling." Sheep don't even bleat at this one. Service *is* an essential component of what we offer. But any librarian who looks at the technological revolution, our competition, the imperative that we invent and provide value-added products, and the state of our information illiteracy and who still insists on intoning the "service-above-all" slogan needs serious employment counseling. Service is for tennis and maitre d's.

# Cut the cuteisms

I learned firsthand about the foolishness of the "Access has replaced owner-ship" cuteism. I made the mistake of announcing this in a meeting at which the organization's information czar, collection-development staff, chair of the library committee, and frontline librarians were in attendance.

I explained the concept to them: You see, inflation and the information explosion conspire to make it impossible for any given library to have everything people want from it. So interlibrary loan was created to operationalize access. Translation: Prey upon larger collections, and thereby relieve the party of the first part from having to own what its clients request. This is in all the articles and textbooks, so I felt pretty safe in repeating the slogan.

Wrong! First, I'll translate the looks I got from the librarians:
- Naiveté, thy name is Curran.
- This is what happens when you let those people out of their ivory-tower cages.
- We gotta start checking ID at the front door again.
- Someone adjust that poor man's slobber cup.

Second, let me caution you against *ever* mouthing the slogans, platitudes, and mindless maxims that substitute for thought and common sense. At the very least, don't suggest to harried interlibrary loan personnel that they will *ever* convince impatient clients that "access has replaced ownership." In a pig's eye (speaking of organs).

# Simplistic sophistry

Slogans are odious because they are one-dimensional and simplistic. They serve us for a second, then leave a nasty residue. And they have opposites—contradictory maxims. "Look before you leap" was okay advice if nobody was shooting at you and there were crocodiles in the castle moat. But subsequent to the invention of the crossbow, "He who hesitates is lost."

Ironically, slogans can elect, then topple, leaders of the free world. So read my lips: It isn't that slogans aren't powerful, it's just that they can't get the real job done. "Access has replaced ownership" is a supply-sider's axiom, not a client's. It is an abstraction that pleases Bibliographic Controlvenators; but in superimposing its doctrine of managerial convenience, it ignores the

7

---

**Know your customers**

Marketers realize they need to do research to know what customers want. They have to know their customers and what appeals to them.

Suggestion: Remember that people born after you aren't reacting the same way you are to many things. If you need to do some homework, just remember that:

**22%** of your potential customers don't remember the American Bicentennial Celebration.

**33%** of the people living in the United States feel that people have always been on the Moon.

**50%** are too young to remember the assassination of John F. Kennedy.

**66%** are not old enough to remember the Korean War.

**70%** don't remember the days "before TV."

**85%** are not old enough to remember the 1929 stock market crash.

The point: Customers are changing. And people who want to serve them have to change too.

*Source: PR Activity Report, August 1993, p.5, citing Fred Newell in Arthur Andersen Retailing Issues Letter, Center for Retailing Studies, Texas A&M University.*

clarion call for libraries to be demand-driven, not supply-driven. Worse, it lures us into polemics when we should be concentrating on providing value-added packages, not musing over some bibliographic conundrum. What's next: "Neither a borrower nor a lender be"?

Admonitions alone won't feed the bulldog, however, so I am including some wise sayings you can memorize and repeat to help you keep from speaking in slogans:

- Repeat a platitude, expect an attitude.
- Declare a dictum, reside in hickdom.
- Mouth a cliché, you're passé.
- Proverb, schmahverb.

*Source:* Charles Curran, "Down with Slogans," *American Libraries* 24 (December 1993): 999–1000.

# Forming a foundation

*by Faye Clow*

**BEFORE TAKING THE LEGAL STEPS** to actually organize or establish a foundation for a public library, it is wise to take time to do some planning, decision making and educating. The success of a foundation hinges on the performance of the library in the community, the support of the staff and board of trustees for a foundation, and the careful choice of persons to serve as the board of the foundation.

Public libraries approach this planning component in different ways. At the very least, staff meetings to educate library personnel on the idea should be held. Staff are often the first people approached by the public for information. The library board must also be fully informed and enthusiastic. In addition to acceptance of the concept, the library should identify its roles and develop a mission statement and strategic plan. A long-range plan can help identify library needs and provide a sense of purpose to the foundation.

## Choosing the board

Once the library staff and trustees "know their library" they can begin to think about an initial organizational meeting and the appropriate choice of persons to serve as foundation board members. It is essential that foundation board members be influential residents of the community, able to garner financial support from their contacts and from business and industry, able to personally give financial support, and able to command respect for the library. Ideally, the foundation board will have equal representation with respect to gender, include such professions as a lawyer or accountant, and be representative of the community in such areas as age, race and political affiliation.

It is important to public libraries to communicate clearly to and maintain good relations with the appropriate governing body. Consider including an elected official, such as a city council member, or appointed official such as a finance director, on the foundation board. This removes the impression that the library is hoarding dollars or withholding financial information. It ensures that at least one member of the governing body will understand library needs at budget presentation time.

Another group to consider is the local Friends of the Library. If an active group exists in the community, consider whether the foundation should be created by the Friends with strong Friends membership on the foundation board, or whether the foundation would function better as an independent association. At the very least, consider appointments of Friends as well as members of other civic groups with strong ties to the library.

A decision will also have to be made as to the number of foundation board members and how many, if any, library trustees will be on the foundation board. Some public libraries have only trustees on the foundation board, some have a mix of community people and trustees, some have no trustees. Each public library must look at its situation and service areas and decide what is best for itself, but it would be difficult to justify a foundation board with no community representation except for trustees. The more people involved with and aware of the library, the more support for the library.

The size of the foundation board is optional. Again, it is advantageous to have influential people involved in the library. Some boards are as small as seven, some as large as thirty-five. Consider your facility and community and decide on a manageable and reasonable number.

## Organization meeting

Once the staff and library board have settled on a list of potential foundation board members, it is time to invite them to an organizational meeting. This is a vital moment in the life and success of a foundation. First impressions last. At this time the staff and trustees should present the roles, mission and plan of the library. Outline the needs of the library, as well as the role a foundation and its board can play in fulfilling those needs. Point out how valuable this coalition would be to the community. Be prepared. The people invited to serve are the best the area has to offer and their questions will be intelligent ones. Finally, before adjournment gain a commitment from each individual candidate to serve on the foundation board.

## Articles of incorporation

At this time the incorporation process can begin. To become a foundation, an organization must first incorporate as a nonprofit corporation with the state. A nonprofit corporation is a corporation which does not distribute any income or profit to its members, directors or officers. In order to incorporate, articles of incorporation must be filed with the Secretary of State. To draft this document and others, it is advisable to utilize the city attorney or a lawyer of your choice. An excellent source for model documents and advice of all kinds regarding the process of organizing a foundation is *Planning Tax Exempt Organizations* by Robert Desiderio and Scott Taylor.

Articles of Incorporation should be brief and contain only the most essential facts about the organization. These include the following:

- *Name of the corporation.* Usually it is the name of the library followed by the word "foundation." However, it is not necessary to use "foundation." Some public libraries use "Friends of . . ."

- *Duration of the corporation.* In most cases the duration is perpetual.
- *Purpose of the corporation.* Here it is important to use the language needed later by the Internal Revenue Service: The purpose of the corporation shall be to operate exclusively for charitable, scientific, and educational purposes as a nonprofit corporation.
- *Address of corporation.*
- *Management of corporation.* Include the number of board members and a statement to the effect that the affairs of the foundation will be controlled and determined by the bylaws.
- *Name of registered agent.* As this is a new organization, this is often the library director.
- *Names and addresses of the initial board.*
- *Hold harmless clause.* Protection for board members against legal claims.
- *Provision of distribution of assets upon dissolution.* Usually given to the library.

Each state's regulations may be slightly different so each public library should check with the Secretary of State to determine exact requirements, filing procedures and filing fee. Sometime after filing you will receive a Certificate of Incorporation authorizing you to transact business as a nonprofit corporation.

The next step is to file a Form SS-4 with the Internal Revenue Service. This is an application for an employer identification number which you will need for filing for tax exempt status. The IRS will assign you a number and send you notification of the number. This identification will be used on all business accounts, tax returns and related documents. The granting of the number does not mean you have gained tax exempt status.

## Bylaws

Bylaws flesh out provisions of the Articles of Incorporation and are therefore more lengthy. They are the guidelines and procedures according to which the foundation will operate. Bylaws explain the following:

- *Location of corporation.*
- *Members.* A foundation may decide to have members in addition to the Board of Directors. If so, this clause should include: qualifications for membership, rights of membership, terms, how members can resign or be terminated and related matters.
- *Meetings.* This is the place to explain such things as: when regular meetings occur, how to call a special meeting, how directors are notified, how action is taken, what a quorum is, and proxy voting.
- *Board of Directors.* Describe its powers, number of members, tenure and qualifications. If they must be residents of the library service area, say so. Include such things as when they meet, attendance requirements, how vacancies are filled, and manner of acting.
- *Officers.* List officer's titles, methods of election, term of office, removal from office, how to fill a vacancy, number of terms able to serve and other relevant information.
- *Executive director.* Many foundations appoint an executive director or financial development officer to promote the organization.
- *Committees.* Most foundations have permanent committees such as a development or fund-raising committee, an investment committee, or a marketing committee. Committee composition, duties and responsibilities should be described here.

- *Fiscal year.*
- *Dues.* Use only if you have made the decision to have members other than a Board of Directors.
- *Books and records.* Describe what books and records, such as minutes, will be kept and where they will be kept.
- *Contracts, loans, checks and deposits.* Include such items as authorization for entering into contracts, restricting loans to certain situations, and establishing who can pay bills or make deposits.
- *Dissolution.* Explain what happens if the foundation disbands.
- *Amendments.* Establish provisions for changing the bylaws.
- *Rules of order.* Consider adoption of guidelines such as *Robert's Rules of Order* for governing meetings.
- *Waiver of notice.* It is prudent to include a provision for an alternative to issuing notices required elsewhere in the bylaws.
- *Indemnification.* This clause states that directors will be held harmless or protected from legal responsibility for the actions of the organization.

This document should be written in consultation with an attorney. It must be prepared in time for discussion and adoption at the first meeting of the foundation following the organizational meeting.

## Applying for tax exempt status

Once the organization has incorporated with the state, received an employer identification number, and adopted bylaws, it is ready to file for recognition of exemption from federal income tax. The magic number at this juncture is 501(c)(3). This is the pertinent section of the IRS code that will give the library foundation all the advantages outlined earlier, including tax deductibility for its donors. To apply, fill out IRS Form 1023. This can be done while waiting for certification from the state and should be done by or reviewed by an attorney. The form asks the following:

- Signature of authorized person
- Employer Identification Number
- Previous tax returns (only if the organization has been in operation for a while)
- Balance sheet of receipts and expenditures for current and preceding three years or a proposed two-year budget
- Description of anticipated activities
- Articles of Incorporation
- Bylaws

7

This form is filed with the district IRS office. Even if the application is thoroughly completed, it is not unusual for the IRS to ask for additional information. Supply what is requested and wait for their reply. Expect to wait five to six months for the IRS to respond with the Letter of Determination. This is not a problem because the tax exempt status is retroactive. It is also common, especially for new foundations, to receive a temporary determination or, as the IRS terms it, an "advance ruling period." After this period, perhaps eighteen months, a determination is made as to whether the requirements have been met in actual performance. In any event, the public library foundation can expect a declaration of tax exemption six to twenty-four months after organizing.

*Source:* Faye Clow, *Forming and Funding Public Library Foundations* (Chicago: ALA Public Library Association, 1993). 31p.

## Fundraising and urban libraries

A 1993 fundraising survey of 63 library members of the Urban Libraries Council revealed the following financial facts:

### Endowments
- 59% of the responding libraries have endowments.
- Urban libraries reported $136.5 million in endowments.
- $8,573,000 endowment income was used in the last fiscal year.

### Foundations
- 44% of responding libraries have foundations.
- 64% of the foundations were formed in the 1980s.
- Of the libraries not now having foundations, 36% indicate that they plan to form them in the next 1–4 years. Only 12% indicated they never plan to form foundations.
- 54% of the foundations in the survey are governed by foundation boards which overlap in membership with library boards.
- 75% of the foundations have staff, 54% have two or fewer staff people, 14% have none.

### Friends
- 92% of the reporting libraries have Friends groups.
- Friends groups reporting on the survey raised $2.6 million in the previous year.

### General fundraising
- 75% of the reporting libraries indicated they are actively engaged in raising funds from the private sector.
- 70% reported their levels of fundraising have increased in the last ten years. Nineteen percent said levels of fundraising activities were about the same, and none reported they had decreased.
- 76% indicated they expected the levels of fundraising activities to increase in the next 5–10 years. Only one library reported expecting it to decrease.
- Reporting libraries raised $2.4 million in private funds in the previous year.

### Who does fundraising?
- 85% of the library directors.
- 47% of the boards of trustees.
- 45% of the foundation boards.
- 75% of the Friends groups.

*Source: Fund Raising and Financial Development Survey Results*
(Evanston, Ill.: Urban Libraries Council, December 1993). 469p. Reprinted with permission.

# TECHNOLOGY 8

## "Low" technology

*by Charles E. Farley, Jr.*

WHEN I EARNED MY MS IN LIBRARIANSHIP from Western Michigan University in 1971, TV media laboratories were considered the technological wave of the modern library's future. At the time, well before VCRs and laser discs, going to the library to watch educational videos seemed pretty advanced, daring, bold.

By current standards, it's about as daring as a brown tweed jacket and about as bold as a pair of wingtips. Today, this technology is an artifact, a curiosity, even an embarrassment, like the clothing and hairstyles of the 1960s. But it does remind us how transient the technology of the moment really is. It reminds us that in a few short years the CD-ROM databases that we're wide-eyed about today will seem like quaint collections of so many scratchy 45s.

Disillusioning, yes. But time—even in small doses—can do peculiar things. Not that long ago, a Democratic candidate for president could enter an election and, with one hand on the Bible, talk sincerely about coming out of it with a victory. Not that long ago, Frank Sinatra elicited the same sort of parental scowls as we see produced now by Metallica.

Change is something you'd think we'd be accustomed to, especially in the waning years of the 20th century, when new technologies sprout like potholes in the central New York spring. At no time in history has so much change occurred so rapidly. And nowhere are the changes in libraries more powerfully documented than in the pages of the product catalog my company, Gaylord Information Systems, has been producing since the turn of the century.

Browsing through these old catalogs is amusing, intriguing, and ultimately a bit disturbing. All these changes, and to what end?

Leafing through these old catalogs one cold, quiet Syracuse evening, after everyone else had left the office, I was struck by the scores of products that (like old friends) had changed, the dozens that had quietly disappeared, the many others that I no longer even recognized. On page after page they appeared, like silent rows of tombstones.

Suddenly—overcome by a feeling of fleeting professional mortality—I called out into the darkness beyond my lone fluorescent tube: "What lasts?"

**Library Bureau Patent Diamond Frame Steel Stack**
is adjustable, indestructible, ornamental, removable, perfectly lighted, well ventilated, and simple in construction. Single wall sections erected for wall spaces, or double floor sections as shown above.
**IT IS IN USE IN OVER 100 LIBRARIES.**
*Correspondence invited with all libraries requiring Shelving. Designs and estimates on application.*
**LIBRARY BUREAU,**
BOSTON, 530 Atlantic Avenue.

Like Poe upon a midnight dreary, I think I heard an answer. I think it came from the brittle old pages themselves. Okay, so maybe not from the pages themselves.

And no, there wasn't any ominous bird perched above my chamber door. Still, the products in these pages told me something that I think is vitally important to all of us. Let's turn to them briefly while I explain this revelation.

## Remembering a trusty friend

In every edition of these product catalogs, even the newest, I found the venerable card catalog. We all know it well. Quartered light oak. Antique finish. Little brass pull handles. Made to last.

From the dawn of our profession as a profession—days when the best way to get from here to there was on the back of a horse—the card catalog was the library's basic "system," the "database" that centralized information on the holdings of libraries large and small. Who among us cannot recall the school librarian (in my case, Mrs. Dalton) conducting an "orientation" for the third grade class—a process that began, naturally and inevitably, with the card catalog.

As I paged my way back in time, I realized that the card catalog, to most of us, is a special sort of product. The card catalog was there for us in grade school. It was there for us in high school. It was there in college. Indeed, the card catalog is more to us than just a reference tool; for my generation, at least, it's a widely shared cultural experience, like puberty or chicken pox.

Even through the 1960s and 1970s, the card catalog was still the faithful spaniel that you could rely on, more or less, to locate a book. In a concession to modern tastes, the cabinets began to appear in different finishes: walnut, dark maple, honey maple, even vinyl. The cabinet designs were modernized, too, and now came in an array of heights, widths, and depths. But card catalogs, like wheelbarrows and sewing machines, were pretty much the same as they'd always been.

Today, of course, computers have come to do what the card catalog used to do. Today, every second-grader is computer literate, undaunted by function keys, cursors, menus, and all the accoutrements of the public access catalogs. Today—the realization made me shudder as I sat hunched in the gathering darkness—the card catalog may finally be ready to receive its last rites.

## Paging further back

**8**

The old product catalogs also reminded me that a similar evolution has occurred among the products we use to circulate books, and now tapes and videos and software.

Nowadays, even in most small libraries, barcodes and laser scanners are the tools of the check-out process. No need for handwriting. No need for key strokes. And no room (ahem) for human error.

Laser scanners and barcodes are the highly evolved descendants of crude, manual charging methods that are almost too painful to consider. Here we must fight a pitch-pine torch and peer backward into the Cro-Magnon period of library products. In these dark days (gasp!) we find only handwritten date slips and manual circulation records—the technological equivalent of rubbing two sticks together to start a fire.

The technology was refined considerably during the 1930s and 1940s, when various types of charging machines—the first ones purely mechanical, the later models electronic—were developed to automate the check-out process. Remember your library card with the little metal plate? That plate, of course, was a prime component of the new charging machine technology of the 1930s.

But another page had yet to be turned before I reached the oldest library products of all . . . and found what I think I'd really been looking for.

## The fossils of our profession

In the earliest catalogs (turn-of-the-century and nineteen-teens vintage), I uncovered the really old products—the pottery fragments and cave drawings of a time when the world was truly a different place. It may have been the best of times; it may have been the worst of times. I suspect a little more of the latter. It was an era, in any event, when libraries operated less like Ferraris and more like the Niña, the Pinta, and the Santa Maria.

These were days long before gigabytes and nanoseconds—nay, almost before electricity itself—a primitive, hunter-gatherer period which featured library products that in today's market would be rendered extinct before the end of the current quarter.

Engraved brass shelf labels whose messages were never expected to change. Call numbers that were hand-lettered in real gold leaf. Combination pencil/date stamps ("the lightest on the market"). Bookbinders' supplies (special threads, needles, glues, clamps, awls, knives, and so forth) that rivaled a country doctor's set of instruments. Posters drawn and lettered by hand, right on the premises. "Overdue" postcards that could be mailed for a penny. Relics. Arrowheads. Ghosts.

One after another they appeared before me, like the faded renderings of early presidents. As I viewed the procession, I indulged a yearning for earlier, simpler tunes (if not kinder, gentler ones).

## Bookbinders' thimbles

And then came the revelation. Between the products of the 1990s and the products of the Gay Nineties, as much as they had changed, I perceived a dim kinship, less a family resemblance than a spiritual likeness. I saw them all suddenly as working toward the same end, all as individual threads in a common fabric.

What did our hot new networking software have in common with an embossing stamp the size of a truck jack? What relation was there between these advanced new antitheft systems and these odd-looking bookbinders' thimbles?

They were all related in one single, central respect. All of the products in the catalogs there before me—those of steamboat days and those of the Concorde—shared a common purpose: to help librarians help people find and use information. This was the constant, the one thing that had endured. "What lasts," I recalled the poet Charles Wright saying, "is what you start with." And that, for all of us in libraryland, past and present, is an unflagging commitment to improving access to information.

Not exactly nirvana, I admit. Not exactly the discovery of the Holy Grail. But, hey. It made me feel better somehow. It made me feel like I'd regained some little something I'd lost, or remembered something I'd lost sight of. With my heels on the desk, I basked for a while in a warm fondness for past times.

In a while, I closed the old catalogs and took them back to the storage room where they could continue their process, briefly interrupted, of quietly gathering dust. Then I turned off the lights, locked the doors, and headed for home, without further thought—at least for that night—about the new technologies tomorrow might bring.

*Source:* Charles E. Farley, Jr., "What Lasts Is What You Start With," *American Libraries* 23 (October 1992): 794–98.

# Typewriters

*by Michael Stuart Freeman*

EARLY TYPEWRITERS (BEFORE 1867) failed because they could not type as fast as a person could write, but by the middle of the 1870s, with the introduction of the so-called "advanced" design typewriter, which offered individual typebars, each carrying a single type and each operated by a single finger, the machine came into its own. The typewriter was introduced in this country at the same time libraries adopted card catalogs, but the two innovations—which to 20th-century librarians seem to go hand in hand—usually involved separate decisions for libraries. Libraries began acquiring typewriters in the 1880s, and from the 1890s through the first decade of the 20th century, many librarians commented in the library press about various features and the utility of individual brands. But many libraries did not purchase their first machine until much later—as late as the 1920s in some cases. In the meantime, practitioners skilled with pen and ink serviced card catalogs. The reasons so many libraries continued to use handwritten catalogs are worth examining.

The cost of equipment aside, librarians had reservations about using typewriters, and so did the general public. In the 1880s, it was considered insulting to use typewriters for private correspondence. It was thought, for instance, that a typewritten letter from a man was not really personal because it would generally have required a professional operator's help to produce.

Some librarians also considered the typewriter to be ill-suited to library work. Typewritten cards "lacked character" and the typewriter produced letters with "disconnected, jerky style," lacking the "ease and expressiveness" that the same author's handwriting might have possessed. However, the reservation based on aesthetics runs counter to the arguments of writers on library handwriting. The so-called library hand was not an art form, but a highly disciplined system. Debates about the use of the joined or disjoined hand did not concern beauty, but speed and legibility. The differences between letters were to be accentuated, but uniformity in letter size, slant, blackness of line, and spacing was considered essential. The mixing of styles, shading, and fine strokes—characteristic of "beautiful" penmanship—was discouraged. Good library handwriting was to be, as one librarian stated in 1885, "as near to type as possible." The disjoined hand, though 25% slower to produce, was preferred by library educators because it looked more like print.

There was concern that the typewritten product would be prone to errors because "the cataloguer's mind would be concentrated as much on the manipulation of the keys as the contents of the book." Also, this big machine was thought to disturb the comfort of the cataloger. Catalogers were used to spreading books out on a desk in order to digest their contents, but the typewriter made this difficult:

> The book must either be taken up in the hands or placed at the side of the machine and the body twisted in order to look at it. In the case of an ordinary octavo, this may not occasion much inconvenience, but the case is otherwise with stout quartos or folios.

The worry about typewritten errors persisted. In 1914, William Warner Bishop, in his *Practical Handbook of Modern Library Cataloging*, recommended

8

that the typewriter be used for simple cataloging where speed is required, but for "recondite books," found in research libraries, where "judgment, accuracy, and selection are the important factors" (and where speed is of secondary importance), he recommended the "ancient practice of writing the original card by hand with the pen."

Another objection to the typewriter had to do with the quality and longevity of the product. How permanent were typed catalog cards? Would they fade with time? This concern was so great in 1900 that a librarian in Albany, New York, subjected typewritten cards to sunlight, rain, heat, and even boiling. The results proved that ink from the typewriter was quite sturdy and could be removed only with strong chemicals.

A skilled operator could type much faster than he or she could write, but the advantage of the typewriter in producing cards was less clear cut. There were about a dozen typewriter brands employed in library work at the turn of the century, but some were clearly not manufactured with card typing in mind. Some machines could not adequately keep cards from shifting position when the platen revolved; others could not provide uniform spacing, were incapable of handling card stock, or would bend the card so badly that they were permanently misshapen. Finally, it was quite a few years before typewriters had all the keys desired by librarians for card production.

Clearly, some librarians disliked typewriters because they were machines, but others believed, as did Bishop, that there were some instances when the pen better suited the catalog card. Even in an ideal situation, the typing of cards required many steps: inserting the card into the machine, setting the margins, rolling the platen to the correct position on the card, and typing the text. For added entries where no more than one line (and in many cases just one word) was to be inserted on the top of the card, the typewriter was clearly inefficient and some libraries continued to handwrite this information on printed Library of Congress cards many years after they had integrated typewriters into normal operations.

Typewriters changed work procedures and the workforce within libraries, though the transition was rarely noted in the library literature. The typewriter required skilled workers and, at least at the outset, libraries would have had fewer typists than those skilled in library hand. As one librarian stated in 1907, "If the typist is ill or absent, the catalogue must wait." We can imagine that the typewriter set up new ways of differentiating staff, with implications for wages and the potential for intergenerational friction, but the record is not rich in this area. Library educators, though, for years advised new library school students to learn to use the typewriter because it would enhance their chances of finding employment.

Library hand continued to be supported by the profession. The New York State Library School published a library handwriting guide for its students as late as 1916, and even in 1930, cataloging textbooks urged library students to acquire proficiency in the art. Haverford College produced cards with pen and ink until 1915, and I can still remember the supply closet at the Dartmouth College Library in 1975, with its array of old fountain pens, ink holders, and supply of ancient nibs, all unused for years—a monument to a past age.

*Source:* Michael Stuart Freeman, "Pen, Ink, Keys, and Cards: Some Reflections on Library Technology," *College & Research Libraries* 52 (July 1991): 328–35.

# High Technology

# Paper is best except . . .

*by Michael Buckland*

A DOCUMENT ON PAPER, such as a letter or a book, is unquestionably extremely convenient to use compared with other media such as microfilm or floppy disks, at least for most purposes. But, even if we were firmly agreed that paper were the best medium for documents, it is increasingly clear that there are significant exceptions to this rule. Electronic documents, with or without the generation of paper copies, become preferable in the following instances:

1. When documents are highly *volatile*. For example, it is unwise to depend on printed paper versions of highly change-able material such as airplane schedules, stock prices, and currency exchange rates.

2. When *manipulation* of the document is desired. No one would want to have to transcribe (and possibly mistranscribe) printed numerical data for statistical analysis if the data were already available in electronic form. Similarly, when a text is to be modified, a bibliog-raphy revised, or the layout rearranged, the availability of an electronic copy in a standard format for word processing can dramatically reduce the work involved compared with having only a typed or handwritten copy.

3. When *scanning* for names or for particular words or phrases in a lengthy document. Trying to find mention of some thing or person in, say, a multivolume printed work or the run of a periodical is very tedious and error-prone. No one now would want to compile a concordance "by hand" anymore: The first step in concordance making now is the creation of an electronic copy of the text.

4. When light use of *remote material* is needed. For a thorough reading of a document that is not available locally, obtaining a paper copy by interlibrary loan would probably be preferred. If, however, use were light—to check here and there in the document or to skim the document superficially to see whether or not a more careful reading would be warranted—rapid access by telecommunications to an electronic copy could be attractive.

5. When rapid *communication* is desired, especially within a dispersed group that is not conveniently available at the same time and place. The use of electronic mail has considerable advantages over ordinary mail and, for some purposes, over the telephone.

Note that these examples do not include the usual notion of solid, system-atic, consecutive reading. They could be regarded as exceptional cases around the fringes of "normal" use of documents, but in some circumstances, as when geographically separated quantitative researchers collaborate, these excep-tions could add up to substantial amounts of activity and a significant propor-tion of total use. Electronic documents add new possibilities for the use of texts and, in this regard, constitute an enhancement that is valuable in its own right.

8

## Reinventing the library

What are we to do with a document in electronic form? There is little choice but to do the same as we do with a paper document or with a microfilm document:

- Catalog it and, as with manuscripts, pay careful attention to which version or state of text it is.
- Store it in some accessible place.
- Give it a call number.
- Ensure that pertinent bibliographic and location data are accessible in or through bibliographic databases.

There seems no real alternative. Given that electronic documents exist and are becoming progressively more important, to ignore them would be to provide a progressively less complete library service. A library administration might choose to retain an exclusive concentration on paper, microfilm, and other localized media, but that would mean that access to electronic documents would have to be found through other channels, such as the computer center. The result would be a split in the provision of library service: the library providing access to only some kinds of documents and another organization providing the balance of the library service—access to electronic documents.

The significant difference with an electronic document as compared to a paper document is that if you have the call number it should be possible, from any workstation, to gain access to it remotely, view it, download it, and use it. Think how much simpler and quicker it would be if librarians and, even better, library users could obtain their own interlibrary loans (now, technically, copies) on a self-service basis, requiring the tolerance but not the time or energy of the staff of the library from which it is obtained. This change would be rather like the change from having closed library stacks, in which library employees had to fetch each book for users, to open stacks in which library users could obtain and examine books by themselves. Similarly, in the Electronic Library, library staff would be mainly concerned with creating and sustaining the system so that users could serve themselves.

Self-service, however, is a mixed blessing. It assumes standardized, intelligible procedures, presupposes some expertise on the user's part, and may make it less easy for the service providers to know what is going well and what is not going well. Yet it may be the only affordable way to support large-scale library use.

## Prior experience

The change from the Automated Library to the Electronic Library is an extension of the same changes that have characterized the shift from the Paper Library to the Automated Library:

- standardization of data;
- remote access to files;
- the linking and combining of files;
- access to numerous different files from the same terminal;
- increased cooperative use of shared files;
- discontinuation of numerous, more-or-less duplicative local files;
- greater capability for doing things to and with the (computer-based) files; and
- increased vulnerability to technological failure.

Hardly recognized is the fact that many librarians and library users, particularly in academic and special libraries, already do have extensive experience with the Electronic Library through their use of online bibliographies. This is because bibliographies tend to occupy an ambivalent position: They are acquired and used primarily to provide access to other documents, but a bibliography is itself a kind of document. Bibliographies added to library collections are library materials. For more than twenty years there has been a steady shift toward searching bibliographies online as well as or instead of on paper. Although not usually viewed as such, this is an early, incomplete manifestation of the Electronic Library with which there is already substantial experience and familiarity. Hence we should expect the future expansion of the Electronic Library to be an expansion of what is already familiar.

*Source:* Michael Buckland, *Redesigning Library Services: A Manifesto*
(Chicago: American Library Association, 1992).

# What are clients and servers?

*by Gary Lee Phillips and Stuart W. Miller*

THE CONCEPT OF A CLIENT/SERVER architecture is a key element of the open system approach. In this type of design, system functions are divided and each unit is classified as either a client (requester of information or services) or a server (provider of information or services). In other words, a server stores and manages data while a client provides access to the data.

This division can apply to both hardware and software, so client software can run on a workstation with server software running on a larger computer. In such a case, a communications link—most commonly a LAN—is necessary for both parts to talk to each other.

To a great extent, the client/server model was developed by IBM and is now known as OSI, the Open System Interconnection. OSI is a widely recognized model for network structure and evolved from IBM's work to create a proprietary network for linking IBM computers to each other. While not a formal standard, OSI has been followed by many hardware and software vendors in developing systems.

The OSI model uses the concept of layers to separate functions from each other. Each layer in an OSI system is devoted to fulfilling one of seven major functions: physical, data link, network, transport, session, presentation, and application.

The idea behind the OSI model is that if you design each piece of a system to perform one of these functions, you can design and maintain the system more efficiently—a change or enhancement needed in one layer does not necessarily affect any of the other layers.

While not conforming strictly to the OSI model, client/server software designers use the same concept of dividing functions; in other words, access to and presentation of data (the client) becomes separate from the storage and management of data (the server). Each part has a different function to perform.

By designing both the client and the server to use a standard communication method, it is possible to create them as separate applications that share information freely with each other. Using a standard communication method permits individual client or server applications from separate vendors to work together. Client/server design also lets you mix and match, change, or upgrade each part independently from the other.

As long as an effective communication channel exists between the two

8

parts (or applications), the client and server don't need to reside on the same machine or run on the same hardware architecture or operating software environment. For example, a client can be a bibliographic retrieval program that runs on a microcomputer in a faculty office, while the associated server can be the cataloging subsystem at the university library.

The same client software can be used, through the same or a different communication line, to search bibliographic databases provided by a commercial vendor in a remote city. The user sees a single interface and uses a single command system—the need we identified as a result of implementing open systems.

Individual users may choose different client environments to obtain access to the same server. This allows not only individual preferences for "point and click" with a mouse rather than typed commands, but could also support custom interfaces.

To help you visualize the functions of the client and server portions of a system, imagine a take-out counter in a Chinese restaurant. The customer or patron is a user. The customer communicates a dinner order in English to the order-taker (the client) who translates it into a dinner check in Chinese.

In this case, written Chinese is the standard format for requests and the written check is the communication medium. The order-taker sends the check to the kitchen, where it is read by the cook (the server). The cook prepares food

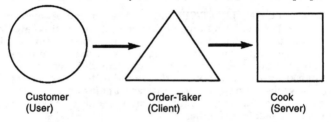

| Customer | Order-Taker | Cook |
| (User) | (Client) | (Server) |

from the restaurant's storage area (acting as a database would in the software system) and delivers the dinner in standard packages marked with Chinese characters. The order-taker returns these packages to the customer, adding any notations or explanations in English.

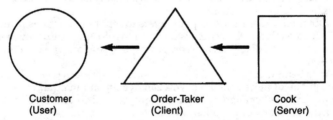

| Customer | Order-Taker | Cook |
| (User) | (Client) | (Server) |

The customer in our example does not need to know any Chinese, nor anything about the actual source or preparation of the food. Likewise, the cook (server) does not need to know any English, nor anything about either the customer or the order-taker (client).

Now think of a library patron at a terminal or workstation. The patron formulates a request in some query language understood by the workstation (client) which translates it into an information request in a standard format (for example, Z39.50) understood by the information source (server).

Upon receiving the standardized request (perhaps via a LAN), the source retrieves the appropriate data, packages the bibliographic information or text in a standard form, and ships it back to the workstation. The client workstation presents this information in a format that the patron can easily process.

The patron may speak Spanish and the client software may provide help screens and accept commands in that language, but the server software doesn't need to know the patron's language or command formats. Obviously, the potential for flexibility in such a system greatly surpasses the old "integrated" interfaces of earlier library systems. And just as obvious is that the client and the server perform different functions and are co-dependent.

To use our Chinese restaurant analogy again, if the cook (the server) is unavailable, the order-taker (the client) can take the customer's order but cannot deliver any food since the cook is not there. In the library, the patron can use the client to send a search but no results will come back unless the server is up and running.

One client can be used to communicate with several different servers. In academic institutions, for example, clients could be used to query local resources that include the bibliographic database created for the library's holdings; citation databases; locally created and locally mounted databases; and other resources (full text, numeric, and image databases).

All of these resources could be on the same or different servers—a fact that is transparent to the end-user who does not need to know where any database is as long as it is accessible. By the same token, the same client could also provide access to remote resources on servers located off-site at other cooperating institutions, accessible via a LAN or WAN.

Given the various types of data stored on servers, clients usually handle similar types of data but have the flexibility to act as a bridge to other, related data. Providing there are appropriate interconnections and a workstation with the necessary peripherals, a client could allow the user to search for and display a local bibliographic record for a score in the library, with an option to display an image of the score or hear a sound recording of a performance of the score—a "multimedia" client.

Similarly, a server that stores one kind of data can be linked to a server with another type of data. To continue the above example, the library's bibliographic database could reside on one server with links to two other servers—the musical score image server and a sound recording server. This permits the seamless user interface. On the other hand, there might be three separate clients for searching the three servers, each with its own way of linking (or not) to the other two.

*Source:* Gary Lee Phillips and Stuart W. Miller, *Open Systems, Client/Server, and Your Library* (Evanston, Ill.: NOTIS Systems, Inc.; Provo, Utah: Dynix Marquis, 1994). 15p. Reprinted with permission.

8

# Zen in the art of troubleshooting

*by Terry Ballard*

"TERRY, COULD YOU COME OVER and look at this?" As university systems librarian I hear such requests seven times in an average day. Five or six of these can be handled in seconds because they are common mishaps and the solutions are in my bag of tricks. But once or twice a day, I face the unknown and must solve a problem with a machine I know little about that won't perform a work procedure that I know nothing about.

Although I nod reassuringly as a colleague describes the problem, secretly I am terrified. My problem-solving reputation is on the line. Clinging to the proper state of mind is crucial. According to Zen masters, such things cannot be written. However, Westerners rely on words, so here is a list that describes this state of mind:

1. The problem *can* be solved;
2. It is my job to solve it, so the buck stops here.
3. Once it is solved, that will be one more thing that I know how to do.

## The first tier

Suppose the message on the screen reads "!!@Memory device hung on line 44. Buffer overload exceeds density threshold." No cursor is visible and pushing the escape key does not work. The first tier of problem solving is simply turning the machine off and then on again to let it reboot. The second step is checking all of the cables. Anything that connects one part of the computer to another can shut down the whole operation if it is just a tiny bit unplugged. The final step on the first tier is turning the tables on the person reporting the problem—asking a lot of questions that are a variation on the theme of "Where does it hurt?" Caution is necessary in this questioning because it is easy to be led astray by wrong assumptions made by the person describing the problem, and a wrong turn may lead light years away from the solution.

## Zen and the limber mind

That is where Zen comes into the picture. My wife frequently kids me about my habit of reading about Eastern religions. "You're not a Zen Buddhist. What do you think you're doing?" she'll say. Reading such material keeps my mind limber, I reply. Besides, following the Zen principle of nonattachment is a reminder to be slightly suspicious of all incoming information.

Those pitfalls are there even when I should know better. Recently, I was asked to look at an OPAC terminal that had gone completely blank. "This happened right after I swivelled the machine. I think I've ruined one of the cables on the back," said the reference librarian. Turning the power off and on got no response. Then I checked the power cable on the back and found that the plug was not fully seated. Seating the plug produced a cursor, but no menu screen appeared. I went to another terminal to restart the port the malfunctioning terminal was assigned to. When I got back, I saw the welcome sight of the menu. However, the machine still would not accept commands. At that point, I accepted my colleague's notion that she had broken the cable.

The terminal sat unused until the Zen side of my nature dreamed up one more thing to check. Sure enough, the phone plug that connected the keyboard to the CRT had not clicked into place. Now the terminal works just fine.

## Wading into the unknown

Sometimes the problem does not have any easy solution. Returning to the example of the error message "!!@Memory device hung . . . ," suppose that rebooting the machine brings up the same message. At that point it is time to look at the documentation of the malfunctioning equipment. Most documentation has a deservedly bad reputation, but chances are that there will be a short chapter on troubleshooting. With any luck, the problem will be described and a simple solution offered.

If the documentation doesn't help, there is little to lose by taking a risk or two; it's time to wade methodically into the pool of the unknown. This usually means altering the configuration settings on the malfunctioning terminal or printer. There are thousands of permutations and combinations, so it is important that I resist the temptation to change more than one thing at a time. This is the same principle that cave explorers follow when they mark their passage. Some changes will almost certainly make the machine act worse than

## Parallels between Zen masters and systems librarians

| | Zen Master | Systems Librarian |
|---|---|---|
| GOAL | Satori—the state of perfect enlightenment. | Solving the problem so I can go back to reading my e-mail. |
| METHODS | Meditate to achieve a blissful state. | Play with things until they start working. |
| | Think about Zen koans: impossible sounding puzzles that lead to a state of no-mind. | Read the manual: impossible sounding directions that lead to the state of no-luck. |
| | Being hit with a stick. | Hitting the computer with a stick. |
| | Fasting. | Eating. |
| SURVIVAL | Going into the village with a rice bowl and begging. | Going to the peer review committee and getting tenure. |
| SECRETS | Share your knowledge with a select group of young monks. | Let your secrets go to the grave with you. |

it did before, so I need to know how to put things back. Some intuitively talented troubleshooters break this rule and get away with it, but they aren't sure what action ultimately solved the problem.

Another example from my personal Hall of Pain concerns the transfer of records in our cataloging department. I had set up our OCLC terminals with function keys that automatically send a two-screen record to our local system. Sometimes a record would hang up after the first screen was accepted.

I couldn't solve the problem, so I put it out of my mind. Months later the problem came up again. I asked a library assistant to show me another example. "But you said it was impossible to fix," she reminded me.

In half an hour we had isolated the problem and fixed it. The system had received the information but did not know it. The fix was just a matter of sending the interface unit something that would satisfy its search for a second screen without adding anything to the record. With intermittent problems, the main challenge is finding out what the problem really is. Once you find out what is different about the thing that malfunctions, it is usually easy to fix.

## Accepting uncertainty

Sometimes things will return to normal before you figure out what went wrong. I call this the "uncertainty factor" and have learned to just accept it. A problem is quickly forgotten unless the machine does the same again within a few days. I don't feel that I have to know every aspect of a problem—especially if the problem disappears.

Often after quick fixes, people ask how I did it. I mutter about fooling with the connections and prodding the thing. "But I did that!" they exclaim, and then they wonder if my job has an element of magic. It is useful for people to believe this. There seems to be a greater chance of success if the person believes that the machine will work as soon as I look at it. However, I must guard against believing my own clippings.

The solutions for long-term problems often prove to be simple—so simple that I could kick myself later. One of my favorites was a machine in the acquisitions department that could not be used for check-ins. When the check-in box appeared, the data would start to fall apart. We checked the settings repeatedly, and they were identical to the other machines in acquisitions, even though the balky machine was an earlier model.

Swapping cables with the machine on the next desk didn't help, proving that the problem was with the machine itself. In desperation, I tried changing the terminal emulation. This seemed to affect the check-in boxes. The machine could not handle the terminal emulation it was running, but our acquisitions system couldn't run anything else. Finally, the terminal was swapped with one linked to the cataloging and circulation system, which can be set at VT100 terminal emulation. It has worked perfectly ever since.

When a piece of equipment is broken, the only procedure is to send it out for repair. However, I have found that only one percent of my cases need to be sent out. As someone with no technical background and little formal education in computer science, I feel pretty good about that score. The point is not that I am an extraordinary troubleshooter—it's that if I can learn to do this anybody can.

## Buddha-nature

I could offer more examples, but more might cloud the issues and thus tell you less. The above statement is similar to a Zen koan, a kind of puzzle Zen masters give to students to make them think beyond their normal frame of reference and to drive them crazy. The modern equivalent is minimalist comic Steven Wright's story about buying a cordless extension cord.

One of the most famous Zen koans is the question, "Does a dog have Buddha-nature?" I suggest you meditate on these questions: Does a systems librarian have Buddha-nature? Does a computer? But first, you must hear the rest of the famous koan concerning dogs: "If you answer yes or no, you lose your own Buddha-nature."

*Source:* Terry Ballard, "Zen in the Art of Troubleshooting,"
*American Libraries* 25 (January 1994): 108–10.

# How to select CD-ROM software

*by Stephen Bosch, Patricia Promis, and Chris Sugnet*

WITH THE ADVENT OF ELECTRONIC FORMATS, the selection process has become more complex. Added to the traditional criteria associated with collection development policy and user needs are new concerns related to technology, costs for the same information in different formats, additional staffing needs, and additional user demands. Some of the issues and questions a library should address are outlined below.

## Policy concerns

The criteria for selecting material in electronic format should reflect the library's own collection development and acquisitions policies.

It is very important to have written procedures for selecting electronic resources. It could become necessary to have different procedures for every type of format available.

Licensing constraints and limitations on the use of the data imposed by vendors, publishers, or producers should be addressed in the process of selection.

User and programmatic needs are a prime consideration. Special attention could be given to products that provide coverage of underrepresented or high-priority subject areas.

Selection procedures and criteria should be evaluated and revised regularly.

Public demand for and use of current printed versions are sometimes good indicators of the need for the electronic product.

The reputation of the publisher and producer should be investigated. Request a list of current customers from the publisher and contact those that seem to have the most in common with your library. Sometimes networks, consortia, and state libraries serve as clearing houses for information on new products.

Assess the comprehensiveness and scope of the data's coverage, and data and indexing accuracy. Reviews are helpful in this area.

Another important concern is the timeliness of updates or cumulations.

Evaluate the relative difficulty of using the printed version versus the electronic counterpart.

There are no standards addressing the preservation of electronic media yet. The selector must evaluate the durability of the medium and what the cost/benefit trade-off will be between immediate usefulness and potential degradation of electronic data.

## Service concerns

The selection criteria should conform with the institution's general plans for establishing a computerized information environment.

Public service staffing and training levels should be evaluated in light of the additional information services available to patrons.

User-friendly features such as online tutorials should be available.

The user documentation should be accurate, easy to use, comprehensive, and cost-effective.

The impact on current library staffing and training, such as cataloging and processing subscriptions in different formats, should be carefully assessed.

Effectiveness of data retrieval software (the search engine) should be appraised.

Product evaluation, such as reviews, user studies, and product demos should be consulted.

The availability of printing facilities (remote or connected directly to each work station) should be considered.

## Technical concerns

A crucial concern relates to the necessity for technical support and maintenance of the product.

The evaluation of software should focus on issues that include menu-driven vs. command-driven feature, override capability in the program's command structure, short initial learning curve, security (tampering and viruses), compatibility with existing hardware and software medium.

The hardware related concerns include reliability, maintenance, compatibility with peripherals, flexibility for other uses or networking, security from theft and tampering.

Compatibility with existing systems in the library and with the systems used by the parent organization's community should be a consideration.

The environmental and spatial requirements for equipment and workstations need special consideration.

## Cost considerations

Short-term preservation benefits of optical disk technology are apparent.

If print sources or other formats are discontinued there may be savings. Duplication of information in several formats usually results in higher costs. Package discounts are sometimes available when retaining the subscription to the paper or alternate (i.e., microfiche) format.

There are cost differentials between online and CD-ROM options.

Information may be available in more cost-effective electronic formats.

Purchase or lease options need to be studied.

Plan for any additional costs for future updates or upgrades.

There may be additional start-up and maintenance costs that are not reflected in the invoice for the information product. These could include site preparation and hardware shipping and installation.

Consider the shelf life of the product's storage medium and replacement costs.

Explore the availability of vendor/publisher discounts for hardware and software packages (bundles) associated with the product.

*Source:* Stephen Bosch, Patricia Promis, and Chris Sugnet,
*Guide to Selecting and Acquiring CD-ROMs, Software, and Other Electronic Publications*
(Chicago: ALA Association for Library Collections and Technical Services, 1994). 48p.

# Cumulative trauma disorders increase

A MAJOR INCREASE IN THE INCIDENCE of cumulative trauma disorders such as shoulder, neck, and hand (wrist) injuries has been reported especially among computer and other office workers. According to Michael J. Smith, professor, Department of Industrial Engineering, University of Wisconsin-Madison, research and experience have shown that the level of psychological distress in an organization influences the reporting and seriousness of these disorders. In addition, the ergonomic design characteristics of the workstation, equipment, and work environment are risk factors in worker-cumulative trauma.

Cumulative trauma relates primarily to musculoskeletal disorders, such as muscle weakness and dysfunction; tendon, ligament, or nerve damage; lower back pain; and upper extremity trauma. Ergonomics (or designing the proper "fit" between workers and jobs) involves many disciplines, including biomechanics, business management, engineering, medicine, physiology, psychology, and sociology.

## Causes

According to Smith, research indicates that ergonomics accounts for 25% of the cumulative trauma cases, psychosocial aspects contribute to another 25% of the cases, and approximately 50% are related to undefined aspects, which may include individual susceptibility, off-worksite issues, etc.

Work elements that can cause problems include task requirements and environmental effects, such as glare and noise, workstation, and technology design. Task risk factors in cumulative trauma syndrome can include the extent to which there is frequency of action, duration of exposures, posture of wrists and hands, and the force used in keyboard input.

The interaction between behavior, demands of work, and stress influences how one feels about work and pain. Individual susceptibilities such as circulatory problems, diabetes, arthritis, acute injuries, menopause, and obesity can aggravate and affect cumulative trauma syndrome. Psychological disturbances include mood disturbances, fears, attitudes, and normal daily hassles. Longer-term psychological problems might involve anxiety and depression, poor attitudes and lack of motivation, unemployment fears, and phobias to technology (techno-stress). Long-term stress can lead to cardiovascular diseases, digestive disorders, chronic fatigue syndrome, and psychoses.

## Reducing job stress

Job stress factors that can potentially cause problems include the extent of workload pace demands, the content of jobs (cycle time, variety), amount of control over task decisions and participation, organizational interface (e.g., supervision and company policies), career issues such as job loss and lack of advancement, resources (e.g., sufficiency of tools and materials), rewards (pay, recognition), supports (socialization, coworker support, culture), and roles (responsibilities, contributions).

Smith urged organizations to look at job elements as a system that includes the environment and facilities, tools and technologies, tasks, organizational structure, and individual skills and abilities. All jobs have stress, but the challenge is to keep the stress level manageable and help employees learn to live with it. Removing risk factors can be accomplished by addressing physical ergonomic issues, excessive demands, poor content, low control, career limitations, poor supervision, and lack of support. To balance job factors and minimize stress, one needs to look at the job as a whole and provide good elements to counteract the bad. One can reduce the frequency of repetitive action (i.e., slow down the process), rotate to jobs with fewer repetitions, and redesign work methods (e.g., use of optical scanning instead of keyboard operations where possible). In any work redesign, the major points to address are both the physical dimensions of work and the psychological ones.

## Repetitive strain injuries in Colorado, 1990

Carpal tunnel syndrome. Eye strain and radiation associated with computer monitors. Muscular-skeletal injuries. Repetitive motion injuries. Cumulative trauma disorders. These are the workplace diseases of the 1990s. A cursory review of news and business magazines revealed articles on all of these topics. Perhaps the most inclusive name for them is "repetitive strain injuries" (RSIs). In fact, this was the terminology used in a July 1990 *Library Journal* article entitled "The Light at the End of the Carpal Tunnel." This article reports the results of a February 1990 survey of the nation's largest libraries on this topic. At the request of one of Colorado's larger public libraries, that survey was replicated and expanded during November 1990 with Colorado public libraries employing 10 or more full-time equivalent staff. This is a report of the findings.

The percentages of libraries reporting cases of RSI were virtually the same for Colorado and the United States. Forty-five percent of libraries in the national sample reported them; 44% in the Colorado sample. The incidence of RSIs, however, was twice as high for Colorado as for the United States. Nationwide, 17 libraries reported 49 cases, while, in Colorado, eight libraries reported 48 cases. That makes an average of six cases per Colorado library compared with an average of three cases per U.S. library.

Out of seven types of tasks associated with RSIs, the four leading ones for Colorado libraries were: working at computers or terminals and shelving library materials (tied for first place), charging out library materials, and

**8**

preparing and/or repairing library materials. Other tasks reported once each were: answering telephones, driving bookmobiles, and performing custodial duties.

Out of six possible treatments of RSIs, seven libraries reported that staff with RSIs take medication (e.g., muscle relaxants, anti-inflammatory drugs). Tied for second place were physical therapy, rest, and use of braces. Two libraries reported cases of RSI which were treated surgically, and one reported use of eyeglasses with special lenses.

Colorado libraries reported purchasing a wide variety of ergonomic furnishings and equipment to minimize RSIs. In rank order, these include chairs, step stools and monitors, desks/work stations, keyboards, single-face half book trucks, and foot rests and anti-glare screens.

Colorado libraries reporting and not reporting RSIs differ significantly only on purchases of special computer monitors and keyboards. Libraries reporting RSIs were more likely to have made such purchases than those not reporting RSIs.

National figures available for three of these choices suggest that Colorado libraries are being more responsive to the problem than libraries nationwide. Three out of four Colorado libraries reported purchasing adjustable chairs compared with one out of four nationally. Two out of five Colorado libraries reported purchasing adjustable desks/work stations compared with one out of six nationally. And, one out of three Colorado libraries reported purchasing adjustable keyboards compared with one out of eight nationally.

Colorado libraries reported providing several types of training to reduce RSIs. Almost half train staff in preventive practices, more than a quarter train staff in the use of adjustable chairs and desks/workstations, one out of six provides exercise training for staff, and one out of ten trains supervisors in how to detect early signs of RSI.

Compared with public libraries nationwide, Colorado libraries are more than twice as likely to provide such training in general and more than four times as likely to provide training in preventive practices.

Asked about specific policy or job structure changes relating to RSIs, a third of Colorado libraries reported that they encourage staff to vary tasks more frequently and one out of six reported permitting more job rotation. Notably, no Colorado libraries reported changing personnel policies to permit more frequent breaks. Three libraries reported planning RSI-related policy changes for implementation in 1991.

While only one out of six libraries nationwide reported changing policies or job structures or providing training programs related to RSIs, half of Colorado libraries (9 out of 18) report such changes. Two of the state's libraries even reported having outside consultants perform workstation assessments for their staff.

Several questions are raised by this study. How many of the differences between the Colorado and U.S. samples can be attributed to when they were surveyed? Notably, media reports on RSIs have been frequent during the interim between the two surveys. To what extent is the higher incidence of RSIs among Colorado library personnel attributable to increased awareness of them? To what extent is the increased incidence of RSIs attributable to the "Marcus Welby" syndrome (i.e., the tendency to contract any popular disease with whose name and symptoms one becomes acquainted)?

Continued research is needed to answer these questions.

*Sources:* "Cumulative Trauma Disorders Increase," *Library Personnel News* 8 (January-February 1994): 2-3; "Repetitive Strain Injuries among Personnel in Large-Staff Public Libraries in Colorado, 1990," *Fast Facts: Recent Statistics from the Library Research Service* (Library Research Service, Colorado State Library), December 17, 1990, pp. 1-8.

# Internet software tools for libraries

*by Mary E. Engle, Marilyn Lutz, William W. Jones Jr., Genevieve Engel*

A FEW INDUSTRIOUS INTERNET USERS have written software to make it easier to use the directories of online library catalogs. These software programs allow you to search the directories alphabetically or by geographic location, and pull up the logon and search instructions contained in the directory.

The programs vary in extent. Some merely help you browse the directories' contents, while some actually initiate the Telnet connection for you. This section provides a brief overview of these programs and tells you how to obtain them for free over the Internet.

## HYTelnet

HYTelnet, a program that runs on many types of computers, makes it easier to reach the principal Internet-accessible library catalogs and databases. It is designed specifically for users who access the Internet using the Telnet program via modem or serial line. On personal computers, it is a memory-resident program (Terminate and Stay Resident—TSR), which is to say that, once you run HYTelnet, it exists in the background of your computer session, and is invoked when you wish to use a remote library database. To invoke the program, press the control (CNTL, CTRL, etc.) and Backspace keys simultaneously and follow the directions. A slightly different version exists for UNIX machines.

HYTelnet contains a database of Internet sites available by Telnet; the most recent version even handles the Telnet connection for you to library catalogs, Free-Nets, campus-wide information systems (CWIS), and library bulletin board systems. You can customize the program relatively easily to add new sites to its list using standard word processors, as long as they are capable of producing ASCII output files.

HYTelnet currently knows about online library catalogs in the following countries/regions:

- North America, including Canada, Mexico, and the United States
- Europe, including Scandinavia, Austria, Belgium, Denmark, Finland, France, Germany, Iceland, Ireland, Italy, Netherlands, Norway, Spain, Sweden, Switzerland, and the United Kingdom
- The Middle East: Israel
- Asia/Pacific, including Hong Kong, New Zealand, Taiwan
- Australia

HYTelnet is available for IBM PC, Unix and DEC VMS systems. You can test drive the UNIX version of HYTelnet by Telneting to access.usask.ca (IP address 128.233.3.1). Login as *hytelnet*.

HYTelnet is available for anonymous FTP from access.usask.ca in the directory pub/hytelnet. The DOS version can be found in the directory pub/hytelnet/pc as file hyteln63.zip. Be sure to look at the directory listings with the *ls* command for the most recent version (for example, hyteln63.zip represents version 6.3. There may be later versions available, indicated by higher numbers). This file is archived using the ZIP utility so you must set the mode to "binary" before transferring the file. (Type *binary* at the FTP prompt.) Before you will be able to use it on your local computer, you will need to uncompress it with an unzip program.

HYTelnet was originally developed by Peter Scott (scott@sklib.usask.ca) at the University of Saskatchewan in Canada. The UNIX version was written by Earl Fogel, also of the University of Saskatchewan.

## CATALIST

CATALIST is a DOS program based on Windows Version 3.0 that presents a hypertext version of the OPAC directory *UNT's Accessing On-Line Bibliographic Databases*, commonly called the "Barron Guide" after its author Billy Barron. It is designed to run in a window by itself or alongside the window you use to connect to a remote OPAC.

CATALIST searches the Barron guide alphabetically by name or by geographic location. It provides instructions on how to access the catalogs you select, but it currently does not handle the Telnet connection for you. You will need to start a communications program separately, establish the connection to the host you use to access the Internet (if dial-up), Telnet to the remote catalog, and login.

After you login to the remote catalog, you can return to the CATALIST window for searching instructions and a notebook facility that allows you to make personal notes, including copying whole screens using the Windows Clipboard facilities, that will be retained and associated with the appropriate catalog.

CATALIST is available free of charge from the following two anonymous FTP sites:

| | | |
|---|---|---|
| zebra.acs.udel.edu | directory: | pub/library |
| vaxb.acs.unt.edu | directory: | library/catalist |

The readme.txt file provides detailed information on how to get and extract the CATALIST program. As a software program, CATALIST must be transferred in binary mode. Type *binary* at the FTP prompt before you issue the *get* command.

Richard H. Duggan of the English Department at the University of Delaware developed CATALIST. You can contact the author at the Internet address duggan@brahms.udel.edu or the BITNET address FCA02040@UDELVM.

## LIBTEL

LIBTEL is a shell script for UNIX and VMS systems that helps you access most of the OPACS and databases listed in the *Directory of Internet-Accessible Library Catalogs and Databases*. LIBTEL uses a menu-based approach to connect to over 200 library catalogs, databases, and bulletin boards on the Internet.

LIBTEL requires that you use the program TN3270, a Telnet adaptation that handles IBM 3270 terminals. You can also get a copy of TN3270 from the same FTP server from which you get LIBTEL—samba.oit.unc.edu in the directory publtn3270 as the filename disttn3270.unc.tar.Z.

LIBTEL also requires that your UNIX or VMS host machine run the domain name server program BIND (also known as DNS or name service) for LIBTEL to use to establish remote connections.

LIBTEL includes some interesting services such as the Ham Radio Call Book, the Geographical Nameserver, and the Weather Server, as well as several Free-nets, a number of bulletin boards, and library catalogs in seven countries.

You can take LIBTEL for a test drive before you obtain it for your local machine via Telnet.

- Telnet to the host launchpad.oit.unc.edu
- Login as *bbs*
- Follow the instructions to get an ID.
- At the main menu, select: *9* (Online Information Systems)

You can set up an account for yourself by typing in your first and last name at the appropriate prompt.

LIBTEL is available via anonymous FTP from the host samba.oit.unc.edu in the directory pub/docs as filename libtel. Both the UNIX and VMS versions are also available on the host vaxb.acs.unt.edu in the directory library as filename libtel (UNIX version) and libtel.com (VMS version).

LIBTEL was originally developed by Terry Mancour (mancour@samba. oit.unc.edu), Tom Snee, Paul Jones (pjones@mento.oit.edu) and Dan Mahone (who wrote the first version).

Below is a sample interaction with the University of North Carolina system laUNChpad, which puts you into the LIBTEL program:

```
                    Welcome to laUNChpad,
        the Internet Service Mediator laUNChpad 2.0 running on
                        launchpad.unc.edu
              at the University of North Carolina at Chapel Hill
              Courtesy of the Office of Information Technology


                    ABOUT THE NEW LAUNCHPAD:


        HELP can be found by typing h, help, or ? at any laUNChpad
        menu. More extensive HELP files and documents can be found in
        5. Download files section. You may use the simple ASCII dump to
        display the files on your screen. This system keeps track of
        users by their first and last names.
        Your name? Daniel Urmann
        That name isn't familiar. Would you like to open an account as
        'Daniel Urmann'? yes
        What kind of terminal do you use? [vt100] vt100
        Slowly adding you to the system mail file. Please be patient


           Main Menu

           1. Network News
           2. Electronic mail
           3. On-line Information Systems (LIBTEL)
           4. Topical document search (WAIS)
           5. Download files
           6. Find user
           7. User Options
        (? or h)elp, (q)uit. ==> 3
```

8

Internet Accessible Libraries and Information Systems

| (NA) | North American Region | (MISC) | Miscellaneous Services |
|------|----------------------|--------|----------------------|
| (EUR) | European Region | (BBS) | Other Bulletin Boards |
| (ANZ) | Pacifica Region | (NOT) | Notes on Libtel (Please Read) |
| (ASA) | Asian Region | (CTP) | Contemporary Poetry |
| (ME) | Middle-Eastern Region | (EXIT) | Go Back to the BBS |

To return to this screen during search press 'ctrl G'
Where would you like to go? **not**

---

LUX   Welcome to LIBTEL!   LIBERTAS

Libtel is an information resource access system that allows you, the User, to visit University libraries and information systems worldwide from the comfort of your own cubicle. Organized by geographical location, simply use the menus to travel to the area you wish to search and then choose your destination library or information resource.

Unfortunately, due to the occasionally unreliable nature of the Internet (as well as local systems) some services will be unavailable from time to time. Should this occur, simply try again later.

Should you have any problems with the program, or are aware of inaccuracies or new services that you think should be added, simply drop a line to the Libtel operator at:

Libtel@lambada.oit.unc.edu

Thank you for using Libtel, and the BBS.
[Please hit Enter to continue]

## LIBS

Like LIBTEL, the LIBS program operates in conjunction with the St. George OPAC directory but runs only on UNIX and VMS systems. LIBS uses a menu approach to help you select and connect to remote library resources (it establishes the Telnet session for you). LIBS also presents information on searching the remote service *before* it establishes the connection. Since this information disappears once the remote system is in control, you may wish to write down the instructions or follow along using a print copy of the St. George directory. Below is a sample of the opening menu of LIBS.

To take LIBS for a test drive, Telnet to the host vax.sonoma.edu and login as username *libs*. Since the service is intended for the faculty, students, and staff of Sonoma State University, please only use LIBS on this machine for evaluation purposes. If you like the program, you are encouraged to get a copy of it for yourself.

The LIBS software is available free of charge via anonymous FTP from the host sonoma.edu in the pub directory as filename libs.com. Remember to use binary mode for the transfer (type *binary* at the FTP prompt before the transfer).

Mark Resmer, Director of Computing and Telecommunications at California State University (resmer@sonoma.edu) originally developed this useful program. Here are the LIBS opening screens:

```
LIBS-Internet Access Software v2.0 (beta)
Sonoma State University, Sept 1992 (information omitted)
Copyright (c) 1991-92, Mark Resmer

On-line services available through the Internet:

1  United States Library Catalogs
2  Library Catalogs in other countries
3  Campus-wide Information Systems
4  Databases and Information Services
5  Wide-area Information Services
6  Information for first time users

Press RETURN alone to see previous menu
Press Control-C Q <return> to exit at any time

Enter the number of your choice:  4
```

```
Information services/databases in the following areas are
accessible:

1  Agriculture
2  Arts/Humanities
3  Business/Economics
4  Education
5  Scientific
6  Weather/Time/Earthquakes
7  Other Services

Press RETURN alone to see previous menu
Press Control-C Q<return> to exit at any time
Enter the number of your choice:  3
```

```
The Pennsylvania State Data Center maintains this
database of population and economic statistical data which
includes, among other things, the Commerce Business
Daily. EDIN is accessible through the EBB service of Penn
State.

Note the following instructions carefully
Once you are connected:
Type: info <return> at the first prompt
Type: EDIN <return> at the next prompt
Press Control-C Q <return> to exit at any time
Do you want to connect now? (Y or N):
```

8

Source: Mary E. Engle, Marilyn Lutz, William W. Jones Jr., and Genevieve Engel,
Internet Connections: A Librarian's Guide to Dial-up Access and Use
(Chicago: ALA Library and Information Technology Association, 1993). 166p.

# Telecommunications terms you may not be familiar with

*by George S. Machovec*

**ACID.** An abbreviation for "atomicity, consistency, isolation and durability."

**ARIADNE.** The Greek communications network offering data communications to academic and research institutions throughout Greece.

**Atomic action.** An operation or task which must be fully completed or else not done at all.

**Basket.** A collection of services which can be offered for one group price.

**Blanca.** One of five gigabit network research testbeds for NREN. It is a U.S. coast-to-coast testbed that will provide implementation fabric for atmospheric modeling and an experimental multimedia digital library.

**Broadcast storm.** The uncontrolled dumping of data onto a network saturating the circuit.

**Cheapernet.** A name variation for Thin Ethernet.

**Coloured Book.** The set of communications protocols developed by the Joint Academic Network (JANET) which are widely used in Britain, Ireland, Australia and New Zealand. Although based on the OSI Reference Model, many of the protocols predate OSI.

**Dark fiber.** Fiber optic cable which has been deployed but is not yet in use.

**Despotic network.** A network in which the timing of all network traffic is governed by one master clock.

**Erlang.** A unit of measurement for rating telecommunications traffic and use demand. One erlang is the intensity at which one traffic path would be continuously occupied (e.g., one call per minute, one call per hour). An erlang equals 36 ccs (36 hundred call seconds) which represents full-time use of a conventional telecommunications traffic path.

**IMHO.** An abbreviation for "in my humble opinion."

**Interlocation trunking.** Communications switching equipment which connects telecommunications channels from two or more different locations.

**Jabber.** Noise on a network caused by the random transmission of data due to a malfunction.

**Jitter.** A signal impairment in which data are coming too fast or too slow in the slots allocated in a circuit.

**Judder.** The lack of uniform scanning on a telefacsimile picture.

**Leaky PBX.** A PBX that allows private-line traffic (tie-line) to access the local telephone exchange, or vice versa.

**MOO Gopher.** A Gopher client developed at Mankato State University which enables more than one person to view a Gopher listing and allows more than one user, through messaging, to instruct and lead one or more users through GopherSpace.

**Nonreturn to Zero (NRZ).** An encoding method used for signaling in which the binary representations of zero and one are indicated by a positive or negative voltage on a line. This method has no neutral or rest position.

**Sliding windows.** A technique used in some file transfer protocols in which information is sent at the same time it is being received, thus using less time waiting for the other modem to reply. Protocols using this technique are faster.

**Snow removal.** The ability in some telecommunications software packages to eliminate flickering from a screen should it occur.

**Virtual.** Something that appears to exist but does not.

*Source:* George S. Machovec, *Telecommunications, Networking and Internet Glossary* (Chicago: ALA Library and Information Technology Association, 1993). 124p.

# Little-known NETs

*by Jim Michael and Carol Hole*

HERE IS A COLLECTION of whimsical networks for highly specialized users.

| | | |
|---|---|---|
| SonNET | — | poets |
| GnatGNET | — | entomologists |
| ButterflyNET | — | see GnatGNET |
| NETthirty | — | accounts receivable clerks |
| KnessetNET | — | Israeli politicians |
| NyetNET | — | Russian dissidents |
| ClariNET | — | woodwind musicians |
| BasiNET | — | parents of newborns, or big band fans |
| NETwork | — | people who are mad as hell and not going to take it any more |
| GarNET | — | rockhounds |
| GraNET | — | see GarNET |
| NitNET | — | picky people |
| DebtNET | — | junk bond dealers |
| NET(NOT!) | — | *Wayne's World* fans |
| EtherNET | — | anesthesiologists who don't mind trademark infringement |
| PeaNET | — | Charles Schulz fans |
| NothingbutNET | — | basketball stars |
| BonNET | — | milliners |
| InnerNET | — | TM practitioners |
| FishNET | — | anglers |
| HairNET | — | beauticians (some prefer Wash 'n' setNET) |
| CoroNET | — | bluebloods |
| CabinNET | — | cruiseline bookings |
| JetNET | — | airline bookings |
| DragNET | — | the FBI |
| BetNET | — | gamblers |
| VetNET | — | veterinarians |
| CastanetNET | — | flamenco dancers |
| ForgetNET | — | amnesiacs |
| MarionNET | — | puppeteers |

8

*Source:* "Little-known NETs," *American Libraries* 24 (May 1993): 375.

# Public library Internet connections

*by Charles R. McClure, John Carlo Bertot, and Douglas L. Zweizig*

IN EARLY 1994 THE U.S. NATIONAL COMMISSION on Libraries and Information Science conducted a survey of public libraries to determine the level of their involvement with the Internet. The following paragraphs detail the state of public library Internet connections, including the number of public libraries connected to the Internet, the average number of Internet addresses per library, the type of Internet connection libraries have, and the type of network connection provider libraries use.

## Public libraries connected to the Internet

Of all public libraries, 20.9% currently possess an Internet connection. In general, as the public library population of legal service area increases, so does the percentage of libraries possessing an Internet connection. Thus, 77.0% of public libraries with populations of legal service areas above one million are connected to the Internet, while only 13.3% of public libraries with populations of legal service area below 5,000 are connected to the Internet. The percentage of libraries connected to the Internet also varies by geographic region. Public libraries in the West show the greatest percentage of Internet connections (28.2%), while libraries in the Midwest show the smallest percentage of Internet connections (15.4%).

On average, each connected library has 4.14 individual Internet accounts, with libraries that have populations of legal service areas of under 5,000 possessing an average of 1.63 Internet accounts per library, and libraries that have populations of legal service areas of greater than one million possessing an average of 44.48 Internet accounts. The average of Internet accounts varies little by geographic region. The figures do indicate, though, that public libraries in the West have the highest number of average Internet accounts with 5.28, followed by public libraries in the South with 4.68, public libraries in the Midwest with 3.76, and public libraries in the Northeast with 3.74.

Urban libraries have a considerably higher percentage of Internet connections, 78.9%, than do rural libraries with 16.8%. Moreover, urban libraries possess a higher average number of Internet addresses, with 20.84, than do rural libraries, with 1.90. The percentage of Internet connections increases as average library material expenditures increase, with 83.5% of public libraries incurring material expenditures in excess of $1 million connected to the Internet and 13.5% of public libraries incurring material expenditures of less than $50,000 connected to the Internet. Similarly, the percentage of Internet connections increases proportionally with average library operating expenses. Indeed, 83.4% of public libraries that have operating expenditures in excess of $5 million have Internet connections, while only 11.5% of libraries with operating expenditures of less than $100,000 have Internet connections.

## Type of network connection and connection provider

The most common type of public library Internet connection is VT-100 terminal access (47.1% of library connections), followed by e-mail gateway (13.9%), and dial-up Serial Line Internet Protocol (SLIP)/Point-to-Point Protocol (PPP) connection (11.8%). As such, most public libraries that connect to the Internet do so with the most basic of available connection types. It is interesting to note that 11.2% of library respondents with Internet connections do not know the type of Internet connection their library possesses, with the percentage of those not knowing the library's type of Internet connection increasing as library population of legal service area decreases. In general, larger libraries possess Internet connections that allow full Internet services access through the use of direct connect and SLIP/PPP connections. Public libraries in the West possess higher instances of direct connect and SLIP/PPP Internet connections, with 12.7% and 16.8% respectively.

Percentages of connection type for urban and rural libraries vary only by the percentage of direct connect and SLIP/PPP connections. Urban libraries have considerably greater percentages of direct and SLIP/PPP Internet connections than do rural libraries, with 17.9% and 23.0% respectively.

A majority of public libraries, 31.2%, access the Internet through a state library network, with 18.8% using other network providers, 14.4% using commercial providers, and 14.0% using local educational organizations. Within the "other" category, public libraries indicate that they gain network connectivity predominantly through CLASS providers and regional library consortia. In general, as library population of legal service area increases, so too does public library reliance on commercial and local educational institutions for Internet connections, with public libraries serving populations of under 5,000 using commercial providers for Internet connection 5.9%, public libraries serving populations of over one million using commercial providers 21.9%, public libraries serving populations of under 5,000 using local educational organizations 9.3%, and public libraries serving populations of over one million using local educational organizations 24.0%. As library population of legal service area decreases, however, public library reliance on statewide library networks for Internet connection increases, with public libraries serving populations of over one million using statewide library networks 16.6%, and public libraries serving populations under 5,000 using statewide networks 41.1%. In general, network connection provider does not deviate significantly by geographic region. A notable exception is public libraries located in the South. The data show that southern public libraries utilize local educational organizations and OCLC regional library networks in greater proportion than libraries located in other geographic regions.

In looking at network connection providers by urban and rural library categories, the data show that urban libraries primarily use commercial providers for Internet connectivity with 25.3%, followed by local educational organizations with 22.3%, and statewide library networks with 15.7%. Rural libraries, on the other hand, predominantly use statewide library networks for Internet connectivity with 35.6%, followed by "other" with 17.8% (generally library consortiums or CLASS providers) and commercial providers with 12.8%.

*Source:* Charles R. McClure, John Carlo Bertot, and Douglas L. Zweizig, *Public Libraries and the Internet: Study Results, Policy Issues, and Recommendations* (Washington, D.C.: National Commission on Libraries and Information Science, 1994). 62p.

# TurboGopher: Internet access on the Macintosh

*by Edward J. Valauskas*

**8**

ON MY MACINTOSH DESKTOP, AMID THE CLUTTER of ordinary icons for hard disks, HyperCard stacks, spreadsheets, and word processing documents, is an unmistakable image of a gopher. I double-click on this icon, and a brief screen flashes by with another gopher image, informing me that I've connected to the University of Minnesota and its Computer & Information Services. The entire transaction happens so quickly that there is no time to stare at the rotating hands of a Macintosh "watch" nor step away for coffee.

The first screen offers me a view of ten folders and an icon with a question mark; the question mark gives me a way of locating more information. One folder is labeled "Information About Gopher." Scanning through its contents, I can learn more about Gopher, access archives, report troubles, and learn how to hook my own electronic files into the Gopher universe.

## Exploring the Internet with Gopher

Though I am tempted to open a "Fun & Games" folder—which contains folders entitled "Humor," "Movies," "Music," and "Recipes"—I decide to dive into the folder called "Libraries." Inside I find folders identified as "Electronic Books," "Library Catalogs via Telnet," "Library of Congress

Records," "Newspapers, Magazines, and Newsletters," and "Reference Works."

"Reference Works" allows me to open *Roget's Thesaurus* and the *CIA World Fact Book for 1991*. If I needed to locate the latest facts on conditions in Thailand or Egypt, I can open the most recent U.S. State Department Travel Advisory. Can't remember the area code for Silicon Valley? I can just type in "San Jose" and see the answer (408) on the screen. Need a definition for a Gopher? I see an icon labeled "Webster's Dictionary" so I try to access it. My request bombs—access is only available to users on the campus of the University of Minnesota. It is not technology at fault, merely the legalities of licensing the availability of a copyrighted file.

I decide that I need to check on the latest receipts in the Library of Congress. Opening a file billed as "Search Library of Congress Records 12-91 to Present," a dialog box appears on the screen, prompting me to locate documents containing a string of words or characters of my choosing. Feeling a need to know more about this virtual mammal doing my bidding over the network, I type in the word *gopher*. A bibliographic record for Jack Schaefer's *Conversations with a Pocket Gopher* appears, published in 1993 in Santa Barbara, California, by the Capra Press. The information was loaded from a Cataloging In Process (CIP) file created in June 1992.

## Gopher-ing to library catalogs—and joke books

Another folder indicates I can access many libraries across the network. No longer do I have to experiment with online catalogs and their dial-in procedures. Gopher understands my impatience and gives me an ever-so-polite prompt to reach a library catalog a few miles away or on the other side of the globe. I decide to track down the availability of Jack Schaefer's books at a library in my old neighborhood in Chicago. I scroll through the list of icons in the "Library Catalogs via Telnet" folder until I reach the one with the label "University of Chicago." I double-click, and a dialog box informs me that I need to log on as "lib48." I hit <Return> and I see the familiar script indicating that I am in one of the University of Chicago computers. I type *lib48* and tap <Return>, and find the usual brief prompts before me. Entering *Schaefer*, I locate a copy of his *An American Bestiary* in the Harper Library on the Midway. With the call number in hand, I leave the South Side and return to further adventures with my close electronic friend, Gopher, on the network.

Going into the Colorado folder, I can scan the holdings of any number of libraries through CARL. I decide to check the tables of content for a few of my favorite journals. I ask CARL to give me access to "Uncover." In answer to my request, I see a note indicating that some features of CARL are available only to those with valid accounts. I know that and at the "Uncover" prompt, I plug in my password. In a few screens, I am scanning the contents of several magazines for articles. I remember that a patron asked me to locate an article by a colleague in a recent, but unspecified, issue of a physics review journal. I scan a year's worth of tables of content but find no sign of his colleague in print. I note the evidence of the search in a word processing document, and send him an electronic note via QuickMail indicating my futility in the search, and asking for other suggestions. I also think about other electronic approaches, via more staid databases available in other, more traditional electronic ways.

Curious about the "Electronic Books" folder, I open it and notice immediately, through another folder, the availability of the opera of Lewis Carroll as well as Thomas Hardy's *Far from the Madding Crowd*, Herman Melville's *Moby Dick*, and Willa Cather's *O Pioneers!* Enthralled by anything related to a gopher, I decide to search the texts of the available classics for references to my animal. The results of my search are posted quickly.

I end this Gopher session by pulling in a few lawyer jokes for my barrister relatives, and scan the dessert file for a new brownie recipe. As I leave Gopher on my mundane desktop, I imagine a few other folders that I need to explore, a few more queries to post, and holdings to check in other libraries. I never quite imagined that the future would be called "Gopher," but the monikers "wheel" and "hammer" probably bothered their inventors, too. Gopher is the network future—immediately gratified in a search in a foreign library catalog, in an issue of the latest electronic journal, in savoring a few sentences from Lewis Carroll. "The time has come, the Walrus said, to talk of many things." Even gophers.

## Gopher: What it is and is not

Documents in Gopher's own files explain how it works. Essentially, Gopher transparently links together groups of file servers, each with their own collections of folders and files. I access one folder, which may be located on one computer, track through several files in search of a document, locate it and print it. I return to my desktop and enter another folder, which may, or may not, be on another computer, and start the process again. I do not know where my searches and folder sifting takes me, nor does it matter.

Gopher handles the details that I've always hated. The process is invisible to me at my keyboard. And if it's invisible, it's magic. Suddenly I have a MARC record in one hand, and a weather report in the other; two computers next to each other or on different continents. It doesn't matter to me. More importantly, I have the information I need (oh, ok, and another recipe, too), more quickly and accurately than with any other process of Internet weaving. Gopher takes the world and puts it on my desktop. You can discover more details about Gopher via anonymous FTP to boombox.micro.unm.edu.

Gopher works well on the Macintosh, but "client" programs work on all sorts on computers from DOS to UNIX boxes. Your computer needs to be hooked into the Network, not your local print-spooling kind but the Big Show—the Internet. If your computer has an IP address—for example, boombox.micro.unm.edu also is known by its IP number 134.84.132.4—then you're all set for a small virtual mammal to go to work for you.

The acronym IP stands for Internet Protocol, a mechanism for addressing your computer so mail and other messages can find their way to you. Imagine how difficult it would be to live in an apartment with no number, in a building on a street with no name, in a city absent in any atlas. Speculate on how someone could send you a postcard without an address. Without an IP number, your electronic mail would furtively scout through the ether with no success. In the case of e-mail, dead letters do not vanish into an electronic sack, but ping your unlucky correspondents with the blaring command *Address unknown*.

Once you are properly connected, have an IP address, and the Gopher client ready to go on your desktop, you are ready to begin. Now come your own adventures in answering old problems differently and trying new processes once thought too cumbersome, except for the most experienced net hands.

Gopher on the Macintosh has been improved by the Minnesota team in a version known as TurboGopher. TurboGopher is fast in that it displays on your screen results as quickly as possible, while in the background it still works on completing the search. A directory cache also helps accelerate the entire process. Unlike other applications, Gopher is not a hog on memory or computing cycles and freely shares your Macintosh with other applications. I can run this form of access to multiple library catalogs at my reference desk, and keep open a database with my own library catalog, and a word processing document all at the same time.

## Gopher and WWW

Gopher is significantly different in how it works from the World Wide Web (WWW). WWW takes advantage of hypertext to link documents. The creation

**8**

of links means that you can more easily scan and search large files of documents. Using a single interface reduces the possibility of missing a file, but in that difference, Gopher finds many more adherents.

I usually search at the reference desk for discrete, very specific kinds of information. I am not looking for an all-encompassing survey of every aspect of knowledge on a given subject. Gopher lends itself to fact-finding missions rather than encyclopedic expeditions. If I need one isolated and perfectly finite verification of a fact, there is no need to scour the electronic universe for every shade of interpretation of that fact.

Gopher's philosophy also means that anyone can set up a server and load their documents, without the need for exotic blueprints for pointers and connectors. To Gopher searchers, your text file will be just fine if it contains the exact tidbit they're looking for on their fact-shopping trip. It is no wonder Gopher is becoming increasingly popular; some servers see a transaction every second. In spite of their differing philosophies, it is possible to access WWW and WAIS information from the Gopher perspective.

## Growing Gophers

The growing use of Gopher and other access tools means that traffic on our electronic networks will continue to climb exponentially. Given the number of computers in the world, and the fact that many are isolated from surveys and other kinds of censuses by security practices and other firewalls, there is no accurate number of machines available over the global networks. One 1992 estimate by John Quarterman looked at the major networks—BITNET, Usenet, FidoNet, UUCP, the Internet, and the IP Enterprise—and derived a total of 1,626,585 computers. Another survey by Mark Lottor, of SRI International in Menlo Park, California, also as of July 1992, indicates that there are 992,000 computers with IP addresses. Gopher's ease of use and functionality will add to the number of clients and servers available, and push these counts even higher.

We are on the verge of realizing that some ancient predictions about computers will come true. Soon it may no longer matter what kind of box we are using or accessing, what kind of file or what version of software was used in making it available to us, or at what distance—in human terms—a server is positioned. I won't have to remember commands, addresses, or character strings that never quite made sense to me. I won't be penalized even if I accidentally type a wrong character or an erroneous case for a character in an address.

Gopher makes information access more human by hiding the inhuman aspects of using a computer, making it invisible to my desire to locate a fact as quickly and as accurately is possible. Is my Mac really an information appliance? If that means that I no longer fight with local library systems, with idiosyncrasies of different computers, with the ways in which pages appear, then Gopher has indeed created an information appliance.

With the appearance of more servers and more documents the true restraints will not be technology or our imaginations, but copyright, licenses, and the boundaries of human law over intellectual property. Gopher, and programs like it, will accelerate our reanalysis of the legal restraints to electronic information. If Gopher's arrival means the speedy resolution of copyright between publishers, libraries, and their community of patrons, its value will be measured long after my computer is extinct. It will liberate in a way its inventors never envisioned—a beneficial fate proving serendipity's role in anything of value. Gopher will have a most prosperous life as the catalyst for our ways of access in what remains of this decade and into the next century as well.

*Source:* Edward J. Valauskas, "TurboGopher: Internet Access with Ease on the Macintosh," *Online,* March 1993, pp. 87–89. Reprinted with permission.

# 84 library uses for the Internet

*by George M. Eberhart*

THE INTERNET IS SO FLUID and wide-ranging that it is hard to imagine confining a list of relevant library uses to a mere 84, especially since librarians' needs are also vastly fluid and wide-ranging. However, that's never stopped me before. So in this list I will include areas that may not be your usual roadside attractions along the infobahn, as well as the more frequented data watering holes. Basic commands are followed by //, then addresses, paths, or menu choices.

## Computers

**Displaying Asian documents** on a PC, Mac or X-window system. [Chinese] gopher// gopher.ccu.edu.tw I →About the Gopher →About this Gopher ; [Chinese] ftp// nic.funet.fi I path: /pub/culture/chinese/* ; [Korean] ftp// ftp.kaist.ac.kr I path: /pub/hangul/readme.faq ; [Japanese] gopher// bash.cc.keio.ac.jp I →Japanese →How to read Japanese files

**UNIX computers.** gopher// gopher.fsl.orst.edu I →Other Sources of Information →Hugo's Lore-House →Where the Sun Doesn't Shine & Other Bottomless Pits →The Logintaka–or–How to Become a UNIX Wizard

## Education

**AskERIC.** Internet-based question-answering service for teachers, librarians, and administrators. AskERIC staff respond within 48 working hours. gopher// ericir.syr.edu I →News and Information about ERIC and AskERIC →The AskERIC Service for Educators

**Distance Education Database.** Provides listings of available courses by subject or intended audience. telnet// ndlc.occ.uky.edu I login: ndlc

**Higher Education Resources and Opportunities (HERO).** Scholarships, grants, research opportunities. telnet// fedix.fie.com I login: new

**United States Department of Education.** Includes USDE/OERI publications, educational software, Goals 2000 documents, USDE programs and phone directory. gopher// gopher.ed.gov

**United States National K12 Gopher.** New educational applications for students and teachers. gopher// copernicus.bbn.com

## Humor

**Ambrose Bierce's Devil's Dictionary.** Wry, turn-of-the-19th-century humor that is still apropos for the turn of the 20th. ftp// ftp.std.com I path: /obi/ Ambrose.Bierce/The.Devils.Dictionary.Z ; gopher// ftp.std.com I →OBI The Online Book Initiative →The Online Books →Ambrose Bierce →The Devil's Dictionary

**Amusing tests and quizzes.** ftp// quartz.rutgers.edu I path: /pub/humor/ Tests/* ; gopher// quartz.rutgers.edu I →Humor →Tests

**ASCII cartoons.** gopher// pfsparc02.phil15.uni-sb.de I →fun →cartoons

**Callahan's bar.** Puns and banter. newsgroup// alt.callahans

**Jive server.** Send a short message to this server and within minutes, you will receive its translation into jive. mail// jive@ifi.unizh.ch

**Library humor.** Includes bumperstickers, lightbulb jokes, subject headings. gopher// snymorva.cs.snymor.edu I →Library Services →Library Humor

**Mystery Science Theatre 3000.** If you're a fan of this series on the Comedy Channel. newsgroup// rec.arts.tv.mst3k

8

**Smiley dictionary.** Identifying those strange Internet faces :-> gopher// pfsparc02.phil15.uni-sb.de I →fun →cartoons →Smilies :-)

## Internet help

**EFF's Guide to the Internet.** Everything from e-mail to MUDs. ftp// ftp.eff.org I path: /pub/Net_info/EFF_Net_Guide/netguide.eff

**Electronic Frontiers Foundation.** New communications technologies and access. ftp// ftp.eff.org I path: /pub/eff/* ; gopher// gopher.eff.org

**FAQ lists.** Lists of frequently asked questions available. newsgroups// alt.answers, comp.answers, misc.answers, news.answers, rec.answers, sci.answers, soc.answers, talk.answers

**Information Resources: The Internet and Computer-Mediated Communication,** by John December. Lists pointers to information describing the Internet, networks, and computer-mediated communication. gopher// gopher.fsl.orst.edu I →Other Sources of Information →Hugo's Lore-House →Where the Sun Doesn't Shine & Other Bottomless Pits→Information Sources: The Internet and Computer-Mediated Communication

**International e-mail access.** International country codes and network status. gopher// gopher.psg.com I →Networking Computers →Connectivity →International Connectivity →FAQ: International E-mail Accessibility

**Internet access** no matter where you are. newsgroups// alt.internet. access.wanted, alt.internet.services

**Internet hunt.** Monthly questions about finding information on the Internet. ftp// ftp.cni.org I path: /pub/net-guides/internet.hunt

**Internet Mall.** Shopping on the info-highway. ftp// ftp.netcom.com I path: / pub/Guides/Internet.Mall

**Internet Monthly Report.** News from Internet organizations and research groups. ftp// venera.isi.edu I path: /in-notes/imr/* ; mailing list// subscribe: imr-request@isi.edu I address: cooper@isi.edu

**Inter-network mail guide.** How to e-mail from one network to another. ftp// csd4.csd.uwm.edu I path: /pub/internetwork-mail-guide ; finger// yanoff@csd4.csd.uwm.edu ; newsgroup// alt.internet.services

**Most comprehensive gopher server.** gopher// english-server.hss.cmu.edu

**People on the Internet.** How to find people's e-mail addresses. mail// dalamb@qucis.queensu.ca I Body: Send How to find people on the Internet ; gopher// yaleinfo.yale.edu I →Browse YaleInfo →People on the Internet ; mail// nic@vnet.ibm.com I Body: whois *lastname, firstname*

**Posting to newsgroups by e-mail** if you don't have netnews or Usenet. mail// *newsgroup*@cs.utexas.edu

**Special Internet Connections,** by Scott Yanoff, is a collection of useful and intriguing Internet areas. ftp// csd4.csd.uwm.edu I path: /pub/inet.services. txt ; gopher// gopher.uwm.edu I →Remote Information Services →Special Internet Connections (Yanoff List)

**Surfing the Internet,** an introduction for librarians by Jean Armour Polly. ftp // nysernet.org I path: /pub/resources/guides/surfing.2.0.3.txt ; gopher // nysernet.org I →Special Collections: Internet Help →Surfing the Internet

**Tips for finding Internet resources (ann-lots).** mailing list// subscribe: listserv@vm1.nodak.edu I address: ann-lots@vm1.nodak.edu

**University of Michigan subject-oriented Internet resource guides.** ftp// una.hh.lib.umich.edu I path: /inetdirsstacks ; gopher// gopher.lib. umich.edu I →What's New & Featured Resources →Clearinghouse for Subject-Oriented Internet Resource Guides

**Zen and the Art of the Internet,** by Brendan Kehoe, covers the Internet basics. ftp// csn.org I path: /pub/net/zen

# Law

**Bureau of Justice Statistics** documents.gopher// uacsc2.albany.edu ⏐ →United Nations Justice Network →Bureau of Justice Statistics Documents

**Freedom of Information Act.** How to use it. ftp// ftp.spies.com ⏐ path: /Gov/ foia.cit ; gopher// wiretap.spies.com ⏐ →Government Docs →Citizens Guide to Using the FOIA

**Government Accounting Office reports.** ftp// ftp.cu.nih.gov ⏐ path: gao-reports ; gopher// wiretap.spies.com ⏐ →GAO Transition Reports

**Legal Directory.** Contains biographical information on attorneys and law firms in the United States. gopher// wld.westlaw.com

# Libraries

**Acquisitions Librarians Electronic Network (ACQNET),** an irregular newsletter for collection development and serials management. mail// cri@cornellc.cit.cornell.edu ⏐ Body: Subscribe ACQNET

**African-American studies and librarianship (afas-l).** mailing list// subscribe: listserv@kentvm.kent.edu ⏐ address: afas-l@kentvm.kent.edu

**ALA Washington Office Newsletter (alawon).** Up-to-date information on legislation affecting libraries. e-serial// subscribe: listserv@uicvm.uic.edu ⏐ address: fdk@alawash.org

**American Library Association.** gopher// gopher.uic.edu ⏐ →The Library →American Library Association

**Health science libraries.** newsgroup// bit.listserv.medlib-l

**Libraries in society.** Notes, comments. newsgroup// soc.libraries.talk

**Library catalogs online.** Worldwide list. gopher// gopher.lib.umich.edu ⏐ →Library Catalogs

**Library of Congress.** LC's public access catalog, and much more. gopher // marvel.loc.gov ; telnet// locis.loc.gov

**National Information Infrastructure.** The future of information and telecommunications. gopher// iitf.doc.gov

**Public-Access Computer Systems News (pacs-l).** End-user computer systems in libraries. e-serial// subscribe: listserv@uhupvm1.hh.edu ⏐ address: libpacs@uhupvm1.bitnet ; newsgroup// bit.listserv.pacs-l

**Public libraries.** newsgroup// bit.listserv.publib

**Reference questions,** problems, anecdotes, research (librefed). newsgroup// bit.listserv.libref-l

**Reference questions—extra hard (stumpers-l).** mailing list// subscribe: listserv@crf.cuis.edu ⏐ address: stumpers-list@crf.cuis.edu

**Reviews and book news.** mailing list// subscribe: booknews @columbia.ilc.com ⏐ address: listserv@columbia.ilc.com ; newsgroup// rec.arts.books

**Special collections and the book trade.** newsgroup// bit.listserv.exlibris

**Support staff.** newsgroup// bit.listserv.libsup-l

# Miscellany

**Almanac of events,** a daily list of birthdays and other historical events. Sports schedules. finger// copi@oddjob.uchicago.edu

**Area codes.** gopher// gopher.gsfc.nasa.gov ⏐ →Virtual Reference Shelf →U.S. telephone areacodes

**Bruce Sterling articles.** gopher// gopher.well.sf.ca.us ⏐ →Cyberpunk and Postmodern Culture →Bruce Sterling

**Copyediting.** Editing and proofreading tips. mailing list// subscribe: listserv@cornell.edu ⏐ address: copyediting-l@cornell.edu

**Music fun.** Lyrics, gif files, etc. ftp// cs.uwp.edu ⏐ path: /pub/music/*

**8**

**Postcard collectors.** Many of them collect library postcards. newsgroup //bit.listserv.postcard

**Shorter Oxford Dictionary.** ftp// ftp.white.toronto.edu |path: /pub /words/sodict.gz

**Telephone numbers.** Provides complete name, address and phone number. mail// info@ameri.com |Body: Request report on *name*.

**White House.** mail// president@whitehouse.gov ; mail// vice.president @whitehouse.gov

**ZIP codes.** gopher// gopher.uoregon.edu |→Geographic & Travel Information →U.S. ZIP Code Directory (search by city or ZIP)

## News

**Daily Report Card News Service.** National update on America's education goals. gopher// goldmine.cde.ca.gov |→Daily Report Card News Service

**Consumer Price Index.** gopher// infopath.ucsd.edu |→News & Services →Economic... →Price and Productivity...

**Economic Bulletin Board.** Current economic information, including Census, Bureau of Labor Statistics, Treasury news. gopher// infopath.ucsd.edu |→News & Weather →National News →Electronic Bulletin Board

**Hot business news.** newsgroup// clari.biz.urgent

**Odd happenings,** such as "hitman died of heart attack" and "Mt. Everest to get toilet." newsgroup// clari.living.bizarre

**Stock market summary report.** telnet// a2i.rahul.net |login: guest

**White House press releases.** mail// almanac@esusda.gov |Body: subscribe wh-summary ; gopher// gopher.tamu.edu |→Browse Information by Subject →Government Information →Information from the White House

## Science and medicine

**AIDS information.** newsgroup// sci.med.aids ; mailing list// subscribe: aids-stat-request@wubios.wustl.edu |address: aids-stat@wubios.wustl.edu

**Botany database.** 100,000 records in Type Specimen Register for the U.S. National Herbarium. gopher// smithson.si.edu |Botany at the Smithsonian Institution →Type Specimen Register

**Earthquake information.** finger// [Wash., Ore.] quake@geophys. washington.edu ; [Alaska] quake@fm.gi.alaska.edu ; [world] quake@ gldfs.cr.usgs.gov ; [central U.S.] quake@slueas.slu.edu ; [Nev.] quake@ seismo.unr.edu ; [Utah] quake@eqinfo.seis.utah.edu ; [Northern Calif.] quake@ andreas.wr.usgs.gov ; [Southern Calif.] scec.gps.caltech.edu

**Mammal database.** All known mammals. gopher// smithson.si.edu |→Vertebrate Zoology at the Smithsonian Institution

**NASA news.** finger// nasanews@space.mit.edu

**Natural resources librarians and information specialists discussion group (natreslib-l).** mailing list// subscribe: annhed@cc.usu.edu |address: natreslib-l@cc.usu.edu

**Skymap** for anyplace on earth from 4000 B.C. to 8000 A.D. gopher// oak.oakland.edu |→OAK Software Repository →pub →msdos →astrnomy →skymap21a.zip, skymap21b.zip

**University of Illinois Weather Machine.** For weather-related documents and National Weather Service reports. Includes severe weather bulletins worldwide. gopher// wx.atmos.uiuc.edu

## Social sciences and history

**Africana (africa-l).** mailing list// subscribe: listserv@brufmg.bitnet |address:

africa-l@brufmg.bitnet

**Electric Mystic's Guide to the Internet,** by Michael Strangelove. Bibliography of electronic documents relevant to religious studies. gopher// nysernet.org |→Reference Desk →200-Religion →Electric Mystic's Guide ; gopher// gopher.lib.umich.edu |→Humanities Resources →Philosophy and Religion →Electric Mystic's Guide

**Feminist,** owned by the ALA Feminist Task Force. mailing list// subscribe: listserv@mitmva.mit.edu | address: feminist@mitmva.mit.edu

**Historical costumes,** courtesy of the Society for Creative Anachronism. gopher// gopher.univ-lyon1.fr |→Usenet→Usenet FAQs (news.answers)→crafts-historical-costuming

**National Archaeological Database.** 100,000 archaeological reports searchable by keyword, author, location, publication date. telnet// cast.uark.edu | login: nadb

**Soviet archives.** ftp// seq1.loc.gov | path: /pub/soviet.archive/* ; gopher// gopher.virginia.edu |→Library Services →University Library Collections →Alphabetic Organization →Soviet Archive Exhibit, Library of Congress

# Developing the National Information Infrastructure

IN SEPTEMBER 1993 THE AMERICAN LIBRARY ASSOCIATION and the Council on Library Resources sponsored a forum in Washington, D.C., on Telecommunications and Information Infrastructure Policy. During its discussions the group, composed of representatives from 15 national library and information associations, reached a consensus on key principles and questions that must be used to guide the development of plans for the evolution of the National Information Infrastructure (NII)—also called the national data highway.

The major principles identified during the forum discussion were:

- First Amendment;
- Privacy;
- Intellectual Property;
- Ubiquity;
- Equitable Access;
- Interoperability.

8

### First Amendment/Intellectual freedom

1. Access to the NII should be available to all regardless of age, religion, disability, sexual orientation, social and political views, national origin, economic status, location, information literacy, etc.

2. The NII service providers must guarantee the free flow of information protected by the First Amendment.

3. The NII should support and encourage a diversity of information providers.

4. Individuals should have the right to choose what information to receive through the NII.

### Privacy

1. Privacy should be carefully protected and extended.

2. Comprehensive policies should be developed to ensure that the privacy of all people is protected.

3. Personal data collected to provide specific services should be limited to the minimum necessary.

4. Sharing data collected from individuals should only be permitted with their

informed consent.

5. Individuals should have the right to inspect and correct data files about themselves.

6. Transaction data should remain confidential.

**Intellectual property**

1. Intellectual property rights and protections are independent of the form of publication or distribution.

2. The intellectual property system should ensure a fair and equitable balance between rights of creators and other copyright owners and the needs of users.

3. Fair use and other exceptions to owners' rights in the copyright law should continue in the electronic environment.

4. Compensation systems must provide a fair and reasonable return to copyright owners.

**Ubiquity**

1. Libraries in every community should preserve and enhance their traditional roles in providing public access to information regardless of format.

2. Network access costs for libraries, educational organizations, government entities and nonprofit groups should be stable, predictable and location insensitive.

3. Resources must be allocated to provide basic public access in fostering the development of the information infrastructure.

**Equitable access**

1. The NII should support and encourage a diversity of information providers in order to guarantee an open, fair, and competitive marketplace, with a full range of viewpoints.

2. Diversity of access should be protected through use of nonproprietary protocols.

3. National and international interoperability standards should be adopted to promote diversity and an open playing field.

4. Access to basic network services should be affordable and available to all.

5. Basic network access should be made available independent of geographic location.

6. The NII should ensure private, government and nonprofit participation in governance of the network.

7. Electronic information should be appropriately documented, organized and archived through the cooperative endeavors of information service providers and libraries.

**Interoperability**

1. The design of the NII should facilitate two-way, audio, video and data communication from anyone to anyone easily and effectively.

2. The NII must support maximum interoperability and utilize both national and international standards.

3. A transition phase should provide compatibility between leading-edge technology and trailing-edge technology to allow users reasonable protection from precipitate change.

4. Interoperability standards should be encouraged and tied to incentives for the use of those standards in awards for Federal funding.

5. Federal government information dissemination programs should adhere to interoperability standards.

6. Principles of interoperability should require directory and locator services and nonproprietary search protocols as well as a minimal set of data elements for the description of databases.

*Source: Principles for the Development of the National Information Infrastructure*
(Chicago: ALA Telecommunications and Information Infrastructure Policy Forum, 1993). 55p.

# ISSUES

9

**Intellectual Freedom / Access**

# The Library Bill of Rights

THE AMERICAN LIBRARY ASSOCIATION affirms that all libraries are forums for information and ideas, and that the following basic policies should guide their services.

1. Books and other library resources should be provided for the interest, information, and enlightenment of all people of the community the library serves. Materials should not be excluded because of the origin, background, or views of those contributing to their creation.
2. Libraries should provide materials and information presenting all points of view on current and historical issues. Materials should not be proscribed or removed because of partisan or doctrinal disapproval.
3. Libraries should challenge censorship in the fulfillment of their responsibility to provide information and enlightenment.
4. Libraries should cooperate with all persons and groups concerned with resisting abridgment of free expression and free access to ideas.
5. A person's right to use a library should not be denied or abridged because of origin, age, background, or views.
6. Libraries which make exhibit spaces and meeting rooms available to the public they serve should make such facilities available on an equitable basis, regardless of the beliefs or affiliations of individuals or groups requesting their use.

## Interpretations (summaries)

**Free access to libraries for minors.** Denying minors access to certain library materials and services available to adults is a violation of the Library Bill of Rights. Librarians and governing bodies should maintain that parents—and only parents—have the right and responsibility to restrict the access of their children to library resources.

**Labeling.** Describing or designating certain library materials by affixing a prejudicial label to them or segregating by a prejudicial system is an attempt to prejudice attitudes and, as such, is a censor's tool; such practices violate the Library Bill of Rights. A variety of private organizations promulgate rating systems and/or review materials as a means of advising either their members or the general public concerning their opinions of the contents and suitability or appropriate age for use of certain books, films, recordings, or other materials. For the library to adopt or enforce any of these private systems, to attach such ratings to library materials, to include them in bibliographic records, library catalogs, or other finding aids, or otherwise to endorse them would violate the Library Bill of Rights.

**Access for children and young people to videotapes and other nonprint formats.** Recognizing that libraries cannot act *in loco parentis*, policies that set minimum age limits for access to videotapes and/or audiovisual material and equipment with or without parental permission abridge library use for minors. Nevertheless, ALA acknowledges and supports the exercise by parents of their responsibility to guide their own children's viewing, using published reviews of films and videotapes and/or reference works that provide information about the content, subject matter, and recommended audiences.

**Expurgation of library materials.** Expurgation of any parts of books or other library resources by the library, its agent, or its parent institution is a violation of the Library Bill of Rights because it denies access to the complete work, and, therefore, to the entire spectrum of ideas that the work was intended to express.

**Diversity in collection development.** Librarians have a professional responsibility to be inclusive, not exclusive, in collection development and in the provision of interlibrary loan. Access to all materials legally obtainable should be assured to the user and policies should not unjustly exclude materials even if offensive to the librarian or user. A balanced collection reflects diversity of materials, not equality of numbers. Collection development responsibilities include selecting materials in the languages in common use in the community which the library serves. Collection development and the selection of materials should be done according to professional standards and established selection and review procedures.

Librarians have an obligation to protect library collections from removal of materials based on personal bias or prejudice, and to select and support the acquisition of materials on all subjects that meet, as closely as possible, the needs and interest of all persons in the community which the library serves. This includes materials that reflect political, economic, religious, social, minority, and sexual issues.

**Evaluating library collections.** Evaluation of library materials is not to be used as a convenient means to remove materials presumed to be controversial or disapproved of by segments of the community.

**Challenged materials** which meet the criteria for selection in the materials selection policy of the library should not be removed under any legal or extralegal pressure.

**Restricted access.** Attempts to restrict library materials violate the basic tenets of the Library Bill of Rights. Policies to protect library materials for reasons of physical preservation, protection from theft or mutilation must be carefully formulated and administered with extreme attention to the principles of intellectual freedom.

**Meeting rooms.** Libraries maintaining meeting room facilities should develop and publish statements governing use. These statements can properly define time, place, or manner of use; such qualifications should not pertain to the content of a meeting or to the beliefs or affiliations of the sponsors. If meeting rooms in libraries supported by public funds are made available to the general public for non-library sponsored events, the library may not exclude any group based on the subject matter to be discussed or based on the ideas that the group advocates. A publicly supported library may limit use of its meeting rooms to strictly "library related" activities, provided that the limitation is clearly circumscribed and is viewpoint neutral.

**Exhibit spaces and bulletin boards.** Libraries maintaining exhibit spaces and bulletin boards for outside groups and individuals should develop and publish statements governing use to assure that space is provided on an equitable basis to all groups that request it. A publicly supported library may limit use of its exhibit space to strictly "library related" activities, provided that the limitation is clearly circumscribed and is viewpoint neutral. Libraries may include in this policy rules regarding the time, place, and the manner of use of the exhibit space, so long as the rules are content neutral and are applied in the same manner to all groups wishing to use the space.

**Library-initiated programs as a resource.** A policy on library-initiated programming should set forth the library's commitment to free access to information and ideas for all users. Library staff select programs based on the interests and information needs of the community. Libraries serving multilingual and multicultural communities make efforts to accommodate the information needs of those for whom English is a second language.

**Access to resources and services in the school library media program.** Members of the school community involved in the collection development process employ educational criteria to select resources unfettered by their personal, social, or religious views. Students and educators served by the school library media program have access to resources and services free of constraints resulting from personal, partisan, or doctrinal disapproval and which reflect the linguistic pluralism of the community. School library media professionals resist efforts by individuals to define what is appropriate for all students or teachers to read, view, or hear.

**Universal right to free expression.** The American Library Association believes that freedom of expression is an inalienable human right, necessary to self-government, vital to the resistance of oppression, and crucial to the cause of justice, and further, that the principles of freedom of expression should be applied by libraries and librarians throughout the world.

*Source:* ALA Office for Intellectual Freedom, *Intellectual Freedom Manual* (Chicago: American Library Association, 1992, 4th ed.). 283p.

# The freedom to read

**THE FREEDOM TO READ** is essential to our democracy. It is continuously under attack. Private groups and public authorities in various parts of the country are working to remove books from sale, to censor textbooks, to label "controversial" books, to distribute lists of "objectionable" books or authors, and to purge libraries. These actions apparently rise from a view that our national tradition of free expression is no longer valid; that censorship and suppression are needed to avoid the subversion of politics and the corruption of morals. We, as citizens devoted to the use of books and as librarians and publishers responsible for disseminating them, wish to assert the public interest in the preservation of the freedom to read.

We are deeply concerned about these attempts at suppression. Most such attempts rest on a denial of the fundamental premise of democracy: that the ordinary citizen, by exercising critical judgment, will accept the good and reject the bad. The censors, public and private, assume that they should determine what is good and what is bad for their fellow citizens.

We trust Americans to recognize propaganda, and to reject it. We do not believe they need the help of censors to assist them in this task. We do not believe they are prepared to sacrifice their heritage of a free press in order to be "protected" against what others think may be bad for them. We believe they still favor free enterprise in ideas and expression.

We are aware, of course, that books are not alone in being subjected to efforts at suppression. We are aware that these efforts are related to a larger pattern of pressures being brought against education, the press, films, radio, and television. The problem is not only one of actual censorship. The shadow of fear cast by these pressures leads, we suspect, to an even larger voluntary curtailment of expression by those who seek to avoid controversy.

Such pressure toward conformity is perhaps natural to a time of uneasy change and pervading fear. Especially when so many of our apprehensions are directed against an ideology, the expression of a dissident idea becomes a thing feared in itself, and we tend to move against it as against a hostile deed, with suppression.

And yet suppression is never more dangerous than in such a time of social tension. Freedom has given the United States the elasticity to endure strain. Freedom keeps open the path of novel and creative solutions, and enables change to come by choice. Every silencing of a heresy, every enforcement of an orthodoxy, diminishes the toughness and resilience of our society and leaves it the less able to deal with stress.

Now as always in our history, books are among our greatest instruments of freedom. They are almost the only means for making generally available ideas or manners of expression that can initially command only a small audience. They are the natural medium for the new idea and the untried voice from which come the original contributions to social growth. They are essential to the extended discussion which serious thought requires, and to the accumulation of knowledge and ideas into organized collections.

We believe that free communication is essential to the preservation of a free society and a creative culture. We believe that these pressures towards conformity present the danger of limiting the range and variety of inquiry and expression on which our democracy and our culture depend. We believe that every American community must jealously guard the freedom to publish and to circulate, in order to preserve its own freedom to read. We believe that publishers and librarians have a profound responsibility to give validity to that freedom to read by making it possible for the readers to choose freely from a variety of offerings.

The freedom to read is guaranteed by the Constitution. Those with faith in free people will stand firm on these constitutional guarantees of essential rights and will exercise the responsibilities that accompany these rights.

We therefore affirm these propositions:

1. **It is in the public interest for publishers and librarians to make available the widest diversity of views and expressions, including those which are unorthodox or unpopular with the majority.**

Creative thought is by definition new, and what is new is different. The bearer of every new thought is a rebel until that idea is refined and tested. Totalitarian systems attempt to maintain themselves in power by the ruthless suppression of any concept which challenges the established orthodoxy. The power of a democratic system to adapt to change is vastly strengthened by the freedom of its citizens to choose widely from among conflicting opinions offered freely to them. To stifle every nonconformist idea at birth would mark the end of the democratic process. Furthermore, only through the constant activity of weighing and selecting can the democratic mind attain the strength demanded by times like these. We need to know not only what we believe but why we believe it.

2. **Publishers, librarians, and booksellers do not need to endorse every idea or presentation contained in the books they make available. It would conflict with the public interest for them to establish their own political, moral, or aesthetic views as a standard for determining what books should be published or circulated.**

Publishers and librarians serve the educational process by helping to make available knowledge and ideas required for the growth of the mind and the increase of learning. They do not foster education by imposing as mentors the patterns of their own thought. The people should have the freedom to read and consider a broader range of ideas than those that may be held by any single librarian or publisher or government or church. It is wrong that what one can read should be confined to what another thinks proper.

3. **It is contrary to the public interest for publishers or librarians to determine the acceptability of a book on the basis of the personal history or political affiliations of the author.**

A book should be judged as a book. No art or literature can flourish if it is to be measured by the political views or private lives of its creators. No society

**9**

of free people can flourish which draws up lists of writers to whom it will not listen, whatever they may have to say.

**4. There is no place in our society for efforts to coerce the taste of others, to confine adults to the reading matter deemed suitable for adolescents, or to inhibit the efforts of writers to achieve artistic expression.**

To some, much of modern literature is shocking. But is not much of life itself shocking? We cut off literature at the source if we prevent writers from dealing with the stuff of life. Parents and teachers have a responsibility to prepare the young to meet the diversity of experiences in life to which they will be exposed, as they have a responsibility to help them learn to think critically for themselves. These are affirmative responsibilities, not to be discharged simply by preventing them from reading works for which they are not yet prepared. In these matters taste differs, and taste cannot be legislated; nor can machinery be devised which will suit the demands of one group without limiting the freedom of others.

**5. It is not in the public interest to force a reader to accept with any book the prejudgment of a label characterizing the book or author as subversive or dangerous.**

The idea of labeling presupposes the existence of individuals or groups with wisdom to determine by authority what is good or bad for the citizen. It presupposes that individuals must be directed in making up their minds about the ideas they examine. But Americans do not need others to do their thinking for them.

**6. It is the responsibility of publishers and librarians, as guardians of the people's freedom to read, to contest encroachments upon that freedom by individuals or groups seeking to impose their own standards or tastes upon the community at large.**

It is inevitable in the give and take of the democratic process that the political, the moral, or the aesthetic concepts of an individual or group will occasionally collide with those of another individual or group. In a free society individuals are free to determine for themselves what they wish to read, and each group is free to determine what it will recommend to its freely associated members. But no group has the right to take the law into its own hands, and to impose its own concept of politics or morality upon other members of a democratic society. Freedom is no freedom if it is accorded only to the accepted and the inoffensive.

**7. It is the responsibility of publishers and librarians to give full meaning to the freedom to read by providing books that enrich the quality and diversity of thought and expression. By the exercise of this affirmative responsibility, they can demonstrate that the answer to a bad book is a good one, the answer to a bad idea is a good one.**

The freedom to read is of little consequence when expended on the trivial; it is frustrated when the reader cannot obtain matter fit for that reader's purpose. What is needed is not only the absence of restraint, but the positive provision of opportunity for the people to read the best that has been thought and said. Books are the major channel by which the intellectual inheritance is handed down, and the principal means of its testing and growth. The defense of their freedom and integrity, and the enlargement of their service to society, requires of all publishers and librarians the utmost of their faculties, and deserves of all citizens the fullest of their support.

We state these propositions neither lightly nor as easy generalizations. We here stake out a lofty claim for the value of books. We do so because we believe that they are good, possessed of enormous variety and usefulness, worthy of cherishing and keeping free. We realize that the application of these propositions may mean the dissemination of ideas and manners of expression that are repugnant to many persons. We do not state these propositions in the comfortable belief that what people read is unimportant. We believe rather that what people read is deeply important; that ideas can be dangerous; but that the suppression of ideas is fatal to a democratic society. Freedom itself is a dangerous way of life, but it is ours.

*Source:* ALA Office for Intellectual Freedom, *Intellectual Freedom Manual* (Chicago: American Library Association, 1992, 4th ed.). 283p.

# 11 ways to answer a censor

*by Martha Cornog*

1. No one is forcing you to read *The Limerick* or check it out. We have plenty of other humor books you might like—like the books by Bennett Cerf and Edward Lear.
2. Have you read the entire book? The overall message of Asimov's *The Robots of Dawn* favors caring, committed, loving sex, as deliberately contrasted to the supercasual sex that is the norm on the planet Aurora in the story.
3. Since you think our collection favors only one point of view, we invite you to suggest some books reflecting other sides of the issue. We would be happy to consider them for purchase.
4. *Changing Bodies, Changing Lives* was selected according to favorable reviews and our formal criteria, which include need, demand, quality, and balance. Here's a copy of the criteria. We'll be glad to answer any questions.
5. We agree that the library should reflect community values. However, our community is more varied than you may think, and we have many patrons who wish to read *Playboy*. We cannot remove publications just because they offend some people. If we removed every book or magazine that offended someone, we would serve *no one* in our community.
6. No child is forced to read *Daddy's Roommate*, including your own. You are free to prevent your child from looking at it or checking it out. But not all parents feel as you do. You do not have the right to keep *their* children from reading it.
7. No, your tax dollars did not go toward buying *Intimacy Between Men*. That was paid for by the tax dollars of the people who checked it out over the past few years. You might want to think of your tax dollars buying Paul Cameron's *Exposing the AIDS Scandal*, which takes a point of view closer to yours.
8. If you want to protest the Stephen King books, it's your right as a citizen to circulate petitions and call the mayor. However, the library doesn't respond differently to those who are more vocal than others. We will process your complaint according to our normal reconsideration procedure.
9. When your child finds a book you disagree with, as will surely happen whether or not the library bans *Forever*, you have an opportunity to tell your child about your values and why you think the book is wrong.
10. Whether actions are illegal or not, writing about them is not illegal. As to whether this book is illegal because of obscenity, that is a judgment that would have to be determined by a court of law.
11. We may have to disagree.

*Source:* Martha Cornog, "Is Sex Safe in Your Library? How to Fight Censorship," *Library Journal* 118 (August 1993): 44.

9

# Coping with censors

**WHEN LIBRARIES FOLLOW THE POLICIES AND PROCEDURES** outlined in this Handbook and in ALA's *Intellectual Freedom Manual* (4th ed., 1992), the overwhelming majority of complaints will be resolved without undue controversy, very often to the mutual satisfaction of both the library and the complainant. But sometimes, despite the protections offered by a good materials selection policy and review procedure, a major censorship incident still develops. In such cases, beleaguered librarians, library trustees, or concerned library users may contact the state intellectual freedom committee directly for assistance, or they may be referred to the committee by ALA's Office for Intellectual Freedom (OIF). Sometimes the state committee will learn of an incident independently and approach those affected with an offer of assistance. It is entirely up to the affected library to decide whether to work mainly through members of the state committee, directly with OIF, or through some convenient combination thereof. The library may even choose to reject all outside assistance. In any event, the state committee should maintain close and regular contact with OIF and report all relevant information. Communications failures within the ranks of the anticensorship forces are unnecessary and can be destructive.

When a censorship incident threatens to mushroom into a crisis, everyone involved should observe two basic rules. The first is: Do Not Panic! No matter how belligerent and seemingly unreasonable the complainants may become, no matter how much some local politicians, the media, or assorted independent careerists may distort the issues, the library and its librarians should strive first and foremost to maintain a calm and professional attitude. The library and the state committee should insist that established policies and procedures be upheld. Though a careful and reasoned response should be made to all allegations, efforts should be made to keep the discussion focused on the major intellectual freedom issues. Defenders of intellectual freedom should at all times refrain from making personal attacks on their opponents, no matter how tempting this may become.

The second basic rule is that the person directly involved must always retain the final word. To the state intellectual freedom committee, a local incident may appear to be a golden opportunity to educate the public and promote the principles of intellectual freedom. But to the beleaguered librarian, it may seem like a horrible nightmare, to be resolved in a manner consistent with professional principles, to be sure, but as quickly and quietly as possible. In such instances, OIF, the Freedom to Read Foundation, and the state committees all exist to assist and support the people directly involved. The nature and extent of that assistance and support are ultimately determined by those people. If, for example, a beleaguered librarian wants to avoid statewide or national publicity, nothing should be done to attract such attention.

Although it may be tempting to immediately "pull out all the stops" in meeting a censorship challenge,

**CAUTION!**

SOME PEOPLE CONSIDER THESE BOOKS DANGEROUS

AMERICAN HERITAGE DICTIONARY • THE BIBLE • ARE YOU THERE, GOD? IT'S ME, MARGARET • OUR BODIES, OURSELVES • TARZAN ALICE'S ADVENTURES IN WONDERLAND • THE EXORCIST • THE CHOCOLATE WAR • CATCH-22 • LORD OF THE FLIES • ORDINARY PEOPLE • SOUL ON ICE • RAISIN IN THE SUN • OLIVER TWIST • A FAREWELL TO ARMS • THE BEST SHORT STORIES OF NEGRO WRITERS • FLOWERS FOR ALGERNON • ULYSSES • TO KILL A MOCKINGBIRD • ROSEMARY'S BABY • THE FIXER • DEATH OF A SALESMAN • MOTHER GOOSE • CATCHER IN THE RYE • THE MERCHANT OF VENICE • ONE DAY IN THE LIFE OF IVAN DENISOVICH • GRAPES OF WRATH • THE ADVENTURES OF HUCKLEBERRY FINN • SLAUGHTERHOUSE-FIVE • GO ASK ALICE

BANNED BOOKS WEEK—CELEBRATING THE FREEDOM TO READ

this may be detrimental. Too many false alarms make it difficult to mobilize broad support when it is truly needed. Outside involvement may also force people and institutions into dogmatic positions from which they find it difficult to compromise or retreat. It is never useful to needlessly place people in positions in which they will "lose face" by backing down.

Each censorship incident has its own peculiar history. The library and its defenders must generally plot their strategy and tactics on a case-by-case basis. The following principles, however, are generally applicable:

- If the issue involves a local library, be sure that all staff members are kept fully abreast of the situation as it develops.
- Make sure that all members of the library's governing body are kept informed about the incident. Use this opportunity to educate or reinforce their beliefs about the principles of intellectual freedom in libraries.
- Confer with the president and/or the entire executive board of the state library association and keep them advised about the progress of the situation.
- The library's ongoing program of public education about the principles of intellectual freedom should be intensified. All library staff, governing board members, media representatives, and concerned library users should receive a copy of the Library Bill of Rights and those of its interpretations which are relevant to the issue at hand.
- If national, state, or even local media become involved, all media statements should be centrally coordinated. The state library association and its intellectual freedom committee should be certain that all public statements have been cleared in principle with the affected library or librarians. In dealing with the media, it is important to stress the principles involved in the incident, to point out the implications of censorship for First Amendment freedoms, and to emphasize the library's responsibility to provide access to information for all members of the community it serves.
- If radio or television talk shows or interviews are scheduled, library supporters should be alerted so that individuals may attend or even participate. The procensorship forces should not be permitted to "stack" the audience or otherwise dominate media coverage, thereby giving the false impression that they represent the majority.
- Lines of communication to the complainants should always remain open, no matter how strained the situation becomes. The freedom to read is not negotiable, but an acceptable and principled solution to a crisis is better attained through dialogue than confrontation.
- If legal action is threatened the library's legal counsel should be so advised at once. If the library does not have legal counsel, assistance can be obtained with the advice of the Freedom to Read Foundation. Attorneys for the Foundation are available to consult with local counsel.
- When the incident is settled, a responsible representative of the library—and, if appropriate, the state committee—should write or personally thank the media representatives, organizations, legislators, officials, board members, and other individuals who came forward in support of intellectual freedom. If the issue is unresolved, these supporters should be kept advised of the situation. After the challenge is resolved, key members of the library staff, the governing body, members of the state committee, and others intimately involved with the incident should meet to summarize how the issue was handled and consider how the procedure may be improved in the future.

9

## Coping with stress

In these pages the importance of maintaining a calm approach and professional response in the face of challenges has been repeatedly emphasized. Yet this is easier said than done. A beleaguered librarian, surrounded by angry protesters who may consider the librarian a "communist pornographer" and more, may well find a professional demeanor difficult to maintain. And members of state intellectual freedom committees may find the calm handling of crises elusive when they try to respond to repeated media inquiries from sources ranging from national television networks to the *Mudville Post* and still meet all their other professional responsibilities. Working for intellectual freedom can be extremely stressful. Coping with stress is itself an important part of defending libraries and librarians against censorship.

Members of state intellectual freedom committees need not be psychologists, but in providing assistance to librarians involved in censorship incidents and in coping with the strains of activism oneself, personal concern, common sense, and knowledge of some basic facts about stress are useful. Stress may result from either positive or negative stimuli. It may take physical, emotional, psychological, or social forms, and it may be mild or severe, chronic or acute. Stress is never the product solely of external stress factors, but arises from the reaction of individual personality characteristics to environment.

Most people can recognize when they are experiencing stress, but cannot so easily identify its cause. A person in the midst of a stressful struggle against censorship may not immediately recognize that it is the demands of this involvement which lie at the root of the stress being felt. People involved in working for intellectual freedom should be aware that increased stress can be one perfectly normal and controllable byproduct of their work.

Constructive strategies for coping with stress are geared toward confronting the problem and dissipating its effects. We may not always be able to control the stress factors in our lives, but we can control how they affect us. Here are a few proven, commonsense ideas for managing stress:

- Maintain good health habits, especially during times of crisis. Eat a well-balanced diet, get plenty of sleep, and exercise regularly.
- Take time to get organized. Determine priorities and concentrate on them. Set reasonable demands for yourself and learn to delegate or postpone responsibilities when necessary.
- Get better acquainted with yourself. Acknowledge your successes. Recognize that mistakes do not make you a failure.
- Decompress. Allot time to yourself each day. Experiment with relaxation techniques and give them a chance to work.
- Be creative and vary your routine.

Most of all, keep in mind two very important facts. First, what you are doing is right. Intellectual freedom is worth defending. The problems that arise and the mistakes you may make are secondary. Second, you are never alone. There is support out there for intellectual freedom. Not only do the great majority of Americans back the efforts of libraries to defend intellectual freedom, the library profession stands behind its commitment to intellectual freedom with a full program of support. In particular, beleaguered librarians and those working for intellectual freedom should never forget that ALA's program of assistance is always available to them.

*Source: Intellectual Freedom Manual* (Chicago: American Library Association, 4th ed., 1992). 283p. "Coping with Stress" adapted from the Salt Lake City Public Library's Orientation Program, prepared (1980) by the Staff Development Advisory Committee in conjunction with Jed L. Erickson, ALSW, director, Salt Lake Mental Health Crisis Intervention, University Hospital, University of Utah.

## Top 10 list of silly and illogical reasons to ban a book

10. **An unofficial version of the story of Noah's Ark will confuse children.** *Many Waters,* by Madeleine C. L'Engle, was challenged in 1991 at the Hubbard (Ohio) Library because it alters the story of Noah's Ark, making it secular and confusing children. *Newsletter on Intellectual Freedom,* September 1991.

9. **A female dog is called a bitch.** In 1990 Mary O'Hara's *My Friend Flicka* was pulled from 5th- and 6th-grade optional reading lists in Clay County (Fla.) schools because the book uses the word "bitch" to refer to a female dog, as well as the word "damn." *Newsletter on Intellectual Freedom,* January 1991.

8. **It may lead to pornography.** Maurice Sendak's *In the Night Kitchen* was challenged at the Elk River (Minn.) schools in 1992 because reading the book "could lay the foundation for future use of pornography." *Newsletter on Intellectual Freedom,* March 1993.

7. **One bunny is white and the other is black.** *The Rabbit's Wedding,* by Garth Williams, was transferred from the open shelves to the reserved shelves at the Montgomery (Ala.) Public Library in 1959 because an illustration shows a black buck rabbit with a white doe rabbit. Such miscegenation, stated an editor in Orlando, was "brainwashing . . . as soon as you pick up the book and open its pages you realize these rabbits are integrated." The Montgomery *Home News* added that the book was integrationist propaganda obviously aimed at children in their formative years. Jonathan Green, *The Encyclopedia of Censorship* (Facts on File, 1990).

6. **Little Red Riding Hood's basket contains a bottle of wine.** *Little Red Riding Hood,* by the brothers Grimm, was banned in 1990 by two California school districts—Culver City and Empire—because an illustration shows her basket with a bottle of wine as well as fresh bread and butter. The wine might be seen as condoning the use of alcohol. *Newsletter on Intellectual Freedom,* July 1990.

5. **It's a real "downer."** Four members of the Alabama State Textbook Committee in 1983 called for the rejection of the *Diary of Anne Frank* because it is a "real downer." *Newsletter on Intellectual Freedom,* March 1983.

4. **Tarzan was not married to Jane.** Edgar Rice Burroughs's *Tarzan* was removed from the Los Angeles Public Library in 1929 because Tarzan was allegedly living in sin with Jane. Randy F. Nelson, "Banned in Boston and Elsewhere," in *The Almanac of American Letters* (William Kaufmann, 1981).

3. **The least suspicion of controversy.** Dee Brown's *Bury My Heart at Wounded Knee* was removed in Wild Rose, Wisc., in 1974 by a district administrator because the book was "slanted" and "if there's a possibility that something might be controversial, then why not eliminate it." *Newsletter on Intellectual Freedom,* November 1974.

2. **Responsible for an epidemic of rapes.** *Arabian Nights, or The Thousand and One Nights,* a collection of ancient tales from the Middle East that includes "Ali Baba and the 40 Thieves" and "Aladdin and His Magic Lamp," was confiscated in 1985 in Cairo, Egypt, on the grounds that it contains obscene passages that posed a threat to the country's moral fabric. The public prosecutor demanded that the book be "burned in a public place" and said that it was the cause of "a wave of incidents of rape which the country has recently experienced." *Index on Censorship,* June 1985.

1. **Encourages children to break dishes.** Shel Silverstein's *A Light in the Attic* was challenged in 1985 at the Cunningham Elementary School in Beloit, Wisc., because the book "encourages children to break dishes so they won't have to dry them." *Newsletter on Intellectual Freedom,* July 1985.

*Source:* Robert P. Doyle, *Banned Books: 1994 Resource Guide* (Chicago: American Library Association, 1994). 130p.

**9**

# Policies on access to library materials, services and facilities

THE AMERICAN LIBRARY ASSOCIATION'S Intellectual Freedom Committee recommends that publicly supported libraries use the following guidelines, based on constitutional principles, to develop policies, regulations and procedures. All library policies, regulations and procedures should be carefully examined to determine if they may result in denying, restricting or creating barriers to access. If they may result in such restrictions, they:

1. should be developed and implemented within the legal framework that applies to the library. This includes: the United States Constitution, including the First and Fourteenth Amendments, due process and equal treatment under the law; the applicable state constitution; federal and state civil rights legislation; all other applicable federal, state and local legislation; and applicable case law;
2. should cite statutes or ordinances upon which the authority to make that policy is based, when appropriate;
3. should be developed and implemented within the framework of the Library Bill of Rights and its Interpretations;
4. should be based upon the library's mission and objectives;
5. should only impose restrictions on the access to, or use of library resources, services or facilities when those restrictions are necessary to achieve the library's mission and objectives;
6. should narrowly tailor prohibitions or restrictions, in the rare instances when they are required, so they are not more restrictive than needed to serve their objectives;
7. should attempt to balance competing interests and avoid favoring the majority at the expense of individual rights, or allowing individual users' rights to interfere materially with the majority's rights to free and equal access to library resources, services and facilities;
8. should avoid arbitrary distinctions between individuals or classes of users, and should not have the effect of denying or abridging a person's right to use library resources, services or facilities based upon arbitrary distinctions such as origin, age, background or views;
   [In the Library Bill of Rights and all of its Interpretations, it is intended that: "origin" encompasses all the characteristics of individuals that are inherent in the circumstances of their birth; "age" encompasses all the characteristics of individuals that are inherent in their levels of development and maturity; "background" encompasses all the characteristics of individuals that are a result of their life experiences; and "views" encompasses all the opinions and beliefs held and expressed by individuals.]
9. should not target specific users or groups of users based upon an assumption or expectation that such users might engage in behavior that will materially interfere with the achievement of substantial library objectives;
10. must be clearly stated so that a reasonably intelligent person will have fair warning of what is expected;
11. must provide a means of appeal;
12. must be reviewed regularly by the library's governing authority and by its legal counsel;
13. must be communicated clearly and made available in an effective manner to all library users;

14. must be enforced evenhandedly, and not in a manner intended to benefit or disfavor any person or group in an arbitrary or capricious manner;

[Libraries should develop an ongoing staff training program designed to foster the understanding of the legal framework and principles underlying library policies and to assist staff in gaining the skill and ability to respond to potentially difficult circumstances in a timely, direct and open manner. This program should include training to develop empathy and understanding of the social and economic problems of some library users.]

15. should, if reasonably possible, provide adequate alternative means of access to information for those whose behavior results in the denial or restriction of access to any library resource, service or facility.

*Source:* ALA Intellectual Freedom Committee, *Guidelines for the Development and Implementation of Policies, Regulations and Procedures Affecting Access to Library Materials, Services and Facilities,*
June 28, 1994.

# When are library records confidential?

WHILE WE ALL KNOW THE IMPORTANCE of maintaining the confidentiality of library records, sometimes requests come in that may seem quite reasonable. It is important to remind ourselves of the many situations in which it is not appropriate to reveal information about library records. The University of Illinois at Urbana-Champaign has a task force chaired by circulation librarian Merri Hartse developing a policy on the confidentiality of library records. Part of their policy document includes the following examples of requests for library information that are confidential and must *not* be honored:

### Circulation and patron records

1. A request for the circulation records of a faculty, student, staff or other library card holder by someone else.
2. A request by a faculty member for the identities of students who borrowed reserved items.
3. A request to review the circulation records of a student suspected of plagiarism.
4. A request to see interlibrary loan borrowing records.
5. A request for addresses, phone numbers, I.D. numbers or other personal information contained in the patron database.
6. A request to see a list of individuals who are not members of the university community but who have been granted library borrowing privileges.
7. A request by a parent for information such as fines or other fees by the library to Student Accounts Receivable without the student's permission.

### Other examples

1. A request for the name of the person who has signed out a particular item.
2. A request to review past use of study room, listening room, study carrel or CD-ROM work station.
3. A request to reveal the nature of a patron's reference request or database search.
4. A request for the names of persons who have used audiovisual materials.
5. A request for a list of items photocopied for or faxed to a particular patron.

9

6. A request for a list of suggested acquisitions submitted by a particular patron.

7. A request from law enforcement authorities for the identity of anyone conducting research on a particular subject.

*Source:* "When Are Library Records Confidential?"
*College & Research Libraries News* 53 (February 1992): 129.

Patron Behavior

# Policies on user behavior and library usage

LIBRARIANS ARE FACED WITH PROBLEMS of user behavior that must be addressed to ensure the effective delivery of service and full access to facilities. Library governing bodies must approach the regulation of user behavior within the framework of the ALA Code of Professional Ethics, the Library Bill of Rights and the law, including local and state statutes, constitutional standards under the First and Fourteenth Amendments, due process and equal treatment under the law.

Publicly supported library service is based upon the First Amendment right of free expression. Publicly supported libraries are recognized as limited public forums for access to information. At least one federal court of appeals has recognized a First Amendment right to receive information in a public library. Library policies and procedures that could impinge upon such rights are subject to a higher standard of review than may be required in the policies of other public services and facilities.

There is a significant government interest in maintaining a library environment that is conducive to all users' exercise of their constitutionally protected right to receive information. This significant interest authorizes publicly supported libraries to maintain a safe and healthy environment in which library users and staff can be free from harassment, intimidation, and threats to their safety and well-being. Libraries should provide appropriate safeguards against such behavior and enforce policies and procedures addressing that behavior when it occurs.

In order to protect all library users' right of access to library facilities, to ensure the safety of users and staff, and to protect library resources and facilities from damage, the library's governing authority may impose reasonable restrictions on the time, place, or manner of library access.

## Guidelines

The American Library Association's Intellectual Freedom Committee recommends that publicly supported libraries use the following guidelines, based upon constitutional principles, to develop policies and procedures governing the use of library facilities:

1. Libraries are advised to rely upon existing legislation and law enforcement mechanisms as the primary means of controlling behavior that involves

public safety, criminal behavior, or other issues covered by existing local, state, or federal statutes. In many instances, this legal framework may be sufficient to provide the library with the necessary tools to maintain order.

2. If the library's governing body chooses to write its own policies and procedures regarding user behavior or access to library facilities, services, and resources, the policies should cite statutes or ordinances upon which the authority to make those policies is based.

3. Library policies and procedures governing the use of library facilities should be carefully examined to ensure that they are not in violation of the Library Bill of Rights.

4. Reasonable and narrowly drawn policies and procedures designed to prohibit interference with use of the facilities and services by others, or to prohibit activities inconsistent with achievement of substantial library objectives, are acceptable.

5. Such policies and the attendant implementing procedures should be reviewed regularly by the library's legal counsel for compliance with federal and state constitutional requirements, federal and state civil rights legislation, all other applicable federal and state legislation, and applicable case law.

6. Every effort should be made to respond to potentially difficult circumstances of user behavior in a timely, direct, and open manner. Common sense, reason and sensitivity should be used to resolve issues in a constructive and positive manner without escalation.

7. Libraries should develop an ongoing staff training program based upon their user behavior policy. This program should include training to develop empathy and understanding of the social and economic problems of some library users.

8. Policies and regulations that impose restrictions on library access:

a. should apply only to those activities that materially interfere with the public's right of access to library facilities, the safety of users and staff, and the protection of library resources and facilities;

b. should narrowly tailor prohibitions or restrictions so that they are not more restrictive than needed to serve their objectives;

c. should attempt to balance competing interests and avoid favoring the majority at the expense of individual rights, or allowing individual users' rights to supersede those of the majority of library users;

d. should be based upon actual behavior and not upon arbitrary distinctions between individuals or classes of individuals. Policies should not target specific users or groups of users based upon assumption or expectation that such users might engage in behavior that could disrupt library service;

e. should not restrict access to the library by persons who merely inspire the anger or annoyance of others. Policies based upon appearance or behavior that is merely annoying or which merely generates negative subjective reactions from others, do not meet the necessary standard unless the behavior would interfere with access by an objectively reasonable person to library facilities and services. Such policies should employ a reasonable, objective standard based on the behavior itself;

    f. must provide a clear description of the behavior that is prohibited so that a reasonably intelligent person will have fair warning and must be continuously and clearly communicated in an effective manner to all library users;

    g. to the extent possible, should not leave those affected without adequate alternative means of access to information in the library;

    h. must be enforced evenhandedly, and not in a manner intended to benefit or disfavor any person or group in an arbitrary or capricious manner.

The user behaviors addressed in these guidelines are the result of a wide variety of individual and societal conditions. Libraries should take advantage of the expertise of local social service agencies, advocacy groups, mental health professionals, law enforcement officials, and other community resources to develop community strategies for addressing the needs of a diverse population.

*Source: Guidelines for the Development of Policies and Procedures Regarding User Behavior and Library Usage, ALA Intellectual Freedom Committee, 1993.*

# Hostile patron situations

### by Morell D. Boone, Sandra G. Yee, and Rita Bullard

ON OCCASION, STUDENTS WILL BE FACED with "problem patron" situations. This may arise because of the students' inability to satisfy the patrons' needs, either because the rules prevent it, or because of lack of knowledge. Under these situations frustrated patrons often exhibit rude, obnoxious behavior. Students need to be trained to deal with problem patrons in an effective yet disarming way. This requires training the students in the fine art of dealing with difficult situations. A short training session could provide enough basic techniques for students to get through a difficult situation. Again, role playing is an excellent way to practice the techniques that can be described and given to the students in writing.

1. If a patron becomes irate and loud while you are dealing with him or her, attempt to determine the cause of the problem and to find a solution. While doing this, remain attentive and pleasant.
2. Lower your voice. Speak quietly. Very often the patron will become quieter if they are interacting with someone who is speaking quietly.
3. Listen attentively and take notes. Nod your head to indicate you understand. Empathize with the patron, but do not agree that library rules are stupid, etc. Keep your integrity.
4. Do not take the problem as a personal attack. However, if the patron becomes abusive while no supervisory staff are on duty, call security. (Supervisors: always provide to the students quick access to security personnel and let your security personnel know when you will have students alone.)
5. Use all information available to you and as much decision-making power as is allowed you to attempt to solve the problem. Use the problem-solving techniques that you have practiced. Offer to turn the matter over to your supervisor. If the supervisor is on duty, find him or her immediately. If no supervisor is on duty, take down complete information including: the patron's name, address, and phone number; the nature of the problem; what kind of solutions you have offered; the date and time of the encounter; and your name. (Supervisors: provide

forms for your student assistant to fill out giving the necessary information. This will provide the student assistant a guideline to follow, the patron will know his or her complaint is being taken seriously, and a form will cover the areas of information necessary for the report.)

Sometimes patrons can be calmed by simply listening to them. Other times, it is impossible to satisfy an irate patron. Do the best you can and then turn the situation over to a supervisor. In some cases, patrons cannot be given the results they would like to see.

*Source:* Morell D. Boone, Sandra G. Yee, and Rita Bullard, *Training Student Library Assistants* (Chicago: American Library Association, 1991). 110p.

# Difficult people

*by Paul John Cirino*

WHEN YOU ARE DEALING WITH PEOPLE who are difficult, you will see an infinite variety of unhealthy behaviors displayed. These behaviors are motivated by indecision, doubt, fear, anxiety, feelings of inadequacy, guilt, supersensitivity, hostility, and resentment. Whether they are members of the staff or the public, these people must be dealt with. You and your supervisors have to develop the mental reflexes to see a punch coming and diffuse its power. Here are some of the punches that may be thrown your way:

1. **Critics.** The world is full of critics. We even pay some of them to tell us what movies to see, books to read, and restaurants to visit. The critic that is tough to deal with is the one who must offer a negative opinion on everything, whether it is warranted or not. Most critics are frustrated doers who are controlled by fear of failure.

2. **Aggressors.** These people attempt to get their way with all the grace of an elephant in heat. Aggressors have a burning desire to dominate and control others. They don't know the difference between aggressiveness and assertiveness.

3. **Gossips.** These people think of themselves as the sole source of information. You usually get a much embellished rumor, instead of real information.

4. **Moralists.** These people take it upon themselves to tell other people how to live their lives. Moralists see everything as black and white, good or bad, and only they know which is which. Moralists like to tell you how to do everything, including living your own life, and are absolutely convinced of their righteousness.

5. **Martyrs.** These people manipulate others by setting themselves up as sacrificial lambs. Their primary weapon is guilt. The moralist tells you when to feel guilty, while the martyr uses guilt in a covert manner. Martyrs let you know what they have sacrificed for your good, and then are very annoyed when you don't do what they want you to do because of the supposed guilt that you should be experiencing.

6. **Steamrollers.** Don't anybody stand in their way. They interrupt conversations and demand attention in their childlike attempts to control situations.

7. **Bombs.** This is an explosion waiting to go off. Their goal is to frighten you into giving them their way. You must give every matter the same prominence and urgency that these people think it should have.

They are very intense and quick to lose their tempers. They are unpredictable, to say the least.

8. **Whiners.** These people find everything wrong and say so repeatedly. Nothing is ever done right. The way things used to be done was always better.

9. **Yes people.** These people agree with everything and everybody. Performance rarely measures up to promises.

10. **Braggarts.** These people always exaggerate their deeds in an effort to make others feel smaller.

There are infinite varieties of these difficult types. Here are some strategies that you can use to deal with them, and keep your own sanity:

1. Develop your skills as an effective communicator. Good communications will help to prevent unnecessary conflicts.
2. Never act defensive.
3. Be assertive, but not aggressive. You don't need to dominate the other party to resolve conflicts.
4. Understand that you have been picked as a target, either randomly, or more likely, because the difficult person fears your talents and abilities.
5. Never retaliate. Don't give these people a hard wall to hit against. Most will be diffused by lack of resistance.
6. Always remain cool, calm and collected. Your body language should indicate clearly that you are in control.

The neurotic behavior of difficult people is something that is part of life. Leaders must not involve themselves in the unhealthy game playing of these people. It takes more than one person to play the game, so why waste your time and energy needlessly by playing? As a leader, you don't have the time to devote to such counterproductive pastimes. Agree politely with difficult members of the public. Avoid becoming embroiled in the games of difficult members of the staff. Your calm handling of the conflicts created by these people will win you the respect of the vast majority of your staff and public who are really quite nice to deal with. Why let a few jerks spoil it for everyone? If you want to succeed as a leader, you and your supervisors must demonstrate great skill in dealing with difficult people. Constant training and positive reinforcement are in order. You should develop sensitive antennae, not horns.

*Source:* Paul John Cirino, *The Business of Running a Library* (Jefferson, N.C.: McFarland & Co., 1991). 173p. Reprinted with permission.

# Sexual harassment issues

OUTLINED BELOW IS A "Suggested Model for Addressing Sexual Harassment Issues in Libraries" developed by the American Library Association Committee on the Status of Women in Librarianship. It is the Committee's belief that developing effective workplace sexual harassment policies enables management to set a tone that ensures all persons are treated with dignity and respect in the workplace, and encourages internal resolution when a problem arises.

The committee recommends that you adapt this model to your local setting. To be effective this policy should be separate and distinct from other policies, and should be updated annually by a letter from top management that reviews the steps to be taken to report instances of sexual harassment and emphasizes that sexual harassment will not be tolerated.

# Suggested model for addressing sexual harassment issues

1. **Purpose:** The purpose of this policy is to state clearly that (name of library) prohibits sexual harassment and to set forth procedures by which allegations of sexual harassment may be filed, investigated, and resolved.

2. **Policy Statement:** Sexual harassment of staff members or applicants for employment by library supervisors and/or staff is unacceptable behavior and will not be tolerated or condoned. The library will take appropriate corrective action to remedy any situation which is brought to its attention.

3. **Definition:** Sexual harassment is defined by the Equal Employment Opportunity Commission as follows:

> Unwelcome sexual advances, requests for sexual favors, and other verbal or physical conduct of a sexual nature constitute sexual harassment when: (1) submission to such conduct is made either explicitly or implicitly a term or condition of an individual's employment; (2) submission to or rejection of such conduct by an individual is used as the basis for employment decisions affecting such individual; or (3) such conduct has the purpose or effect of unreasonably interfering with an individual's work performance or creating an intimidating, hostile, or offensive work environment.

No absolute standards exist for determining whether certain incidents are sexual harassment or are simply reflections of personal or social relationships. Each situation must be looked at individually. Telling a sexual joke to a group of coworkers may be acceptable in many instances. If it is done repeatedly, however, with the knowledge that it causes embarrassment and discomfort to some people in the group, it may constitute sexual harassment. Asking a coworker for a date may be considered sexual harassment if this causes any negative consequences in the terms and conditions of employment.

Sexual harassment clearly exists whenever a person is asked for sexual favors in exchange for a promotion or any other job benefit, or whenever a person is threatened with demotion or termination for rejecting a sexual advance. Displaying sexual pictures, making sexual comments or propositions, leering, squeezing, pinching or touching of any kind are considered sexual harassment if done in such a way as to embarrass, humiliate or cause discomfort to others.

4. **Violations:** Any staff or supervisor who violates this policy will be subject to discipline up to and including discharge.

5. **Complaints or Questions:** Each library may have an established procedure to follow regarding the handling of complaints or questions. The library would insert that procedure here. For those libraries which may not have procedures established, the following may give some guidance:

> Any questions regarding this policy should be addressed to the (whoever is in charge of personnel or human resources). Any staff member who feels that he/she is a victim of sexual harassment (including but not limited to, any of the conduct listed above) by any supervisor or staff member should immediately bring the matter to the attention of his/her supervisor or designated person or persons in the Personnel or Human Resources Office. A staff member who is uncomfortable for any reason in bringing such matters to the attention of his/her supervisor, or is not satisfied after bringing the matter to the attention of his/her supervisor, should report the matter to the designated person or persons in the Personnel or Human Resources Office. Where investigation confirms the offensive behavior, prompt corrective action will be taken.

9

6. **Investigation.** Each library may have an established procedure for investigations, either under collective bargaining agreements or library regulations or policies. For those libraries which may not have such procedures established, it is recommended that such a procedure should be set up to handle complaints or sexual harassment and other complaints and/or grievances.

7. **No Reprisals:** Libraries may have such a policy in place; it would be inserted here. For those libraries which may not have an established policy, it is recommended that such a policy be established whereby staff members reporting incidents of sexual harassment will be protected from reprisals in any form.

*Source: Suggested Model for Addressing Sexual Harassment Issues in Libraries*
*(Chicago: ALA Committee on the Status of Women in Librarianship, 1990). 2p.*

# Guidelines regarding thefts in libraries

## What to do before a library theft occurs

**Library security officer (LSO).** Appoint a senior library staff member as Library Security Officer (LSO) who has delegated authority from the library and the institution to act on their behalf working with the institution's legal counsel and security force.

**Security planning group.** Form a group made up of the LSO and other appropriate personnel to develop a specific plan of action to follow when a theft is discovered. This may be a part of the institution's disaster plan or a separate plan.

**Publicity.** Establish liaison with the institution's public relations office so that timely and accurate announcements can be made to the press when a theft is discovered.

**Law enforcement.** Establish contact and foster good working relations with law enforcement agencies—institutional, local, state, and/or federal—to determine who will be called and under what circumstances. The library should maintain a list of contacts in each level of law enforcement and discuss the plan of action with each. (See pp. 438–39 for "Networking Resources Directory for Protection and Recovery.") The value of materials or other circumstances will dictate which law enforcement agency will handle the case: for example, the FBI may be involved if the total dollar amount of the theft exceeds $5,000, and the U.S. Customs or Interpol may be involved if stolen items are suspected of being smuggled into or out of the country.

Work with the library's institutional administration to ensure support for the prosecution of thieves. This support may range from an active willingness to participate in the collection of evidence to be turned over to the district attorney or U.S. attorney for further consideration, or it may involve direct participation in the prosecution by the institution.

Work with appropriate institutional, local, and state groups to lobby for strengthening of state laws regarding library thefts and for diligent prosecution of such crimes.

**Other outside contacts.** Establish liaison with local rare book, manuscript, and second-hand dealers to inform them of the library's collecting areas. Thieves sometimes try to sell stolen property quickly, and dealers with knowledge of the library's collections can recognize, or at least be suspicious of, materials they know the library collects which are offered to them.

Report the name of the LSO to the ACRL/RBMS Security Committee and note changes. The RBMS Security Committee will compile a list of the LSOs annually. The list will be available from the ALA/ACRL office and will be forwarded to the Antiquarian Booksellers Association of America (ABAA).

Establish liaisons with appropriate Internet listservs and national stolen and missing book databases so that thefts can be reported immediately upon discovery.

**Preventive measures in the library.** Implement the RBMS "Guidelines for the Security of Rare Book, Manuscript, and Other Special Collections" (1990) available from the ALA/ACRL office and published in *College & Research Libraries News* 51 (March 1990): 240–44.

Coordinate work in the library to assure that unique ownership marks appear on the institution's holdings, providing proof that materials, if stolen, belong to the library. The RBMS Security Committee urges the use of its marking guidelines for rare materials. (Contact the ALA/ACRL office for this document.) The committee also recommends recording distinctive characteristics of individual copies in cataloging notes as another means of identifying appropriate items.

When providing complete catalog records at point of receipt is not possible, maintaining a brief record of ownership is recommended. It should contain brief author/title description and identifying characteristics. These records of purchase or gift and ownership are especially important when materials are going to be added to a cataloging backlog.

Eliminate cataloging backlogs. While this may seem to be a daunting task in many libraries, it is an essential step in the establishment of a secure library collection. Use the catalog record to describe physical characteristics that distinguish the library's copy (i.e., binding, marks of previous ownership, and completeness). Create machine-readable records for local public access. Report the library's holdings to the national-level bibliographic databases. Participate in broad-based bibliographic projects providing data and information about the library's copies that serve to help distinguish between editions, issues, and states.

Conduct regular inventories of both cataloged and uncataloged collections. This task is most effectively performed by staff working in teams, and conducted on a random basis. Proceeding through the collection in a predictable method is not wise as it may allow for the replacement of materials temporarily removed or stolen. An inventory of shelf list cards to be taken simultaneously is also recommended, if this is not already a part of the procedure being followed. Again, while the task seems overwhelming for libraries large and small, the committee recommends that libraries make a beginning.

Follow the hiring and other management practices recommended in "Standards for Ethical Conduct for Rare Book, Manuscript, and Special Collections Librarians, with Guidelines for Institutional Practice in Support of the Standards," 2nd edition, 1992, available from the ALA/ACRL office and published in *College & Research Libraries News* 54 (April 1993): 207–15.

Review materials in the library's general collections and open stacks for consideration of transfer to special collections or to a caged, limited access area of the library. The ACRL/RBMS transfer guidelines, "Selection of General Collection Materials for Transfer to Special Collections," 2nd edition,

**9**

available from the ACRL office and published in *C&RL News* 54 (December 1993): 644–47, will help the library identify candidates for transfer. Some libraries have identified rare materials in the open stacks in the course of projects, such as reporting to the English Short Title Catalogue or working through a collection development policy using the Research Libraries Group Conspectus. While the task seems overwhelming for libraries large and small, the RBMS Security Committee recommends that libraries make a beginning.

A recent theft may give an indication of an area which may be the target of future theft or mutilation. If it is appropriate, transfer materials intellectually or physically related to those already stolen or mutilated. Categories of such materials may but will not necessarily include periodicals, related imprints, or related subject matter.

## Checklist of what to do after a theft occurs from a library

**Notification.** Notify the LSO and appropriate library administrators upon suspicion that a theft has occurred.

**Discovery of theft and collection of evidence.** Evidence of intrusion connected with missing library materials.

Indication that patron, staff member, or other has stolen books or manuscripts.
Apprehension of person(s) in act of theft.
Discovery of systematic pattern of loss.
Recovery of materials stolen from library.
Other evidence.

**Evaluation.** The LSO must evaluate evidence with administration, law enforcement personnel, library security group, and legal counsel as appropriate, and determine a plan of action.

**Actions.** Take inventory and compile a list of missing items.
Notify appropriate stolen and missing book databases and other appropriate networks.
Notify local booksellers and appropriate specialist dealers.
Request action from law enforcement agencies.
Request action from legal authorities.
Transfer vulnerable items to a more secure location, if appropriate.

**Publicity.** LSO, administration, law enforcement, and public relations officer plan appropriate publicity strategy.

LSO or public relations officer prepares news releases to alert staff and community to problems and action.

LSO or public relations officer handles inquiries from news media.
LSO's coordination of staff efforts should include:

- compilation of inventories
- arrangement for appraisals of loss or recovery
- preparation of communications to staff about progress on case
- maintenance of internal records of actions followed during the progress of case

## Networking resources directory for protection and recovery

*The AB Bookman's Weekly,* Jacob L. Chernofsky, Editor & Publisher, P.O. Box AB, Clifton, NJ 07015; (201) 772-0020; fax: (201) 772-9281. (Publishes a missing books column at reduced rates.)

**ABAA National Office,** Liane Wood-Thomas, Executive Director, 50 Rockefeller Plaza, New York, NY 10020; (212) 757-9395. (Circulates lists of missing materials to membership.)

**ABAA Security Committee,** Ron Lieberman, Chair, R.R. 1, Box 42, Glen Rock, PA 17327; (717) 235-2134; fax: (717) 235-8042.

**ACRL/RBMS Security Committee,** Susan M. Allen, Chair, Director of Libraries

& Media Services, Kalamazoo College Library, 1200 Academy Street, Kalamazoo, MI 49006-3285; (616) 337-7149; fax: (616) 337-7143; e-mail: sallen@kzoo.edu. (Compiles incidents of theft list; LSO list.)

**Archives and Archivists.** To subscribe send the message: Subscribe Archives <your first name your last name> to: archives@miamiu.acs.muohio.edu. (Listserv for archivists.)

**BAM-BAM,** Katharine and Daniel Leab, P.O. Box 1236, Washington, CT 06793; (212) 737-2715. (Compiles missing materials list.)

**EXLIBRIS.** To subscribe send the message: Subscribe exlibris <your full name> to: listserv@rutvm1.bitnet or: listserv@rutvm1.rutgers.edu. (Listserv for rare books and manuscripts librarians.)

**IFAR,** International Foundation for Art Research, Constance Lowenthal, 46 E. 70th St., New York, NY 10021; (212) 879-1780. (Newsletter includes a column listing missing materials.)

**Interpol/USNCB,** Angela Meadows, U.S. Department of Justice, 10th & Pennsylvania Ave., N.W., Washington, DC 20530; (202) 272-8383; fax: (202) 272-5941. (Circulates information internationally.)

**National Stolen Art File,** Interstate Theft Unit, FBI Headquarters, Washington, DC 20535; (202) FBI-3000. (Database of stolen artifacts; will add books soon. Cannot be queried directly; work through local law enforcement.)

*Source:* "Guidelines Regarding Thefts in Libraries: Draft Version," *College & Research Libraries News* 55 (May 1994): 289–94.

# Library security: The Blumberg legacy

### by J. Steve Huntsberry

[The author, a Washington State University police sergeant, has been commended by various library-related organizations for his diligence in pursuing an investigation that led to the March 1990 arrest of Stephen Blumberg, convicted as the principal in a $20 million, coast-to-coast theft of rare books, manuscripts, and artifacts. At the time of his arrest, Blumberg, whose career as a rare book and manuscript thief spanned more than 20 years, was found to have more than 19 tons of library and archival material from more than 280 universities stored in an Ottumwa, Iowa, house. It was the largest such seizure in the FBI's history.

Huntsberry, a detective on the WSU police force, entered the case in 1988 when he was assigned to investigate the December 1987 theft of $500,000 in rare books from WSU's Holland Library. Huntsberry put in long hours of his own time on the case, sending out teletypes and tracking down leads. Finally, a break came when Blumberg, using an alias, was arrested for trespassing and possession of burglary tools at the University of California-Riverside library. Also in Blumberg's possession was a schedule of the Holland Library's business hours. He was released shortly after the arrest, but not before he was photographed and fingerprinted. Huntsberry pursued fingerprint checks in several states, including Minnesota, where a positive identification was made of Stephen Blumberg. The case was turned over to the FBI which arrested Blumberg after the March 1990 raid of his Ottumwa house.]

WHEN TELLING THE STEPHEN BLUMBERG theft story at seminars and library conventions across the United States, I find that although the investigation makes an interesting narrative, it has recently been the "lessons learned" that have been the focus of interest among librarians. "What type of alarm system should we install in order to protect our valuable books and documents?" "Is this alarm system better than that system?" "Should we install the Acme Model X, Triple Secret, Anti-Intruder Destructo of All Alarm Systems Package?" I respond, "Why not! If you have the financing to accommodate state-of-the-art technology—go for it!" But in unfortunate reality, who among us has the luxury to throw money at security systems?

## Any alarm system can be defeated

The reality is that any system can be defeated, albeit some more easily than others. The dedicated thief—for example, Blumberg—will get you if he wants you bad enough. It makes little sense to rely on a foot-thick steel door when it is latched with a dimestore lock. One is reminded of the unscalable, impenetrable wall. The initial impression by the amateur is that access is impossible. The serious thief studies the problem and determines that the wall is only 50 feet long and therefore may be bypassed by a quick jog to the left or right. The amateur may be deterred but the professional will scoff.

## A Blumberg lesson

If Blumberg taught us anything, it was that a book thief will travel the path of least resistance. A thief will strike at an area that allows the most direct and unencumbered access to his goal and, just as important, immediate and easy retreat from the scene. When considering the best way to protect a collection, it is simply not enough to install the biggest and the best. As any military strategist will indicate, once the enemy compromises the Maginot Line you have lost the battle.

## Multiple security systems

I suggest that multiple systems be employed to impede a would-be thief and that care be taken to make it as difficult to leave the facility as it was to enter. Certainly go for the best that you can afford, but do not rely solely on one deterrent. Blumberg's methods of operation illustrate the rationale of this concept. He would familiarize himself with the physical layout of the victim institution. It is obvious from the number of victims (280 plus) that few gave him much worry. Considering his twenty successful years in the stolen book business, it was, apparently, not especially difficult for Blumberg to determine the weaknesses in the defenses of his victims.

A simple technique used by Blumberg was to obtain keys to the areas in which he was interested. Blumberg understood that one did not have to breach an alarm system to steal a key. Once the key was his, many of the sophisticated alarm systems could be bypassed. Some security systems are not set up to counteract a keyed entry. If a $30,000 alarm system can be defeated by a $5 key, then part of the security system had better be strict key control.

One can only speculate as to Blumberg's method of obtaining critical library keys. As I mentioned in *Art Documentation News* (Winter 1991), it appears that he would simply observe the library staff members and target any who were careless about key control. Once the key was in his possession he was frequently able to bypass the security measures successfully. A master key afforded Blumberg legitimate access to the areas selected to be victimized.

Although at the time of his arrest Blumberg was in possession of several keys to various libraries, only one, Clarke Library in Los Angeles, discovered the keys missing in time and bothered to re-key the facility. Sadly, a Washington State University sub-master key was among Blumberg's collection, but no record exists of a WSU staff member reporting the loss or theft of the key—a serious breakdown in security control. I suspect that the facility would not have re-keyed regardless, due to the expense.

## A sad fact

It is a sad fact that had Blumberg been caught stealing the keys, he probably would have escaped with a mere apology. The beauty of Blumberg's modus operandi is that, taken separately, none of the violations, up to and including the theft of books or documents, is regarded by the law enforcement community, the public at large, and some library professionals as a serious crime. Each facet of the theft, unless the thief is apprehended with significant quantities of valuable books and documents on the way out, is usually regarded as a "slap on the wrist" infraction and does not generate much concern. Unfortunately, separate elements of what may constitute a major book theft occur daily at most institutions and are generally accepted as part of the cost of doing business.

Equally depressing is that there are usually no mechanisms in place to connect elements of crimes and detect significant theft patterns. Not many librarians or police officers become excited over the isolated theft of a magazine, newspaper or book by a physically unimposing, perhaps scholarly looking patron. Librarians and law enforcement personnel rarely understand each others' roles and responsibilities in the event of a reported theft. Even more discouraging is that a dozen thefts could be handled by a dozen different police investigators with no hope of any connecting conclusions being drawn or patterns observed. Lamentably, a significant number of librarians would prefer to deny that they are even victims when a theft occurs.

## What can we do?

Two actions come immediately to mind. Each operation could be the sole topic of an article such as this but I will abbreviate here for expediency. First, each institution, according to its security budget, should devise its defense in a concentric circle configuration.

**The Bulls-eye concept.** The theory is to make access to valuable assets increasingly difficult as the value of the item increases. Keep in mind that the dedicated thief will get you if he has the time. The idea is to impede and frustrate the suspect so that he either becomes discouraged or makes a mistake. The perimeter of the circles of protection should begin on the outside of the structure housing the collection. As the thief moves closer to the heart of the collection, it should become more and more difficult to penetrate the defenses. This also requires increasingly smaller areas to protect. Logically, the closer to the asset, the more sophisticated, expensive and numerous should be the devices in place to protect the material. It is crucial that once the circles of security have been put in place, there is no simple way to circumvent, confuse the response of, or deactivate security defenses. Ideally, by the time the dedicated would-be thief has penetrated all of the circles of protection, the police would be waiting in the center with congratulations for his perseverance—and handcuffs.

**Not all alarms are electronic.** Second, the primary deterrent to library theft must come from the staff and patrons of the facility. If the books and documents are to remain intact and available to the public, then the people who have custody must take a personal stake in the collection. The people in the trenches including circulation personnel, custodians, temporary assistants, and concerned patrons—all must assume this personal attachment to the collection. They all must assume at least a partial security capacity while performing their everyday tasks. They can provide extra sets of security eyes and ears if they are conditioned and trained to be alert to the environment around them.

Unfortunately, there are too few library cops in the stacks. Although I have found numerous individuals who take library theft and security seriously (the majority tend to be mid-level professionals), it seems that many library personnel, the ones who deal with the patrons on a daily basis, do not have the necessary passion for the significance of the treasures in their workplace. They have *a job* in a library, but are not aware of what is going on around them. Training should be provided to library staff so that they can recognize actual and potential library theft and mutilation.

Blumberg was brought to task by a few concerned and dedicated library professionals who cared enough to take the extra step. It was not a library director who remembered a suspect description flyer when Blumberg was arrested at the University of California at Riverside; it was Sharla Desens, the night circulation desk worker. It was not the head of special collections at Washington State University who recalled a missing incunabulum at a department meeting; it was the Rare Book Reading Room attendant, Julie King. Even these dedicated few would have been crying in the night if there had not been someone to collect, coordinate and evaluate the pieces of information. Fortunately, the pieces came together in the Blumberg incident.

## Teamwork and communication are the keys

There is no reason why a general protective consciousness cannot be developed that will address the problems of book theft and library security on a national level. There is no reason why the concept of security in depth cannot be incorporated. These concepts have their beginnings in isolated instances— Blumberg and Shinn. Truly, it requires a dedicated effort on the part of library and law enforcement professionals and concerned library patrons collectively striving to maintain a precious heritage. These groups need to know and understand one another. *They need to work together!* Surely, the reward is well worth the struggle.

*Source:* J. Steve Huntsberry, "Library Security: The Blumberg Legacy," *Journal of Information Ethics* 1 (Fall 1992): 46–50. Reprinted with permission.

# Workplace violence

SEVERAL ORGANIZATIONS HAVE COMPLETED studies of workplace violence. They show that what was once uncommon if not unthinkable is becoming a reality. Violence against employers is one of the most rapidly increasing crimes, according to Joseph L. Kinney who coauthored a study for the National Safe Workplace Institute. The National Institute of Occupational Safety and Health (NIOSH) also released a study which noted that homicide is the leading cause of death in five states (Alabama, Connecticut, Maryland, Michigan, and South Carolina) and in Washington, D.C. The NIOSH study also noted that workplace homicide is the leading killer of working women.

The Society for Human Resource Management (SHRM) recently completed a survey of its members on the topic of workplace violence. The SHRM survey reported that slightly more than one-third of the respondents had experienced incidents of workplace violence in their companies. Seventy-five percent of the incidents were fistfights, 17% were shootings, 6% were sexual assaults, and 8% were stabbings. Fifty-four percent of the violent acts were committed by one employee against another employee, 13% were committed by an employee against a supervisor, and 7% were committed by customers against employees.

## Workplace violence follows a pattern

What may seem like random, senseless acts actually fall into patterns. There is a profile of both the type of organization that is likely to harbor violent employees and a profile of the employee who is likely to react violently. According to the National Safe Workplace Institute study, the characteristics of a violence-prone workplace are:

- chronic labor management disputes
- frequent grievances filed by employees
- extraordinary number of injury claims
- understaffing or excessive demands for overtime
- many stressed workers
- authoritarian management

The profile of the violent employee is:

- usually a white male in his 30s or 40s
- has lost his or her job or believes that job loss will happen soon
- finds personal identity mainly through job
- has a history of people problems—trouble with workers, supervisors, or both
- is usually a loner
- may also be undergoing private stress such as divorce or death in the family
- has difficulty accepting authority
- has a tendency to blame others for his or her problems
- threatens coworkers or supervisors
- may have a history of substance abuse
- has a fascination with weaponry
- has a history of depression, paranoia, and violence or encounters with violence
- frequently talks about past incidents of violence

## How to prevent workplace violence

Even though a profile of the violent employee exists, experts agree that it is difficult to predict which employees will actually follow through on their potential for violence. Most experts advise changes in the workplace culture as the best precaution. According to a report issued by the Northwestern National Life insurance Company, the best ways to prevent workplace violence are:

- foster a supportive, harmonious work environment
- train supervisors and employees on conflict resolution
- develop effective policies to protect employees from harassment
- establish grievance procedures
- provide counseling through an employee assistance program
- implement effective security procedures
- establish a crisis plan

## Contact

The National Institute of Occupational Safety and Health for the report *Fatal Injuries to Workers in the United States, 1980-1989: A Decade of Surveillance.*

  National Safe Workplace Institute, Courthouse Place, 54 W. Hubbard St., Suite 403, Chicago, IL 60610, for the report *Breaking Point: The Workplace*

9

*Violence Epidemic and What to Do about It.*

The Northwestern National Life Insurance Company, P.O. Box 20, Minneapolis, MN 55440-0020 for the report *Fear and Violence in the Workplace.*

The Society of Human Resource Management, 606 N. Washington, Alexandria, VA 22314, for information on its survey on workplace violence.

*Source:* "Agencies Study Workplace Violence," *Library Personnel News* 8 (May-June 1994): 2–3.

# Legislation

# How to contact your legislator

**Personal visits.** Face-to-face discussion is the most effective means of communication, and essential to the establishment of a solid working relationship if you do not already know each other. A meeting is more easily arranged early in a session, before pressures build up.

All legislators have one or more district offices. Visits there will often be more convenient for you than in Washington. Members of Congress return periodically (check with the district office), during Congressional recesses, and between sessions.

Constituents are always welcome in Washington. Be sure you have a firm appointment. Use the district office to make local or capitol appointments. (Get to know district staffs: secretaries and administrative assistants. Close working relationships will benefit in many ways.)

Take along others—library director, trustee, Friend, representative of a community organization, citizen activist. Keep the delegation small enough for an easy exchange of viewpoints with the legislator. Leave your card and any written information you may have prepared. Follow up with a letter of appreciation for the time given to you, and include any additional information suggested by the visit.

**Telephone calls.** Once you have the acquaintance of your representative, telephone calls are appropriate and easy. Make them sparingly to the legislator, whose time is heavily occupied. (Regular contact with staff is possible and desirable.) Telephone to ask support before a hearing or floor vote; to ask for help with legislative colleagues; or to convey urgent local concern. Judge how far to pursue by the reaction. Remember that it is more difficult for a legislator to temporize in a conversation than by letter.

**Letters, letters, letters.** These are the chief fuel powering any legislative vehicle. They are read. They elicit responses. They represent votes. (Each letter writer is deemed to represent several like-minded if less highly motivated constituents.) Letters may be formal or informal, typewritten or handwritten. They should be composed by you, giving your reasons for your position (and giving the legislator reasons to support it). If you are asking support for a particular bill, cite it by number and author, and give its title or subject matter.

**Telegrams, mailgrams, and fax.** These are fast, easy ways to communicate with legislators when the need for action is critical: just prior to a committee or floor vote. Use Western Union's nationwide toll-free telephone number: (800) 325-6000. Various low rates are available.

### Five basic rules for effective communication

1. **Be brief.** A legislator's time is limited. So is yours.
2. **Be appreciative.** Acknowledge past support, and convey thanks for current action.
3. **Be specific.** Refer to local library and district needs.
4. **Be informative.** Give reasons why a measure should be supported.
5. **Be courteous.** Ask; do not demand or threaten. Be positive but polite.

Where possible use your official letterhead. If this is not in order, and you write as an individual, use plain white bond paper, and give your official title in parentheses following your signature as a means of identification and to indicate your competency to speak on the subject.

1. Your legislators like to hear opinions from home and want to be kept informed of conditions in the district. Base your letter on your own pertinent experiences and observations.

2. If writing about a specific bill, describe it by number or its popular name. Your legislators have thousands of bills before them in the course of a year, and cannot always take time to figure out to which one you are referring.

3. They appreciate intelligent, well-thought-out letters that present a definite position, even if they do not agree.

4. Even more important and valuable to them is a concrete statement of the reasons for your position—particularly if you are writing about a field in which you have specialized knowledge. Representatives have to vote on many matters with which they have had little or no firsthand experience. Some of the most valuable information they receive comes from facts presented in letters from people who have knowledge in the field.

5. Short letters are almost always best. Members of Congress receive many, many letters each day, and a long one may not get as prompt a reading as a brief statement.

6. Letters should be timed to arrive while the issue is alive. Members of the committee considering the bill will appreciate having your views while the bill is ripe for study and action.

7. Don't forget to follow through with a thank-you letter.

*Source:* ALA Washington Office.

# Intellectual property

9

**THE FOLLOWING STATEMENT OF PRINCIPALS** was developed by the Association of Research Libraries and endorsed in 1994 by the American Library Association and other concerned groups.—*GME.*

The genius of United States copyright law is that it balances the intellectual property rights of authors, publishers, and copyright owners with society's need for the free exchange of ideas. Taken together, fair use and other public rights to utilize copyrighted works, as established in the Copyright Act of 1976, constitute indispensable legal doctrines for promoting the dissemination of knowledge, while ensuring authors, publishers, and copyright owners protection of their creative works and economic investments. The preservation and continuation of these balanced rights in an electronic environment are essential to the free flow of information and to the development of an information infrastructure that serves the public interest.

The United States and Canada have adopted very different approaches to intellectual property and copyright issues. For example, the Canadian Copyright Act does not contain the special considerations for library and educational use found in the U.S. Copyright Act of 1976, nor does it place federal or provincial government works in the public domain. Because of these differences, this statement addresses these issues from the U.S. perspective.

Each year, millions of researchers, students, and members of the public benefit from access to library collections—access that is supported by fair use, the right of libraries to reproduce materials under certain circumstances, and other related provisions of the copyright law. These provisions are limitations on the rights of copyright owners. The loss of these provisions in the emerging information infrastructure would greatly harm scholarship, teaching, and the operations of a free society. Fair use, the library, and other relevant provisions must be preserved so that copyright ownership does not become an absolute monopoly over the distribution of and access to copyrighted information. In an electronic environment, this could mean that information resources are accessible only to those who are able to pay. The public information systems that libraries have developed would be replaced by commercial information vendors. In the age of information, a diminished scope of public rights would lead to an increasingly polarized society of information haves and have-nots.

Librarians and educators have every reason to encourage full and good-faith copyright compliance. Technological advancement has made copyright infringement easier to accomplish, but no less illegal. Authors, publishers, copyright owners, and librarians are integral parts of the system of scholarly communication, and publishers, authors, and copyright owners are the natural partners of education and research. The continuation of fair use, the library and other relevant provisions of the Copyright Act of 1976 applied in an electronic environment offer the prospect of better library services, better teaching, and better research, without impairing the market for copyrighted materials.

Although the emerging information infrastructure is raising awareness of technological changes that pose challenges to copyright systems, the potential impact of technology was anticipated by the passage of the Copyright Act of 1976. Congress expressly intended that the revised copyright law would apply to all types of media. With few exceptions, the protections and provisions of the copyright statute are as relevant and applicable to an electronic environment as they are to a print and broadcast environment.

The research library community believes that the development of an information infrastructure does not require a major revision of copyright law at this time. In general, the stakeholders affected by intellectual property law continue to be well served by the existing copyright statute. Just as was intended, the law's flexibility with regard to dissemination media fosters change and experimentation in educational and research communication. Some specific legislative changes may be needed to ensure that libraries are able to utilize the latest technology to provide continued and effective access to information and to preserve knowledge.

The Association of Research Libraries affirms the following intellectual property principles as they apply to librarians, teachers, researchers, and other information mediators and consumers. We join our national leaders in the determination to develop a policy framework for the emerging information infrastructure that strengthens the Constitutional purpose of copyright law to advance science and the useful arts.

## Statement of principles

1. **Copyright exists for the public good.** The United States copyright law is founded on a Constitutional provision intended to "promote the progress of Science and Useful Arts." The fundamental purpose of copyright is to serve the public interest by encouraging the advancement of knowledge through a system of exclusive but limited rights for authors and copyright owners. Fair use and other public rights to utilize copyrighted works, specifically and intentionally included in the 1976 revision of the law, provide the essential balance between the rights of authors, publishers and copyright owners, and society's interest in the free exchange of ideas.

2. **Fair use, the library, and other relevant provisions of the Copyright Act of 1976 must be preserved in the development of the emerging information infrastructure.** Fair use and other relevant provisions are the essential means by which teachers teach, students learn, and researchers advance knowledge. The Copyright Act of 1976 defines intellectual property principles in a way that is independent of the form of publication or distribution. These provisions apply to all formats and are essential to modern library and information services.

3. **As trustees of the rapidly growing record of human knowledge, libraries and archives must have full use of technology in order to preserve our heritage of scholarship and research.** Digital works of enduring value need to be preserved just as printed works have long been preserved by research libraries. Archival responsibilities have traditionally been undertaken by libraries because publishers and database producers have generally preserved particular knowledge only as long as it has economic value in the marketplace. As with other formats, the preservation of electronic information will be the responsibility of libraries and they will continue to perform this important societal role.

The policy framework of the emerging information infrastructure must provide for the archiving of electronic materials by research libraries to maintain permanent collections and environments for public access. Accomplishing this goal will require strengthening the library provisions of the copyright law to allow preservation activities that use electronic or other appropriate technologies as they emerge.

4. **Licensing agreements should not be allowed to abrogate the fair use and library provisions authorized in the copyright statute.** Licenses may define the rights and privileges of the contracting parties differently than those defined by the Copyright Act of 1976. But licenses and contracts should not negate fair use and the public right to utilize copyrighted works. The research library community recognizes that there will be a variety of payment methods for the purchase of copyrighted materials in electronic formats, just as there are differing contractual agreements for acquiring printed information. The research library community is committed to working with publishers and database producers to develop model agreements that deploy licenses that do not contract around fair use or other copyright provisions.

5. **Librarians and educators have an obligation to educate information users about their rights and responsibilities under intellectual property law.** Institutions of learning must continue to employ policies and procedures that encourage copyright compliance. For example, the Copyright Act of 1976 required the posting of copyright notices on photocopy equipment. This practice should be updated to other technologies that permit the duplication of copyrighted works.

6. **Copyright should not be applied to U.S. government information.**

The Copyright Act of 1976 prohibits copyright of U.S. government works. Only under selected circumstances has Congress granted limited exceptions to this policy. The Copyright Act of 1976 is one of several laws that support a fundamental principle of democratic government—that the open exchange of public information is essential to the functioning of a free and open society. U.S. government information should remain in the public domain, free of copyright or copyright-like restrictions.

7. **The information infrastructure must permit authors to be compensated for the success of their creative works, and copyright owners must have an opportunity for a fair return on their investment.** The research library community affirms that the distribution of copyrighted information that exceeds fair use and the enumerated limitations of the law require the permission of and/or compensation to authors, publishers, and copyright owners. The continuation of library provisions and fair use in an electronic environment has far greater potential to promote the sale of copyrighted materials than to substitute for purchase. There is every reason to believe that the increasing demand for and use of copyrighted works fostered by new information technologies will result in the equivalent or even greater compensation for authors, publishers, and copyright owners. The information infrastructure, however, must be based on an underlying ethos of abundance rather than scarcity. With such an approach, authors, copyright owners, and publishers will have a full range of new opportunities in an electronic information environment and libraries will be able to perform their roles as partners in promoting science and the useful arts.

*Source:* Association of Research Libraries, 1994.

# The National Education Goals

**By the year 2000 . . .**
1. All children in America will start school ready to learn.
2. The high school graduation rate will increase to at least 90 percent.
3. American students will leave grades four, eight, and twelve having demonstrated competency in challenging subject matter including English, mathematics, science, history, and geography; and every school in America will ensure that all students learn to use their minds well, so they may be prepared for responsible citizenship, further learning, and productive employment in our modern economy.
4. U.S. students will be the first in the world in science and mathematics achievement.
5. Every adult American will be literate and will possess the knowledge and skills necessary to compete in a global economy and exercise the rights and responsibilities of citizenship.
6. Every school in America will be free of drugs and violence and will offer a disciplined environment conducive to learning.

*Source: National Goals for Education* (Washington, D.C.: Executive Office of the President, 1990), pp. 4–4

---

### What is illiteracy?

Harvard University reading researcher Jeanne Chall has identified three levels of illiteracy that need to be addressed:

1. The totally illiterate group reads below the fourth-grade level and cannot get information from printed sources.
2. The functionally illiterate group reads between the fourth- and eighth-grade levels and has trouble coping well in today's society.
3. The marginally literate group reads between the eighth- and twelfth-grade levels, but is at a competitive disadvantage in a technological society.

*Source:* "Community Information Section," *Public Libraries* 31 (July/August 1992): 240.

---

### Are libraries losing the game?

**Home video games** are a $5.5-billion-a-year industry.

That's almost four times the $1.5 billion spent annually on the curricular resources in public and private school libraries.

That's more than five times the $1.0 billion spent annually for educational and research materials for college and university libraries.

That's almost eight times the $0.7 billion spent annually on the information, literature, and lifelong learning materials available in public libraries.

Or, to total it up, 72% more than the $3.2 billion total for materials for all of these types of libraries.

*Source:* "Are Libraries Losing the Game?" *Fast Facts: Recent Statistics from the Library Research Service* (Library Research Service, Colorado State Library), no.75 (January 7, 1994).

---

# The Environment

## The recycling librarian: 50 things you can do to save the earth

*by Madelene Barnard*

9

1. Bring your own coffee cup to meetings. Don't use styrofoam cups.
2. Recycle your old magazines and catalogs. Cut them up for bookmarks, or use them for children's crafts, or donate them to the local animal shelter for litter or cage lining.
3. Participate in your community recycling program. For example: collect and recycle office paper, or place a recycling bin by the office and public access copiers.
4. Reuse the backside of computer paper as scrap or additional printout.
5. Use fax post-it notes—you save using a cover sheet.

6. At your next meeting/luncheon/program do a trash demo. Collect all the refreshment trash and sew it up on one big piece of string. This makes a powerful visual. It makes us stop and "rethink, reuse, and recycle." Tie this in with an environment program offered at your library.

7. Reuse all packaging material and don't purchase styrofoam popcorn or peanuts. Contact your suppliers, let them know you don't want such packaging. Several packaging material substitutes you can use are plain popped popcorn, peanut shells, and old crumpled-up paper. If you can't reuse your styrofoam packaging, perhaps a local recycling company will accept them.

8. Don't use balloons for children's activities. Balloons can be harmful to wildlife. Children can make animal masks from old folders, receive a seedling to grow from a local nursery—there are many green alternatives!

9. Participate in your community's Earth Day fair with a library booth. Hand out a local reference guide/flyer/bookmark created by your library.

10. Save paper. Reuse the envelopes for each interlibrary loan that comes through the mail and mark it with the title for the book. When the time comes to return it, there's no frantic hunt for a comparably sized envelope—plus the canceled postage will tell you how much it will cost to ship the book back to its home library.

11. Consolidate your names for vendor/catalog mailing lists. Why receive multiple copies when only one will do? In addition, eliminate excess junk mail by writing to the Mail Preference Service, Direct Marketing Association, 6 E. 43rd Street, New York, NY 10017.

12. Supermarkets recycle plastic bags—why not libraries? Have a bin at your library entrance for patrons to drop off excess plastic bags. Provide another filled bin for the circulation desk to dole out on rainy days.

13. If you don't like the idea of plastic bags, why not barcode and check out your library logo canvas bags? Attach a luggage tag with a laminated barcode and check it out with your patron's books. A great idea for any online circulation system.

14. Need to cut corners on your magazine subscriptions? Have patrons donate their subscriptions through an arrangement with the Friends of Library or a subscription service.

15. Coordinate your book sale with recycling awareness. When patrons turn in a recyclable glass bottle or aluminum can, he or she can receive a credit toward your book sale. Moreover, encourage a local business to pledge matching funds for the library's collection development drive.

16. Be an environmental sponsor. Get the library involved with a roadside or coastal cleanup through your local adopt-a-highway/road/shore programs! Participate in the Audubon Christmas bird count! Adopt a local endangered species as a library mascot.

17. Have an Ecolympics like Harvard University. They had 12 dorms competing for a prize by cutting their steam, gas, water, oil and electricity bills. The students not only saved 30% by turning off lights, but also took shorter showers to conserve water (a total of $100,000 savings a month). The prize: free Ben & Jerry's ice cream (this company donates 1% to charity). Have an office supplies Ecolympics with your city government agencies or promote a recycling contest within the schools.

18. Donate excess magazines and paperbacks to soup kitchens, nursing homes, youth centers, library book sales, not-for-profit hospital waiting rooms, library sale racks, teacher/student associations, mental institutions, correctional institutions and jails, senior citizen centers, public transportation waiting rooms, mobile home/retirement community clubhouse/reading rooms, local charities, or children's departments (to cut up for pictures and projects). Call it the Recycled Reading Program.

19. Before cutting up or donating your magazines use the pictures, local-interest stories, company profiles, and biographies for your vertical file.

20. Is your office supply budget nonexistent? Solicit slightly used office supplies and equipment from local businesses. For example—hardly used pencils, folders, old computers.

21. Provide environmental education programs, storytime, bus trips and/or reader advisory services. Encourage local environmental organizations, clubs, and schools to participate. They can provide a wealth of information and be very enthusiastic.

22. Encourage awareness of Arbor Day. North Indian River County Public Library did tree plantings. For a free brochure of what you can do for the environment write: Trees for America, The National Arbor Day Foundation, Nebraska City, NE 68410.

23. Use recycled products such as paper towels, toilet tissue, computer and office supplies, and nontoxic cleaners.

24. Print your library newsletter on recycled paper with soy ink.

25. Practice healthy and helpful book cleaning tips from Heloise. For example: To restore sheen to old books use a piece of white bread as a cleaner.

26. Provide an environmental science collection or a directory of special libraries with federal and state environmental libraries, databases, and clearinghouses.

27. Need a new book display? Recycle your local bookstore's cardboard displays (called dumps), which most booksellers throw away after their marketing promotions.

28. Don't know what to do with those empty poster tubes? Use them as shelf filler to push small books up to the front.

29. For tax time, keep a looseleaf of reproducible tax forms. Only provide multiple copies for those in high demand (1040 EZ). This eliminates leftovers. Why order a supply if there isn't a demand?

30. Subscribe to newsletters and journals that focus on environmental issues.

31. Develop a book club focusing on environmental literature (fiction and nonfiction). Suggested titles: *Silent Spring* by Rachel Carson; *Ecotopia* by Ernest Callenbach; *Time's Arrow* by Martin Amis; *Nature's End* by Whitley Strieber; *O-Zone* by Paul Theroux.

32. Looking for other sources listing children's science projects and activities? Try these offerings from Teacher's Ideas Press, a division of Libraries Unlimited: *Consider the Earth: Environmental Activities for Grades 4-8*, by Julie M. Gates; *Nature Puzzlers*, by Lawrence E. Hillman; *Bags Are Big: A Papercrafts Book*, by Nancy Renfro; *Beautiful Junk: Creative Classroom Uses for Recyclable Material*, by Karen Brackett and Rosie

9

Manaley; and *Garbage Games: Language and Math Games Using Recycled Containers*, grades 1-4, by Betty Isaak. These books allow children to learn about science and the importance of recycling.

33. Don't rely only on the major publishing companies for your collection development. Order from small presses, too. There are many environmental science titles to choose from. To aid in the selection try the Small Press Center, 20 W. 44th St., New York, NY 10036, (212) 764-7021.

34. When possible, car pool to work/conference/workshops and other library functions. If you are only a few blocks away, bicycle or walk over. It does wonders for your circulatory system.

35. Develop a nature corner/room/seasonal display to educate children as well as adults. The Manatee County Public Library (Bradenton, Florida) has a nature discovery room filled with "hands on" displays, and parent and child exploratory boxes. They even have dinosaur teeth! This fascinating room has volunteers available to answer the public's questions and seasonal exhibits for all ages. A similar display may be a worthwhile endeavor for your library to explore.

36. Bring your lunch in a cotton sack. Demco and other vendors offer cloth lunch bags with a library theme, as well as other environmentally oriented products.

37. Provide a recycling or conservation suggestion box at the circulation desk and the staff lunch room.

38. Limit the number of printouts at your public access terminals. Conservation is the word.

39. Green up your library! Place some flowering plants by the reference desk. Hang some ferns in the reading room. Perhaps the local nursery would like to recycle or donate some of their foliage which is not selling. Environmental interior decorating not only makes the library a more welcoming place to visit, but also helps reduce office pollution. For more information, contact Foliage for Clean Air Council, 405 N. Washington St., Falls Church, VA 22046; (703) 241-4004.

40. There is no longer a U.S.S.R. What do you do with those out-of-date maps? One retailer has converted them into wrapping paper. You may think of other possibilities.

41. Don't discard last year's reference source. Ask yourself, can this be part of my circulating collection? Can I donate this to the Friends' Book Sale? Even better, would another library want it? The Tampa Bay Library Consortium collects such reference sources for its Reference Book Clearinghouse. It's an informal setup. The clearinghouse not only helps to recycle valuable books, but also aids in resource sharing.

42. Recycle those catalog cards. Many of us use them as scrap. Think of other creative uses. Donate your cards to the local art school's classes for sculpting or use the backside for flashcards.

43. Is your library changing from phonographic records to CDs? What will you do with those plastic phonograph record sleeves? Recycle or convert them to other library uses. They could be used for pouches to store your data files or vertical files.

44. Do you need little prizes for your children's summertime reading club? Ask patrons to bring the prizes in their cereal boxes to the library. Most consumers discard these items. Are there any other free items you can think of?

45. Another community collection could be old eyeglasses. Set up a collection box and donate them to a local charity in need. Can you think of other items to recycle?

46. What do you do with the extra boxes after your new books have arrived? Set up a freebie table for the public. You can place items there you would otherwise throw out, but other people could use. This can be very popular during the holidays when people are shipping gifts.

47. Inquire at your local post office about their undeliverable magazines. Offer to take these discardable materials. The address labels can be quickly peeled off. These magazines can be used within the library or donated elsewhere as "Recycled Reading."

48. When you are the last one to leave the room, turn off the lights. Install "occupancy sensors" in rooms that are infrequently used. Saving on lighting and other electricity not only is cost-effective, but environmentally sound.

49. Are you remodeling the library or planning a new building? In addition to cost factors, look into environmental factors. Your choice of building materials and the way you dispose of the construction wastes affect the environment. For more information, write to the American Institute of Architects, 1735 New York Avenue, N.W., Washington, DC 20006; (202) 626-7300. Ask about their "Environmental Resource Guide."

50. Celebrate Earth Day every day!

*Source:* Madelene Barnard, "The Recycling Librarian," *Florida Libraries* 35 (May 1992): 81–83.
Reprinted with permission.

## Ethics

# Standards of ethical conduct for rare book, manuscript, and special collections librarians

SPECIAL COLLECTIONS LIBRARIANS hold positions of trust involving special responsibilities for promoting scholarship by preserving and providing access to the records of knowledge in their care. Such librarians, in implementing the policies of their institutions, must accept and discharge these responsibilities to the best of their abilities for the benefit of their institutions and the publics those institutions serve.

The maintenance of public trust is essential to the effective function of a special collections library and special collections librarians must scrupulously avoid weakening this trust. They must act with integrity, assiduously avoiding activities that could in any way compromise them or the institutions for which they work. They must particularly guard against personal conduct

9

or procedures within their libraries that may lead to conflict of interest—a condition which arises when an employee's personal or financial interest conflicts or appears to conflict with that employee's official responsibility. Special collections librarians should not reverse, alter, or suppress their professional judgment in order to conform to a management decision, but they must be accountable for making themselves familiar with and adhering to institutional policies as well as applicable laws.

It is in the public interest and the institution's interest that special collections librarians engage in the full range of professional and personal scholarly activities. However, in doing so, librarians must remember that their first responsibility is to carry out fully and conscientiously the duties of the position held in the library. Special collections librarians must avoid actual or potential conflicts of interest and misuse of the library's name, reputation, or property.

These Standards of Ethical Conduct are designed to help in the application of these principles to situations in which extraordinary care must be taken to avoid conflicts of interest. The standards identify certain categories of activity, such as dealing, which are unethical because by their very nature they cannot avoid an appearance of conflict of interest. In other areas of conduct, where judgment is required to guide individual behavior, the standards are illustrative, not comprehensive. The standards assume that the librarian will act in accordance with the spirit as well as the letter of this document.

## Personal collecting

The acquiring, collecting, and owning of books and manuscripts by special collections librarians is not in itself unethical. These activities can enhance professional knowledge and judgment and are not to be discouraged. Ethical questions can arise, however, in personal collecting. Extreme care is required whenever a librarian collects items similar to those being acquired by the institution and some institutions will choose to restrict or prohibit personal collecting. Special collections librarians must keep the appropriate administrative personnel of the library informed in a timely way about their personal collections and collecting activities.

In the course of personal collecting activities, special collections librarians may wish to make occasional sales or trades to upgrade their collection or may wish to dispose of a collection en bloc. Because questions of title and conflict of interest may be raised by such sales or trades, it is incumbent upon the librarian to inform the library administration of proposed sales and trades and to present to any potential purchaser evidence of clear title or, failing the existence of a title document, a personal affidavit affirming ownership.

Special collections librarians must not use their library affiliation to promote any personal collecting activities. They must not, for example, take advantage of discounts offered on their own purchases in return for institutional orders.

Special collections librarians must not compete with their institution, in fact or in appearance, in any personal collecting activity. The library's collecting needs always come first.

Extraordinary care must be taken to avoid any possible confusion between personal and institutional collecting. To this end, personal orders for books or other items of the kind collected by the library must be placed from a home or other nonlibrary address and invoiced and delivered to that address. In addition, great care must be taken to avoid any possible confusion of ownership. Only those personal books and similar items which special collections librarians find necessary to their work should be brought into their offices. Each item should be marked for personal identification before introduction into the library, and inspected when brought in and when removed.

## Personal dealing

Special collections librarians must avoid any activity which appears or has the potential to place their personal gain above the best interests of the employing institution. Therefore, it is unethical for special collections librarians to engage in any dealing of books, manuscripts, and other library materials.

Dealing is here defined as the regular purchase, sale, or trade of library materials for profit. Upgrading of a personal collection (see previous section) is not dealing. Special collections librarians must also not be party to the recommending of materials for purchase by institutions or collectors if they have any undisclosed financial interest in these materials, nor may they accept any commission or undisclosed or otherwise compromising gift from any seller or buyer of such materials.

## Appraisals

Appraisal is here defined as the determination of the monetary value of an item or collection of items. Valuation of materials for internal administrative purposes is not considered appraisal.

In the course of working with donors, special collections librarians are often required to advise on market value of books and manuscripts. Although it is proper to assist in the use of reference tools for this purpose, special collections librarians must not appraise any rare book, manuscript, or special collections materials, either for compensation or pro bono. Identification, authentication, and description (areas related to appraisal), when pursued as outside activities, must be subject to clearly defined library policy.

## Gifts, favors, discounts, and dispensations

Special collections librarians must not accept gifts, loans, or other dispensations, or things of value that are available to them in connection with their duties for the institution. Salaries together with standard related benefits should be considered complete remuneration for all library-related activities. Gifts include discounts on personal purchases from suppliers who sell items or furnish services to the library, except where such discounts regularly are offered to the general public.

Personal gifts may originate from individuals who have a potential financial or other interest in the library. In such instances the librarian is obliged to disclose the circumstances fully to the library director.

## Outside activities

Special collections librarians have the same right as other professional persons to engage in personal research and outside employment in accordance with announced institutional and library policy statements.

**Personal research.** Personal research and publishing by special collections librarians is to be encouraged in the institutional interest of furthering scholarship in fields supported by the library's holdings. It is not unethical for a librarian to use the library's research holdings for personal research and publication on the same terms as others using the same holdings. Any perception of possible conflict of interest can be avoided by making this activity known publicly or by notification to the proper administrative authority. It is, however, unethical for a librarian to make use of special personal access to, or nonpublic information about, the library's research holdings to further personal research and publication in unfair competition with members of the public research community.

The proprietary interest of both library and librarian in copyrights, royal-

9

ties, and similar properties should be in conformity with stated general institutional policy.

**Outside employment.** All outside employment activity must be undertaken within the fundamental premise that the librarian's first responsibility is to the library, that the activity will not interfere with the librarian's ability to discharge this responsibility, and that it will not compromise the library's professional integrity or reputation. Reference to the librarian's official position within the library should be avoided or made only sparingly in connection with outside activities.

Certain types of outside employment, including teaching, lecturing, writing, and consulting, can be of benefit to both the institution and the employee by stimulating professional development. Consequently, special collections librarians should be encouraged in these activities. In academic institutions, policies often regulate outside employment and consulting by faculty and staff; special collections librarians should be governed by these same policies.

Special collections librarians often will be considered representatives of their institutions while they are engaged in activities or duties similar to those they perform for their library, even though their work may be wholly independent of the institution. In other instances a librarian's activities outside the institution may bear little relation to the functioning of a library. In either case, special collections librarians must disclose to the library director or other appropriate superior the facts concerning any planned outside employment or consulting arrangements.

**Personal use of library resources.** Prior approval must be obtained for any contemplated use of the library's research facilities, staff assistance, or property such as stationery, telephones, copying machines, computer time, or objects from the collections in connection with outside efforts. Arrangements should also be made to reimburse the institution for such use under the guidance of institutional policy.

No special collections librarian should use at home any object or item that is part of the library's collections or under the guardianship of the library and which is not normally made available for home use by members of the public, or use any other property, supplies, or resources of the library except for the official business of the institution. To the extent that circumstance or special policies warrant exceptions, the circumstances or policies should be a matter of written record.

## Confidentiality

Special collections librarians, whose work involves knowledge of the work of researchers, the library's relations with donors and booksellers, and other matters of a confidential nature, must exercise care in respecting the privacy of this information.

In accordance with American Library Association policy (S52.4, Confidentiality of Library Records), special collections librarians must keep confidential information about the activities and research of their readers which they gain in performance of their duties. Exceptions may be made to this provision in cases where, for the advancement of scholarship, the reader has signed a written agreement to waive any claim to confidentiality in general or in specific instances.

*Source:* "Standards for Ethical Conduct for Rare Book, Manuscript, and Special Collections Librarians, with Guidelines for Institutional Practice in Support of the Standards, 2d Edition, 1992," *College & Research Libraries News* 54 (April 1993): 207–15.

# LIBRARIANA 10

# Quotes about libraries and books

I have always had a special affinity for libraries and librarians, for the most obvious reasons. I love books. (One of my first jobs was shelving books at a branch of the Chicago Public Library.) Libraries are a pillar of any society. I believe our lack of attention to funding and caring for them properly in the United States has a direct bearing on problems of literacy, productivity, and our inability to compete in today's world. Libraries are everyman's free university.

—John Jakes, in the afterword to *Homeland* (1993)

A man should keep his little brain attic stocked with all the furniture that he is likely to use, and the rest he can put away in the lumber room of his library, where he can get it if he wants it.

—Sherlock Holmes, in Arthur Conan Doyle's
"The Five Orange Pips" (1892)

I've been drunk for about a week now, and I thought it might sober me up to sit in a library.

—unnamed guest at one of Gatsby's parties,
in F. Scott Fitzgerald's *The Great Gatsby,* chap. 3 (1925)

Libraries are reservoirs of strength, grace and wit, reminders of order, calm and continuity, lakes of mental energy, neither warm nor cold, light nor dark. The pleasure they give is steady, unorgastic, reliable, deep and long-lasting. In any library in the world, I am at home, unselfconscious, still and absorbed.

—Germaine Greer, "Still in Melbourne, January 1987,"
in *Daddy, We Hardly Knew You* (1989)

No place affords a more striking conviction of the vanity of human hopes than a public library.

—Samuel Johnson, in *The Rambler,*
no.106 (March 23, 1751)

. . . my library
Was dukedom large enough.

—Prospero, in William Shakespeare's
*The Tempest,* Act I, scene 2

Here Greek and Roman find themselves
Alive along these crowded shelves;
And Shakespeare treads again his stage,
And Chaucer paints anew his age.

—John Greenleaf Whittier, "The Library," stanza 7.

She'll always be high on nerves and low on animal emotion. She'll always breathe thin air and smell snow. She'd have made a perfect nun. The religious dream, with its narrowness, its stylized emotions and its grim purity, would have been a perfect release for her. As it is she will probably turn out to be one of those acid-faced virgins that sit behind little desks in public libraries and stamp dates in books.

—Raymond Chandler, *The High Window* (1943)

Fact is Our Lord knew all about the power of money: He gave capitalism a tiny niche in His scheme of things, He gave it a chance, He even provided a first instalment of funds. Can you beat that? It's so magnificent. God despises nothing. After all, if the deal had come off, Judas would probably have endowed sanitoriums, hospitals, public libraries or laboratories.

—The Curé de Torcy, in Georges Bernanos's
*The Diary of a Country Priest,* chap. 2 (1936)

A well-chosen library has innumerable dishes, and all of admirable flavor.

—William Godwin

---

Baseball books are all wonderful . . . Football books are a waste of paper. For some reason baseball fans read and football fans drink beer and raise hell. Basketball sucks and hockey can be slow. But always buy golf books, any damn golf book that comes through the door . . . Buy anything on horses or auto racing. Buy billiards and chess, the older the better, but don't ever buy a bowling book.

—Ruby Seals, in John Dunning's
*Booked to Die,* chap. 20 (1992)

---

. . . the chaos in the Net felt like having one of life's underpinnings knocked out. What had been a well-ordered, if undisciplined, ruckus of zines, holochannels, SIGs, and forums had become a rowdy babel, a torrent of confusion and comment, made worse because in order to be noticed each user now sent out countless copies of his messages toward any node that might conceivably listen.

—David Brin, *Earth,* Part X (1990)

---

We know by one's reading
His learning and breeding;
By what draws his laughter
We know his Hereafter.
Read nothing, laugh never—
The Sphinx was less clever!

—Ambrose Bierce, *The Devil's Dictionary* (1911)

---

Reader placid and bucolic,
Sober, guileless man of the good,
Fling away this saturnine book,
Orgiastic and melancholic.

—Charles-Pierre Beaudelaire,
"Epigraphe pour un livre condamné" (1857)

---

Seems like she forgot all about the library that she told her old man now.

—The Beach Boys, "Fun Fun Fun" (1963)

---

"Well, you've got your way now," the librarian said to Kornhoer as they approached. "When'll you be putting in a mechanical librarian, Brother?"

"We find hints, Brother, that once there were such things," the inventor growled. "In descriptions of the *Machina analytica,* you'll find references to—"

"Enough, enough," the abbot interposed . . .

—Walter M. Miller Jr., *A Canticle for Leibowitz,*
chap. 14 (1959)

---

"This is silly," he said, and did as I asked. People started to cluster around the computer. Toomy sat down next to Jonathan and headed for the keyboard—and Mary Kay took it away from them both. "This is my pidgin," she said firmly, and they relinquished it. (Mary Kay is one of the secret masters of the world: a librarian. They control information. Don't ever piss one off.)

—Spider Robinson, *The Callahan Touch* (1993)

---

Twenty-two acknowledged concubines, and a library of sixty-two thousand volumes, attested the variety of his inclinations; and from the productions which he left behind him [Emperor Gordian the Younger], it appears that the former as well as the latter were designed for use rather than ostentation.

—Edward Gibbon, *Decline and Fall of the Roman Empire* (1776)

---

**10**

Rock's the best possible of worlds. You get to go on stage, turn up the amplifiers, go wang wang wang, and make a fool of yourself. Compare that to being a librarian.

—Frank Zappa

# Words beginning with "bibl-"

THE FOLLOWING LIST consists of words deriving from the Greek words *biblion* (papyrus reed) and *biblos* (book). Egypt exported papyrus for writing material to Greece and other regions through the Phoenician port of Byblos (modern Jubail, Lebanon), from which comes the root word *bibl-*, the source of both Bible and bibliography.—*GME.*

**Bible,** n. The sacred scripture of Christians, comprising the Old Testament and the New Testament.

**bible,** n. Any book or reference work accepted as authoritative, informative, and reliable.

**bible,** n., v.t. In TV series production, the general outline of plots and character development prepared before the first program of the season.

***Bible-back,** n. A round-shouldered person; or a pious and/or sanctimonious person.

***Bible bug,** n. An insect that makes a chirping, shrilling, or clicking sound.

**Bible paper,** n. Thin, lightweight, bright, opaque, durable paper for Bibles or reference books. Originally made from vegetable fiber in China and Japan, though erroneously thought to come from India.

**Bible style,** n. A flexible, round-cornered, leather binding.

***bible-tripe,** n. (Northumbrian dial.) The third stomach of a ruminant, so called from the similarity of its folds to the leaves of a book.

**Bibler,** n. A student or reader of the Bible.

***bibler,** n. Six cuts on the back as punishment.

***bibler,** n. (Scots.) Senior boy in a school.

**biblet,** n. (Obsolete.) A book or library.

**biblia abiblia,** n. Books that are of no humanist interest; irrelevant materials brought together in one volume, simply to make a book.

**Biblia pauperum,** n. Medieval picture books containing illustrations of scriptural subjects.

**Biblián,** n. Town in Ecuador, northeast of Cuenca.

**Bibliander,** n. Greek surname of Theodor Buchmann, 1500?–1564, Swiss theologian and Oriental scholar.

**biblic,** adj. biblical.

***biblic,** n. In medieval universities, the lowest grade of bachelor of theology.

**biblical,** adj. Pertaining to the Bible or the era and region in which events of the Bible took place.

**biblicism,** n. Adherence to the letter of the Bible.

**biblicist,** n. One who so adheres.

***biblid,** n. A bibliographic identification code established by the International Standards Organization (ISO) for contribution to serials and monographs with several authors.

***bibling-rod,** n. A wand with four apple twigs twisted together at the end that is used to administer a beating.

***biblio,** n. A bibliographical note in a book, usually on the reverse of the title page.

***biblioanomaly,** n. Any event, behavior, condition, or discovery regarding books or libraries that does not conform to prevailing world views. Weird book stuff in general. *George Eberhart.*

***bibliochresis,** n. The use of books.

**biblioclasm,** n. Destruction of books.

**biblioclast,** n. A person who mutilates or destroys books.

***bibliofame,** n. Renown as a bibliographer. *Norman Stevens.*

---

*New to this edition of *The Whole Library Handbook.*

**bibliofilm,** n. A microfilm used to photograph the pages of valuable books.

**bibliogenesis,** n. Production of books.

**bibliognost,** n. One versed in knowledge about books.

**bibliogony,** n. The art of producing and publishing books.

**bibliograph,** v.t. To put in a bibliography.

**\*bibliograph,** n. A graph of any curve that describes Bradford's law of scattering, named after science librarian Samuel Clement Bradford.

**\*bibliographee,** n. The person about whom a bibliography has been written.

**bibliographer,** n. An expert in bibliography.

**bibliographic, bibliographical,** adj. Pertaining to bibliography.

**\*bibliographic center,** n. An organization, often a department of a library, which maintains a collection of reference books from which it is possible to give information concerning the availability of books.

**Bibliographic Classification,** n. A classification system devised by Henry Evelyn Bliss, first published in outline form in 1910, characterized by the organization of knowledge consistent with scientific and educational consensus.

**bibliographic control,** n. Complete bibliographic records of all bibliographic items published; standardization of bibliographic description; providing physical access through consortia, networks, or other cooperative endeavors; or providing bibliographic access through compiling and distributing union lists and subject bibliographies and through bibliographic service centers.

**bibliographic coupling,** n. The theory that if any two scientific papers contain a citation in common, they are bibliographically related.

**bibliographic database,** n. A database consisting of computer records that represent works, documents, or bibliographic items.

**bibliographic description,** n. The description of a bibliographic item, divided into specific areas, such as title, edition, publication, etc.

**\*bibliographic index,** n. A systematic list of writings or publications.

**\*bibliographic information,** n. The details concerning a publication that are sufficient to identify it for the purpose of ordering or locating it.

**bibliographic instruction,** n. An information service to a group, which is designed to teach library users how to locate information efficiently.

**bibliographic item,** n. A document or set of documents in any physical form, forming the basis for a single bibliographic description.

**bibliographic network,** n. A network established and maintained for the sharing of bibliographic data through the use of a standard communication format and authority control.

**bibliographic record,** n. A record of a bibliographic item that comprises all data contained in or accommodated by a bibliographic format such as MARC.

**bibliographic reference,** n. A set of bibliographic elements essential to the identification of a work.

**bibliographic search,** n. The process of identifying a work and obtaining bibliographic data about it through a systematic search of bibliographic tools and other sources.

**bibliographic service center,** n. An organization that serves as a distributor of computer-based bibliographic processing services.

**\*bibliographic unit,** n. Any document, part of a document, or several documents, that are treated as a bibliographic entity.

**bibliographic utility,** n. An organization that maintains online bibliographic databases, enabling it to offer computer-based support to users.

**\*bibliographic volume,** n. A publication distinguishable from other publications by virtue of having its own title page, half title, cover title, or other means of establishing its separate identity.

**bibliographical ghost,** n. A work or edition of a work, recorded in bibliographies or otherwise mentioned, of whose existence there is no reasonable proof.

**10**

**bibliographical note,** n. Text set apart from the text of a document, which contains a reference to one or more works used as sources.

**\*bibliographical scatter,** n. The appearance of an article on one subject in a periodical devoted primarily to another subject.

**\*bibliographical strip,** n. The contents of a part of a periodical.

**\*bibliographical tool,** n. A publication used by a bibliographer in the course of her work.

**\*bibliographical warrant,** n. The basing of book classification according to the actual groupings into which books tend to fall for use, ignoring minute classes for which there is no literature, but including composite classes for which there is a literature.

**\*bibliographing,** n. The act of consulting bibliographies.

**bibliographize,** v.t. To make a bibliography of.

**bibliography,** n. The study of books as physical objects; the art of correctly describing books; or, a list of works, documents, or bibliographic items, usually by author, subject, or place of publication.

**\*bibliography of bibliographies,** n. A bibliography that describes bibliographies.

**\*biblioholic,** n. One afflcited with biblioholism. *Tom Raabe.*

**\*biblioholism,** n. The habitual longing to purchase, read, store, admire and consume books in excess. *Tom Raabe.*

**biblioklept,** n. A person who steals books.

**bibliokleptomania,** n. Obsessive stealing of books.

**bibliolater, bibliolatrist,** n. A book worshiper.

**bibliolatry,** n. Extravagant devotion to or dependence upon books.

**\*bibliolite,** n. Certain laminated schistose rocks, otherwise called bookstones.

**bibliologist,** n. One versed in bibliology.

**bibliology,** n. The study of books, embracing knowledge of the physical book in all its aspects, such as paper, printing, typography, illustration, and binding.

**bibliomancy,** n. Divination by means of a book, especially the Bible, opened at random to some verse or passage, which is then interpreted.

**bibliomania,** n. Excessive fondness for acquiring and possessing books.

**bibliomaniac,** n., adj. Characterized by bibliomania.

**bibliomanian, bibliomane,** n., adj. Bibliomaniac.

**bibliometrics,** n. The use of statistical methods in the analysis of a body of literature to reveal the historical development of subject fields and patterns of authorship, publication, and use.

**\*biblionarcissism,** n. The art of convincing others that you are more bookish than you really are. *Tom Raabe.*

**\*biblionomy,** n. The body of laws or perceived knowledge pertaining to bibliography and/or librarianship. *Norman Stevens.*

**bibliopegic,** adj. Related to the binding of books.

**bibliopegist,** n. A bookbinder.

**bibliopegy,** n. The art of binding books.

**bibliophage, bibliophagist,** n. An ardent reader.

**bibliophilately,** n. The study of books and libraries on postage stamps. *George Eberhart.*

**bibliophile,** n. A person who loves or collects books.

**bibliophile binding,** n. A binding, usually ornate, such as that which might be used by a bibliophile.

*Bibliophile de la vieille roche,* n. (French.) A book collector of the old school whose interests ranged widely and who did not specialize.

**\*bibliophile edition,** n. A specially printed and bound edition of a book published for sale to bibliophiles.

**Bibliophile Jacob,** n. Pseudonym of Paul Lacroix, 1806–1884, French scholar.

**bibliophilism, bibliophily,** n. A love of books.

**bibliophobe,** n. A person who hates, fears, or distrusts books.

**bibliophobia,** n. Dislike of books.

**bibliopoesy,** n. The making of books.

**bibliopole, bibliopolist,** n. A bookseller, especially a dealer in rare or used books.

**bibliopolic, bibliopolar,** adj. Pertaining to booksellers.

**bibliopolism,** n. The trade or art of selling books.

**bibliopoly, bibliopolery,** n. The selling of books.

**bibliopsychology,** n. Study of authors, books, and readers, as well as their interrelationships.

**bibliort,** n. Something other than a bookmark used by people to mark a place in a book—ticket stub, laundry list, etc. *Paul Dickson.*

**bibliosoph,** n. One who knows about books.

**bibliotaph,** n. A person who caches or hoards books.

***bibliotaphy,** n. Burying books to ensure their safekeeping. *Tom Raabe.*

**bibliothec,** n. A library.

**bibliotheca,** n. A library or collection of books.

***bibliothecal bibliography,** n. The phase of bibliography concerned with the collection, preservation, and organization of books in libraries.

**bibliothecal classification,** n. A classification system devised for arranging library materials.

**bibliothecary, bibliothecarian,** n. A librarian.

**bibliotheke,** n. A library.

*Bibliothèque bleu,* n. (French.) Popular pamphlets with blue wrappers.

**bibliotherapist,** n. One who practices bibliotherapy.

**bibliotherapy,** n. The use of reading materials in a program of directed reading that is planned and conducted as an auxiliary in the treatment of mental and emotional disorders and social maladjustment.

**bibliothetic,** adj. Pertaining to or based on the placing or arrangement of books.

**bibliotics,** n. The analysis of handwriting and documents for authentication of authorship.

***bibliotime,** n. A season, occasion, or appointed hour for reading books. *Norman Stevens.*

**bibliotrain,** n. Railroad car converted into a mobile library.

**Biblis,** n. Town in Germany, north of Mannheim.

***biblist,** n. One who makes the Bible the sole rule of faith.

**Byblia,** n. A woman who fell in love with her brother Caunus and was changed into a fountain near Miletus. Ovid, *Metamorphoses.*

**Byblos,** n. Ancient Phoenician city known for exporting Egyptian papyrus; modern Jubail in Lebanon, 20 miles north of Beirut.

# Librarians on stage and screen

*by Frederick Duda*

THE FIRST EDITION OF *The Whole Library Handbook* included a list of librarians and library assistants in movies. This listing expands on the first with 44 new citations, including several from the stage. There are scores of movies that have passing scenes in libraries. I have included a few of these if the incident amused me (for example, James Stewart in *The FBI Story;* Ingrid Bergman in *Spellbound*) or it involved a particularly blatant stereotype (as in *Sophie's Choice*). *Editor's Note:* Frederick Duda is the author of *Bib/Triv: Profundities, Banalities, and Trivialities in Libraryland* (McFarland, 1992).

10

1932—**No Man of Her Own;** Carole Lombard as Connie Randall, public librarian.

*1934—**Imitation of Life;** Fredi Washington as Peola Johnson, who lies to her mother about having a night job in the library (see 1959 remake below).

* 1938—**Scandal Street;** Louise Campbell as Nora Langdon, public librarian.

1940—**The Philadelphia Story;** Hilda Plowright as Quaker librarian.

1941—**Citizen Kane;** Georgia Backus as Bertha Anderson, manuscripts librarian, Thatcher Memorial Library.

1942—**Quiet Please, Murder;** George Sanders as Fleg, library thief; Frank O'Connor as library guard.

1943—**The Human Comedy;** Adeline De Walt Reynolds as children's librarian.

1943—**Shadow of a Doubt;** Eily Malyon as librarian, Santa Rosa (Calif.) PL.

* 1944—**It Happened Tomorrow;** John Philliber as Pop Benson, a newspaper librarian who befriends Dick Powell. After Pop dies, his ghost returns to give Powell copies of the next day's paper for three successive days.

1945—**Adventure;** Greer Garson as Emily Sears, San Francisco PL.

* 1945—**Spellbound;** on the lam in New York City, Ingrid Bergman as Dr. Constance Peterson is considered harmless by a hotel detective (Bill Goodwin) because he thinks that she looks like either a librarian or a schoolteacher.

1945—**A Tree Grows in Brooklyn;** Lillian Bronson as children's librarian.

1946—**The Big Sleep;** Carole Douglas as librarian, Hollywood PL; Dorothy Malone as antiquarian bookseller.

1946—**Good News;** June Allyson as Connie Lane, student library assistant, Tait College Library.

* 1946—**Happy Birthday;** (Broadway comedy, 1946–47); Helen Hayes as public librarian Addie Bemis, a teetotaler, who finds romance in the Mecca Cocktail Bar in Newark, N.J. (Hayes won a Tony award for her performance in 1947, the first year Tonys were awarded.)

1946—**It's a Wonderful Life;** Donna Reed as Mary Hatch, Bedford Falls PL (in alternate life).

* 1947—**So Well Remembered;** Martha Scott as public librarian Olivia Channing, who appears to be meek but turns out to be aggressive and ruthless.

* 1949—**All the King's Men;** the Willy Stark Library is featured in a "March of Time" style newsreel.

* 1950—**The Asphalt Jungle;** Sam Jaffe as inmate "Doc" Erwin Riedenschneider gets to work in the prison library for good behavior.

1951—**Katie Did It;** Ann Blyth as Katherine Standish, librarian.

1952—**The Thief;** Ray Milland as Allan Fields, atomic spy and library user.

* 1955—**Desk Set;** (Broadway comedy, 1955–56); Bunny Watson (Shirley Booth) and her assistants confront automation in a radio and TV reference library (see 1957 movie version below).

* 1956—**The Man Who Never Was;** Gloria Grahame as librarian Lucy Sherwood has a pivotal role in convincing a Nazi agent of the legitimacy of a bogus allied plan to invade Greece, not Sicily.

1956—**Storm Center;** Bette Davis as Alicia Hull, public librarian; Kim Hunter as Martha Lockridge, assistant, then acting librarian; Kevin Coughlin as Freddie Slater, young adult reader and arsonist.

1957—**Desk Set;** Katharine Hepburn as Bunny Watson, research librarian for a communications firm; Joan Blondell as Peg Costello, and Dina Merrill as Sylvia, library support staff; Spencer Tracy as Richard Sumner, automation consultant.

---

* New to this edition of *The Whole Library Handbook.*

* 1957—**Interlude;** June Allyson as Helen Banning shelves books in the American Cultural Center in Berlin.
* 1959—**The FBI Story;** Jimmy Stewart as Chip Hardesty kisses a librarian (Vera Miles) in the stacks.
* 1959—**Imitation of Life;** Susan Kohner as Sarah Jane Johnson, a singer and dancer in a strip joint, who tells her mother that she has a job cataloging books in the library at night.
* 1959—**Web of Evidence;** Vera Miles as librarian Lena Anderson helps Paul Mathry (Van Johnson) clear his late father of murder.
* 1960—**The Tell-Tale Heart;** Laurence Payne as Edgar Marsh dreams he is a crippled librarian.
  1961—**Breakfast at Tiffany's;** Elvia Allman as librarian, New York PL.
* 1961—**Return to Peyton Place;** Robert Sterling as Mike Rossi, school principal, is fired for refusing to remove Allison Mackenzie's (Carol Lynley's) racy novel from the school library.
* 1962—**Murder, She Said;** Stringer Davis as Mr. Stringer, the village librarian, appears as Miss Marple's friend in this and the other Margaret Rutherford interpretations of Agatha Christie's sleuth.
  1962—**The Music Man;** Shirley Jones as Marian Paroo, librarian, River City (Iowa) PL.
  1962—**Only Two Can Play;** Peter Sellers as John Lewis, librarian, Swansea Library.
  1962—**Rome Adventure;** Suzanne Pleshette as Prudence Bell, assistant librarian in a girls' school.
* 1962—**That Touch of Mink;** honeymooners are interrupted in Al's Motel in Asbury Park, N.J., by Philip Shayne (Cary Grant), who leads Mr. Smith (John Fiedler) to believe that he had an affair with Mrs. Smith (Barbara Collentine). After Grant departs, Mr. Smith says to his wife, "You librarians live it up pretty good." Mrs. Smith later tries to convince her husband that there was no other man in her life until he walked into the library.
  1963—**Cleopatra;** Rex Harrison as Julius Caesar, library arsonist, Alexandria, Egypt; Elizabeth Taylor as Cleopatra, intellectual freedom advocate.
* 1963—**Spencer's Mountain;** James MacArthur as Clayboy Spencer fails to negotiate a higher salary to run the local library.
  1964—**7 Faces of Dr. Lao;** Barbara Eden as Angela Benedict, public librarian.
  1966—**The Spy Who Came in From the Cold;** Claire Bloom as Nan Perry, librarian and Communist; Richard Burton as Alec Leamas, library assistant and spy.
  1966—**You're a Big Boy Now;** Peter Kastner as Bernard Chanticleer, library page, New York PL; Rip Torn as Bernard's father, I. H. Chanticleer, rare book librarian, New York PL; Karen Black as Amy and Tony Bill as Raef, library assistants, New York PL.
* 1967—**The Whisperers;** Dame Edith Evans as Mrs. Maggie Ross, a lonely old lady who spends lots of time reading the daily papers and warming her toes in the library.
  1969—**Goodbye, Columbus;** Richard Benjamin as Neil Klugman, library assistant, Newark (N.J.) PL.
* 1970—**The Dunwich Horror;** Sandra Dee as Nancy Walker and Donna Baccala as Elizabeth Hamilton, student assistants, Miskatonic University Library; Toby Russ as a librarian.
  1970—**Love Story;** Ali McGraw as student assistant, Radcliffe College Library.
* 1971—**Making It;** Doro Merande as high school librarian Ms. Hobgood tells a student that books by D. H. Lawrence are not for general distribution.
* 1973—**Soylent Green;** in 2022, Detective Thorn (Charlton Heston) and Sol Roth (Edward G. Robinson) find out that librarians have all the power because they are the only ones who have information or know how to get it.

10

1974—**Mr. Sycamore;** Jean Simmons as Estelle Benbow, librarian.

* 1974—**Norman Conquests;** (Broadway play, 1974–75); Tom Courtney as Norman, a drunken librarian who spends his time trying to seduce his wife and sisters-in-law.

* 1975—**Rollerball;** Sir Ralph Richardson as an absented-minded Swiss librarian.

1976—**All the President's Men;** Jaye Stewart as library clerk, Library of Congress; Robert Redford as Bob Woodward and Dustin Hoffman as Carl Bernstein, LC researchers.

* 1976—**Logan's Run;** Peter Ustinov as the Old Man explains what a library is to Logan (Michael York).

* 1978—**Debbie Does Dallas;** stodgy librarian Mr. Biddle has to put up with sex in the stacks.

1978—**Foul Play;** Goldie Hawn as Gloria Mundy, librarian, San Francisco.

1978—**Movie, Movie;** Trish Van Devere as Betsy McGuire, public librarian.

* 1979—**Escape From Alcatraz;** Clint Eastwood as inmate Frank Morris works in the Alcatraz library.

* 1982—**Hammett;** Marilu Henner as a sexy San Francisco librarian.

* 1982—**Sophie's Choice;** Meryl Streep as Sophie Zawistowska, a Polish immigrant, seeks a book by the American poet Emily Dickinson, though she pronounces the name "Emil Dickens." A prissy, surly male librarian played by John Rothman is in no mood to provide reference service and tells her there is "no American poet named Dickens."

1983—**Something Wicked This Way Comes;** Jason Robards Jr. as Charles Halloway, librarian, Green Town (Ill.) PL.

* 1984—**Cal;** Helen Mirren as Marcella, an attractive widow who works in a library in Northern Ireland.

1984—**Ghostbusters;** Alice Drummond as librarian, New York PL; John Rothman as library administrator, New York PL; Ruth Oliver as library ghost; Bill Murray as Peter Venkinan, library ghost exterminator.

1985—**Bridge Across Time;** (made for TV); Adrienne Barbeau as Lynn Chandler, head librarian, Lake Havasu City PL, Arizona.

1985—**Maxie;** Mandy Patinkin as Nick, rare book librarian, San Francisco PL; Valerie Curtin as Ophelia Sheffer, supervising librarian and sexual harasser, San Francisco PL.

* 1985—**Wetherby;** Dame Judi Dench as Yorkshire librarian Marcia Pilborough.

1986—**The Name of the Rose;** Volker Prechtel as Malachia, monastery librarian, unnamed Benedictine abbey in Italy, 1327; Michael Habeck as Brother Berengar, assistant librarian.

1986—**Off Beat;** Judge Reinhold as Joe Gower, library assistant by day, dancer by night.

* 1987—**Prick Up Your Ears;** Gary Oldman as British playwright Joe Orton vandalizes a public library and gets kicked out by the librarian.

*1987—**Wimps;** Freshman wimp (Louie Bonanno) helps quarterback woo library clerk Roxanne (Deborah Blaisdell, aka X-rated star Tracey Adams).

* 1989—**Dr. Jekyll and Mr. Hyde;** (Ridiculous Theatrical Company, Off Broadway play); a psychotic killer (who never appears on stage), formerly a mild-mannered librarian, dismembers 16½ bodies because he suffers from quantum synaptic dualism.

1989—**Major League;** Rene Russo as Lynn Westland, special collections librarian, Cleveland (Ohio) PL.

* 1990—**The Handmaid's Tale;** Natasha Richardson as Kate wins a game of Scrabble. The Commander (Robert Duvall) says, "I knew you would be good at this. You used to be a librarian."

1990—**Personal Ads;** (made for TV); Jennifer O'Neill as killer reference librarian.

* 1990—**Stanley & Iris;** Dortha Duckworth as a Waterbury (Conn.) public librarian who shushes Robert DeNiro for reading out loud.

1990—**Stephen King's It;** (made for TV); Tim Reid as Mike Hanlon, librarian, Derry (Me.) PL.

* 1992—**The Baltimore Waltz;** (Off-Broadway play); an elementary school teacher named Anna (Cherry Jones) learns that her brother, a young San Francisco librarian named Carl (Richard Thompson) is ill with AIDS.

* 1992—**Forever Young;** while Daniel McCormich (Mel Gibson) is researching microfilm in the library, his 10-year-old friend Nat (Elijah Wood) sees a girl he has a crush on. Nat says, "I'm in a library on a Saturday. She'll think I'm a geek."

* 1992—**The Gun in Betty Lou's Handbag;** Penelope Ann Miller as children's librarian Betty Lou confesses to murder to get the attention of her policeman husband; Marian Seldes as head librarian Margaret Anderson believes that "The best effect of any book is that it be returned unmutilated to its shelf."

* 1993—**The Countess Alice;** (Masterpiece Theater, PBS); Connie (Zoe Wanamaker), a childless, aging librarian who is bored with her job, puts cheap tea in Fortnum and Mason tins to keep up appearances for her mother (Wendy Hiller).

* 1993—**Demolition Man;** Lanita Huxley (Sandra Bullock) informs John Spartan (Sylvester Stallone), who had been cryogenically frozen for 36 years, about the Arnold Schwarzenegger Presidential Library, named after the first President not born in America.

* 1994—**Party Girl;** Mary (Parker Posey) is a high-life flake who finds fulfillment in a public library (shot in the Jersey City, N.J., PL).

* 1994—**With Honors;** Simon (Joe Pesci), a homeless man, lives in the basement of the Harvard library.

# Haunted libraries

*by Dennis William Hauck and George M. Eberhart*

**GRAVEYARDS AND STATELY MANSIONS** are not the only places you might meet with an apparition or ghost. A respectable number of libraries in the United States harbor a haunt or two. Here is a partial list, culled primarily from Dennis Hauck's *The National Directory of Haunted Places*, and augmented with some follow-up interviews and research of my own.—*GME.*

**Dover Public Library,** Highway 8, Dover, Delaware. In a hatbox in the library's technical services area rests a skull that supposedly belongs to a notorious female outlaw named Patty Cannon, who was arrested in April 1829. The owner of a tavern in Sussex County, Cannon was involved in illegal slave trading and was responsible for at least one murder, but before she could be executed she took a fatal dose of poison in her jail cell. She was buried in a potter's field, but her bones were dug up later and remained in private hands for many years. In the early 1960s the skull was loaned to the Dover Public Library, where it still resides. Contrary to some accounts, there are no reports of ghostly phenomena associated with the skull, according to library director Bob Wetherall.

**The Rotunda of the U.S. Capitol Building,** Washington, D.C. A male librarian haunts the rooms west of the Rotunda, where the Library of Congress was earlier housed. The man died before he could fetch the money he had hidden there. When the Library was moved

10

The Willard Library in 1890.

in 1897, workers discovered nearly $6,000 stashed between the pages of books.

**The Willard Library,** 21 First Ave., Evansville, Indiana. The ghost of a woman wearing a grey veil is still seen in this Gothic library building. The first sighting took place around 1936 when the janitor for the building encountered a female figure as he was firing the furnace in the basement early in the morning. When he flashed his light up and down the apparition, it disappeared. Since then, janitors, staff, and patrons of the library have reported sensing the Lady-in-Grey—sometimes only as a cold spot or an odor of perfume—near the elevator, near the restrooms, or in the Children's Room, which moved to the basement in the 1940s. Margaret Maier, who served as children's librarian until her death in 1989, saw the Lady-in-Grey on many occasions since the late 1950s. When the Children's Room was remodeled in 1985, Maier claimed that the ghost moved home with her, where she was seen by her sister and nephew as well. The apparition returned to the library when the remodeling was complete. Current director William Goodrich said that the specter appeared once on a security monitor placed near the restrooms. One of the most recent experiences occurred in 1992 when a child came into the Children's Room and asked who was the lady sitting in the peacock chair—he then went on to describe a figure resembling the late Margaret Maier in the chair, with another ghostly shape behind her.

**Roy O. West Library, De Pauw University,** Greencastle, Indiana. The ghost of James Whitcomb, governor of Indiana from 1843 to 1848, protects a special collection of books he donated to the library in 1852. He left instructions in his will that the Whitcomb Collection should never leave the library building, and it soon became common knowledge that anyone who dared to do so could be assured of a visit by his ghost. One student, who took a copy of the poems of Ossian to his room, found himself awakened by Whitcomb's figure at the foot of his bed. The specter pointed its finger at the terrified student and chanted, "Ossian! Ossian! Who stole the Ossian?" After the figure faded, the student stayed awake all night and returned the book to the library the first thing next morning. When the collection moved to its current location in 1956, rumors of the ghost continued. However, since the books are in the library's special collections division it is unlikely that they will be removed. (I tried to persuade one staff member to take the Ossian home with her over the weekend as an experiment, but she flatly refused.—*GME*.)

**Brucemore Mansion,** Cedar Rapids, Iowa. A strange, groaning presence has been detected in the library of this 1886 home. Objects move by themselves and sometimes untraceable laughter is heard. At the turn of the century, a University of Chicago professor was called in to investigate. He confirmed the presence of the paranormal and wanted to remain in the house for several months to study it. The owners refused, however, fearing that news of the haunt would leak out.

**Cedar Rapids Art Museum** (prior to 1985 the Cedar Rapids Public Library building), Cedar Rapids, Iowa. At 10:30 one morning in the late 1960s, a reference librarian at the Cedar Rapids PL noticed one of her regular patrons walking down from the balcony where current newspapers were kept. Elizabeth Schoenfelder, who later served as head of adult services at the library, said that the patron (whose name was Hazel or Helen) passed only 15 feet away from her. The odd thing was that, although Hazel had little money, on this particular morning she was wearing a new brown dress, an unusual amount of makeup, and sported a brand new permanent. A circulation attendant also saw her in the library, and another employee noticed Hazel afterwards at a park bench where she used to wait for a bus. When the afternoon paper arrived, Schoenfelder was shocked to see that Hazel had died of suffocation during a fire at her apartment building around 4:00 that morning. A later check with the family indicated that they had bought Hazel a new brown dress for her to wear in the coffin. One-time apparitions seen shortly before or after a person's death are well-known to parapsychologists, who call them "crisis apparitions." Schoenfelder's explanation is a simple one: "Hazel just didn't realize she had died, so she went to the library as usual, which was a second home to her."

**Salem Athenaeum Library**, Salem, Massachusetts. While still a young author, Nathaniel Hawthorne encountered the ghost of an elderly minister every day for a week here.

**Moriarity House**, Goodrich Avenue, St. Paul, Minnesota. The ghost of a former owner haunted this house from 1965 to 1968. Within a few weeks after moving into the two-story brick house, Dick Gibbons and his wife Valjean realized they had an uninvited houseguest. A rocking chair in the library started moving at regular intervals, their dog chased an invisible presence up the stairs, and objects started disappearing. Neighbors confided that the house had been haunted since the death of the previous owner, Mrs. Moriarity.

**Bernardsville Public Library**, 2 Morristown Road, Bernardsville, New Jersey. The female ghost here was so active that the staff issued it a library card. Jean Hill, Local History Room volunteer, said that "she was not put on our computer with the rest of us mortals, but her card is always available should she choose to use it!" Phyllis Parker's specter was first encountered in January 1877 in a private residence that is now part of the library. The building had been converted from a tavern that was built during the  Revolutionary War. The old Vealtown Tavern was the scene of a tragic love affair between the innkeeper's daughter and a tenant, Dr. Byram. In January 1777, Dr. Byram was revealed to be the British spy Aaron Wilde and executed by General Anthony Wayne. His body was delivered to the tavern to await burial in the morning. Not knowing what was in the large pine box, Phyllis opened it with a hatchet. On seeing the corpse she became hysterical and suffered a nervous breakdown. Her screams are sometimes heard in the old section of the library, which consists of a meeting room and a public reading room (where the incident with the casket occurred). Beginning in 1974, employees started seeing apparitions of Phyllis moving through the front rooms of the library. An attempt to pick up ghostly noises on audiotape was made in 1987, and the ambiguous sounds recorded can be played back by patrons in the Local History Room. In November 1989 a small child saw a lady in a long white dress in the reading room and said hello to her.

**Sunnyside**, Tarrytown, New York. The ghost of Washington Irving appeared at his former home several years after his death in 1859. Three witnesses saw his apparition walk through the parlor and disappear into the library. In the 1860s his ghost also roamed through stacks of books at the old Astor Library, which stood at Lafayette Place in Manhattan and was where Irving wrote "The Legend of Sleepy Hollow."

**New Hanover County Public Library**, 201 Chestnut St., Wilmington, North Carolina. The second-floor wing of this library is haunted by the ghost of a short woman, who some believe to be a patron who frequented the Local

10

History Room. The phenomena started in 1982 or 1983, not long after the library moved into the building, a former department store. Her form has been seen by several employees in the past few years. Beverly Tetterton, the local history librarian, said that some mornings she has found files spread on a reading room table when she is certain she had put everything away when locking up the previous evening. Sometimes people report the sounds of pages turning—subtle rustling noises that a "librarian would recognize as the sounds of doing research," according to Tetterton. The ghostly phenomena have also been attributed to the inhabitant of a home that stood on the site before the department store was built. He was killed in a duel in the 19th century, but his ghost was allegedly heard pacing in the house for many years.

**Hinckley Library,** Ridge and Center Roads, Hinckley, Ohio. This 1845 structure once belonged to the family of Vernon Stouffer, founder of the hotel and food corporation that bears his name. In 1973 the building, which had been boarded up for years, was acquired by the Friends of the Hinckley Library and renovated. During the renovation, library employee Elaine Vanderschreier was driving past one evening when she saw a light on in the hallway and a young woman in an old-fashioned blue dress who was sitting on the stairs. A few days later another staff member glanced into the same hallway and noticed a man wearing a hat peering at her through the bars of the stairway—she investigated, but no one was there. Others have felt an odd presence in the upper rooms, occasionally paper clips fly through the air without anyone throwing them, and a workman once saw a ghostly figure on the basement stairs. Possibly the ghost is Dr. Nelson Wilcox, a pioneer school teacher whose Civil War–era log cabin stood on the site. (Perhaps the young girl was his sister Rebecca.)

**Pendleton Public Library,** 214 N. Main St., Pendleton, Oregon. The ghost of Ruth, a Pendleton librarian, is said to haunt this building, formerly the Umatilla County Library. In the 1940s or 1950s Ruth was working one Sunday when the library was closed and she became very sick. (She did not take poison, as some accounts have asserted.) She was discovered the next day and taken to a nearby hospital where she died. The library staff attribute to Ruth's ghost the occasionally reported odd noises, books falling off shelves, lights

turning on spontaneously, toilet tanks flushing on their own, and windows opening.

**Linderman Library,** Lehigh University, Bethlehem, Pennsylvania. A cantankerous ghost pesters students and staff at this academic library. He is thought to be an elderly gentleman who frequented the library and was a general nuisance.

**Easton Public Library,** Church and 6th Streets, Easton, Pennsylvania. During construction of this building in 1903, workers uncovered a cemetery containing the graves of 514 people. Most of the bodies were moved to other cemeteries, but at least 30 were left unclaimed. Two prominent former citizens, Elizabeth Bell "Mammy" Morgan and William Parsons, were reburied on the library grounds. (Parsons, an early surveyor, is buried on the front lawn, while Mammy Morgan is buried on the west lawn underneath a large marker in the shape of an Indian mortar.) The other corpses, and any unidentified pieces of bodies, were unceremoniously dumped into an underground concrete vault on the property. Today, the library is haunted by the misplaced souls. Doors slam shut and open suddenly, filing cabinet drawers swing open for no reason, and unseen hands run through the hair or touch the shoulders of patrons and staff. Over the years, people have reported the ghost of Mammy Morgan roaming the grounds.

**Heyward House,** 31 Legare St., Charleston, South Carolina. James Heyward's ghost walks in the library of his Charleston home. The young man died in 1805 in a hunting accident. His rifle went off and the bullet severed his jugular vein. His apparition, clad in a green hunting coat, has been seen several times by later owners of the house.

**Hampton Plantation,** 1950 Rutledge Road, McClellanville, South Carolina. Among other ghostly phenomena experienced in Hampton House, built in 1735 by a Huguenot family, are the sounds of a man's sobbing and a chair that rocks itself in the downstairs library.

**Thomas Hughes Free Public Library,** Central Avenue, Rugby, Tennessee. Historic Rugby was a utopian community founded in 1880 by the English social reformer Thomas Hughes. The ghost of Eduard Bertz, the librarian who organized the collection in 1881–1883, has been sensed during the twilight hours in the library. The original 7,000 volumes of Victorian literature are still housed there.

**Houston Public Library,** Julia B. Ideson Building, 500 McKinney Ave., Houston, Texas. Ghostly music was heard drifting through the building in the 1960s. The notes always started in the basement, then drifted, turning off and on until they reached a crescendo in the balcony before fading away. The music allegedly came from the violin-playing ghost of a man named Cramer, who was janitor of the library from 1921 to 1936. When the library moved into its present building in 1926, Cramer moved into the basement. After regular hours in the library, he would walk from floor to floor through the building, into the stacks and up to the balcony just outside the main reading room, where he would sit and play his violin for hours. Since the library now closes at 6:00 p.m. and the staff does not stay after hours, there is no one around late at night to hear the music—if indeed it still can be heard.

**Fort Concho Museum,** East Avenue D, San Angelo, Texas. Construction on this remote outpost started in 1867. The fort was abandoned in 1889 and the individual buildings were turned into private homes shortly after. The museum library, formerly Officer's Quarters #7, is supposedly haunted by the ghosts of several transients who were murdered in the building in the 1890s. Lights have been seen inside the building when no one was there, eerie footsteps have been heard, and doors slammed. One library staff member said that when she worked in the building known as Officer's Quarters #9, an invisible presence locked her out several times by latching the 19th-century lock (not the modern deadbolt).

**Blandfield Mansion,** Essex County, Virginia. This 18th-century mansion is haunted by the ghosts of several members of the Beverley family. A male figure haunts the downstairs library.

**Edgehill,** Highway 17, Warrenton, Virginia. The ghost of Colonel William Chapman, second-in-command of the infamous Mosby's Rangers, returns to haunt his former home. Chapman's apparition has been seen in the library, and he is thought responsible for opening locked doors and making loud noises late at night. The house was built in 1840 by James Eustace Jeffries, the father of Chapman's wife Josephine.

**Stratford Hall,** Westmoreland County, Virginia. Ghosts of the family of Robert E. Lee haunt this estate, built in the 1730s by Thomas Lee. The ghost of his father, Light-Horse Harry Lee, has been seen at a desk in the library.

10

**Rocky Mountain High School,** Byron, Wyoming. This combination elementary and high school building was the scene of a paranormal occurrence in 1952 or 1953. At that time the library was located where the weight and wrestling room is today. The school superintendent at the time, Harold Hopkinson, was working late in the office next to the library when he heard footsteps coming down the hall and going up the short staircase to the library. He heard the library door open and close. Hopkinson's curiosity was rekindled several minutes later when he heard the library door open and close again. This time he got up and looked out into the hall. "As I stood there looking," Hopkinson said, "those footsteps went right past me and *there was no one there.* I heard them continue down the stairs towards the front door, which I heard opening. . . . I didn't dream it. There really was something walking on that old floor, which used to creak in a certain way." Hopkinson said that his predecessor refused to go to that part of the building after dark, and so did he at least for some time after the incident. Hopkinson said he was not aware of any other paranormal occurrences in the school afterwards.

**Sweetwater County Library,** 300 N. First Street East, Green River, Wyoming. Parapsychological phenomena have occurred in this building almost from the day it opened in 1980. Lights go on and off for no reason and unexplainable voices and flapping sounds reverberate through the building at night. Library director Patricia LeFaivre said that her staff has seen dots of light dancing on the walls inside the closed art gallery room in such a way that ruled out an external light source like car headlights. Once, a steel-spring gate at the entrance to the library started spinning wildly with no one near it. At least two electic typewriters in the library have been seen to type on their own; there was no paper loaded at the time, so if these were messages they were lost. (The library staff experimented by leaving paper in the typewriters overnight, but no phantom typing occurred.)

Maintenance people have reported strange goings-on at night. One reported seeing a "form" out of the corner of her eye sitting in the Multipurpose Room; when she looked at it directly it shot into the air and hit the ceiling with a loud "pop" before vanishing. Staff and patrons report thumps and bumps and phantom voices calling their names. One day the interlibrary loan librarian turned away briefly from her computer terminal—when she looked back she saw her full name spelled out on the screen. On another occasion a librarian and a custodian were both in the building early when they heard the sound system come on spontaneously; the system, which had been shut down for the night, is controlled from the circulation area and there was no one in sight. Another incident involved an attendent in the Financial Office who came in to work on the weekend when the library was closed. He brought his dog for company, but the animal lay down in front of the office door and growled continuously.

The library was built on top of a cemetery that dates from the 1860s. The graves were moved in the 1920s, but unearthed bodies started turning up on the property in the 1940s. In 1983, three more unrecorded graves were discovered during the construction of a retaining wall. During work on the foundation in 1985, the coffin of a small child was found.

*Sources:* Dennis William Hauck, *The National Directory of Haunted Places* (Sacramento: Athanor Press, 1994), 402p.; Gloria Brown, "Haunted Hinckley," *Ohio Libraries,* April 1993, pp. 30–31; Eileen Luz Johnston, *Phyllis—The Library Ghost?* (Newark, N.J.: The author, 1991).

# Biblioanomalies from the pages of *Fortean Times*

*FORTEAN TIMES,* SUBTITLED "The Journal of Strange Phenomena," is a British magazine of news, reviews, and research on strange behavior and experiences, scientific and historical mysteries, prodigies and portents. Formed in 1973 to continue the work of the iconoclastic American philosopher and collector of curiosa, Charles Hoy Fort (1874–1932), *Fortean*

*Times* treats weird occurrences and coincidences with an open mind and abundant humor. The editor, Bob Rickard, identified most of the items summarized here specially for *The Whole Library Handbook 2.—GME.*

**Nearly a Fortean death.** The sort of nightmare demise that has inevitably, and with a fleeting anxiety, occurred to those of us whose muse condemns us to toil in book-lined pits became a pressing possibility for 86-year-old Anthony Cima of San Diego. During a small earthquake at 8:46 a.m. on July 15, 1986, Cima was trapped when thousands of his beloved books came tumbling down. He was pinned for 12 hours, barely able to breathe and unable to call for help, before other residents in his hotel realized he was missing. He was taken to the University of California-San Diego Medical Center, where he spent a month in intensive care and soon resolved to sell off most of his 10,000 volumes. *San Francisco Chronicle,* August 9, 1986.

A similar tragedy was the death of a 70-year-old Long Island woman, Eleanor Barry, who was suffocated in her bedroom on December 18, 1977, when one of the many towers of books, old newspapers, and clippings fell, knocking others down and pinning her to the floor. *Minneapolis Star,* December 21, 1977.

More recently, lawyer Donato Causarano, 33, was working in his office in Arezzo, Italy, on the weekend of April 1–2, 1989. He reached up to place the last file on a year's worth of paperwork, and was instantly buried under five tons of the stuff. Firemen took four hours to dig him out. *London Daily Mirror, Daily Express,* April 3, 1989.

Carole Webb, 22, took a book off a shelf in the publishing warehouse in which she worked, in Abingdon, Oxfordshire, and was promptly buried beneath an avalanche of books weighing 20 tons. By luck she was not seriously injured, but needed rescuing by firemen and treatment in an Oxford hospital. *London Sun,* July 22, 1987.

Two young men and a woman in the French town of Blanc-Mesnil suffered a "novel" death when shelves holding "tons" of books collapsed on them in the

10

warehouse of EuroDispatch, a distribution firm. One of the men was the son of the boss who had begun a temporary job the day before while waiting to take up military service. *London Independent*, September 14, 1989.

**Librarians and ball lightning.** In the groves of Academe the existence of ball lightning is still debated. Editor Bob Rickard, in the course of locating possible photographs of ball lightning for a book, inquired at the National Meteorological Library at Bracknell. Stunned with a mixture of disbelief and amusement, a librarian told him: "You won't find anything on ball lightning here. We don't believe in it." How Fort would have chuckled!

**Homing books.** Mrs. S. C. M. Hill of London wrote to the *Sunday People* on July 27, 1980: "My mother bought some children's books at a jumble sale, intending to read them to my young niece when she came to stay. Later when she examined one of the books more closely, she saw my name and address on the fly-leaf, written by me when I was five, 25 years ago. There was also a half-finished letter that I had been writing to an aunt, still between the pages."

And Mrs. E. Owens, of Bristol, wrote to the *Sun* of June 22, 1980: "My brother wrote from Canada asking if a book of his was still around at home. It wasn't—we thought it had been sent to a jumble sale years earlier. A week later in a second-hand book shop I spotted a copy of the book my brother wanted. Opening it to see the price I found his name on the fly-leaf."

**Death by murder mystery.** As members of the Mystery Writers of America were giving readings in the Barnes and Noble store at Broadway and 83rd Street, New York, an unidentified elderly woman sat dead, apparently of natural causes, in a chair for four hours before anyone noticed. Soledad Santiago, author of *Nightside*, said: "Somebody put a blanket over her. All you could see were her big rubber boots." *New York Post*, February 16, 1994.

**Lost father found in a library.** Wilf Hewitt, 86, a widower of Warwick Street, Southport, wanted to look through an electoral roll in Southport Library, and asked the woman opposite whether she would be much longer. Vivien Fletoridis replied that she was looking for a man named Hewitt. She was his daughter, whom he had not seen for 46 years. Wilf had had a wartime love affair with Vivien's mother, who had died in 1983. Their daughter was adopted in 1941 and went to Australia with her foster parents in 1954, where she now has a husband and two grown-up children. In July 1987 she traveled 13,000 miles to track down her family. She traced her two brothers and sister through an agency, and then set out to find her father. *London Daily Express*, July 24, 1987.

**Two for the books.** Officials at the Philadelphia State Library discovered a book left in a manila envelope on December 30, 1985. It was a volume of Townsend's *Collection*, published in 1657, detailing the Cromwellian laws passed in the previous year, and was one of the books purchased for the General Assembly under the direction of Benjamin Franklin sometime between 1745 and the American Revolution. The book had vanished from the library between 1823 and 1900.

The chief librarian at Wilberforce University in Ohio was looking through old books and found a copy of *Scriptores reis Rustica (Writings about Country Life)* printed by Dionysius Bertochus of Bologna in 1496. The 300-page volume had been rebound using the original wooden covers. There were a few wormholes and a few pages missing. No one could guess how it had come there. *Harrisburg Patriot*, January 1 and March 22, 1986.

**Rent-a-read.** Bibliophiles in Ulm, Germany, who wish to give their personal libraries that enviable "well-read" look can hire a professional "reader," who will turn down corners, leave theatre and cinema tickets as bookmarks, make marginal notations, and underline significant passages. Prices are assessed according to quantity of books and Behandlungsintensität, a useful word meaning roughly "degree of intensity of handling." *Manchester Guardian*, August 8, 1992.

**The Kirchentellinsfurt Syndrome.** Contributed by Nigel Pennick. The recent expansion of copyright protection in British courts might be seen as a petty and mean way of squeezing more money from a captive audience. But its implications are far greater than mere greed. It could give muscle to the Kirchentellinsfurt Syndrome. This is the insidious process of removing from museums all those objects that in some way challenge the status quo, leaving only those artifacts, specimens, and works of art approved of by the proprietors or that reinforce their world-view. The "offending" objects are hidden away and eventually forgotten or destroyed. In this manner, everything left on display in the museum is reduced to a carefully controlled spectacle.

The syndrome is named after a German museum which epitomizes the phenomenon. The schloss at Kirchentellinsfurt, near Baden-Württemberg, once possessed a wonderful "Cabinet of Curiosities" of more than 80,000 weird and wonderful items: mutant animals, the staves of cunning men, mummified rats, magical objects, alrauns, odd stones, and other undefinable things of interest. But when a new curator took over, more than 75,000 priceless and curious objects, many of which had Fortean connotations, were stowed away in packing cases—the intermediate staging point to the trash dump. The removal of all things deemed weird in the new curator's opinion projects a false impression that the world is normal, all is known, and everything is under control.

**British bibliography.** There follows a gleaning of curious titles from that great happy hunting ground of the bibliomaniac, *The British Library Catalogue of Printed Books to 1975*. Contributed by Paul Sieveking.

**BETHELL** (A. J.) — From Cleopatra to Christ. [Arguing that the former was the latter's mother.] 4 vol. [*London*, 1921.] fol. *Typewritten.*

**BUM,** ANTON — Handbuch der Massage und Heilgymnastik für praktische Ärtze ... pp. x. 456. *Berlin, Wien; Wien* [printed], 1902. 8°.

**COLES** (RICHARD BERTRAM) and **KINMONT** (PATRICK DAVID CLIFFORD) — Skin Diseases for Beginners, *etc.* pp.43 *H.K. Lewis & Co.: London*, 1957. 8°.

**COLLINS** (SEWELL) — The Rubáiyát of a Scotch Terrier ... With drawings by the author. *Grant Richards: London*, 1926. 8°.

**EDISON PORTLAND CEMENT COMPANY.** — The Romance of Cement. pp.128 *Livermore & Knight Co.: Providence*, [1926.] 4°.

**EJACULATIONS.** Ejaculations to be used by a Woman during the time of her Labour. *London*, 1853. *a card* 4°.

**F., J. G.** — How I lived on 4 ¾ d. a Day. By a woman who now realizes that she has hitherto eaten too much. (By J.G.F. [i.e. Janetta Griffiths Foulkes.]) pp.11 *Truelove & Bray: London,* [c. 1912.] 8°. *A letter from the Ministry of Food to the author is inserted.*

**FIVE HUNDRED HOUSEHOLD HINTS.** — Five Hundred Household Hints. By 500 Housewives. pp.121 *Country Life: London*, 1926. 8°.

**FOWL DECEIVER.** *See* POOF. The Fowl Deceiver. A lay of the Inventions Exhibition, *etc.* [1885.] 4°.

**FREAKS.** *See* NEW YORK, *City of.—Freaks.*

**GANNETT** (WILLIAM CHANNING) — Blessed Be Drudgery ... With preface by the Countess of Aberdeen. 1897. *See* BOOKS. WORTHY BOOKS. vol.1. 1897, *etc.* 8°.

**HARRIET,** *Aunt.* "Chains for the Neck." A text-book of heavenly truths ... for the young. [Compiled by Aunt Harriet.] *London*, [1867.] 16°.

**10**

HENDY (David Ponting) — Thirty-six reasons for believing in Everlasting Punishment. pp.15  *Marshall Bros.: London; Bishop's Stortford* [printed]. 1887. 8°.

HERNAN (W. J.) — Laundry Lists with detachable counter-checks in French, Spanish, Portuguese, German, Italian, including vocabularies and necessary phrases with phonetic spelling. *Eyre & Spottiswoode: London,* [1909.] fol. *Part of a series entitled: "What you want to say and how to say it."*

HOLYOAKE (George Jacob) — Public Performances of the Dead, *etc. London,* [1865.] 8°.

HOWSON (Geoffrey) — Handbook for the Limbless. Edited by G. Howson. Foreword by John Galsworthy. pp.225 *Disabled Society: London,* [1922.] 8°.

HUTCHINSON (Raymond Charles) — Food for Survival after a Disaster. [With plates.] pp.90 *Melbourne University Press: Carlton,* 1959. 8°.

KUENKEL (Fritz) — Let's be Normal! The psychologist comes to his senses . . . Translated by Eleanore Jensen. pp.299 *Ives Washburn: New York,* 1929. 8°.

KURRENS (Calamus) *pseud.* — Some advice to the people! Be not conceited; beware of humbugs; hate cant; restrain your tongues; amend your ways; and hang together! With sundry other odds and ends of counsel, loosely appended to the second edition of "My Dog Bruce"; in many respects a very irregular poem; by the Rev. C. K. *London,* 1847. 8°.

LEAKE (Frederic) — Historic Bubbles. pp.217 *Suckling & Galloway: London* [*America* printed], 1896. 8°.

OLISAH (Sunday Okenwa) — The way to get money. The best wonderful book for money mongers. By the Master of Life (Okenwa Olisah). *Onitsha: Okenwa Publications,* [1963?]

OMER (Lewis) — Hand Grenade Throwing as a College Sport. pp.9  *A.G. Spalding & Bros.: New York, Chicago,* [1918.] 8°.

Source: Fortean Times, nos. 26 (Summer 1978), 31 (Spring 1980), 39 (Spring 1983), 44 (Summer 1985), 47 (Autumn 1986), 48 (Spring 1987), 49 (Winter 1987), 51 (Winter 1988/89), 52 (Summer 1989), 53 (Winter 1989/90), 62 (April 1992), and 66 (December 1992/January 1993). The editors can be reached at Box 2409, London NW5 4NP, England; e-mail: bobr@forteana.win-uk.net. U.S. subscriptions are handled by Fenner, Reed & Jackson, P.O. Box 754, Manhasset, NY 11030. Illustrations by Hunt Emerson.

# Beasts in the library

### by Nouleigh Rhee Furbished

EXCEPT FOR THE FEW LIBRARIANS and libraries that proudly boast of library cats, and may even belong to the Library Cat Society (P.O. Box 274, Moorhead, MN 56560), libraries have not been particularly hospitable to the presence of animals, pigeons, or other creatures on or about their premises. Creative suggestions for the appropriate use of our fellow creatures in libraries have, in a few cases, offered a picture of what life in libraryland might be like if we were more sympathetic, or at least less hostile, to other forms of life in our work environment—especially in terms of their ability to help protect our collections.

### The British Museum

One of the few true stories that deals with the protective role of animals in the library was originally told by Ernest Rhys in his autobiography and then retold by Barbara McCrimmon in *Richard Garnett*, her biography of that distinguished Librarian of the British Museum. One day Rhys was startled when a mouse darted between his feet while he was using the catalogue at the British Museum. Seeing Dr. Garnett nearby, Rhys reproached him. Garnett slyly replied, "Do you know we were much troubled by mice last autumn. They infested what we sometimes call the catacombs downstairs and nibbled the bindings of the great old tomes in calf. So we decided to get a pussy. Well, we got a tomcat, and one day a reader went downstairs to look up one of the big folios, pulled it out from its place, and pussy on the lookout for mice went through the gap behind the books. The readers presently replaced the big folio without noticing what had happened, and some months later it was decided to clean out the shelves down there and, lo and behold, at the back of the lowest shelf was found a skeleton. You see, the mice had eaten poor pussy." Perhaps the ignominious failure of that experiment served to impede our further efforts to use animals in libraries to supplement overworked and underpaid staff.

## Buchstickumhunds

Charles Wegener, a distinguished faculty member at the University of Chicago, has suggested an alternative approach to protecting that library's collections with the use of dogs. A brief story in the University of Chicago *Maroon* for April 1, 1981, attributed to N. Crymon, announced "Library Adopts Draconian Security Measures." In that tale Hooper Draco, newly appointed associate director for security and information control, described his discovery of the dogs. "What dogs, we asked. 'Nice little  dogs—the Buckstickumhund, you know. Quiet little animals, look a bit like the giant Sumatran rat, have a nose for thirty-five different kinds of binding glue. They'll sit at the control desk and sniff out smugglers. It's a little unfortunate, public-wise, that they were bred by the Gestapo for finding readers—but it isn't fair to hold that against the pooch.' We asked about expense. 'Oh no, cheapest thing we could do. Only need three of them; great stamina, work seven shifts on a bone and a couple of doggy vitamins. Of course we may have a problem with students trying to feed them—make friends you know, and sneak out a codex or two while the dog is licking his chops—or her chops I should say, mostly the best of them are bitches. They make lovely pets when off duty, so to speak; we've arranged for them to live in with a sociologist and a chemist—had to find homes without any books, of course, so as not to distract the dogs.'" Alas, the Buckstickumhunds seem to have quietly disappeared from the scene.

## Cockroaches

Efforts to control the spread of food and drink in libraries, a largely unsuccessful battle fought mainly against student users of academic libraries, often focus on another aspect of protecting and preserving library collections. One poster campaign succinctly describes why eating and drinking are forbidden in the library: "Residue from food and drink attracts cockroaches, silverfish, rodents, and other pests that feed on books and paper, thus endangering the research collections. Insect and rodent infestations also make it unpleasant to work and study in library buildings."

A short poem by Art Waugh in the April 1979 issue of *Top of the Stacks*, the newsletter of the Florida International University Library, graphically de-

10

scribes one not entirely satisfactory approach to cockroach control in the tropical climate of the south where those beasts thrive.

### Euthanasia

I surprised
gargantuan roach
with Raid

which drove him
to running insane
around the [library]

moments before
I philosophically
squashed him.

But Raid and other chemical products are no longer to our liking. The same sign that describes the evil creatures that food attracts reminds users that the only means of ensuring a pest-free environment is regular fumigation that, in turn, is itself highly undesirable because of the potential health risks associated with the use of toxic chemicals. Animal activists might object to Waugh's approach of simply squashing cockroaches.

## Geckos

Still many libraries, especially those in warmer climates and/or those where the food and drink battle is being lost, remain infested with cockroaches and other equally undesirable creatures. What is to be done?

A story in the November 12, 1990, *New York Times* at first glance, seems to offer a new alternative. It described how geckos, small nocturnal lizards from Southeast Asia, as natural predators of cockroaches have been snapped up— so to speak—for just that purpose by many people. A Tokay gecko, the most popular of the lot, that costs between $15 and $25 may consume up to 200 cockroaches a day. That works out to $.000034 per cockroach over the first year which is a true bargain since a gecko's lifespan typically exceeds one year.

The appearance of that story quickly came to the attention of the library and preservation community. Within a day of its appearance, Shard Frackenthal suggested that geckos might indeed control the cockroach problem in libraries but that substantial questions such as the gecko's appetite for binding cloths, glues, and paper as well as the long-term effects of library dust on gecko breeding patterns needed further study. Almost instantaneously, the University Library Planning Discussion electronic bulletin board (libpln-l@qucdn.bitnet) took up the cry as part of its continuing discussion of the food and drink problem in libraries. The hunt was on.

One respondent reported that a similar story on the Cable News Network (CNN) had indicated that the use of geckos in warehouses to control cockroaches had been so successful that the owners had, in turn, to buy cockroaches to feed the geckos. Another worried about the quantity of gecko droppings, and the damage they might do, and asked if they could be trained to use a litter box. He had probably not seen the article, "The Defecatory Consequence of Warm-Bloodedness in Dinosaurs," by C. Richard Tracy and Judith Sugar in *The Journal of Irreproducible Results* 35 (November/December 1990): 24–25, that, indirectly, provides a great deal of useful information on the relatively small quantity of droppings produced by lizards. That same respondent also wondered about what the institution's liability might be if a reader were to suffer a heart attack when approached by a gecko in the stacks. A larger problem was identified by a respondent who thought it might be best to purchase only geckos of the same sex to avoid establishing a gecko colony that might eventually overrun the library or, worse yet, simply die out after consuming all of the cockroaches. Did, someone else asked, dead geckos attract more cockroaches? If not, perhaps, vultures?

Finally, of course, there is the inevitable problem of escalation in the food chain. What happens when the geckos get out of control? Do you illegally import mongooses to control the geckos? If you do you might, incidentally, destroy your chance of ever being appointed Librarian of Congress. In any case, you might then have to find a fiercer predator to control the mongooses. Before you know it you have to hire Arnold Schwarzenegger as Associate Director for Security and Predator Control along with his Buchstickumhunds. There go your savings!

It's cheaper, in the long run, to forget the geckos. Besides, what purchasing agent, especially in a public institution, is going to approve a purchase order from the library for geckos? Either ban food and drink, fumigate periodically, or learn to live with and love the cockroaches. Perhaps, with some thought, they can be trained to perform a useful library service.

*Source:* The author is preservation officer at the Molesworth Institute and, as such, is heavily influenced by the philosophy of Norman Stevens.

# Ten commandments for borrowers of books

### by Henry T. Coutts

"Who goeth a-borrowing goeth a-sorrowing"

1. Thou shalt not buy what thou canst borrow.
2. Thou shalt take care of thine own books, for thy babies and thy puppies will find as much delight in borrowed books as playthings.
3. Thou shalt not cut the leaves of a book with a butter-knife, nor decorate the margins with jam in imitation of the old illuminated manuscripts.
4. Remember that the most artistic form of appreciation is to repair the torn leaves of a book with postage-stamp edging, and to arrange the red and green lines alternately.
5. Honor the opinions of an author as expressed in his book, but shouldst thou disagree with his views, pencil thine own notes in the margins. By so doing thou wilt not only give evidence of thy vast learning, but will irritate subsequent readers who will, unmindful of thy superior knowledge, regard thee as a conceited ass.
6. Thou shalt choose thy books from amongst those most worn. Shouldst thou be dissatisfied with their contents thou wilt have the pleasure of knowing that many of thy neighbors have been "had" likewise.
7. Thou shalt consult the librarian when thou knowest not what thou requirest. Should he be unable to assist thee, substitute "in" for "con."
8. Thou shalt not pay fines on principle (current cash is much preferred).
9. Thou shalt not bear false witness against the library assistant, saying: "He taketh the best books and reserveth them for his friends."
10. Thou shalt not covet the books that thy neighbor hath appropriated.

10

*Source:* Henry T. Coutts, *Library Jokes and Jottings* (Grafton and Company, 1914).

# The word "library" in 85 different languages

| | | | |
|---|---|---|---|
| Afrikaans | biblioteek | Spanish | biblioteca, fem. |
| Albanian | bibliothekë | Swahili | maktaba |
| Arabic | ḥizâna-t kutub | Swedish | bibliotek, neut. |
| Armenian | qradun | Syrian Arabic | maktabe |
| Baluchi | kytabjah | Tagalog | aklatan |
| Basque | liburutegi | Tahitian | paepae buka |
| Breton | levraoueg, fem. | Tibetan | kun-dga-ra-ba |
| Bulgarian | biblioteka | Turkish | kütüphane |
| Catalan | biblioteca | Ukrainian | biblioteka |
| Cornish | lyverjy,-ow,masc. | Vietnamese | thụ viện |
| Czech | knihovna | Visayan | pamasahonan |
| Danish | bibliotek, neut. | Welsh | llyfrgell |
| Dutch | bibliotheek, com. | Xhosa | indlu yeencwadi |
| Egyptian (ancient) | st n 3š' w | Zulu | iqoqolamabhuku |

—GME

| | |
|---|---|
| Egyptian Arabic | kutubhâna |
| Esperanto | biblioteko |
| Estonian | biblioteek |
| Fijian | vale ni wilīvola |
| Finnish | kirjasto |
| French | bibliothèque, fem. |
| German | Biblioŧhek, fem. |
| Greek | βιβλιοθηκα |
| Hausa | labùrarè, masc. |
| Hawaiian | he waihona puke |
| Hmong | tsev khaws ntawv |
| Hungarian | könyvtár |
| Icelandic | bókasafn, neut. |
| Ido | biblioteko |
| Indonesian | perpustakaan |
| Iraqi Arabic | maktaba |
| Italian | biblioteca, fem. |
| Japanese | toshokan |
| Kikuyu | mabukumongañĩtio gĩkundi |
| Konkani | pustakañsāl,neut. |
| Lao | hohng sai muit |
| Latin | bibliotheca, -ae, fem. |
| Latvian | biblioteka |
| Lithuanian | knygynas |
| Malay | khizanah kitab |
| Marshallese | ḷāibrāre |
| Moroccan Arabic | mektaba |
| Norwegian | bibliotek |
| Polish | biblioteka, fem. |
| Portuguese | biblioteca, fem. |
| Romanian | bibliotecǎ |
| Russian | библиоте, fem. |
| Serbo-Croatian | knjižnica, fem. |
| Slovak | knižnica, fem. |
| Slovenian | knjižnica |

The Rosetta stone.

## But could they shelve?

Persian vizier Abdul Kassem Ismail (938–995) traveled with 400 camels that bore his 117,000-volume library everywhere he went. The animals were trained to walk in an order that ensured the books' alphabetical arrangement.

Source: *Adlibs*, June 1990, Metropolitan Library System of Oklahoma

ቤት ፡ መጻሕፍት **Amharic**

**Khmer** បណ្ណាល័យ

مَكْتَبَة، دارالكُتُب؛ مجموعة
كُتُب؛ سِلْسِلة كُتُب **Arabic**

**Korean** 도서관

*Գրադարան* **Armenian**

**Marathi** ग्रन्थालय

পুস্তকসমূহ **Bengali**

**Persian** مجموعهٔ کتاب ـ

စာကြည့်တိုက် **Burmese**

**Punjabi** ਲਾਇਬ੍ਰੇਰੀ

大学图书馆 **Chinese** 图书馆

𓉘𓏲𓏭𓏤 **Egyptian**

**Sanskrit** पुस्तकसङ्ग्रह

પુસ્તકાલય **Gujarati**

**Sindhi** لائبريري

סִפְרִיָּה **Hebrew**

**Tamil** புத்தகசாலை

पुस्तक संग्रह **Hindi**

**Thai** ห้องสมุด

Leabarlann **Irish**

ביבליאָטע'ק **Yiddish**

大学図書館 **Japanese**

10

# Worst serial title changes, 1991–1994

## 1994

### Here's Looking at You Award

To the *Journal of Refractive and Corneal Surgery*, for changing from the *Journal of Refractive Surgery*, and *Refractive and Corneal Surgery;* and then combining the two into the current title. This title has left many medical librarians searching for a pair of trifocals.

### Honorary "Greased Pig"Award

While at Annual Conference in Miami Beach on the beautiful Atlantic Ocean, we can not neglect *Atlantic Monthly* for their inability to get a handle on their title. *Atlantic Monthly* has dropped "monthly" twice in its long history, for a total of five title changes. We're hoping that they don't move to San Francisco—we'd hate to see what they'd do with the Pacific.

### Give the Kids a Chance Award (aka Give the Librarians a Chance Award)

Two journals have the honor of sharing an award this year: *Archives of Pediatrics and Adolescent Medicine* (formerly *American Journal of Diseases of Children*) and *Journal of Child and Adolescent Psychiatric Nursing* (formerly *Journal of Child and Adolescent Psychiatric and Mental Health Nursing*).

### Shockingly High Frequency Award

We would like to honor the Institution of Electrical Engineers for 11 separate title changes during 1994. Unfortunately, we are sure they will continue shocking us with future changes.

### Students Choice Award

To the student newspaper at Louisiana State University. The title began as *The Almagest*, changed to *The Sentinel* from November 1993 to April 1994, and after a student poll changed back to *The Almagest*. So who says we're the only ones that care about title changes?

### The Incredible Shrinking Title Award

To *Public Utilities Reports Fortnightly*, which became *Public Utilities Fortnightly* and has now been downsized to *Fortnightly*. Anything smaller and it just might disappear entirely.

### Award of Distinction

To the *Journal of Scholarly Publishing*. According to the publishers, "Not every change we've introduced will seem an improvement to everyone" (we agree) and "we hope that through the *spirit* with which *Scholarly Publishing* was founded will be a constant, connecting the journal's past with its future." Unless of course, you shelve by title, and then never the two shall meet.

### Short-Term Title Award

With the topic of health care leading everyone's agenda, we are proud to present the *PRIDE Institute Journal of Long Term Home Health Care*, now known as *The Journal of Long Term Home Health Care: The PRIDE Institute Journal*.

### Too Many Changes Are Hazardous to a Serials Librarian's Health Award

In clear violation of this warning the Pennsylvania Department of Health has presented us with *Health Risk Behaviors of Pennsylvania Adults, Behavioral Health Risks of Pennsylvania Adults, Health Risks of Pennsylvania Adults*, and finally, *Behavioral Health Risks of Pennsylvania Adults*.

### Sorely Needed Change Award

Lest you think all we do is criticize, we want to thank *Advances in Wound*

*Care,* formerly *Decubitus,* for healing the wounds of incomprehensible title changes.

### Snake in the Grass Award

To the *Journal of Interlibrary Loan, Document Delivery and Information Supply,* formerly the *Journal of Interlibrary Loan,* for borrowing bad publication practices and delivering unnecessary title changes.

### Worst Serial Title Change of 1994

To *Barron's* for returning to its original title after a brief 52-year experiment as *Barron's National Business and Financial Weekly.* After 52 years, couldn't they have waited for a new volume to make the change?

# 1993

### No-Nonsense Award

To *Brain, Mind and Common Sense.* Over the last few years this title changed from *Brain Mind Bulletin* to, most recently, the *New Sense Bulletin.* In selecting an appropriate award for this title, we also considered the "NuisanceAward."

### Too Many Pralines Award

Presented with pride to the *Journal of Diabetic Complications* for making the daring move to the new title *Journal of Diabetes and Its Complications.* Thank you for not complicating matters more by changing the numbering as well.

### Bourbon Street Award

Reserved for *Applause/Best Plays Theater Yearbook of . . . ,* which recently changed from the *Burns Mantle Theatre Yearbook of . . . ,* after it had already changed titles *five* times before with equally entertaining and significant changes.

### Muddy Waters Award

In honor of the Mississippi Delta blues great Muddy Waters, this award goes to *Piano & Keyboard, the Bimonthly Piano Quarterly.* The publisher changed this title from the more distinguished *Piano Quarterly* in order to publish more issues per year—too bad it wasn't done more clearly.

### New World Order Award

To *Country Reports,* for all of its changes this last year due to the changing world around them. Let's hope they can keep the countries in the *same* order from one issue to the next, which appears to be a problem for them now.

### Long Overdue Award

To *OCLC Systems and Services* (published by Meckler) for changing from *OCLC Micro,* reflecting the need of OCLC users to talk about more than just their micros.

### Hands Across the Sea Award

Bestowed upon the *European Journal of Cancer* for two reasons—one being that it's European and "across the sea," of course. The other is what prompted the nomination, which came to us from a library in Geneva, Switzerland. This fine journal split into two sections (after only recently appearing to have changed its title to *EJC* ), one of which is simply called "Part A." Very distinctive, Part A.

10

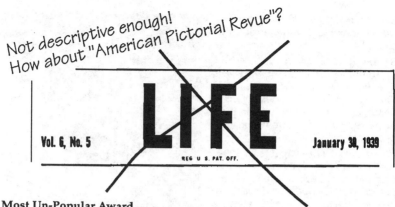

Not descriptive enough!
How about "American Pictorial Revue"?

LIFE

Vol. 6, No. 5

REG U S. PAT. OFF.

January 30, 1939

### Most Un-Popular Award

To *Popular Photography* for suddenly changing its numbering system from vol. 100, no. 4 (April 1993), to vol. 51, no. 1, with the May 1993 issue. All this grief for us and our patrons just so they could reflect the number of years of publication in their numbering. Thank you, Ziff-Davis. We are not amused.

### Inadvertent Snake in the Grass Award

We usually have a Snake in the Grass Award, but this year we must alter it to bestow this upon *JASIS*, whose editor wrote to us to note a typographical error and save us from title change misery. He also asked that we not give him the Snake in the Grass Award, so we didn't. We thank you and honor you with this special award, Donald Kraft, editor of *JASIS*. At least *you* care!

### Worst Serial Title Change of 1993

To *Broadcasting and Cable Yearbook*. Bowker has had this title for two years and has already published it under two different titles: the above and *Broadcasting and Cable Marketplace*. For a publication that has had more title changes than we care to discuss, we ask Bowker to pick one and stick with it, *please!* The Title Change Police *will* be watching!

## 1992

### Frequent Offenders Award

To Prentice Hall for changing *Lawyer's Weekly Report* to *Lawyer's Tax Weekly* in August 1991 and then to *Tax Advisor's Letter* in February 1992. Warning: the next time it will be Alcatraz.

### It Should Be Miller Time Award

In recognition that ALA is about to begin the "Marilyn Miller Reign," this award goes to Harcourt Brace Jovanovich for changing *Millers Comprehensive GAAP Guide* to *HBJ Miller Comprehensive GAAP Guide*.

### Schizophrenia Award

To *Progress in Experimental Personality Research*, which changed to *Progress in Experimental Personality & Psychopathology Research*. We hope it doesn't split next.

### Golden Gate Bridge Award

For the title changes from *Engineering Issues* to *Issues in Engineering* to *Journal of Professional Issues in Engineering*, and finally *Journal of Professional Issues in Engineering Education and Practice*, this award goes to the American Society of Civil Engineers with the suggestion that they exercise some quality control and build a permanent title.

### Mixed Metamorphosis Award

To *American Journal of Anatomy* for changing a distinctive title that had survived 91 years to *Developmental Dynamics,* a vague, "lost in the fog" kind of title.

### Prima Donna Award

To the Kiplinger Washington Agency for taking the widely known title *Changing Times* and changing it to *Kiplinger's Personal Finance Magazine.* We wonder if new yuppie subscriptions can possibly make up for the loss in recognition and revenue at newsstands.

### Pinnacle Award

From the country that has *the* Library Association comes a title change worthy of a Hands Across the Sea Award. To Times Newspapers Ltd. for changing its 20-year-old title *The Times Higher Education Supplement* to simply *The Higher,* the Pinnacle Award honors ultimate silliness.

### Phoenix from the Ashes, or the Politically Correct Award

To *The Bureaucrat* for its change to *Public Manager.* But remember, old bureaucrats never die—they are just reborn with new titles.

### Lifetime Achievement Award (the first!)

To IEEE for numerous silly and unnecessary title changes, resulting in repeated nominations over many years, and in recognition of this year's nominee, the change from *IEEE LCS* to *IEEE LTS.* What an honor!

### Special Recognition

To the publishers of *In Health,* who promised that the most recent title change to *Health* was the last we would see. Alice Stanglin of Richland College Library was so moved that she submitted "A Periodical Clerk's Lament" or "Magazine Hades (I would say Hell but I'm too much of a lady)."

> Woe unto me and woe unto you
> Our *Health* is gone and our *In Health* too!
> For *Health* has been bought by *In Health* you see
> (Remember, it's the former *Hippocrates!*)
> But the *Health* that we had is really no more
> And our *In Health* too is really out of the door!
> 'Cause a new *Health* is here to replace the old
> But it's really *In Health* if the story be told!
> If by now you're thinking your "health" is not normal
> The attached letters prove that and make it all formal!

### Snake in the Grass Award

To the Maine State Library, the Maine Library Association, and the Maine Educational Media Association for their joint responsibility for a sequence of title changes the Awards Committee characterized as "a serial librarian's nightmare." Beginning in 1991, *Downeast Libraries* changed three times to *Downeast Libraries & Mediacy, Maine-ly Libraries,* and finally, *The Maine Entry.*

### Worst Publisher of the Year Award

To Tolley's Publishing for apparently working through the list of titles they issue and adding Tolley's to each of them, as in *Tolley's Journal of Child Law, Tolley's Journal of Media Law and Practice,* etc., etc.

### Worst Serial Title Change of 1992

To Rohrich Press of Akron, Ohio, for changing the *Blue Book of Sr. College, University and Junior and Community College Athletics* to *Blue Book of College Athletics for Senior, Junior & Community Colleges,* its third title change in four years. All of the changes have simply "stir-fried" the same seven or eight words (senior, junior, college, community, blue book and athletics) into new and different "winning" combinations.

10

## 1991

As we enter the 1990s, we would like to repeat Mrs. Eleanor Mitchell's "Lullaby for Little Periodicals":

Dear Periodicals be still,
Don't change your names again until
I've made your latest names all clear.
Couldn't you wait at least a year?

Dear little quarterlies be good.
If you must change your size you should
Give the matter a lot of thought
So that you'll look the way you ought.

Little Weeklies just you rest,
Staying the way you are is best.
If you must change to Monthlies, then
Don't change back to Weeklies again.

Just you be tranquil little pets.
Just be good; don't cause regrets.
Oh, my darlings, great and small,
I would like to suspend you all.

### Snake in the Grass Award

As if it wasn't bad enough when the *RTSD Newsletter* changed to the *ALCTS Newsletter*, this year *American Libraries* decided to upgrade their cover image by removing the volume number and the ISSN, thus endearing themselves once again to serial librarians and check-in staff everywhere across America.

### Eager Beaver Award

To the Optical Society of America for changing *Optics News* to *Optics and Photonics News*. As one member explained: ". . . the word 'Photonics' was scribbled in . . . by some eager beaver who did not even consult the advisory committee or its chairperson." Not knowing how to undo the numbering change as the new title started with volume 1, the Society has, fortunately, decided to let the title change stand.

### Gone with the Wind Award

To Family Media Inc., publishers of *Science Digest*, who chose not to honor the old tradition of "if it ain't broke, don't fix it" and instead fell prey to the yuppie trend, improving their title to *Breakthroughs*.

### Udderly Ridiculous Award

To Coulter Publishing Co. for changing *Dairy Field* to *Dairy Field Today* and back to *Dairy Field*. Ice scream, you scream, we all scream at the *Dairy Field* publishers.

### You Are Special Award

To all publishers of special issues and especially those who give them seasonal dates, we hereby present the Fred Rogers of PBS "You Are Special Award." OK, publishers, can you spell special? What does special mean and how special can something that comes out regularly really be?

### Look Before You Leap, and Hands Across the Water Awards

In 1990, the *British Journal of Experimental Pathology*, after 70 years of publication, wanted to shed its British image. It thereby changed its name to *Journal of Experimental Pathology*. After publishing three issues under this new name, it realized that there already was a periodical with the same name. It then hastily changed its name to *International Journal of Experimental Pathol-*

*ogy.* In recognition of its efforts, Blackwell Scientific Publications is presented with this dual honor.

**Visionary Award**

To Academic Press. In 1983, *Computer Graphics and Image Processing* changed its title to *Computer Vision, Graphics, and Image Processing.* This change gave a futuristic vision to the publication. In 1990, the journal split to form two new titles: *Computer Vision, Graphics, and Image Processing: Image Understanding* and *Computer Vision, Graphics, and Image Processing: Graphical Models and Image Processing.* What we thought was improvement of vision in 1983 turned out to be double vision problems in 1990. Hopefully this myopia will end soon.

**We No Longer DO Maintenance Award**

To Madisen Publication Division for changing *Park Maintenance and Grounds Management* to *Park and Grounds Management.*

**Worst Serial Title Change of 1991**

To the Foundation Center for *Grants for International and Foreign Programs,* which flip-flopped to *Grants for Foreign and International Programs* for no other reason than to make it impossible to shelve for those of us who shelve alphabetically.

*Source:* ALA Association for Library Collections and Technical Services.

# Famous librarians' favorite books

**WHAT DO PROMINENT LIBRARIANS** have to say about their favorite books? In 1994 a second group of library leaders was polled on their preferences (supplementing the choices of those surveyed in 1990 for the first edition of *The Whole Library Handbook*)—publications that have given them great enjoyment or have significantly affected their professional or personal lives and philosophies. We defined the term "book" as loosely as possible, so that they could have the widest latitude to include such widely disparate media as 15th-century incunabula, nonbook materials, Ph.D. dissertations, oral histories, dramatic performances, or entire runs of periodicals. Here are the results, in their own words.—*GME.*

**LARRY X. BESANT,** Director of Libraries, Morehead State University, Morehead, Ky.

1. Plato, *The Republic* (ca. 380 B.C.). I had the good fortune to study *The Republic* just before library school. Two questions remain: Could the allegory of the Cave (Book VII) refer to library science? And what the heck is a "uniform entry"?

2. Philip Wylie's books and stories, especially *A Generation of Vipers* (1942).

3. Lecomte de Nouy, *Human Destiny* (1947). I still quote his theory of early education to my children and grandchildren.

4. Thornton Wilder, *The Bridge of San Luis Rey* (1927).

5. *Chemical Abstracts* (1907–   ) and all the other abstracting and indexing services. Their metamorphosis from paper journals to fancy database businesses mirrors the evolution of American librarianship.

6. Everything by and about Jack London. I began my collection at the urging of friend and mentor Hugh Atkinson. He believed that librarians who collected books were better for it and kept them from going nuts.

7. *Worm Runners Digest.* Check it out.

8. Gene Fowler's biographies and novels. If you've never heard of him, start with his autobiography, *A Solo in Tom-Toms* (1946).

**10**

9. *The Houston Post Stylebook* (1963), written by the *Post's* resident genius of the day, Hubert Mewhinney, who also wrote *A Manual for Neanderthals.* We need a similar stylebook for the Internet.

**HIRAM L. DAVIS,** Deputy Librarian of Congress.

1. Robert A. Bone, *The Negro Novel in America* (1968). Pointed me to a body of unknown literature and served as a counterpoint to my English major.

2. *Bottom Line Personal Newsletter,* bimonthly, edited by Martin Edelston, New York. Excellent for keeping up to date on a broad range of topics.

3. *Communication Briefings Newsletter,* monthly, edited by Encoders, Inc., N.J. Must reading for anyone who must achieve results by working through others.

4. John J. Gabarro, *The Dynamics of Taking Charge* (1987). Helped me to understand the process of influencing people and achieving results.

5. Edward Gross and Paul V. Grambsch, *University Goals and Academic Power* (1968). Not widely read by many administrators, but it provided the theoretical model for my doctoral dissertation (not widely read either).

6. E. J. Josey, *What Black Librarians Are Saying* (1972). As an African American, this book helped me to connect with librarianship in my early years.

7. Douglas J. MacGregor, *The Human Side of Enterprise: 25th Anniversary Printing* (1985). Helped to shape my style of management. I re-read it often.

8. Gerard I. Nierenberg, *Fundamentals of Negotiating* (1973). Provided a name and context for what I was or should have been doing and how to do it more effectively. A continually useful source.

9. Margaret J. Wheatly, *Leadership and the New Science* (1993). Changed my perception of management and brought me into the 21st century.

10. *Three Negro Classics* (1965), which included Booker T. Washington's *Up from Slavery* (1901), W. E. B. Du Bois's *The Souls of Black Folk* (1903), and James Weldon Johnson's *The Autobiography of an Ex-Colored Man* (1912). I am only now beginning to appreciate the profound influence that this single volume had in instilling in me the values of self-worth and determination.

**CAROL HENDERSON,** Director, ALA Washington Office.

1. Conrad Richter, *The Trees* (1940). The first of a trilogy of novels that gave me a vivid sense of what my home state of Ohio was like when the first settlers crossed the Ohio River.

2. Laura Ingalls Wilder, *Little House on the Prairie* (1935). This book and others in the series have wonderful family associations because they held my daughters (and husband) enthralled during read-aloud sessions on long car trips to visit relatives in Ohio.

3. Joanna L. Stratton, *Pioneer Women: Voices from the Kansas Frontier* (1981). This book was a gift from my mother and left us both in awe of what my great-grandmother endured as a settler in the Kansas-Nebraska territory.

4. Percy Bysshe Shelley, "Ozymandias" (1818). A perfect poem that still has the power to elicit shivers.

5. Elizabeth W. Stone, *American Library Development: 1600–1899* (1977). I was impressed by the sweep of this chronology when I was in library school. Many Catholic University students contributed to the work and Betty Stone used it in her teaching.

6. Clifford A. Lynch, *Accessibility and Integrity of Networked Information Collections* (contract background paper BP-TCT-109, for the U.S. Office of Technology Assessment's Telecommunication and Computing Assessment Program, 1993). An excellent summary and discussion of policy issues—I always find Cliff helpful on technology policy.

7. Fred W. Weingarten, "NREN and the National Infrastructure: Policy Decisions for Libraries," in *Principles for the Development of the National Information Infrastructure,* proceedings of the ALA Telecommunications and Infor-

mation Infrastructure Policy Forum, September 8–10, 1993. A commissioned background paper by a technology policy wonk who writes with clarity and creativity.

8. *ALA Washington Newsletter* and *ALA Washington Newsline* (ALAWON). Ongoing print and electronic publications of the ALA Washington Office. These are so much a part of my life that no such list would be complete without them!

**BEVERLY P. LYNCH**, Dean and Professor, UCLA Graduate School of Library and Information Science, Los Angeles, Calif.

1. *The A.M.C. White Mountain Guide: A Guide to Trails in the Mountains of New Hampshire* (Boston: AMC, in continuously revised editions). This guide remains the model against which I measure all other trail guides. Without it I would never have hiked in these wonderful mountains.

2. *Blueprints for Modern Living: History and Legacy of the Case Study Houses*, catalog of an exhibition at the Museum of Contemporary Art, Los Angeles (MIT Press, 1989). This exhibit portrayed one of Southern California's major contributions to architecture. The catalog includes photographs and architectural drawings, and provides an excellent description of this program.

3. Bernard DeVoto, *The Year of Decision 1846* (1961 ed.). With an introductory essay on the author by Catherine Drinker Bowen.

4. Antonio Frasconi, *Known Fables* (1964). This, my first Frasconi book, started me on my Frasconi collection.

5. John Milton, *Paradise Lost* (1667). I go back time and again to this poem, particularly to Milton's portrayal of Eve.

6. Charles Perrow, *Complex Organizations: A Critical Essay* (1972). I was a student of Perrow's when he was writing this book. More than any other sociologist, he has influenced my thinking about organizations.

7. Dorothy Sayers, *The Nine Tailors* (1934). But all of her Lord Peter Wimsey mysteries are favorites of mine. Wimsey is a great English character, and one of my favorite detectives.

8. William Landram Williamson, *William Frederick Poole and the Modern Library Movement* (1963). Williamson's biography of Poole introduced me to one of the giants of librarianship, and provided the model I was seeking of excellent research and fine writing in librarianship.

9. James Q. Wilson, *Bureaucracy* (1989). Wilson's book was one of the texts I used in the 1993 UCLA Senior Fellows program. The fellows (who, I am told, read it to each other while at the beach!) found it as important as I did in furthering our understanding of libraries as organizations.

10. William Butler Yeats, *Collected Poems* (definitive edition, with author's final revisions, Macmillan, 1958). In 1961 I made a pilgrimage to Yeats's grave in Drumcliff churchyard. On his tombstone, at his command, was inscribed:

> Cast a cold eye
> On life, on death.
> Horseman, pass by!

(From "Under Ben Bulben," 1938)

**JAMES RETTIG**, Assistant Dean of University Libraries for Reference and Information Services, College of William and Mary, Williamsburg, Va.

1. Carl Sandburg, *Chicago Poems* (1916). What Chicago native does not respond instinctively to these immemorial opening words of Sandburg's "Chicago"?

> Hog Butcher for the World,
> Tool Maker, Stacker of Wheat,
> Player with Railroads and the Nation's Freight Handler;
> Stormy, husky, brawling,
> City of the Big Shoulders.

10

Despite being more than 50 years old at the time, *Chicago Poems* vividly captured the reality of that vibrant American city and ignited a high school junior's love of literature that still burns with a "hard, gemlike flame." Friends at the time surely tired of my recitations of passages from this slim volume and the prairie poet's *Complete Poems*, but I still read them with enjoyment.

2. F. Scott Fitzgerald, *This Side of Paradise* (1920). I still remember the early autumn evening when I came upon this in a used book shop in downtown Milwaukee. A college freshman at the time, I read this through in one sitting, fascinated by undergraduate protagonist Amory Blaine. Thank goodness the infatuation passed and I soon matured more than poor Amory, trapped in his fictional universe! Nevertheless, several years ago when strolling for the first time across the enchanting, fairy tale-like Princeton campus haunted by Fitzgerald, I recalled the final passage and, in spontaneous tribute to Amory, recited it:

> He stretched out his arms to the crystalline, radiant sky.
> "I know myself," he cried, "but that is all."

3. William Shakespeare, *Sonnets* (1609). Who cares about the controversies about the identity of Mr. W.H.? Who cares about the authorship claims on behalf of Bacon and others? The sonnets are English poetry at its most sublime. Sonnet 116 read by a friend at my wedding supplemented the Scripture readings and helped place a personal stamp on a beautiful ceremony and celebration.

> "If this be error and upon me proved,
> I never writ, nor no man ever loved."

4. Thomas Merton, *The Seven Storey Mountain* (1948). Another of Merton's books, *Faith and Violence*, appeared as a required text on a course syllabus during my sophomore year in college. I responded to his strong voice, was hooked, and next read his pious, somewhat prim but authentic autobiography, *The Seven Storey Mountain*; and since then I have read many more of his books. Despite the flaws of that autobiography, in it and in all of Merton's other writings his unwavering search for God's will in his life shines through brightly, even in his darkest moments. His brave quest stands as an example worthy of emulation and his unreserved self-disclosure of his extraordinary spiritual life makes him one of this century's few genuine heroes.

5. James A. H. Murray, et al., editors, *The Oxford English Dictionary* (1888–1928). Since my early teen years I have carried on a never-ending, sometimes tempestuous romance with words and the English language. English can be a cruel, taunting lover when the words just won't trip off the tip of one's fingers onto the computer screen; English can also give feelings of unalloyed ecstasy when one finds the *mot juste* (a term sufficiently anglicized that it

appears in the *OED*) and conveys a thought or feeling with crystalline clarity or palpable immediacy. And all of these words and innumerable more to explore in the future are in the bountiful *OED*, now more enticing than ever on CD-ROM.

6. James Beard, *The James Beard Cookbook* (1959). A gift from my mother when I was a college student moving into a typical student apartment, this paperback, redolent with possibilities far exceeding my culinary talents at the time and now yellowed with age and use, was my first cookbook. I have acquired dozens more since, some with a more health- and weight-conscious approach than the rotund gourmand took several decades ago,

but when I bake brownies from scratch, I still turn to his sinfully rich recipe for the chewiest, choclatiest brownies I have ever tasted.

7. James Joyce, *Ulysses* (1922). No other book so artfully, so deftly, so seductively, so maddeningly weaves webs of words to capture and convey "the incredible modality of the visible," "the ineluctible modality of the audible," and more through the lives of Leopold Bloom and others on a single day in Dublin. I am far from being the perfect reader Joyce envisioned—an insomniac who reads nothing but Joyce; but during my last semester in college and the next year in graduate school I was immersed in Joyce, particularly in *Ulysses*, under the tutelage of a wise, witty professor who did approximate Joyce's ideal reader. ". . . and yes I said yes I will Yes."

8. S. R. Ranganathan, *The Five Laws of Library Science* (1931). Frances Neel Cheney has called him "the sainted Ranganathan." Indeed, and one who through his prophetic five laws—that like all true prophecies, are ever renewed and ever deepened in meaning even as times change—should inspire every reference librarian. When I was head of the reference department at the University of Illinois at Chicago, Beverly Lynch once called the reference desk and asked one of the reference librarians to look up Ranganathan's Five Laws. She didn't have to look it up: I had talked about the Five Laws so much that everyone in the department knew them by heart! May every reference librarian ever know them by heart and, more importantly, *take* them to heart!

9. *The Chicago Manual of Style* (14th ed., 1993). As author or editor I often have questions about how best to present a text so that the reader will understand authorial intent as clearly as possible. "Chicago" has come through for me time after time through the three editions I have used, each better than the one before it. True, there are certainly more interesting and more entertaining reference books, but few as useful or indispensable to me.

10. James Rettig, ed., *Distinguished Classics of Reference Publishing* (1992). My pride in this collection of histories of landmark reference works, and my pride in the 31 others who contributed chapters, was confirmed when ALA conferred the G. K. Hall Award for Library Literature on this book. It was a team effort and every coach should be as fortunate as I was to be able to pick his own team and then watch it achieve a level that exceeds one's very high expectations for so very talented an assemblage.

**MARIA B. SALVADORE**, Coordinator, Children's Service, District of Columbia Public Library, Washington, D.C.

1. Maya Angelou, *Wouldn't Take Nothing for My Journey Now* (1993). This personal journey speaks to a wide audience.

2. Dorothy Butler, *Babies Need Books* (1980) and *Cushla and Her Books* (1979). Her lucid writing forcefully describes the power of books.

3. Langston Hughes's poetry (so much and too many titles to list) conveys more than the form would seem to allow.

4. Frances Clark Sayers, *Summoned by Books* (1965). This woman's essays and speeches are as timely today as when they were first written.

5. Maurice Sendak, *Where the Wild Things Are* (1963). Most readers empathize with Max's frustrations in this short, satisfying adventure in pictures and words.

6. E. B. White, *Charlotte's Web* (1952). One of the most powerful and touching novels ever written for any age.

**JOEL SHOEMAKER**, Library Media Specialist, Southeast Junior High School, Iowa City, Ia.

1. Henry David Thoreau, *Walden* (1854). "Do we ride upon the railroad or does it ride upon us?" still seems a seminal thought a quarter century after my first reading it and 140 years after it was written.

10

2. John Steinbeck, *The Winter of Our Discontent* (1961). We all have 'em. Sometimes we get through them.

3. Robert Pirsig, *Zen and the Art of Motorcycle Maintenance* (1974). BMWs, quality, and the human heart illuminated via the open American road.

4. Rex Stout, *The Black Mountain* (1954). Nero must travel to his childhood home in the mountains of Montenegro. Outrageous.

5. J. R. R. Tolkein, *The Hobbit* (1937). Becoming almost scriptural now as I reread it with my own children.

6. David James Duncan, *The River Why* (1983). Coming of age in the Northwest. The most beautiful woman in the world, naked in a tree. That will always stay with me.

7. Richard Wright, *Native Son* (1940). See through Bigger's eyes, walk in his shoes, feel with his heart, get caught up in his despair, *then do something!* Racism must die.

8. Kevin W. Kelly, *The Home Planet* (1988). Get the big picture from those who know first-hand.

9. Larry Watson, *Montana 1948* (1993). My favorite book from last year. Simple, direct, and powerfully evocative of a time, place and ethos.

10. Stewart Brand, ed., *The Last Whole Earth Catalog* (1971). "Access to Tools" could be a subtitle for librarianship, couldn't it?

**NORMAN D. STEVENS**, retired Director, University of Connecticut Library, Storrs.

1. *Punch and Judy*. In my youth, before television, one of my joys was to play with a complete set of Punch and Judy puppets in the attic. It was from that classic puppet-show tale that I first learned that humor can carry with it a message even, at times, a grim one.

2. Stephen W. Meader, *The Long Trains Roll* (1944). It was as a teenager stricken with scarlet fever that I first learned to read. A newly published copy of this classic boy's adventure story, given to me by a rich uncle, set me on the road to reading anything and everything including the adventure, detective, mystery, and spy stories that I still enjoy.

3. Frank R. Stockton, *The Casting Away of Mrs. Locks and Mrs. Aleshine* (1898). In high school a favorite English teacher, who encouraged my reading, recommended this long-forgotten piece of American humor. I remember little about it other than the title but it must have helped shape my interest in humor.

4. Geoffrey Willans and Ronald Searle, *The Compleet Molesworth* (1958). Without their zany tales, which I first read while a Fulbright student in New Zealand in 1954, of Nigel's exploits at St. Custard's, the Molesworth Institute might not exist.

5. Edmund Lester Pearson, "The Librarian," *The Boston Evening Transcript*, March 28, 1906–May 26, 1920. While cultivating my interest in library humor at library school at Rutgers in the mid-1950s, I became acquainted with several of Edmund Lester Pearson's books that included excerpts from his column "The Librarian." That led me to track down and read the column itself that, in turn, shaped my writing style and encouraged me to write library humor.

6. Patrick White, *The Tree of Man* (1956). Family cycle novels, especially those set in Australia, have long had a special fascination for me. White's is one of the best in conveying the message that it is through families that life continues as he concludes "so that, in the end, there was no end."

7. Mark Harris, *Bang the Drum Slowly* (1956). I hope I have learned from this tale of friendship and death, as Henry Wiggen did, to take with me into retirement the idea that "From here on in I rag nobody."

8. David Carroll, *The Year of the Turtle* (1991). My appreciation of his book led me to a personal friendship, and regular correspondence, with David Carroll. His view of the world around us has helped me to become more appreciative of the natural world.

9. Since I continue to read voraciously, I am leaving room for a book that I have not yet read and that may not yet even have been published.

10. I am not a book collector, but I do collect objects in the shape of books as well as figurines, statues and statuettes, postcards, and other ephemera that depict books and reading. One my favorites is a small German bisque figurine that features a mother dog, with stick in paw, leaning over an open book as she teaches her two puppies to read, or bark, "Wau." It demonstrates the universality of the love of books and reading.

**RUTH TOOR,** Library Media Specialist, Southern Boulevard School, Chatham, N.J.

1. Andre Schwarz-Bart, *The Last of the Just* (1960). I've always been intrigued by the legend of the 36 Just Men.

2. Richard Condon's books. Anything from *The Manchurian Candidate* (1959) on, for his skill in cutting through layers to skewer political chicanery.

3. Pat Conroy, *The Prince of Tides* (1986), for its marvelous use of the English language.

4. Harper Lee, *To Kill a Mockingbird* (1960), for its portrayal of life in the South through the eyes of a child.

5. Richard Wurman, *Information Anxiety* (1989), for its discussion of ways to deal with our changing society.

6. *The New York Times.* Although it has changed much over the years, it is still my number one source for what's happening in the world.

7. John Donne, *Devotions upon Emergent Occasions*, Meditation 17 (1624). The quotation "No man is an island intire of itself . . ." has become my creed.

8. William Steig, *Abel's Island* (1976), or any of his other books, for introducing young readers to beautiful language that they no longer hear outside of the classics.

# Famous music librarians' favorite music

**WHAT DO MUSIC LIBRARIANS** listen to in their leisure moments? Four members of the Music Library Association responded to my request for their favorite recordings, compositions, and genres.—*GME.*

**JEANETTE R. CASEY,** Music Information Center, Chicago Public Library, Chicago, Ill.

1. Abdul Tee-Jay's Rokoto, *Kanka Kura* (Rogue Records FMSD 5018, 1990). Terrific energy and mix of instruments! Sentiment brings me back to this recording as well; I came across it while working with two wonderful people in a music library in Australia.

2. Stephane Grappelli, *Compact Jazz* (MPS 8313702). Always brings a smile. Great for relaxing after a day of nightmare patrons.

3. Vladimir Horowitz, *Horowitz at Home* (Deutsche Grammophon 4277722).

4. Sharon Isbin, Larry Coryell, Laurindo Almeida, *3 Guitars 3* (Pro Arte CDD 235).

5. Richard Strauss, *Four Last Songs* (Anna Tomowa-Sintow, H. von Karajan, Berlin Philharmonic; Deutsche Grammophon 4191882). One of my colleagues put it best: "If this is the last thing I hear before I die, surely I will go straight to heaven!"

6. Giacomo Puccini, *Turandot* (Joan Sutherland, Zubin Mehta, London Philharmonic Orchestra, London 4142742).

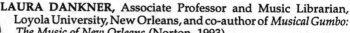

**LAURA DANKNER,** Associate Professor and Music Librarian, Loyola University, New Orleans, and co-author of *Musical Gumbo: The Music of New Orleans* (Norton, 1993).

1. George Gershwin, *Porgy and Bess* (1935). The great American opera, and the Simon Rattle-conducted version starring Willard White and Cynthia Haymon is the definitive performance. As *lagniappe*—as we say "way down yonder"—the work is now available at your local video store as well as in compact disc format. Get both if budget permits.

2. Franz Schubert, *Symphony No. 5* (1816). Especially the first movement, which seems to me the essence of spring, of hopefulness, of youth. The older I get, the more I need those feelings!

3. The Beatles, *Abbey Road* (1969). The famed second side, natch. This will always symbolize the late sixties/early seventies for me. My husband and I played "Here Comes the Sun" on our wedding day.

4. Piotr Ilyich Tchaikovsky, *Romeo and Juliet* (1879). I like my romanticism untainted by Mahleresque cynicism. And the last time that the theme comes back, I always cry.

5. Fats Domino, "Walking to New Orleans" (1960). Had to put at least one "local" down here, or else you'd be disappointed. Seriously, maybe not the finest effort by the Fat Man, but *echt* New Orleans, f'sure.

6. Charles Ives, *Symphony No. 2* (1902). Moving, eclectic, and oh, so American.

**VINCENT PELOTE,** Librarian, Institute of Jazz Studies, Rutgers University, Newark, N.J.

1. All of Louis Armstrong's Hot Five and Hot Seven recordings (1925–28). Armstrong's trumpet playing and singing on these recordings are the embodiment of "hot" jazz. Includes definitive performances of "Heebie Jeebies," "Potato Head Blues," "Struttin' with Some Barbecue," "West End Blues," and other classics.

2. Coleman Hawkins's recordings with the Ramblers, a Dutch swing/dance orchestra, made in the Netherlands on February 4, 1935, August 26, 1935, and April 27, 1937. Tenor sax giant Coleman Hawkins is in excellent form as the featured soloist with this band. Nothing in Hawkins's later discography surpasses his playing on these sides. Performances include "I Wish I Were Twins," "Chicago," "Netcha's Dream," "Original Dixieland One-Step," and others.

3. Fletcher Henderson and His Orchestra's entire output for the Decca label from September 1934. Textbook examples of big band swing before the official start of the "Swing Era." Arrangements are by Fletcher, his brother Horace and Benny Carter. Some numbers like "Wrappin' It Up," "Down South Camp Meeting," and "Big John's Special" were later popularized by Benny Goodman, but these are the definitive interpretations.

4. Anything by alto saxophonist Charlie "Yardbird" Parker.

5. Benny Carter and His Orchestra, *Further Definitions* (MCA/Impulse MCAD-5651). A 1961 session featuring Carter's unique writing for quartet of jazz sax giants (himself, Phil Woods, Charlie Rouse, and Coleman Hawkins). There isn't a weak track on this CD.

6. Wes Montgomery, *The Complete Riverside Recordings* (Riverside 12 RCD-4408-2). Simply the best jazz guitar playing since Charlie Christian's 1939–41 recordings. A 12-CD set of Montgomery's output for the Riverside label (1959–63).

**DON L. ROBERTS,** Head Music Librarian, Northwestern University Library, Evanston, Ill.

1. Indonesian gamelan music. An extremely complex and fascinating genre. The ensembles, which often include all major groups of musical instruments, provide a musical experience equal to that produced by the world's leading symphony orchestras.

2. Gustav Mahler's symphonies. Hearing these remarkable compositions performed regularly for more than 25 years by the Chicago Symphony Orchestra, one of the finest Mahler orchestras, has been a profound revelation.

3. Native American music. The variety, complexity, innovation, and traditionalism found in Native American music has long fascinated me. The best recordings are produced by Indian House and New World Records.

4. Stuart McKay, *Reap the Wild Winds* (RCA Victor LJM-1021, 1954). A recording featuring jazz bassoonist Stuart McKay and an emsemble pioneering new jazz sounds. McKay was an incredible performer, and how can an album go wrong when it contains such tunes as "Fagotte Gavotte," "Newton the Fig," and probably the most extraordinary performance ever recorded of "Take Me Out to the Ball Game."

5. The symphonies of Jean Sibelius. I had the privilege of learning many of these works from conductor Orien Dalley, a student of Sibelius. As a group, the symphonies constitute a major development in the evolution of symphonic form.

6. Richard Wagner's operas. These musical dramas are unparalleled in their integration of music, text, mythology, and human nature. Some people like their Wagner in small doses, but I'm still waiting for an opera house to do a continuous performance of *Der Ring des Nibelungen* followed immediately by *Parsifal*.

---

# Not-really-famous editor's favorite music

I have been collecting all varieties of music ever since I got my first tape recorder in 1963. Public libraries with music collections were primarily responsible for helping me appreciate jazz, classical, and world music in my youth, and it is to them that I attribute my adult obsession with trying to collect samples of as many different musical genres as possible, from abakua to zydeco. So I feel reasonably qualified to append my favorites to those of the famous librarians above.—*GME.*

**Classical.** Bedrich Smetana, "The Moldau," from *Ma Vlast* (1874). Some German students in Munich in 1971 first turned me on to the lilting, swelling, majestic tones of this symphonic ode to a river. Levine's Vienna Philharmonic Orchestra version is said to be one of the best (Deutsche Grammophon 419768-2).

**Avant-garde.** Bernie Krause and Human Remains, *Gorillas in the Mix* (Rykodisc 10119, 1988). You might mistake these compositions for curious yet enjoyable contemporary instrumental tunes—until you realize where the sounds come from. Every single note on this recording was created from the voices of animals—birds, fish, dolphins, elephants, gorillas, tortoises, a parrot named Turkey Corwin, and many others. Krause and friends mixed them so well that you'd never figure it out without the liner notes.

**Pop.** The music of 1947. I began collecting music from this year because it was a significant period in the history of UFOs, another interest of mine. However, it's also important musically because of the transitions taking place in pop, jazz, r&b, and country music. Some wonderfully listenable tunes were released that year: The Sons of the Pioneers, "Will There Be Sagebrush in Heaven?"; Wynonie Harris, "Good Rockin' Tonight"; Louis Jordan, "Barnyard Boogie"; Bing Crosby, "White Christmas"; Jerry Murad, "Peg o' My Heart"; Dizzy Gillespie, "Oop-Pop-a-Da"; Thelonious Monk, "'Round Midnight"; Louis Prima, "Civilization."

**Doo-wop.** The Marcels, "Blue Moon" (Colpix 186, 1961). Fred Johnson's unforgettable "bomp baba bomp" intro and "blue moon" bassline make this the best of the genre.

(continued)

10

**Rhythm and blues.** Lloyd Price, "Stagger Lee" (ABC-Para. 9972, 1959). A good New Orleans r&b ballad, made significant by the fact that I seem to be one of only a handful of people who know when and where Stack Lee actually shot Billy Lyons (I accidentally discovered it a few years ago while going through some old newspapers). The words and music of this song—which has been recorded many times by blues and early jazz artists—have their origins in a ballad first published in the *Journal of American Folklore* in 1911, by which time the original incident had been forgotten.

**Early rock & roll.** *Rock before Elvis* (Hoy Hoy 4050-2, 1993). A two-CD set of 44 proto-rock & roll songs, easily the best ever consigned to disc and all recorded before 1952. Rare recordings by Roy Brown, Joe Turner, Joe Lutcher, Paul Williams, Jimmy Rushing, Jimmy Cavallo, the Treniers, T-Bone Walker, and others. With arguably the first rock & roll recording ever made (Blind Blake, "Hastings Street," 1929) and the first boogie woogie recording (Pine Top Smith, "Pine Top's Boogie Woogie," 1928).

**Rock.** The Doors, complete recordings, 1965–71 (try *The Best of the Doors*, Elektra 960345-2). Sociopolitical poetry with a noir edge. Like Gustave Doré's depictions of Dante's *Inferno*, within each Doors song lies a portent and a curse.

**Blues.** Muddy Waters, master of electric Chicago blues. *After the Rain* (Cadet Concept LPS-320, 1969) is a personal favorite, but his early recordings, in which he transformed acoustic Delta blues into an electrified urban style, and the final albums produced by Johnny Winter, including *King Bee* (CBS BB192, 1981), are intense.

**Cajun.** *The Best of La Louisianne Records* (LLCD 1001, 1990) captures the Cajun sound before it was rediscovered in the 1980s. Alex Broussard, Doc Guidry, Ambrose Thibodeaux . . . these musicians will have you dreaming of bayous and crawfish even if you're in Greenland.

**Country.** Johnny Cash, *At Folsom Prison and San Quentin* (Columbia CGK 33639, 1968). The Man in Black, live, at his grittiest, funniest, and most socially relevant. Every prison library should have this recording.

**Folk.** The Brothers Four, *The Brothers Four* (Columbia 1402) and *Rally 'Round!* (Columbia 1479), both 1960. Lily-white and noncontroversial, but winningly harmonic. Thirty-four years later, I often find myself humming "Eddystone Light," "East Virginia," "Yellow Bird," "Beneath the Willow," and "Blue Water Line."

**Christmas music.** *The Alligator Records Christmas Collection* (ALCD XMAS 9201, 1992). Have a bluesy, soulful holiday season with KoKo Taylor, Son Seals, Charles Brown ("Boogie Woogie Santa Claus"), and other Alligator artists. Honorable mention goes to Phil Spector, *A Christmas Gift for You* (Phil Spector Records D2 4005, 1963), which some have hailed as the first rock concept album.

**Novelty.** Julie Brown, "Earth Girls Are Easy," from *Goddess in Progress* (Rhino RNEP 610, 1984). I have a huge collection of novelty tunes, but this is the only one that makes me laugh *every* time. This mini-album is nearly impossible to find because Warner Brothers bought up all the copies when her movie deal was finalized, but you can still hear it occasionally on Dr. Demento's syndicated radio show. Don't be misled by the insipid version heard in the 1989 movie and soundtrack.

**Jazz.** I like all forms of jazz from ragtime to fusion, but traditional New Orleans jazz has always struck me as the most visceral and joyous genre. Unfortunately, early recordings are often nonexistent or of poor quality. An excellent revival album is *New Orleans Jazz Echoes* (Musical Heritage Society 512449H, 1989), featuring the music of Kid Ory, the Original Dixieland Jass Band, King Oliver, and others, as their improvisations might have sounded when recorded digitally. (Then again, there's Bird.)

**Latin.** Merengue music from the Dominican Republic is fast, exciting, and sensual. Even our cats like to dance to "Soy Chiquito" by Santi y sus Duendes, *"No inventes papito, no inventes"* (Kubaney 0246-2, 1990).

**African.** A hard choice here, but one recording that never fails to mesmerize is Fela Anikulapo Kuti's *Zombie* (CRLP 511, 1976; Celluloid 6116, 1985). Fela sang his songs in broken English rather than Yoruba, which made him popular throughout West Africa. This recording was aimed at the unthinking members of the Nigerian army; however, it has relevance to other cultures including our own.

**Asian.** Ashwin Batish, *Sitar Power* (Batish Records 6001, 1986). Hard-rocking electric sitar, tabla and synthesizer instrumentals that bridge the gap between Ravi Shankar and Eric Clapton. With song titles like "Bombay Boogie," "Raga Rock," and "New Delhi Vice."

# Daffy dissertations

AS THE FOREMOST PUBLISHER OF DOCTORAL DISSERTATIONS, University Microforms International (UMI) publishes over 90% of all U.S. dissertations and thousands of international dissertations yearly. More than one million dissertations and master's theses are included in UMI's database, dating back to the first U.S. dissertation in 1861.

With 35,000 new ones added each year, one might expect to see some intriguing titles or odd topics. Seven dissertations have been written about Elvis Presley (including "Elvis Presley: All Shook Up"). Soap operas have drawn the interest of 24 doctoral candidates (for example, "Life's Little Problems . . . and Pleasures: Watching Soap Operas").

Here are some unusual titles from the UMI dissertation database:

- "Electrical Measurements on Cuticles of the American Cockroach"
- "Determinants of Flossing Behavior in the College Age Population"
- "Classification of Drinking Styles Using the Topographical Components of Beer Drinking"
- "More Fun Than Anything" (about cyclopropenium salts)
- "Creep of Portland Cement Paste"
- "Creepy: An Incremental Secondary Storage Garbage Collector"
- "Garage Sales as Practice: Ideologies of Women, Work and Community in Daily Life (Volumes I and II)"
- "Finger Painting and Personality Diagnosis"
- "Communication Use in the Motorcycle Gang"
- "'Santa Claus': A Mime-Opera Based on The Morality by e.e. cummings"
- "Ritual Drama in American Popular Culture: The Case of Professional Wrestling"
- "Things That Are Good and Things That Are Chocolate: A Cultural Model of Weight Control as Morality"
- "Acute Indigestion of Solipeds"
- "The Making of a Hippie Self"
- "Jock and Jill: Aspects of Women's Sports History in America, 1870–1940"
- "An Adaptive Surfing Apparatus"
- "The Function of the Couch in Stimulating Altered States of Consciousness in Hypnosis and in Psychoanalysis"
- "I Am You, You Are Me: A Philosophical Explanation of the Possibility That We Are All the Same Person"
- "You Can't Just Plug It In: Integrating the Computer into the Curriculum"

In the process of handling hundreds of thousands of manuscripts, UMI Dissertations Publishing staff has discovered unusual acknowledgments and prefaces, such as: "Yes, Mother, I am finally done; and no, Mom, I don't know what good a doctor's degree is either if I can't fix you when you're ill."

Another dissertation author prefaced his work with: "I would like to acknowledge the many years of tolerance exhibited by my parents, who will be the happiest of all, for they now can stop telling their friends, 'The kid is still in school.'"

Children are often mentioned in the foreword. One author wrote: "To my one-year-old son Geoffrey who diligently and enthusiastically tore into this dissertation as I did." Others express remorse at not being able to spend time with their kids. For example: "Dedicated to William, who wrote as an essay

10

for his second-grade teacher: 'I wish my father cood play with me. He uoose to play with me. But you no how they are. They always have to read and rite. He stays lokt up in his room and hrdle comes out to seem me. . . . I ges he likes to be lokt up in his room.'"

Spouses, too, are frequently acknowledged—often fondly and lovingly, such as "To Snugglebunny" or "To my loving, supportive husband." Others opt for humor: "To my wife, good old What's-Her-Name," which, staff members note, has appeared on more than one manuscript. One graduate student, apparently disgruntled at his graduation gift, wrote: "I wish to thank my wife and daughter for the pants. I wanted a camera, but the pants will be fine." Another wrote, "To Clara who couldn't care less."

Perhaps the entire doctoral experience is best summed up by this long-winded acknowledgment:

> If I had a dime for every time my wife threatened to divorce me during the past three years, I would be wealthy and not have to take a postdoctoral position which will only make me a little less poor and will keep me away from home and in the lab even more than graduate school and all because my committee read this manuscript and said that the only alternative to signing the approval to this dissertation was to give me a job mowing the grass on campus but the Physical Plant would not hire me on account of they said I was over-educated and needed to improve my dexterity skills like picking my nose while driving a tractor-mower over poor defenseless squirrels that were eating the nuts they stole from the medical students' lunches on Tuesday afternoon following the Biochemistry quiz which they all did not pass and blamed on me because they said a tutor was supposed to come with a 30-day money-back guarantee and I am supposed to thank someone for all this?!!

*Source:* University Microfilms International press release.

# Classifying librarians

*by Frederick Duda*

A COLLECTION OF favorite library trivia from the author of *Bib/Triv:*

**Acting librarians.** Everyone knows that the late Claudia MacNeil, the actress best known for her stage and screen roles in Lorraine Hansberry's *Raisin in the Sun,* was a licensed librarian in Baltimore before she entered show business. But did you know that Peter Kastner, who played the role of the roller-skating New York Public Library page in *You're A Big Boy Now* (1966), left acting to become a librarian? He is a library/media technician employed by the Cambridge, Mass., Public Schools.

**Angel librarian.** Isadore Gilbert Mudge, the first editor of ALA's *Guide to Reference Works,* served as the model for an angel in several stained-glass windows in the Sage Chapel, Cornell University. The windows were a memorial in honor of Ms. Mudge's grandmother whose second husband, Charles Kendall Adams, was the second president of the University. In later years, Mudge jokingly made note of her early role as an angel.

**Athletic librarian.** Rochester (Mich.) school librarian Laura Sophiea finished third in her age group in Hawaii's 1988 Iron(wo)man Triathalon. She also placed 33rd among 288 female entrants in this grueling event.

**First and last librarians.** Robert B. Palmer was the first and last male to hold the position of librarian at Barnard College (1967–1981), founded in 1899. Charles D. Churchwell was the first and last black to hold the position of librarian of Brown University (1974–1978), founded in 1764.

**Let-there-be-light librarians.** Frank Lloyd Wright designed the E. T. Roux Library (1942–1945), Florida Southern College. The library had high windows to provide natural light, but had no provisions for artificial light. Since it was impossible to read at night or when it rained even in sunny Florida, the librarians provided reading lamps which were always removed when the Master Architect was on campus.

**Librarian lover.** Casanova spent his later years as Count Waldstein's librarian at the Chateau of Dux in, appropriately enough, Bohemia.

**Librarian poet.** Sam Walter Foss (1858–1911) was a poet, librarian of the Somerville (Mass.) Public Library, and columnist for the *Christian Science Monitor*. He was best known for "The House by the Side of the Road" in *Dreams in Homespun* (1898).

**Marryin' a librarian.** Dan Lester (Ph.D./LS) of Boise, Idaho, believes he holds the record for a librarian marrying librarians. All four of his wives had an MLS.

# Test your Bib/Triv knowledge

*by Frederick Duda*

*BIB/TRIV: PROFUNDITIES, BANALITIES, AND TRIVIALITIES* in *Libraryland*, published in 1992 by McFarland & Co., explores the role of libraries and the image of librarians in books, movies, and the media. Although the book deals with substantive issues, it doesn't shy away from the humorous side of our image and the silly things that occur in libraries.

Not surprisingly, what the book reveals about our image is not good. Although on occasion we have been described as efficient, caring, knowledgeable, and, yes, underpaid, the usual stereotypes prevail. Sure, we can—and should—laugh at ourselves. But let's not forget that librarianship continues to suffer from serious misconceptions and has yet to receive full recognition from society. We should take justifiable pride in our labors and know enough about our work and ourselves to recognize the stereotypes for what they are.

Since much of the library profession's substance centers around giving answers, a Q-and-A

SUPERBRAIN KNOWLEDGE

format seemed a fitting way to test librarians' knowledge of their image and the context in which they work. Here's a sample of the 400 such questions contained in *Bib/Triv*; the volume also includes photos, illustrations, a bibliography, and an index.

1. In what 1985 Orion movie does supervising librarian Ophelia Sheffer (Valerie Curtin) begin her sexual harassment of Nick (Mandy Patinkin), her new assistant, by cornering him in the stacks of the San Francisco Public Library and telling him: "Let's not pretend, Nick. Most women avoid married men; I improve them."

10

2. Which of his novels was Samuel Langhorne Clemens referring to when he complained that librarians had arbitrary powers of censorship?
3. What Ivy League chapel has a stained-glass portrait of Columbia University librarian Isidore Gilbert Mudge as a young girl?
4. The Carnegie Corporation of New York gave 1,946 libraries to the United States. What state has the largest number of Carnegie libraries?
5. What New England transcendentalist observed that "Meek young men grow up in libraries"?

6. Maria Mitchell (1818–1889) discovered a comet in 1847 and went on to become the first professor of astronomy at Vassar College. Prior to the Vassar appointment, Mitchell served as head librarian of what town in Massachusetts?
7. Name the Indiana lawyer, novelist, and mother of three who was described in Blackwell's 1988 worst-dressed list as dressing like a 1940's unemployed librarian?
8. What former president of the New York Public Library was Alfred Kazin referring to when he said, "He has a great social gift, which most librarians don't have"?
9. Name the English librarian, poet, and novelist who wrote:

> Sexual intercourse began
> In nineteen sixty-three
> (which was rather late for me)—
> Between the end of the *Chatterly* ban
> And the Beatles' first LP

10. Which of the following Librarians of Congress earned an MLS? a) L. Quincy Mumford; b) Archibald MacLeish; c) Daniel J. Boorstin; d) Luther H. Evans.
11. In what 1956 Columbia movie does Freddie Slater (Kevin Coughlin) set fire to the Kenport Public Library after being tormented by his peers for being the pet of the librarian (Bette Davis)?
12. The circular reading room of the E.T. Roux Library at Florida Southern College was designed with high windows to provide natural light and had no provisions for artificial illumination. Name the master American architect who designed this less than-functional facility, which was built between 1942 and 1945.
13. In fall 1989, it was reported that Pentagon procurement officers allegedly "laundered $35 million for weapons, missile systems, and classified defense projects" through the Library of Congress's purchasing system. Which acronym stands for LC's procurement system? a) FEDLINK; b) LIBPRO; c) LIBLAUN; d) LIBPEN.
14. Which of the following librarians wrote *Women in American Libraries* (1904), which criticized the lack of opportunity for advancement of women librarians? a) Theresa West Elmendorf; b) Tessa Kelso; c) Caroline M. Hewins; d) Mary Salome Cutler Fairchild.
15. In what 1978 20th-Century Fox movie does Betsy McGuire (Trish Van Devere) of "the public liberry" compete with Troubles Moran (Ann Reinking) for the affections of Joey Popchik (Harry Hamlin)?

16. In 1972 the Librarians Anti-Defamation League (LADLE) was founded in New York City to protest an ad depicting librarians as turn-of-the-century old bats. What national food company was responsible for the ad?

17. According to the lyrics of "Marian the Librarian" *(The Music Man)*, what is considered an unforgivable sin in dealing with a librarian?

18. Who was the first African American appointed to direct an Ivy League university library?

19. Name the best-selling horror-story writer who has described himself as an "American literary bogeyman" and who wrote the following as a preface to one of his works: "I feared the old librarian with the blue hair and the cat's-eye glasses who would pinch the backs of your hands with her long, pale fingers and her 'Shh!' if you forgot where you were and started to talk too loud."

20. In which of the following Anne Rice novels does the protagonist muse that "A library was something I could understand. It was the one place in which I still felt the measure of my old sanity"? a) *Interview with the Vampire;* b) *The Feast of All Saints;* c) *The Vampire Lestat;* d) *Cry to Heaven.*

21. Contrary to ALA and LC policy, a clerk (Jaye Stewart) in the Library of Congress gives two reporters information on books charged out to the White House staff. Name the 1976 movie.

22. In what 1959 Philip Roth novella does Neil Klugman describe the lions guarding the steps of the Newark (N.J.) Public Library as suffering a combination of elephantiasis and arteriosclerosis?

23. Name the only member of the House of Representatives of the 102nd Congress who holds a professional library degree.

24. In a 1946 Metro-Goldwyn-Mayer movie, bosun Harry Patterson (Clark Gable) initially considers Emily Sears (Greer Garson) of the San Francisco Public Library "a mild tomato" but he does woo and wed her. Name the movie.

25. In *Black Boy* (1945), Richard Wright describes how he persuaded a white Irish Catholic to get books for him from the Memphis Public Library, which did not serve blacks. Which of the following authors was Wright determined to read through this ruse? a) Harriet Beecher Stowe; b) Sojourner Truth; c) George Washington Carver; d) H. L. Mencken.

26. Which of the following best describes the attitude of the librarian in the 1943 Betty Smith novel *A Tree Grows in Brooklyn?* a) She was aloof to her clientele; b) She hated children; c) She was pettish; d) All of the above.

27. Name the 1988 World Series Most Valuable Player who teammate Mike Sciosia said might have been held back because he looks like a librarian.

28. In a story on the 109th ALA Annual Conference, reporter Steve Johnson of the *Chicago Tribune* noted that at the opening reception librarians "socked away four kegs of beer in 30 minutes." The story

10

mentions that ALA President Patricia Wilson Berger recalled being told once by a hotel official why he liked librarians: "He said, 'You honor your reservations; you go to your meetings so we can clean your rooms; you're relatively quiet; and you drink more than _____.'" Which of the following fills in the blank? a) The Fifth Fleet; b) The American Legion; c) The town of Evanston; d) The American Distillers Convention.

29. In which Howard Breslin novel do we find the following passage? ". . . the librarians are a tribe all their own. They're nice enough, efficient, ready and willing to help you find things, but none of them ever smile. I don't think they go home nights. I think they file each other away on shelves." a) *Let Go of Yesterday;* b) *Autumn Comes Early;* c) *The Tamarack Tree;* d) *A Hundred Hills.*

30. In *Main Street,* Sinclair Lewis's heroine Carol Milford almost drops out of library school to become "one of the young women who dance in cheesecloth in the moonlight" at the Art Institute. However, Carol's commitment to librarianship is reaffirmed after the study of which work? a) *Short-Title Catalogue;* b) *Who's Who in Medicine;* c) *The Cumulative Index;* d) *Genealogies in the Library of Congress.*

31. Name the two-time winner of the Pulitzer Prize for nonfiction (1963 and 1972) who said, "For me, the card catalog has been a companion all my working life. To leave it is like leaving the house one was born in."

32. One night while closing up, Eloise Weldon, assistant librarian of the Millbrook (W. Va.) College Library, who is having an affair with the president of the college, is bludgeoned to death by an avalanche of books. In which crime novel by Dave Pedneau does Eloise meet her ghastly demise? a) *B.O.L.O.;* b) *A.K.A.;* c) *D.O.A.;* d) *P.D.Q.*

33. What 1989 library appointment prompted Jesuit officials to announce that they saw no inconsistency between holding such a position and remaining faithful to the order's vows of "poverty, chastity, and obedience"?

34. "Chistka!" is the Russian term for cleansing. Who undertook the task of "cleansing" libraries of so-called "harmful" books in the Soviet Union in 1920?

35. What gold-plated award was named after librarian Margaret Herrick's uncle?

36. What 18th-century Venetian adventurer and author spent his later years as Count Waldstein's librarian at the Chateau of Dux in, appropriately enough, Bohemia?

37. Name the 20th-century U.S. President whose oldest son married a librarian.

38. In the 1963 Warner Bros. movie *Spencer's Mountain,* starring Henry Fonda and Maureen O'Hara, who played their son Clay Boy, who asked for $20 a week to run the local library, but settled for $10?

## Answers

1. *Maxie*
2. *Huckleberry Finn*
3. Sage Chapel, Cornell University
4. Indiana (164 Carnegie libraries)
5. Ralph Waldo Emerson
6. Nantucket, Mass.
7. Marilyn Quayle
8. Vartan Gregorian
9. Philip Larkin

10. a) L. Quincy Mumford
11. *Storm Center*
12. Frank Lloyd Wright
13. a) FEDLINK
14. d) Mary Salome Cutler Fairchild
15. *Movie/Movie*
16. Nabisco Company
17. Talking out loud
18. Charles D. Churchwell, who was Brown University librarian from 1974–1978
19. Stephen King
20. c) *The Vampire Lestat*
21. *All the President's Men*
22 *Goodbye, Columbus*
23. Major Owens
24. *Adventure*
25. d) H. L. Mencken
26. d) All of the above
27. Orel Hersheiser
28. b) The American Legion
29. a) *Let Go of Yesterday*
30. c) *The Cumulative Index*
31. Barbara W. Tuchman
32. b) *A.K.A. (Also Known As)*
33. The appointment of the Rev. Timothy Healy as president of the New York Public Library
34. Nadezhda Krupskaya (a.k.a., Mrs. Lenin)
35. The Oscar
36. Giovanni Jacopo De Steingált Casanova
37. George Herbert Walker Bush
38. James MacArthur

Source: Frederick Duda, "Test Your Bib/Triv Knowledge," *American Libraries* 23 (June 1992): 463–465.

---

## Library superlatives

**The world's first library in an elevated transit system:** Miami-Dade Public Library System's Porta-Kiosk Library at the Metrorail Civic Center station, which opened in January 1992.

**The nation's most complete repository of written and photographic nudism history:** Library at the Cypress Cove Resort nudist colony, Florida.

**First branch library at a Pizza Hut:** The Eureka (Ill.) Public Library District places 20 books per month in the restaurant for children to read while they are waiting for meals. Waitresses are responsible for removing the books before the food arrives.

**Largest library fine ever collected:** $1,500, paid in 1993 to the College of Wooster Library by a graduate student from the University of Akron who helped himself to some $5,000 worth of library materials from Wooster's unstaffed Chemistry Library.

10

# Billy Wilkinson's ten favorite European library postcards

*by Billy Wilkinson*

**THERE ARE TENS OF THOUSANDS** of library postcards in the world. I asked in the first edition if anyone knew how many. No one ventured an estimate. The Norman Stevens Collection is No. 1 with more than 20,000 cards. I once again tried to persuade the editor into "My Favorite One Hundred Postcards," but he still refuses the space. So a series of selections is in order. Please see the 1991 edition of this volume, pages 459–464, for nine beautiful American postcards and one delightful British one. (You should also see the November 1988 and May 1989 issues of *College & Research Libraries News* for two illustrated articles on exterior and interior views of notable academic libraries.) Selection from such a large number of candidates continues to be most difficult, but here are my ten favorite European ones. As you will see, they are beautiful, baroque, and varied. I could have easily selected "Billy's Best British Library Postcards," or "From Australia to Zambia with Library Postcards" or "Wilkinson's Wild Library Postal Exotica" (leather cards, "hold-to-the-light" postcards in which the windows "glow," metal cards, and other novelties), etc. I am ready for the third edition!

The following are in no particular order—just the fancy of the moment.

In addition to the gracious donors credited, I am also very grateful to Barbara Brown, Julie Casa, Frederick Duda, Judith Holliday, Martha Landis, Jonathan LeBreton, Monty Montee, Louis Silverstein, Judith Sterling, and Norman Stevens. And please send me a library postcard at 234 Highland Ave., Hanover, PA 17331. You will be rewarded with one in return.

**Figure 1.** Trinity College, Wren Library, Cambridge University, Cambridge, England. A distinguished historian and frequent visitor to England advised my wife and me that when we went to London for two weeks' vacation, we should take the train immediately to Cambridge on the first sunny day. He was right! And this postal captures it all: punting and sunbathing on and by the Cam River, and even a willow by Sir Christopher Wren's Library. I have other equally lovely postals of Cambridge—such details as a 17th-century gate by William Partridge on Wren's Library—but they cannot quite compete with the memory of a beautiful May day conjured up by this postcard.

**Figure 2.** Filosofický sál Strahovské knihovny, Prague, The Czech Republic. Jennifer Henderson and the editor brought this 8 ½" x 5 ¾" baroque beauty to me from their visit to the Philosophical Hall of the Strahov Library in Prague. A monastery founded in 1140, it is said to have the best of all views of Prague; straight down the Vltava to the south, with the rooftops and innumerable towers of the city spreading away on either bank of the river. In 1953 the monastery became the National Museum of Czech Literature, housing 130,000 rare books and manuscripts and is undoubtedly the most splendid museum of the forty museums and galleries in Prague today.

**Figure 3.** Helsingfors Universitetsbibliotek, Helsinki, Finland. This large 1982 postcard is a delightful drawing of the Helsinki University Library by Else Ackerman-Hongell and published by Galerie Ackerman. I also have a note card with an elegantly austere drawing done in 1836 by the architect Carl Ludwig Engel, but this contemporary one wins the contest.

**Figure 4.** Radcliffe Camera, Bodleian Library, Oxford University, Oxford, England. I am a sucker for iron grillwork, but the real reason this is one of my all-time favorites is that the idea for a separate library for the undergraduate students at a university has been traced back to the reading room of the Radcliffe Camera. Those of us who were in charge of separate undergraduate libraries in the 1960s in the United States love a little British pedigree for our movement of better library service for undergrads.

**Figure 5.** Library at Ephesus, Turkey. A friend on holiday sailed from Istanbul to Ephesus and sent this card asking if it qualified as a library. The Library at Ephesus naturally was not as famous or as large as the Temple of Artemis (Diana), but this postal qualified as a favorite. The Artemision was one of the Seven Wonders of the World. Excavation at Ephesus began in 1896 and many public buildings including the theatre, the stadium, and this library have been found. All the remains are from the Roman Imperial period.

**Figure 6.** St. Gallen, Stiftsbibliothek, Switzerland. A friend brought me this gorgeous postcard from her Swiss holiday. She declares the St. Gall Abbey Library to be one of the most beautiful research libraries—100,000 plus volumes for use by mediaevalists—that she has ever seen. We should all visit St. Gall.

**Figure 7.** Nationalbibliothek, Vienna, Austria. This is my candidate for most beautiful research library. Perhaps I am unduly influenced by my recent visit to Salzburg and Vienna. As the guidebooks refer to it—the Hofbibliothek Prunksaal—this Grand Hall of the National Austrian Library is one of the most ornate of that most ornate imperial palace, the Hofburg. The Grand Hall was designed by Fischer von Erlach the Elder just before his death in 1723 and completed by his son. It is full-blown High Baroque! Even so, it just barely beats out a postal and personal visit to the Kaisersaal and the frescoed library in the Benedictine Abbey at Kremsmünster, which also has elegant fish basins and splendid baroque statuary with hundreds of mounted antlers and a sensational library. What a combination!

10

**Figure 8.** The Library in Queen Mary's Dolls' House, Windsor Castle, London, England. Friends have diligently searched for and found rare postals showing the libraries in the stately houses of England. I was tempted to include one, but one of those friends and the greatest donor to my postcard collection, James Davis, Special Collections Department, UCLA Library, delighted me even more with this card of the library in a dolls' house in Windsor Castle. He always sends a profusion of library postcards from his travels as well as the most unusual.

**Figure 9.** The Library, seen from the Dining Room, in Sir John Soane's Museum, London, England. I must stop this English and/or interiors kick, but just one more. I have always wanted to turn a house into a museum—even more so after visiting Sir John's house. Every room is a treasure and is full of treasures at No. 13 Lincoln's Inn Fields. He naturally had an elegant library.

**Figure 10.** Universitetsbiblioteket, Carolina Rediviva, Uppsala, Sweden. Uppsala with university libraries! How can I resist ending my ten favorites in any other way than with thousands of students celebrating the coming of Spring—the "Sista april" (the last of April)—in front of the University Library? Gary Menges, Special Collections Department, University of Washington, contributed this Spring frolic to my collection.

# How well do you know your end users?

*by Will Manley*

To:             Members of the American Library Association
From:           The Foolish Activities Round Table
Prepared by:    Will Manley, corresponding secretary
Subject:        You and your end users

**RUMORS OF CONTROVERSY** swirling around the Foolish Activities Round Table are absolutely true. Last month at their spring meeting, a group of old F.A.R.T.ers engaged in a vociferous argument about whether the round table was spending too much time on organizational matters and not enough time on real library issues.

"When's the last time we talked about end users?" challenged Sidney Stonestreet.

"What's an end user?" replied Maxine Merkle.

"That's exactly my point," rebutted Stonestreet. "You're so preoccupied with bureaucratic ego flux that you don't even know that the new term for a library patron is end user, and you've lost sight of the fact that the sole reason we exist is to serve the end user."

A subcommittee was then quickly formed to develop a diagnostic test by which any librarian could determine if he or she had become too remote from the end user. What follows is that test.

10

Simply match the number of the end user with the letter of the request he or she would be most likely to make.

Scoring: Anything less than a perfect score means that you need to spend more time with your end users.

## End users

1. A dittohead.
2. A feminist with an attitude.
3. A person who voted for Pat Buchanan.
4. A recent graduate of an American public school.
5. A yuppie mommy.
6. A member of the Social Responsibilities Round Table.
7. A bald-faced liar.
8. A new sensitive male of the '90s.
9. An off-duty cataloger on the make.
10. A local flasher.
11. A member of the American Civil Liberties Union.
12. A person who has spent too much time waiting in line at the supermarket.
13. A bill collector.

## End-user requests

A. I need a tape recording of live dodo bird sounds.
B. I'm looking for an anti-war, pro-choice, gender-neutral, nondenominational, culturally diverse children's book.
C. Please don't reprimand my daughter. She was not yelling. She was simply exercising her First Amendment rights.
D. Hey, babe, how would you like to go out with me? I know some really creative main entries.
E. I believe that *The Emperor's New Clothes* is a morally objectionable book because it glorifies nudity.
F. My three-year-old is in the middle of her discovery phase. Do you have any books that will give her some good hands-on activities in the area of quantum physics?
G. Why don't you have Madonna's new book *Sex*? Perverts pay taxes too, you know.
H. My objection to *Daddy's Roommate* has nothing to do with homosexuality. I object to the book because the mommy in it is wearing an apron and baking a cake.
I. I need further information on that man in the Philippines who gave birth to a 10-pound chimpanzee.
J. Why does this library have only 53 copies of Rush Limbaugh's new book? It looks to me like you've got a liberal bias.
K. Do you have anything by a contemporary woman novelist that will, you know, speak to me in a very real way?
L. Can you tell me who lives next to Will Manley on Adams Avenue?
M. Do you have *Sex* by Madonna? My next door neighbor asked me to pick it up for him.

## Answers

1J, 2H, 3E, 4A, 5F, 6B, 7M, 8K, 9D, 10G, 11C, 12I, 13L.

*Source:* Will Manley, "How Well Do You Know Your End Users?"
*American Libraries* 24 (May 1993): 425.

# The adventures of Bulldog Hammer, hard-boiled LC reference librarian

## THE BIG SCHLEP
### By Raymond Handler

THE LITTLE GUY WALKED UP to the Research Guidance Office with a tourist shoulder bag and a big smile. His "High-School Volunteers for America" button was as bright as the sun rising on an Iowa cornfield.

"Hi, Mister! My teacher back in Sioux City said I should use our National Library for my high school Science Fair project—I'm researching the effect of milk and cookies on reducing high blood pressure! I only have a couple hours before the bus leaves, but could I check out a few books to take with me?"

I smiled. It was so unutterably droll. Standing there in his neatly-buttoned sport coat he looked like he'd just stepped out of an old Mickey Rooney movie. Still, I had a job to do, and I wasn't one to shirk doing the dirty work. I figured the Joint Committee on the Library was depending on me.

I got up, picked up a policy statement on high schoolers and put my arm around his shoulders, still smiling all the while. I led him to the door, folded up the policy and put it in his coat pocket, and pointed him back the way he came.

"Sorry, kid," I said, "Come back when you're old enough to vote for a Congressman." With that I grabbed him by the scruff of the neck and the seat of the pants, whipped him through the door and heaved him in a high arc into the Great Hall.

He bounced once, skidded a ways and finally stopped about four feet short of my previous record. I always aimed for a spot midway between the Mainz Bible and the Gutenberg and had almost made it once. I have to admit, though, that on that occasion the kid was unusually scrawny and, too, the floor had just been polished the previous night. Still, I thought, a record is a record and every one of 'em was made to be broken. I figured I'd do better the next time.

I went in to the RGO again and put my feet back up on the desk. I looked up at the dome. I had always thought of the Main Reading Room as like the brain of the human race, and seeing the dome was like looking at the inside of its skull. Up on the highest level were History and Art and Philosophy and such like—all pale, motionless and too high up to see very clearly. On the lowest level, though, it was a different realm entirely. There used to be a bunch of law books in between, as if to somehow connect the two levels—but they'd been removed, excised as neatly as in a lobotomy, and now there was nothing but a vacuum between the ideals and the action. And there was plenty of the latter down below, all right—all up close, in living color, and in sharp focus. There was Greed sitting at desk 18, trying to figure out ways to cheat on his

10

income tax; there was Envy sitting at 145, trying to shoot down a colleague's new theory and ruin him for tenure; there was Sloth at 217, plagiarizing an encyclopedia article for a term paper. Over at 83 was Pride, razoring out obscure illustrations that he thought only he could appreciate; and there at 301 was Lust, sending in call slips for dirty books and getting frustrated as hell at all the Not-on-shelf returns. Yeah, down there at the lower level was where the real monuments to humanity were—the live ones with blood surging and eyes bright with purpose. I laughed. It was all so droll.

Just then my little reverie was interrupted by a darkening of the room—for a second I thought the light had gone out, but then I saw a huge silhouette eclipsing the ceiling fixture, and from the shadow a hand the size of a backhoe came reaching down for me.

I felt myself being lifted up by my shirtfront like a rag doll; then I was staring at a face that looked like a cross between King Kong and a Mack truck. The guy was wearing a dark blue coat and a matching wide-brimmed hat; his five o'clock shadow looked like it was made of tire studs and his aftershave smelled like diesel exhaust fumes. Right there I pegged him for a tough customer.

He looked me up and down and back and forth in a kind of puzzled way, like a gorilla encountering some strange new fruit that vaguely resembled a banana. I hoped the resemblance wasn't too strong.

"Are you Bulldog Hammer?"

I said that yes, I was, Sir, and that I might be able to help him better if my feet were down on the ground. It took a few moments for the words to sink in, but finally he seemed to understand. I almost thought I could hear the strains of *Also Sprach Zarathustra* in the background.

My feet were just touching down when he pulled me up again. Now it seemed he had a second idea. I wondered whether his brain or my shirt would wear out first with all this unaccustomed activity.

"I want you should find Velma."

Oh, brother, I thought—another wayward wife. It made me think of all the skiptracing I'd done with the Agency back in L.A. looking for dames who'd discovered the hard way that a wedding band could turn into a boxing ring and that nuptial bells only signalled the start of the first round. I was about to suggest filing a Missing Persons report at the police station when he spoke again.

"She wrote something on computers in libraries."

That brought me up short. The big guy was serious. I got him to put me down and fill in some background. It seems his name was Moose Malone and he'd just gotten out of a seven-to-ten stretch at Leavenworth. While he was there he'd worked in the prison library and he'd grown to like it. Now he thought he'd read up on the new developments so he'd have something to work on when he got back. He was a three-timer already and it seemed not to occur to him that he might avoid returning; he apparently assumed it was just a matter of when. I can't say that I disagreed—I figured this guy was Murder One looking for a place to happen.

I asked him what he did in the library. It turns out he'd put himself in charge of circulation. Sure, I thought, who was gonna argue? He said he'd established real good control of the collection. I asked him if he charged a heavy fine if a reader had books out too long. No, he said, he just broke the guy's legs. I told him that we could use him here and that we had a guy who'd like to talk to him. I was about to send him downstairs but he picked me up again and growled like feeding time was overdue at the ape house.

"I want you should find Velma *now*."

Moose had a small vocabulary, but he could be remarkably expressive within its limitations. I figured I should get busy. It turns out that all he knew was what he'd already told me: just the first name Velma and the fact that she'd written something on library computers. I figured we'd give MUMS a shot.

I walked him over to the RGO terminal. "Here, Moose," I said, "You might want to try one of these computers yourself, just to get the feel of it." He smiled. I'd seen lantern jaws before, but this guy's *teeth* were like lanterns. I told him to just type in "Find Velma" and hit the Enter button.

His fingers pawed the keyboard and the screen responded with DHF 2001L NOT A KNOWN CICS/VS COMMAND. He tried again and got the same response, then again with the same results. The screen was rapidly filling up with DFH 2001Ls; then I saw the reason. His hands were so big that each fingertip was pressing four keys simultaneously. I wondered if ITS had contingency plans for users like this.

Moose was getting hot; his teeth were grinding like millstones. Finally he'd reached the end of his patience and he swung a fist the size of a wrecking ball against the terminal. The machine mewled like a frustrated alley cat in heat and the screen went blank. He hit it again and a mechanical voice from inside said "Stop. Dave. Stop." He whacked it again and it started singing "Daisy, Daisy" in a lower-register voice. At last he brought both fists down on top of it and the whole thing exploded in a shower of electric sparks and green smoke.

Damn, I thought. Why hadn't I ever thought of that?

A second later I was dangling above the ground again, looking into a face with an expression of a Mt. Rushmore head feeling subterranean piles. With some difficulty I finally got him to put me down again—I wondered how Fay Wray handled these situations—and started leading him into the reading room. I figured I should get to another terminal quick and this time do the search myself.

I headed towards Alcove 5; with Moose hovering over me I felt like a balloon tender at a Macy's Thanksgiving Day parade. The terminal near 5 was available; I typed in "Find Velma" and qualified it with computer and library terms. No luck.

The big guy was getting hotter. Since that condition did not bode well for my shirtfront or my legs I quickly ran through the options. *Library Literature* and LISA were out—no indexing by first names, and subject headings would take too long. It had to be a search directly for "Velma"—which meant some other database. I hoped that Dialog wouldn't let me down.

I led him into the back office. When they saw this guy duck his head to get through the doorway, three of the secretaries ran screaming into the far room and slammed the door. Then the Chief stuck his head out, and when he saw the frown on Moose's face he turned white. I hadn't seen him look like that since the time I beat up the State Department Undersecretary who got too pushy in demanding a stack pass.

I logged into ERIC and typed "Select Velma." Moose was breathing heavily over my shoulder, like a sailor coming into a cathouse after eight months at sea. I hoped the confounded database worked, because I didn't want to be the one to tell him that all the girls had just found religion.

The terminal sputtered and whirred like a Mixmaster, chopping up, kneading, dicing, pureeing, and blending all of its little electronic bytes to extrude them into a silicon hors d'ouevre. I wondered if ITS was working on developing machine-compatible people who could just be plugged into terminals and taught intravenously. I figured that was scheduled down the line as Release 500.2.

Just then the machine let out with an electronic burp and its printer started racing as fast as its little bauds could carry it:

10

ED217842. Proceedings of the Preconference on Online Catalogs (Houston, Texas, March 31, 1981). Four papers. The first article on the requirements of online catalogs by Velma Veneziano describes such specific features as comprehensiveness, flexibility, affordability, availability, structured access, user friendliness, level of cataloging, and status information on holdings.

Whew, I thought. Somehow I felt like my legs might not wind up as wishbones after all. I tore off the sheet and held it out to Moose. "It'll be in the Microforms Room," I said, "Just take this over there—" I was interrupted by a huge arm surrounding me like a blanket. "I want *you* should find Velma."

Like I said, Moose was a man of few words, but he had a way with 'em. We both went into Microforms and sat together at a reader-printer, Moose's hand all the while holding on to my back like I was a ventriloquist's dummy. I wondered how I'd look mounted at the Smithsonian next to Charlie McCarthy. I wondered how Moose would look mounted in place of the elephant.

Finally we had a hard copy of Velma's report and as we walked back to RGO the big guy was all smiles. Sure enough, I thought, the National Library had once again come through for the citizenry. When we got back to the door of the Reading Room I told him it made me feel good to see him so happy at finding his Velma. He looked at me and his smile got bigger, gaping like the maw of a hungry garbage truck. He said that wasn't what he was smiling about.

"I seen what you done with that kid before I came in," he grinned. "It looked like fun."

"Well, no, Moose," I said, "fun doesn't enter into it. It's just a job. You see, the Joint Committee on the Library . . ." The backhoe descended again; I felt myself being lifted up and before I knew it I was through the door and sailing out into the Great Hall. My last thought on the way down was that it looked like my skull and the marble floor were about to have it out as to which was harder.

I figure that floor must've won, because it was nearly five minutes before I came to—one of the guards was kneeling next to me and shaking me awake. My head felt like somebody had just bowled a 300 game between my ears. Moose was gone, but from the look on the guard's face I could tell that he was not forgotten.

"Jeeminy, Bulldog, that gorilla was the biggest mug I ever seen! Are you O.K.?"

"Yeah, sure," I said, "I'm O.K.—all in a day's work when you deal with the public." Then I looked around, saw where I was and felt the 10-pins crash one more time.

I was lying midway between the Mainz Bible and the Gutenberg. The big ape had broken my record.

*Source: Library of Congress Professional Association Newsletter*, vol. 15, no.3 (May-June 1983): 5–7. Reprinted with permission. The author wishes to remain anonymous.

# INDEX